NATURE

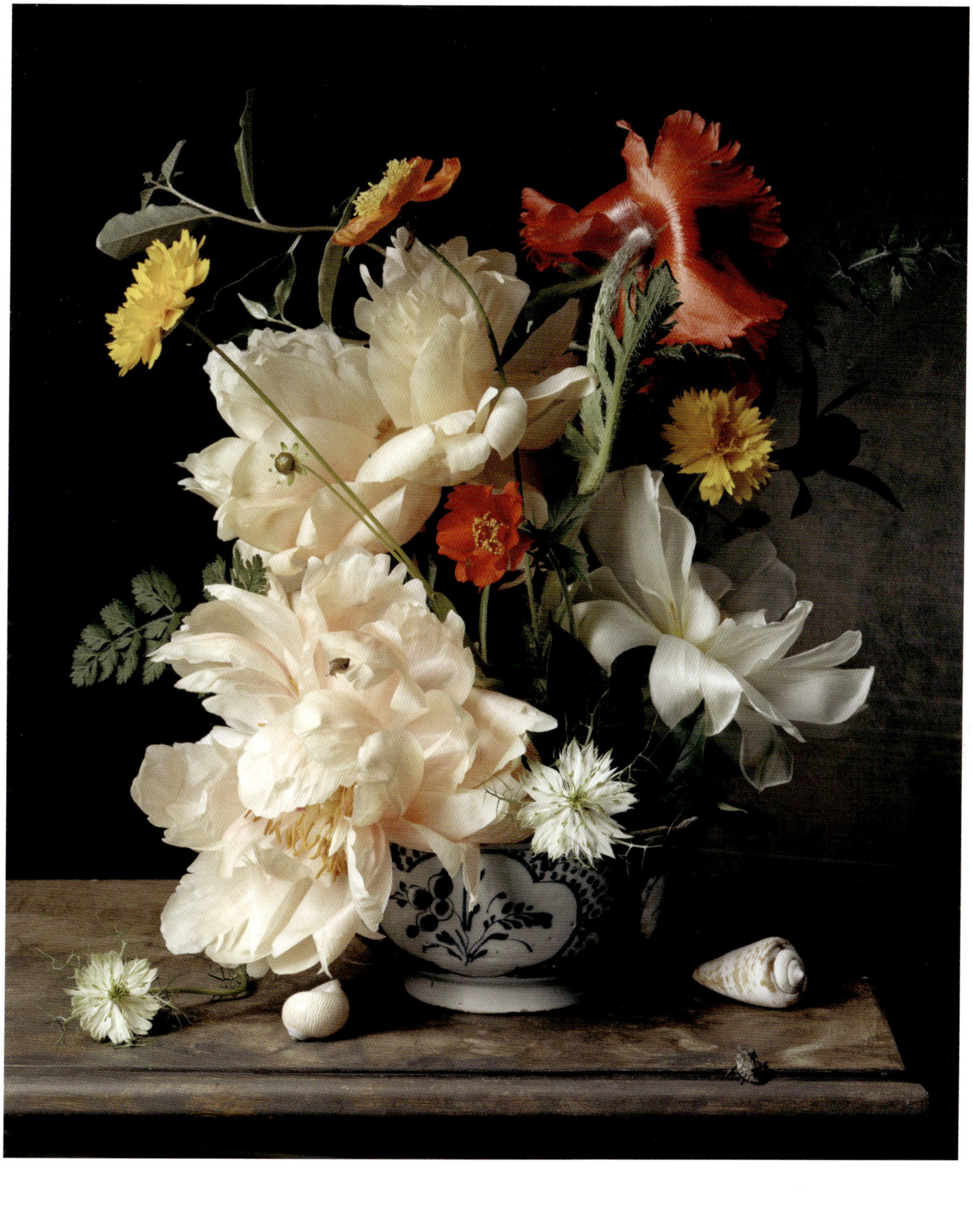

MORTE

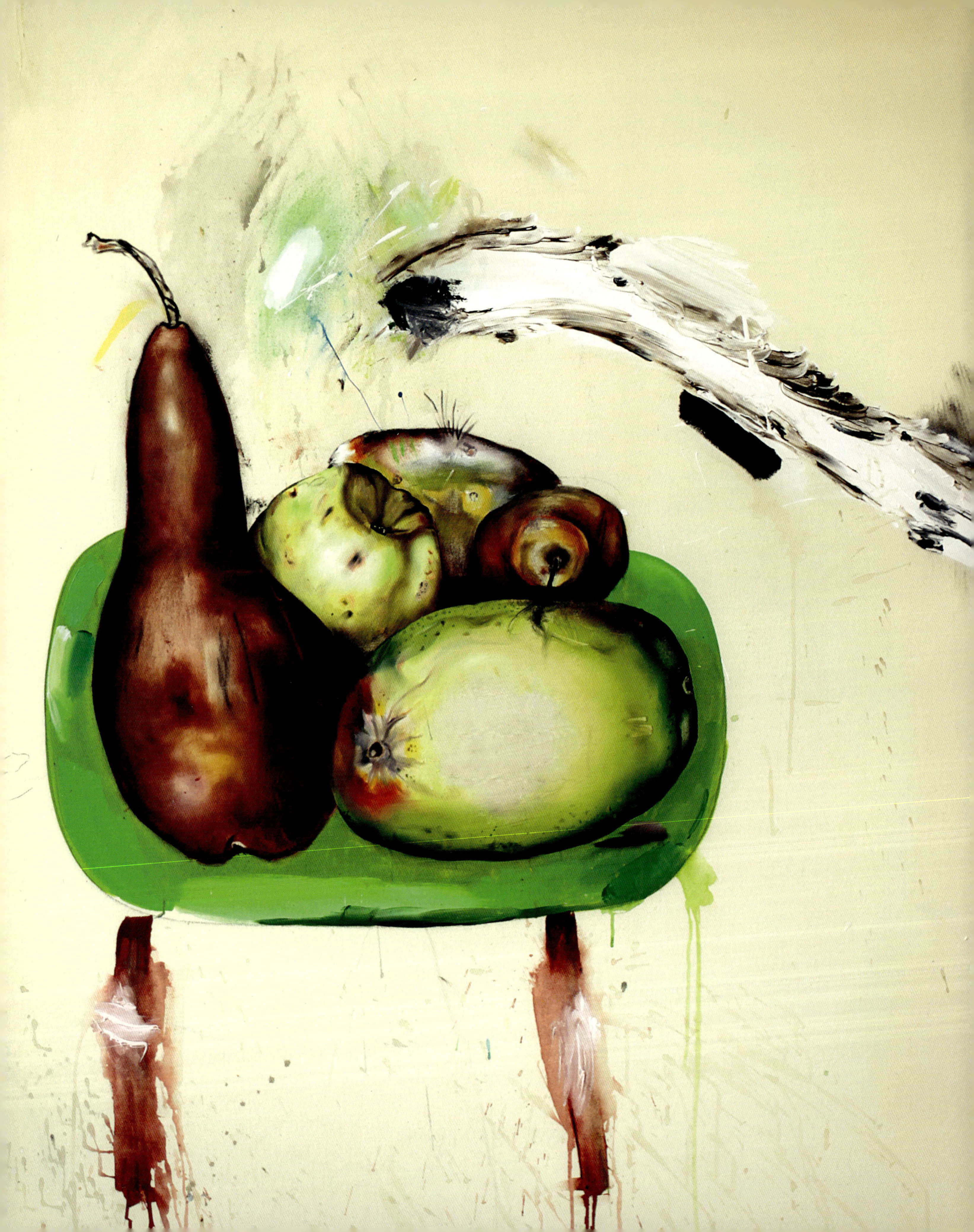

MICHAEL PETRY

NATURE MORTE

Contemporary artists reinvigorate the Still-Life tradition

with 391 illustrations, 366 in colour

Thames & Hudson

CONTENTS

PAGE 1 · Sharon Core
1782, 2011 · archival pigment print

PAGE 2 · Michael Hilsman
Still Life with Pears and Mango, 2011
oil and acrylic on canvas

REVISITING THE STILL LIFE

The still life, or *nature morte,* has been a constant subject throughout the history of art, its significance changing over time. As an independent genre of painting, however, the still life came into its own in the mid-seventeenth century when the Flemish term *stilleven* first came to be applied to oil paintings characterized by their tight focus on an assortment of objects sitting on a flat surface, depicted not as a subsidiary element in a wider narrative but as a subject in its own right. Such paintings had become popular as early as the late fifteenth century but only now did a substantial body of works exist to merit recognition as forming a distinct genre. From *stilleven*, the German *stilleben* and the English 'still life' came into use, but their allusion to still or unmoving nature has never done full justice to the allegorical themes that underpin these works and, ultimately, lend them their gravitas. It would be left to the French, some one hundred years later, to coin the name most suggestive of the layered symbolism of the genre and its poignant reminders of the transience of life and the ever-present threat of death: the still life became known as the *nature morte*, literally 'dead nature'.

The link between the still life and death can be traced all the way back to the paintings that adorn the walls of ancient Egyptian tombs. There, heaps of fruit and other foodstuffs illustrated the bounty that would greet the dead in the afterlife. Similar vignettes feature in the extant paintings and mosaics of ancient Greece. On the walls of ancient Greek dwellings, their presence illustrated the wealth of the inhabitants and the bounty of life. Roman Pompeii is rich in decorative frescoes and mosaic *emblemas* of bowls of fruit, flowers, fish and animals, which indicated the commercial activity, wealth or status of the building's owners [2]. Skulls appear in some of these works, contrasting the transient with the ultimate and reminding viewers that *omnia mors aequat* – death makes all equal [1].

By the early Renaissance, around 1300, assortments of everyday objects were appearing in the religious paintings of Giotto (1267/76–1337) and his contemporaries. Over time these objects had become invested with deep spiritual and allegorical meaning that was easily recognizable to viewers. Early Christians fearing persecution had created a secret language of symbols through which they might connect with other believers. Passed down through the centuries, this language was so well established that all parts of society were familiar with its codes by the Middle Ages. The rose could stand in for the Virgin Mary (as well as the goddess Venus and, by extension, love), as could the lily with its connotations of virginity, purity and justice. The pomegranate, a single fruit containing many seeds, represented the Church; the sunflower, always turning towards the radiance of the sun, divine love and devotion; the fish or lamb was synonymous with Jesus Christ.

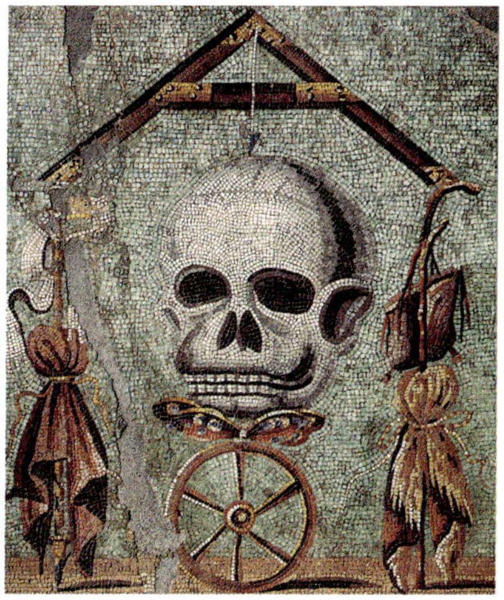

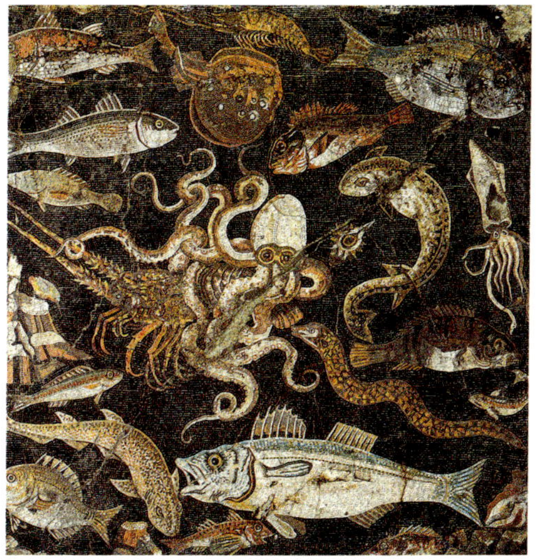

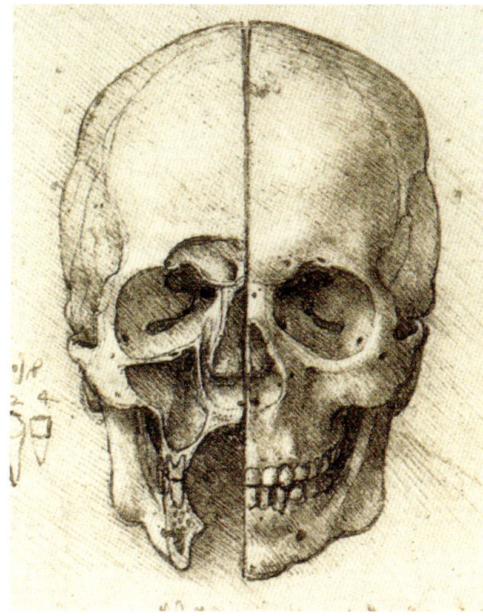

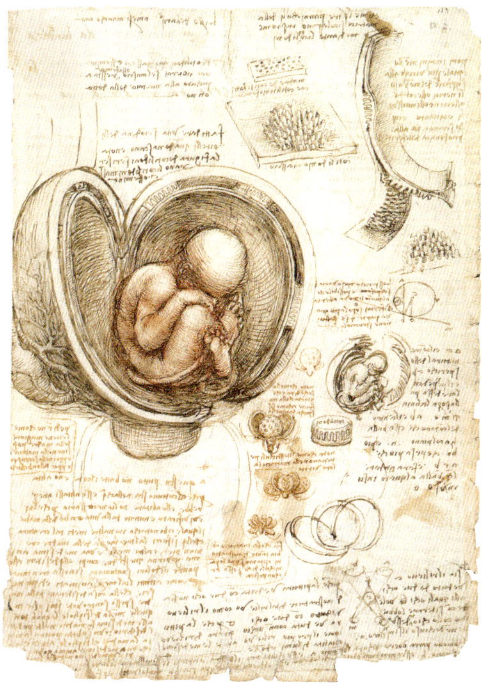

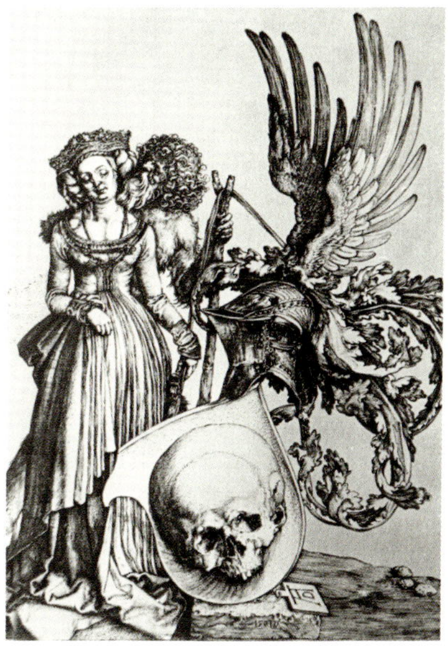

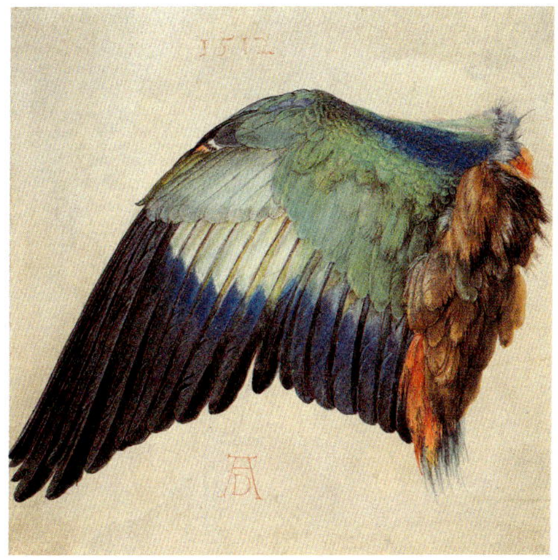

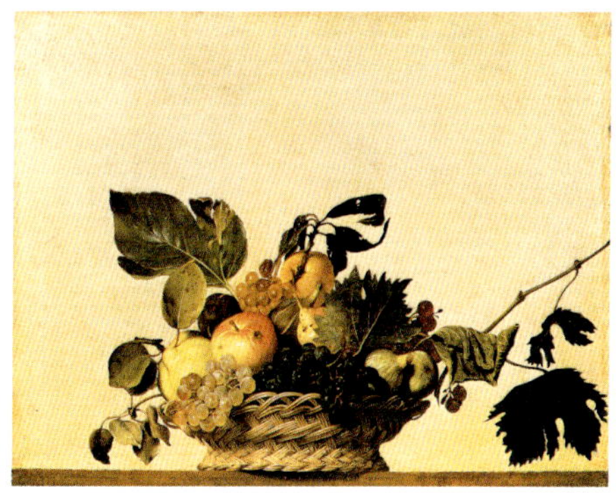

[1] TOP LEFT · **Mosaic with skull and level** · Pompeii, 1st century AD

[2] TOP CENTRE · **Mosaic of sea creatures** · Pompeii, 1st century AD

[3] TOP RIGHT · **Leonardo da Vinci** · ***Anatomical study of the human skull in sagittal section***, 1489 pen and ink over traces of black chalk on paper

[4] BELOW LEFT · **Leonardo da Vinci** · ***Studies of the foetus in the womb***, *c.* 1510–13 · pen, ink and wash over red chalk and traces of black chalk on paper

[5] BELOW CENTRE · **Albrecht Dürer** · ***Coat of Arms with a Skull***, 1503 · engraving on white laid paper

[6] BELOW CENTRE RIGHT · **Albrecht Dürer** ***Wing of a Blue Roller***, 1512 · watercolour and gouache on vellum

[7] BOTTOM · **Michelangelo Merisi da Caravaggio** ***Basket of Fruit***, *c.* 1599 · oil on canvas

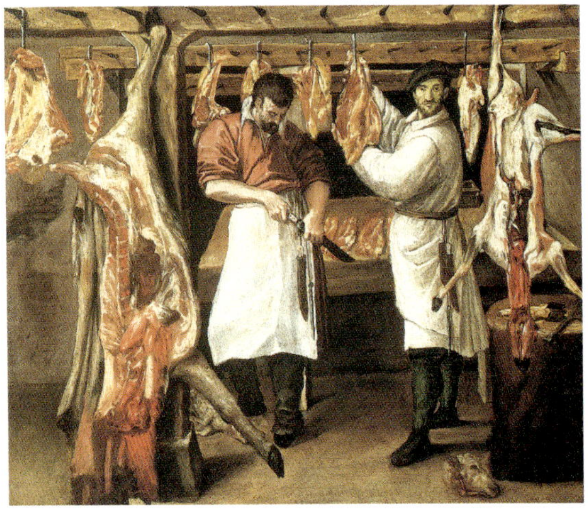

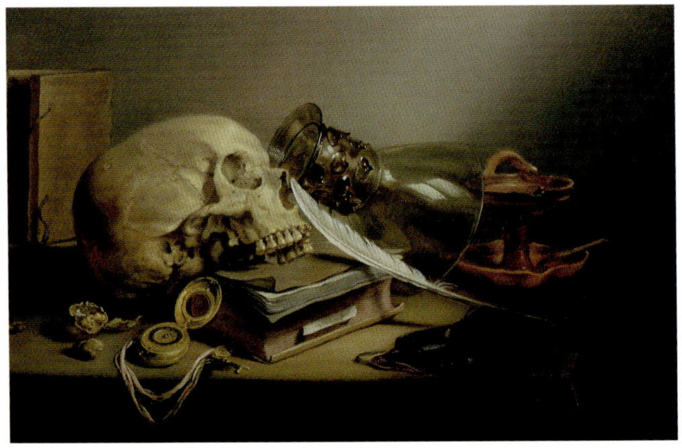

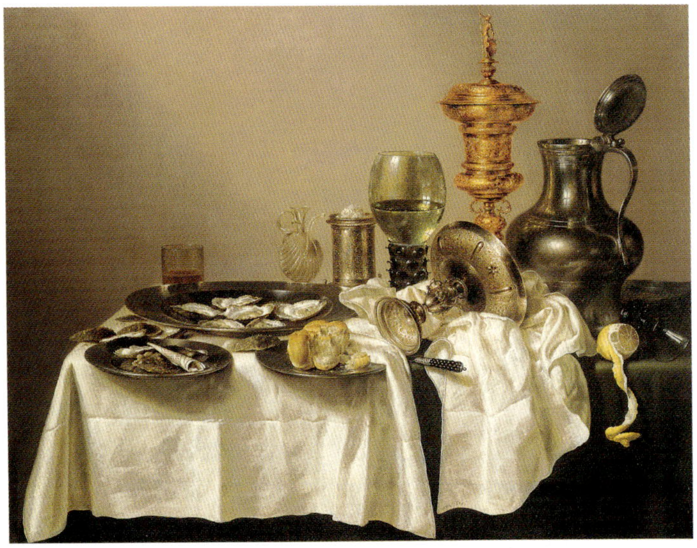

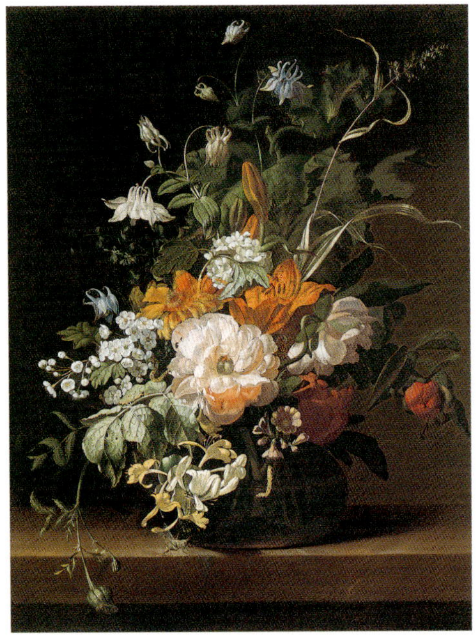

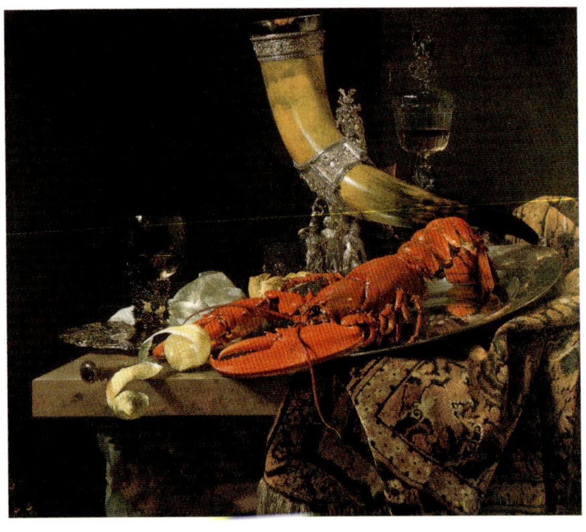

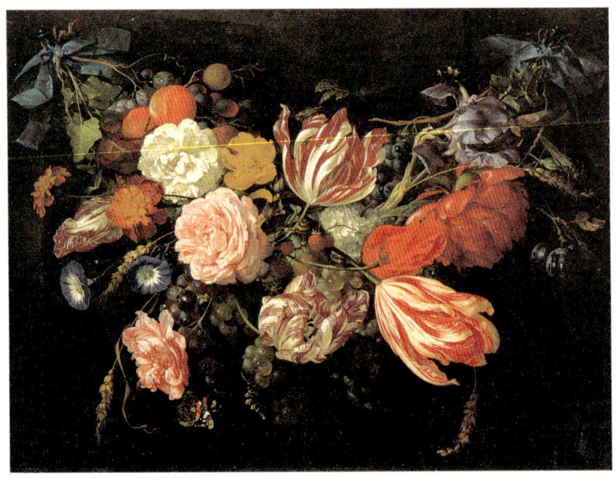

[8] TOP LEFT · Annibale Carracci · *The Butcher's Shop*, *c.* 1583 · oil on canvas

[9] TOP RIGHT · Pieter Claesz · *A Vanitas Still Life*, *c.* 1640 · oil on panel

[10] CENTRE LEFT · Willem Claesz Heda · *Still Life with Gilt Goblet*, 1635 · oil on panel

[11] CENTRE RIGHT · Rachel Ruysch · *Flowers in a Vase*, *c.* 1685 · oil on canvas

[12] BOTTOM LEFT · Willem Kalf · *Still Life with the Drinking-Horn*, *c.* 1653 · oil on canvas

[13] BOTTOM RIGHT · Jan Davidsz. de Heem · *Festoon with Flowers and Fruit*, *c.* 1660–70 · oil on panel

With his razor-sharp mind and surgical clarity of vision, Leonardo da Vinci (1452–1519) was among the first to turn his back on Christian dogma, trusting in the observable and measurable rather than a series of creation myths. His studies of the human body and other natural phenomena focus on mechanical and biological functions as opposed to symbolic or allegorical significance [**3, 4**]. Albrecht Dürer (1471–1528) also sought to deconstruct nature in order to discover its secrets [**6**], though he, like the majority of artists at the time, still utilized symbolism. One finds the same allegorical elements of his famous self-portrait – in which he holds a delicate flower between elongated fingers – in his *Coat of Arms with a Skull*, in which the figure of Death appears in disguise [**5**].

Early paintings in the style of the *nature morte* soon assumed other secular purposes. Wealthy patrons had their portraits painted alongside their possessions to communicate their fortune and power. The Medici dynasty in Florence included what many believe are oranges on their coat of arms; citrus fruits were very rare in Europe at the time and so signalled wealth and influence. Of course, moral and religious symbolism remained. With *The Butcher's Shop*, Annibale Carracci (1560–1609) painted not only an accurate representation of suspended animal carcasses, but also a naturalistic portrayal that reminded viewers of their own essential meatiness [**8**]. The painting acted as a *memento mori*, recalling viewers to their own mortality.

The incredible skill demonstrated in the still lifes of Caravaggio (1571–1610) positioned the form to be of unique merit because it offered a space for artistic experimentation, unlike portraiture, for example. His *Basket of Fruit* is considered one of the most exquisite still lifes of all time for its groundbreaking handling of light (despite its lack of religious content, the painting found its way into the collection of Cardinal Borromeo) [**7**]. The Protestant Reformation and its loathing of the literal depiction of religious subjects ensured that the *nature morte* had come into its own by the early sixteenth century. Following Caravaggio's lead, Dutch and Flemish artists took up the still life with as much zeal as their countrymen did the growing of tulips, embracing with a vengeance the form's potential for conveying allegorical meanings and moralizing messages.

The *vanitas* still life was one of the results. This type of still life featured worldly possessions, as well as flora and fauna, in a commentary that paired symbols of the joys of a life well lived with symbols of death, usually a fresh or rotting skull [**9**]. If not a skull, then a watch, hourglass or burning candle could be inserted into the scene to remind viewers of their own eventual death and to encourage them to uphold their integrity in this world before meeting the harsh judgment of their divine maker in the next. Symbolism infused almost every object featured in these works. Centuries before Damien Hirst (1965–), artists painted butterflies as symbols of transformation and resurrection; ants for hard work (long before Salvador Dalí [1904–89] deployed them as signifiers of the inevitability of change and decay); pearls for virginity; and broken vessels for lost innocence. Flowers, fruit, meat and shellfish, ever on the verge of wilting or spoiling, remained common motifs. Contemporary viewers could read these paintings for their coded meanings as easily as they could read the Biblical scenes that adorned their local church or cathedral.

Rembrandt (1606–69), one of the most outstanding Dutch artists of the period, often experimented with the motifs of the still life, and his *Flayed Ox* takes Carracci's *Butcher's Shop* a step further in terms of realism [**20**]. The starkness of the skinned animal carcass in turn influenced later artists, including Goya (1746–1828) and eventually Francis Bacon (1909–1992). Rembrandt, a master draughtsman, also produced very fine and subtle etchings such as *The Shell* (1650). At the time, shells and other curios were exceedingly popular as decorative objects in Europe – the more exotic the better. A number of women painters also looked to the interior of the home for inspiration. Judith Leyster (1609–60) painted a few highly esteemed works before marriage and domestic duties cut short her career; Rachel Ruysch (1664–1750) managed to continue to paint right up until

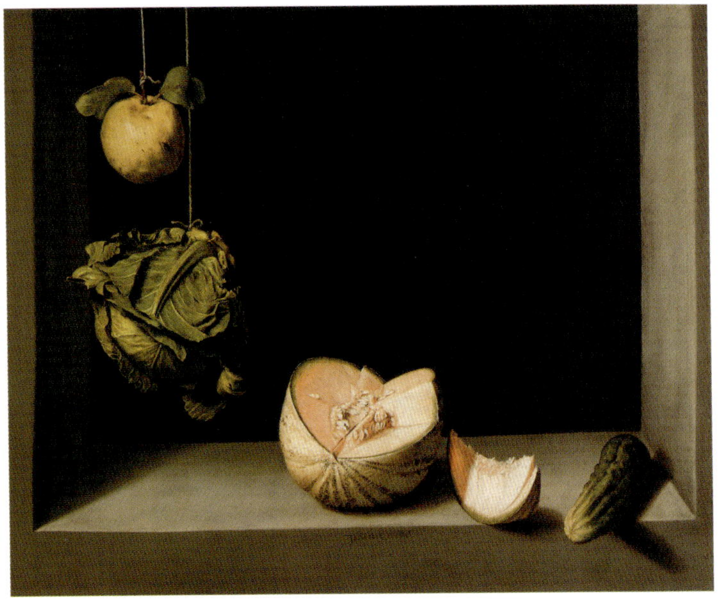

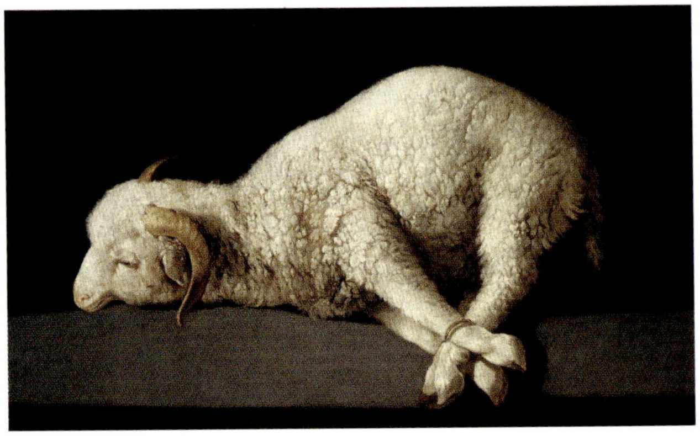

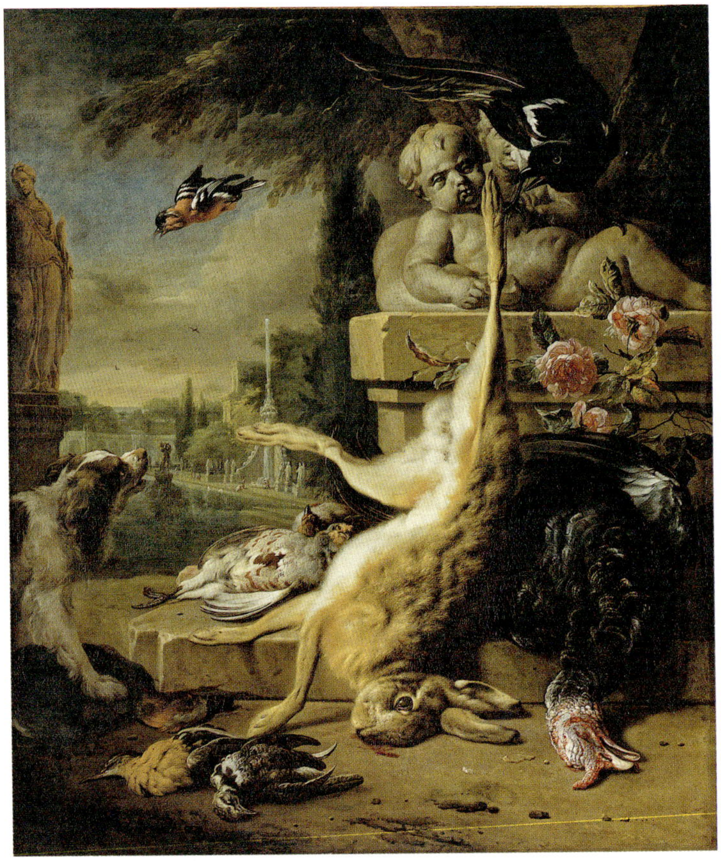

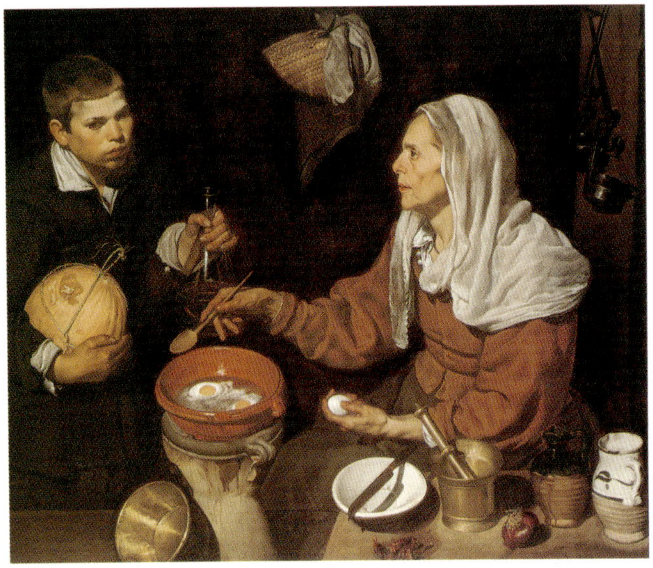

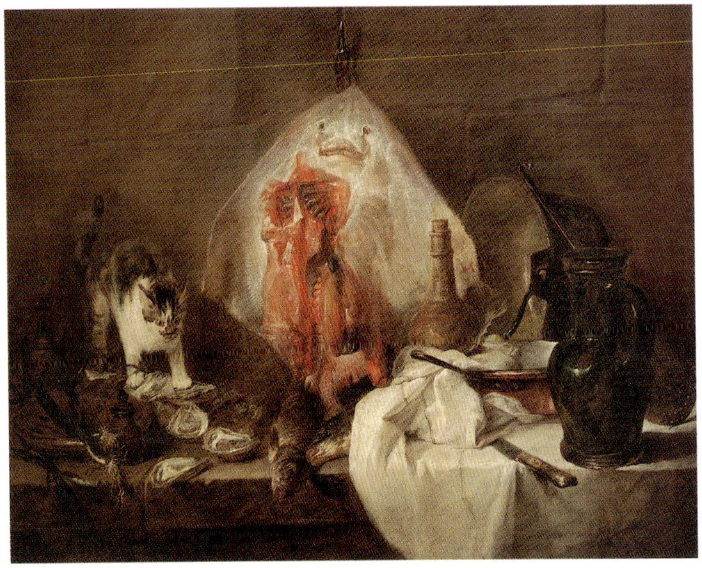

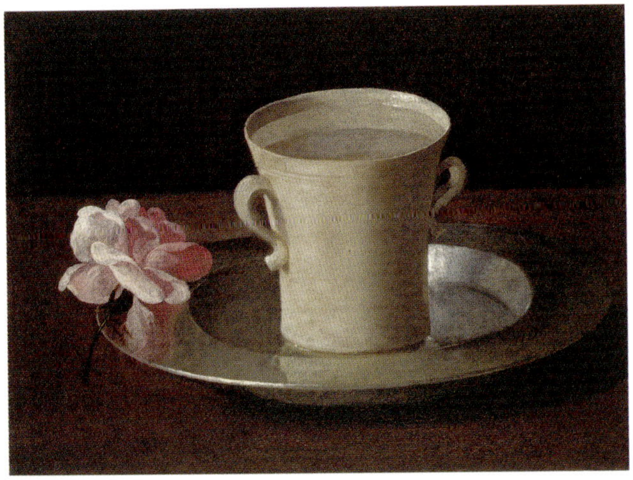

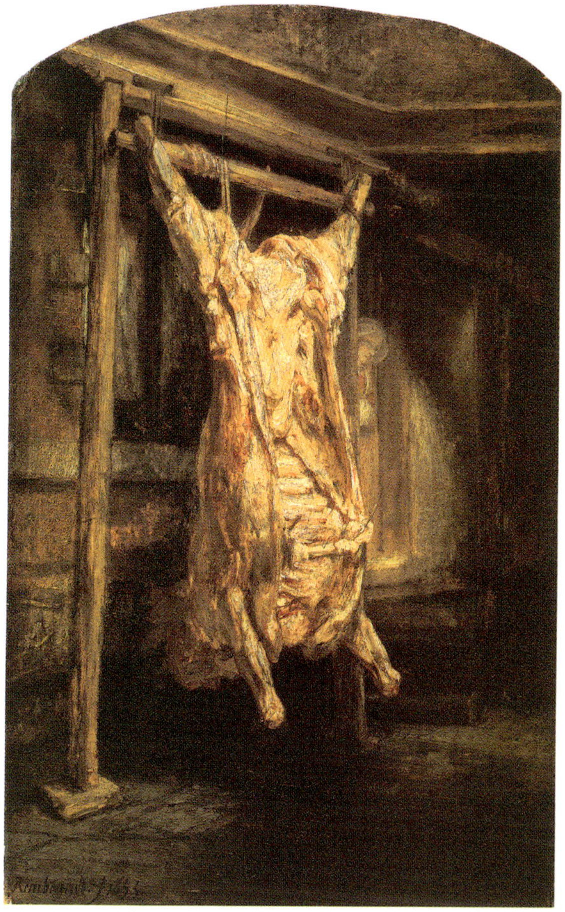

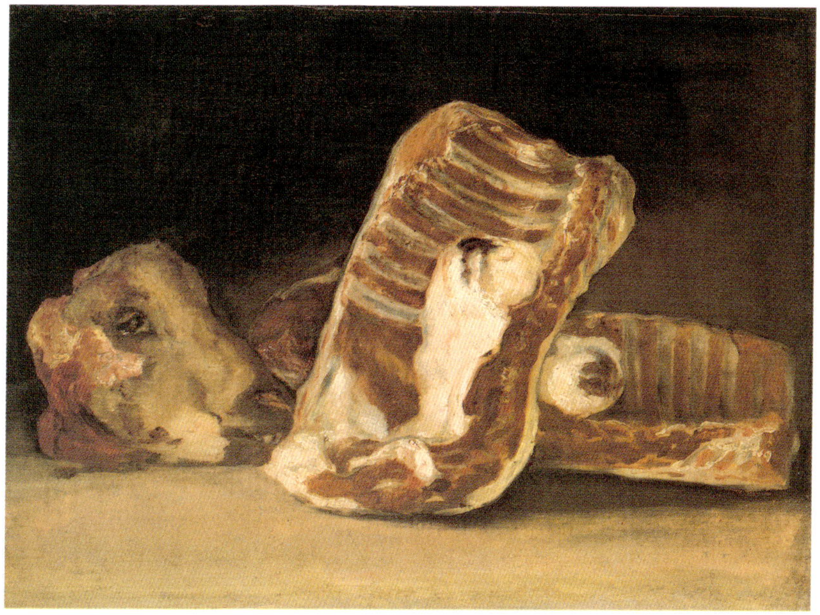

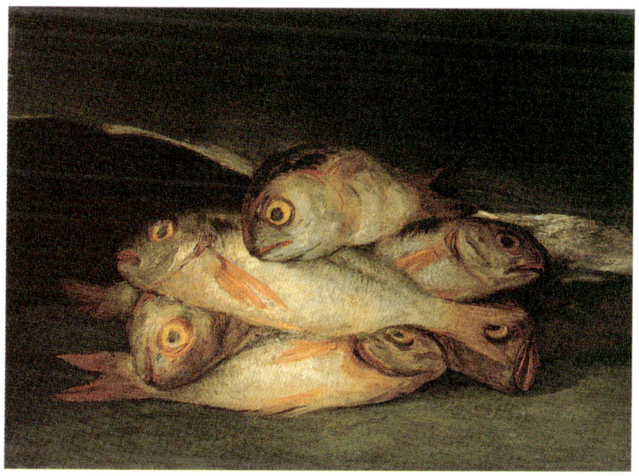

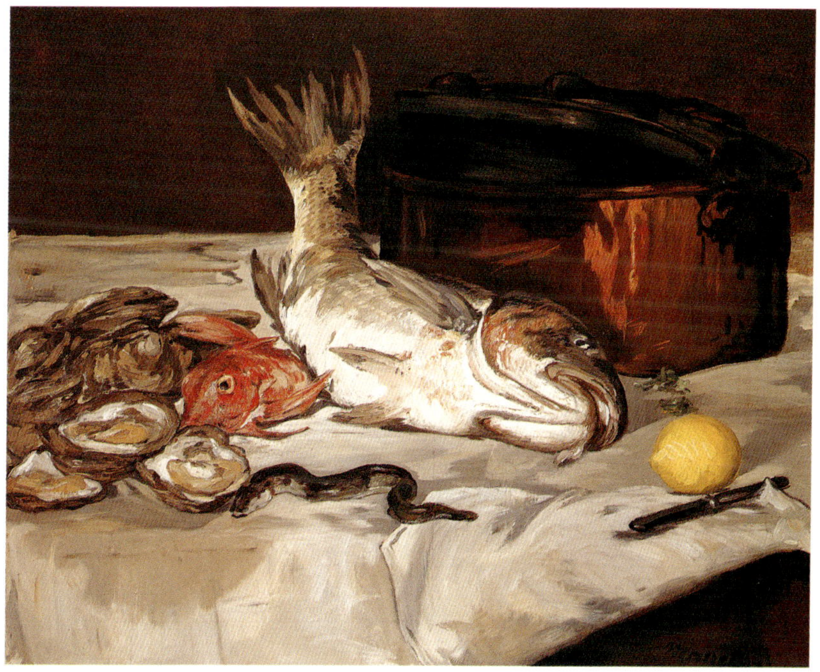

[14] OPPOSITE TOP LEFT · Juan Sánchez Cotán · *Still Life with Quince, Cabbage, Melon and Cucumber*, 1602 oil on canvas

[15] OPPOSITE TOP RIGHT · Francisco de Zurbarán *Agnus Dei*, 1635–40 · oil on canvas

[16] OPPOSITE CENTRE LEFT · Diego Velázquez · *An Old Woman Cooking Eggs*, 1618 · oil on canvas

[17] OPPOSITE CENTRE RIGHT · Jan Weenix · *Dead Hare and Dog*, 1717 · oil on canvas

[18] OPPOSITE BOTTOM LEFT · Jean-Baptiste-Siméon Chardin · *The Skate*, 1725–26 · oil on canvas

[19] OPPOSITE BOTTOM RIGHT · Francisco de Zurbarán *A Cup of Water and a Rose*, *c.* 1630 · oil on canvas

[20] TOP LEFT · Rembrandt van Rijn · *The Flayed Ox*, 1655 · oil on panel

[21] TOP RIGHT · Francisco de Goya · *A Butcher's Counter*, 1810–12 · oil on canvas

[22] BOTTOM LEFT · Francisco de Goya · *Still Life with Golden Bream*, 1808–12 · oil on canvas

[23] BOTTOM RIGHT · Édouard Manet · *Fish* (*Still Life*), 1864 · oil on canvas

her death [11]. It was obviously much more difficult for women to paint at this time and all the more extraordinary that several did manage to do so, including Leyster, Ruysch and Maria van Oosterwyck (1630–93).

From here, still lifes – initially piles of fish or meat, fruit or flowers – became increasingly complex in their composition. Previously artists had predominantly painted works on commission, which limited their creative licence in the composition of the resulting works. Now a new middle-class market existed – typified by the merchant class of the Low Countries – whose purchasers were happy to select from existing works executed to the artist's own preference. Artists took this novel opportunity to experiment with lighting, perspective, texture and colour in these commercial works. They carefully selected and arranged objects into aesthetically pleasing groupings that would allow for the greatest range of tones in the finished work; it was generally believed that the more realistic the rendering, the greater the skill of the artist. These advances in painting techniques meant that the still lifes being produced during the seventeenth century were more convincing than ever before.

It was, perhaps unexpectedly, in Protestant Northern Europe that the *pronk* still life developed, a composition featuring objects chosen as conspicuous indicators of their owner's wealth, for example, gold and silverware, Persian cloth and other rare household goods. In contrast, painters in Catholic Spain, notably Velázquez (1599–1660) and Zurbarán (1598–1664), were creating ever more minimal and emotionally intense works [**14, 15, 16**]. Called *bodegones* – after the Spanish word for pantry or tavern – these humble scenes depicted austerity rather than ostentation, with dead animals instead of cooked meat, and fresh fruit and vegetables as opposed to extravagant desserts.

In the eighteenth century, the emergence of a high bourgeois style saw the decline of overt moral symbolism in painting. Many market-minded painters were producing still lifes, particularly flower canvases, which they did by the cartload in order to meet demand among the rising middle class and the aristocracy. Some artists, such as Jean-Baptiste-Siméon Chardin (1699–1779), combined Rococo excess with the acute observation of natural objects, be they bowls of flowers or, as in *The Skate*, freshly caught seafood [**18**]. The growing influence of the French Academy and its hierarchy of painting genres further sidelined the still life; it came last after, in increasing order of precedence, animal painting, landscape painting, genre painting, portraiture and history painting. The inanimate scenes of the still life, as exemplified by Jan Weenix's *Dead Hare and Dog*, were considered mere technical exercises for the artist looking to practise before making works further up the hierarchy of genres [**17**].

The industrial revolution saw vast numbers of people depart the countryside for the promise of employment in rapidly expanding urban areas. How people lived changed radically, as did their attitudes to the once all powerful forces of Church and State. Seeing freedom and revolution in America and France, individuals elsewhere began to believe that their lives could improve; that it might be possible to enjoy living on the earth, rather than waiting until they were interned in it. This growing consciousness among the educated middle class, if not the majority of people, demanded a new politics as well as a new art. Works such as those by Goya, including *A Butcher's Counter* [**21**] and *Still Life with Golden Bream* [**22**], were clear calls to look upon the abundance yet transience of life without flinching. In Japan, a world away, Katsushika Hokusai (1760–1849) carved out a name for himself as a printmaker and painter. Prints of his flowers such as *Chrysanthemums and Bee* were circulated among European artists, although *The Great Wave at Kanagawa* remains his best-known work [**34**].

In Victorian Britain, the symbolism of objects became both commonplace and banal. The Victorians codified the meaning of flowers as elaborately as the courting rituals of peacocks. Each flower had its own particular meaning so that if a man gave a woman a flower she would likely understand its significance. Red roses spoke of true love; hyacinths

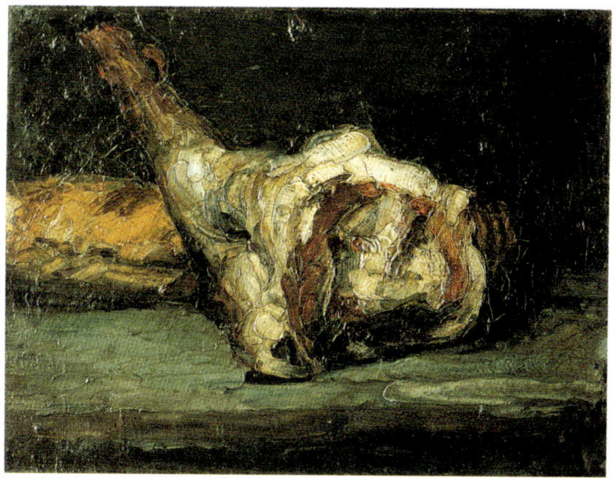

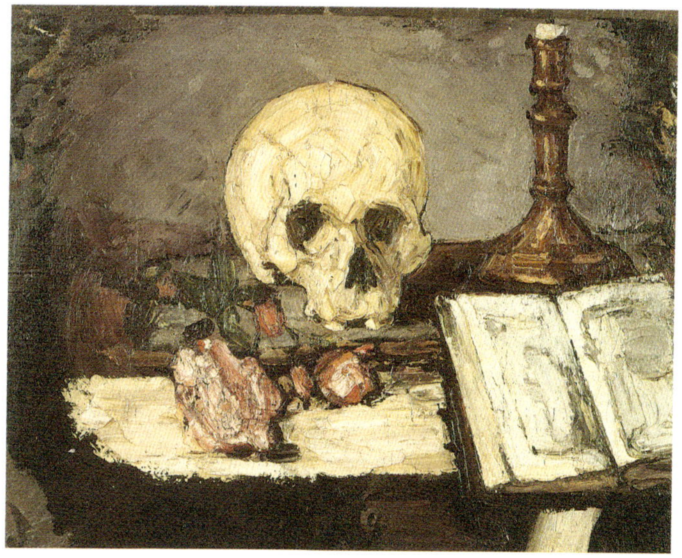

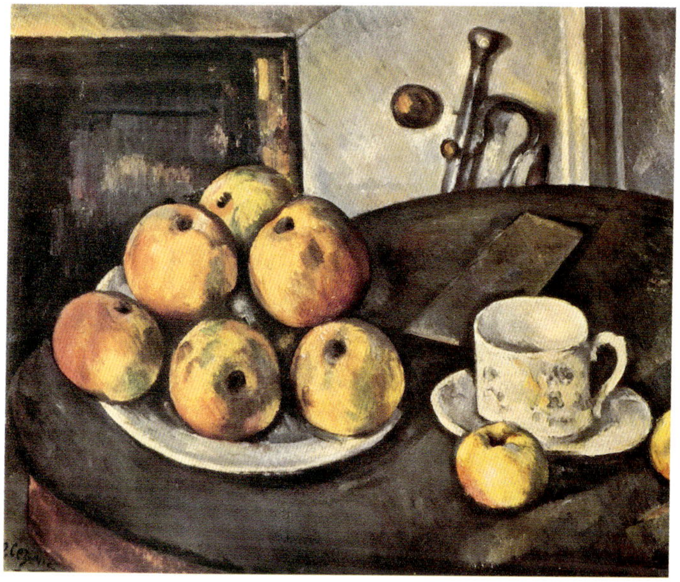

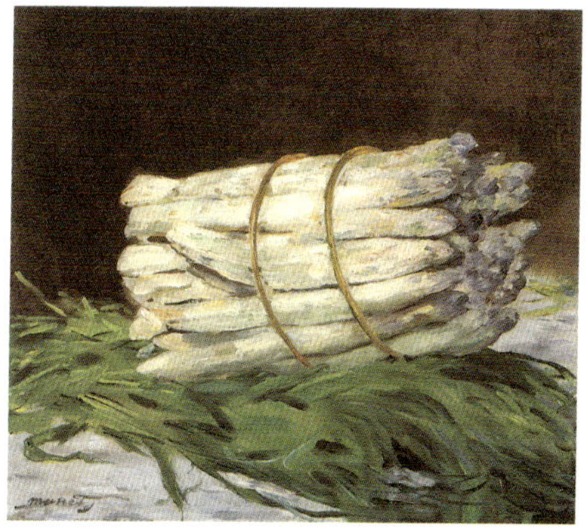

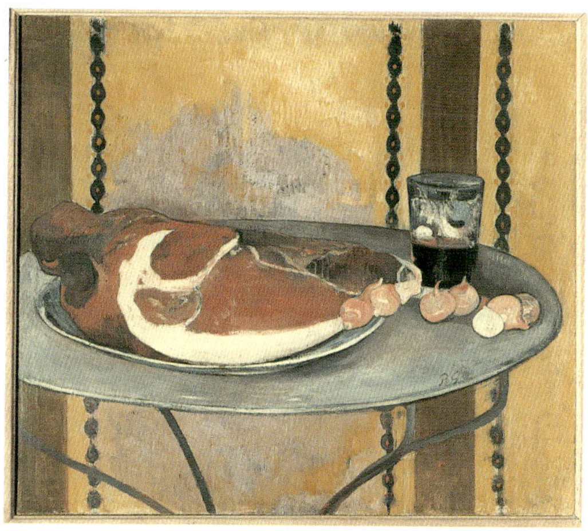

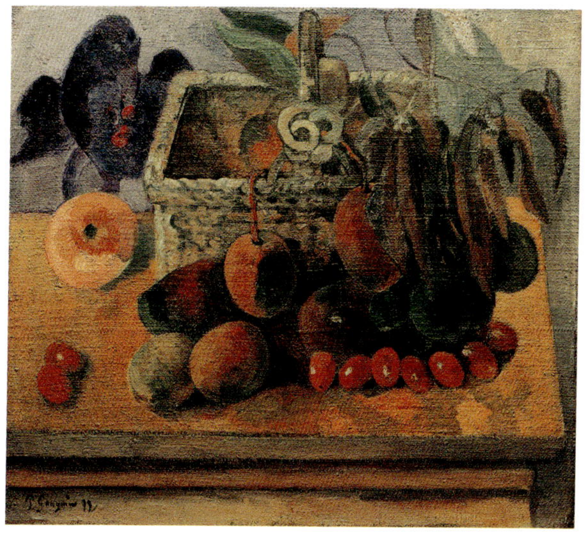

[24] TOP LEFT · Paul Cézanne · *Still Life with Leg of Mutton and Bread*, 1865 · oil on canvas

[25] TOP RIGHT · Paul Cézanne · *Still Life with Skull and Candlestick*, *c.* 1866 · oil on canvas

[26] CENTRE LEFT · Paul Cézanne · *Still Life with Apples*, 1890–94 · oil on canvas

[27] CENTRE RIGHT · Édouard Manet · *Bunch of Asparagus*, 1880 · oil on canvas

[28] BOTTOM LEFT · Paul Gauguin · *The Ham*, 1889 oil on canvas

[29] BOTTOM RIGHT · Paul Gauguin · *Still Life with Exotic Fruit* · oil on canvas

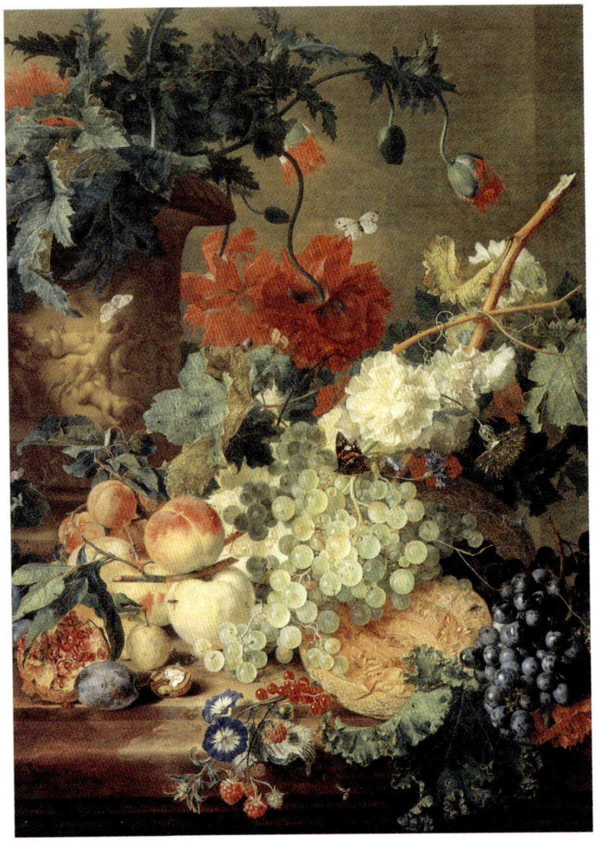

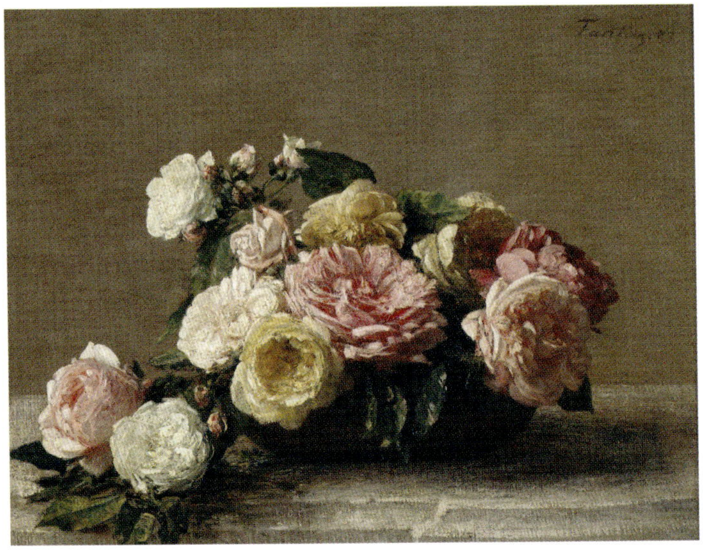

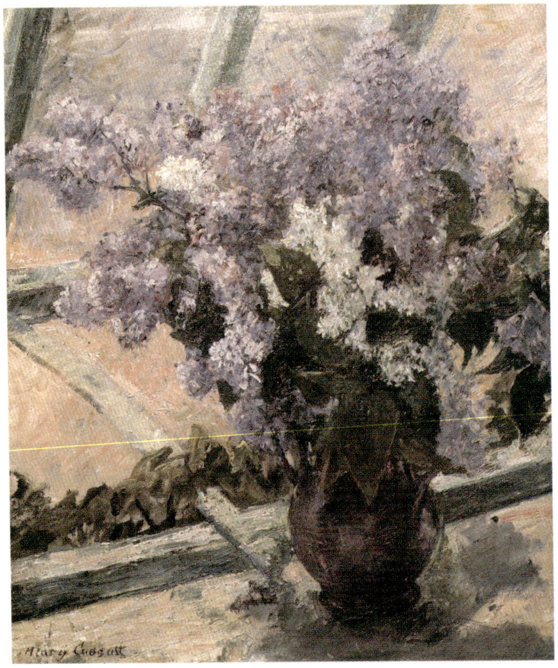

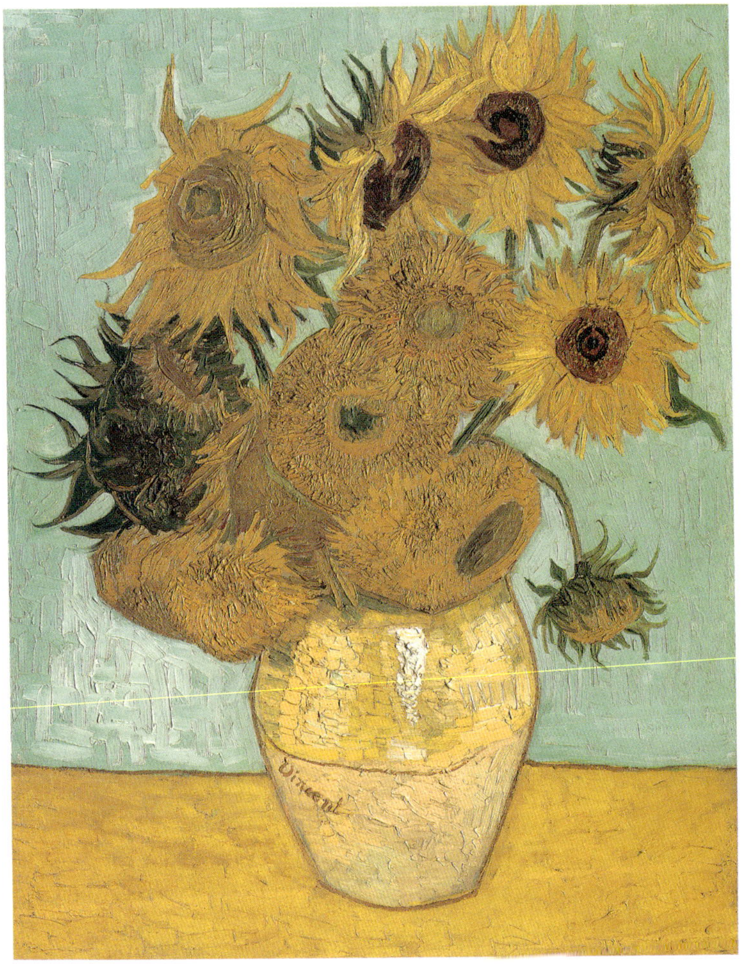

[30] TOP LEFT · Jan van Huysum · *Fruit and Flowers*, early 1720s · oil on mahogany panel

[31] TOP RIGHT · Henri Fantin-Latour · *Roses in a Bowl*, 1882 · oil on canvas

[32] BOTTOM LEFT · Mary Cassatt · *Lilacs in a Window*, *c.* 1880 · oil on canvas

[33] BOTTOM RIGHT · Vincent van Gogh · *Twelve Sunflowers in a Vase*, 1888 · oil on canvas

[34] OPPOSITE TOP · Katsushika Hokusai *Chrysanthemums and Bee*, *c.* 1833–34 colour woodblock print

[35] OPPOSITE LEFT · Édouard Manet · *A Pink Rose and a Yellow Rose*, 1882 · oil on canvas

[36] OPPOSITE RIGHT · Charles Demuth · *Calla Lilies (Bert Savoy)*, 1926 · oil on composition board

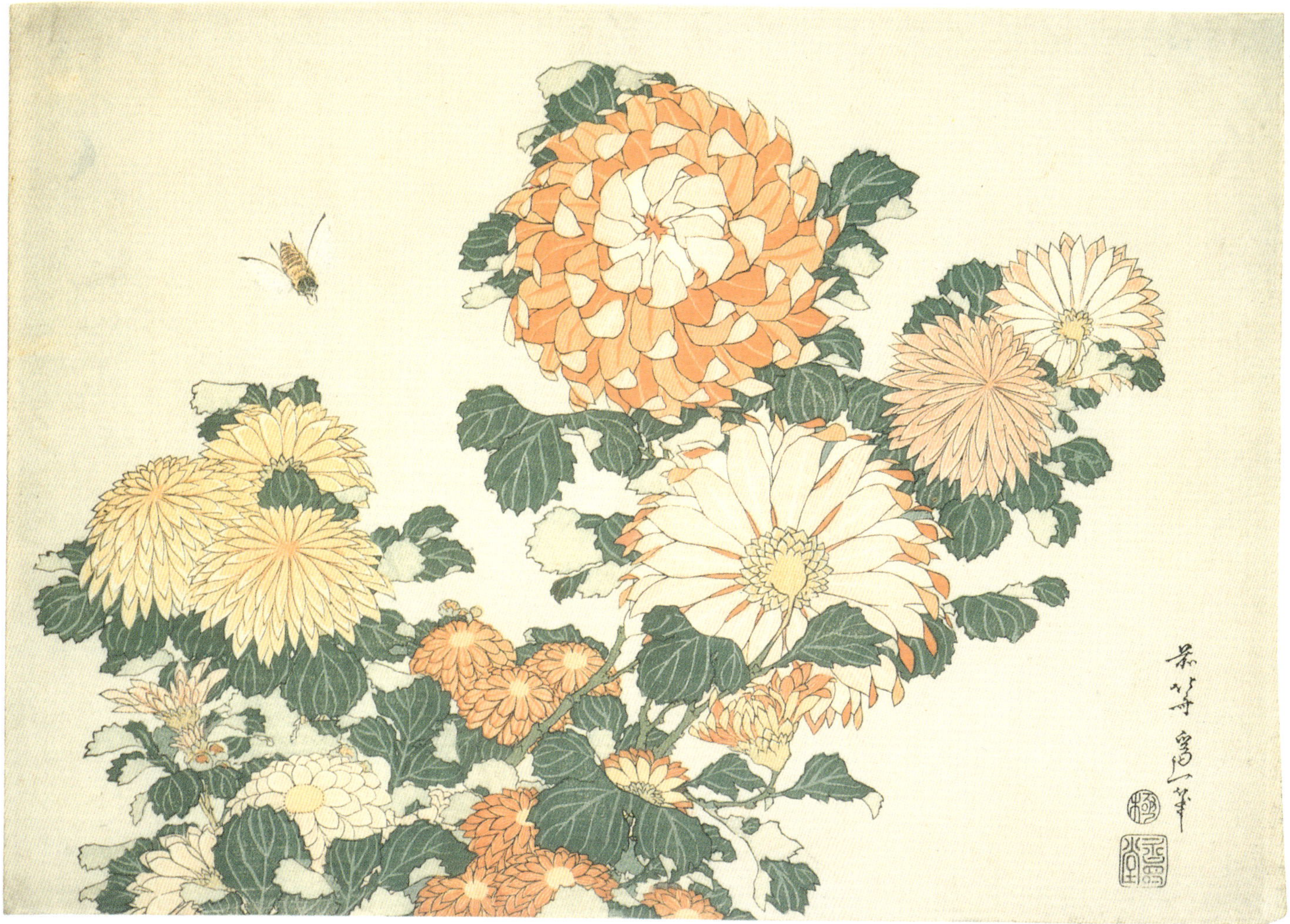

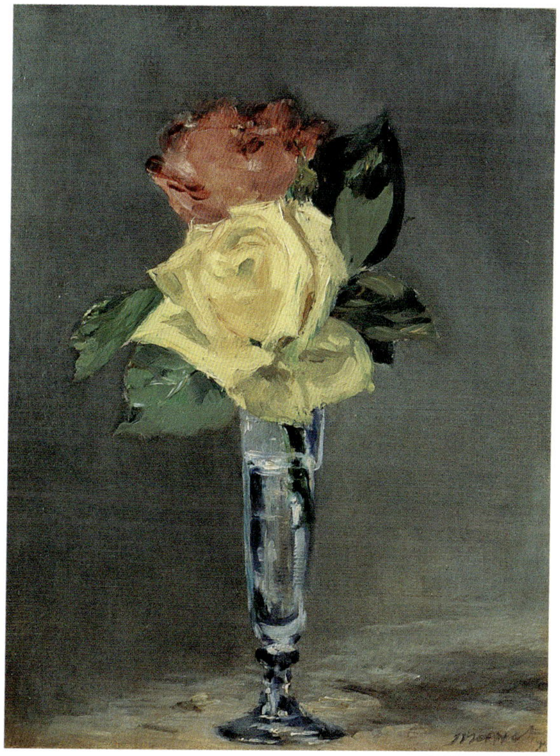

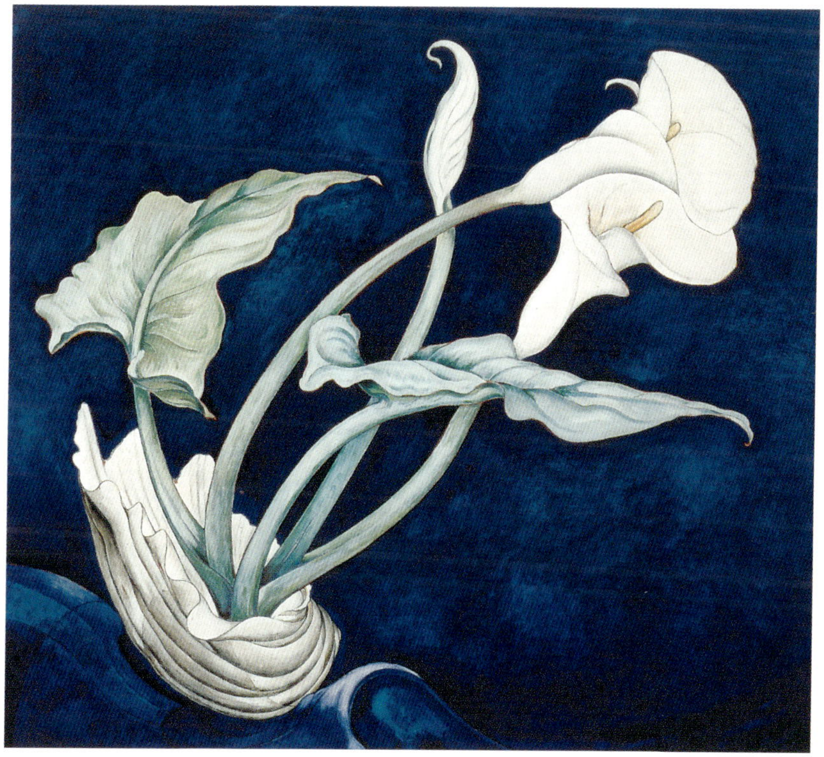

said 'forgive me'. To give a lady a bouquet of sunflowers indicated that the sender thought she was haughty. The floral bouquets of Henri Fantin-Latour (1836–1904), a French painter introduced by James Abbott McNeill Whistler to Britain, proved so popular that few of his works were ever shown in his homeland, where he had virtually no reputation [**31**].

During the second half of the nineteenth century, a new wave of artists in Paris arose to resist the rigid hierarchy of the French Academy and pioneer exciting new stylistic paths for painting. In his paintings of modern life, Édouard Manet (1832–83) blurred the lines between genres. His quiet still lifes include *Fish (Still Life)* [**21**] and *Bunch of Asparagus* [**28**]. The Impressionists' interest in effects of light and their pioneering use of loose brushwork made for some lively object studies. The still lifes of Monet, Renoir and Pissarro are lesser known than their vivid landscapes and portrayals of buzzing Parisian life but offer an intriguing insight into the development of the tradition. Mary Cassatt (1844–1926), an American artist living mainly in France, was one of the few women to exhibit with the Impressionists. Her *Lilacs in a Window* is a rare still life within her *oeuvre* [**32**].

Both reacting against and developing out of Impressionism, Paul Gauguin (1848–1903) enlivened the genre with his bold and vibrant palette. *The Ham* contains echoes of a work by Dutch painter Meijer de Haan (1852–95) while still being executed in the less naturalistic, more primitive style favoured by Gauguin [**28**]. Vincent van Gogh (1853–90) had a stormy relationship with Gauguin and, indeed, the art world in general. He channelled his turbulent emotions into his unorthodox compositions, and his unique style of painting, with its vigorous, swirling strokes, only became widely acclaimed and celebrated after his death. His series of sunflowers are now recognized for their then radical vision [**33**]. Paul Cézanne (1839–1906) also developed a distinctive painting technique with an emphasis on mass and structure that paved the way to abstraction. His career saw him move from making dark and moody works such as *Still Life of a Leg of Mutton and Bread* [**24**] and *Still Life with Skull and Candlestick* [**25**] to the utterly modern and still remarkably fresh *Still Life with Apples* [**26**]. Cézanne's vision of life in the full glare of the sun heralded not only a new century, but also a new way of looking at and making art.

In the first decade of the twentieth century, Paris remained the centre of the art world and was attracting a whole new generation of radical artists. Pablo Picasso (1881–1973) and Georges Braque (1882–1963) took inspiration from Cézanne as they pioneered Cubism in their portraits and still lifes. Under their influence, Juan Gris (1887–1927) and Paul Klee (1879–1940) also experimented with Cubism and, as had their predecessors, found the still life to be an accommodating genre for experimentation [**38, 39**]. These artists predominantly painted still lifes featuring everyday objects; the floral still life had to wait for American artists Georgia O'Keeffe (1887–1986) and Charles Demuth (1883–1935) for a resurgence. Sensually rendered flowers are a central motif in many of their paintings [**36**]. O'Keeffe painted animal bones and Southwestern landscapes, as well as flowers, and in *Ram's Head, White Hollyhock & Little Hills* she combined all three [**37**]. The European artist most closely associated with still-life painting in the twentieth century was Giorgio Morandi (1890–1964). His carefully crafted depictions of bottles – muted tonal poems of greys, creams and every shade of beige that are nevertheless full of life – were a precursor to the minimalism of the 1960s.

As the 1960s began, America came to question itself and its military involvement in Vietnam. Bodies in coffins appeared nightly on the news and a mood of death hovered over the country. In 1964 Andy Warhol and his Factory made over nine hundred prints of *Flowers*, a tight close-up of a bouquet of hibiscus blossoms, which he had appropriated from a photograph taken by Patricia Caulfield (she sued him for its unauthorized use). Warhol reimagined the original source at great scale and in a variety of colour schemes and sizes [**43**]. His *Flowers* are often read as bright, cheerful expressions of the 1960s peace generation, but those close to the artist understood they had a darker resonance.

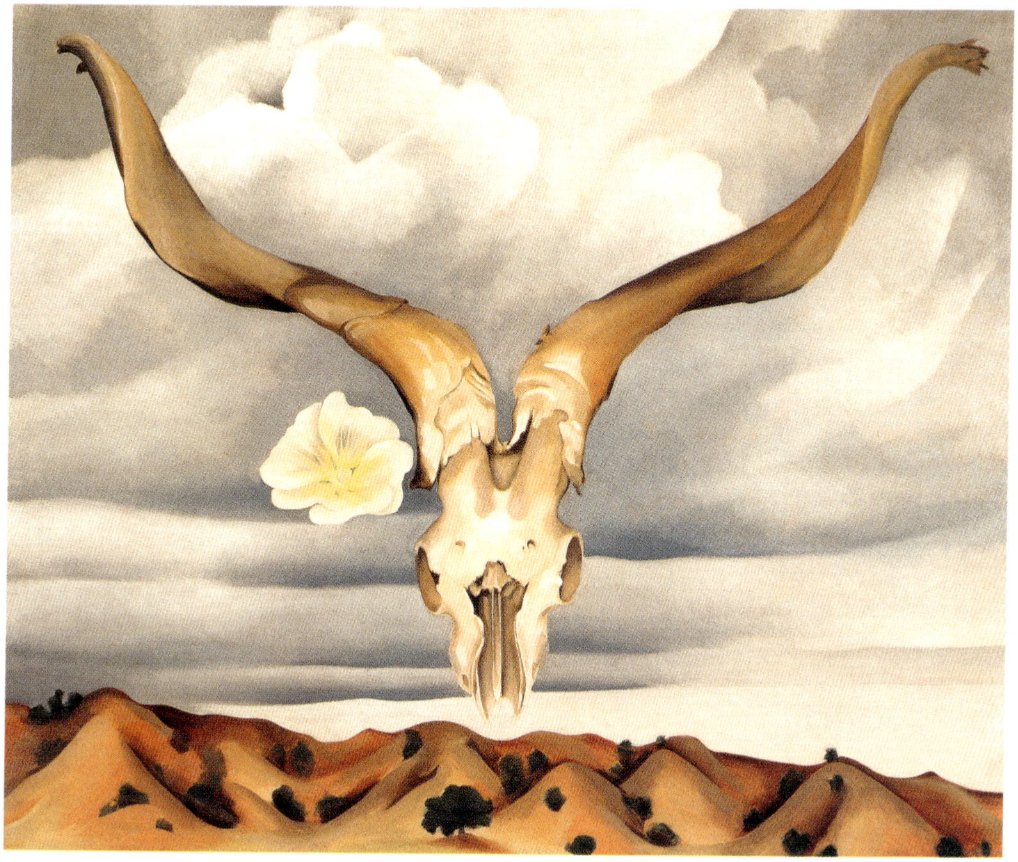

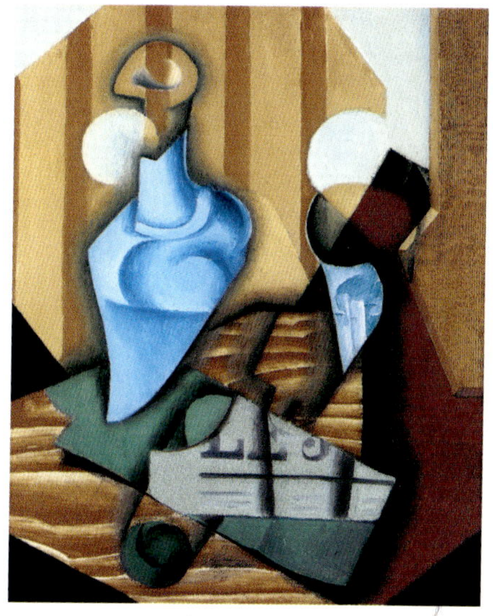

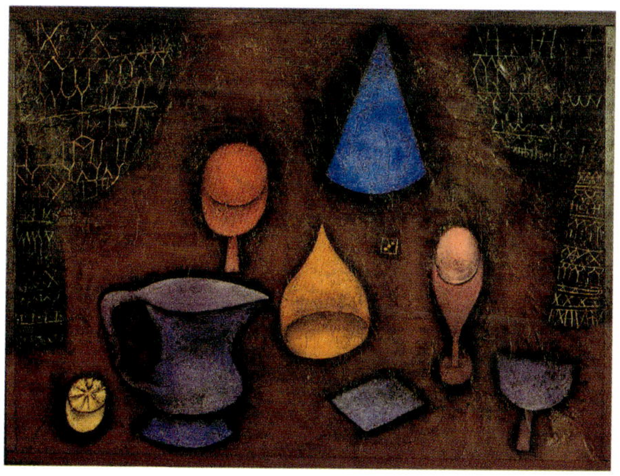

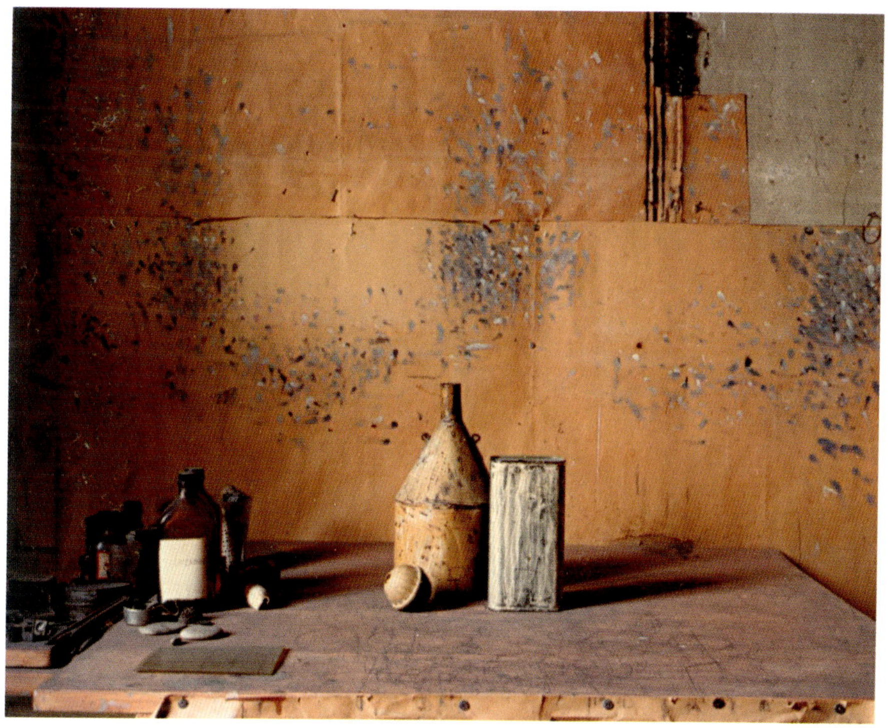

[37] TOP LEFT · Georgia O'Keeffe · *Ram's Head, White Hollyhock & Little Hills*, 1935 · oil on canvas
[38] TOP RIGHT · Juan Gris · *Still Life with Bottle and Glass*, 1914 · oil and collage on canvas
[39] BOTTOM LEFT · Paul Klee · *Still Life (Jars, Fruit, Easter Egg, and Curtains*, 1927 · oil on plaster
[40] BOTTOM RIGHT · Luigi Ghirri · *Bologna – Atelier di Giorgio Morandi*, 1989–90 · project print

In the words of Warhol's assistant Ronnie Cutrone: 'Don't forget, at that time, there was flower power and flower children. We were the roots, the dark roots.... So when Warhol and that whole scene made *Flowers*, it reflected the urban, dark, death side of that whole movement....'

Other major American artists of this generation were working within the tradition of the still life. Ellsworth Kelly (1933–) created a series of *nature morte* studies in the early 1970s. In these superb drawings of leaves and flowers, he removed any residual prettiness or suggestion that nature might be polite or charming, stripping it down to mere pencil lines and making only minimal use of flat colours. What these works have in common is a response to death's immensity as an all pervading background noise to daily life. The second generation Abstract Expressionist painter Joan Mitchell (1925–92) was fascinated by the power of flower imagery, not as domestic décor but as a metaphor for temporality. From 1967 until her death, flowers remained a preferred subject **[43]**. She did not shy away from the comparison of her works with those of Van Gogh and once said, 'If I see a sunflower drooping, I can droop with it...and I draw it, and feel it until its death.' During the late 1970s and 1980s, the New York-based photographer Robert Mapplethorpe revisited the flower as a metaphor for life, love, sex and death. The politics of life and death were very much at play during the Reagan years, what with fears of nuclear engagement with the Soviet Union and the ever-increasing spread of HIV/AIDS. In order to raise national awareness and encourage investment in treatments for the disease, members of the organization ACT UP (AIDS Coalition to Unleash Power) staged die-ins on Wall Street, in churches and at government offices. Mapplethorpe's flowers, frozen in time, remain some of the most important works of the decade **[42]**. These exquisite images of calla lilies, orchids, irises and tulips are often as erotically charged as his more controversial photographs of men engaged in acts of sado-masochism. Both his black-and-white and colour photographs of flowers became powerful reminders of the devastation wreaked by the HIV/AIDS pandemic. Not only did many of the artist's friends die of the disease, and receive their own floral tributes, but Mapplethorpe also succumbed to the illness in 1989.

In the twenty-first century, most contemporary artists are not making overtly political art, or at least less often – Leon Golub was one of the main exceptions – as they know that it is not likely to effect any real change, except possibly to their reputation and the price of their works. Politically charged imagery in art can seem anticlimactic or, worse, trite now that we live in a world of twenty-four-hour news cycles forever showing the very worst that humans can inflict on one another. What images can artists make to confront or compare with the photographs of torture in Abu Ghraib? Amid all this violence, death as the universal human condition has somehow faded from view. Instead death is sensationalized and in the process made alien; it has become the fate of others, the fate of those less fortunate. It is this trend that over the last decade has perhaps prompted so many contemporary artists to turn to the *nature morte* and its more nuanced representation of and allusions to death. Whether consciously or not, many artists are producing works in a variety of media that directly connect with those metaphors first explored in traditional still-life painting. These works, examples of which are collected in the following chapters, each possess a mortal edge (but not a moral one), often velvet-covered and not usually obvious at first sight, but one that hints at death – always around the corner, in the next mark, or slightly out of frame.

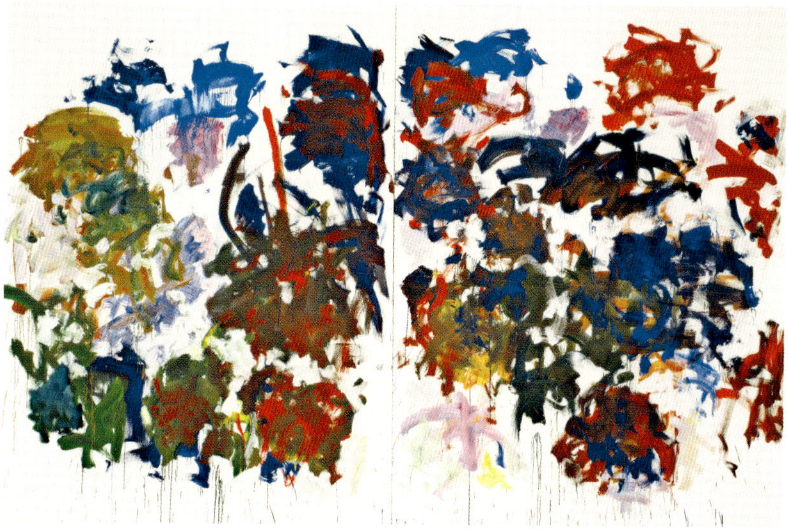

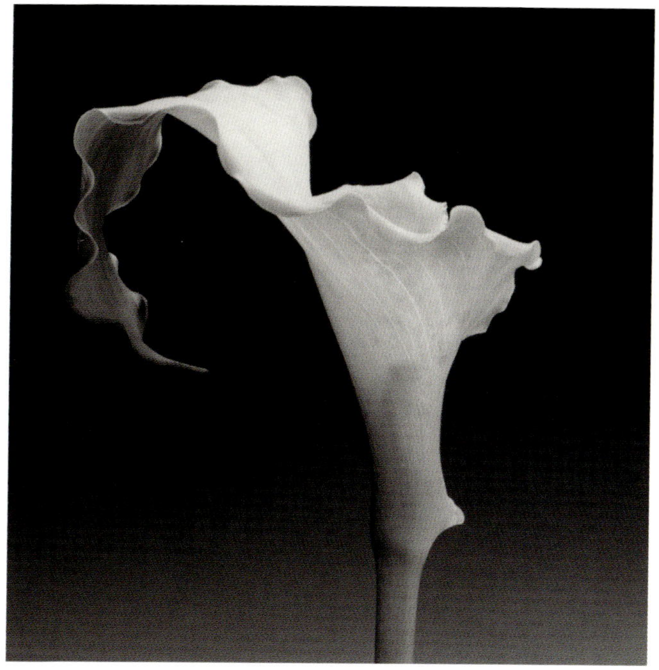

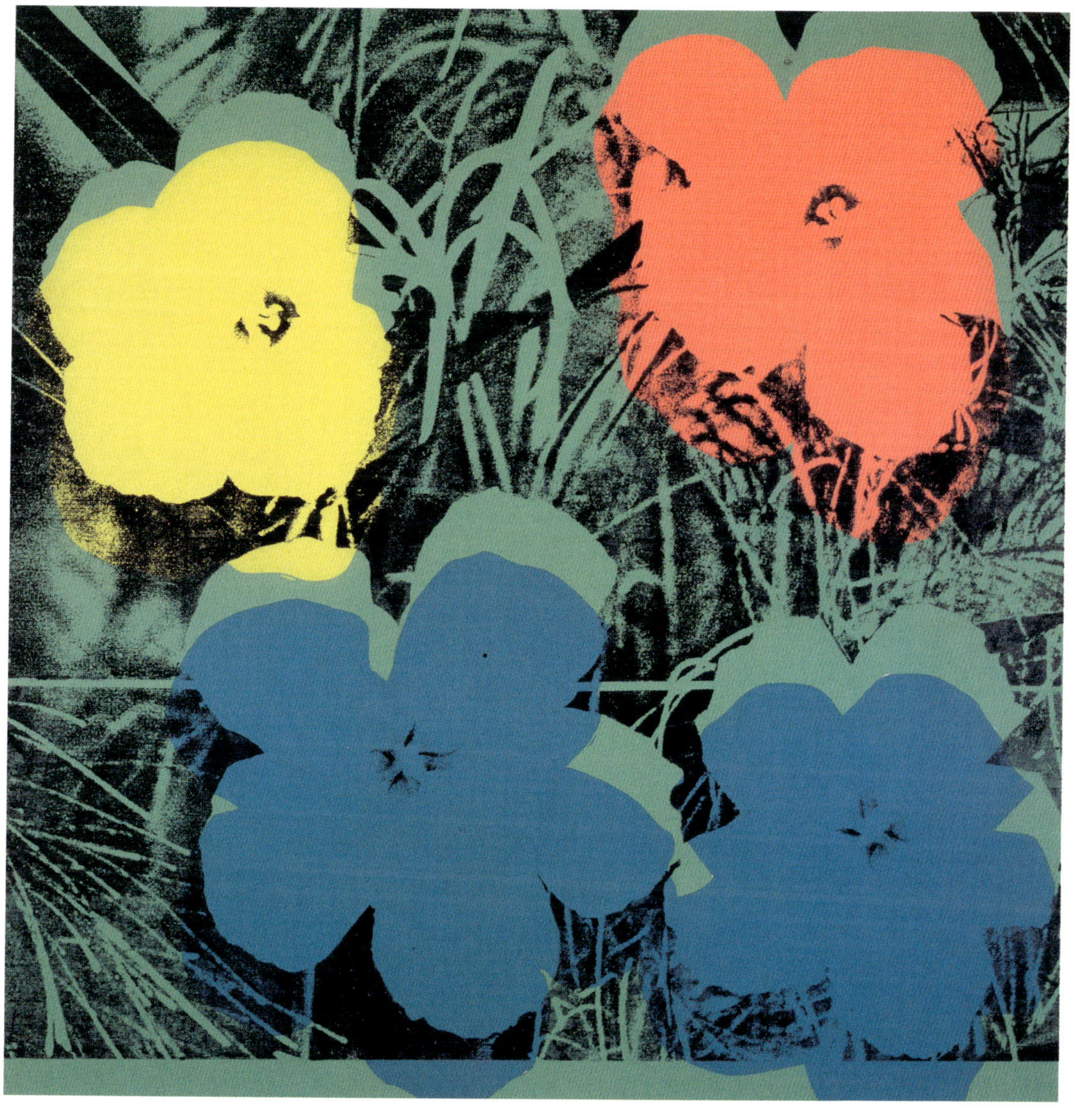

[41] TOP LEFT · Joan Mitchell · *Sunflowers*, 1990–91 · oil on canvas, diptych

[42] TOP RIGHT · Robert Mapplethorpe · *Calla Lily*, *c.* 1988 · gelatin silver print

[43] BOTTOM LEFT · Andy Warhol · *Ten-Foot Flowers*, 1967 · silkscreen ink, acrylic paint on canvas

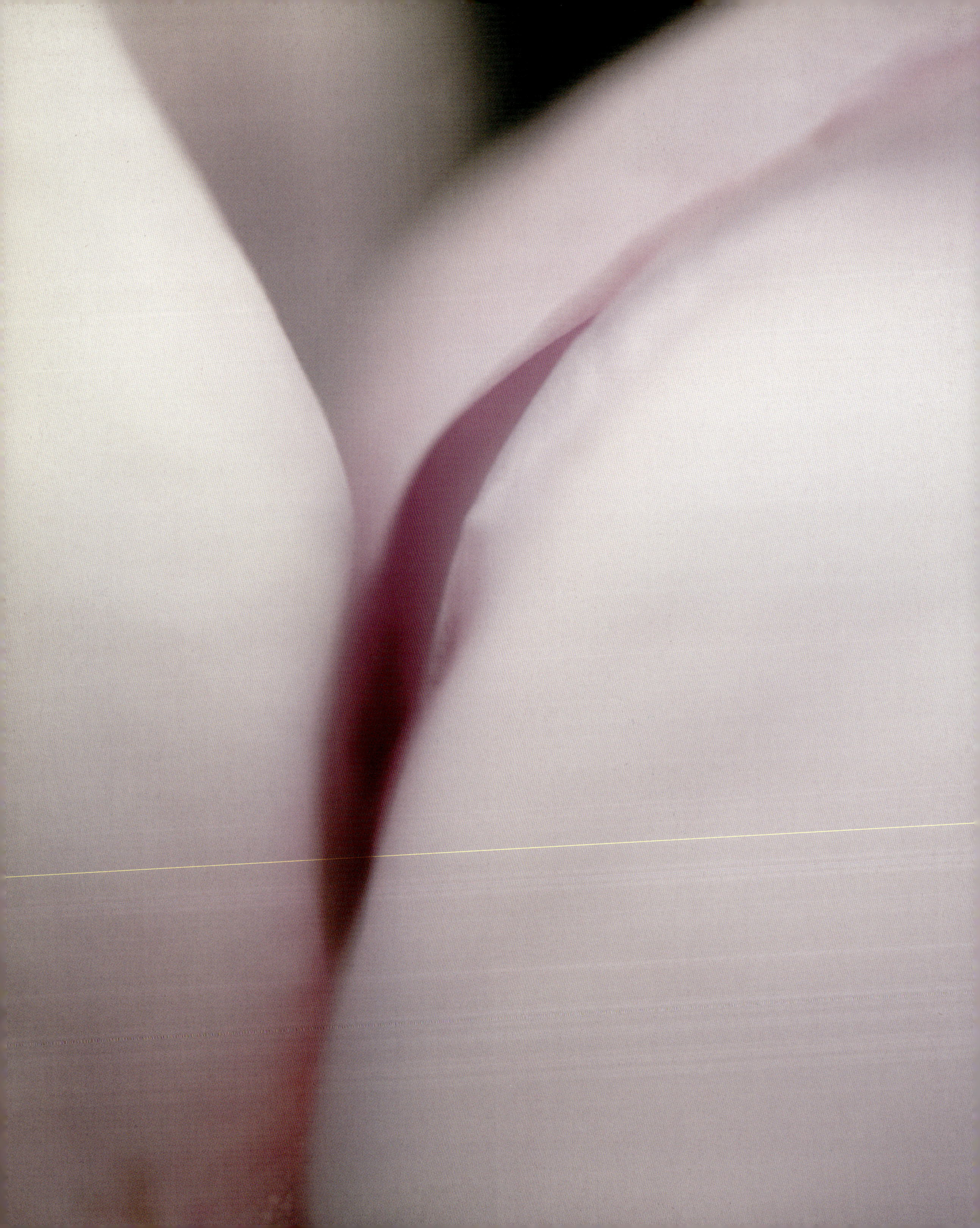

FLORA

FLORA

Love had heard that an immortal language never could die; that,
although silent, it still slept somewhere amongst the flowers...
lost ever since the day when Eve went weeping from
beneath the angel-guarded gates of Eden.

— THOMAS MILLER, *The Poetical Language of Flowers*, 1847

From daffodils in a ceramic vase to elaborate floral bouquets that require their own plinth for display, the arrangement of cut flowers has a long history. In Japan *ikebana*, the art of flower arrangement, has its origins as far as back as the sixth century when Buddhism first arrived in the country. Early floral offerings made to Buddha evolved into artful displays styled for line and form. Hundreds of years on, in the seventeenth century, *tulpenmanie*, or tulip mania, swept through the Netherlands resulting in one of the first speculative bubbles as a single bulb came to cost a small fortune. Since only the very wealthy could afford to have freshly cut bouquets in the home, and only during the flowering season, the floral still-life painting grew in popularity.

Some two hundred years later the Victorians also went flower mad, applying their famed industriousness to the classification and documentation of flora. All that is unpredictable and uncontrollable in nature, they felt, could be made manageable through codification. As a more romantic extension of the work of naturalists, the Victorian cult of florography came into being with its 'language of flowers', in which flowers made up a complex system of codes that allowed lovers to communicate covertly their desires. The only recently opened flower markets in urban centres fuelled this development and, as populations grew and density increased, more affordable pricing made the presence of cut flowers in homes and social venues increasingly commonplace. The movement of flora indoors gained momentum due to industrial pollution. Bringing nature into the parlour was a means to enjoy its beauty without braving the smoke-filled air of the city. Likewise, subdued floral still-life paintings decorated many a home for the same reason.

In the early twentieth century, artists threw off the last sentimental vestiges of Kantian prescriptions for the sublime and beauty (the myth of the artist-genius would also be cast out). Depictions of nature and flora changed drastically as radical avant-garde movements – from Cubism to Dada to Surrealism to Abstract Expressionism – called for a whole new approach to making art. Andy Warhol, followed by Robert Mapplethorpe, brought the depiction of flowers into a new realm, where the political and the personal edged up against one another and new, alternative forms of meaning were possible. It is in their wake that younger artists have taken the representation of flowers into the twenty-first century by embracing an incredible diversity of media. Photography and painting have been joined by sculpture, video and digital work, as well as performance and installation art. Some of these works carry echoes of the historical floral still life, while others share no visual resemblances but retain strong conceptual links to the tradition, such as those by Philip Pirolo, Per Christian Brown and Matts Leiderstam (pages 20, 50, 63 and 69). Other artists have turned to science as a means of moving the still life forward. Rob Kesseler works directly with scientists using electron microscopes to capture artistic (as opposed to purely documentary) images of plant spores and seeds (page 72).

For many contemporary artists, the flower in bloom not only encapsulates the notion of beauty at its peak – that moment before death becomes inevitable and the bruise overtakes the perfect velvet petal – but also alludes to heightened sexual pleasure, if not the orgasm itself. In the works of Marc Quinn and Martin Gustavsson the flower is a graphic embodiment of human desire, a reminder that the instant of greatest pleasure is also the instant of its loss in a never-ending cycle of fulfilment and renewal of sexual longing (pages 24 and 32). Gustavsson brings a queer sensibility to his *Hyacinthos* and Quinn a more heteronormative one in *Under the Volcano. The Slopes of Jan Mayen*; both images still speak the universal language of desire, distilled into each artist's individual visual signature.

Other artists incorporate real flowers and plants into their works to illustrate the effects of the passage of time. Viewers returning to Anya Gallaccio's *Preserve 'Beauty'* or Jeroen de Rijke and Willem de Rooij's *Bouquet IV* will see the flowers begin to alter and fade and, in the case of Gallaccio's installation, ultimately rot in situ (pages 41 and 42). These works foreground loss and track the death of beauty in real time. By contrast, both Mark Wallinger's *Double Still Life* and Hans-Peter Feldmann's *Flower Pot* use artificial flowers to maintain an illusion of eternal perfection (pages 40 and 43). No matter how long or hard we might gaze upon these works they remain the same (assuming they are not allowed to gather too much dust) and, like the flowers in traditional still-life paintings, they do not lose their bloom.

In her book *On Beauty and Being Just* (1999), Elaine Scarry argues that beauty is neither trivial nor corrupt and that such fictive distinctions greatly harm our perception of the world by relegating beauty and denying its power to increase the general good. The elevating power of beauty and aesthetic perfection lies at the heart of the works by David LaChapelle, Sharon Core and Alexander James included in this chapter (pages 52, 56 and 57). The moral imperative that underpinned so many floral still lifes of the past has been subverted in many of the contemporary works here, whether or not they retain and redeploy traditional pictorial strategies or feature entirely new and innovative tropes. Yet all these works still elicit a strong emotional response from viewers – though certainly not a moral conversion. If the devil is in the detail, none of these contemporary works is likely to make it to heaven.

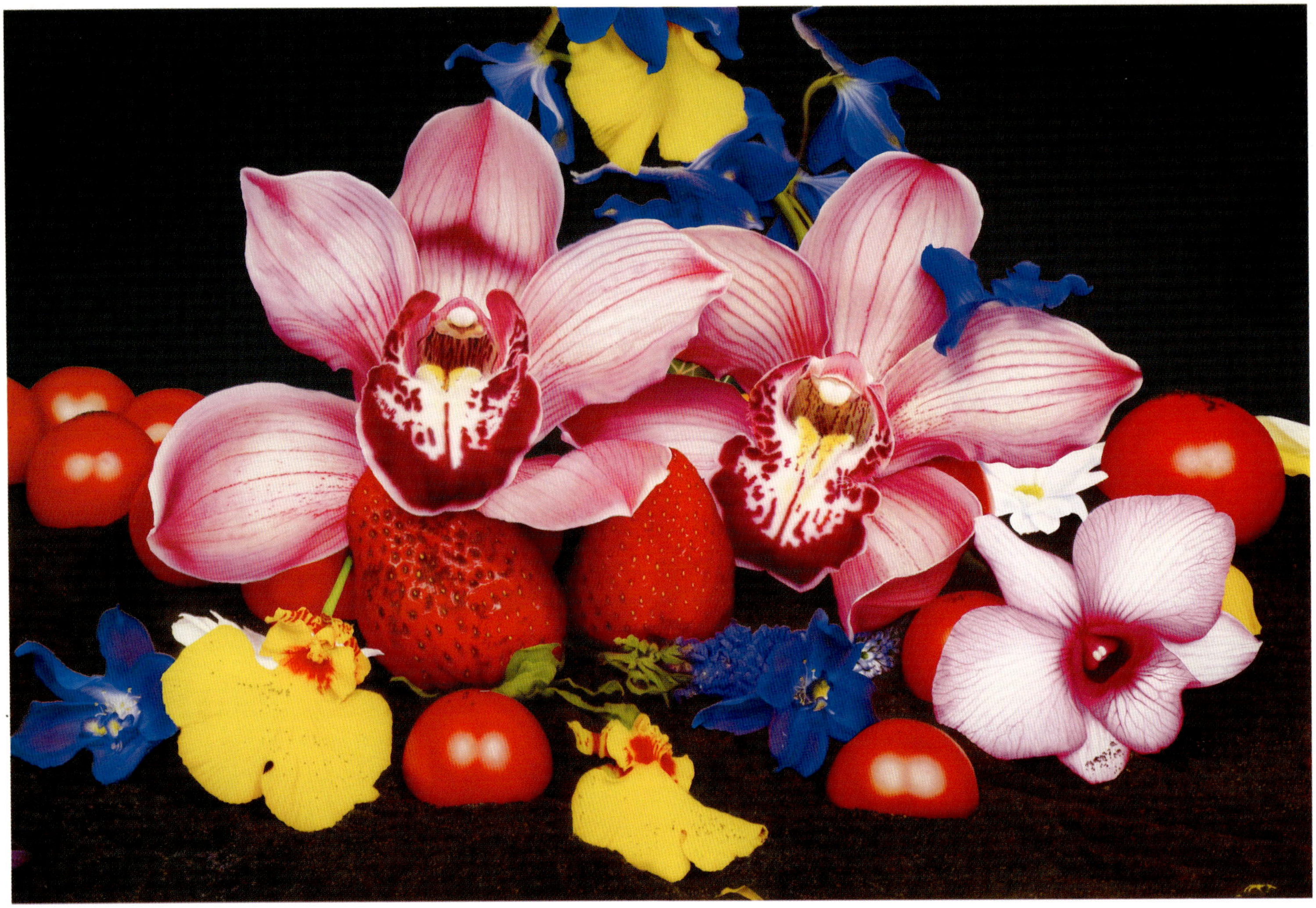

PAGE 20
Philip Pirolo
Angiosperm, Rose 8, 2010
(detail) · photograph

ABOVE
Marc Quinn
Under the Volcano.
The Slopes of Jan Mayen,
2011 · oil on canvas

OPPOSITE
John Currin
Rosebush, 2003
oil on canvas

Marc Quinn's fascination with orchids and their sexual symbolism has meant that these exotic flowers recur throughout his work, including in his *Under the Volcano* series of oil paintings. The orchids in *Under the Volcano. The Slopes of Jan Mayen* overwhelm with their garish perfection, hyperreal colours and size; the painting measures over two-and-a-half by four metres. Its title refers to the volcanic island of Jan Mayen in the Arctic Ocean. Owned by Norway, it has no indigenous human population and visitor numbers are severely restricted to preserve the pristine environment.

Roses and rosebushes popped up in many of the paintings shown in **John Currin**'s 2003 London exhibition. Most frequently, the picturesque flowers served as a backdrop to a posing middle-aged woman, as in *Bent Lady* and *Rachel in the Garden*. *Rosebush* stood apart from the others in depicting a bundle of roses alone, unaccompanied by any human presence. Currin is well known for paintings that reference Renaissance imagery, poses and composition, as well as for his commitment to an idealized contemporary figuration. This particular still life serves as a visual resting point among his other more controversial works.

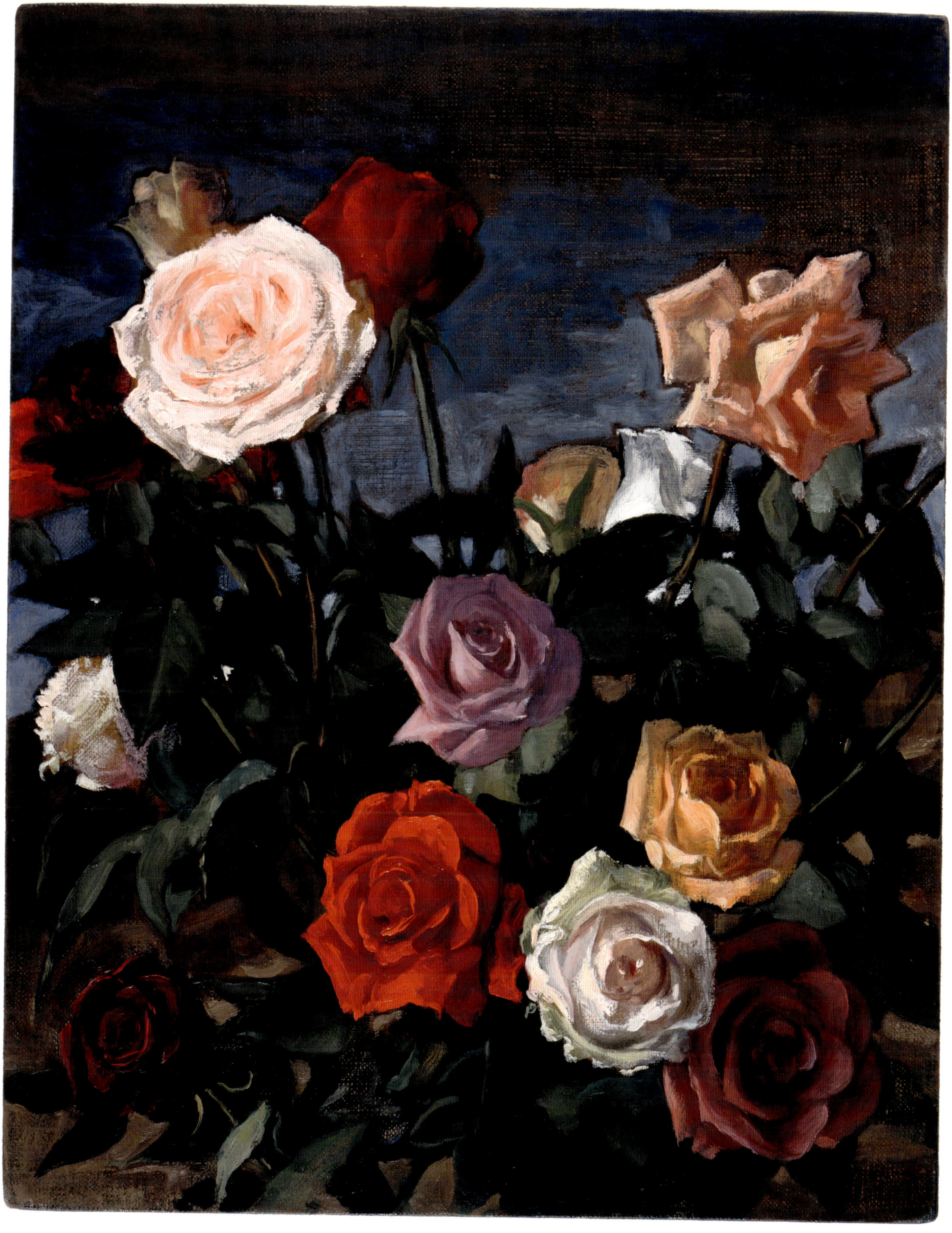

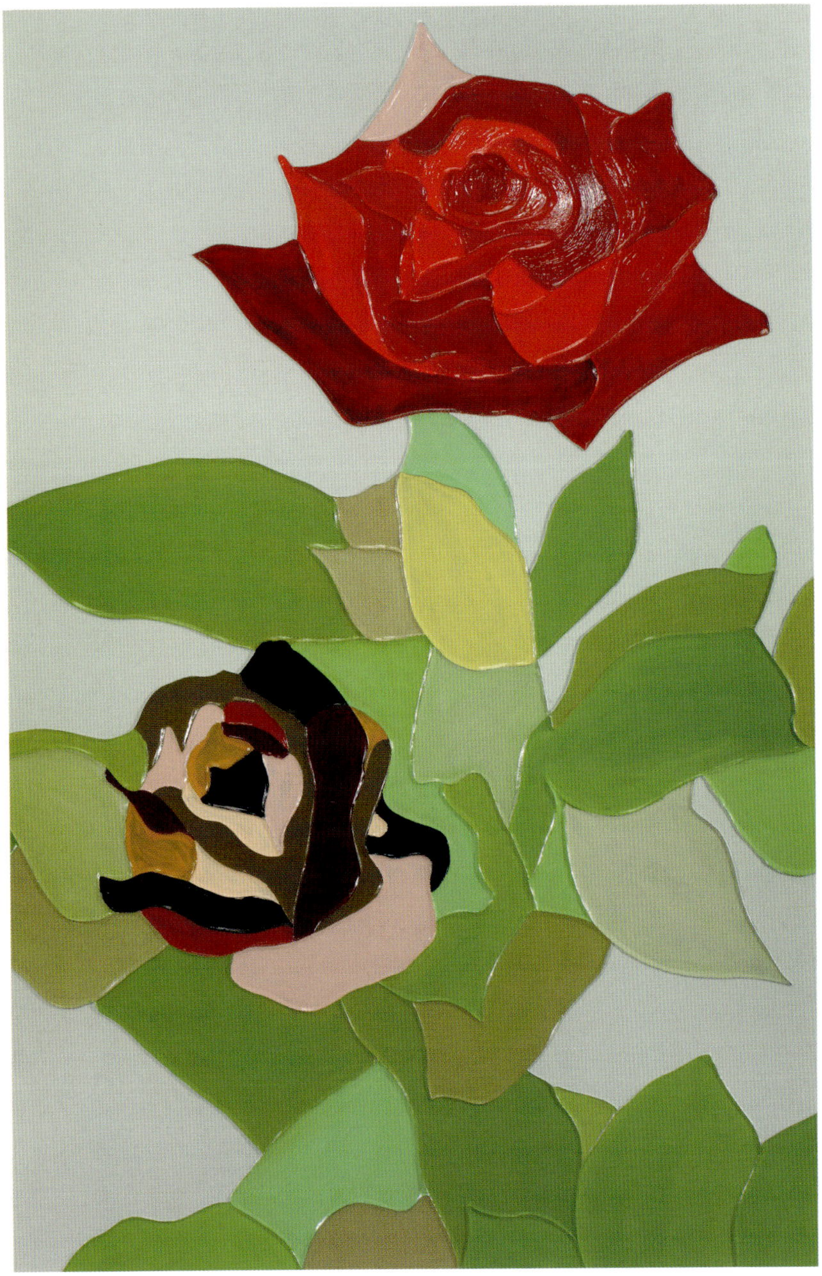

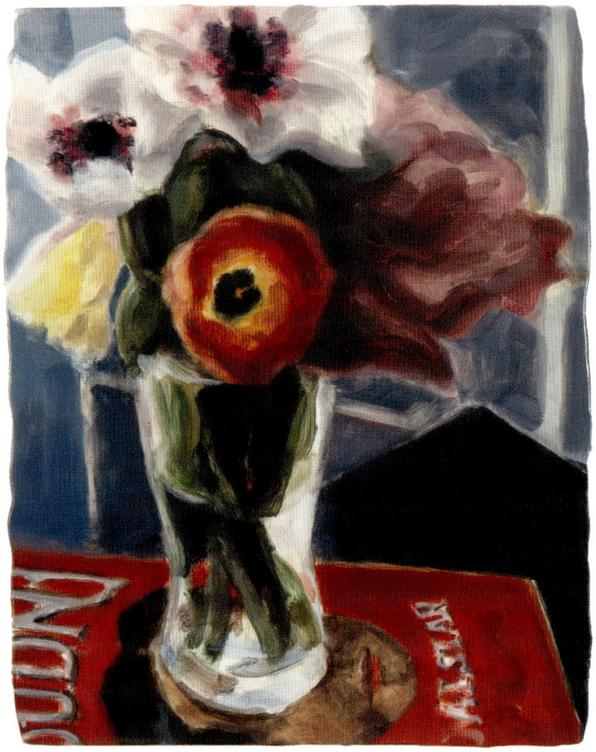

ABOVE LEFT
Gary Hume
***Pink Rent*, 2011**
gloss paint on aluminium

ABOVE RIGHT
Elizabeth Peyton
***Houdini*, 2009**
oil on linen on board

Gary Hume puts 'beauty and life and sex and little moments' at the heart of his work. In a recent series he applied his distinctive style of painting, which involves creating large, flat areas of built-up colour, to a number of seemingly simple close-ups of birds, plants and flowers that offered a fresh take on otherwise age-old tropes. The large scale and visual flatness of the paintings brought the tradition into current contemporary art practice.

Elizabeth Peyton is best known for her stylized portraits of pop culture icons, including rock stars, Hollywood actors and fellow artists. She favours an expressionistic representation of these familiar figures rather than attempting photorealism. For a recent series, she depicted famous individuals alongside house plants and cut flowers in order to explore the psychology and symbolism of these accessories in our lives. In *Houdini* a vase containing a bouquet of flowers sits atop a book on the escape artist, entirely obscuring his eyes and nose.

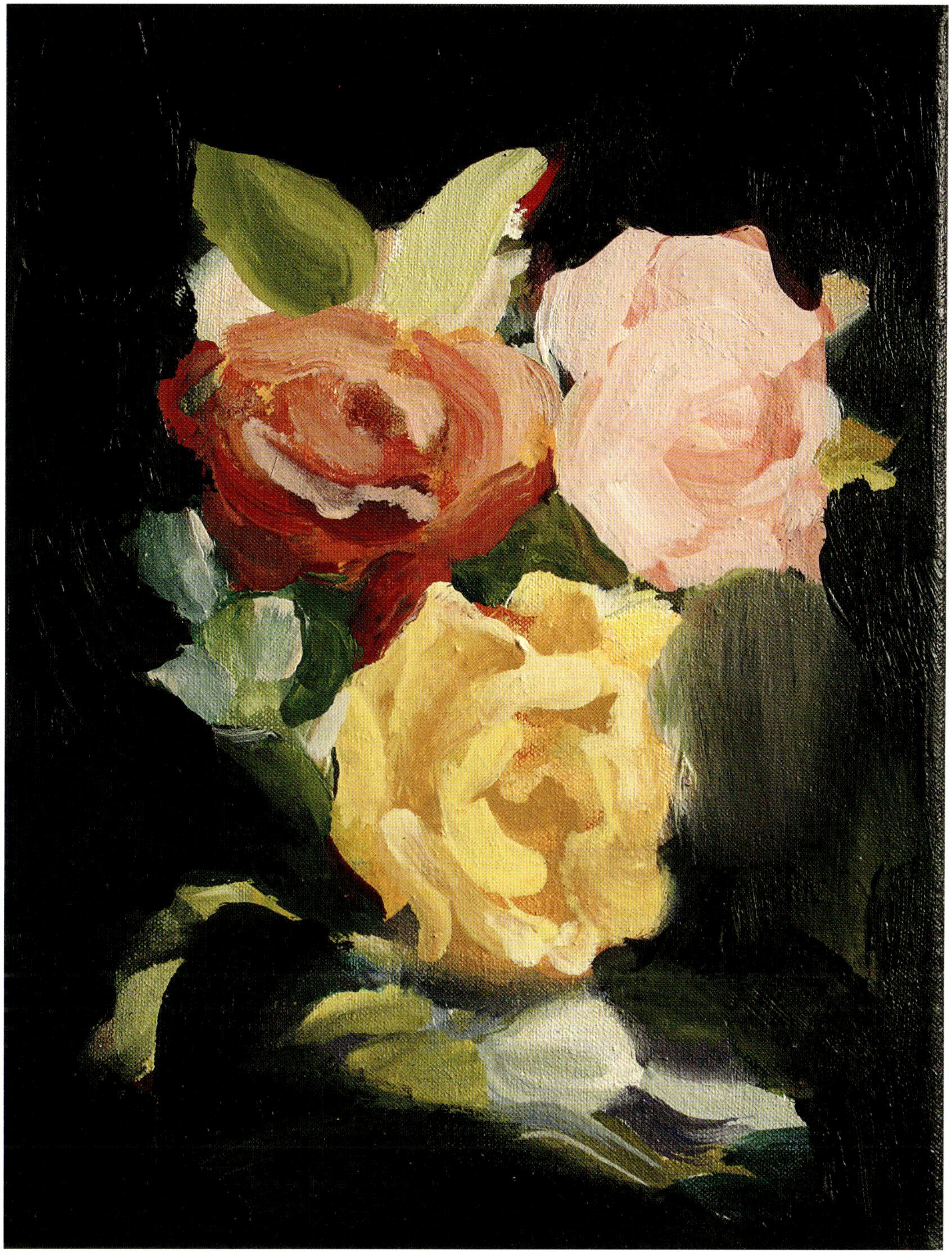

Kim Baker's striking oil paintings take inspiration from the *memento mori* tradition as it evolved in seventeenth-century Dutch still lifes. Her canvases thus feature flowers, birds and insects, the traditional motifs of these earlier works, while retaining a spontaneous technique characteristic of more recent times. Baker often reworks her canvases repeatedly, painting one image on top of another until the finished work tells an additional story: that of its own genesis.

ABOVE
Kim Baker
Untitled 34, 2011
oil on canvas

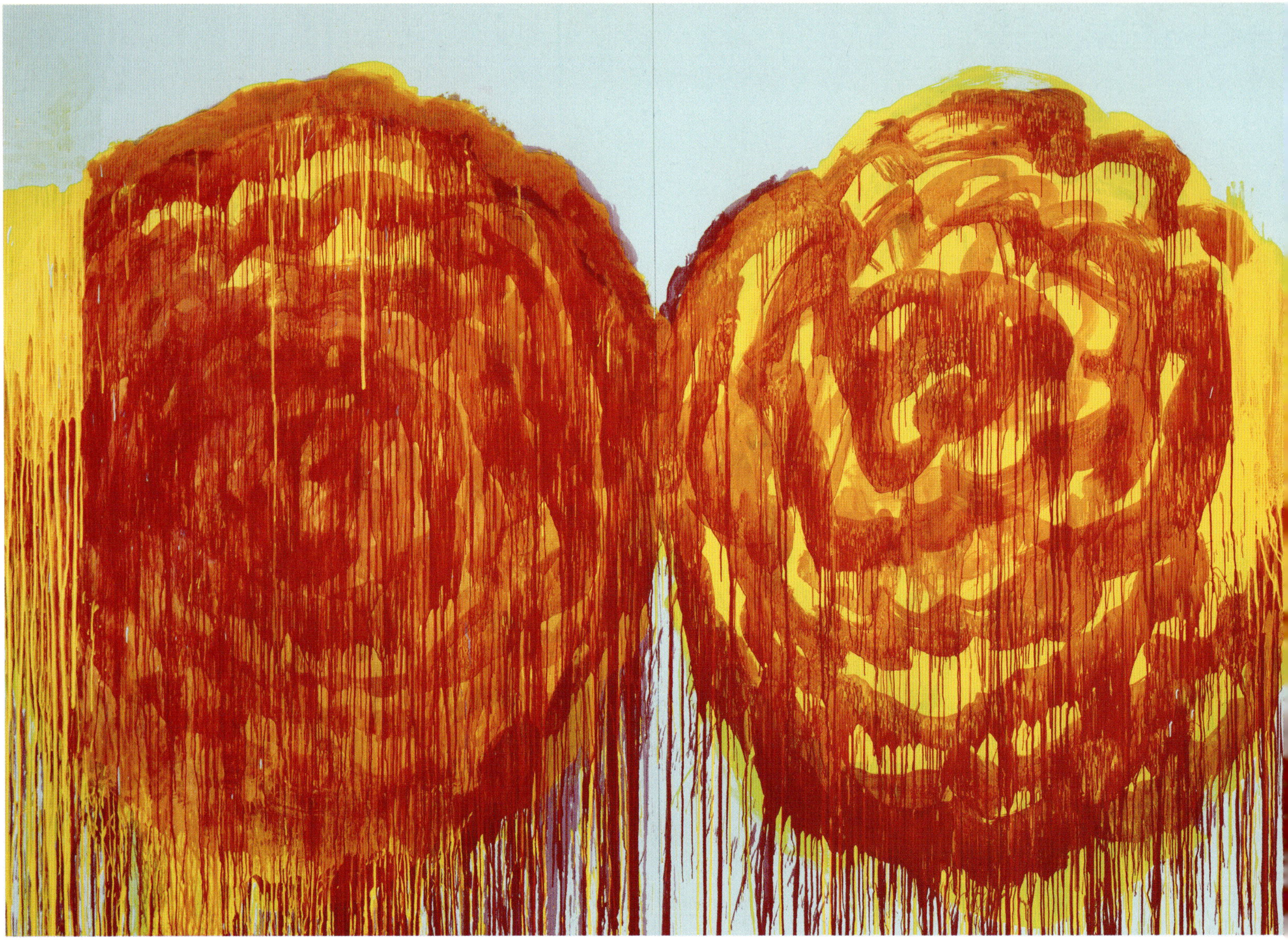

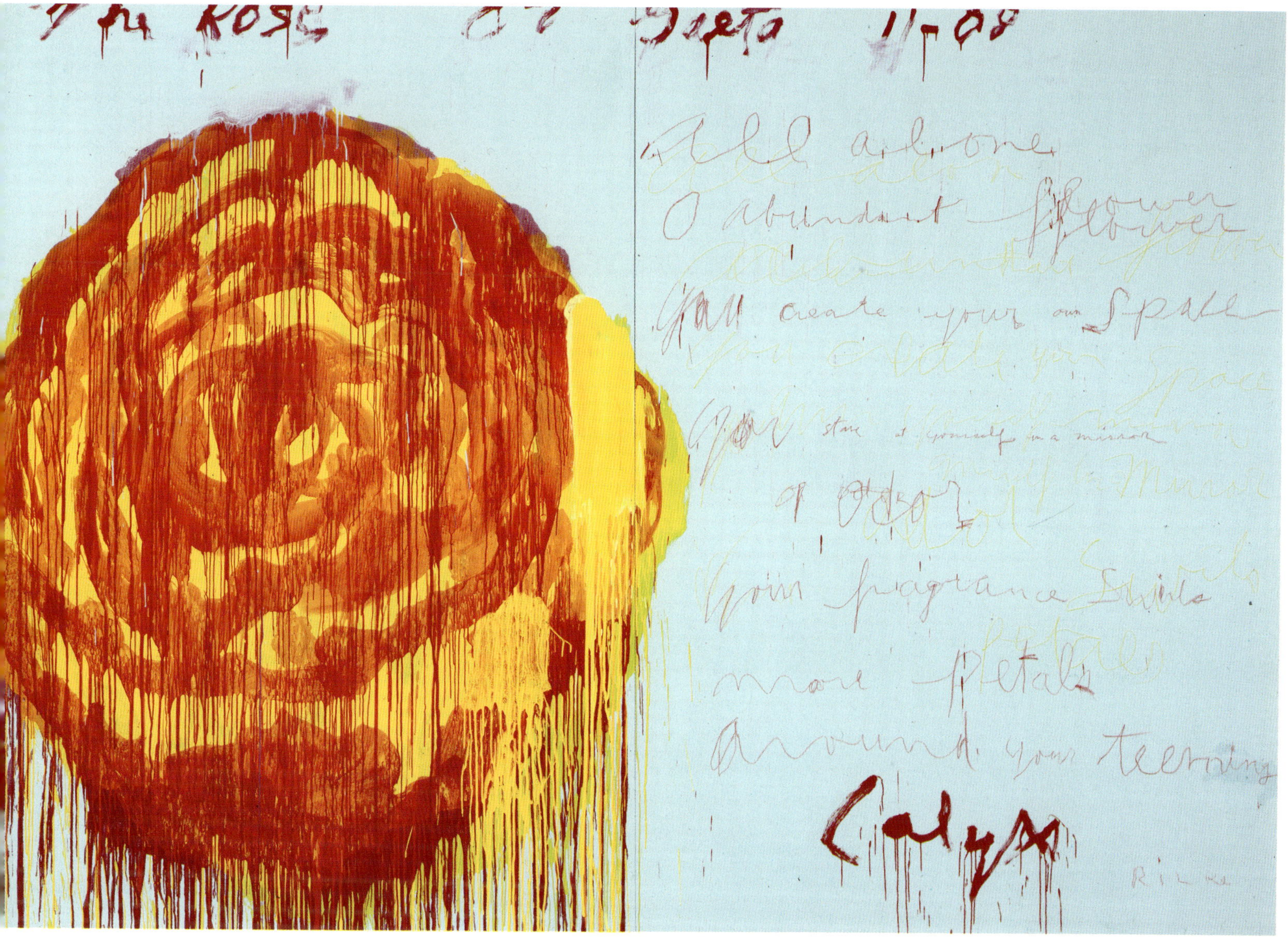

ABOVE
Cy Twombly
The Rose (II), 2008
acrylic on plywood

Towards the end of his long career, **Cy Twombly** painted some of his most expressive and autobiographical works for a series inspired by Rainer Maria Rilke's cycle of poems *The Roses*. Twombly's complex sexuality also played a role: these roses in full bloom speak of youth, love and loss, as well as the imminence of death. Each of the five works in the series consists of four wooden panels, measuring all together some eight by twenty-four metres, and depicts three monumental roses painted in one of five colours (yellow, orange, red, purple or black), with fragments of Rilke's verse transcribed on the fourth panel. *The Rose* series not only continued Twombly's lifelong exploration of Classical ideas and mythology (an interest he shared with Rilke), but also directly referenced Rilke's self-composed epitaph, in which the petals of the rose are linked to the eyelids of the sleeper and the permanent sleep that death ordains.

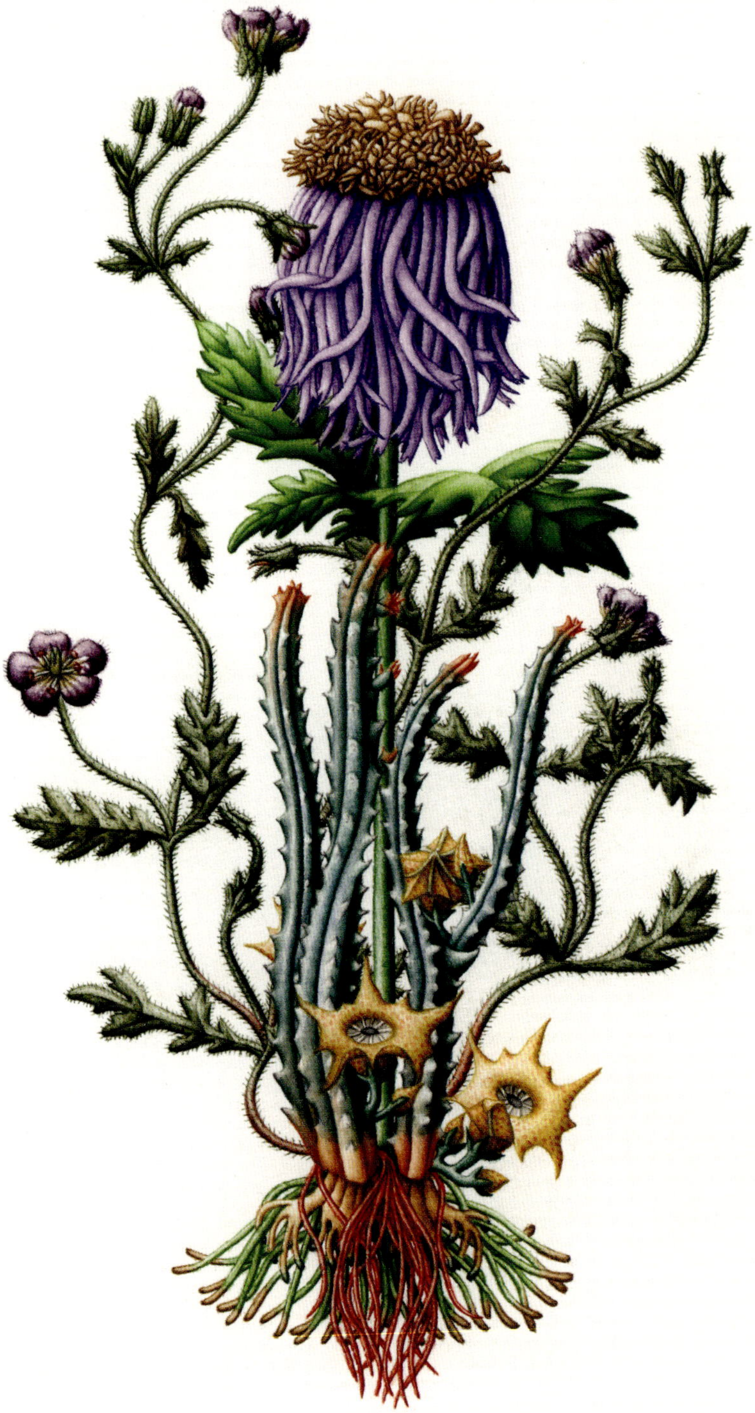

Helena Goldwater's *Show-off* may look as if it has come from the pages of some nineteenth-century compendium of exotic plant species but its precise and scientific observation is in fact completely at odds with its subject; the plants, flowers and weeds that Goldwater delicately depicts in her watercolours grow only in her imagination. Familiar then, yet strange, the works are further complicated by their titles, which invite sexually charged and queer readings. These include *Fleshy Parts* (2009), *Seedy 1* (2007), *Dirty 6* (2007) and *Beast* (2008).

OPPOSITE
Helena Goldwater
***Show-off*, 2006**
watercolour on paper

BELOW LEFT
Nick Fox
***Dreamcatcher* (*chrysanthemum flower no. 5*), 2008**
cut-out acrylic paint pressed between glass

BELOW RIGHT
Robert Brinker
***Chrysanthemum #4*, 2006**
cut magazine centrefold

Nick Fox's *Dreamcatcher (chrysanthemum flower no. 5)* and **Robert Brinker**'s *Chrysanthemum #4* may look similar but there are significant differences in the artists' materials and methods. Fox creates by slowly building up thick layers of acrylic paint on glass, which he then cuts into to make his flowers. Over the top of the layered paint, he paints images copied from pornography that can be discerned only upon close inspection. The meaning of the depicted flower subscribes to the Victorian 'language of flowers'.

Brinker's works are primarily made with paper and collage. His chrysanthemum, cut from the centrefold of an adult magazine, is from a series based around Chinese paper-cutting traditions, also known as 'cut handi-crafts', that he created for an exhibition in Beijing. Brinker noted: 'Since the exhibitions were not government sanctioned, I had some flexibility with regards to censorship.'

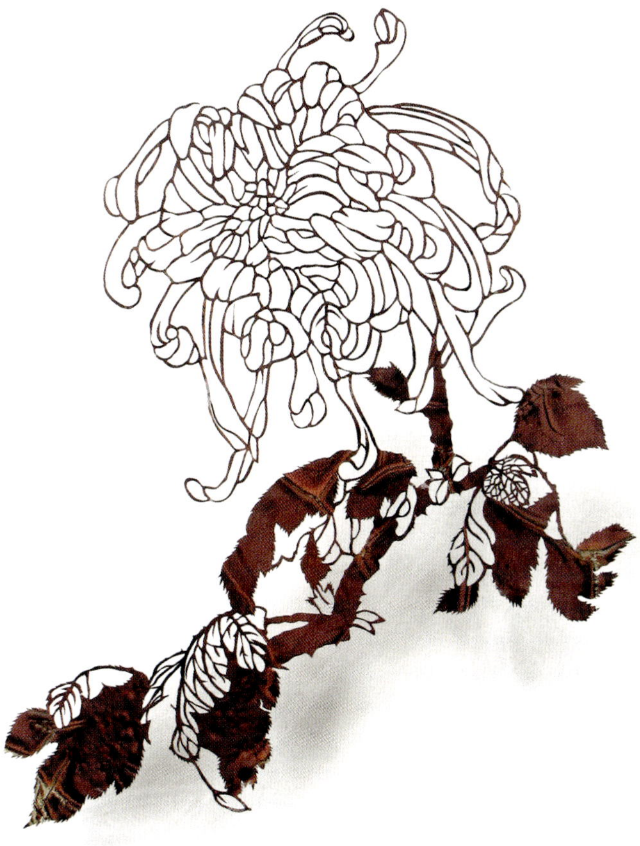

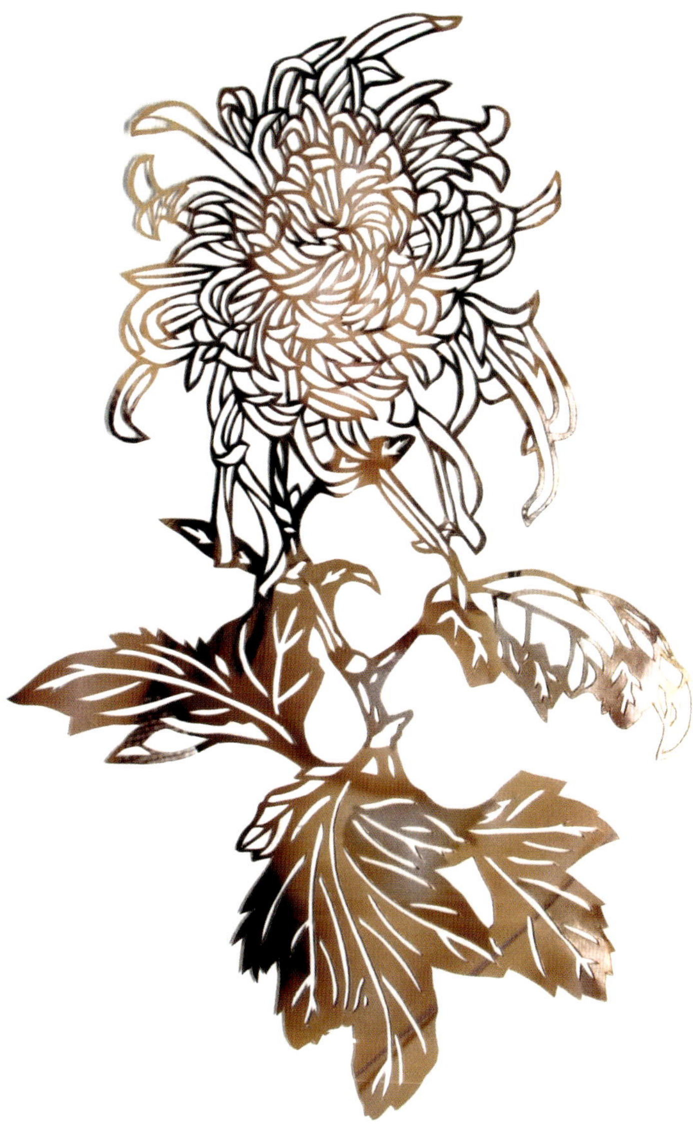

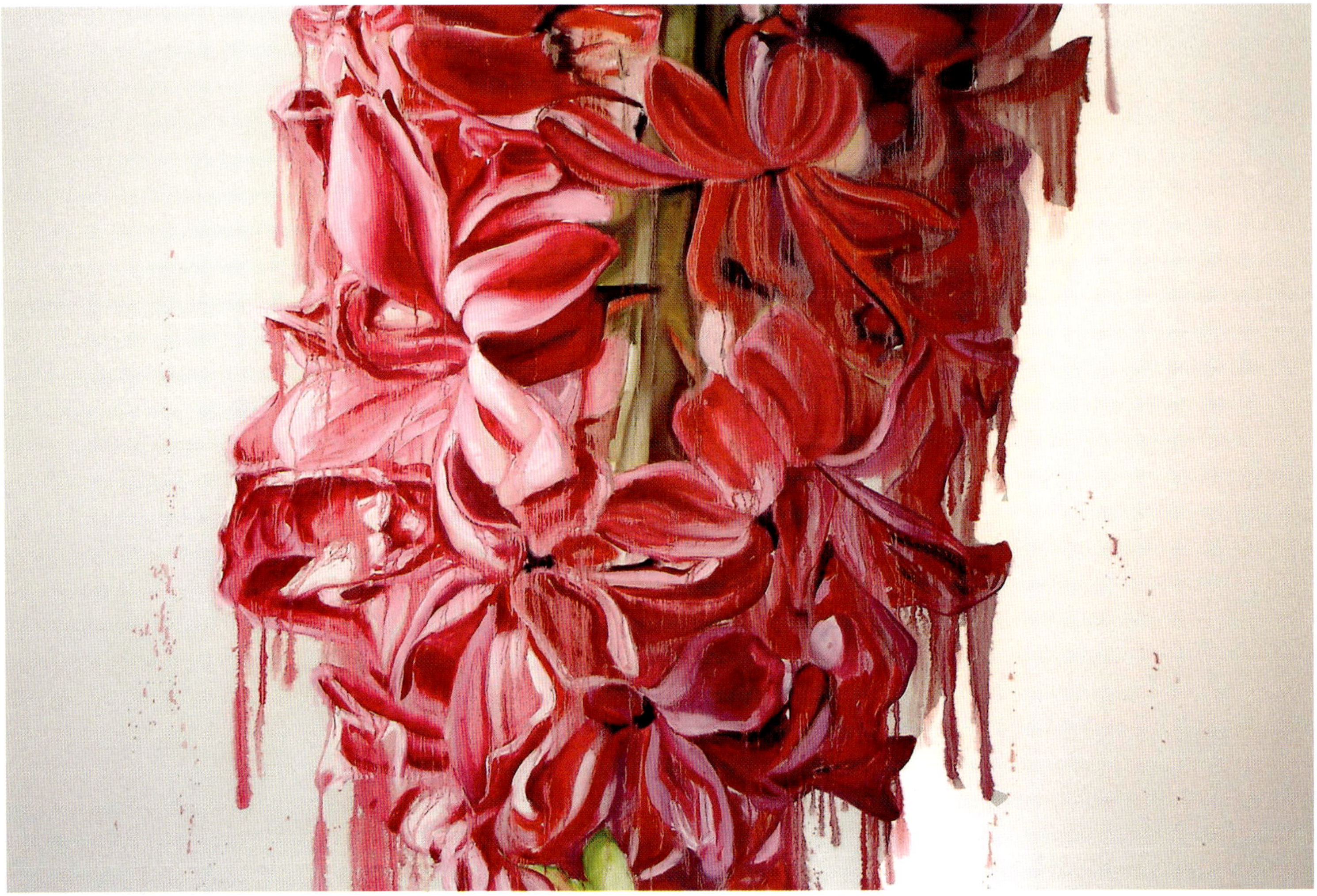

ABOVE
Martin Gustavsson
Hyacinthos, 2006
oil on linen

Martin Gustavsson's large *Hyacinthos* is one in a series of oil paintings of ripe, juicy – indeed dripping – hyacinth flowers, which have been described as pornographic, so erotically charged are they. In Greek creation myths, Hyacinth was a handsome youth whom Apollo, god of the arts, took for his male lover, much to the rage of the wind god Zephyr, who blew a discus thrown by Apollo off course, killing Hyacinth. As Hyacinth lay dying, Apollo transformed his lover's spilled blood into the flower. Eros, death, rebirth and the flower combine to create anew themes often alluded to in earlier still-life imagery.

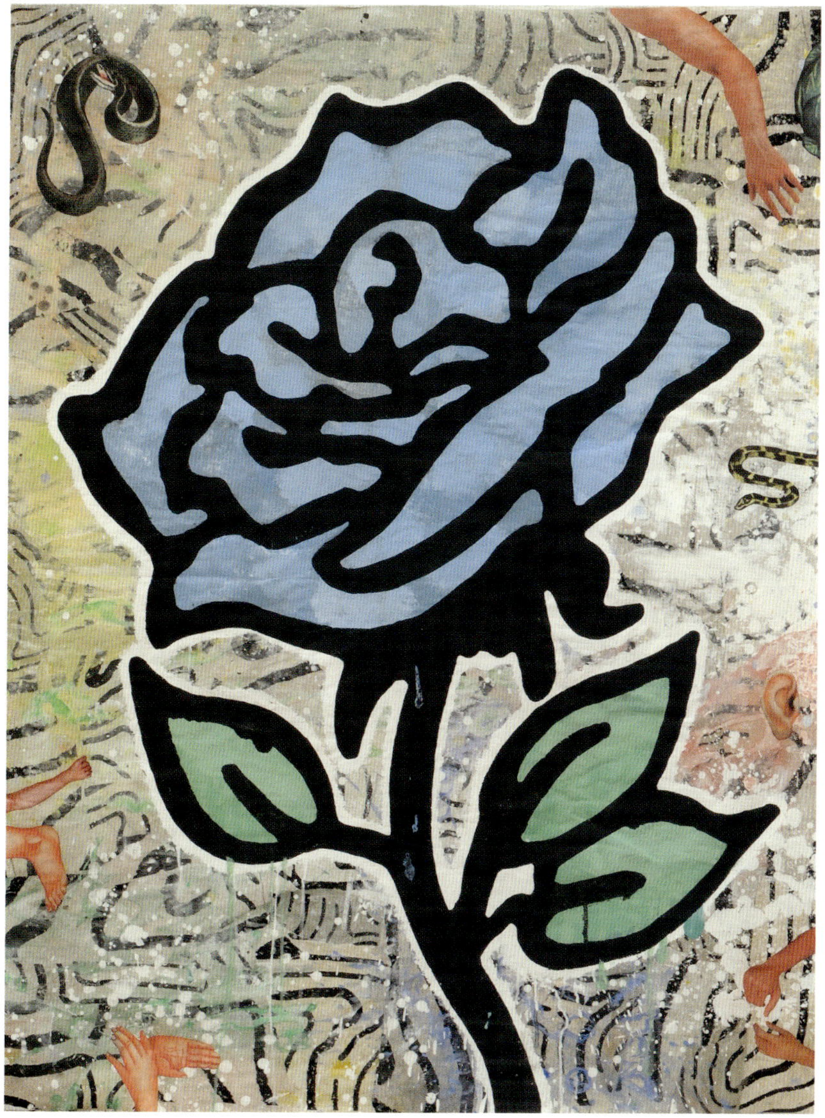

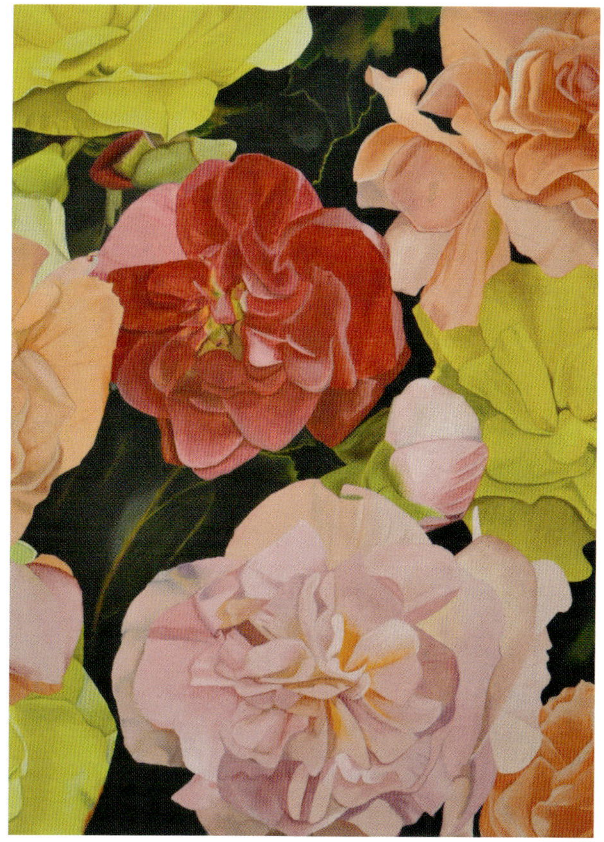

ABOVE LEFT
Donald Baechler
***BLUE ROSE*, 2010**
gesso, flashe and paper collage on paper

ABOVE RIGHT
Marcus Cope
***Various Titles*, 2009**
oil on canvas

For **Donald Baechler** there is 'never an intention of likeness' in his pared-down images. His childlike and child*ish* images drawn from American folk culture are often visually arresting in their simplicity, and he has said he is drawn to minimalism. Yet the works – be they of flowers, trees or candles – retain clear indications of a technical ability that has intentionally been cast aside. These are not cartoons but distinct observations, as in *BLUE ROSE*, which disrupts the picture plane with its physical impossibility (there are no such blooms in nature).

Marcus Cope does not have one distinctive style. Sometimes he paints relatively realistic works, such as those of his *Carrion* series of new and old world vultures; sometimes he paints much more loosely (*I Eat Human*, 2011); sometimes photorealistically, as in *Various Titles*. His aim is to refresh the possibilities of painting, and what it offers younger artists and viewers, while remaining sardonically, even cynically, aware of the medium's limitations in representing reality – failure is built into the attempt.

As part of the 2011 exhibition 'Journey', **Yuken Teruya** spray-painted a series of graffiti flowers directly onto the exterior walls of the Shoshana Wayne Gallery in Santa Monica. Teruya's stencil technique and designs echo the artistic traditions of Okinawa, Japan, his childhood home. *My Vote – Chrysanthemum, Coffee Cup* was a delicate, brightly coloured, yet almost invisible intervention in the urban environment, quite dissimilar in ethos to the much bolder, more disruptive visual language typical of street art. The chrysanthemum may resemble a weed growing out of trash, both real (cigarette butts, chewing gum) and pictorial (empty cups), but it still speaks of beauty and renewal.

Annette Kelm photographs the objects of her still lifes in conventional studio settings that nonetheless provide opportunities for her to continually undermine their visual authority. For *Untitled* (*Tribal*) and *Untitled* (*Flower*) (both 2010) she positioned flowers against surprising, visually intrusive backgrounds. In *Big Print #4* the background itself has become the subject of the photograph. One of a number of floral patterns featured on commercially produced textiles, this work raises a print designed by the early home improvement guru Dorothy Draper to the status of art, making it almost a painting in its own right.

Beatriz Milhazes is a Brazilian artist of the *Geração 80* (80s Generation) that emerged after the fall of the country's military dictatorship in 1985. As in Spain after the death of Franco, a new wave of artists sought to assert themselves in these years and many, including Milhazes, turned to painting. To create her intricate geometric works incorporating natural imagery (flowers, plants and animals) she first paints layer upon layer of acrylic onto a plastic sheet. She then peels off this plastic 'skin' and transfers it to canvas. All this layering and building up (as well as concealing) ties in with the work's title, *Mariposa*, which means moth or butterfly but is also a derogatory term for male homosexuals in much of Latin America.

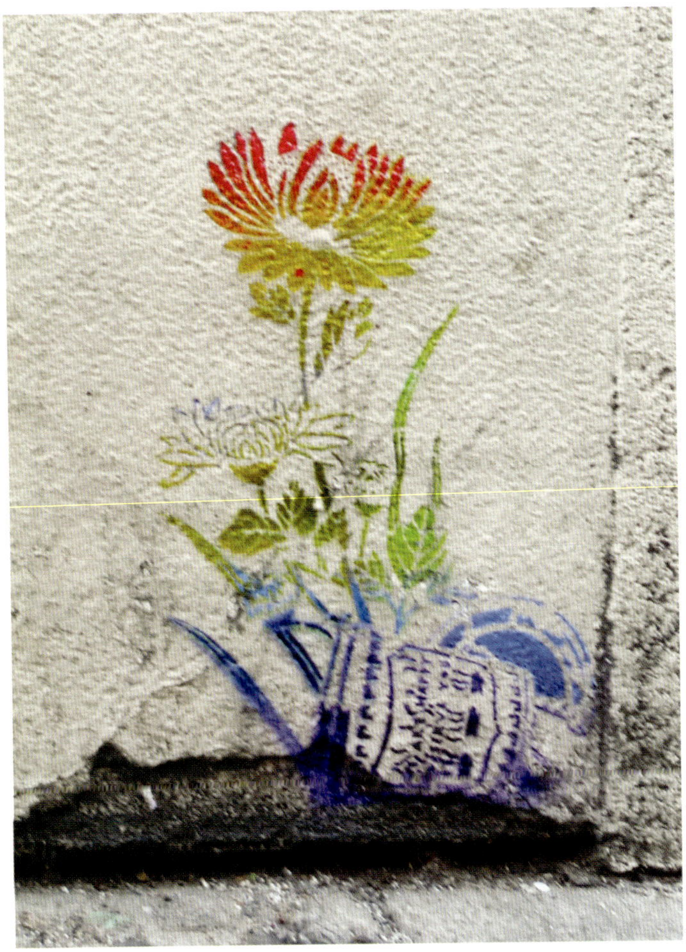

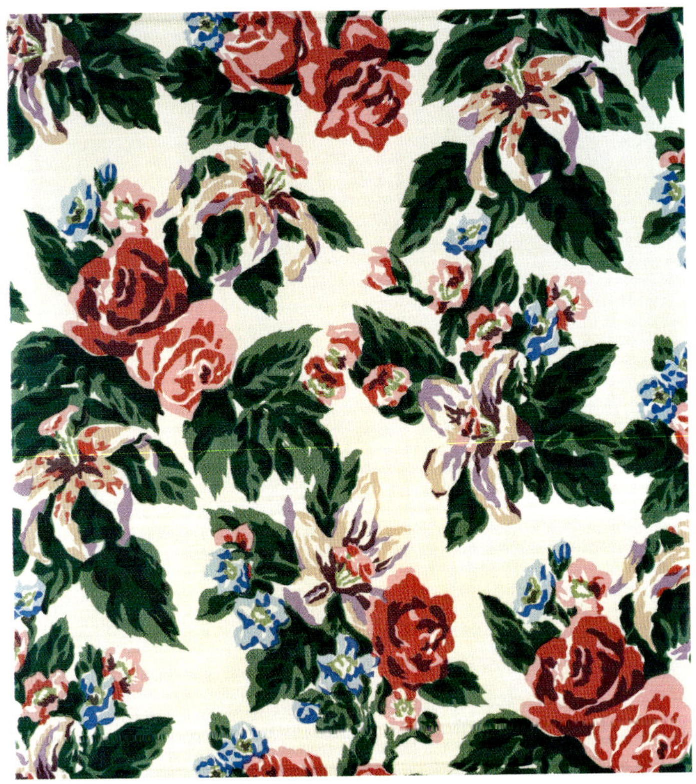

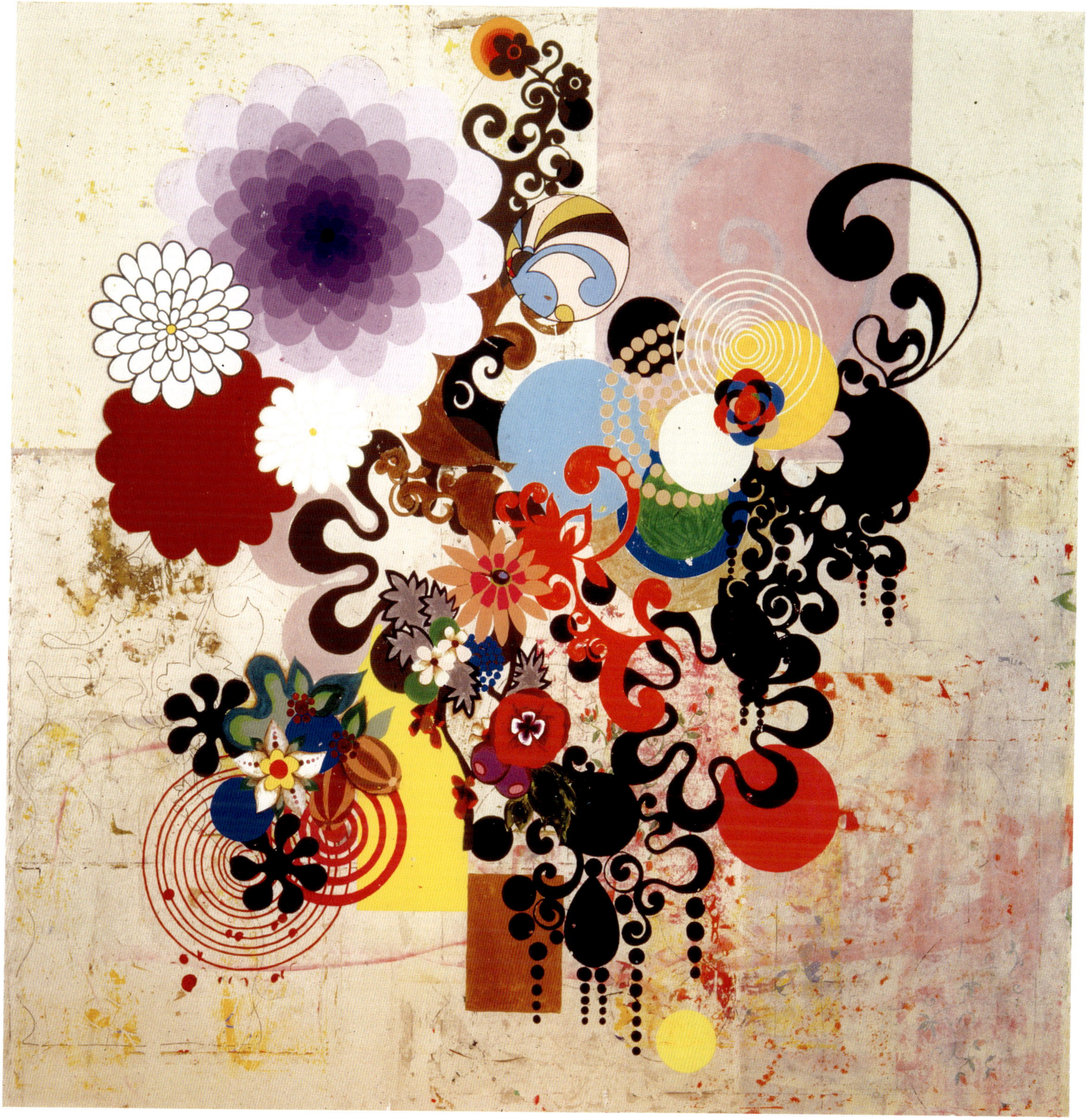

OPPOSITE LEFT
Yuken Teruya · ***My Vote – Chrysanthemum, Coffee Cup***, 2011
spray-paint on concrete

OPPOSITE RIGHT
Annette Kelm · ***Big Print #4 (fazenda lily – white background – cotton fall 1947 design Dorothy Draper, courtesy Schumacher & Co)***, 2007 · C-print

ABOVE
Beatriz Milhazes · ***Mariposa***, 2004
acrylic on canvas

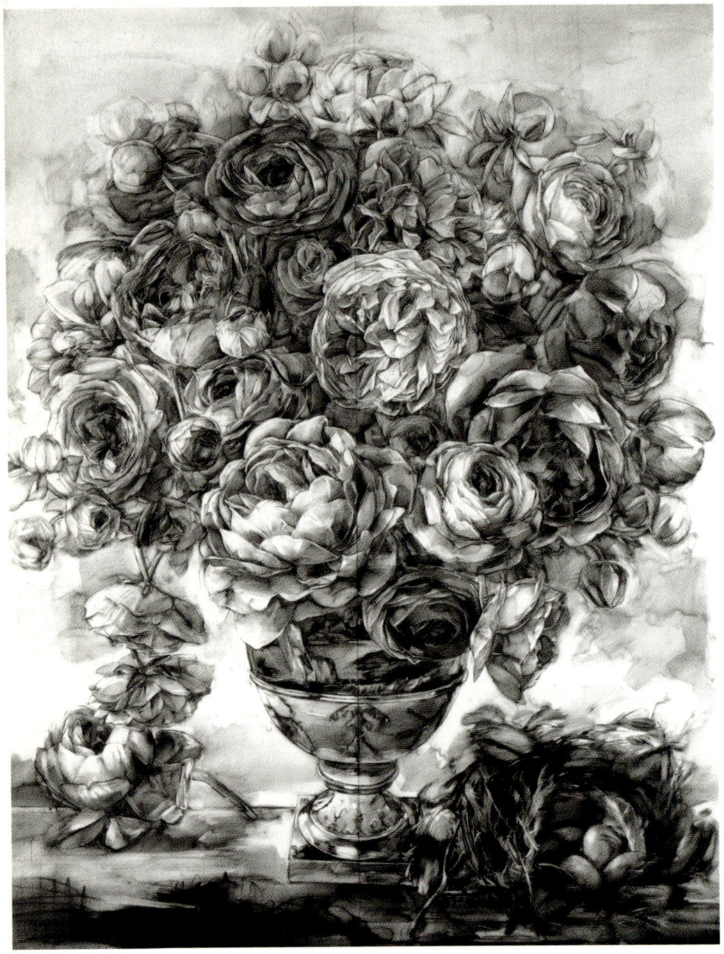

Karin Broker endlessly draws on paper, primed Formica and even found sculptural objects. The resulting works reference Old Master still lifes, but on a vastly different scale. *Domestic Melancholia* is 2.7 metres tall and 2.2 metres wide. Its physical presence is imposing, almost crushing, as the feeling of melancholy so often is.

Paul Evans collaborates with academics, scientists and other artists to explore in his work the contradictions between our human outlook on the world and our animal reactions to it, and how we are the sole creatures that actively harm the planet. He has painted human cells, as well as a series of *Blooms*, and his *Melt* works allude to our potential self-destruction.

The large-scale oil paintings of **Emma Bennett** faithfully depict images of ships, flowers and fruit appropriated from seventeenth- and eighteenth-century Dutch paintings (works by Willem van de Velde, Jan Porcellis, Jan Davidsz. de Heem and Rachel Ruysch) that are now suspended in a dark void. Thus Abstract Expressionism and several centuries of artistic tradition collapse into a single work. Bennett says her paintings can be seen as 'questioning the mercantile value system that has become synonymous with the Dutch Golden Age, and is still prevalent in Western society today'.

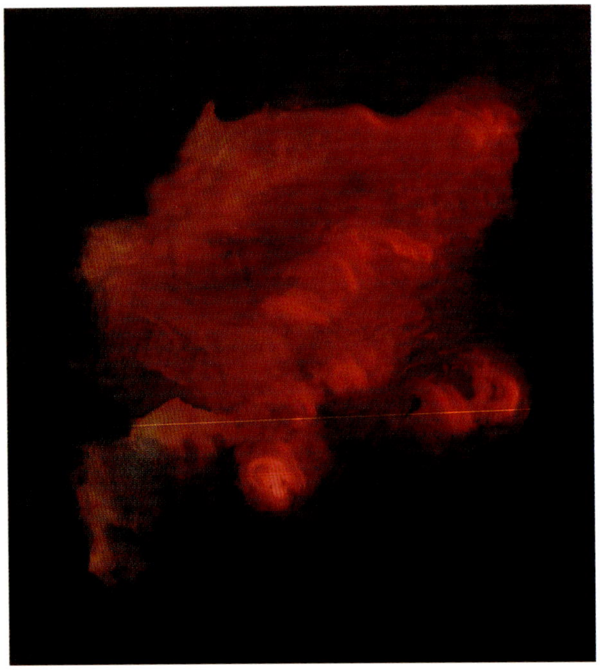

'As it's not about replicating the original, it's odd when people get the wrong idea and want to compare them with the original to see "how well I've done".'

—EMMA BENNETT

ABOVE · Karin Broker · *Domestic Melancholia*, 1997
Conté drawing on Formica

LEFT · Paul Evans · *Bloom (nocturne)*, 2009
oil and mixed media on canvas

OPPOSITE · Emma Bennett · *Stung*, 2011
oil and French enamel on canvas

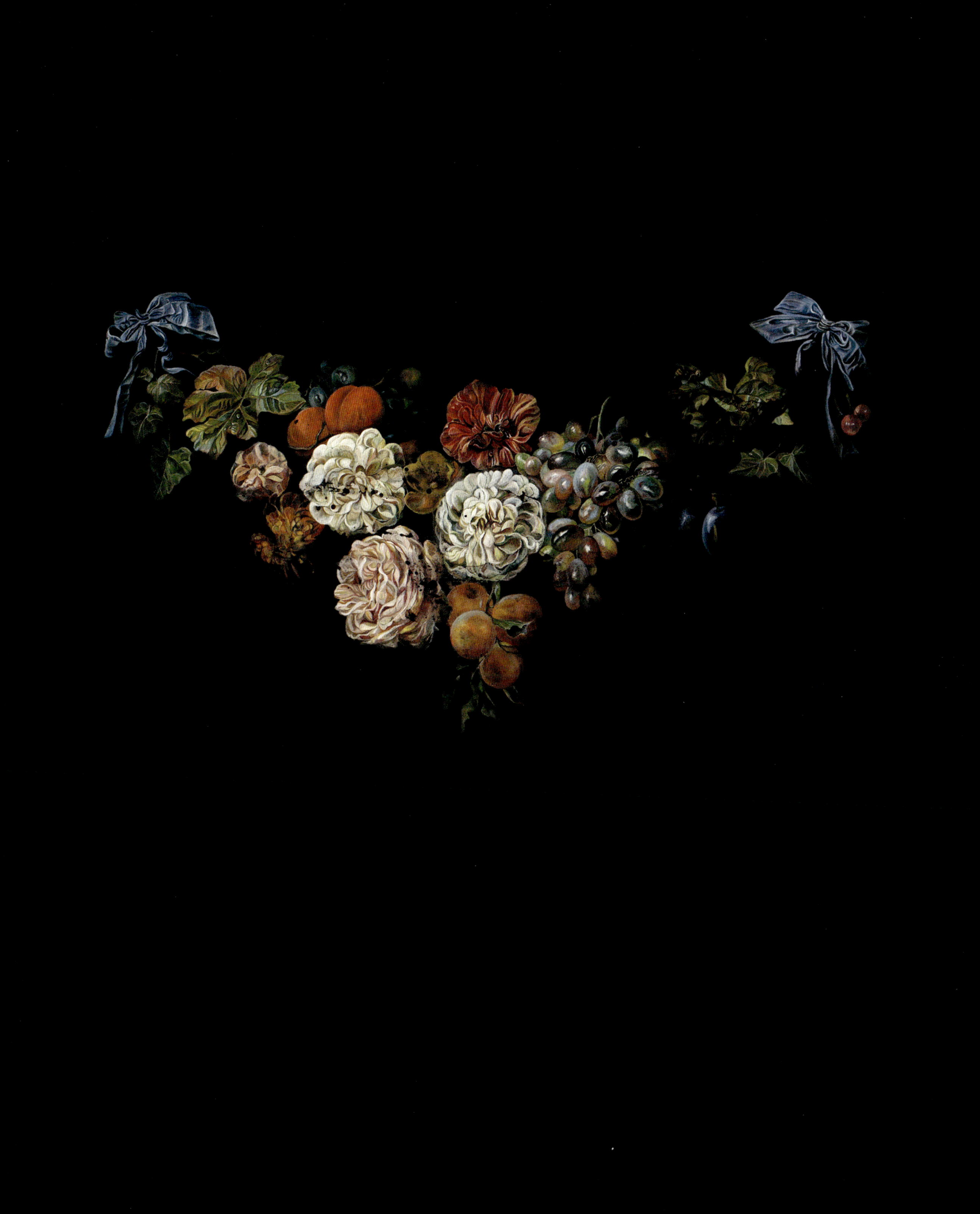

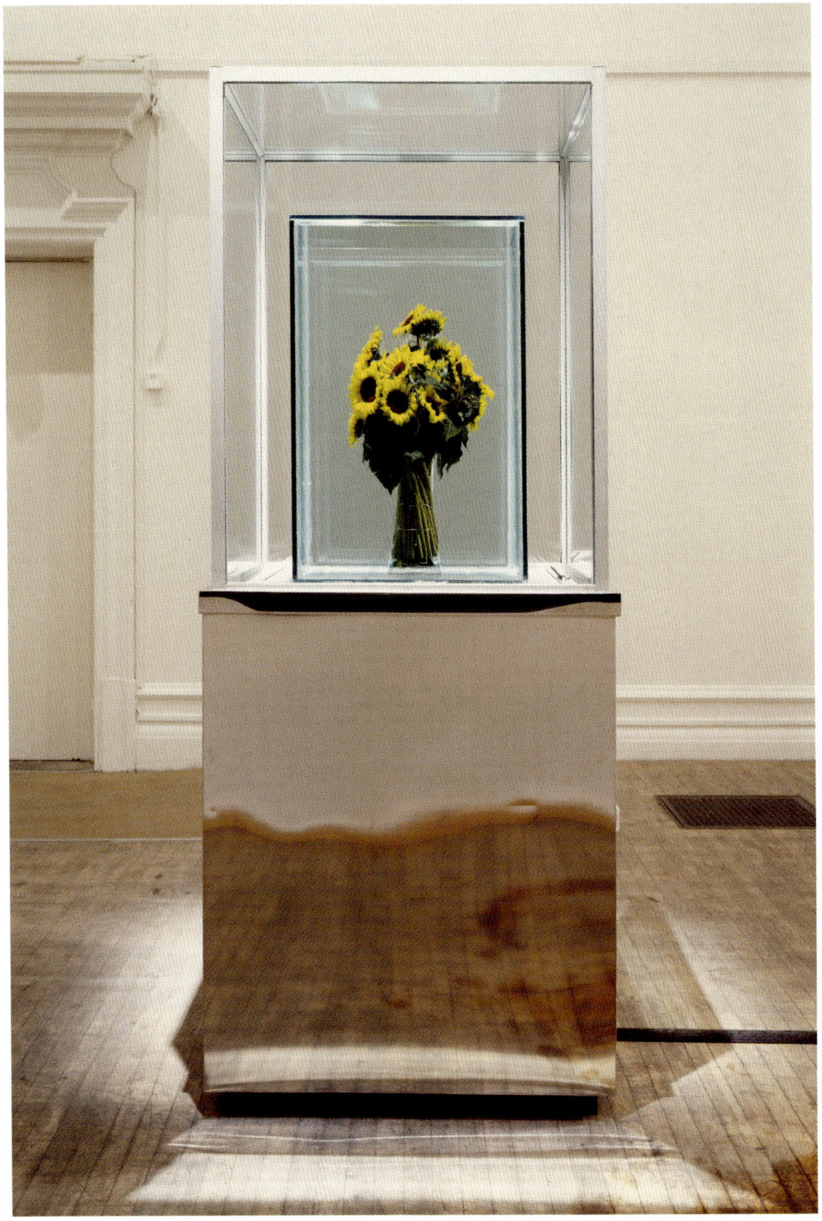

ABOVE
Marc Quinn
Eternal Spring (Sunflower) II, 1998 · stainless steel, glass, frozen silicon, sunflowers and refrigeration equipment

OPPOSITE
Michael Petry
Red Roses, 2009 · blown glass and cut flowers

Marc Quinn has attempted to stop time, or at least halt its harsh aging flow, by freezing pristine sunflower blooms in silicon, whether frozen, as in *Eternal Spring (Sunflower) II*, or liquid, as in *Garden* (2000). 'The flowers, when they freeze, become pure image,' he has said. 'Their matter is dead and they are suspended in a state of transformation between pure image and pure matter.'

Michael Petry's series *The Revenge of the Florist* consists of glass and flower sculptures, and an accompanying photographic series depicting these over time. Curators may either replenish the vessels with fresh flowers or allow them to dry out, but they are never to be shown empty. These complex objects speak a number of languages. The first is the Victorian language of flowers: for example, red roses for true love. The second is the 1970s gay handkerchief code, whereby a man advertised his interest in a particular sexual activity via the colour of his handkerchief (red for fisting). The third is the digital language of the 'web portrait'; the rim of each vessel is Petry's portrait of an anus contributed to the project online. Whether it was the virtual contributor's, or someone else's, remains unknown.

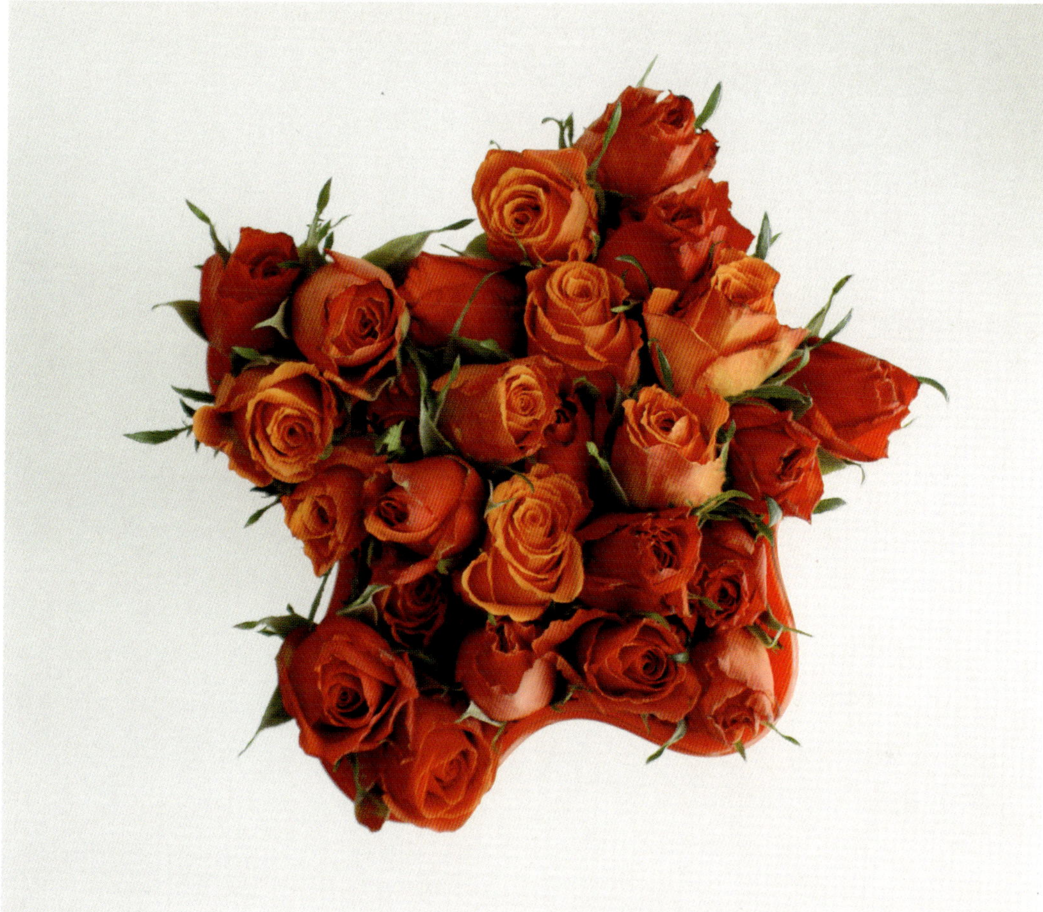

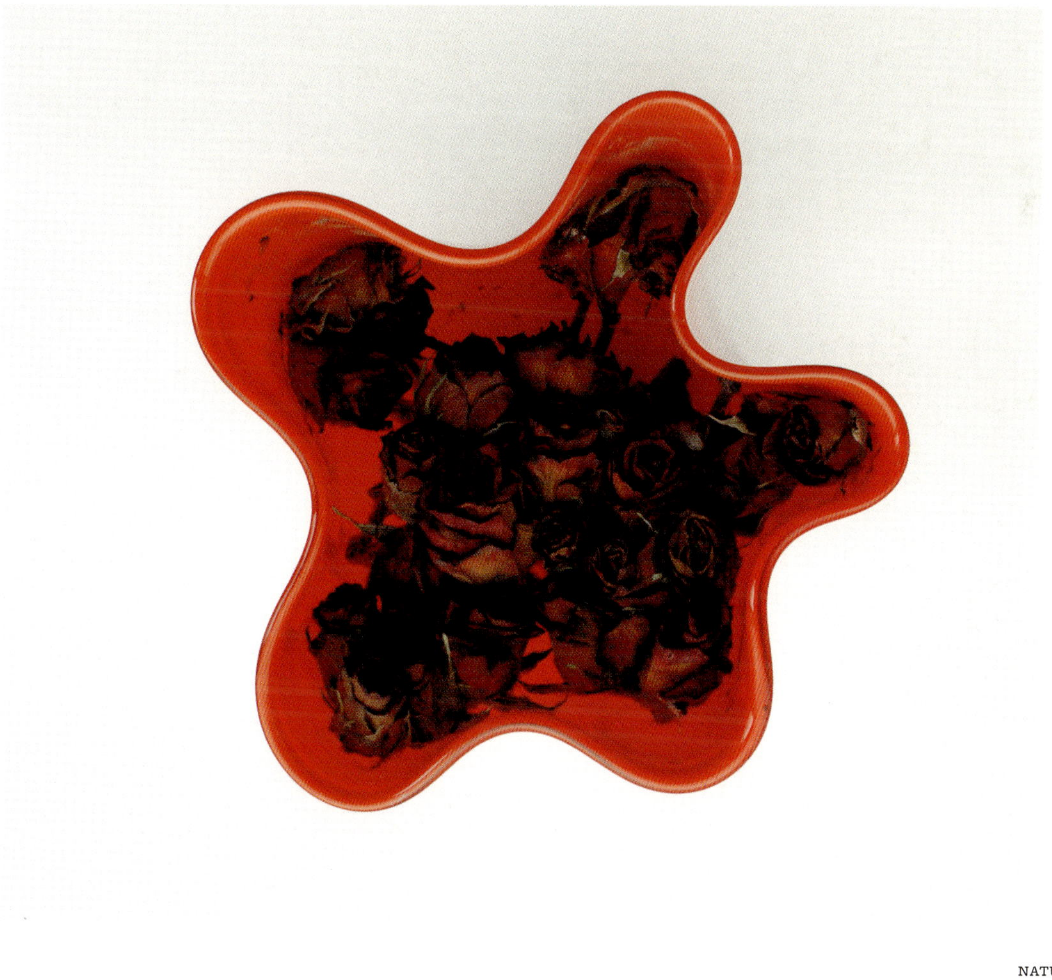

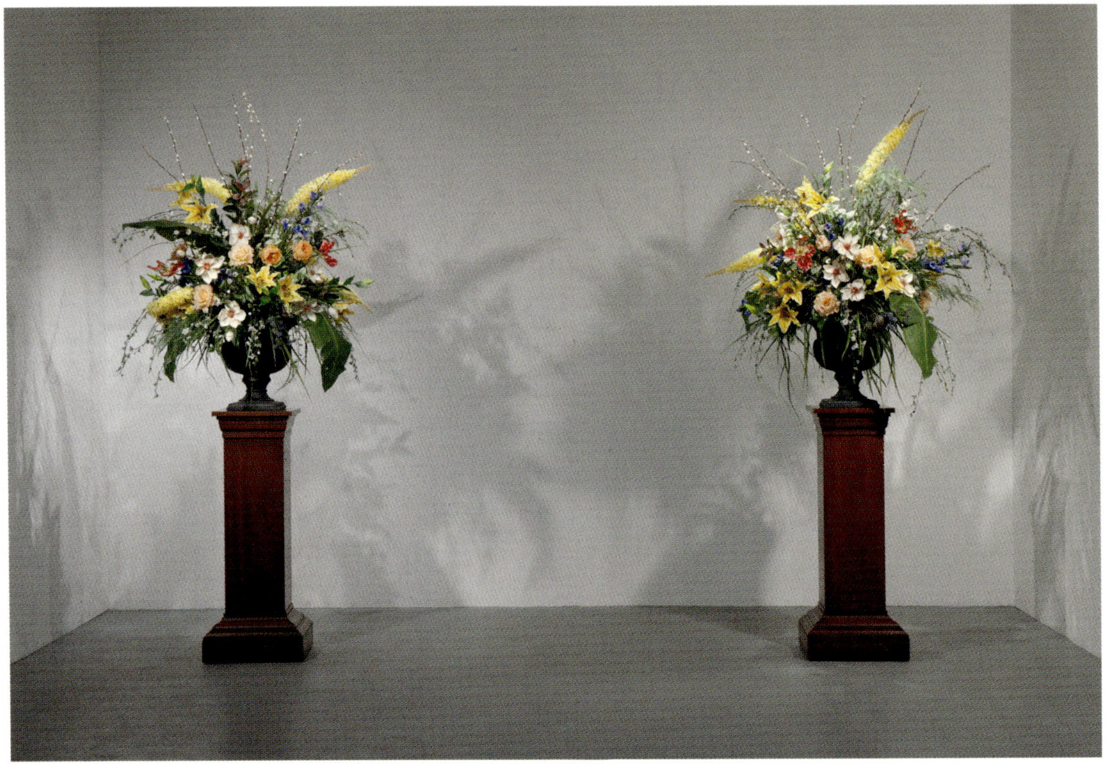

ABOVE
Mark Wallinger
Double Still Life, 2009
silk, plastic urn, lacquered MDF and softwood

OPPOSITE
Anya Gallaccio
Preserve 'Beauty', 1991/2003 · 1,800 red gerbera 'Beauty' and glass

Mark Wallinger's interest in doubling and mirroring is apparent in *Double Still Life*, a sculptural installation that comprises a pair of nearly identical displays of artificial flowers. That the bouquets are *not* exactly the same speaks of the inevitable failure of our human striving for perfection. The work is quietly political in contrast to Wallinger's more overtly political work *State Britain* (2007), which recreated Brian Haw's controversial anti-war protest camp sited opposite the Houses of Parliament in London. *Double Still Life* does not change or decay; its stilled-ness is at the heart of its meaning.

Anya Gallaccio confronts the viewer with the disintegration and decay wrought by time upon the materials that make up her work: fresh flowers wilt, rot and dry out; ice melts away; salt is returned to the sea; unfixed photographs fade in the light. Her *Preserve 'Beauty'*, originally shown at the Karsten Schubert Gallery, London, in 1991, has been re-sited in many versions. At Tate Modern in 1993, four large panels of gerbera flowers were pressed between sheets of glass and left to fade in the gallery. The inherent violence in the death of the flowers, cut in their prime, then doomed to shrivel on view, reminded the viewer of the long tradition of the flower as a metaphor for human beauty, equally doomed and impossible to preserve.

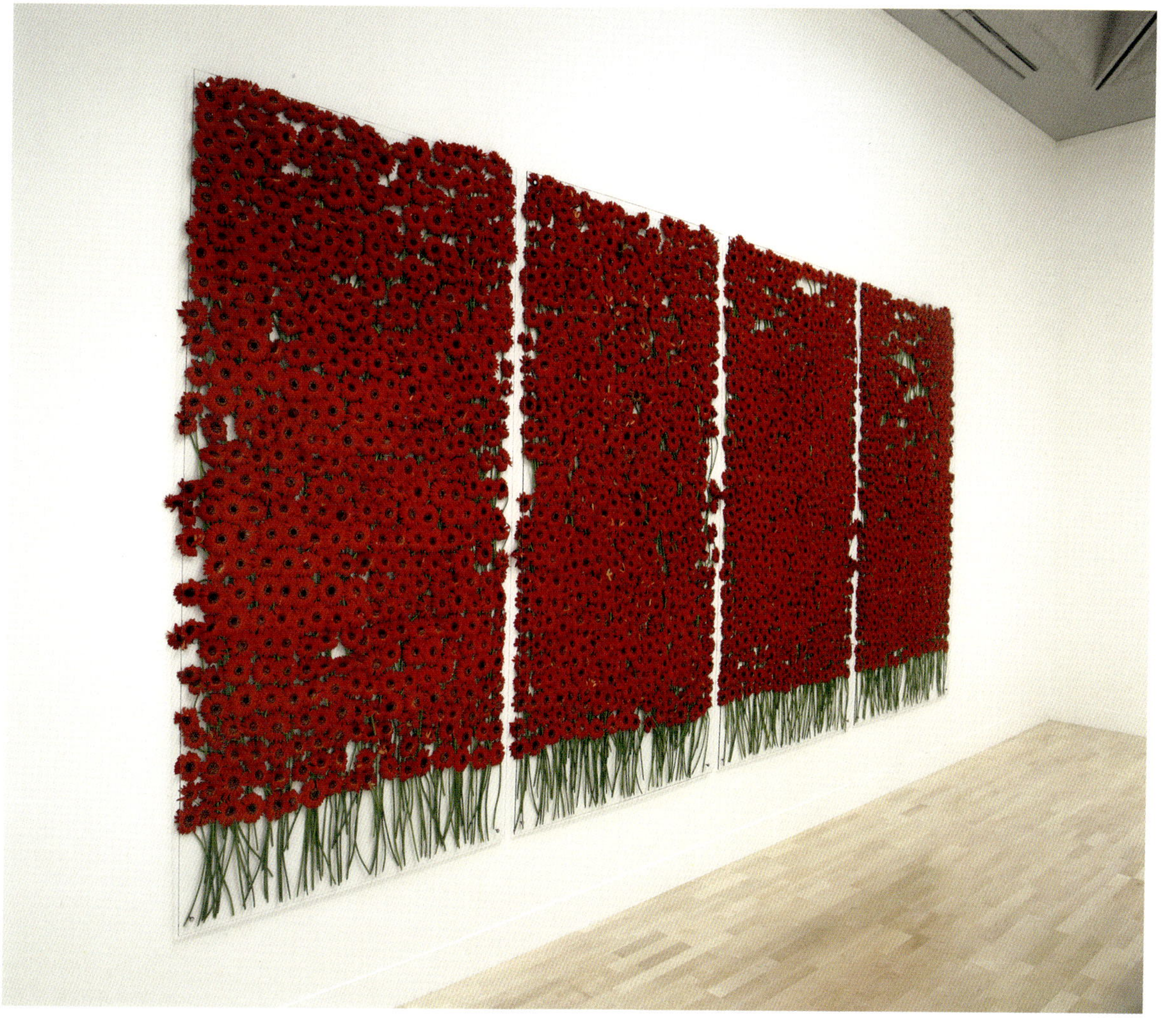

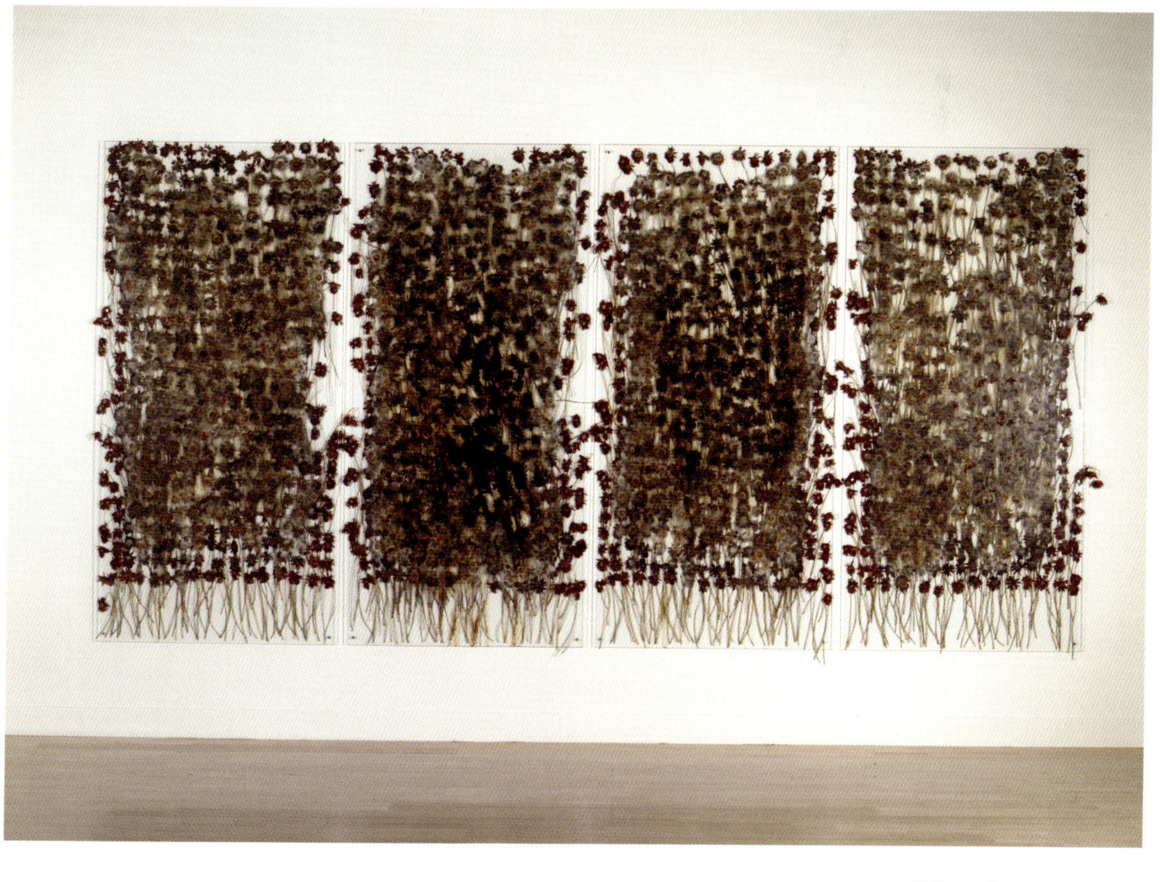

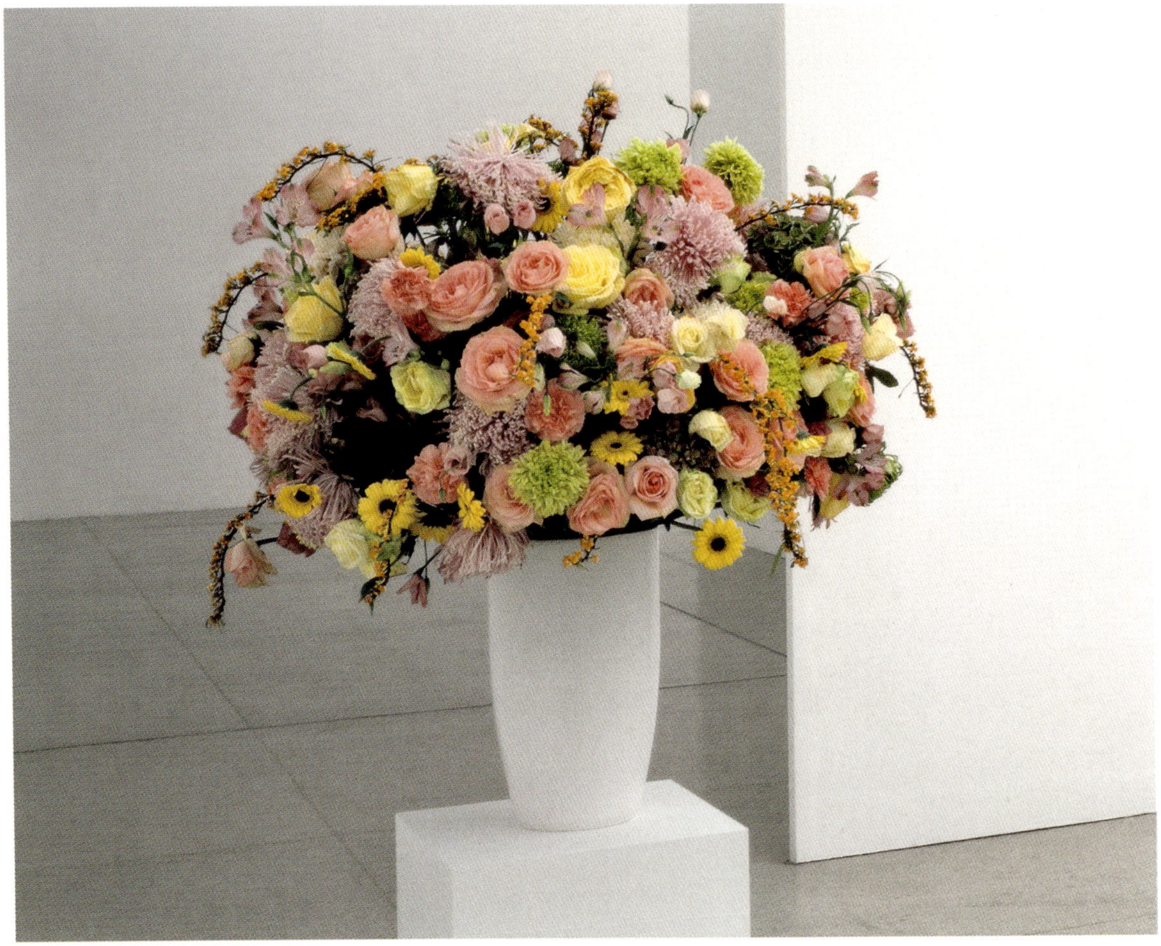

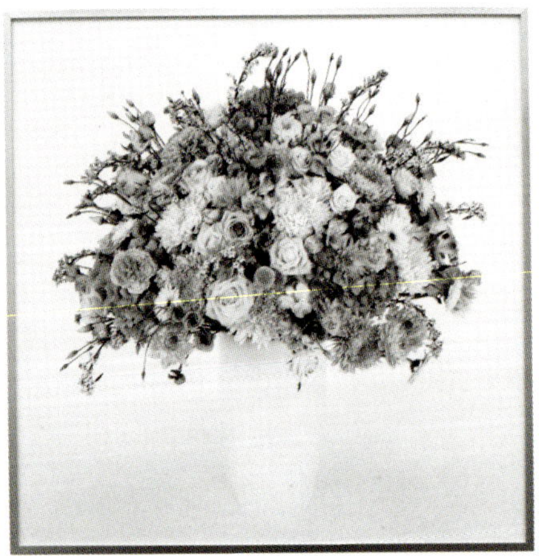

Jeroen de Rijke and Willem de Rooij's *Bouquet IV* consists of both a lavish floral arrangement in a white ceramic vase and a black-and-white photograph of the same. The artist duo work with photography in many ways but always in an attempt to question the difference between what our eyes see and what our brains perceive. Here, the artists explained, the bouquet 'was organized so that its colours in black and white reproduction translate into a relatively small range of grey shades, resulting in an even spread of tones from which high contrasts and extremes on either side of the spectrum are excluded'. The real therefore contrasts with its representation, and while the latter remains constant, the former continually changes.

ABOVE AND LEFT
Jeroen de Rijke / Willem de Rooij
Bouquet IV, 2005
flower arrangement in white ceramic vase; gelatin silver print in aluminium frame

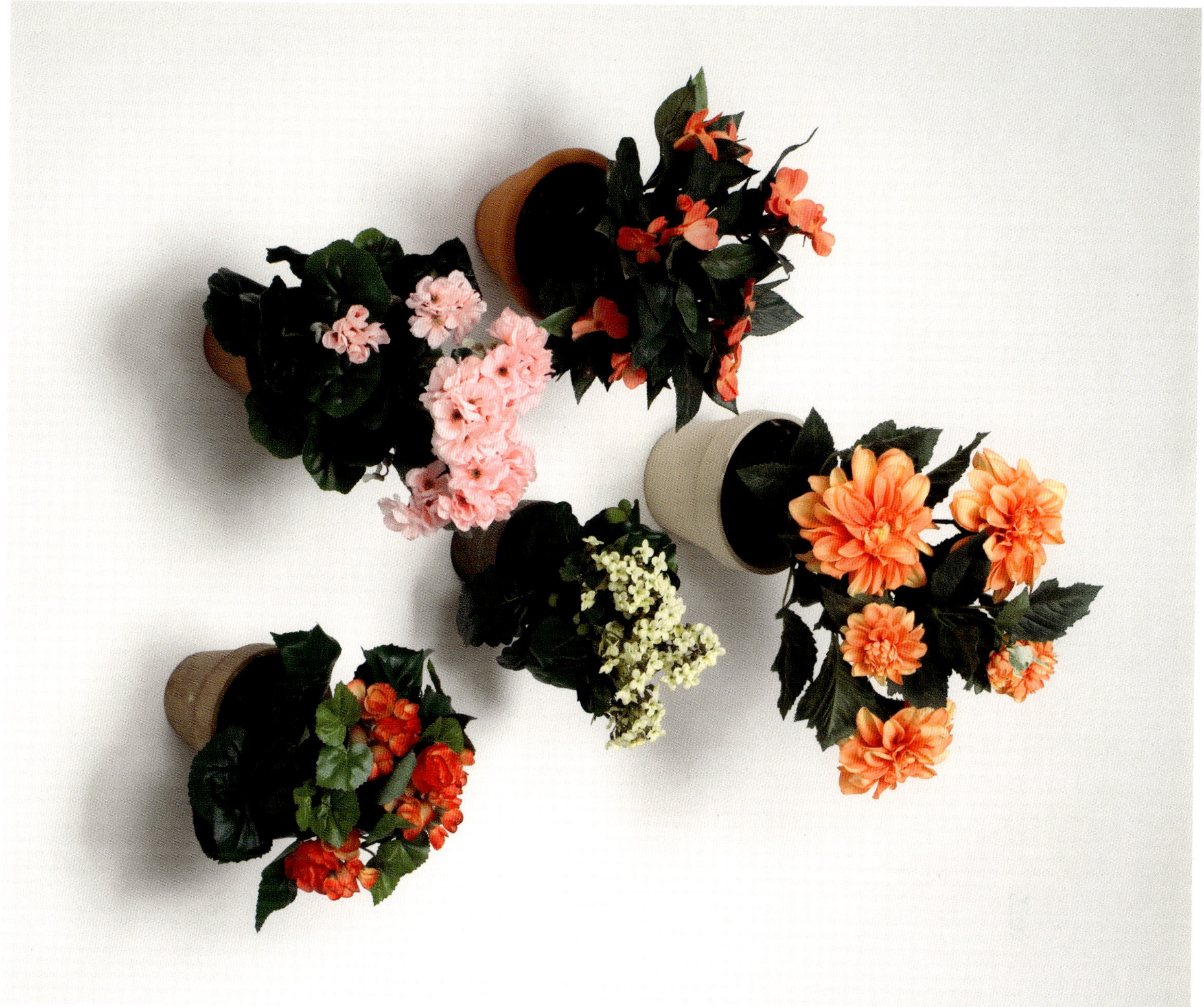

Hans-Peter Feldmann is one of Conceptual art's elder statesmen and his works have taken numerous forms over many years. A recent series of wall-mounted fake flowers in plastic pots is at once a continuation of his investigation of the readymade and colourful Pop art, and a subtle invocation of death. Such artificial flowers are often found on graves. Feldmann turns them into tableaux that allow viewers to contemplate them not as kitsch objects, but as reminders of mortality.

ABOVE
Hans-Peter Feldmann
Flower Pot
mixed media

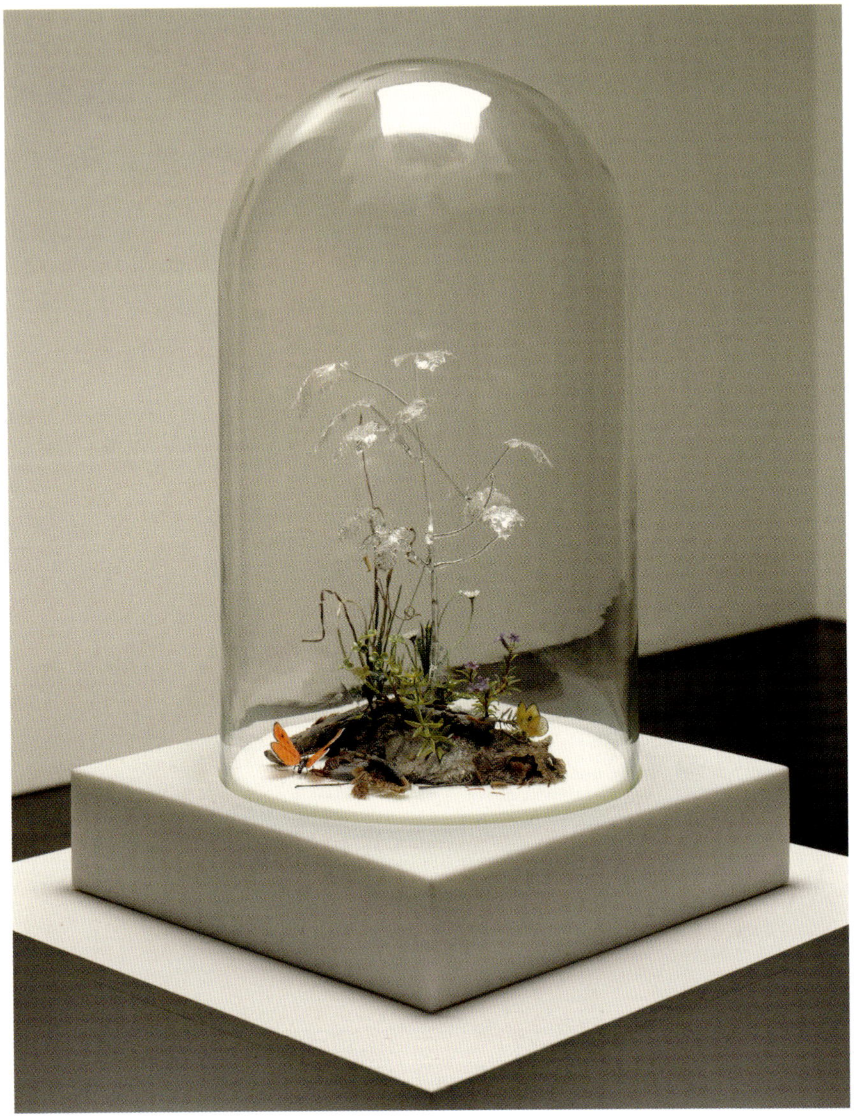

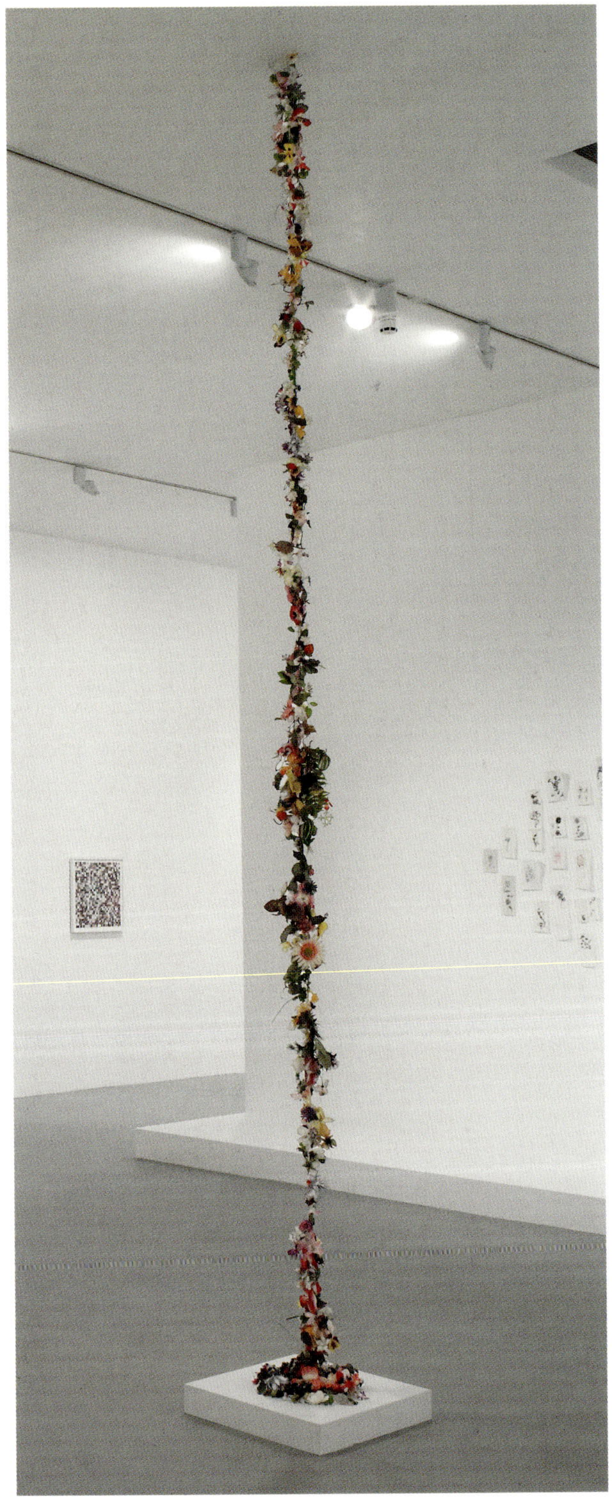

'I think that nature is what gave me my voice, I found my kind of language through nature, first of all through my own understanding of my own nature, my own shortcomings and limitations, and my own wanting to push beyond those limits....'

—JIM HODGES

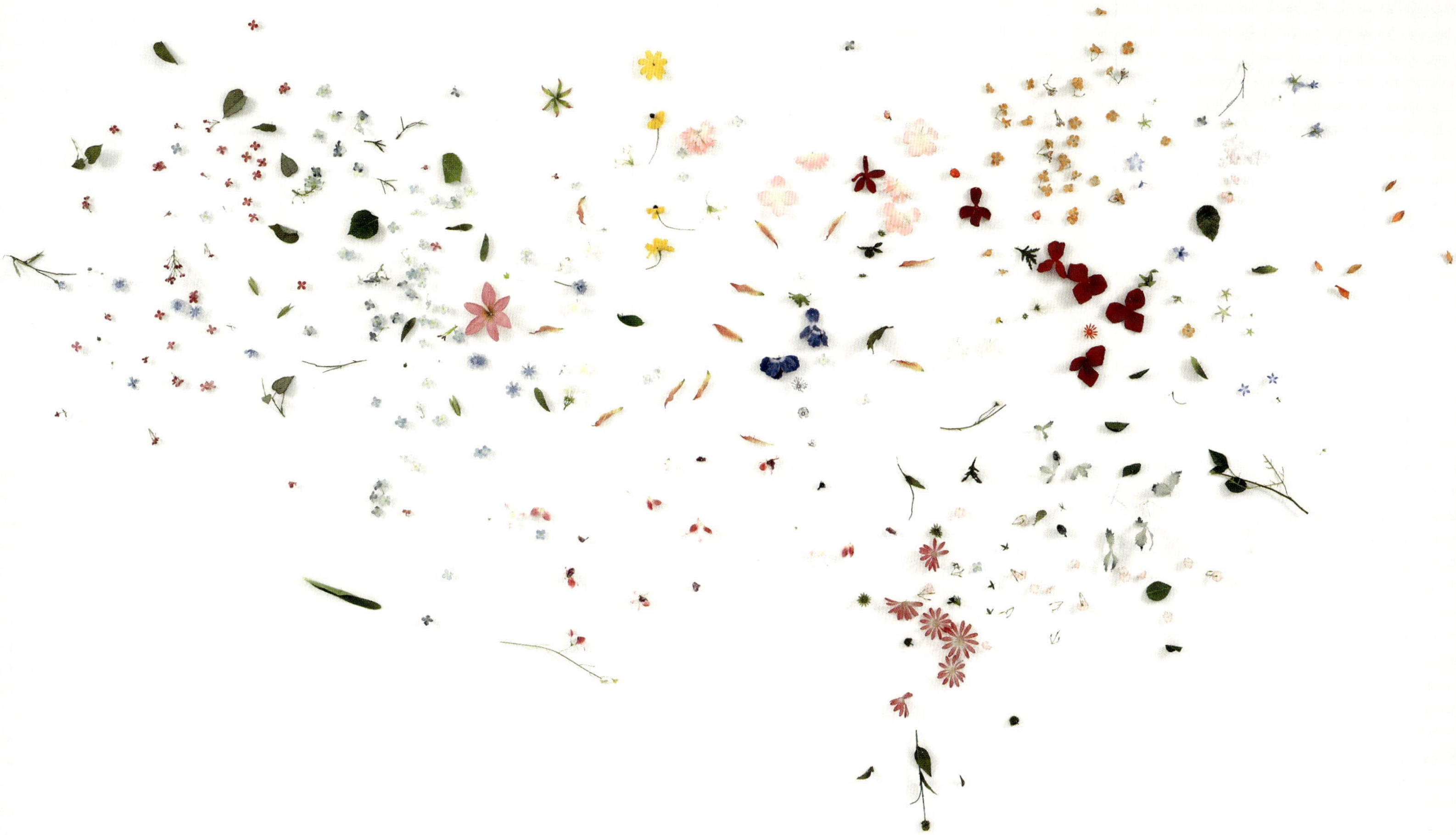

OPPOSITE LEFT
Jim Hodges · *ghost*, 2008
glass sculpture in multiple components

OPPOSITE RIGHT
Jim Hodges · *A Line to You*, 1994
silk, plastic and wire with thread

ABOVE
Jim Hodges · *Changing things*, 1997 · silk, plastic, wire and pins

Jim Hodges is interested in many of the traditional icons of the still life – flowers, butterflies, mirrors, spider's webs. His work is surprising and delicately sculptural. He has stitched together mass-produced silk flowers to form curtains, as in *No Betweens* (1996), and pinned them directly onto the wall in *Changing things*. His work reflects his interest in Jean Genet's 1943 novel, *Our Lady of the Flowers*, which chronicles the down-and-out existence of petty criminals and the fragility of their homosexual lives and loves. In Hodges's work, queerness, transience, mortality and beauty intertwine to elicit an emotional reaction from the viewer, a reminder of joy as well as poignant loss.

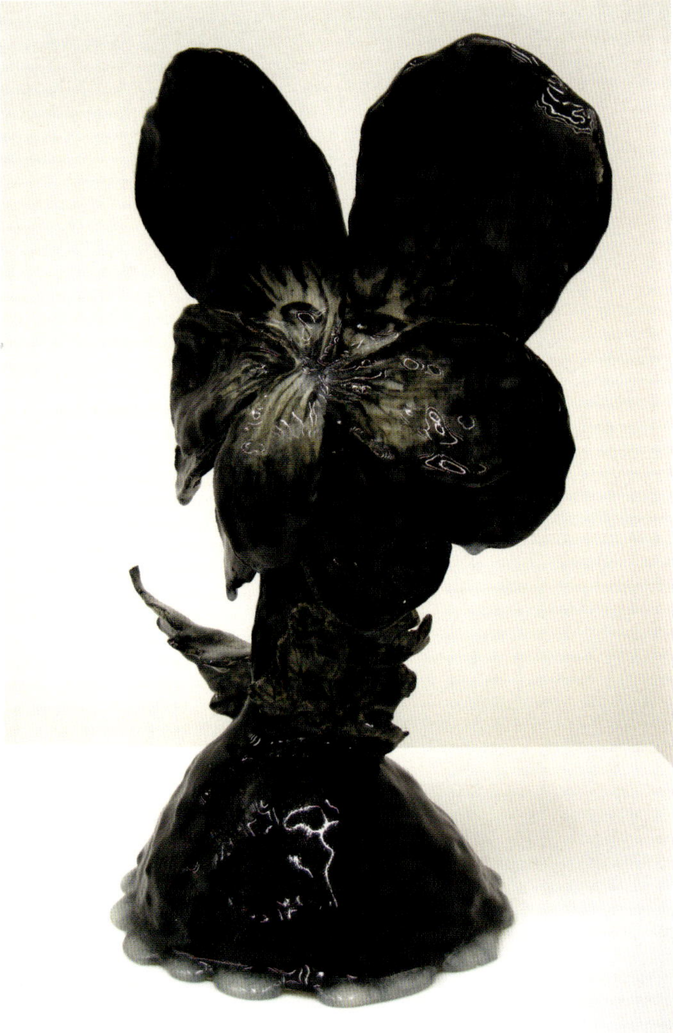

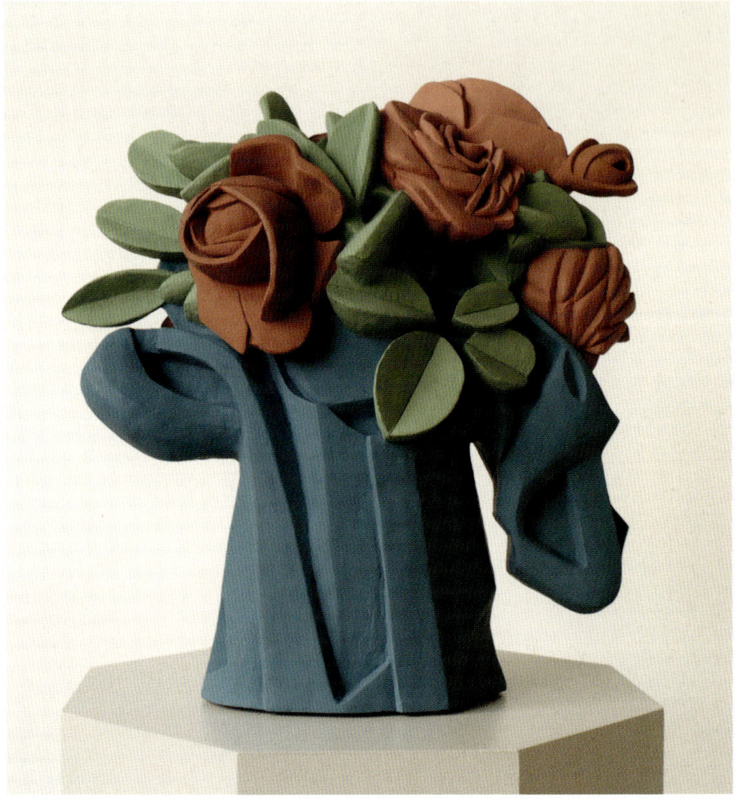

Klara Kristalova uses glazed stoneware to make her disturbing small-scale sculptures that recall Nordic creation myths. Her dark investigations into dreams and memory are often linked to stories of young women who morph into other creatures. A white swan that seems to be calmly floating past is called *Maneater* (2009), while another sculpture of a girl is titled *Becoming a Dog* (2009). Her sinister *Black Pansy* is wholly lacking the cheerful delicacy of this familiar flower.

Marc Quinn's bronze sculpture looks at first glance like a cast of a commonplace potted orchid. But this exotic specimen is made of several different plant species joined together to form a rather attractive, Frankenstein-like whole. A large cucumber hangs vertically from a central stem and the plant has produced tomatoes as well as blooms. Evidencing a high level of sophisticated casting, this work questions what is natural and what is artificial, and reminds us that the plants most familiar to us nowadays are often the products of human intervention. The title points to the impossibility of such a plant existing in this world and, in doing so, speaks of another, more fruitful one.

Georgie Hopton works in a variety of media that feed into each other, including sculpture, painting, photography and performance. Her recent works focusing on floral motifs are no exception. *Flowers in a Bag*, shown atop a polished plinth, resembles many of her paintings and photographs of similar blooms. These subjects tend to come from her own garden: 'I am growing my first flowers, then my first vegetables. They come up out of the ground and they look like sculptures. My relationship with them is not only one of total pleasure but that I am becoming a gardener. This notion in time turns to frustration as I think I am not a gardener, I am an artist. So what the hell is going on here?' This slippage in roles recurs in the works themselves; the sculptures are painterly, the photographs sculptural, the paintings viewed as if through a filter.

ABOVE LEFT · Klara Kristalova · *Black Pansy*, 2009 · glazed stoneware

ABOVE RIGHT · Georgie Hopton · *Flowers in a Bag*, 2007 · acrylic on jesmonite

OPPOSITE · Marc Quinn · *The Nurseries of El Dorado (cucumissativus-paphiopedlium solanumlycopersicumphalenopsispotinaraanthuriumpyrus)*, 2007 · bronze with heat-treated chrome patina

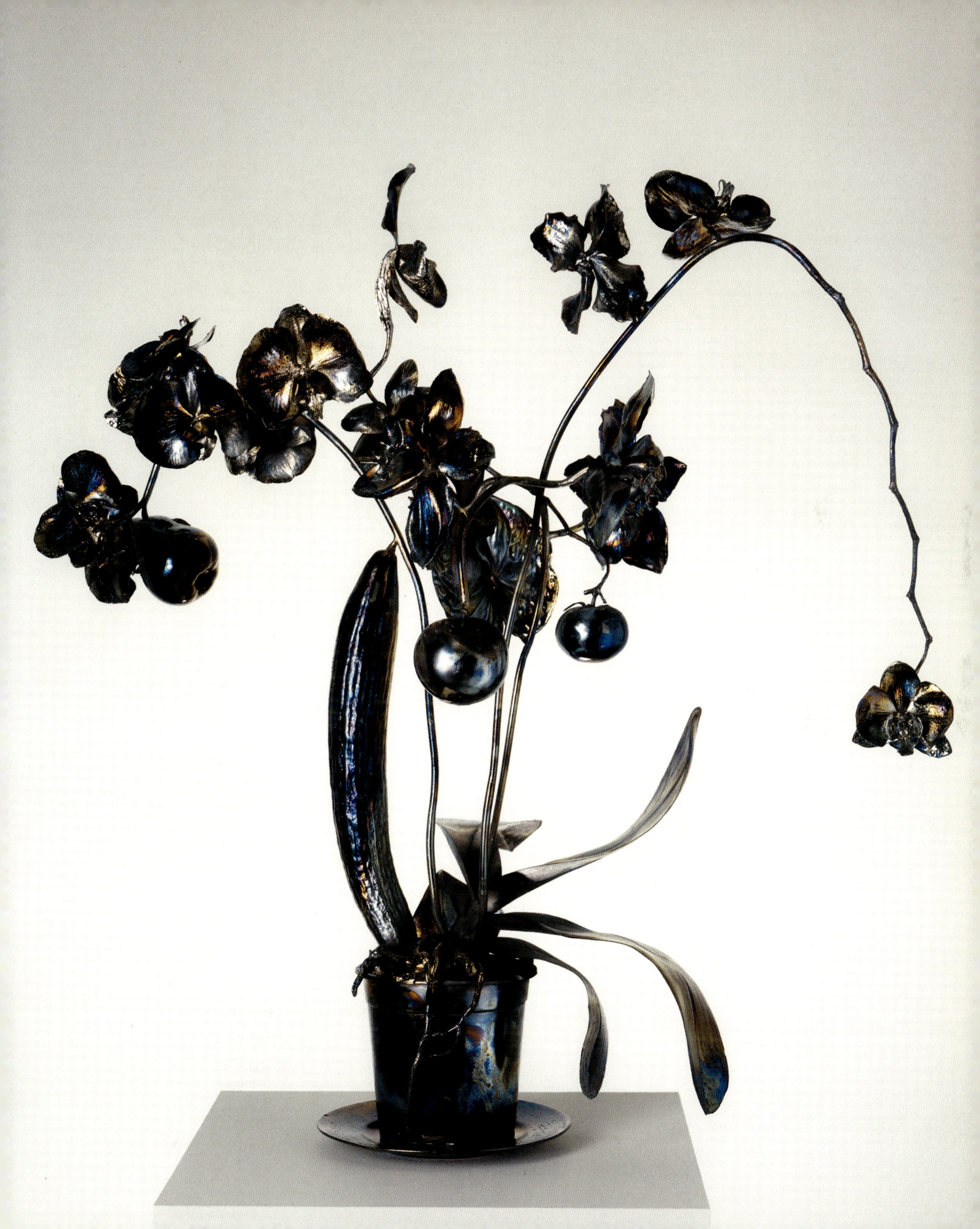

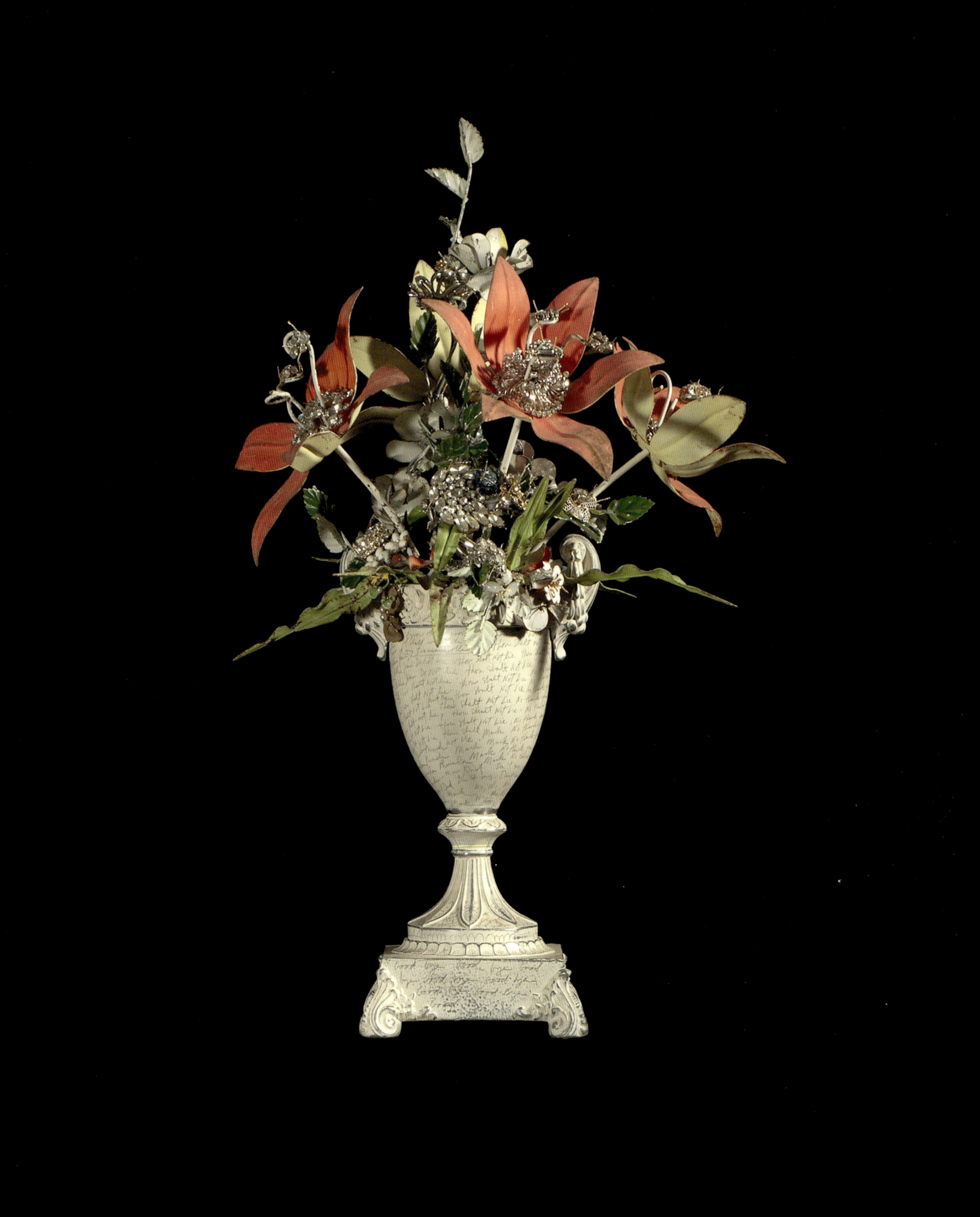

Karin Broker's work touches on femininity, tragedy, gender stereotypes and even happily-ever-afters. The artist adds: 'My work has visually dealt with bad boyfriends, quirky family problems, death and that ever-marching ticking of time called aging.' Working in a variety of media, Broker often turns to the floral still life in works that suggest the possibility of, if not perpetual happiness, then at least détente with the Grim Reaper.

Nicky Deeley's 2009 exhibition 'Ping Ping Ping' featured *Gardens 1 and Gardens 2*, which at first glance appears to be two colourful floral arrangements. Look closer and one finds that these stems are sprouting from the corpses of small stuffed animals (serpents, rats, corporate mascots). These soft fabric forms act as suspended hydroponic gardens, embodying the cycles of nature: life, death, decay and rebirth.

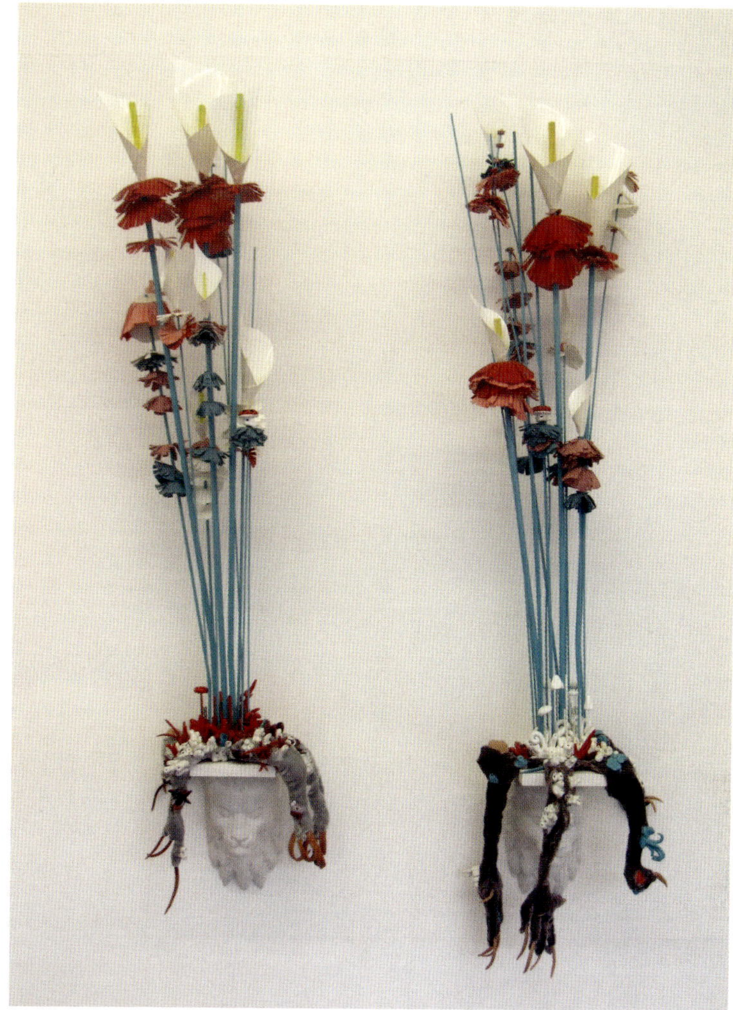

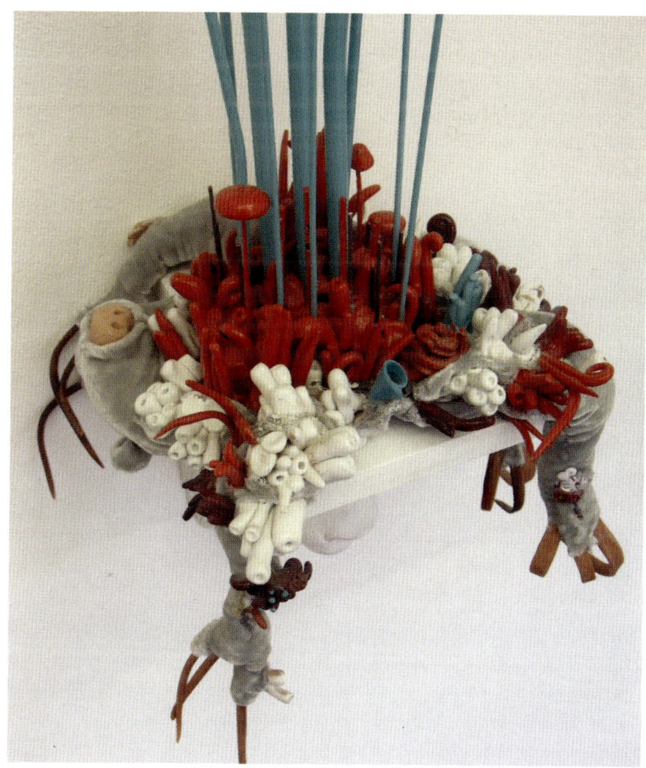

OPPOSITE
Karin Broker
Don't Lie Bouquet, 2005–12
metal, graphite, rhinestones and wire

ABOVE AND RIGHT
Nicky Deeley
Gardens 1 and Gardens 2, 2009
fabric, modelling compound, steel, vinyl, rubber and timber

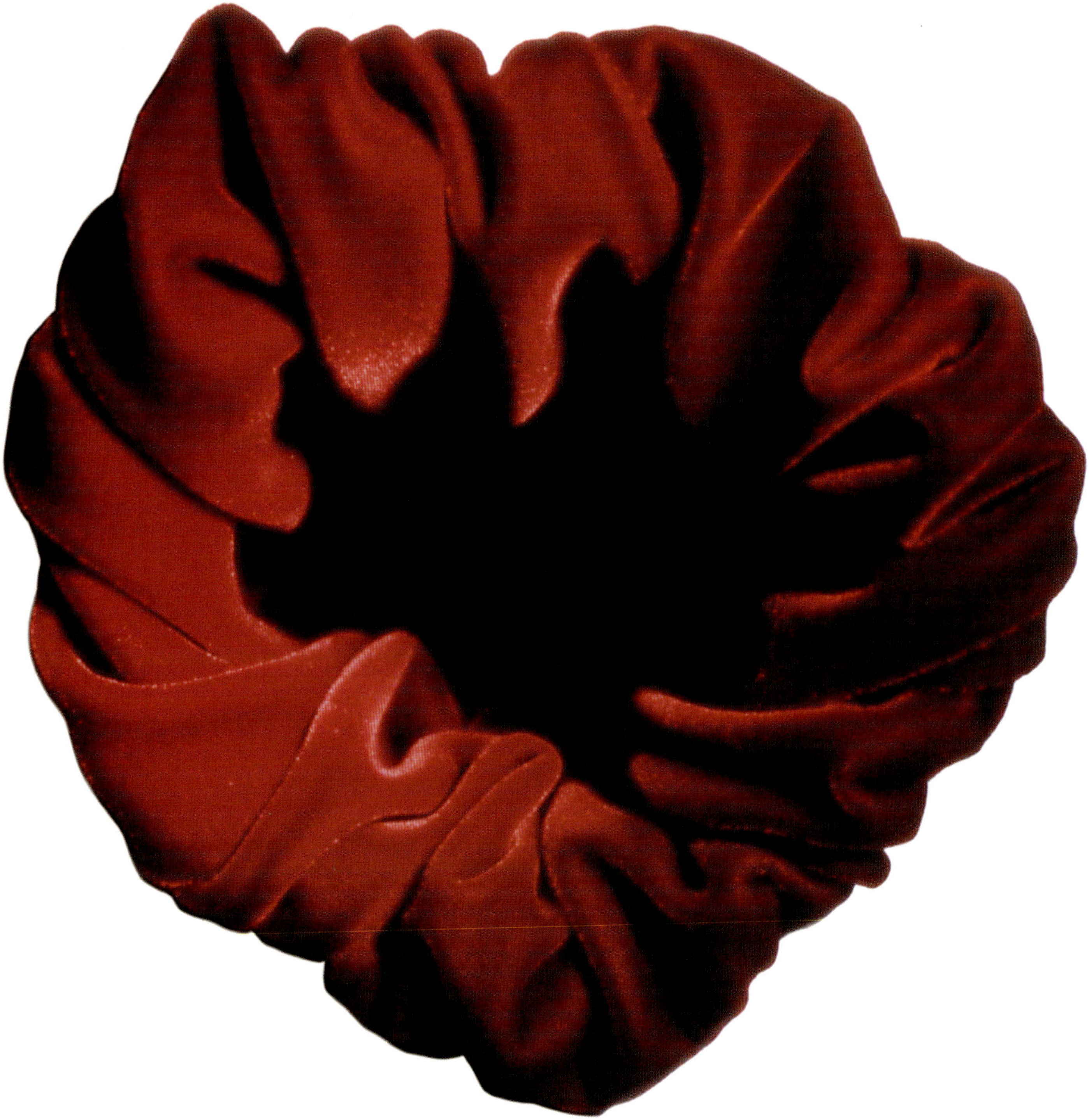

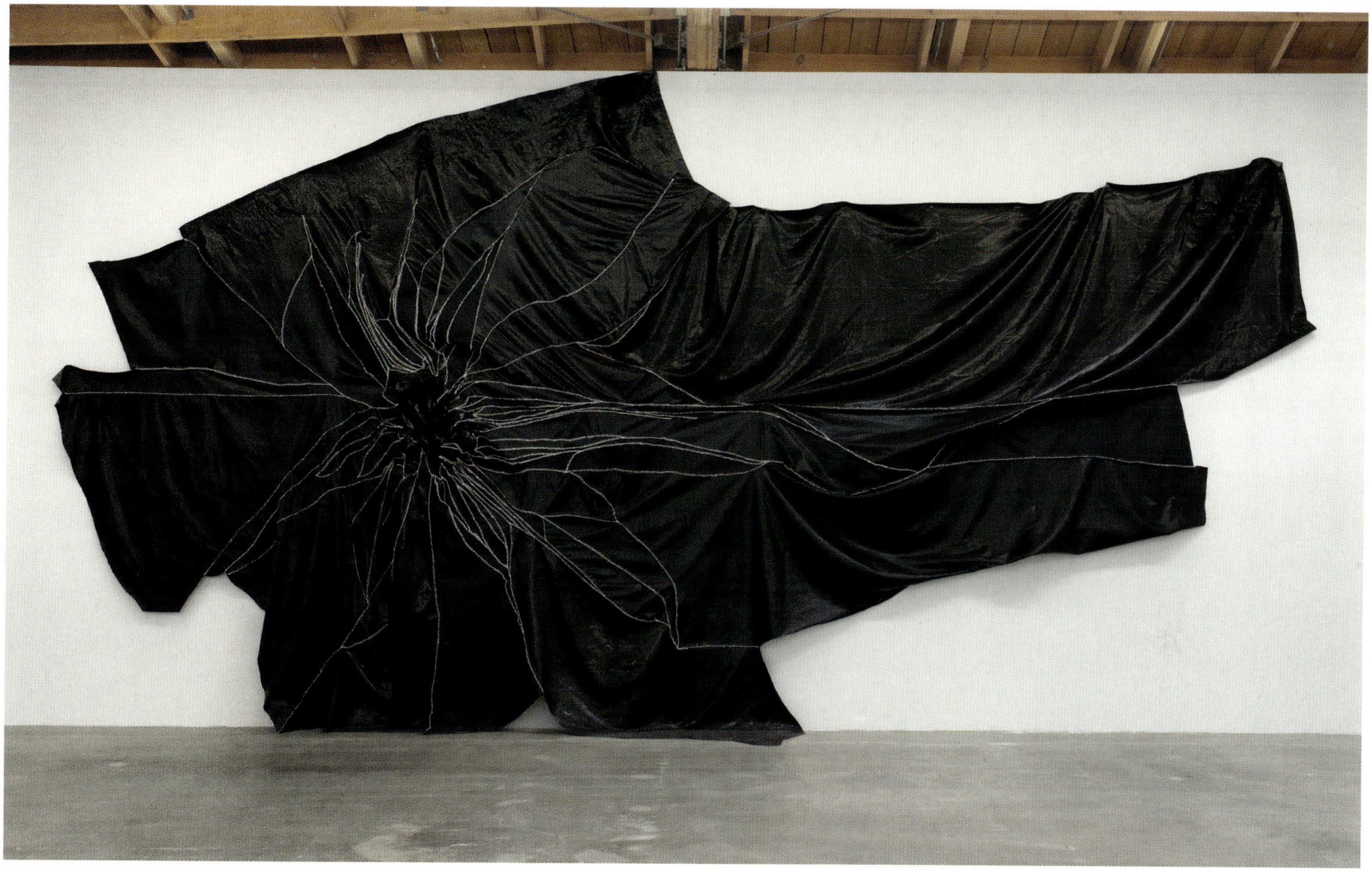

OPPOSITE
Philip Pirolo
Velvet Orifice, 1991
velvet and gallery wall

ABOVE
Rodney McMillian
Untitled, 2010
vinyl and thread

Philip Pirolo's *Velvet Orifice* is an installation of luscious red velvet affixed on and into the wall of a gallery. As with Anish Kapoor's insertions into walls, the first thing that strikes the viewer is the rich colour of the work, but Pirolo's rosebud also speaks of adult sexuality and homosexual desire. The queerness of this unexpected opening continues to resonate in America long after the original HIV/AIDs crisis (when the work was first installed) since same-sex love remains a source of cultural strife.

Rodney McMillian's 2010 show 'Succulent' centred around a large work in black vinyl, hand-sewn with white thread, that covered much of one wall of the gallery space. Surrounded by potted plants, the work resembled both an anus and a flower blossom, with a dark opening at its centre. McMillian is interested in the idea of the home and how cultural, political, racial and personal realities shape our understanding of this concept, as well as loss, absence and the void.

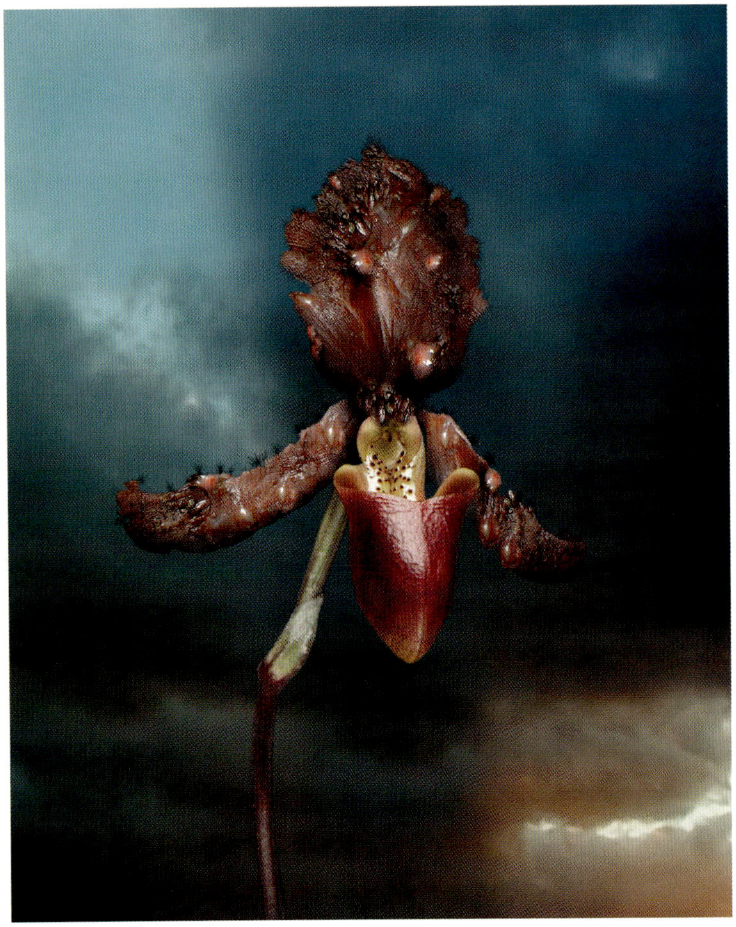

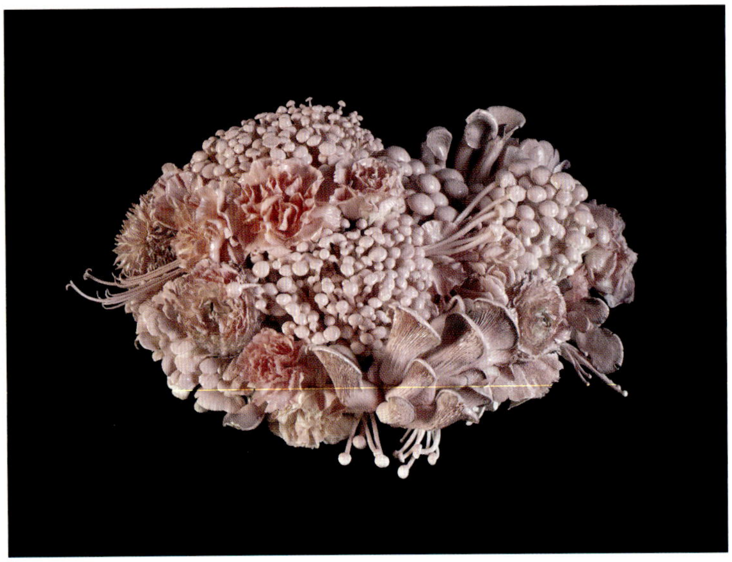

Mat Collishaw's photographic series *Infectious Flowers* appears to document perfect specimens of rare flowers. But on closer inspection it becomes apparent that the flowers' surfaces have been digitally altered: the artist has grafted images of skin diseases onto the petals. Collishaw, like Jim Hodges, has been influenced by the writings of the French novelist Jean Genet. He recalls how, while in prison for a series of minor offenses, the writer 'described his cellmate's wounds and pustules as embellishments. Like flowers or medals adorning a man's jacket. The lines between beauty and repulsion become blurred.'

Saara Ekström photographs constructions of flowers, mushrooms, hair and fruit in order to create formally challenging works with disturbing underlying narratives. In *Breeding*, the flowers resemble not only exotic fungi, but also the internal organs of the human body. Other arrangements of flowers and mushrooms from her *Excess and Ascesis* series look as if they might have been retrieved from a murder scene. Ekström aims to inspire discomfort in the viewer, so that even as the sheer beauty of the image compels the eye, the brain is keen to turn away.

In his 2008–11 photographic series *Earth Laughs in Flowers*, **David LaChapelle** revisits, updates and subverts the classic Dutch formal floral display by including contemporary artefacts and symbols. *Wilting Gossip* ticks all the traditional boxes, with elegant flowers, glowing fruit and flies (even a cockroach), but the bouquet is depicted in a shoddy interior, perhaps a cheap motel room judging by the fan and air-conditioning unit. The still-burning cigarette (a contemporary metaphor for death or, at the very least, cancer) and the naked leg of its owner give an impression of exhaustion. The tabloid newspaper compounds the dingy atmosphere, with its front-page story about Michael Jackson, another contemporary symbol of human fallibility and mortality.

TOP · Mat Collishaw · *Infectious Orchid 2*, 2004 · digital print

ABOVE · Saara Ekström · *Breeding*, 2010 · C-print

OPPOSITE · David LaChapelle · *Wilting Gossip*, 2008–11 · chromogenic print

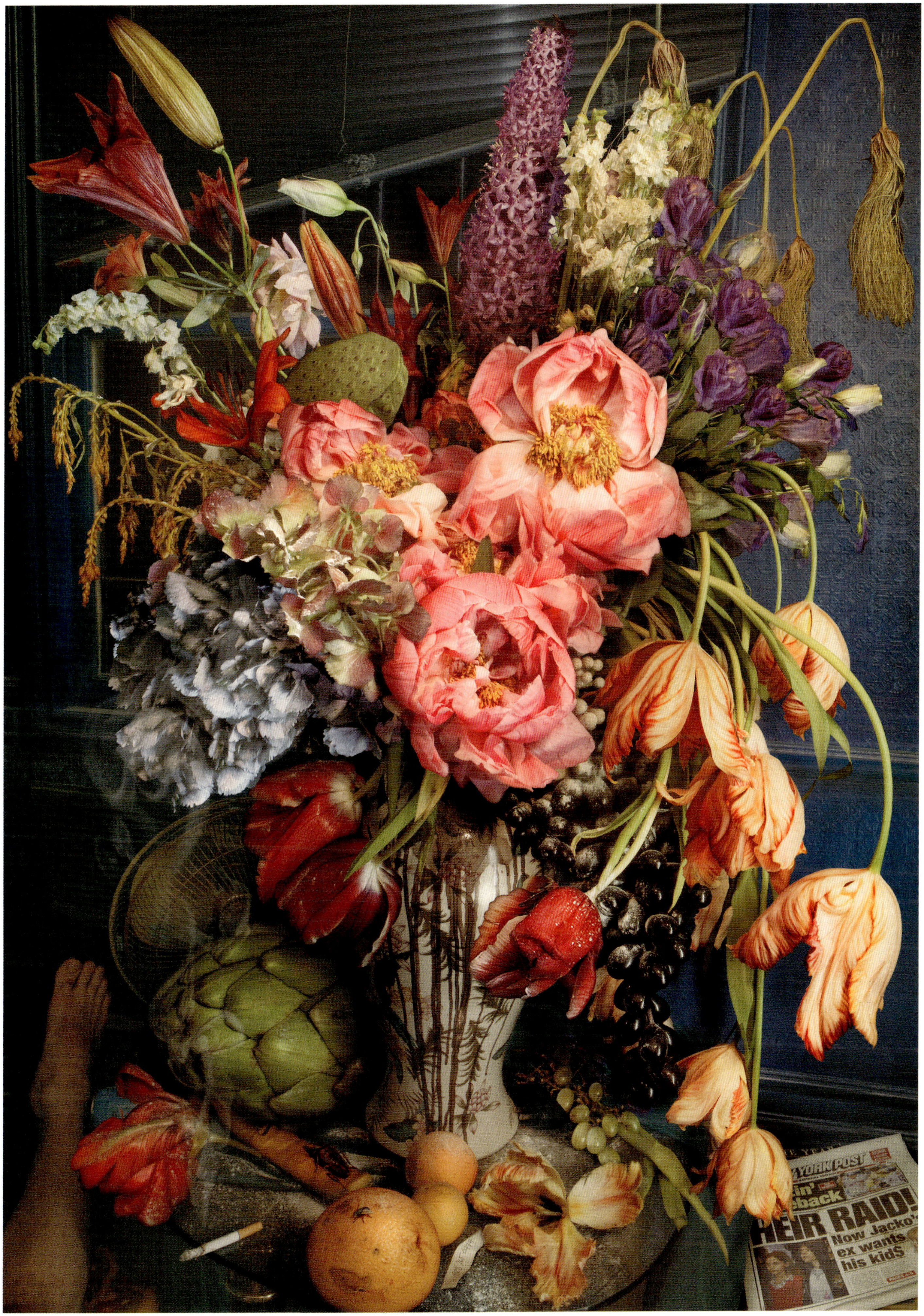
YORK POST
in'
eback
HEIR RAID!
Now Jacko's
ex wants
his kid$

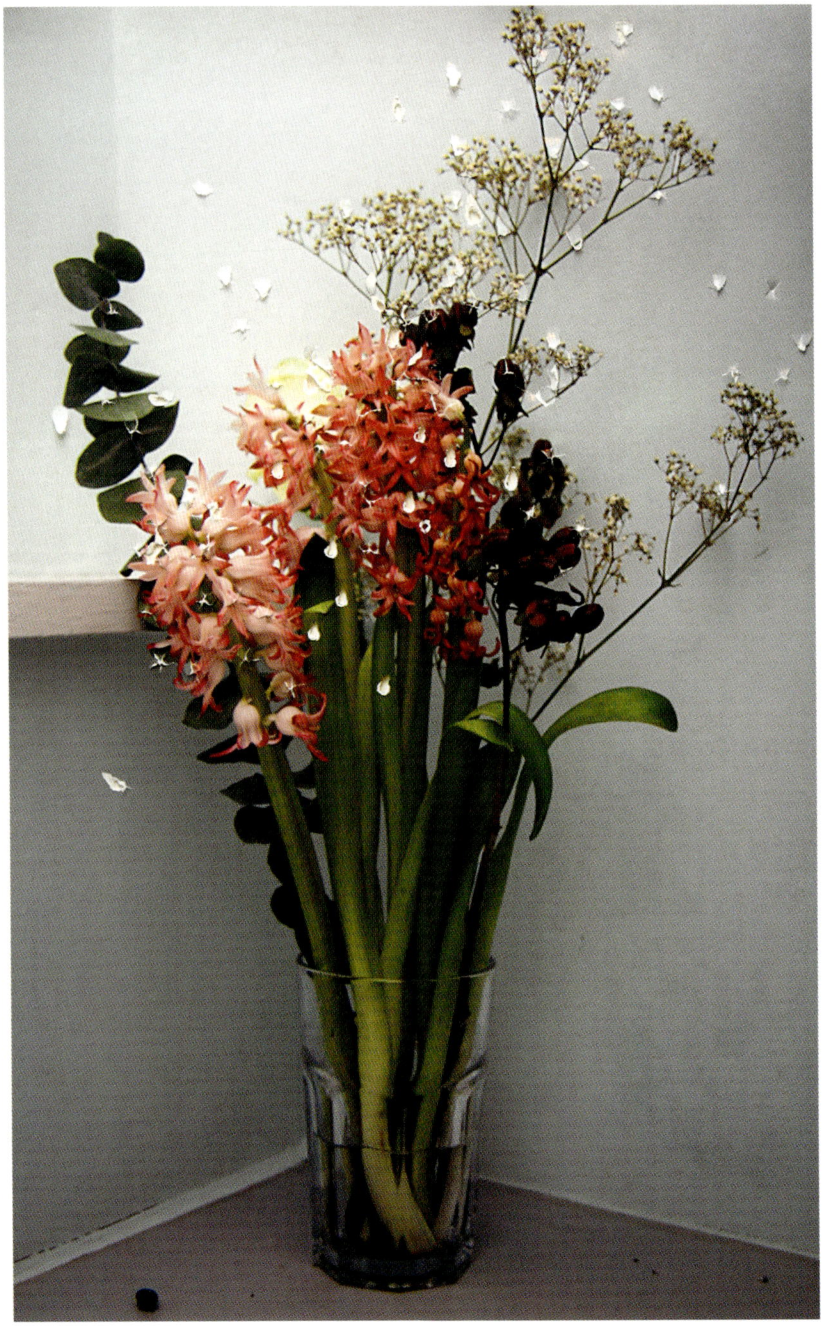

ABOVE
Alana Lake
***Stilleven I*, 2011**
archival digital print

OPPOSITE
Ori Gersht
***Time after Time: Blow up No. 3*, 2007**
light jet print on aluminium

A few flowers sit in a glass of water in what at first glance seems a straightforward floral still life. But there are odd scratches and holes in the surface of the photograph, which one learns the artist **Alana Lake** made by firing a pellet gun at the print. These imperfections interrupt the stilled surface of the image, introducing traces of real physical violence that echo the violence inherent in the photographic process, which ensures that the captured subject remains forever in perpetual stasis.

In a series of large-scale photographs entitled *Blow Up*, **Ori Gersht** documents the instant that a floral arrangement (based on a nineteenth-century still life by Henri Fantin-Latour) explodes. New developments in digital photography allowed the artist to capture the moment in 1/6000 of a second. Gersht contrasts the violence of the explosion with the calm of a traditional still-life painting, though the morbid message remains.

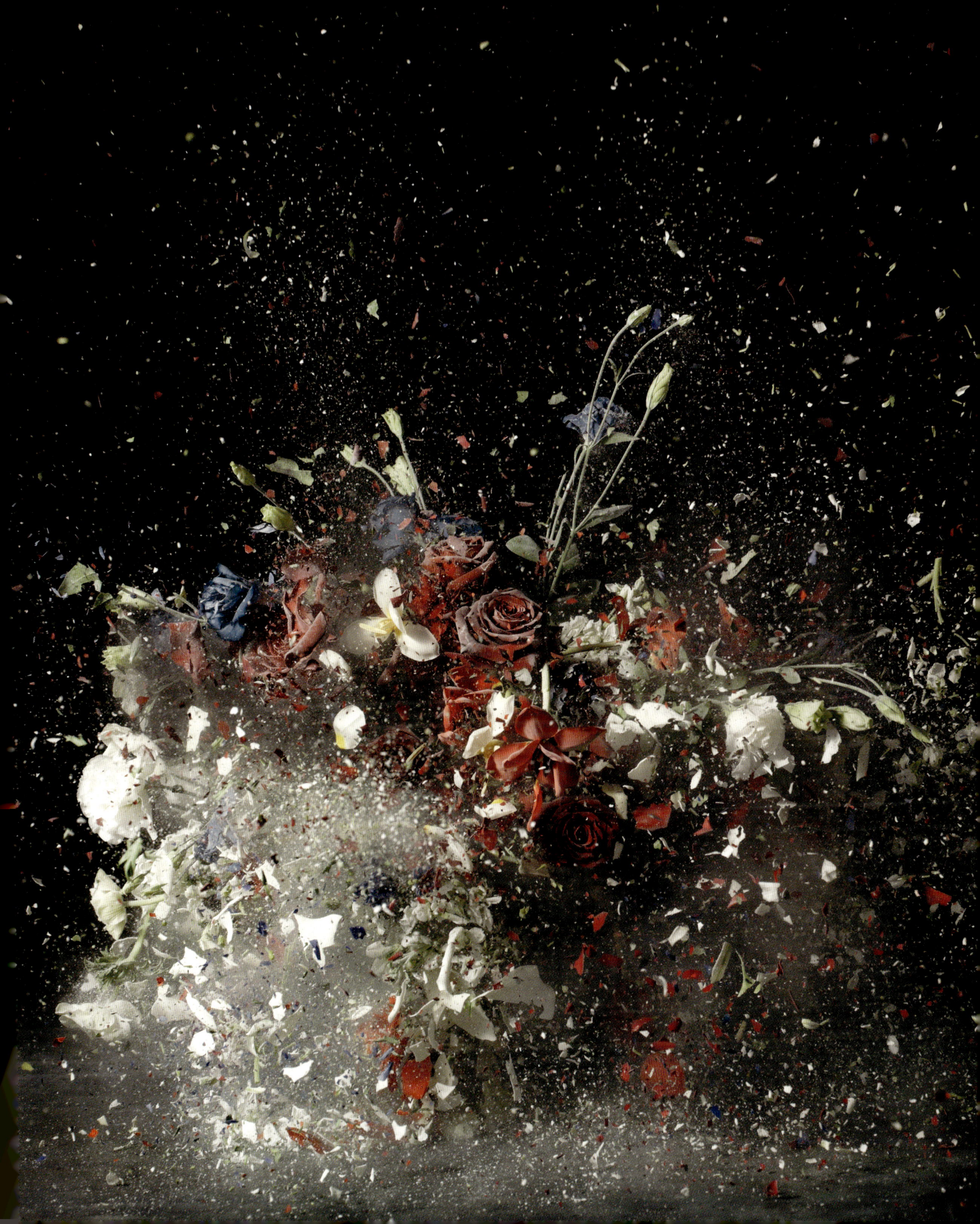

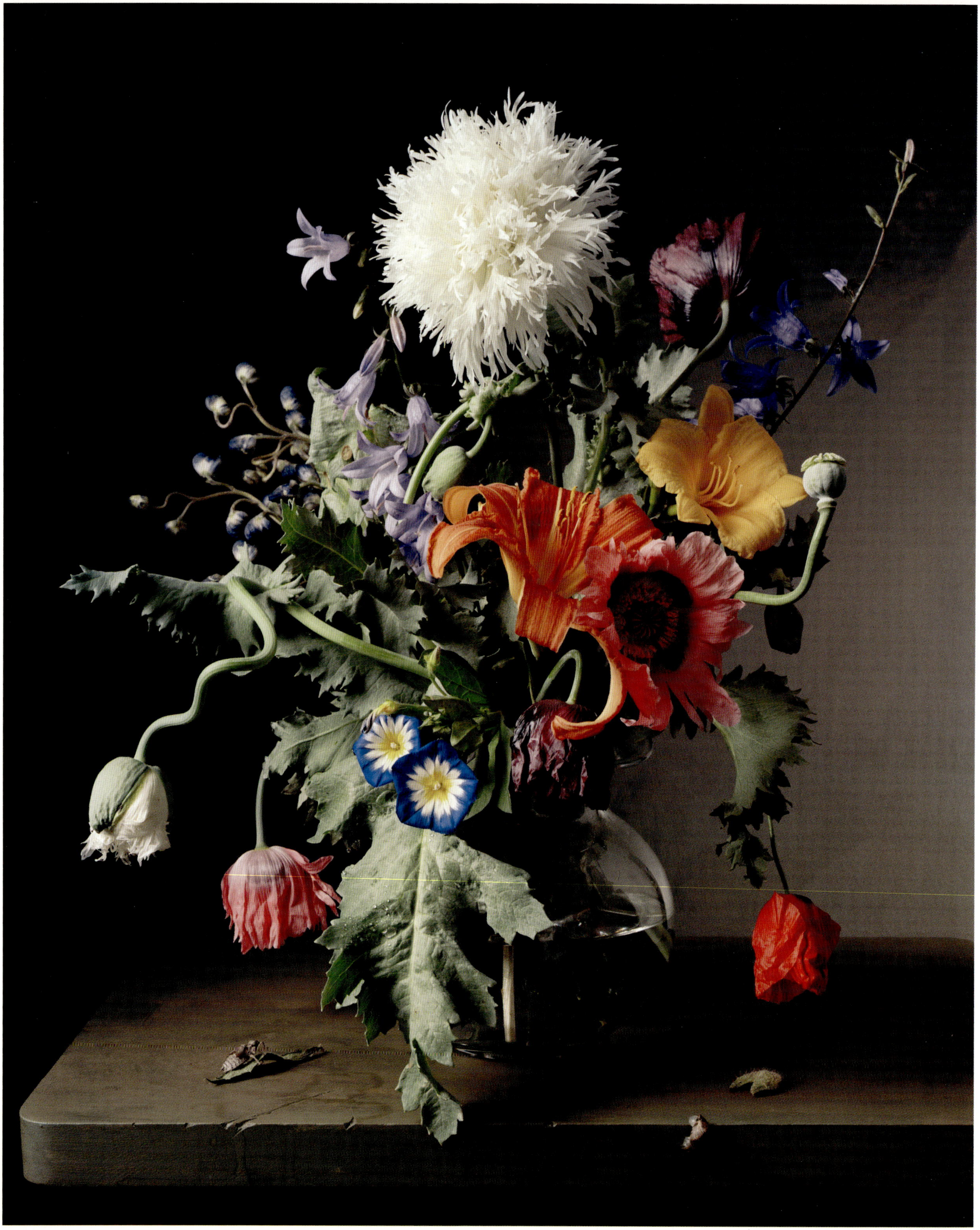

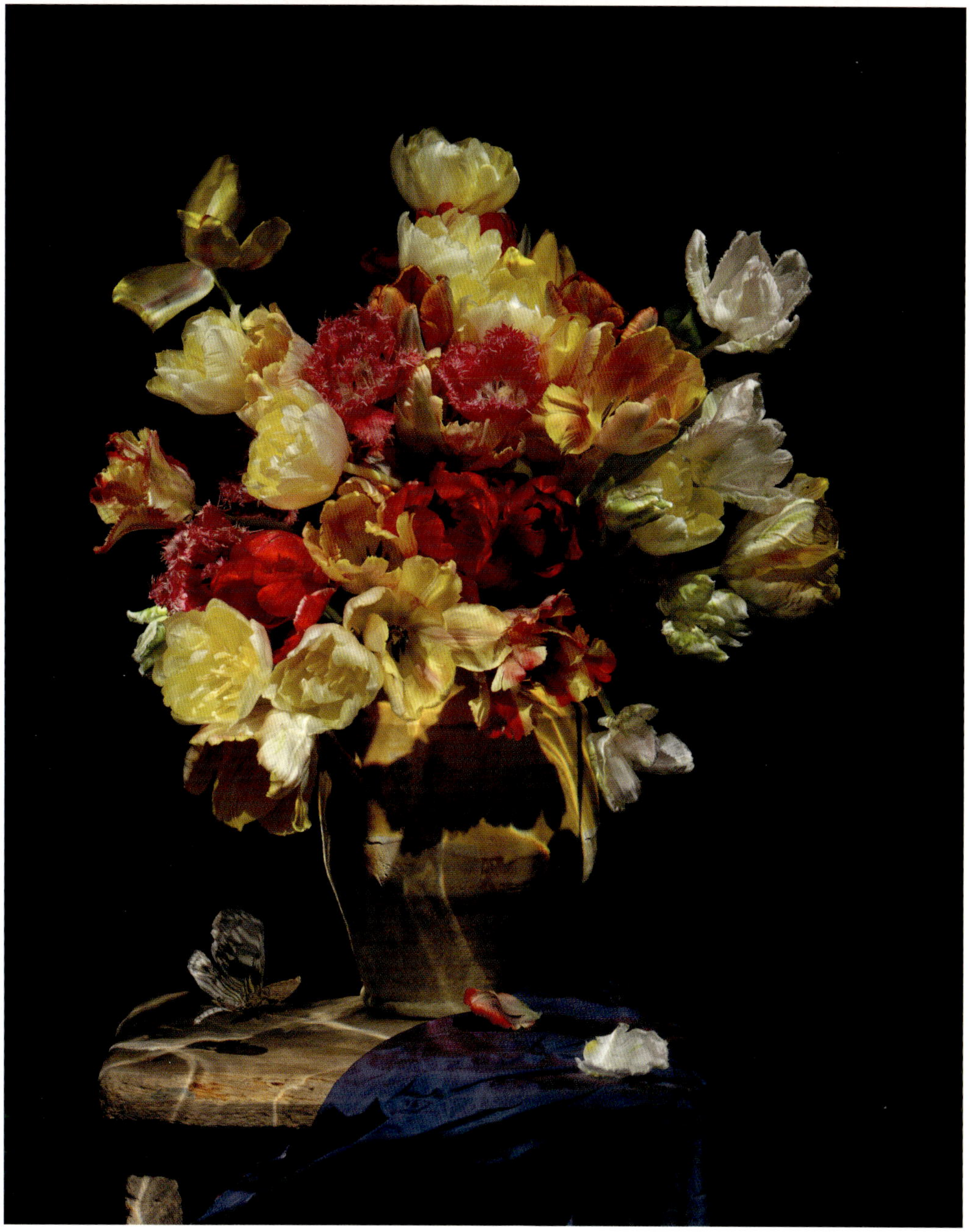

OPPOSITE
Sharon Core · *1665*, 2011
archival pigment print

ABOVE
Alexander James, Distil Ennui Studio · *Vanitas, 'Grace'*, 2011
C-print mounted on polished aluminium

Sharon Core's series *Flowers* consists of photographs that replicate as closely as possible floral still-life paintings from past centuries. Core scrupulously studied the works of Flemish painters Ambrosius Bosschaert and Jan Brueghel the Elder in order to match the light as well as the flowers in her works to the originals. She even grew her own flowers to procure the correct specimens. The title of each work refers to the date of composition of the painting it references. Core's practice questions the traditional supremacy of painting over photography while cleverly revisiting, and revising, the still-life tradition.

Alexander James's '*Grace*', from his *Vanitas* series, depicts an arrangement of tulips that recalls Dutch paintings from the seventeenth century. The difference is that his bouquet has been photographed underwater. Vase and stool sit inside a tank filled with water as light filters gently across the scene, illuminating the individual petals and creating an intense painterly effect. James has captured the contrast of dark and light typical of the Dutch tradition, while making an image that is strikingly contemporary.

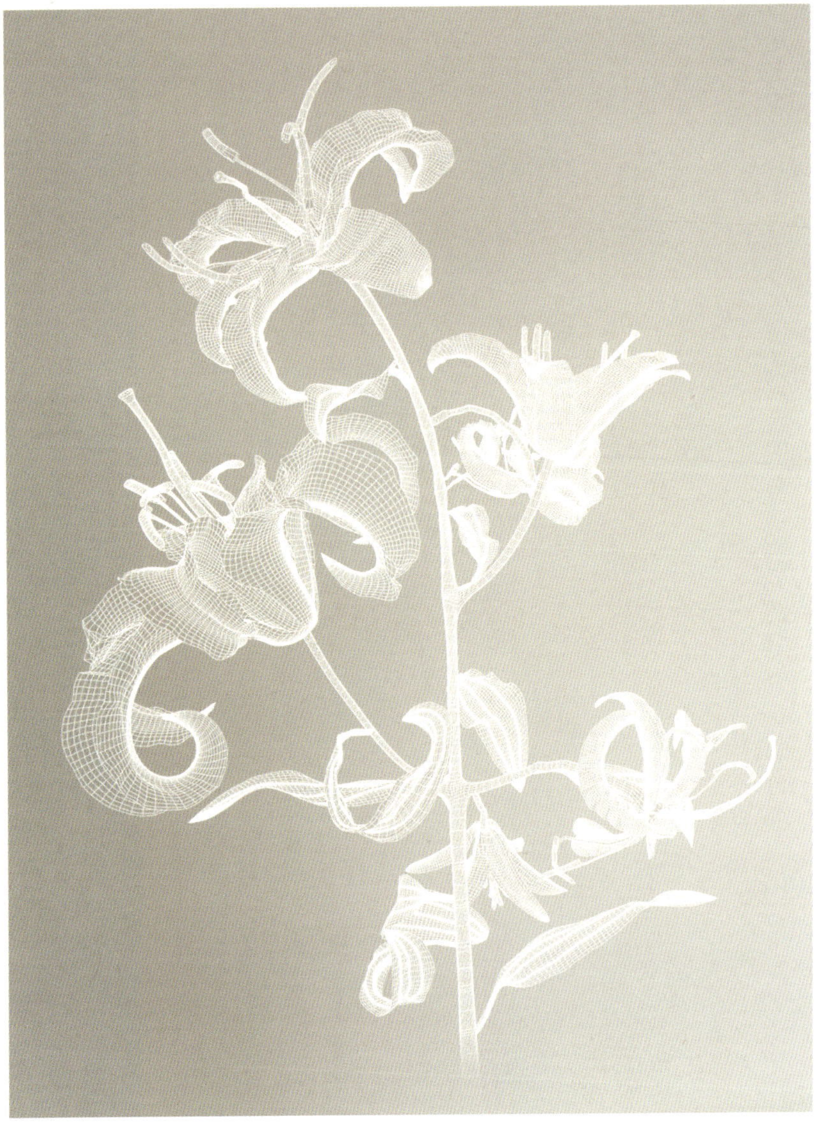

'I draw flowers every day... and I send them to my friends, so they get fresh blooms every morning. And my flowers last.'

—DAVID HOCKNEY

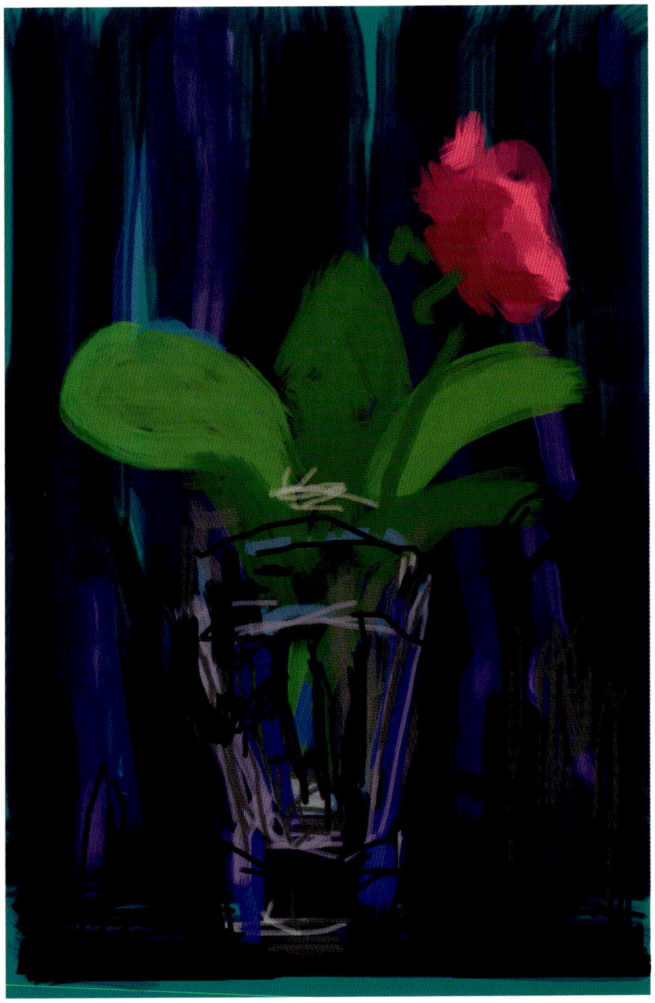

In **Persijn Broersen** and **Margit Lukács**'s *Time and Again*, a digital video projection shows a lily slowly decay and bloom simultaneously. The lily has traditionally been linked with the Virgin Mary and therefore also purity, innocence and majesty. In the installation the flower is formed only of white light upon a gallery wall. There but not there, it is a digital manifestation that lives and dies, and yet never achieves a real existence; instead of DNA it has only digital code.

David Hockney delights in experimenting with new ways of making art. He has been drawing on an iPhone and iPad since they first became available and is fascinated by the possibilities of depicting light on an illuminated screen. He sends his daily drawings of flowers, created using the Brushes application, on to friends.

ABOVE LEFT
Persijn Broersen
& Margit Lukács
Time and Again, 2011
HD video loop

ABOVE RIGHT
David Hockney
Untitled, 30 May 2009, No. 1, 2009
iPhone drawing

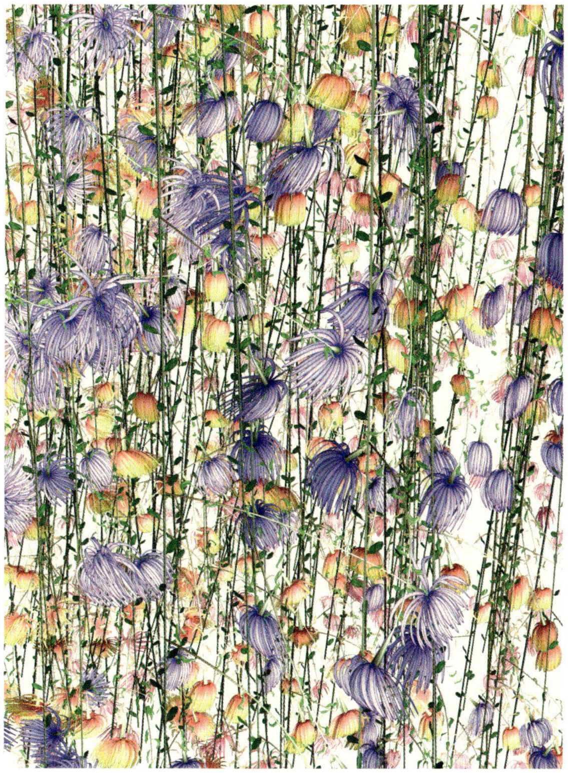

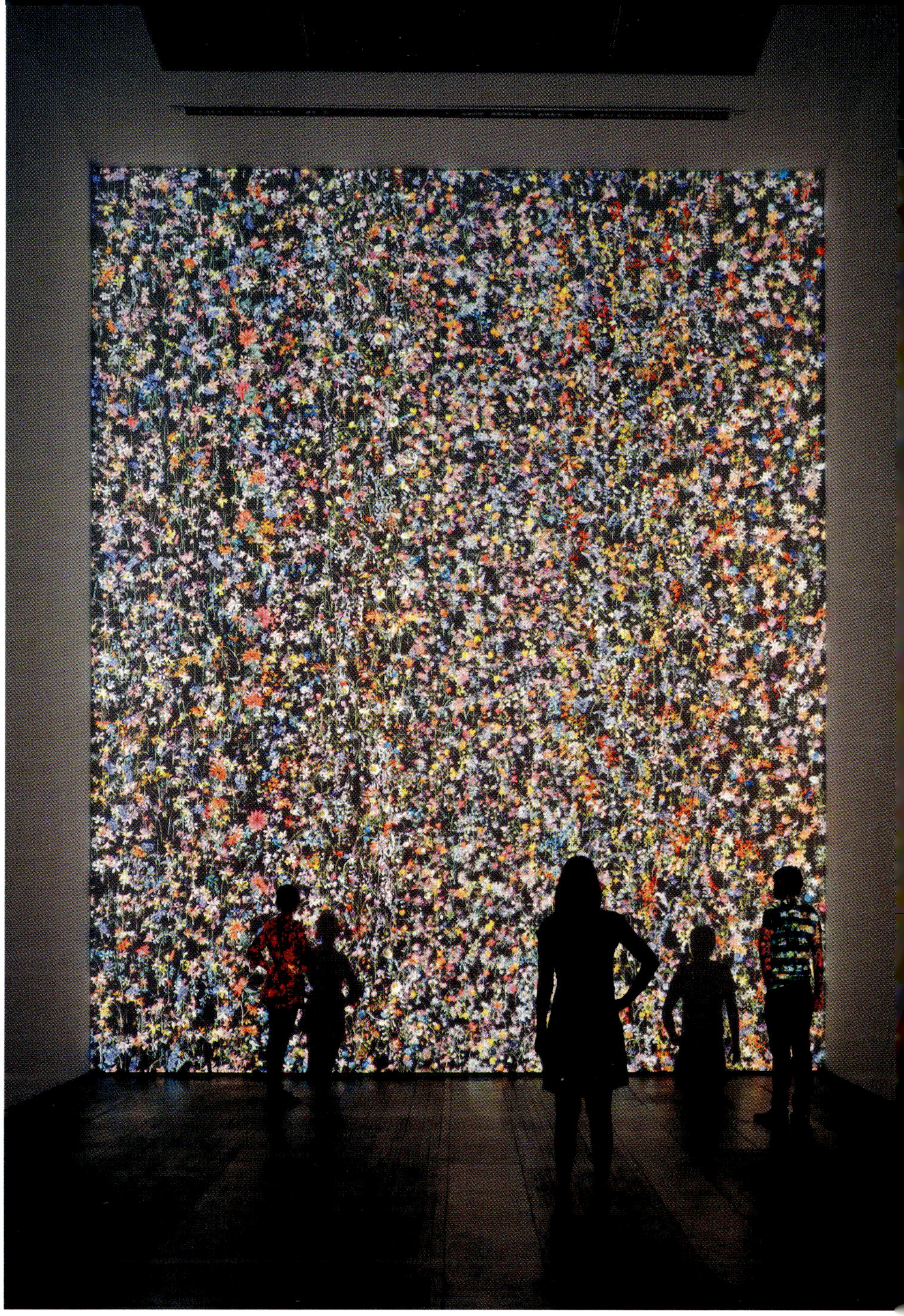

ABOVE LEFT
Jennifer Steinkamp
Rapunzel, 2005–11
5,000+ lumen projectors, computers

ABOVE RIGHT
Jennifer Steinkamp
Daisy Bell, 2008
Mitsubishi projectors, Dell OptiPlex or Logisys computers

Jennifer Steinkamp's digital trees and flowers have been widely exhibited and even crossed over into the fashion world as the backdrop to Valentino's spring/summer 2010 couture show. Her installations *Daisy Bell* and *Rapunzel* are hypnotic works, gently moving and changing through virtual seasons. Her digital tree projection *Mike Kelley* (2007–12) sways in a virtual wind; it was named in honour of her former mentor and now acts as a memorial to the deceased artist. Unlike their organic cousins, these digital flowers will continue to exist so long as there is electricity.

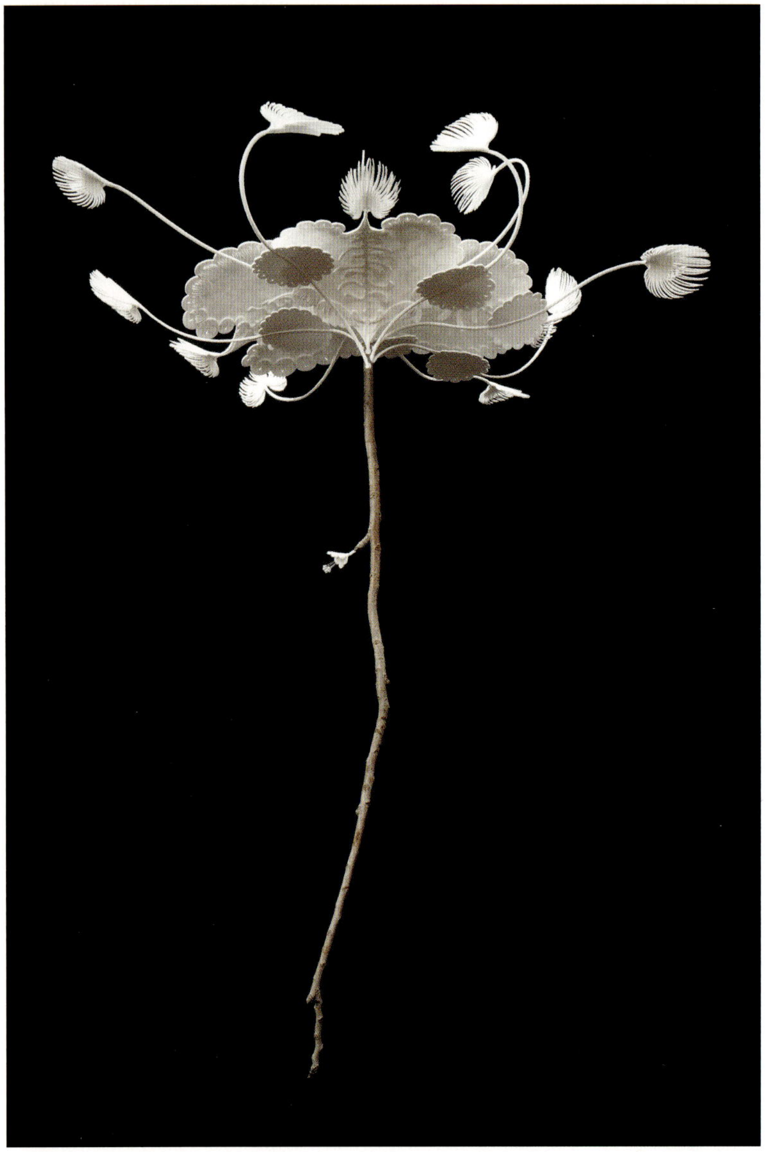

Kana Harada makes sculptures so light and delicate that one can imagine them floating effortlessly in the air, like windblown seed pods or dandelion spurs. Made from ordinary craft foam super-glued together, they nonetheless often appear to be metallic, which further heightens the tension between the natural and the artificial. With titles such as *Summer*, *Into the Garden* and *Dance With Me* (all 2011), these works – though created from long-lasting synthetic materials – capture the fragile impermanence of nature.

For his *still.life.* series, **Ugo Rondinone** selected objects as diverse as potatoes, pieces of bread, cardboard boxes and tree trunks, then had each one cast in bronze before having it painted to resemble as closely as possible the original object. His representations of mainly perishable objects of low value refer back to historical still lifes. They also follow in the tradition of Marcel Duchamp's readymades, despite requiring an immense amount of detailed fabrication work by skilled craftspeople.

Comparable works by **Cecilia Edefalk** and **Jone Kvie** present nature in a similar state of suspended time, as if death were held in check. These roots and trunks cast in bronze or nickel silver will not rot or decay; they seem to have stopped time and so remind the viewer of its passing.

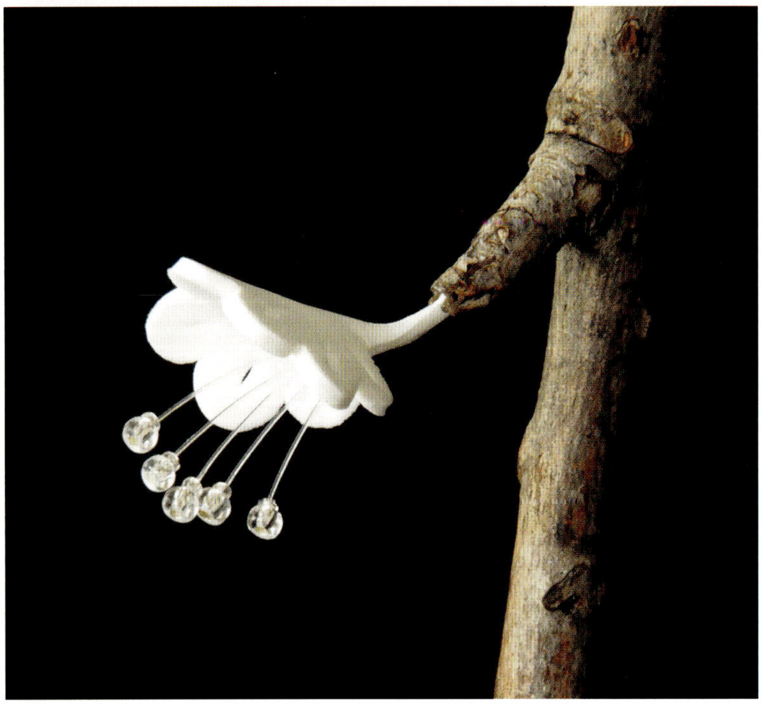

'When it comes to the art historical references in my work...I aim to dissolve the border between nature and culture, extending the metaphor from the sublime to daily life, from the mysterious to the banal.'

—JONE KVIE

OPPOSITE
Kana Harada
Dance With Me, 2011
(details) · hand-cut
white foam sheet and
mixed media

RIGHT
Ugo Rondinone
still.life. (pine tree standing in a corner),
2008 · cast bronze,
lead and paint

FAR RIGHT
Cecilia Edefalk
Weeping Birch Stem,
2010 · bronze

BELOW
Jone Kvie
Untitled, 2009
nickel silver
and black pigment

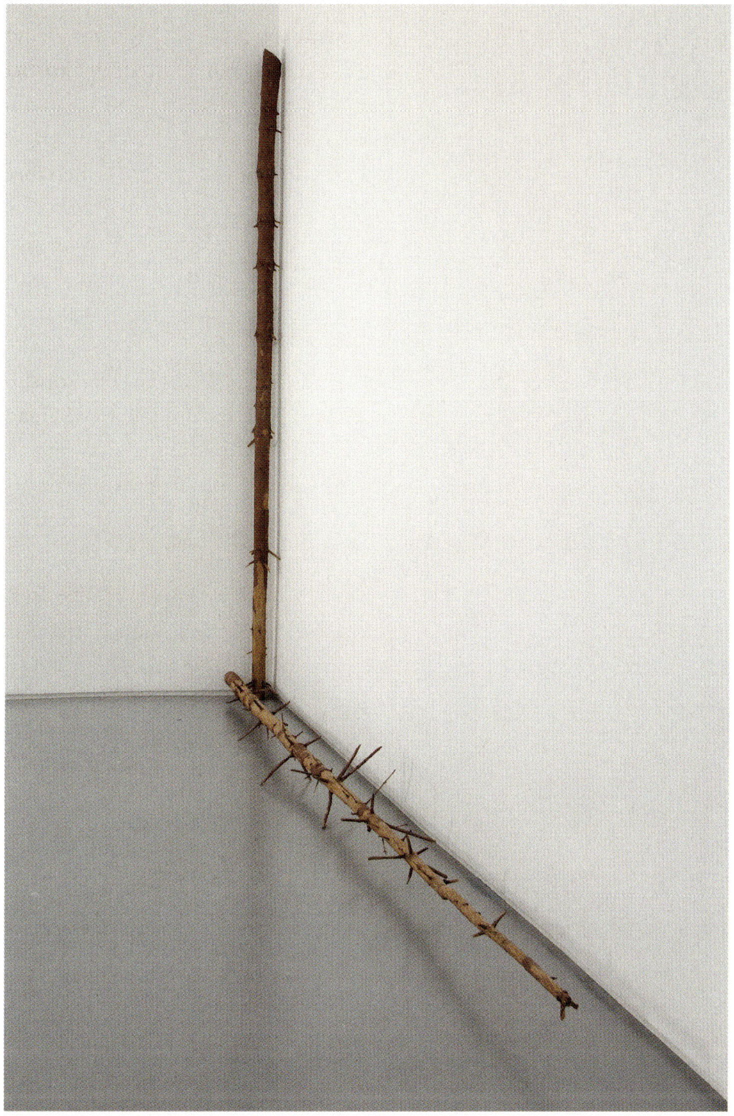

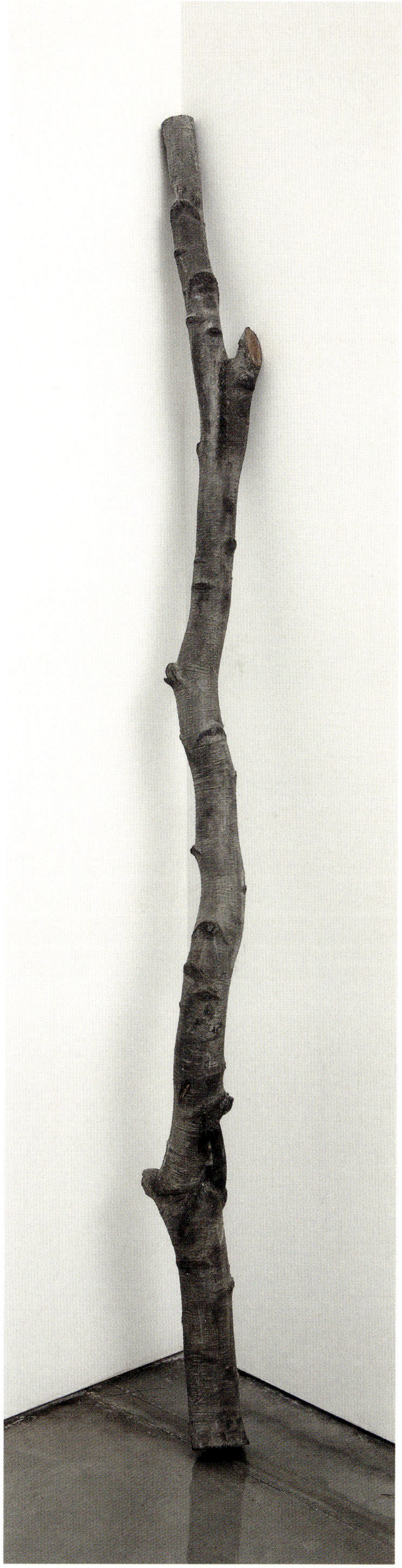

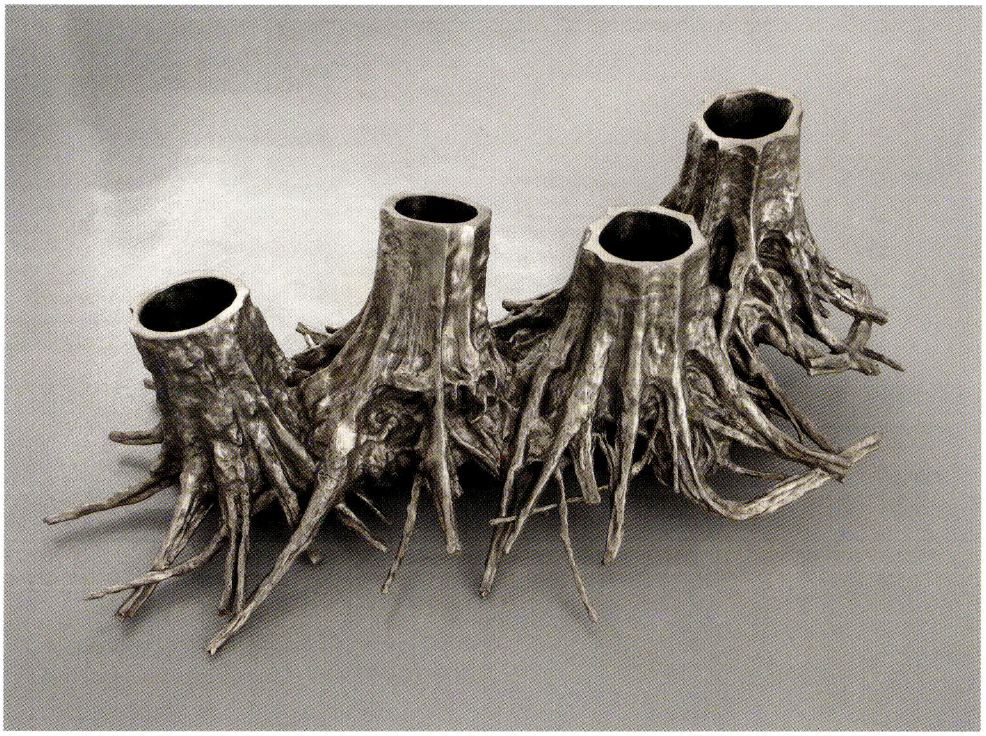

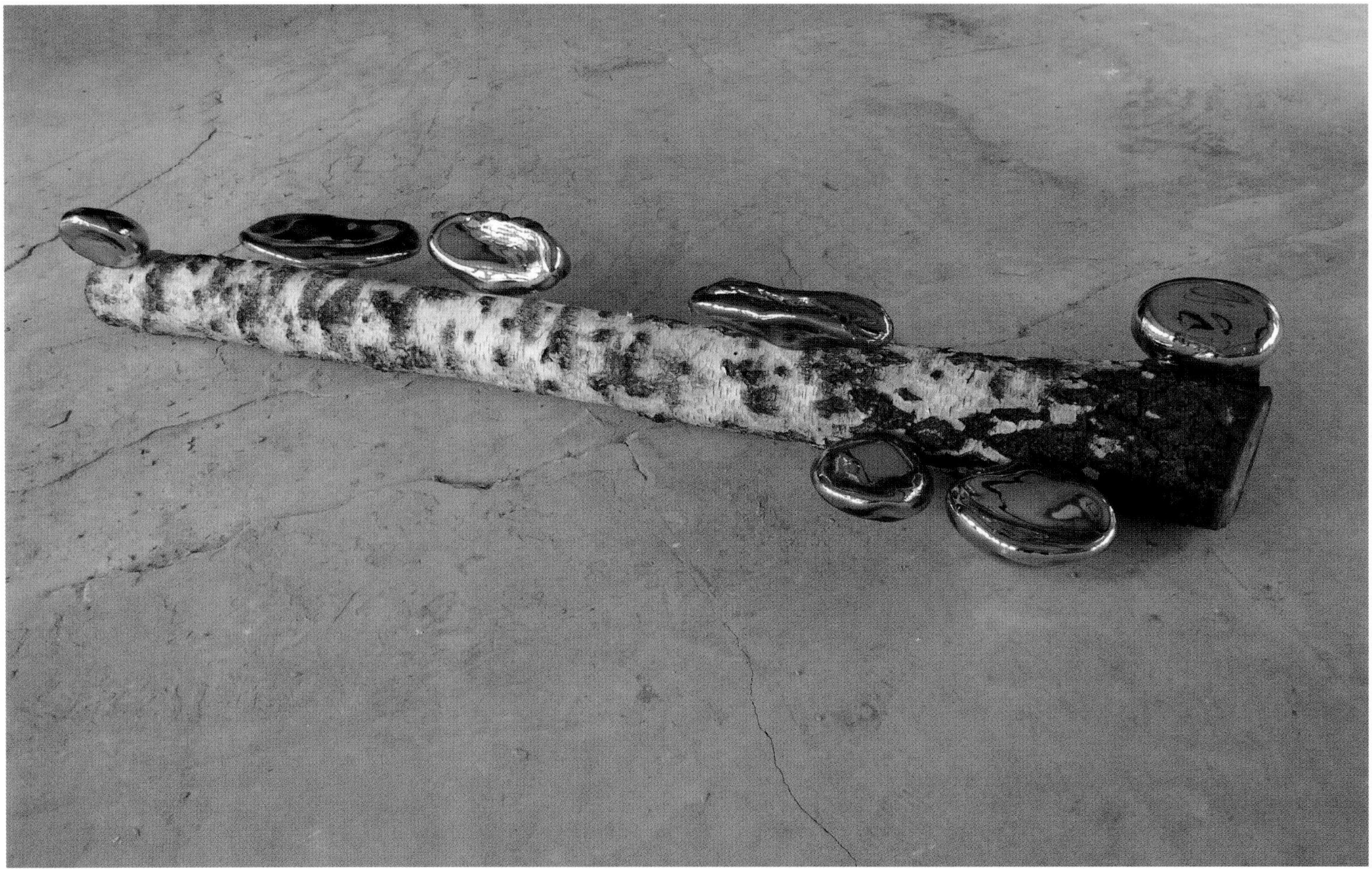

ABOVE
Maria Roosen
***Washed Tree Fluor*,**
2009/11 · glass, mirror and wood

OPPOSITE TOP
Per Christian Brown
***you will still be here when I am gone*, 2011**
C-print

OPPOSITE BOTTOM
Cammie Toloui
***Shadow+Tree*,**
January 1997 · colour transparency film

In **Maria Roosen**'s *Washed Tree Fluor*, purple mushroom-shaped glass forms sprout like fungi from a birch log. With its disconcerting conjunction of the natural and the man-made, this sculptural still life recalls the way that the nutrients in dead plant material are reclaimed by other living things as part of nature's cycle of decay and rebirth. **Per Christian Brown**'s photograph *you will still be here when I am gone* features a large tree in woodland bearing graffiti. The temporary scrawl is transformed into a metaphor for man's limited lifespan and the indifference of the natural world to our attempts to mar or mark it. **Cammie Toloui** brings to the viewer's attention the passage of life and death in nature by photographing the very *un*natural presence of discarded festive fir trees within the urban landscape. Christmas trees casually abandoned as litter appear almost comically misplaced, yet raise serious issues of conservation, consumerism and waste.

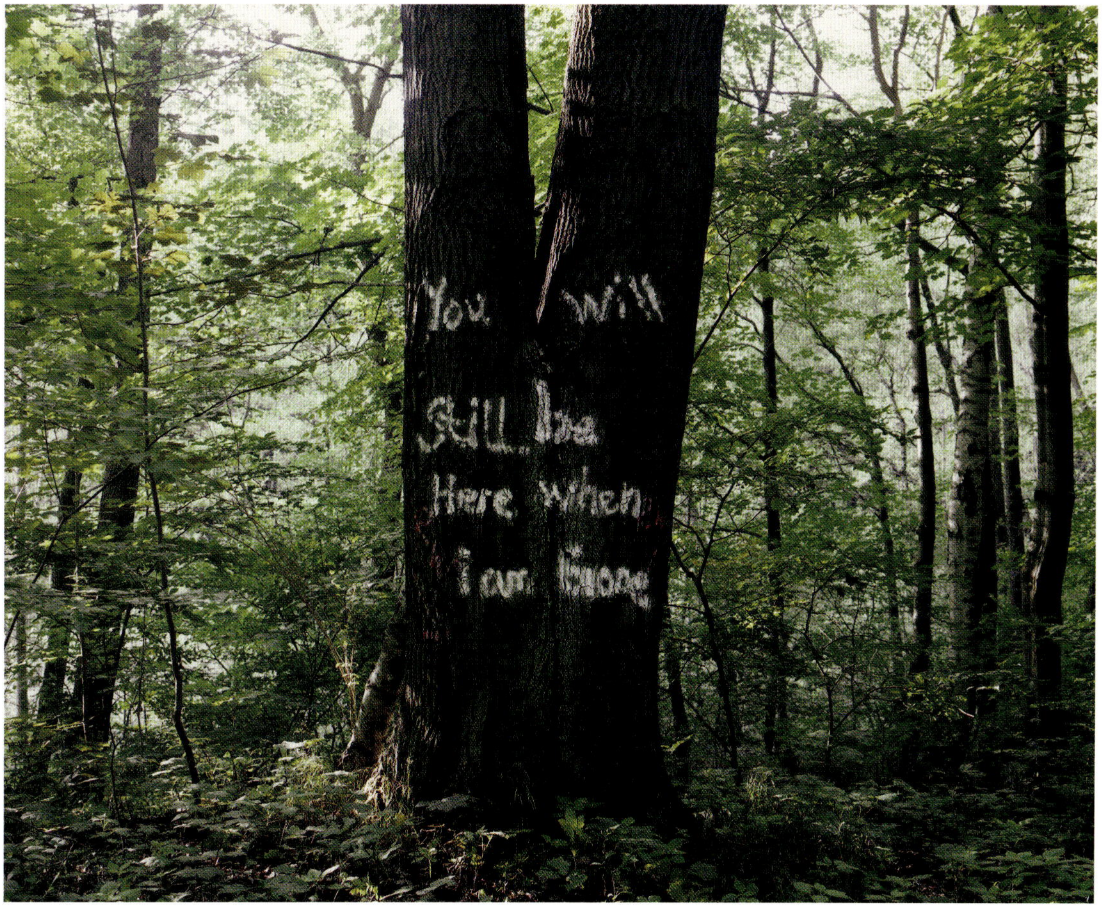
You will
Still be
Here when
I am

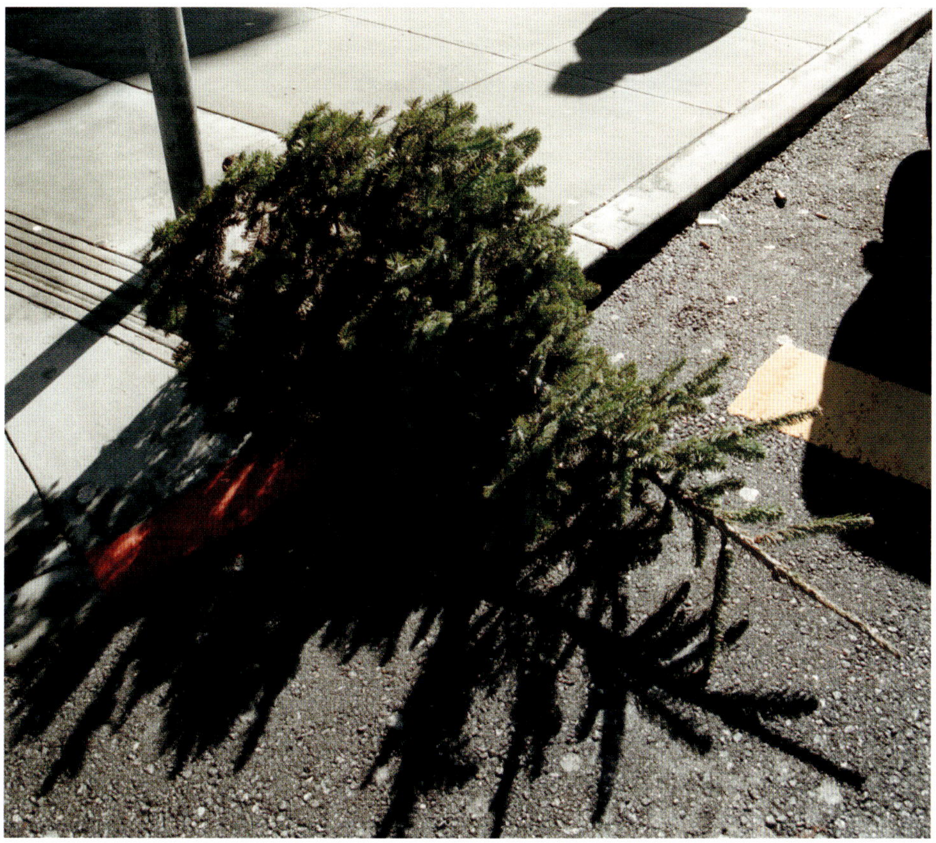

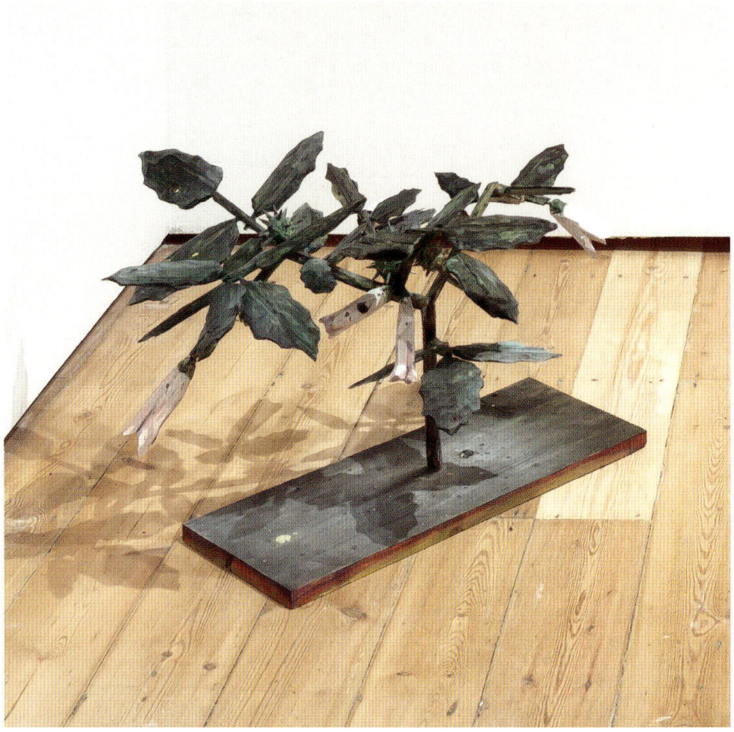

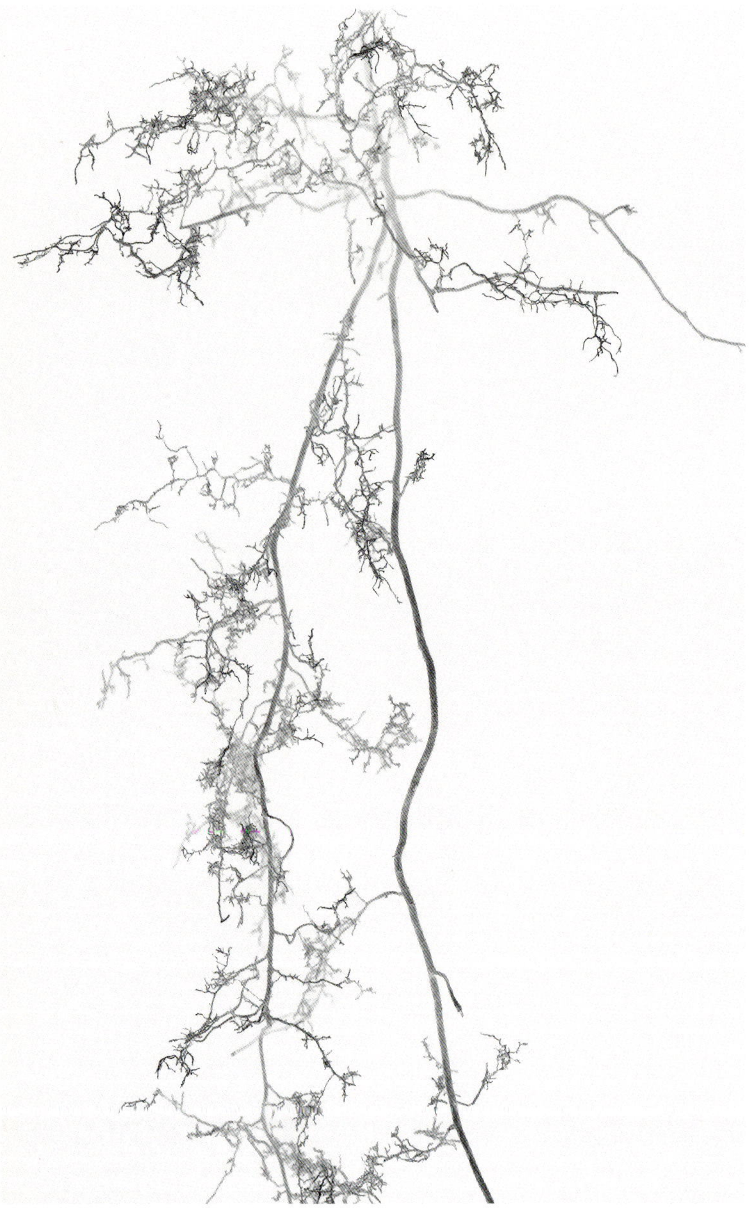

Aidan McNeill's *No.01, (Japanese Knotweed)* is part of her *Non-Native Invasive* series, which considers the havoc wrought by non-indigenous plants on vulnerable ecosystems. The work consists of a print made from a high-resolution scan, provided by the Chelsea Physic Garden, London, that reveals the ghostly roots of Japanese knotweed (*Fallopia japonica*). This invasive species has spread aggressively in parts of North America and Europe since being brought over from East Asia as an ornamental plant during the nineteenth century. The plant is highly destructive, crowding out other species and damaging masonry, paving and concrete.

Mats Adelman's wooden sculpture *Into the Dawn* shares with his other works a rough, faux-naïve aesthetic that recalls painted folk sculpture as much as fine art practice. Adelman combines disparate elements in his sculptures that together question man's relationship with nature and our view of it as either benign or malevolent. Like the man-eating plant in *Little Shop of Horrors*, Adelman's plant has an almost cartoonish quality; perhaps it too might bite.

LEFT · **Aidan McNeill** · ***Non-Native Invasive No.01, (Japanese Knotweed)***, 2010 · C-print

ABOVE · **Mats Adelman** · ***Into the Dawn***, 2010
plant sculpture in wood

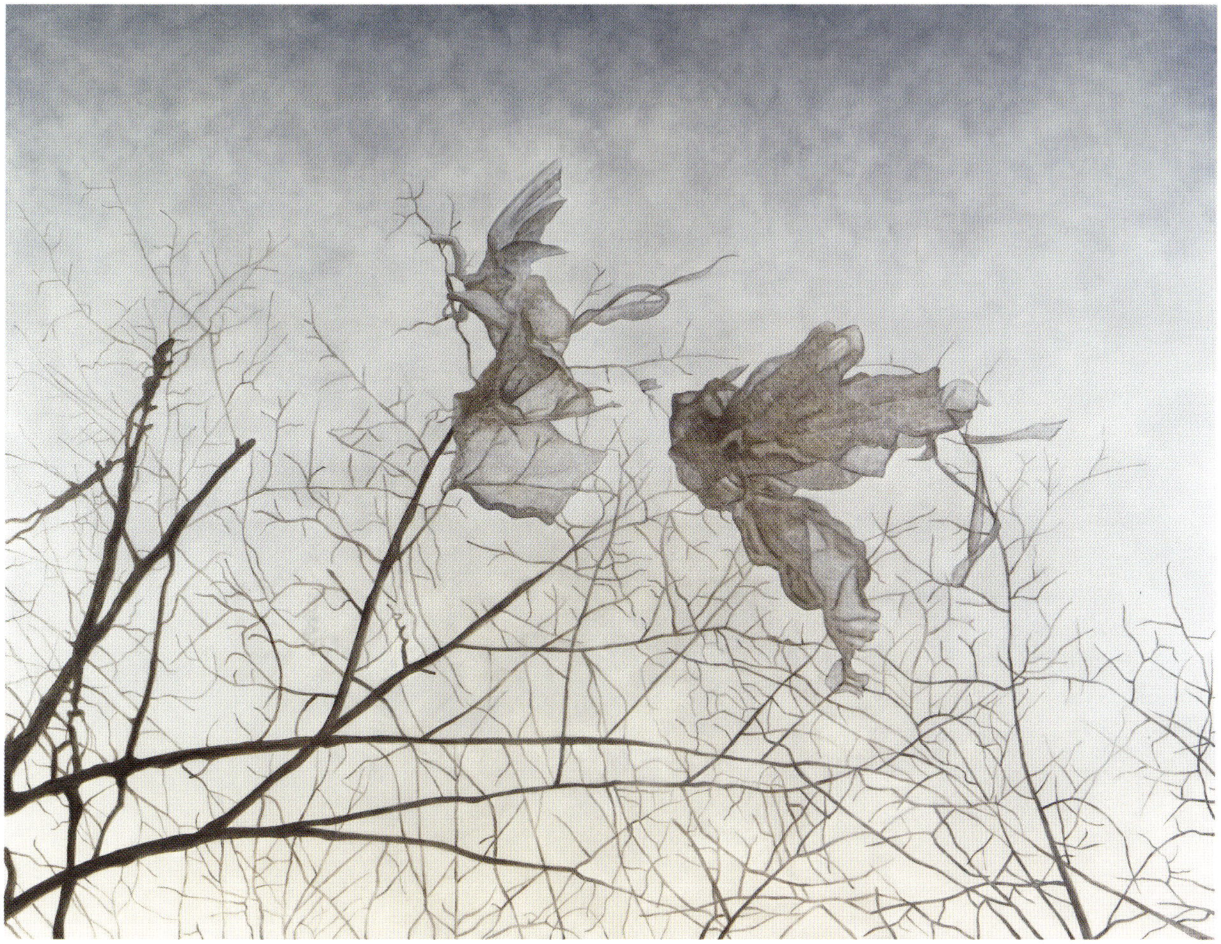

Many artists seek to engage with serious issues within a formal artistic language. **Frank Webster** explored man's often destructive relationship with the natural world in a 2009 series called *In the Landscape of Extinction....* His pitiless images of telephone wires, metal fences or tattered plastic bags caught in a leafless tree offer a harsh vision of where our disregard for nature's essential cycle of life and death has led.

The only signs of life in **Carol Marin-Pache**'s *Evidence no 13* are leaf-shaped stains on concrete pavement blocks – ghostly outlines, soon to fade, as summer's verdancy gives way to winter's bare, lifeless branches. Seasons pass, plants flower and die, and the cycles of nature continue regardless of human presence.

ABOVE · **Frank Webster** · *Plastic Bags*, 2009
acrylic on canvas

RIGHT · **Carol Marin-Pache** · *Evidence no 13*, 2009 · giclée print on watercolour paper

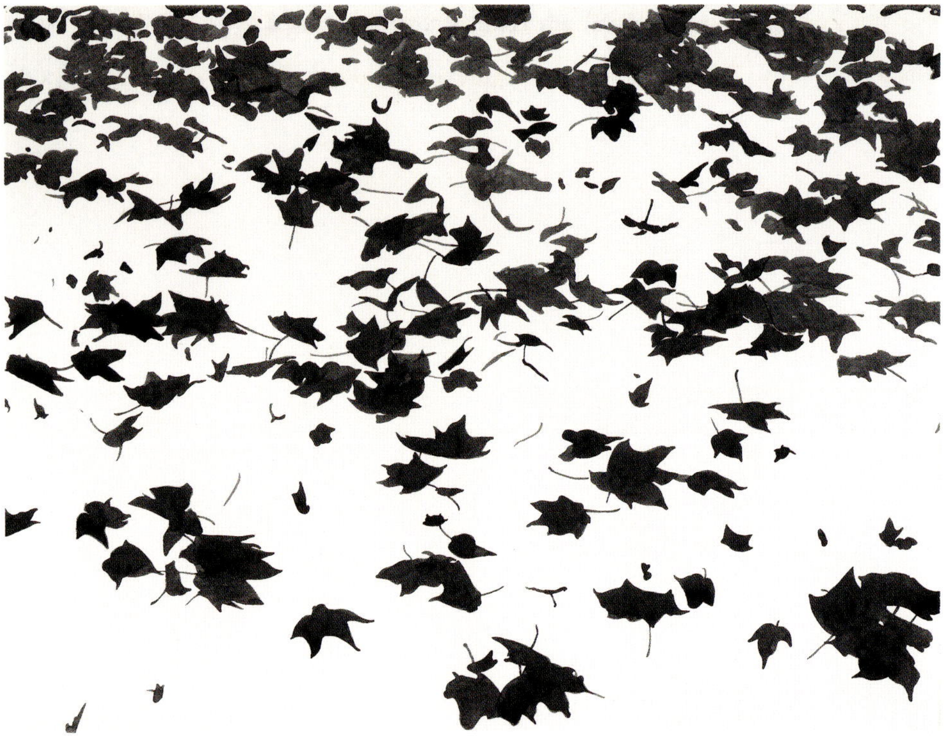

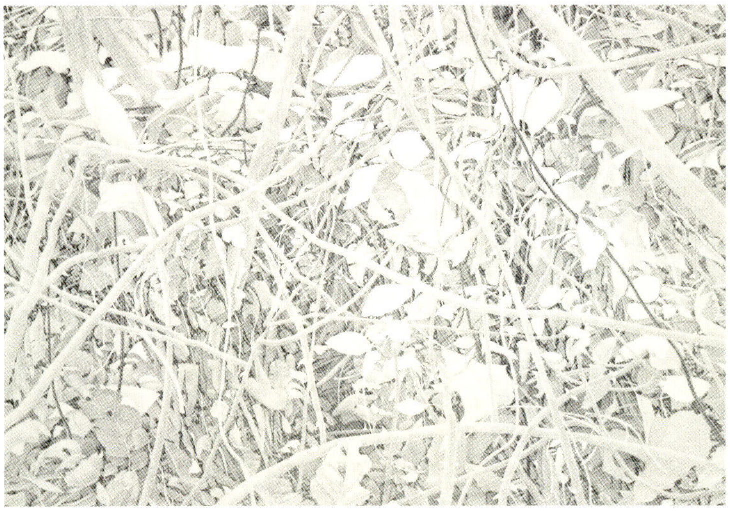

'To look at a painting means that one is taken up with another reality, a pictorial fictive reality, and as such that picture represents an imaginary location....'

—PHILIP TAAFFE

Sue Arrowsmith's *Blowin' In The Wind* depicts a complex pattern of falling leaves, somewhere between shadow and reality. The artist projects photographic images of dense scrubland, flowers or foliage onto a blank canvas, then traces their edges to create web-like works, such as *Cosmos* (2008) or *Swayed* (2009), or fills in the outlines as here. At all times loss is in the air, along with the eternal changing of the seasons. The black on white reads like a newspaper full of portent.

Bill Richards uses various graphite materials to draw his intricate tangles. Each drawing is based on photographs but unlike Arrowsmith he does not project these onto the page; rather they provide inspiration for the basic composition. It often takes him several months to make a single image as a slow meditative process allows him to alter the composition of the drawing as it develops from left to right across the paper. His works hover between abstraction and figuration, and weave into existence a natural world that hints at fear and the darkness of nature.

Patterning and repetition feature in **Philip Taaffe**'s paintings, which incorporate images from other cultures and times (Roman, Islamic, Buddhist, Eastern European) as well as from nature (plants, animals). In *Devonian Leaves II*, leaves rest against an unexpectedly psychedelic marbled background. Intriguingly, the use of repetitive imagery has long been a meditative tool employed in pursuit of altered states of consciousness.

TOP
Sue Arrowsmith
Blowin' In The Wind, 2008 · watercolour on paper

ABOVE LEFT
Bill Richards
Leaves and Branches, 2011 · graphite on paper

OPPOSITE
Philip Taaffe
Devonian Leaves II, 2004 · mixed media on linen

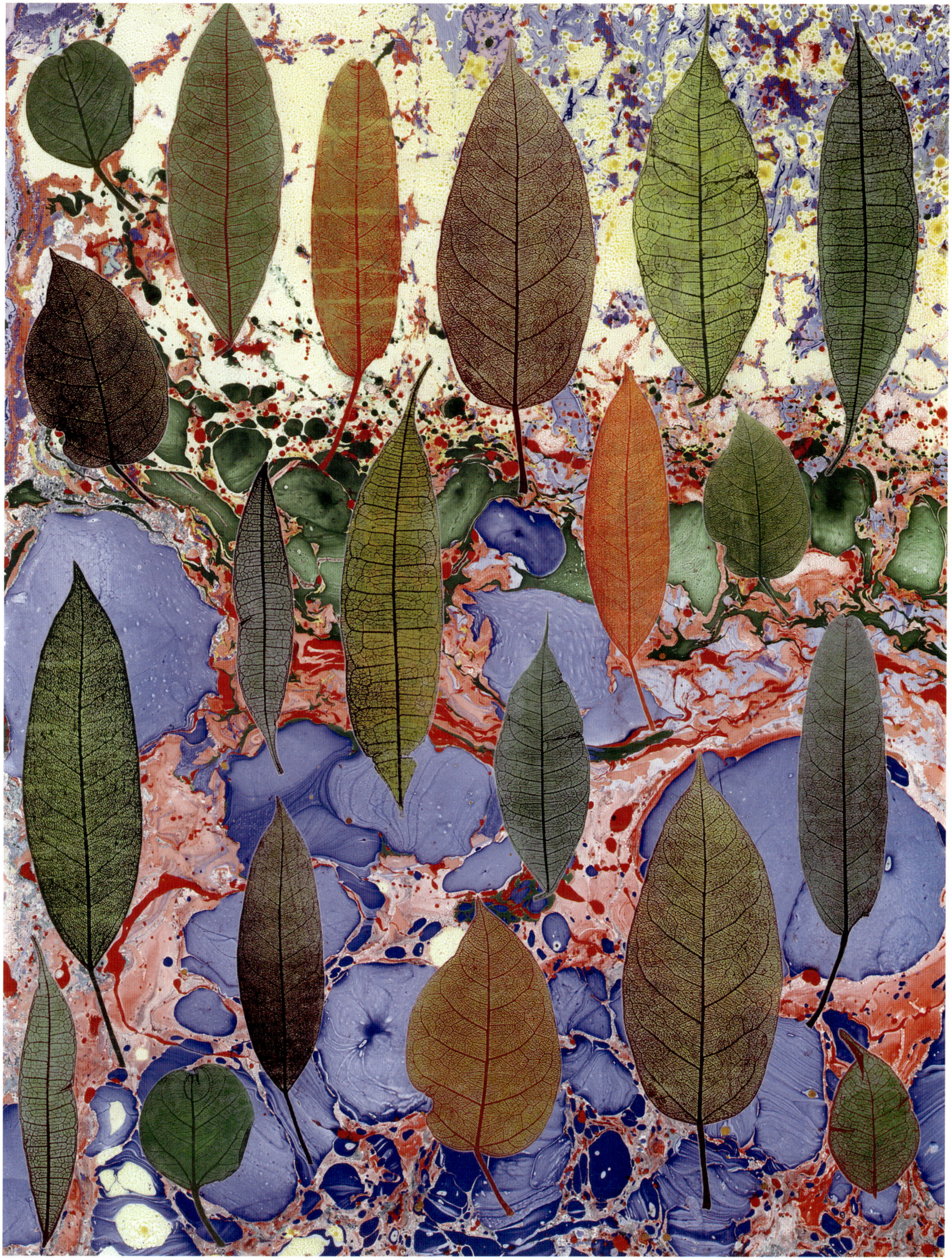

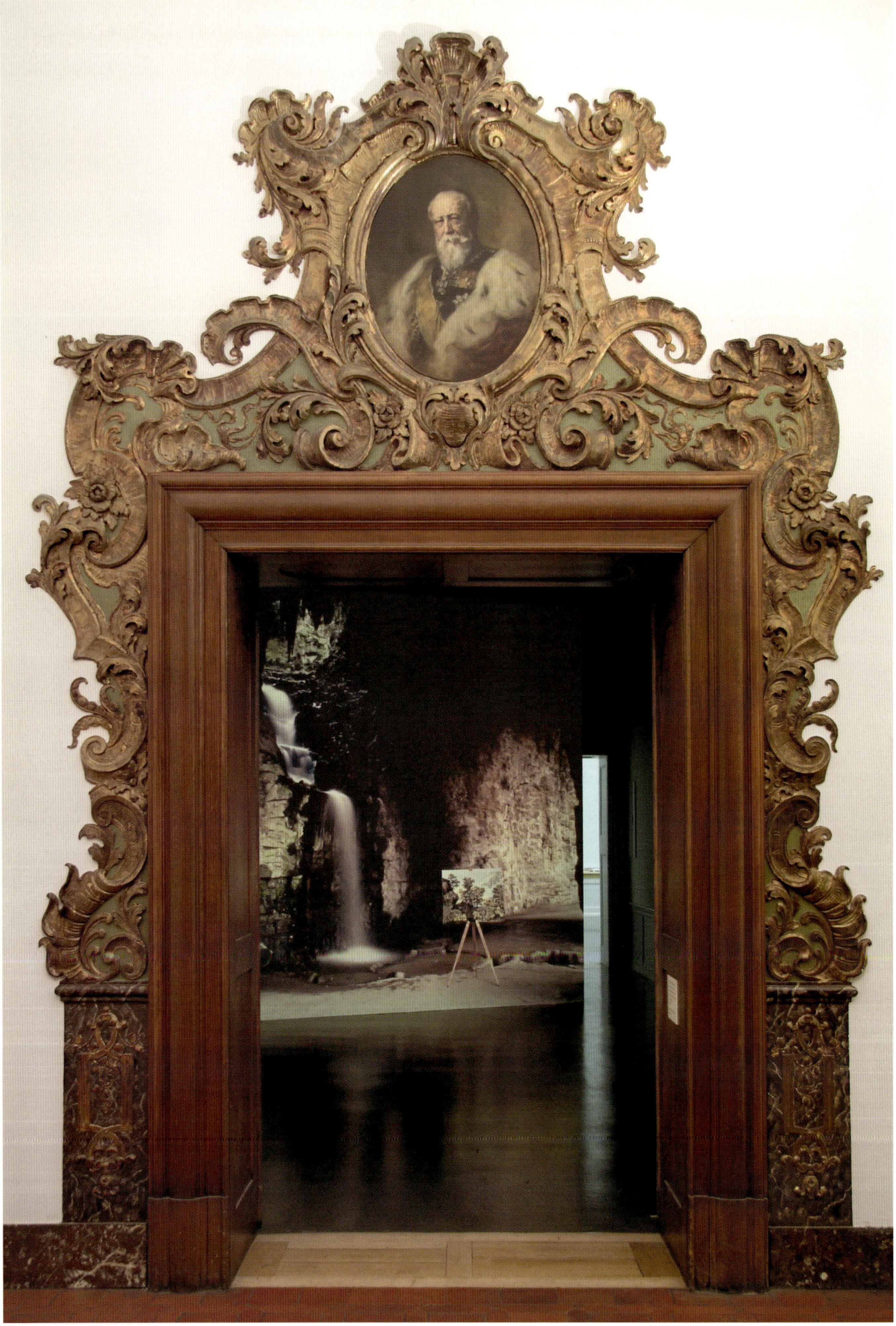

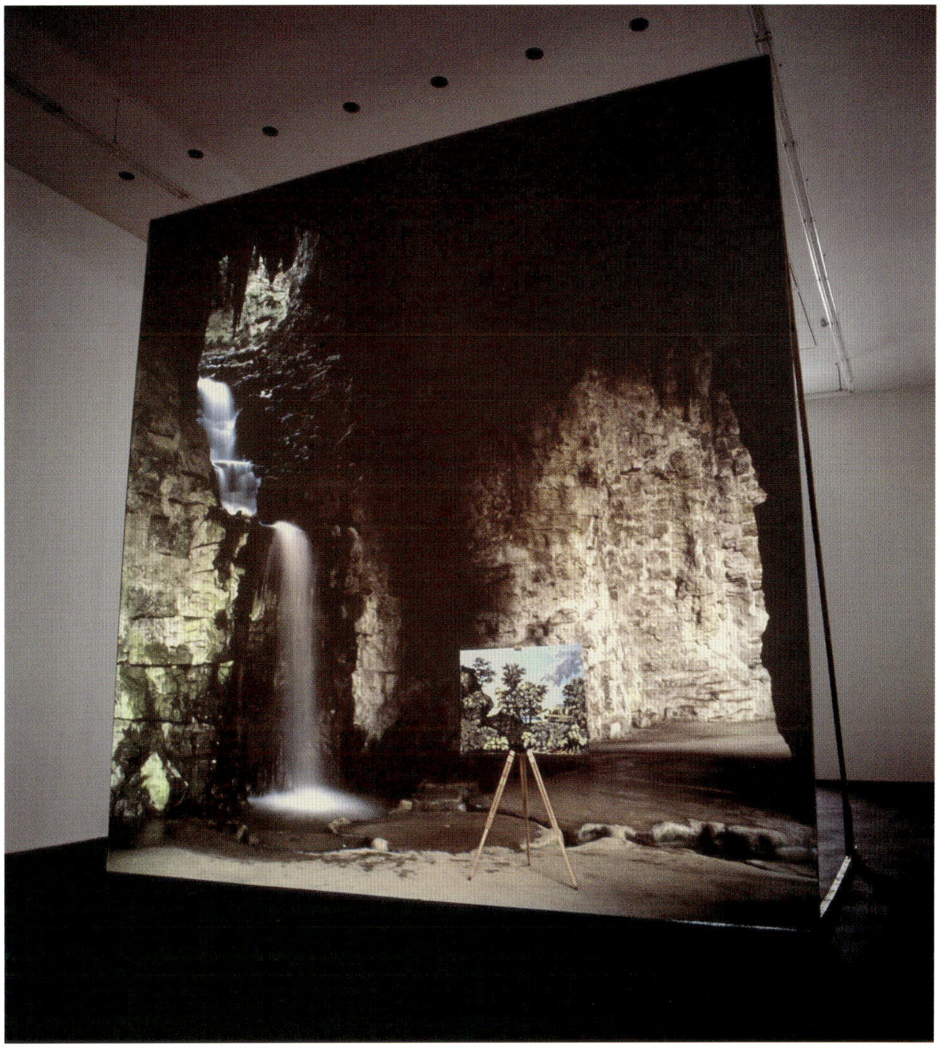

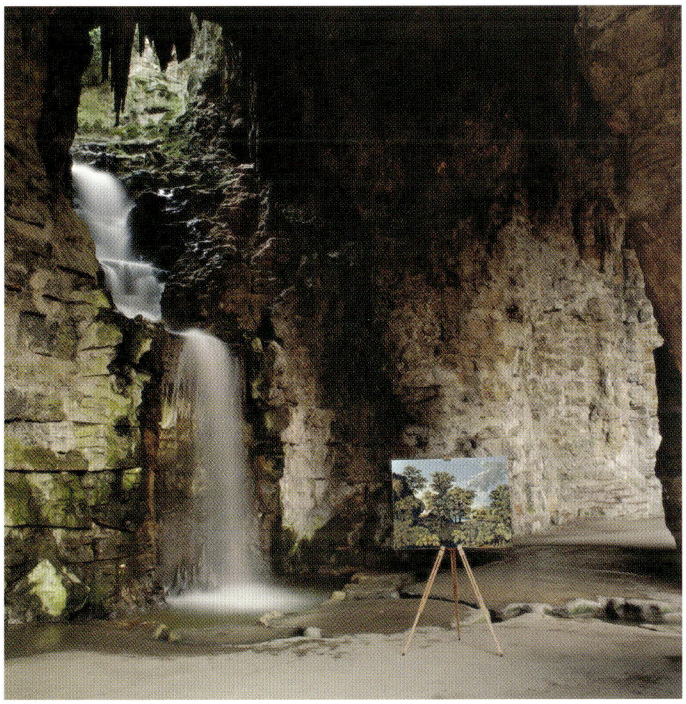

Matts Leiderstam's work instigates repressed readings of the art-historical canon. For his *Returned* series, he painted a copy of Nicolas Poussin's *Spring, or The Earthly Paradise*, which depicts Adam and Eve in the Garden of Eden. He then 'returned' his painting to cruising sites frequented by gay men and photographed it in situ. One of these locations was in the pastoral Parc des Buttes-Chaumont, Paris, which is described in the *Spartacus International Gay Guide* as a place to visit at 'one's own risk'. For his 2007 solo exhibition, Leiderstam projected the photograph onto a large screen that viewers encountered in an otherwise dark space. The work's conflation of time, desire and idealized settings brings into focus the temporality of life.

ALL · Matts Leiderstam · *Paris, 15-03-1999 Returned, Parc des Buttes-Chaumont* (*Made After Nicolas Poussin's Spring or The Earthly Paradise, Rome 1660–1664*), 2000–01
slide projection on a freestanding wall, bench

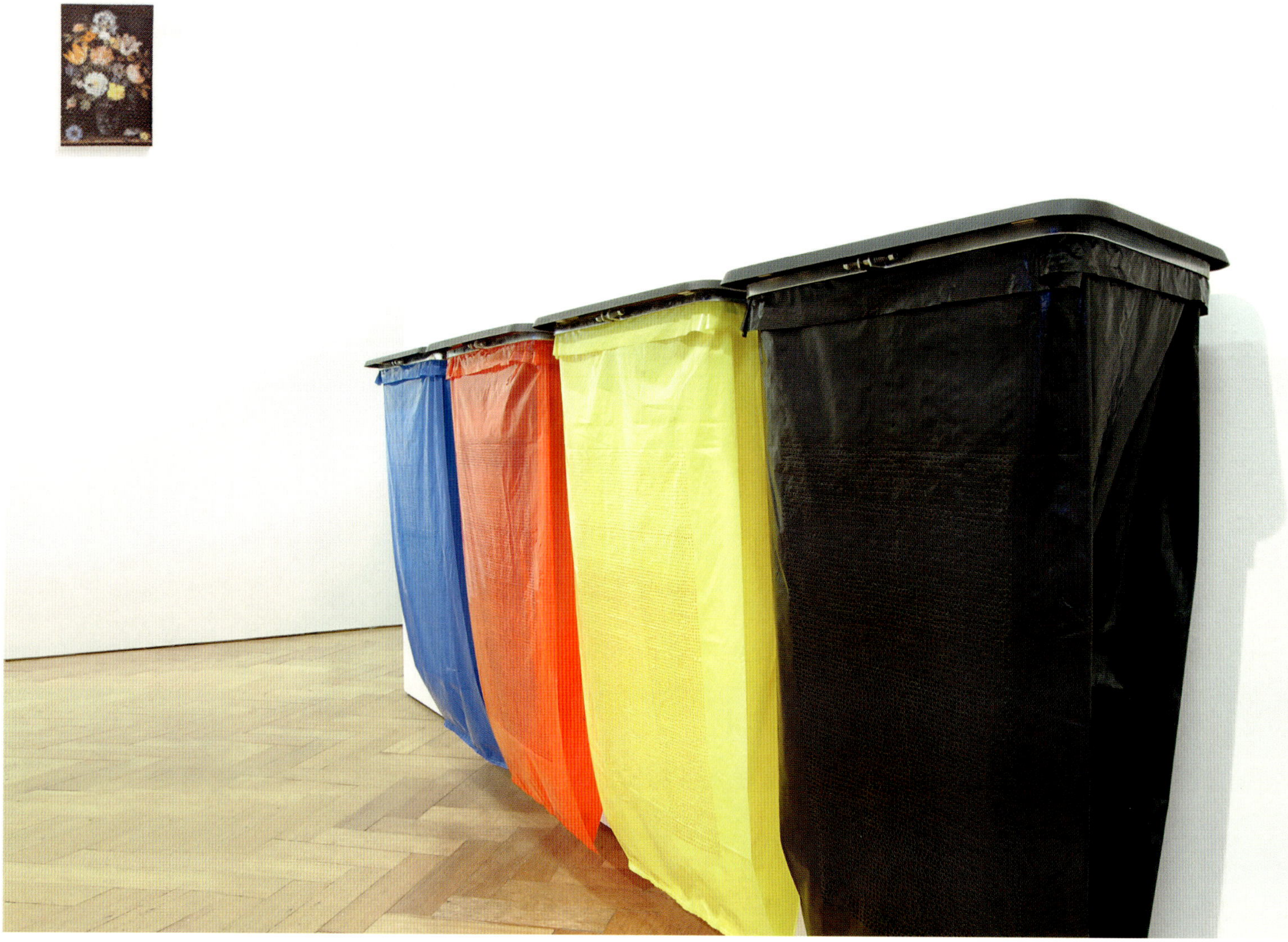

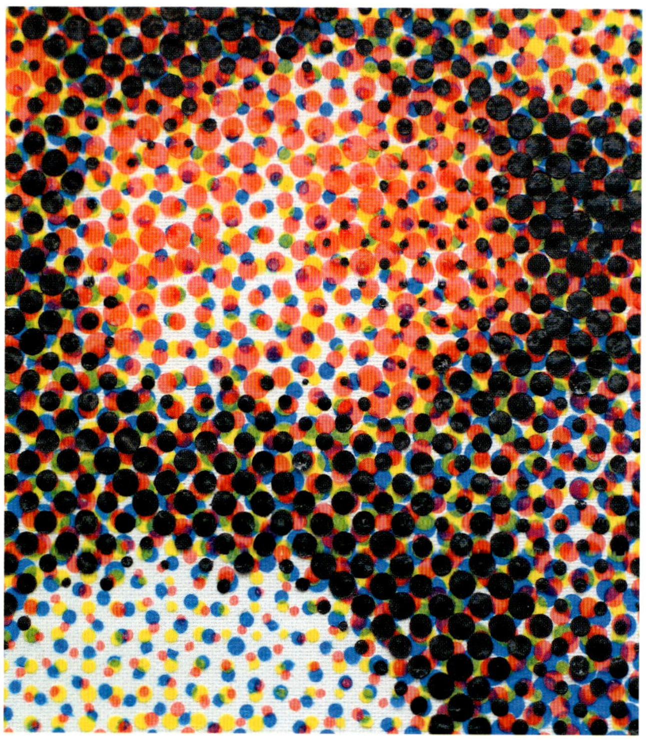

ABOVE AND LEFT
Caroline McCarthy
***Floral Still Life*, 2007**
bin bags on canvas and MDF support, metal brackets

Caroline McCarthy's *Floral Still Life* comprises a small picture of a traditional floral composition and four plastic waste bags, each in one of the four ink colours used in contemporary colour printing (cyan, magenta, yellow and black). McCarthy punched tiny holes out of each of these bags to create thousands of semi-transparent dots with which she then composed the pictorial work using a technique that replicates how colour images are printed in a book or magazine.

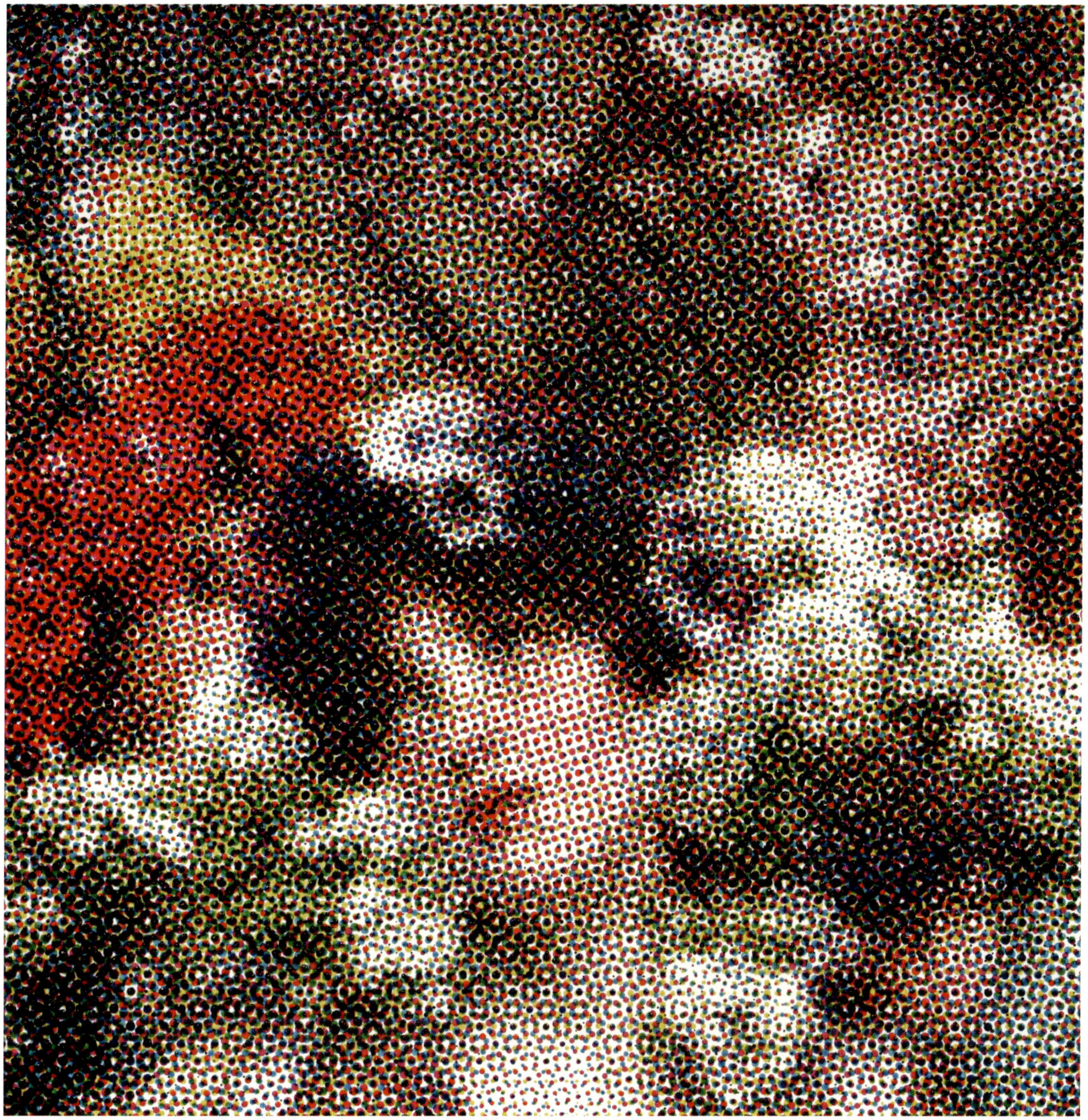

ABOVE
Mark Flores
Spring in Los Angeles
(*After Alma Tadema*), 2009
oil on canvas mounted
on wood panel

Mark Flores walked the length of Los Angeles's Sunset Boulevard (thirty-five kilometres) three times, all the while taking photographs along the way, day and night. The resulting images served as source material for the ninety-nine paintings of his 'Hammer Projects' exhibition (2010). The paintings vary in style from the loosely impressionistic to highly detailed compositions of magnified coloured dots. Flores (which means flowers in Spanish) has also experimented with floral imagery in paintings such as *New Arrangement* (2011), which uses overlapping coloured dots to depict a bouquet of flowers against a black background. Viewed close up, these images disintegrate into abstraction, reinforcing the message of transience traditionally carried by the still life.

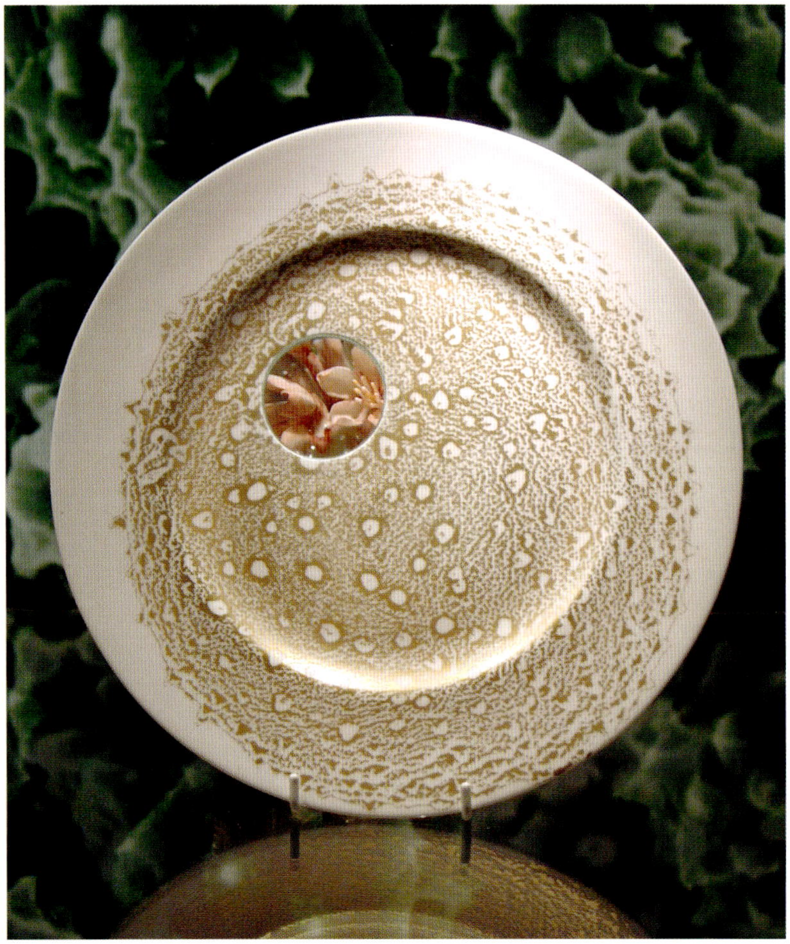

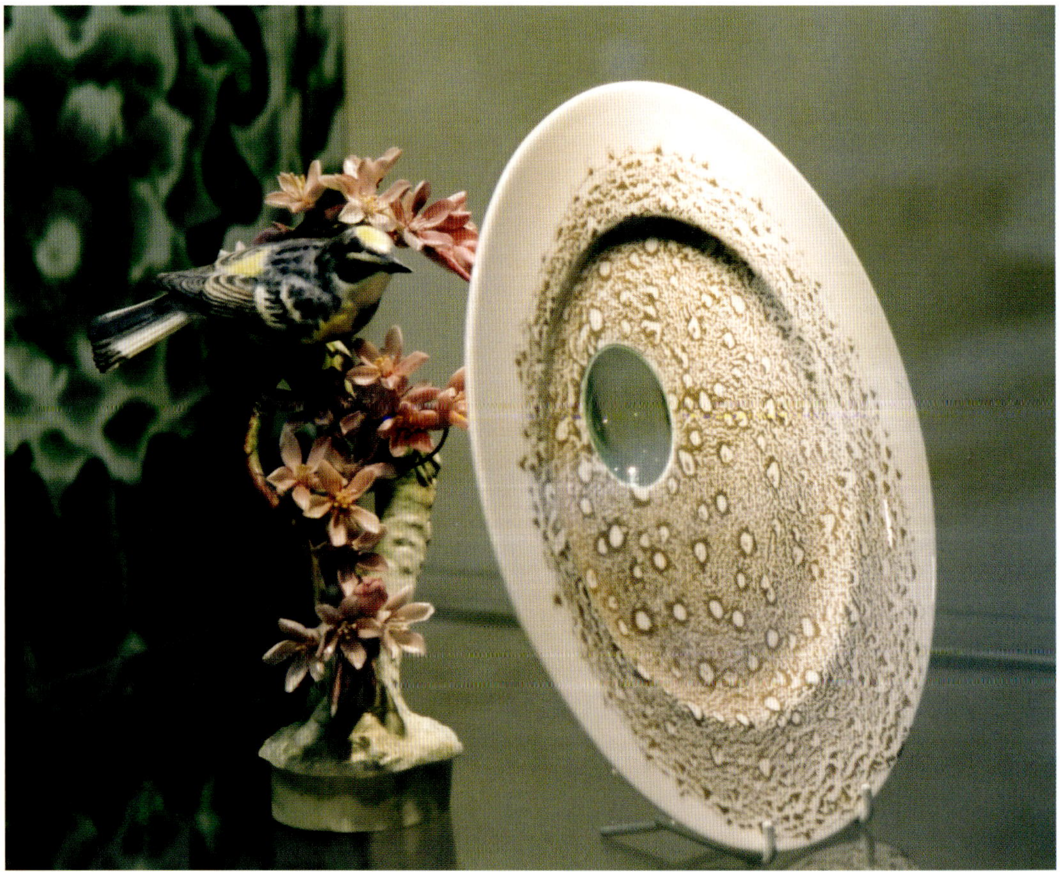

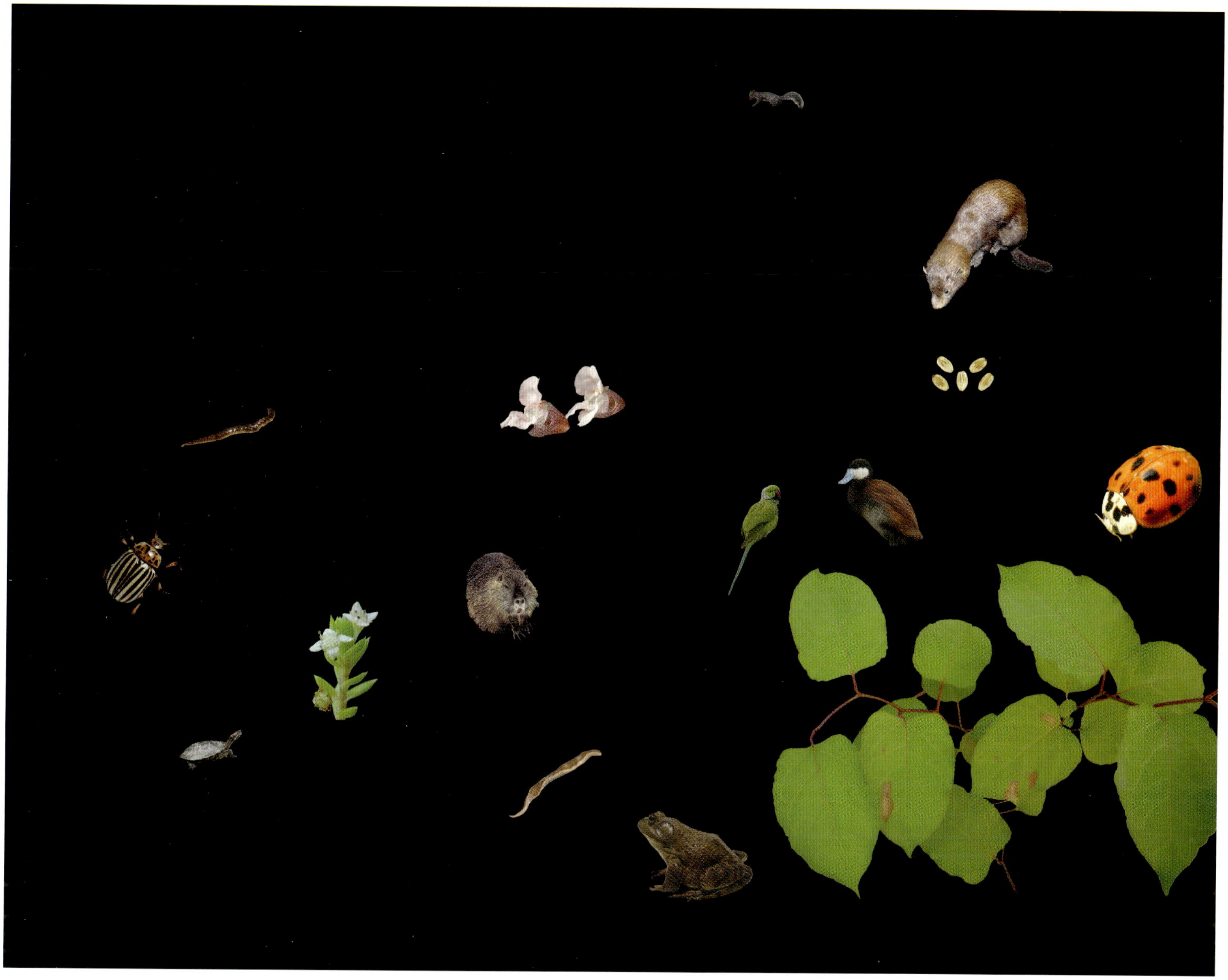

OPPOSITE
Rob Kesseler
On closer inspection, 2001
bone china plate with magnifying lens and gold decal of pollen grain

ABOVE
Aidan McNeill
Australia, India, Japan, New Zealand, North and South America to GB, 2010
C-print

Rob Kesseler uses blank bone china plates from noted English makers, including Wedgwood and Spode, to create works that intermingle the parallel traditions of ceramic and decorative arts. He also collaborates with scientists to reproduce the forms and colours of plants as seen through an electron microscope. *On closer inspection* brings these two interests together. The image of a single grain of pollen is printed in gold onto a plate at a scale vastly larger than real life. Inserted into the hole in the plate is a magnifying glass through which viewers may inspect a nineteeth-century porcelain bird perched among flowers.

Aidan McNeill's *Australia, India, Japan, New Zealand, North and South America to GB* depicts a collection of non-native plant, flower and animal species that have found their way into the United Kingdom. Each poses a threat to local species and has been designated for eradication by the Department for Environment, Food and Rural Affairs. McNeill has grouped these disparate invaders together on a black background, their sizes awkwardly mismatched, in a work that highlights the artificiality of their presence within the same biosystem, and points to the ease with which small interventions can cause immense damage.

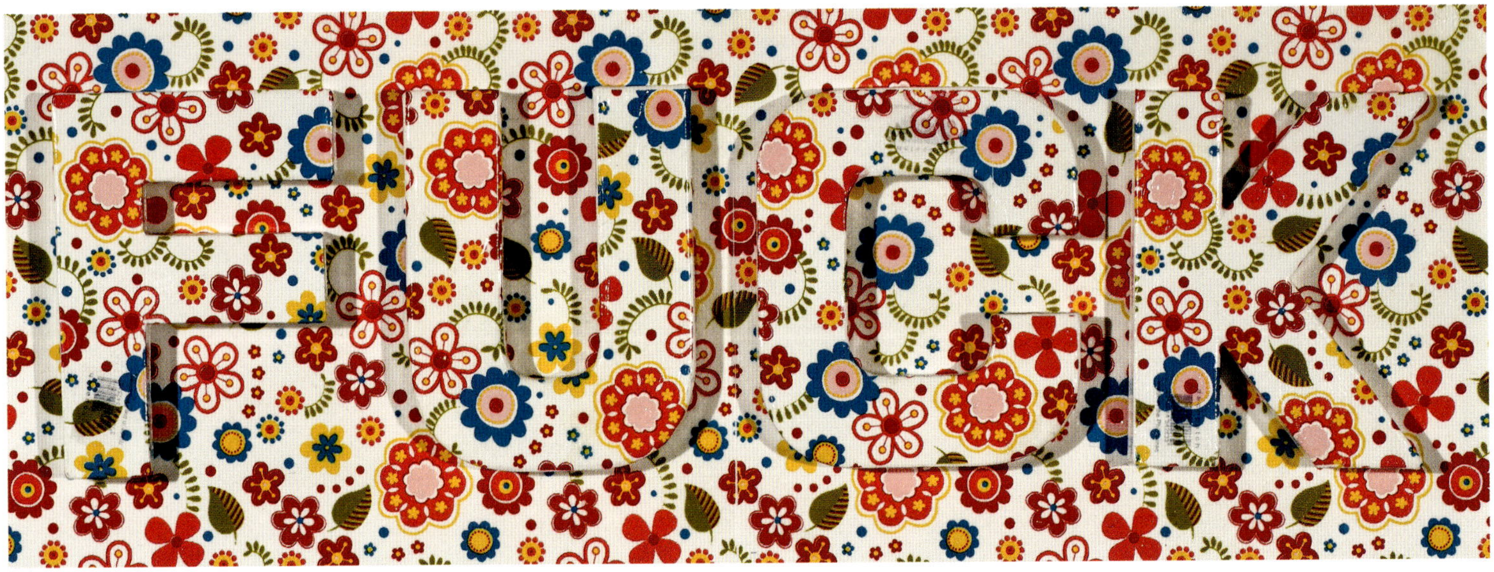
FUCK

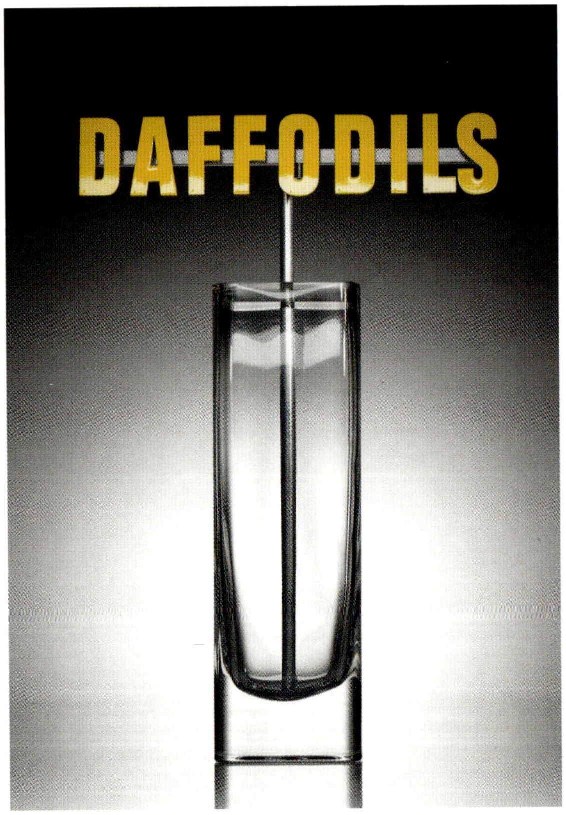
DAFFODILS

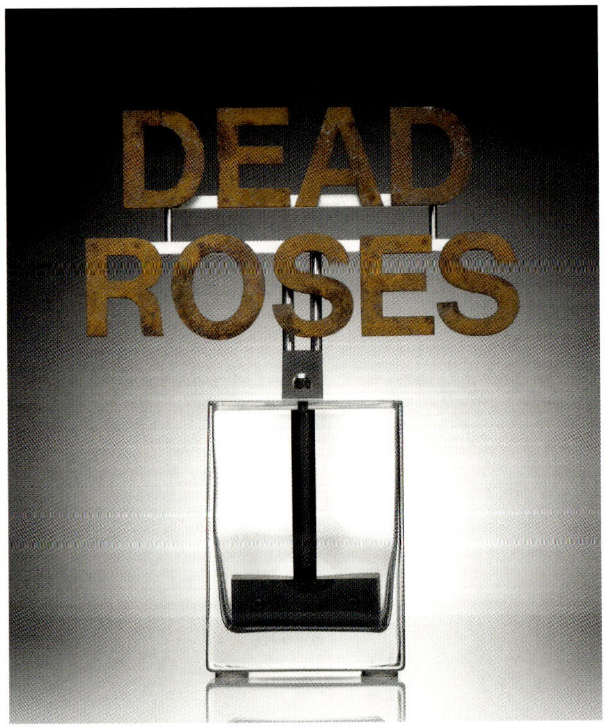
DEAD
ROSES

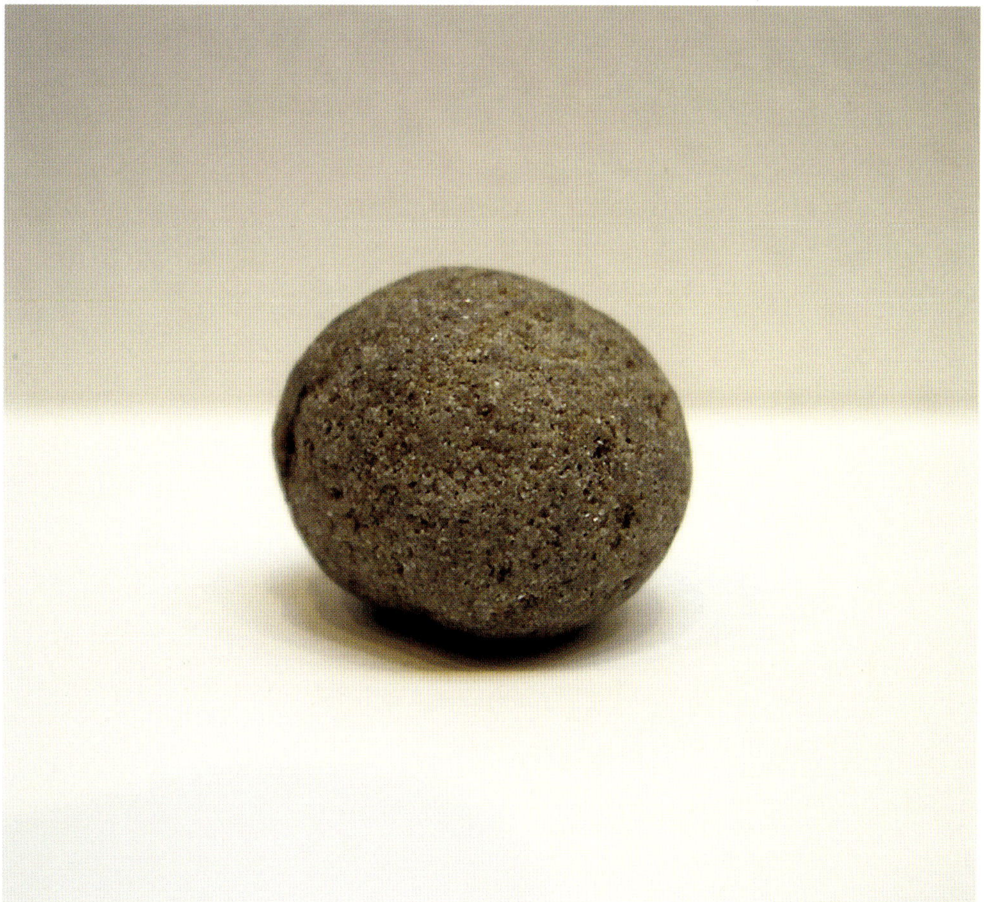

OPPOSITE TOP
Natasha Archdale · ***FUCK***,
2011 · varnished fun and vintage paper

OPPOSITE BOTTOM LEFT
John Kaine · ***DAFFODILS***,
2004 · aluminium, glass, Perspex (acrylic sheet) and automotive cellulose paint

OPPOSITE BOTTOM RIGHT
John Kaine · ***DEAD ROSES***,
2006 · salt-rusted steel, blued steel, aluminium, glass and Perspex (acrylic sheet)

ABOVE
Rob Smith · ***Waterwheel***,
2002 · stone

Natasha Archdale's *4-letter word* series includes pieces that spell out various profanities: *FUCK*, *TWAT* and *NOSH* (the last meaning to perform fellatio). The three-dimensional letters are camouflaged by pretty floral-patterned papers, creating a tangible tension between the innocent visual associations of the printed designs and the adult language.

John Kaine is interested in how visually communicated language differs from spoken or written language. *DEAD ROSES* is spelled out in rusted steel letters that approximate the colour of dried red roses. The letters of *DAFFODILS* are painted a glossy yellow. These economical works bring those flowers into being in the mind's eye, though just as with any organic flowers these images soon fade away, leaving behind only their memory.

To create *Waterwheel* **Rob Smith** installed a homemade waterwheel on a riverbank and placed inside it a rough, craggy piece of rock. The rock was spun around at a much greater speed than it would have been if left in the river, vastly decreasing the time it took to become a smooth, rounded pebble. In effect Smith gave nature a helping hand, hurrying along the passage of time and achieving in a few months an effect that it would have taken the river hundreds if not thousands of years to produce – a timeframe in which any viewer would have aged and died. This simple rock, presented as the final work, stands as a marker for that time lapse. Like a stone marking a grave, it reminds us that geological time is of a different order to human time.

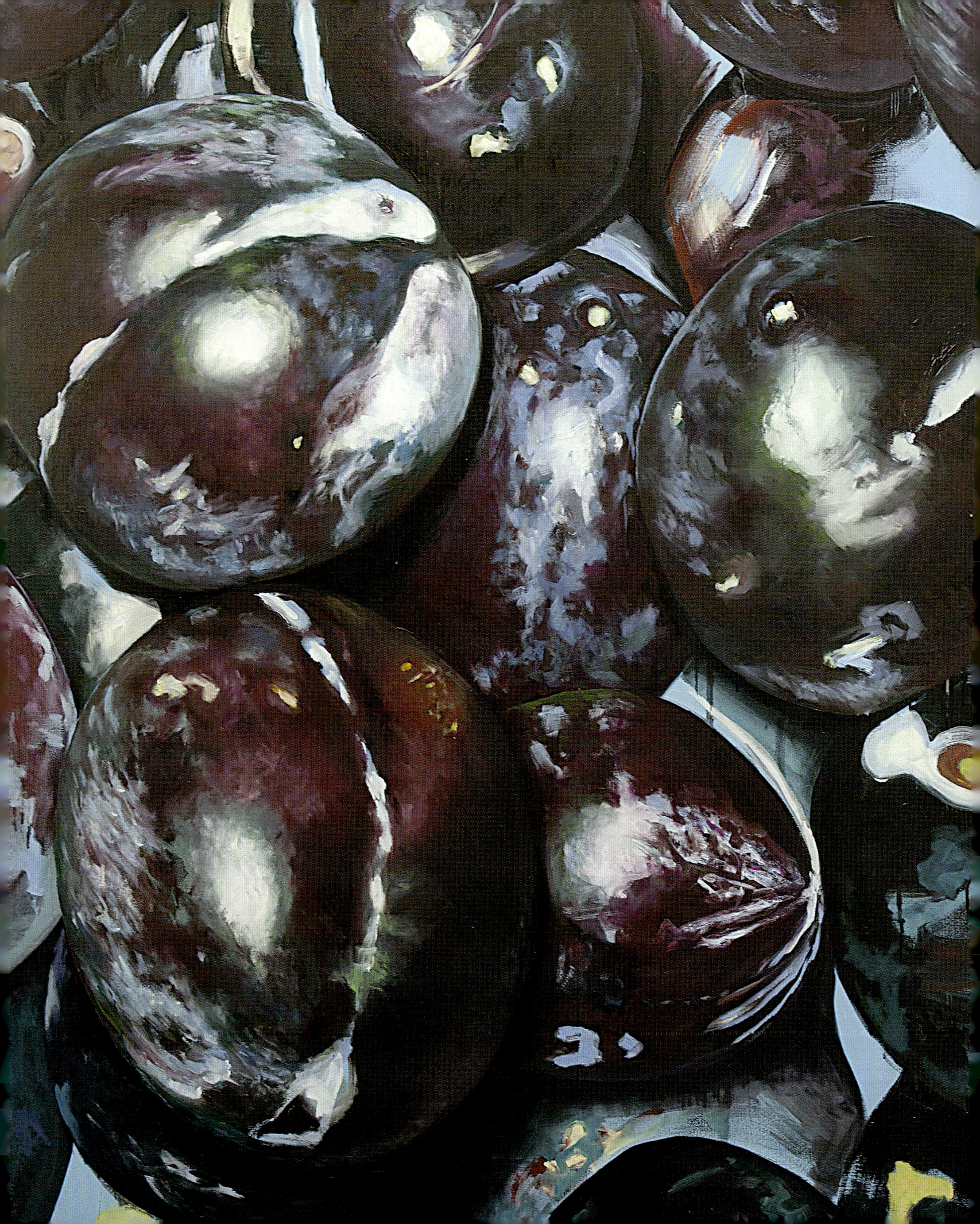

FOOD

FOOD

If music be the food of love, play on;
Give me excess of it, that, surfeiting,
The appetite may sicken, and so die.

—SHAKESPEARE, *Twelfth Night*, 1602

The presence of foodstuffs in the still life initially alluded to both the bounty of the present life as well as the inevitable death and decay of all organisms. In traditional still-life paintings, scenes of food were often split between either sumptuous stagings of ripe fruit or more modest kitchen tableaux featuring game or hewn slabs of meat. But all foodstuffs, whether a glowing peach or a dead hare pinned to a pantry wall, are by their very nature perishable. Fruit and vegetables have only a limited window for consumption before they begin to rot and meat always goes off eventually – even when cured, dried or smoked, the remains of a dead animal cannot be kept forever.

The act of eating certain foodstuffs has also long been a ritual in most human cultures. The Roman Catholic doctrine of transubstantiation, for example, insists that the Eucharist, the offering of bread and wine consumed by believers during Mass, literally transforms into the flesh and blood of Jesus Christ. In many high religious paintings of the Renaissance the visceral suffering of the Son of God and the physical wounds inflicted on his body confront the viewer. With the rise of Protestantism, however, and as more and more congregants became literate and biblical images thus less important in recalling the story of Christ, painters began to expand their repertory of imagery to include still lifes whose symbolism conveyed sacrifice and, if not redemption, the rotting of the flesh.

Visual representations of apples recur frequently in art history, with at least one appearing in almost every religious painting showing the fall of man 'at the hand of a woman', as in Lucas Cranach's *Adam and Eve* (1526). Like a flower in full bloom, a perfectly ripe apple stood to remind viewers that succumbing to temptation had its perils and that though they might be equally pert and polished, soon enough they too would discolour and perish. Contemporary artists such as Christopher Williams, Shirana Shahbazi and Kraig Wilson have captured that delicate moment of ripeness, each in their own particular style updating the tradition for the twenty-first century and moving it forward (pages 80 and 81). The still lifes of Victoria Reynolds, Rigoberto A. Gonzalez and Cindy Wright likewise remind viewers of the frailty of their own flesh and blood but their subjects include close-up depictions of bloody and glistening animal flesh (pages 112, 113, 114 and 115). All animals – including humans – are a source of nourishment for other forms of life, whether bacteria, parasites, worms, or other animals.

Developments in technology have allowed contemporary artists ever more innovative means to translate the power of the still life and its ever-present human concerns – in this case time and its seemingly endless acceleration – for new audiences. Saara Ekström's video *Domestic Nature Morte* documents the rotting of a platter of red plum tomatoes over a period of month (page 129). Projected large against a gallery wall, this process of decay plays over and over again at a greatly increased pace, continuously reminding us that the foodstuffs that sustain life are, like us, subject to disintegration.

Other contemporary artists reinterpret the historical style of Old Master still lifes in what at first glance seems a straightforward and even derivative way. But, in fact, each artist adds their own unique twist. Mat Collishaw's photographic series *Last Meal on Death Row, Texas* features lush piles of food arranged atop a simple table in dark, atmospheric surroundings (page 97). One photograph from the series could almost be the work of Willem Kalf were it not for the fact that burgers and chips were not around during the seventeenth century. Another features a plate of fried eggs in seeming homage to Velázquez, while a group of melons remind us of those painted by Juan Sánchez Cotán. Discounting these images as simple reincarnations of their historical predecessors, however, would be a terrible mistake; each of these meals was prepared at the request of a prisoner on death row, and each work named in their memory. *James Russell* depicts a single apple, *Stacey Lamont Lawton* a jar of pickles, and *David Allen Castillo* a veritable feast of foods guaranteed to clog the arteries (poignantly no longer of any concern to Castillo). In her book *Texas Death Row* (1995), Suzanne Donovan discusses the ritualization of the death penalty in the United States, commenting that 'We crave simplicity in executing justice. But there is nothing simple about what we have created in the ritual of executing men.'

Jorge Diezma makes use of similar imagery to Collishaw in his paintings, though without any backstory. His dark, gloomy staging of a table laden with food in *Bodégon del Limón* deliberately recalls the still lifes of seventeenth-century painters but differs vastly in scale at over eight metres in width (pages 91–94). Diezma's aim is to make the viewer feel they are *within* the work and so his paintings also operate as immersive installations. Alan Salisbury's *Four Hundred Year Old Bread Rolls with reference to works by Pieter Claesz* (1597–1660) also transports viewers back in time while cleverly uprooting them when they learn that to create this one painting Salisbury copied his bread rolls from five separate canvases by the eponymous Dutch master (page 90). Through such twists on tradition, Salisbury, Diezma and the other artists featured in this chapter have deconstructed the depiction of foodstuffs in the still-life tradition and once more made it relevant.

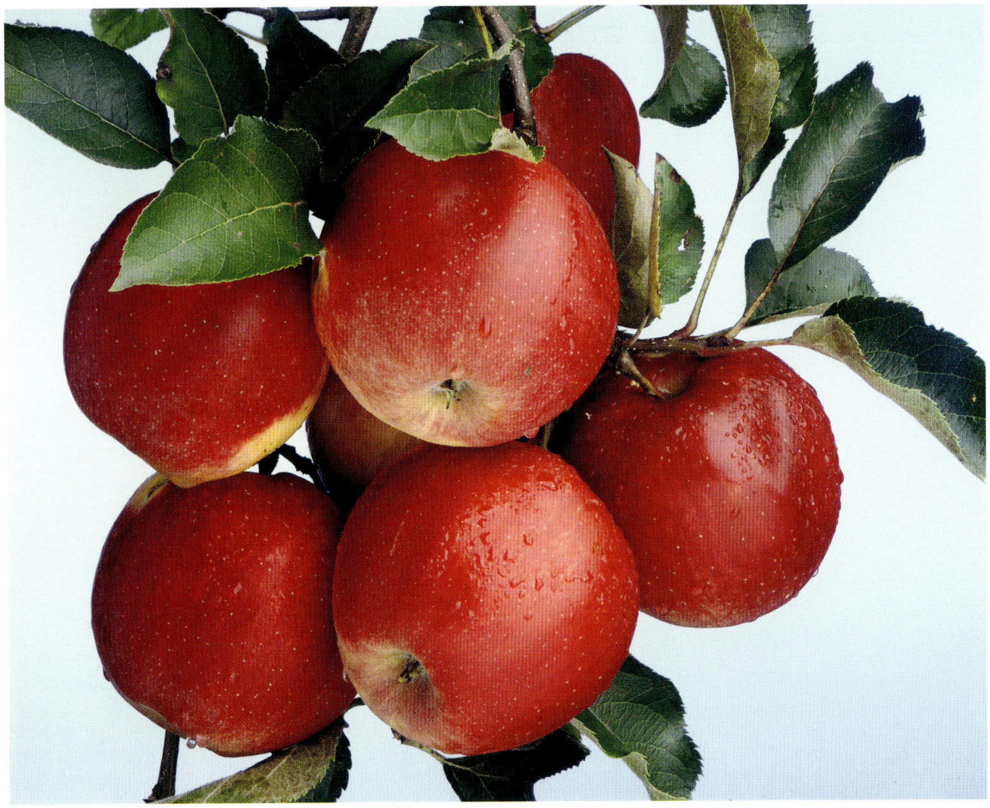

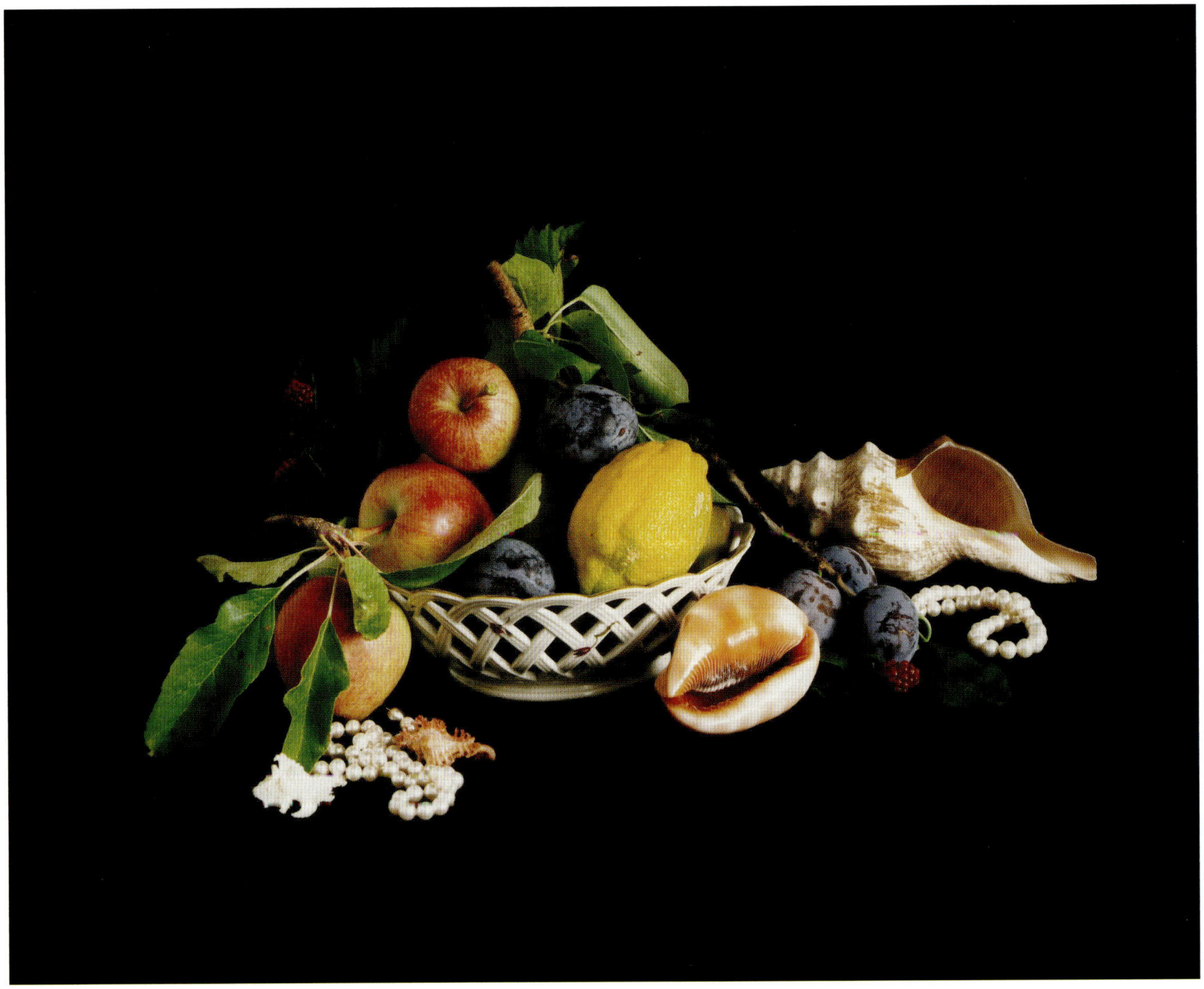

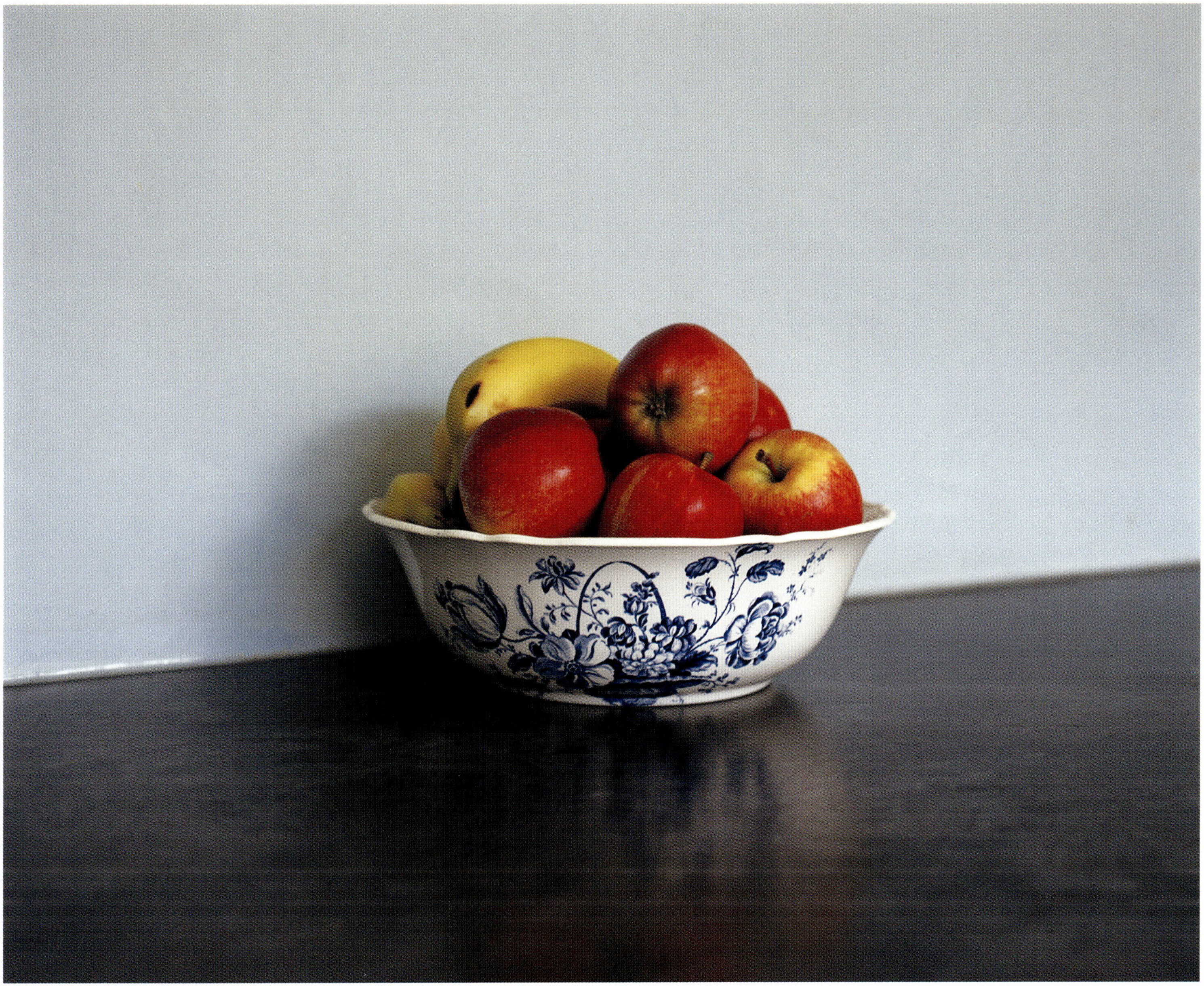

PAGE 76
Martin Gustavsson · *Black Plums*, 2012 (detail) · oil on linen

OPPOSITE TOP
Christopher Williams · *Bergische Bauernscheune, Junkersholz, Leichlingen September 29th, 2009*, 2010 · archival pigment print

OPPOSITE BOTTOM
Shirana Shahbazi · [*Stilleben-26-2008*] C-print on aluminium

ABOVE
Kraig Wilson · *Origin*, 2010
C-print on pearlized paper

In the creation myths of the Abrahamic religions of Judaism, Christianity and Islam it is the apple that led Adam and Eve into disgrace and out of the Garden of Eden. The apple remains the ultimate symbol of human fallibility in the face of temptation, and contemporary artists continue to experiment with this religious legacy. **Christopher Williams**'s dew-dropped apples dangle alluringly from a tree branch, calling out to be plucked and eaten. Shot against a white background, however, they call to mind the superficial perfection found in advertisements as much as any Edenic apples. **Shirana Shahbazi** draws on the still-life tradition – apples perch alongside other fruits in a basket surrounded by shells and pearls – but she updates the imagery by presenting this idealized staging in an all-encompassing blackness. **Kraig Wilson** photographs apples and bananas in a simple china bowl in a clean composition that recalls not only our everyday consumption of these household fruits, but also a nostalgic longing for an age of lost Englishness. With its title, however, *Origin* reminds the viewer of its subject's mythology.

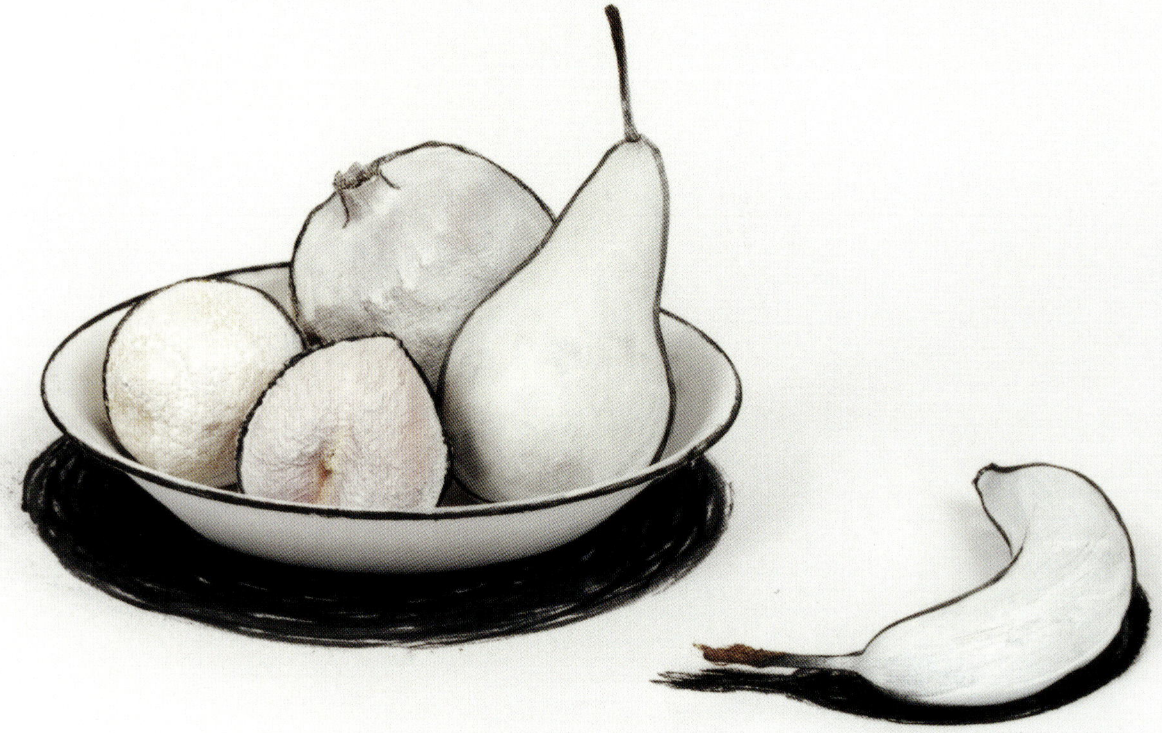

ABOVE
Cynthia Greig
Nature Morte no. 3
(*Gravitational Pull*), 2009
chromogenic print

OPPOSITE
Lisa Milroy
Food, 1999
oil paint on clay

For her *Nature Morte* series **Cynthia Greig** created what she called 'three-dimensional drawings', whitewashing objects and then drawing in black outlines and shadows around them. What appears at first to be a traditional still-life drawing is instead a photographic document of artistic artifice at its most deceptive. Here, the yellow of a lemon, the orange of a peach and the brown of a banana stem seep through the whitewash to assert their innate characteristics. The photograph documents the objects as they appeared, with no additional digital manipulation.

A series of paintings by **Lisa Milroy** from the late 1990s features groupings of food, including melons, Japanese sweets, fast food, fruit and vegetables in a continuation of the artist's earlier explorations of the still life. For *Food*, Milroy applied the motivation behind her paintings to create a three-dimensional installation of painted clay objects, each one painted to approximate an illusion of naturalism that only heightens its artifice.

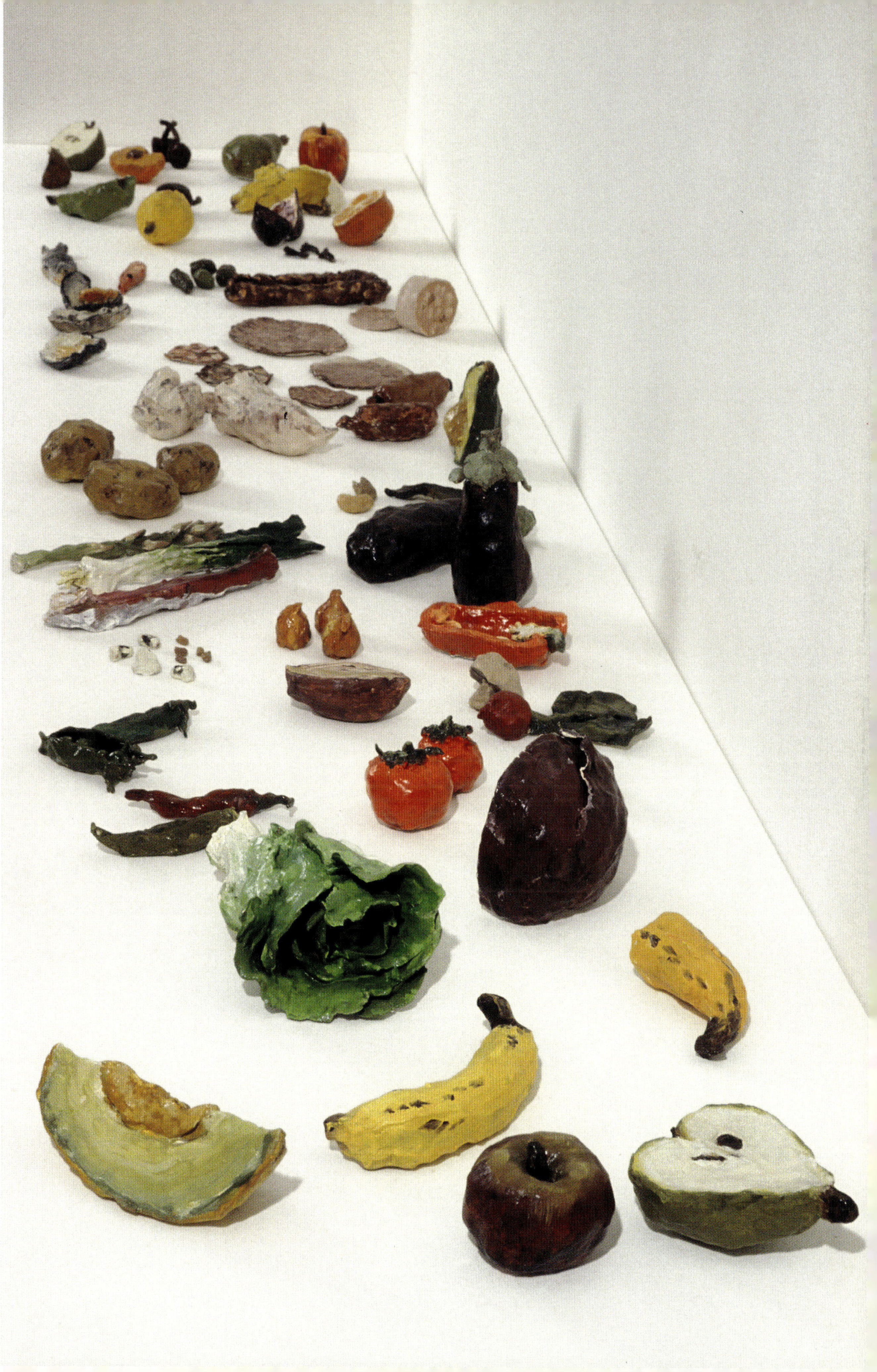

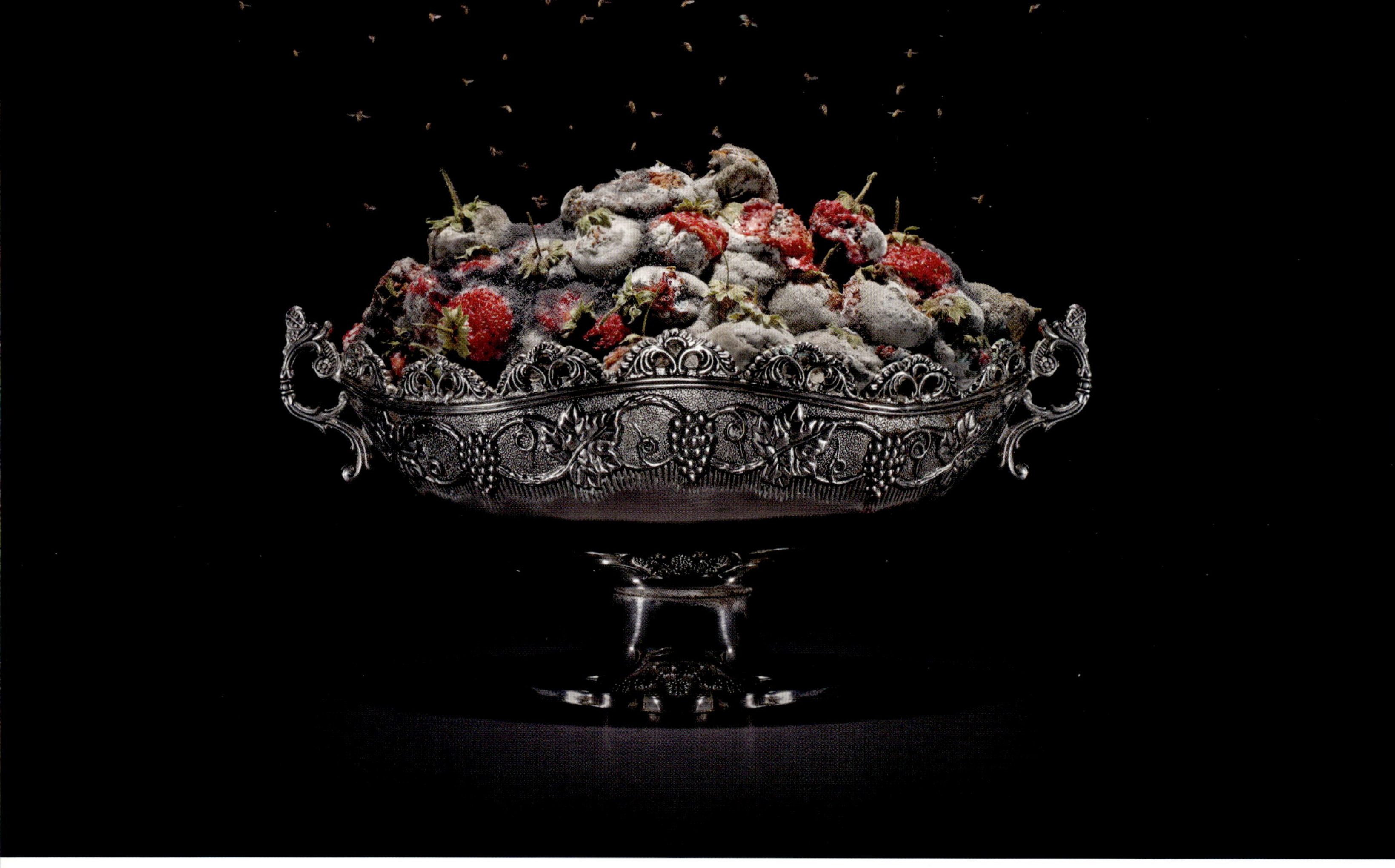

Klaus Pichler entitled his series of photographs of rotting food *One Third* in reference to a UN study that reported that one third of the world's food goes to waste every year. The titles of his elaborate tableaux draw attention to the resources consumed and vast distances travelled in order for the photographed foodstuffs to satisfy consumer tastes.

ABOVE · Klaus Pichler · *Strawberries: Sort: Strawberries 'Elsanta' · Place of production: San Giovanni Lupatoto, Verona, Italy · Transport distance: 741 km · Carbon footprint (total) per kg: 0,35 kg · Water requirement (total) per kg: 348 l · Price: 7,96 € / kg*, 2012 · digital C-print

OPPOSITE TOP · Klaus Pichler · *Capsicum: Sort: Capsicum 'Kapya' red · Place of production: Souk El Khemis, Maroq · Transport distance: 3856 km · Carbon footprint (total) per kg: 0,92 kg · Water requirement (total) per kg: 384 l · Price: 3,98 € / kg*, 2012 · digital C-print

OPPOSITE CENTRE · Klaus Pichler · *Lemons: Sort: Lemons 'Lapithkiotiki' · Place of production: Limassol, Cyprus · Transport distance: 2050 km · Carbon footprint (total) per kg: 0,72 kg · Water requirement (total) per kg: 448 l · Price: 1,99 € / kg*, 2012 · digital C-print

OPPOSITE BOTTOM · Klaus Pichler · *Tomatoes: Sort: Cuore di Bue · Place of production: Albenga, Italy · Transport distance: 1035 km · Carbon footprint (total) per kg: 0,31 kg · Water requirement (total) per kg: 215 l · Price: 0,89 € / kg*, 2012 · digital C-print

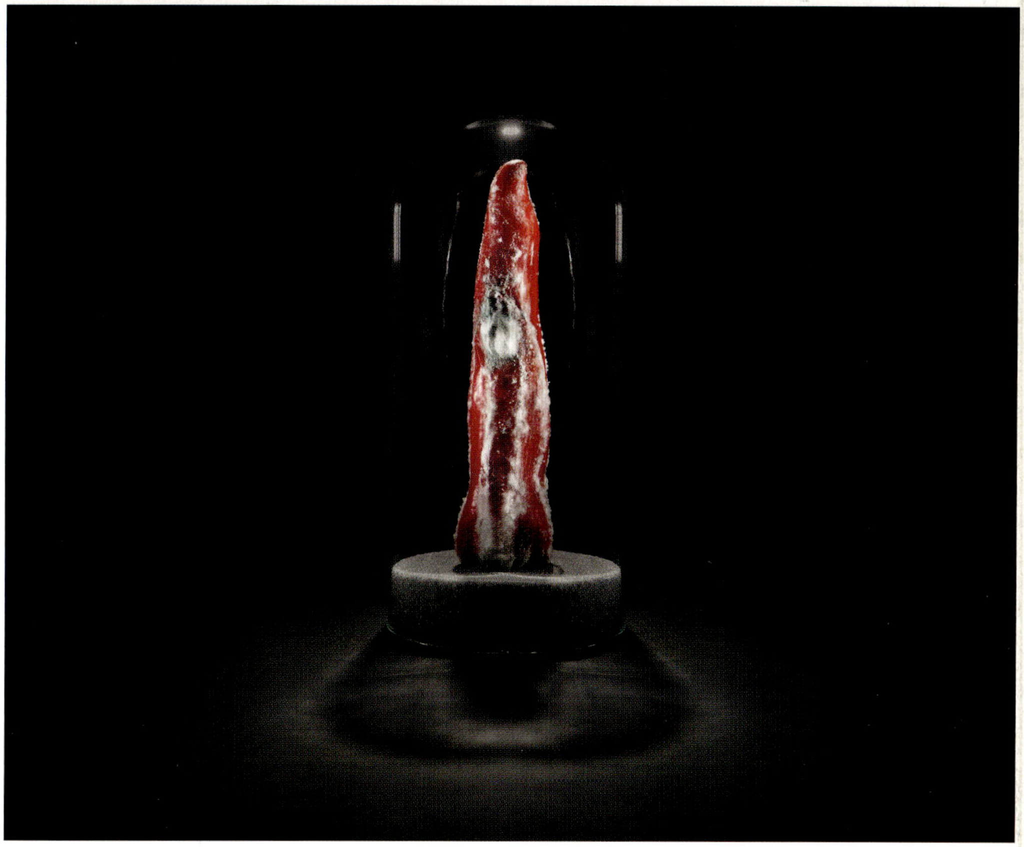

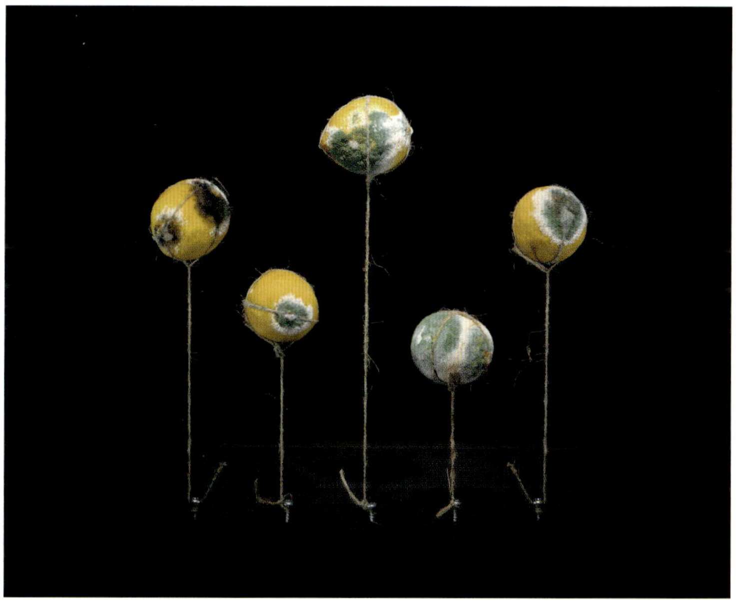

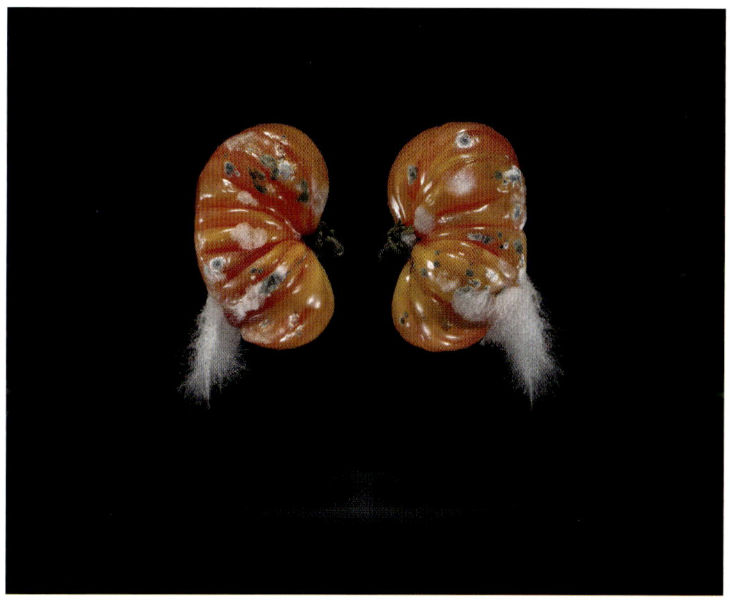

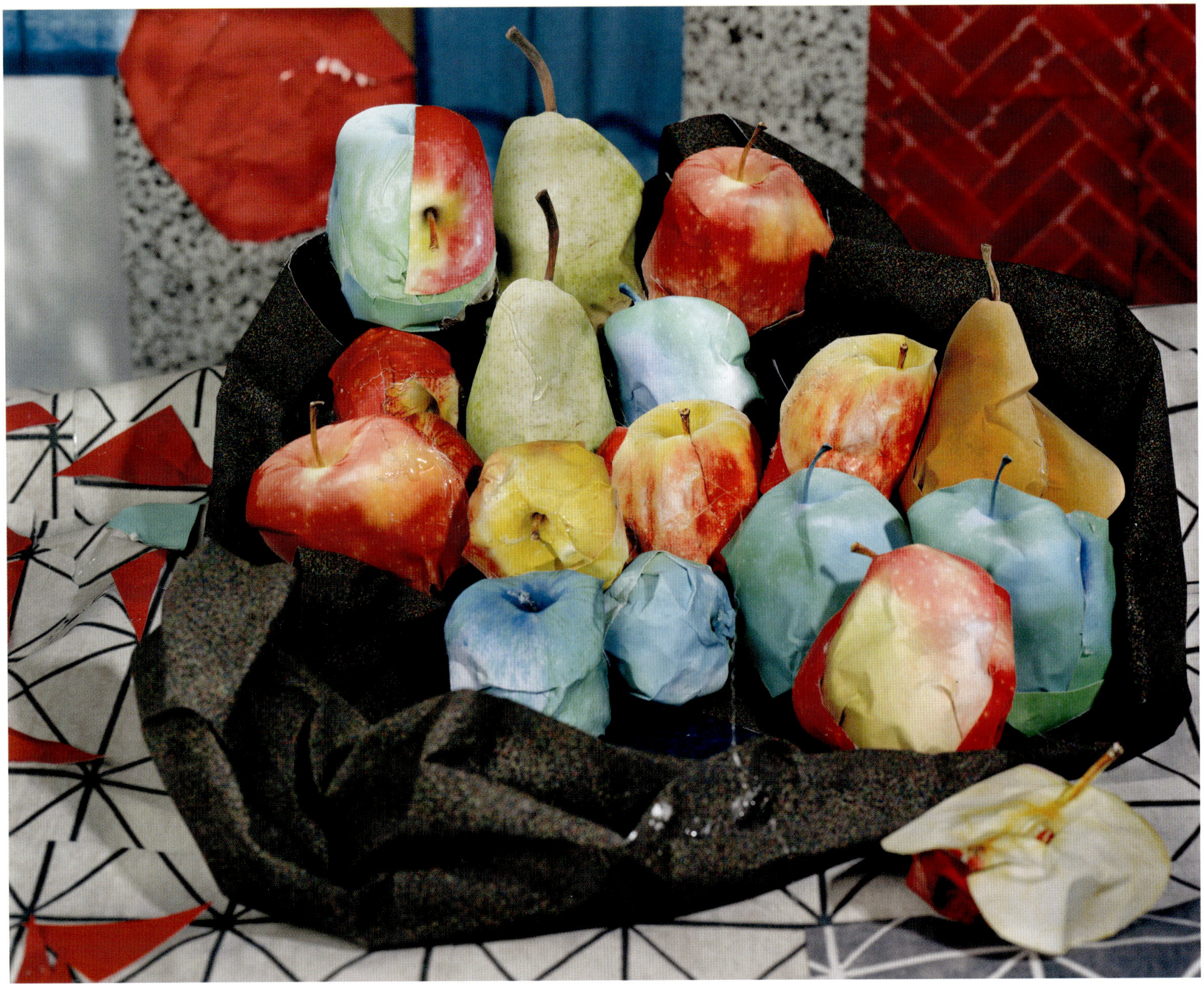

ABOVE
Daniel Gordon
Pink Ladies and Pears, 2012
C-print

OPPOSITE TOP
David Halliday
Carrots, entwined, 2007
archival pigment print

OPPOSITE BOTTOM
David Halliday
Sausage & Eggs, 2007
archival pigment print

From existing images found online and in magazines, **Daniel Gordon** carefully constructs three-dimensional photomontages, which he then photographs. It is these photographic prints that the artist then exhibits, rather than his paper sculptures. Here, a bowl of fruit evokes Cézanne with its disrupted picture plane and angular layering.

David Halliday originally trained as a chef and his personal experience preparing and plating food comes across in still lifes that both defer to and update the tradition. Halliday brings a certain rigour, an almost clinical attention, to these investigations of the commonplace. All of his photographs have been digitally altered in order to be as perfect as possible.

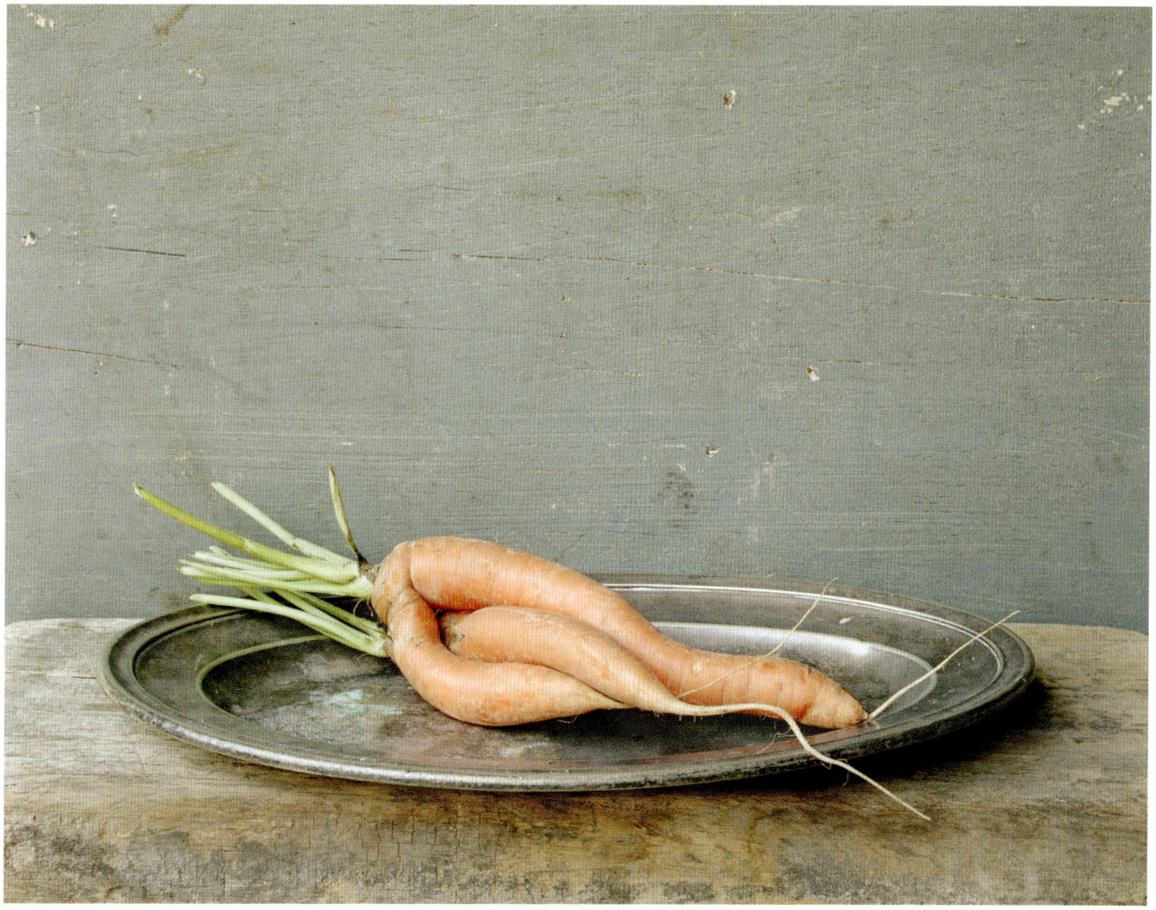

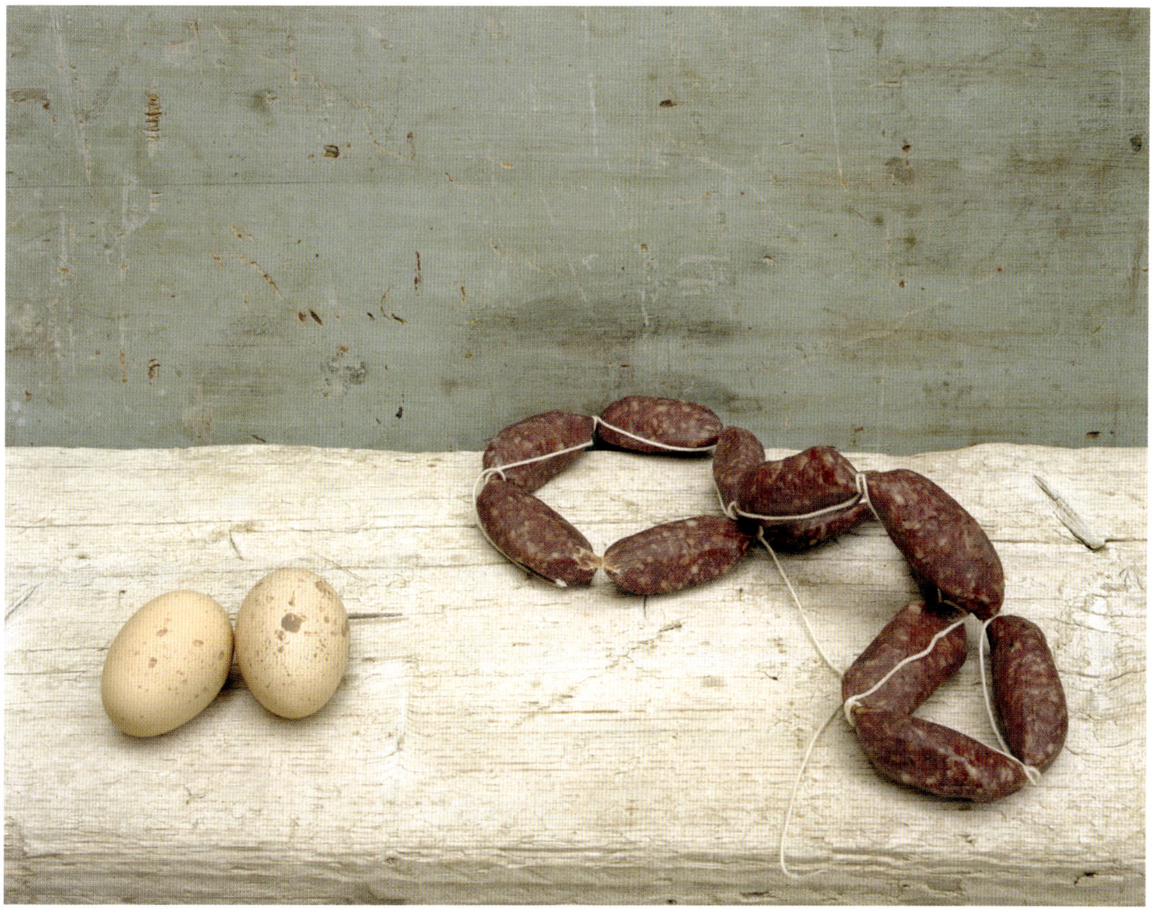

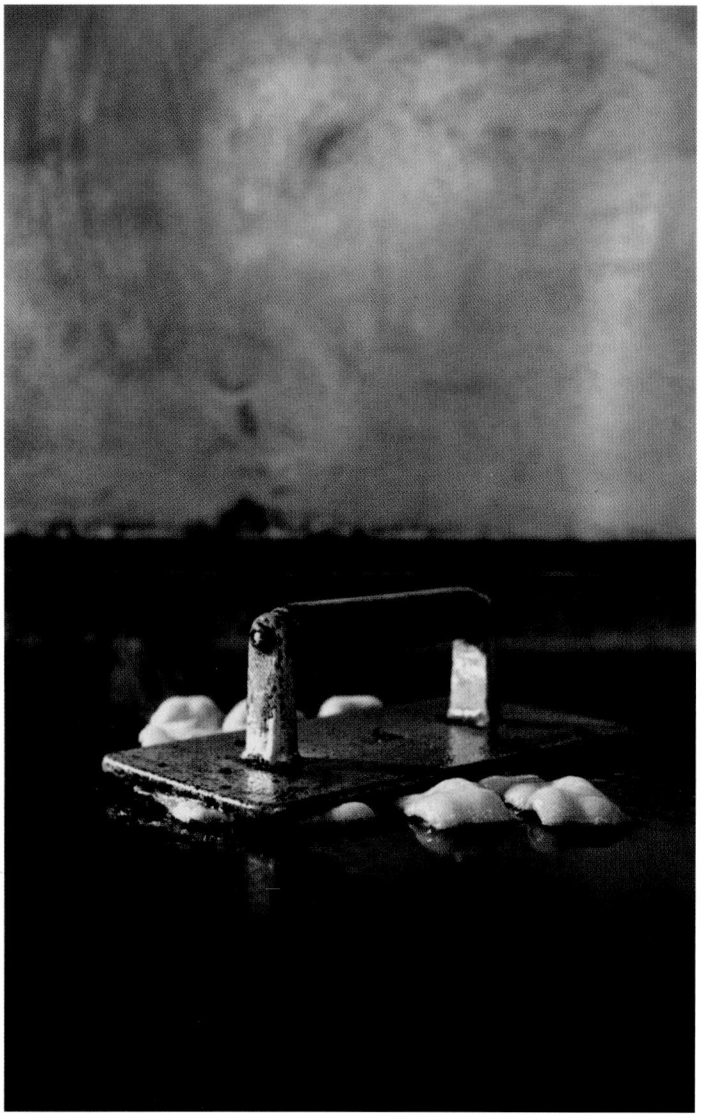

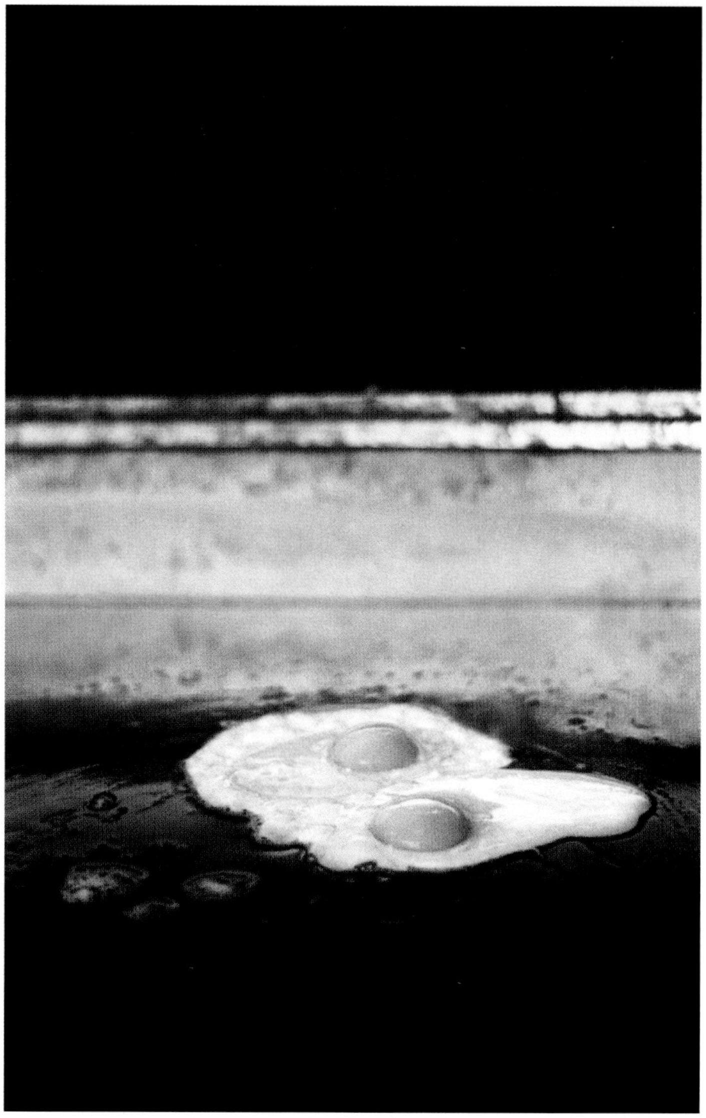

ABOVE LEFT
Kate Joyce
Effuse, 2000
archival pigment print

ABOVE RIGHT
Kate Joyce
Almost, 2000
archival pigment print

OPPOSITE TOP
Ged Quinn
Myth of the Metals, 2012
oil on linen

OPPOSITE BOTTOM
Ged Quinn
Bunker Archeology, 2012
oil on canvas

For her *Aporia* series (2000–06) **Kate Joyce** photographed the grills of American diners during the busy breakfast service. Her black-and-white photographs follow in the footsteps of Diego Velázquez's *An Old Woman Cooking Eggs* (see page 10) and the artistic tradition of celebrating 'low' subject matter or, as Velázquez put it, 'common things'. From Plato's *Meno*, the term *Aporia* refers to the process of learning whereby one unexpectedly discovers one's ignorance of a discipline and so is inspired to pursue greater knowledge. Joyce's photographs invite viewers to contemplate the skills that underpin the chefs' preparations and so to move towards a broader mindset.

Ged Quinn's beautifully painted still lifes come with an unexpected sting. His cakes come in disconcerting shapes modelled on, for example, the grounds of concentration camps, Cold War prisons and the concrete bunkers built by German troops along the coast of Normandy during World War II. In *Bunker Archeology*, a British cherry cake in the shape of a bunker appears to have come under mortar fire, the dark and irregularly placed cherries resembling extensive bomb damage. In *Myth of the Metals*, the cubes of a Battenberg spongecake have also been rearranged to look like a bunker. Quinn likely settled upon this British cake as it recalls another, less traumatic engagement between Germany and Great Britain; it was originally conceived to celebrate the marriage of a granddaughter of Queen Victoria to Prince Louis of Battenberg.

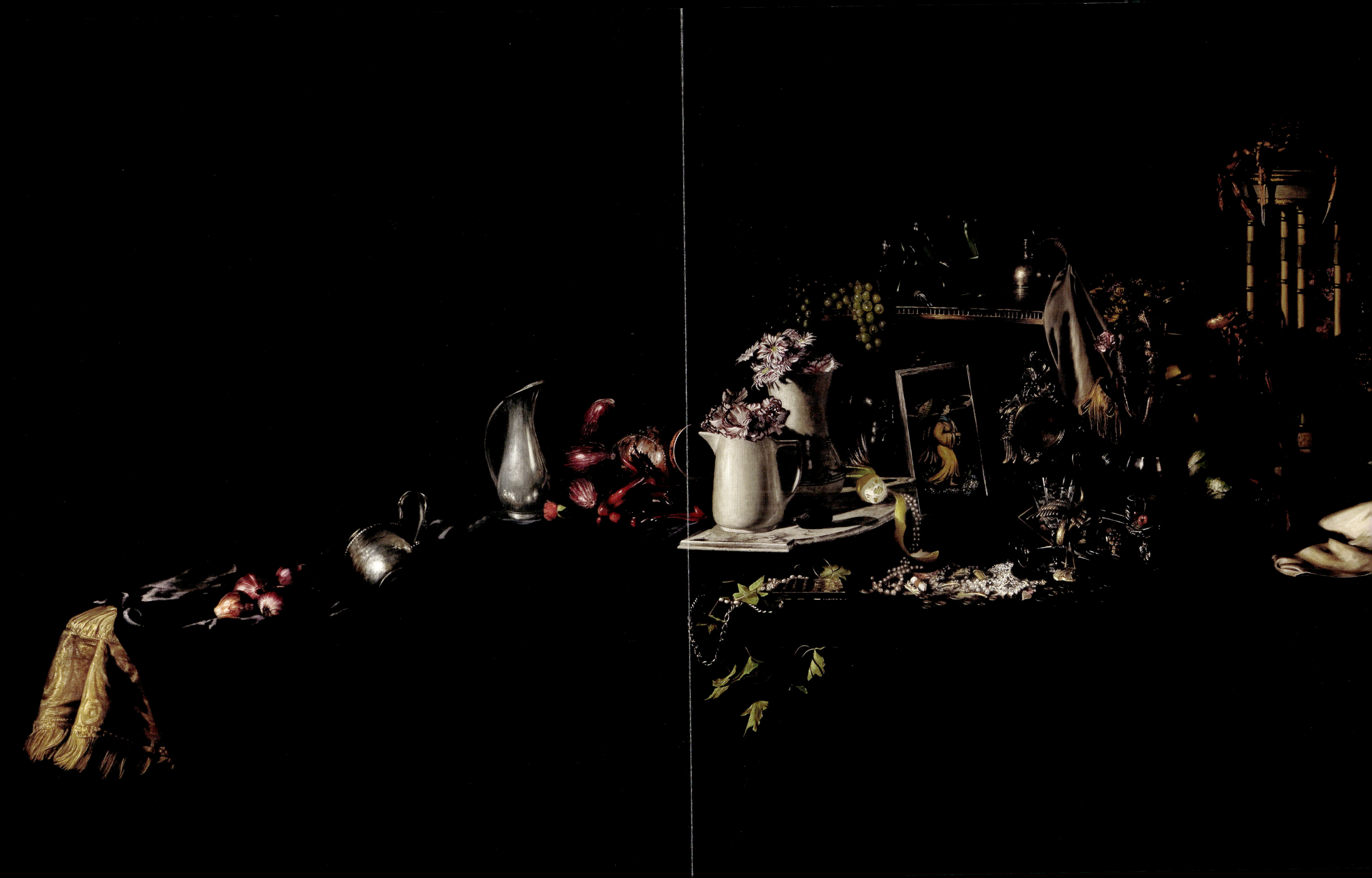

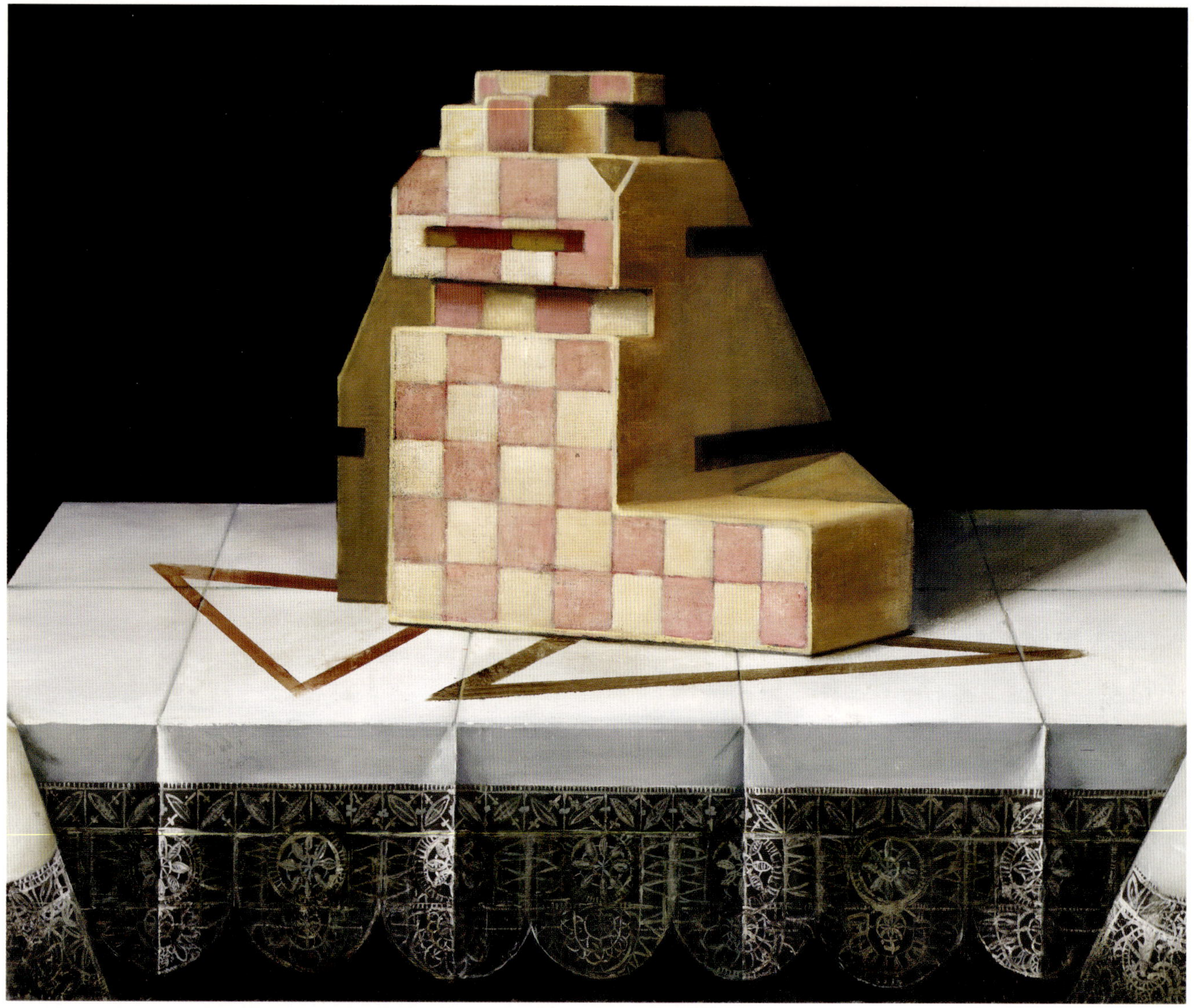

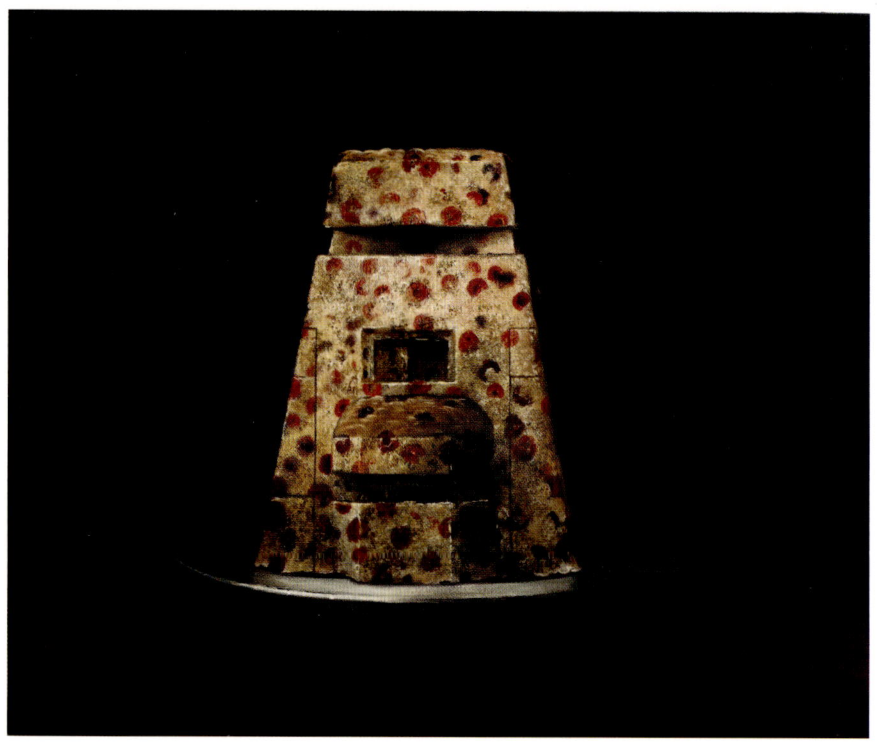

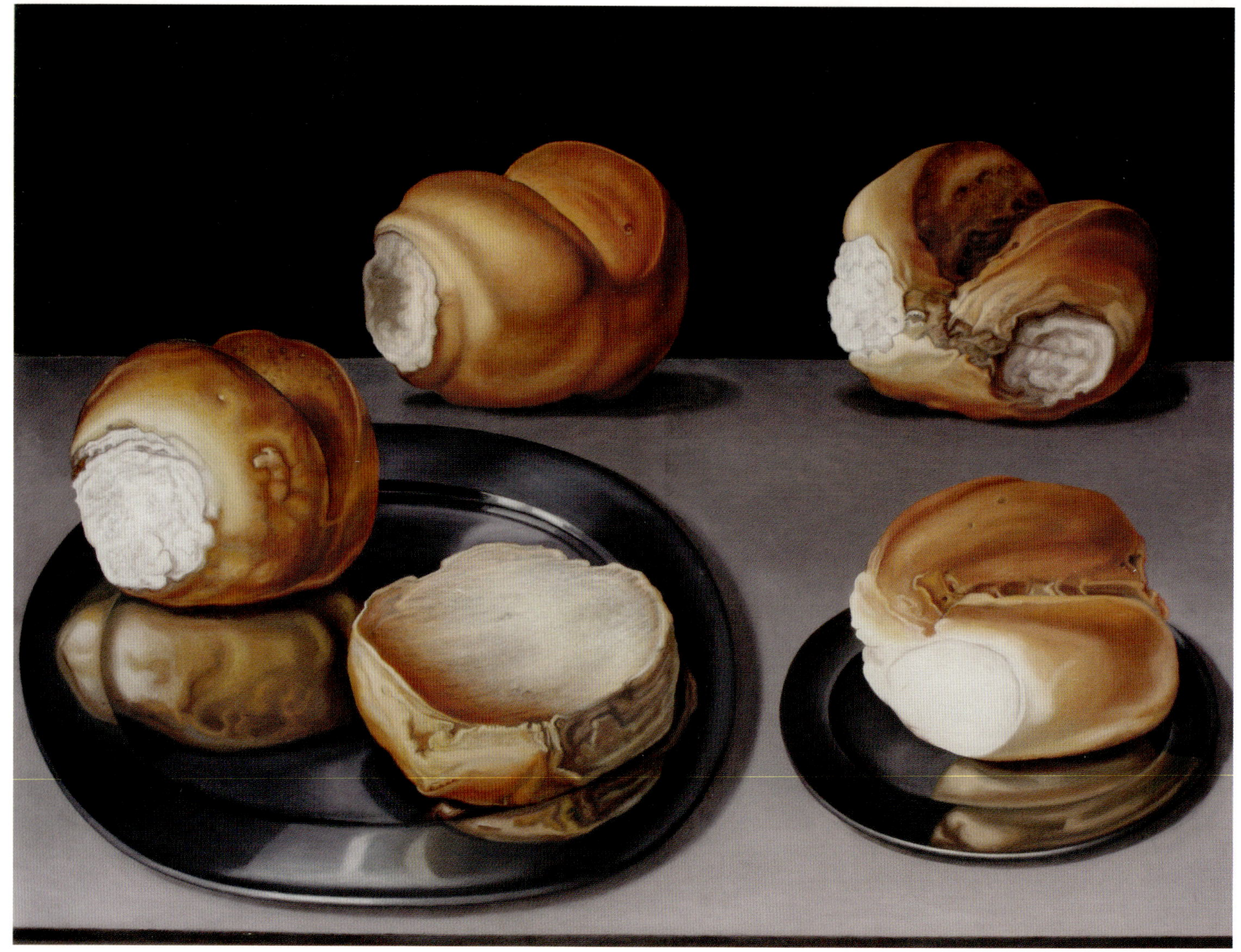

Alan Salisbury turned to the still-life tradition in order to subvert the moral codes so often engrained in paintings of this genre. For *Four Hundred Year Old Bread Rolls with reference to works by Pieter Claesz (1597 to 1660)*, Salisbury carefully copied bread rolls from several of Claesz's paintings into one artfully arranged still life.

Jorge Diezma's huge painting *Bodégon del Limón* appears in reproduction to be a traditional Spanish still life: dark, austere and dense with detail. Diezma was trained as a conceptual artist and taught himself classical painting techniques after leaving formal art education in order to make this and similar works. While they are paintings (oil on canvas) they are first and foremost immersive installations, since they are so large that they envelop the viewer. *Bodégon del Limón* is over eight metres long. One must slowly pass by if not through it, surrounded by the image but never having it fully in one's sights.

ABOVE
Alan Salisbury
***Four Hundred Year Old Bread Rolls with reference to works by Pieter Claesz (1597 to 1660)*,**
2009 · oil on board

INSIDE
Jorge Diezma
***Bodegón del Limón*, 2010**
oil on linen

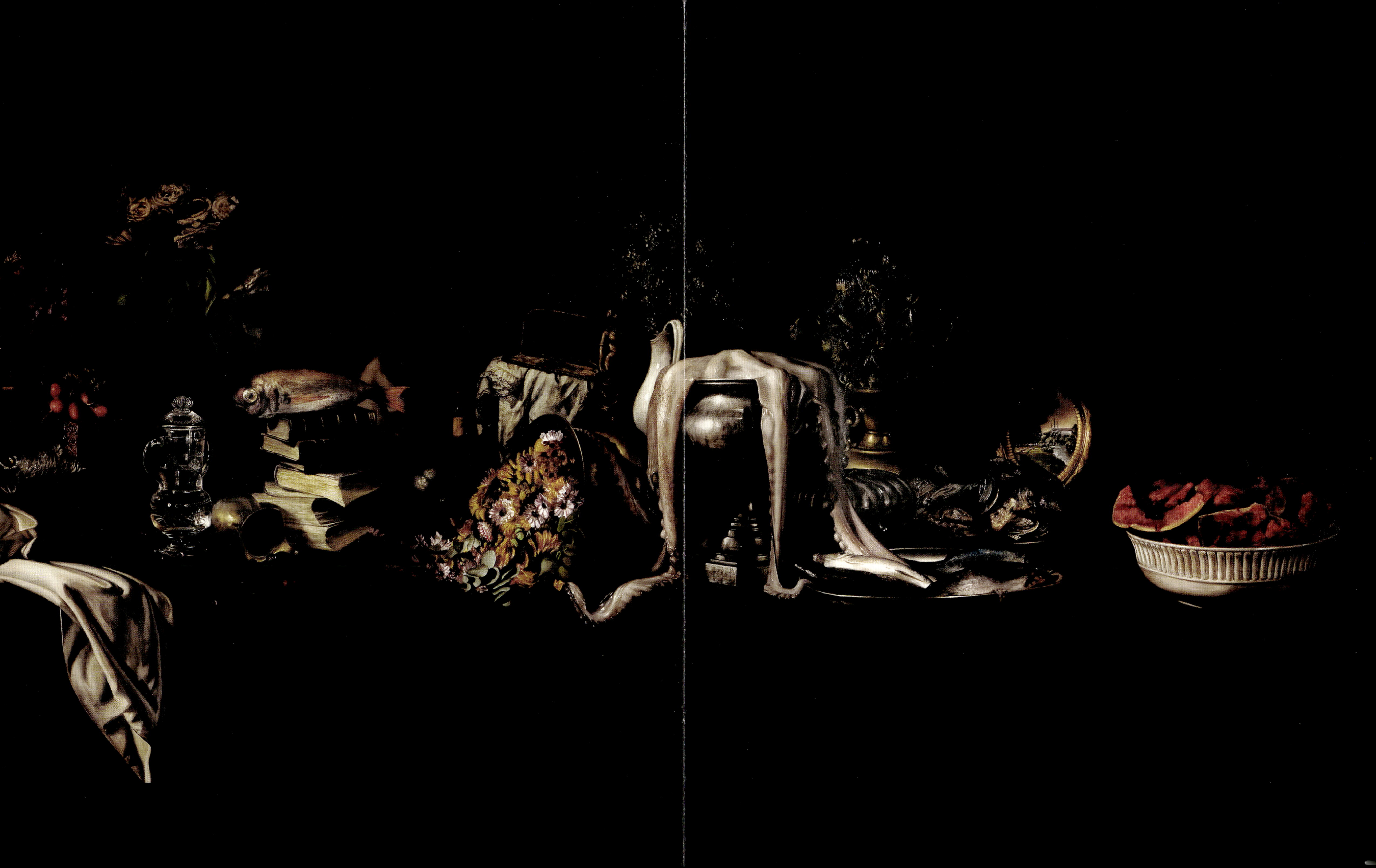

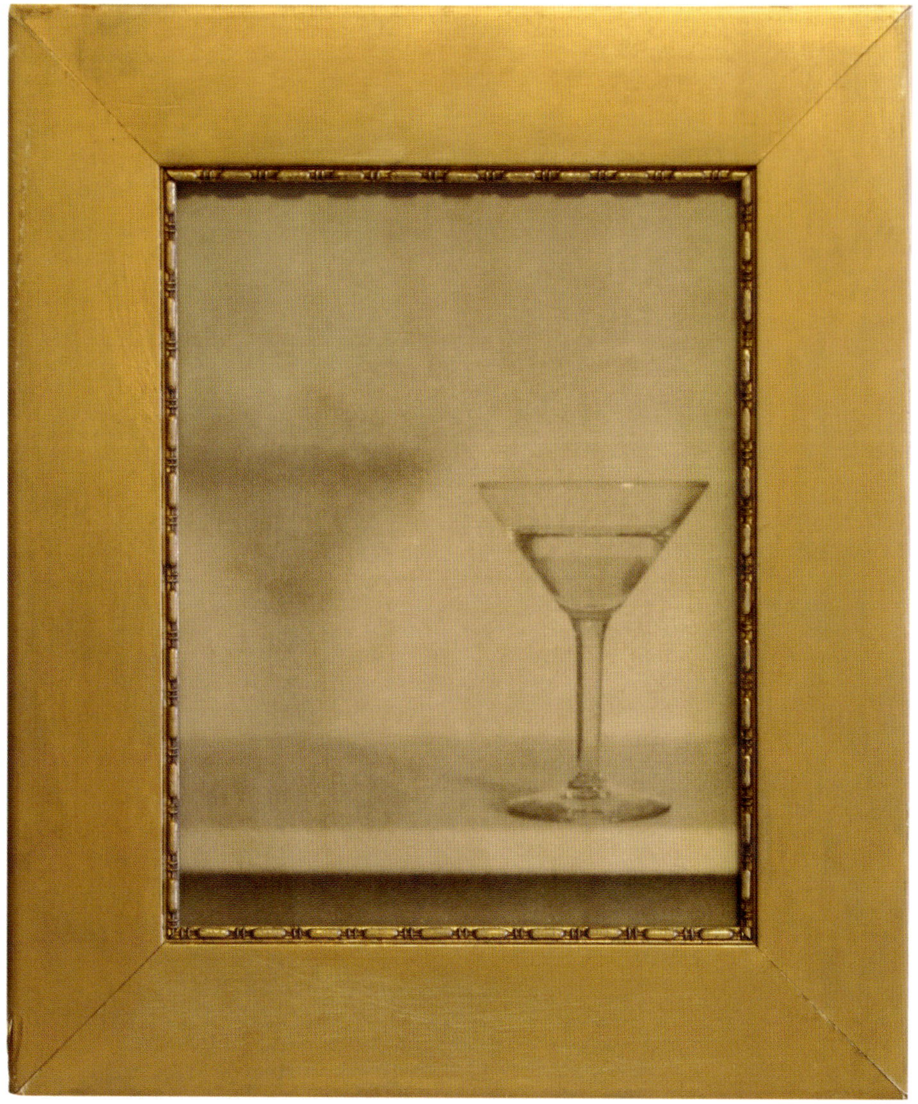

ABOVE
Jefferson Hayman
Martini, 2006
toned silver gelatin print, antique frame

Jefferson Hayman's *Martini* calls to mind an age of smart talk and dry drinks, Noël Coward songs and the Great Depression. The shadow of the drink, however, a barely there stain on the wall, stands in as a symbol for the many types of loss associated with alcoholism: the loss of memory brought on by too much drink, the loss of employment, the loss of dignity.

'I began to think about the idea of leftovers...because it has to do with what you do after the promise, when you realize the promise is not possible. This is fundamental to any utopian notion – the promise and its demise. You can't have utopia without its loss.'

—LAURA LETINSKY

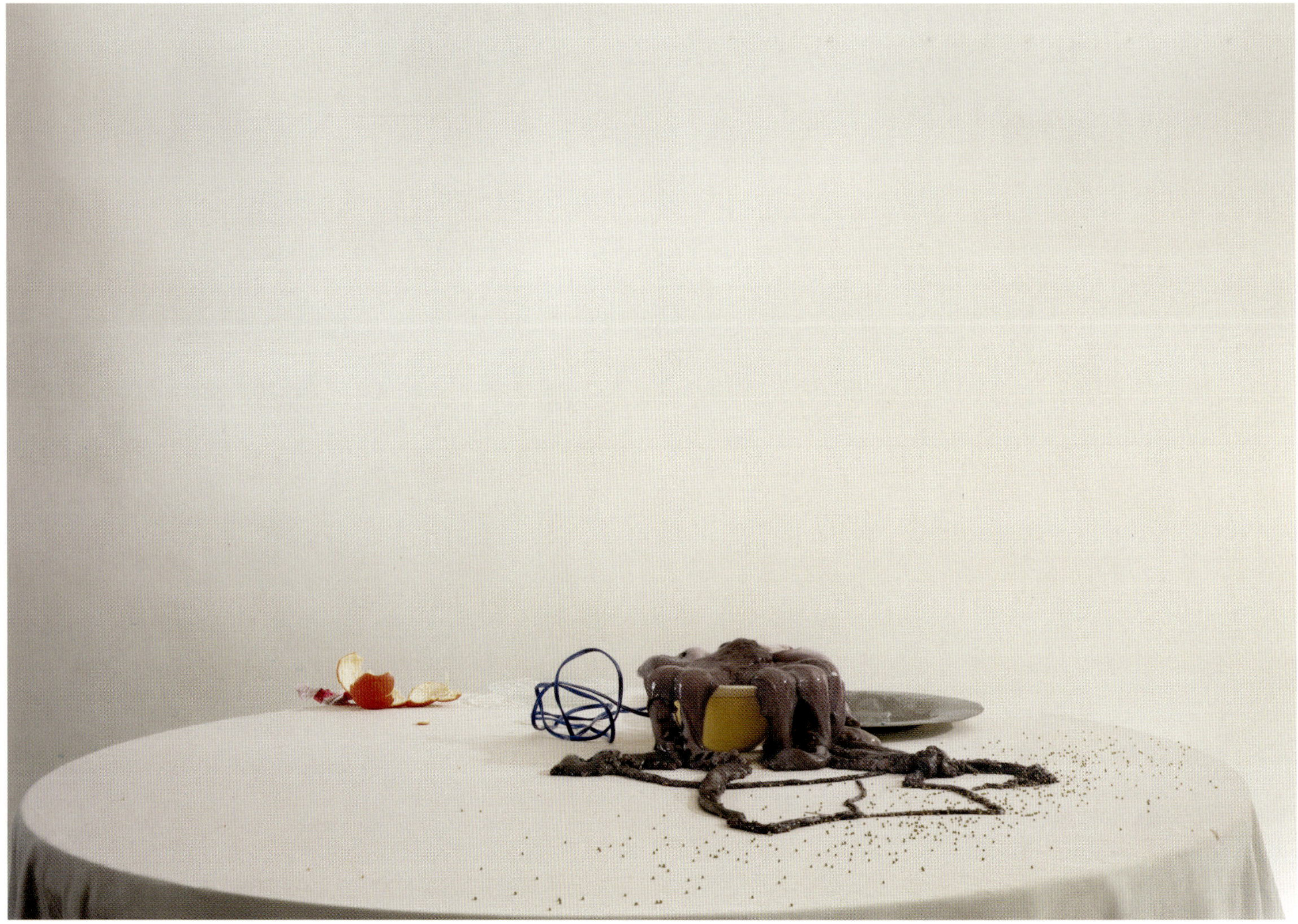

ABOVE
Laura Letinsky
Untitled #28, 2009
C-print

OPPOSITE
Mat Collishaw
Martin Vegas, 2011
C-print

Laura Letinsky's series *The Dog & the Wolf* takes its name from an Aesop fable that explores domesticity versus the untameable and the French phrase *entre chien et loup*, which describes that moment during twilight when distinguishing between the two canines becomes difficult. The festive leftovers captured in the series, the remains of some unknown revelry, were shot with long exposures and so chart this transition from day to night.

Mat Collishaw's startling photographs from his series *Last Meal on Death Row, Texas* were staged to resemble seventeenth-century depictions of food or lavish spreads but actually document the last meals requested by prisoners on death row in the United States. Each work is named after the prisoner who requested the featured dish for their last meal, before being killed by the state.

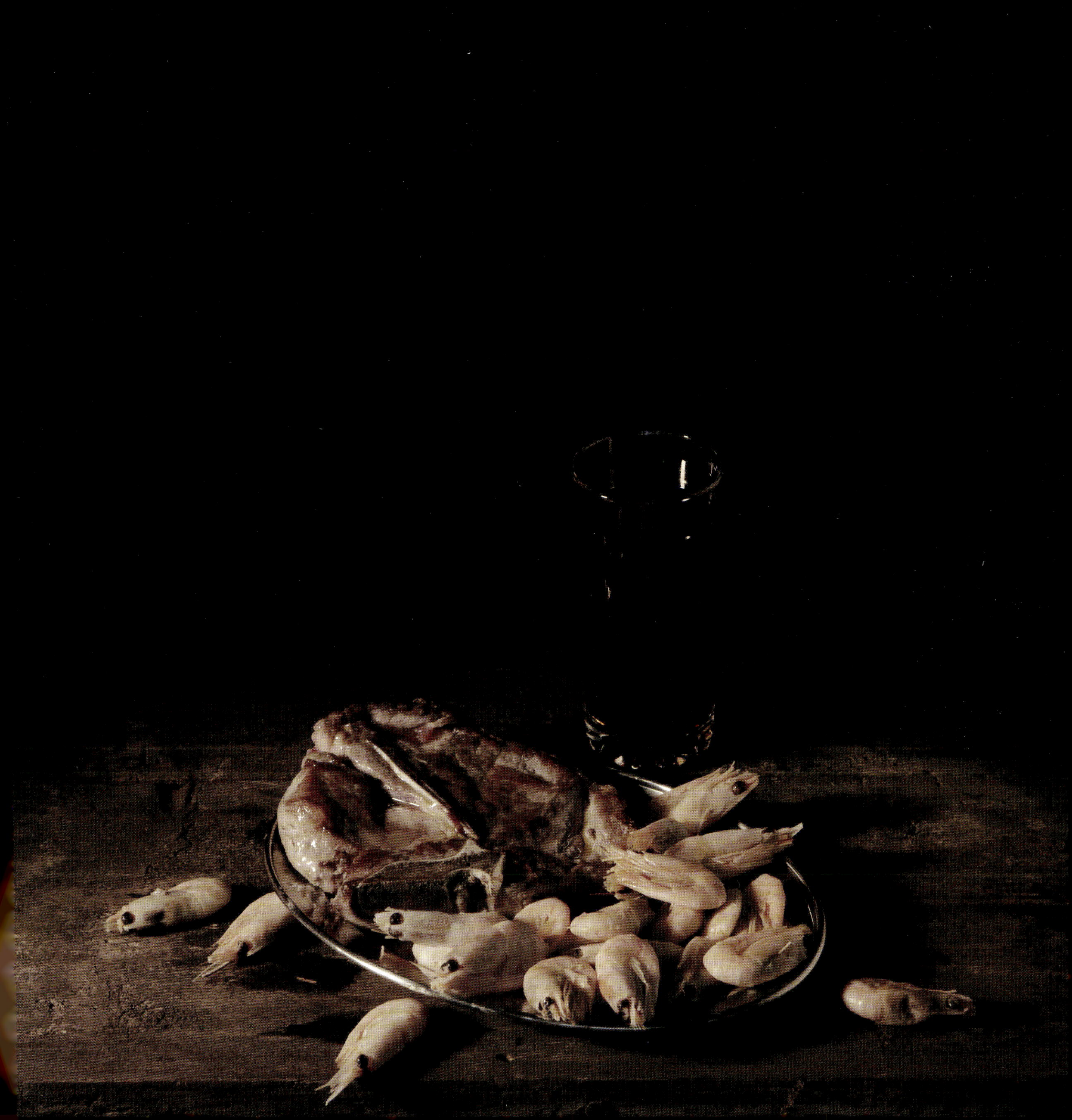

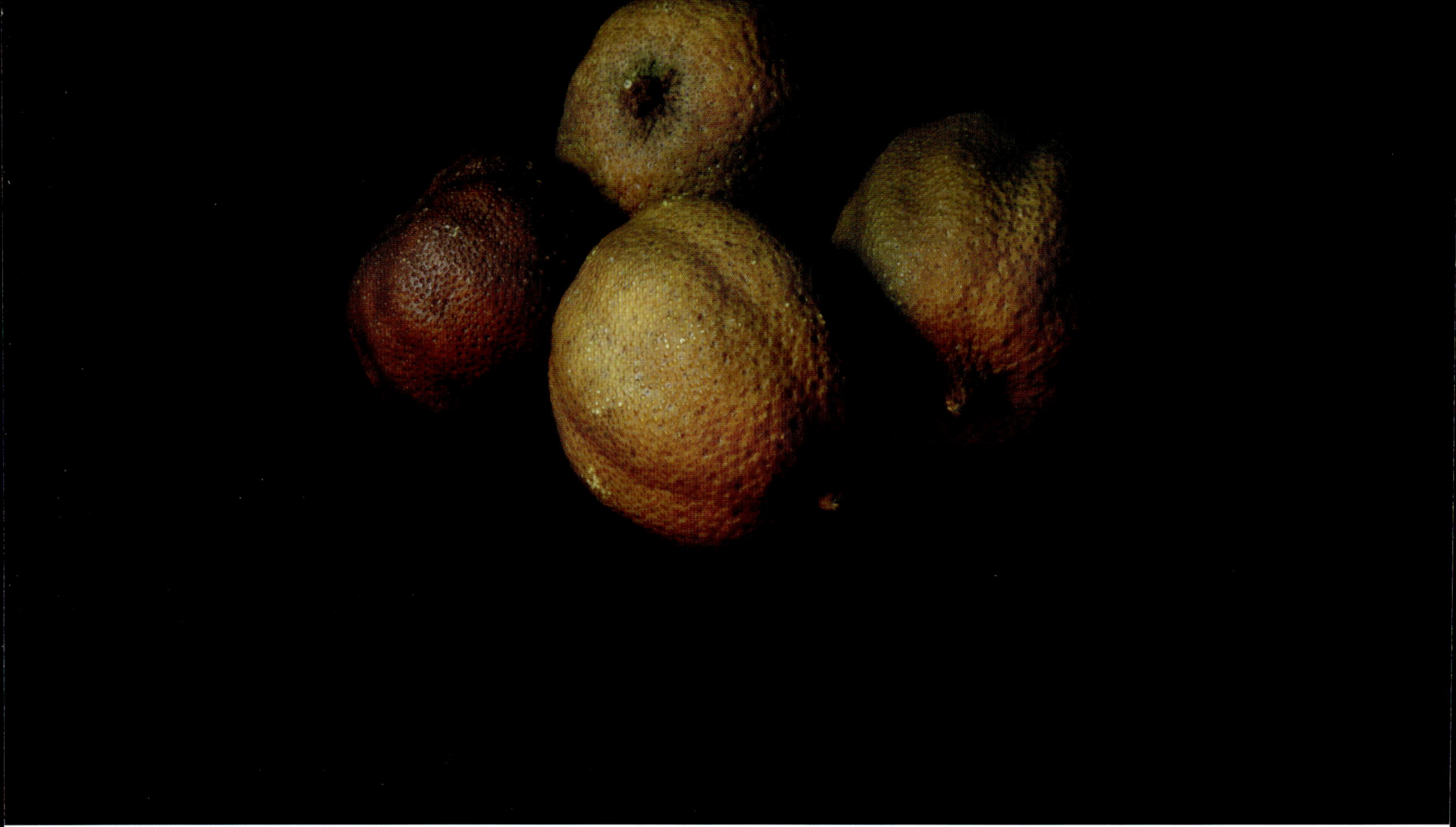

ABOVE
Maciej Urbanek
The Elders, 2012
archival giclée print

OPPOSITE TOP
Janice McNab
The Bloodbathers, 2011
oil on linen

OPPOSITE BOTTOM
Anne-Françoise Couloumy
Réception, 2010–11
oil on canvas

Maciej Urbanek found these forgotten, desiccated lemons and tangerine in his studio and was reminded of 'the old men and women found in the group portraits of Rembrandt and especially Frans Hals'. The leathery fruits recall aging human skin and hint at the decay hidden beneath these shells, the once ripe fruit now despoiled. The artist has written: 'The fruit becomes stand-ins for the body, the substitute that evokes the qualities and characteristics of the old flesh – hardened, shriveled, dry and porous.'

For a series of large paintings called *The Bloodbathers*, **Janice McNab** made what she dubbed 'ice cream monsters' and then photographed them as they slowly melted into forms that recalled both landscapes and the organs of the human body. McNab painted the melting ice cream from this photographic documentation, thereby ensuring the time necessary to capture in paint an otherwise transient moment.

Anne-Françoise Couloumy also charts the passage of time in this rendering of the detritus of a formal banquet. The party is over, the catering consumed, the drinks drunk, the dancers departed. A small wedge of light illuminates the cloth napkins discarded on the table and floor. The night of revelry has passed; a new day has dawned and appetites return.

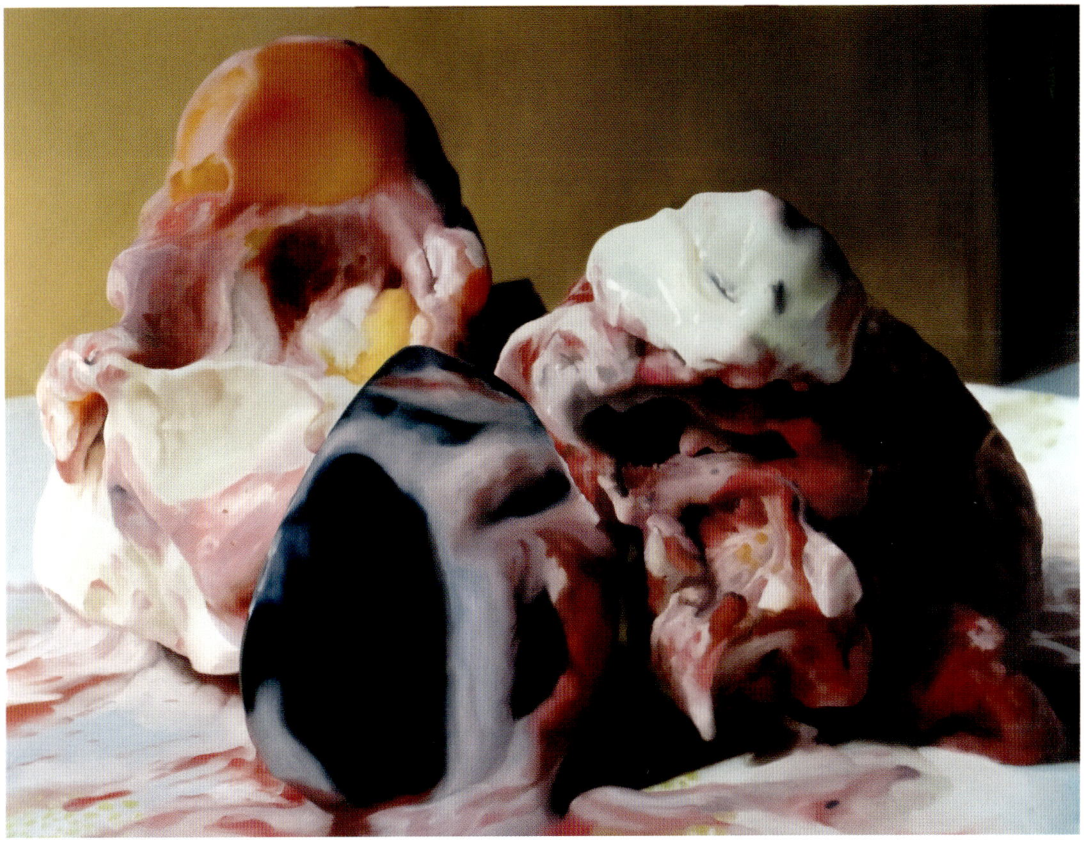

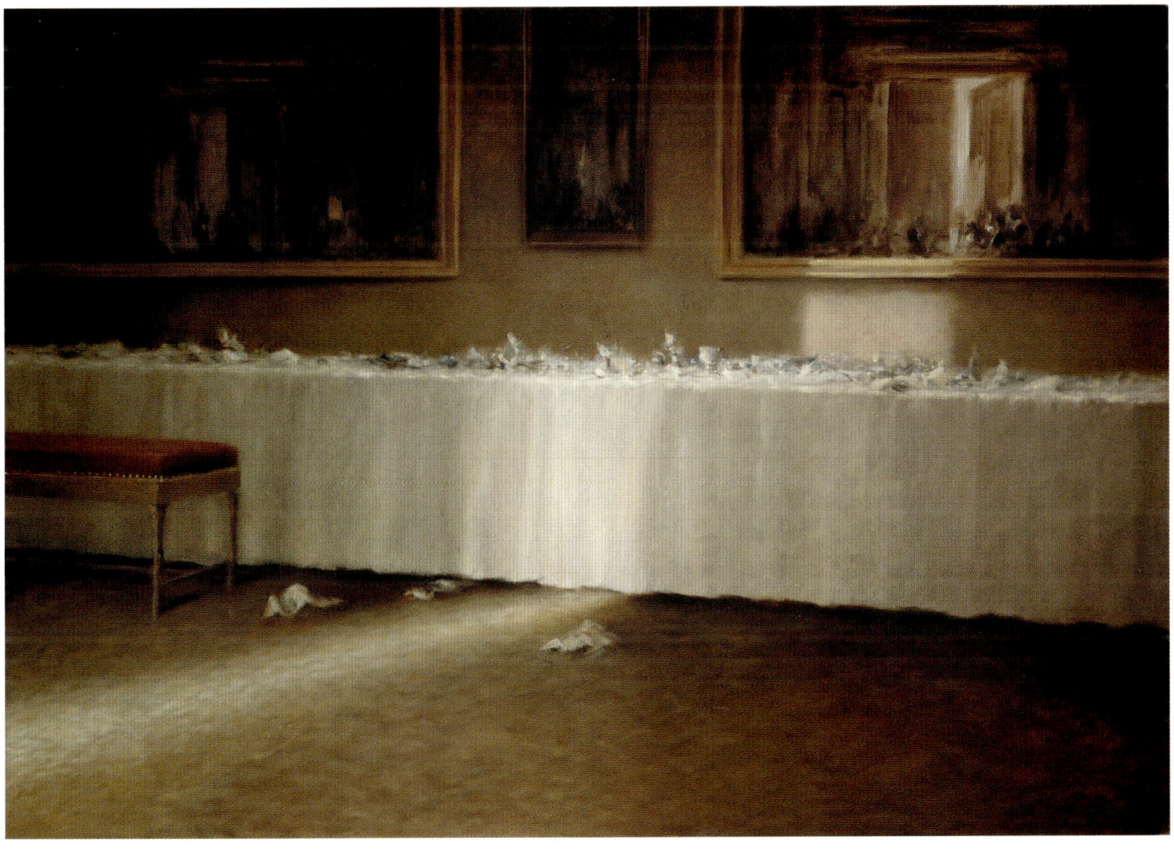

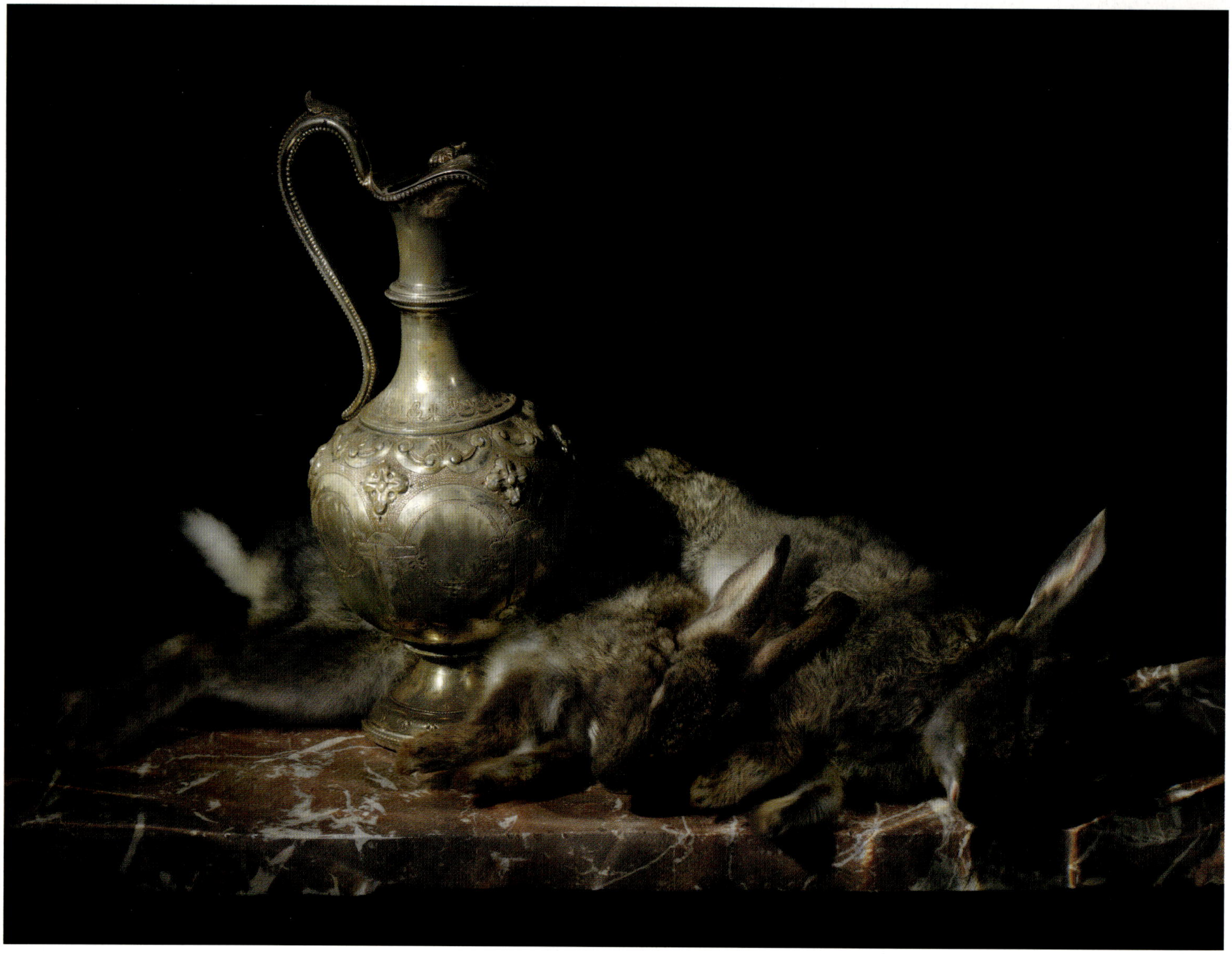

ABOVE
Alexander James,
Distil Ennui Studio
Vanitas, 'Multiply', 2010
C-print mounted on
polished aluminium

OPPOSITE
McDermott & McGough
Tory Fecundity, 1907,
1988 · cyanotype

Alexander James and **McDermott & McGough** conjure in their photographs an idealized time past that overtly situates the works in the painterly tradition of the still life. For his *Vanitas* series, James sought to reproduce the atmosphere of Old Master paintings by photographing studio props and dead animals underwater. The soft refractions of light passing through water lent the resulting images a painterly effect. McDermott & McGough achieved the cyan-blue rinse that veils *Tory Fecundity, 1907* through the Victorian photographic printing process of cyanotype. Their preference for this old-fashioned technique relates to the pair's commitment to living as Victorian gentlemen would, situating their lives in a historical past made present through their collective will. They dress the part, live by candlelight and attribute each of their artworks to a date of manufacture far in advance of their own births.

'I've seen the future, and I'm not going.'

—DAVID MCDERMOTT

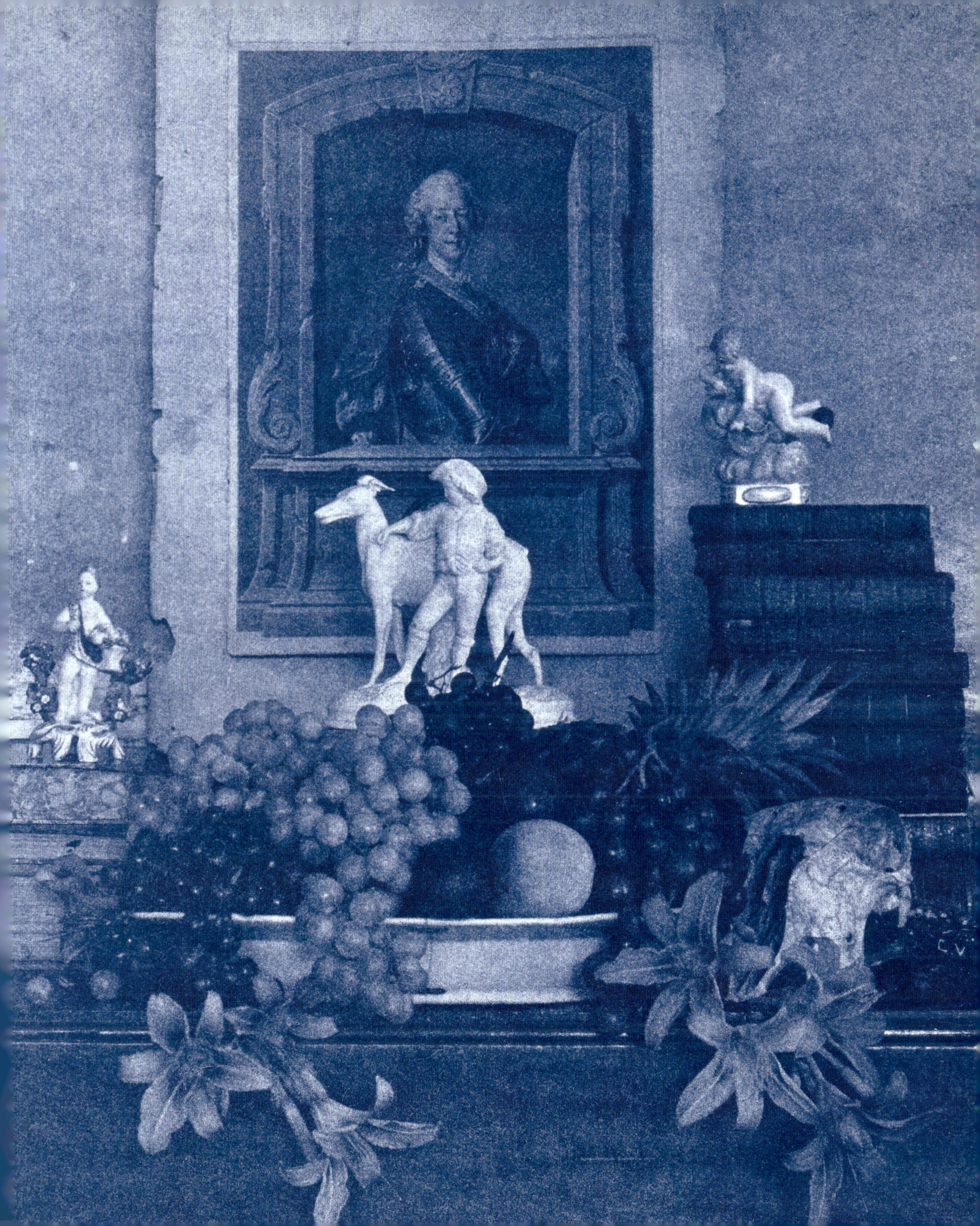
C.V

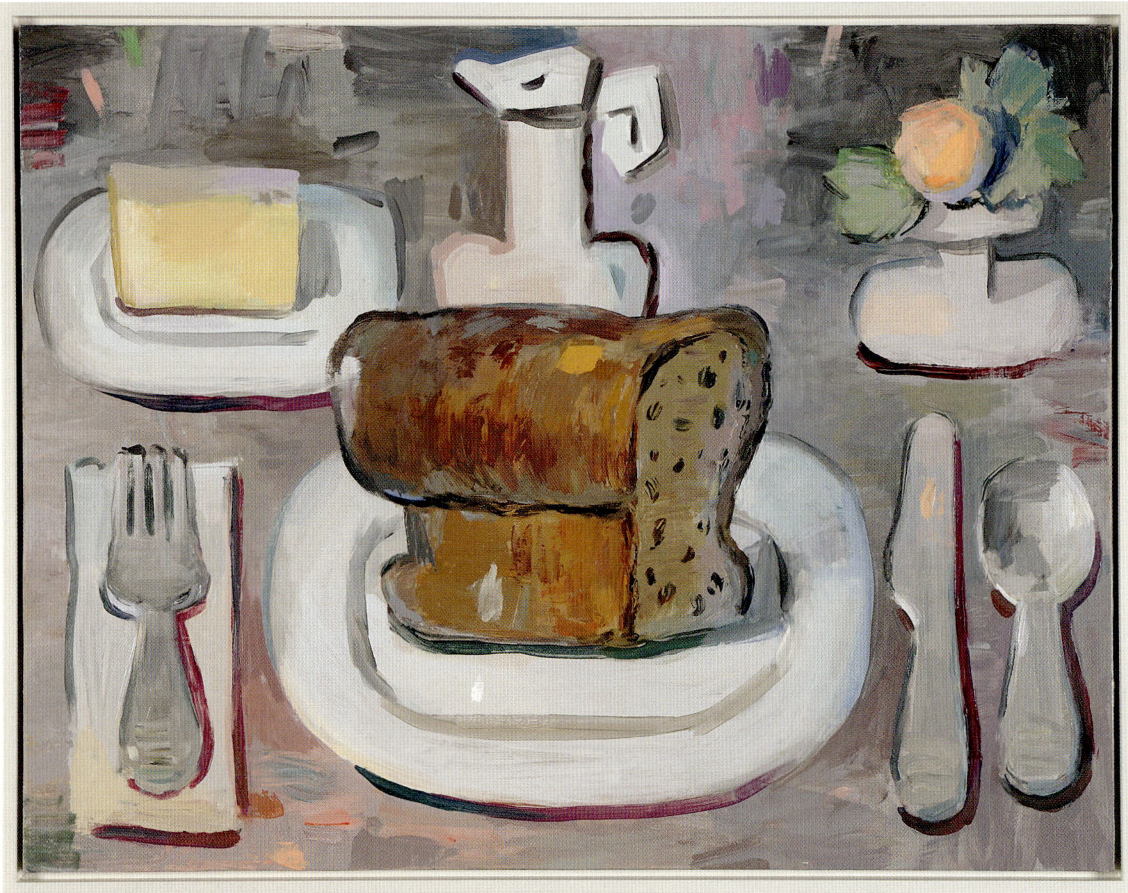

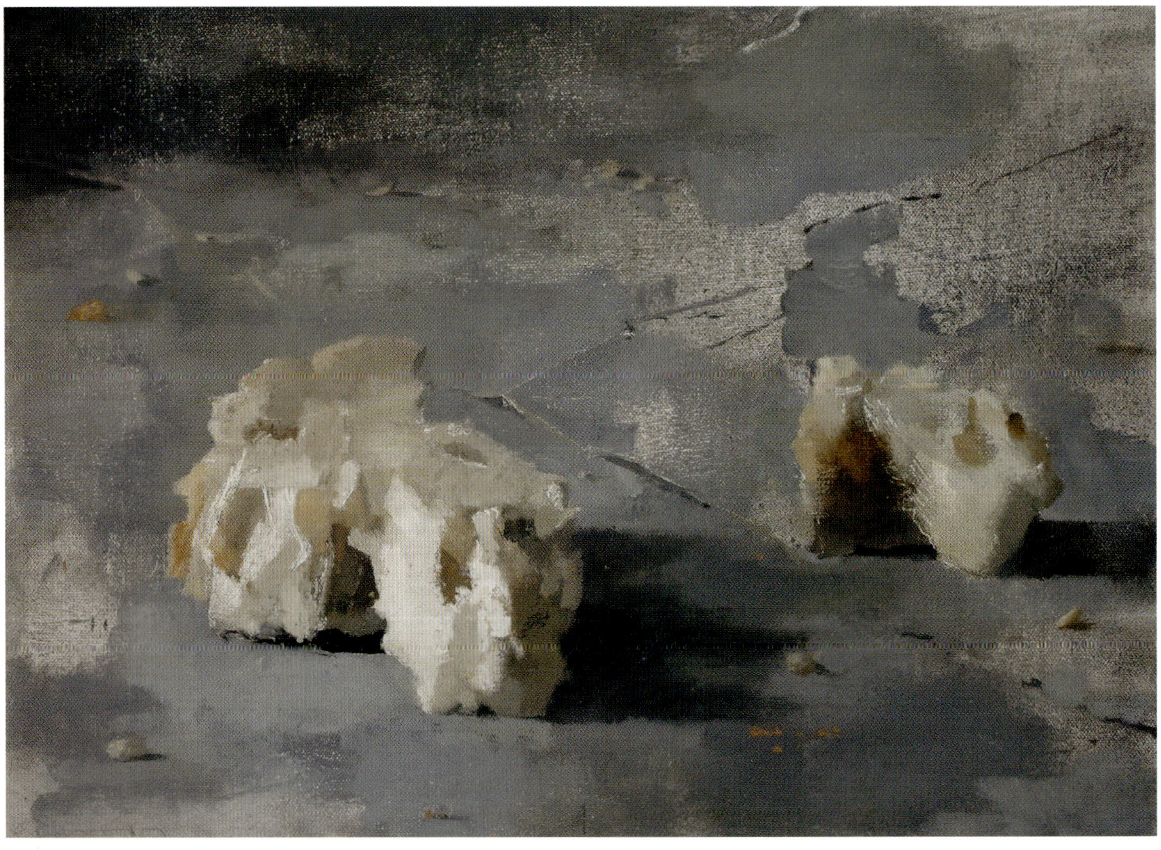

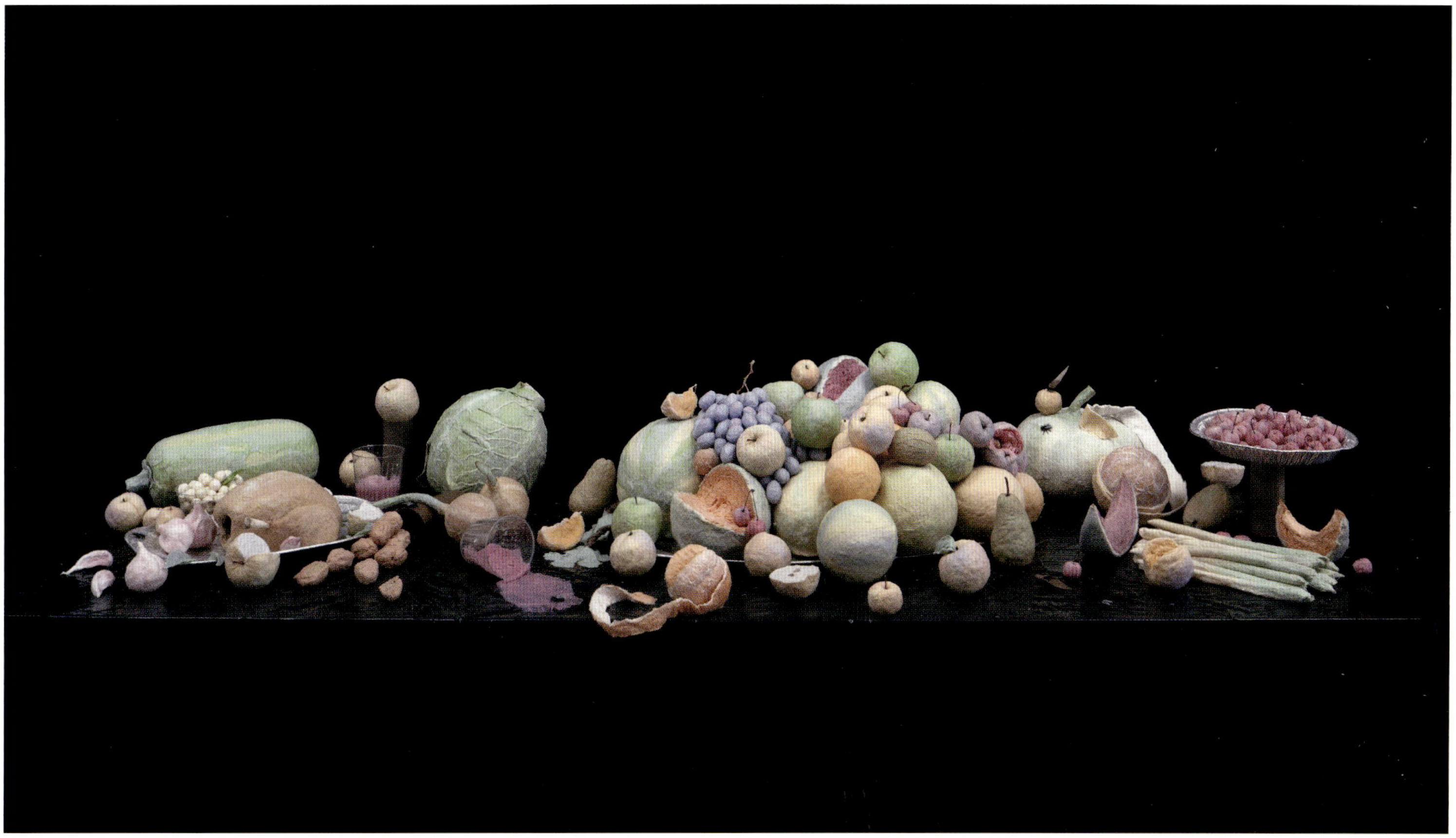

OPPOSITE TOP
Ryan McLaughlin
Dinner Date (Brot), 2010
oil on linen on board

OPPOSITE BOTTOM
Claudia Carr
Seraphim F, 2010
oil on canvas

ABOVE
Caroline McCarthy
The Luncheon, 2002
C-type print

Ryan McLaughlin's *Dinner Date* series depicts individual table settings drawn as if for a child, or perhaps by one. An ungainly chunk of bread perches incongruously atop a white plate in *Dinner Date (Brot)*, hemmed in by oversized flat-handled cutlery. Nothing about the setting or meal seems appropriate for a date. It is this tension between adult narrative and childlike imagery (which draws on earlier artistic traditions, including Cubism) that makes McLaughlin's still lifes at the same time ironic and nostalgic.

Claudia Carr manages to paint still lifes and landscapes simultaneously for her experimentations with scale succeed in transforming everyday detritus – in *Seraphim F*, a small piece of bread – into strange, unfamiliar terrains. At once intimate (as if the viewer's head were resting on the table) and heroic (at a glance the view could be mistaken for a war-torn landscape), *Seraphim F* benefits from an ambiguity of scale that intrigues and transforms the image into something much more complex than genre painting.

Caroline McCarthy is interested in the processes involved in the creation of art and how they are similar and dissimilar to commercial production. *The Luncheon* presents a classic still life: a banquet table spread out with a wide variety of meat, fruit and vegetables. These components, however, are made from an altogether surprising medium: McCarthy carefully chooses from the commercially available ranges and colours of toilet paper to build them up, before staging and photographing them in a tableau as close in resemblance to a traditional painting as possible.

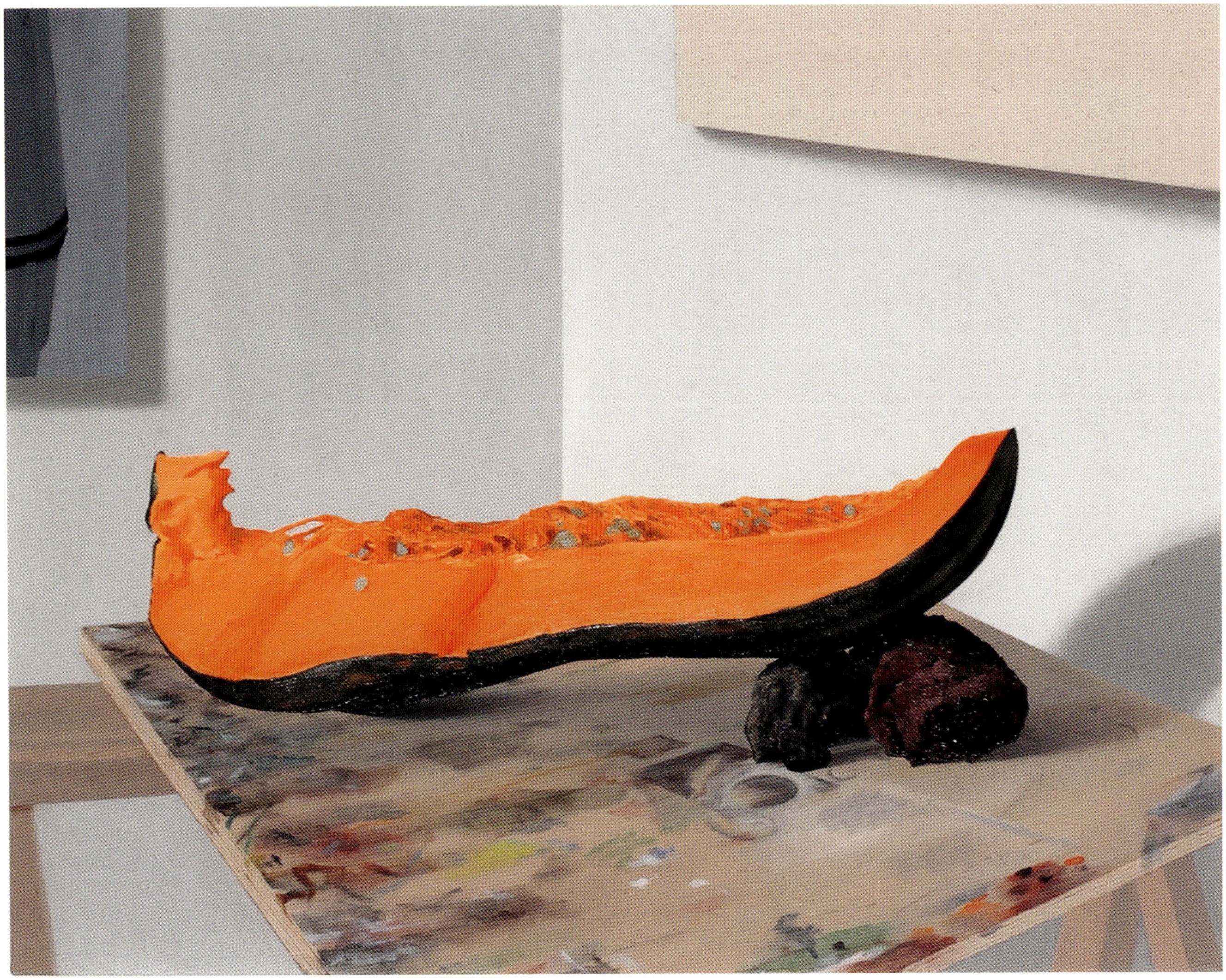

Pádraig Timoney has no immediately recognizable visual style, but builds each painting conceptually, creating not a visual but a conceptual whole. Some works are almost abstract, others photorealistic. In *Imagine this pumpkin is a superhuge concrete boat that has crashed into a small volcanic island in the bay of Naples, knocking the top off it and causing an eruption*, we do indeed see a slice of pumpkin balanced in what is clearly a studio and being painted like a traditional still life. Yet the painting's title transforms it into a conceptual call to the viewer to imagine imminent doom.

Timoney's work is quite different from that of **Craig Wylie** and **Maryam Amiryani**, who work with foodstuffs in a more everyday but no less interesting manner. Wylie often gives his paintings of fruit names at odds with their imagery: a bowl of red apples is *Nightclubbing* (2011), two pears sitting quietly next to a blurred lemon is *Quantum Leap* (2008) and a bowl of bright oranges is called *Blue*. Wylie paints from his own photographs as viewed on his laptop and as prints, bringing the backlit glow of the screen and the natural light that falls on the physical photographs into the final painted version. Amiryani's *Fish* represents her dedication to a minimalist evocation of daily life. She employs the traditional colours and pictorial forms of her native Iran in an effort to slow down the viewer's eye and mind and so force them to contemplate the moment, and in doing so to see the moment pass – the basis of traditional still life.

ABOVE

Pádraig Timoney · ***Imagine this pumpkin is a superhuge concrete boat that has crashed into a small volcanic island in the bay of Naples, knocking the top off it and causing an eruption***, 2005 · oil on canvas

OPPOSITE TOP

Craig Wylie · ***Blue***, 2010 · oil on canvas

OPPOSITE BOTTOM

Maryam Amiryani · ***Fish***, 2010 · oil on linen

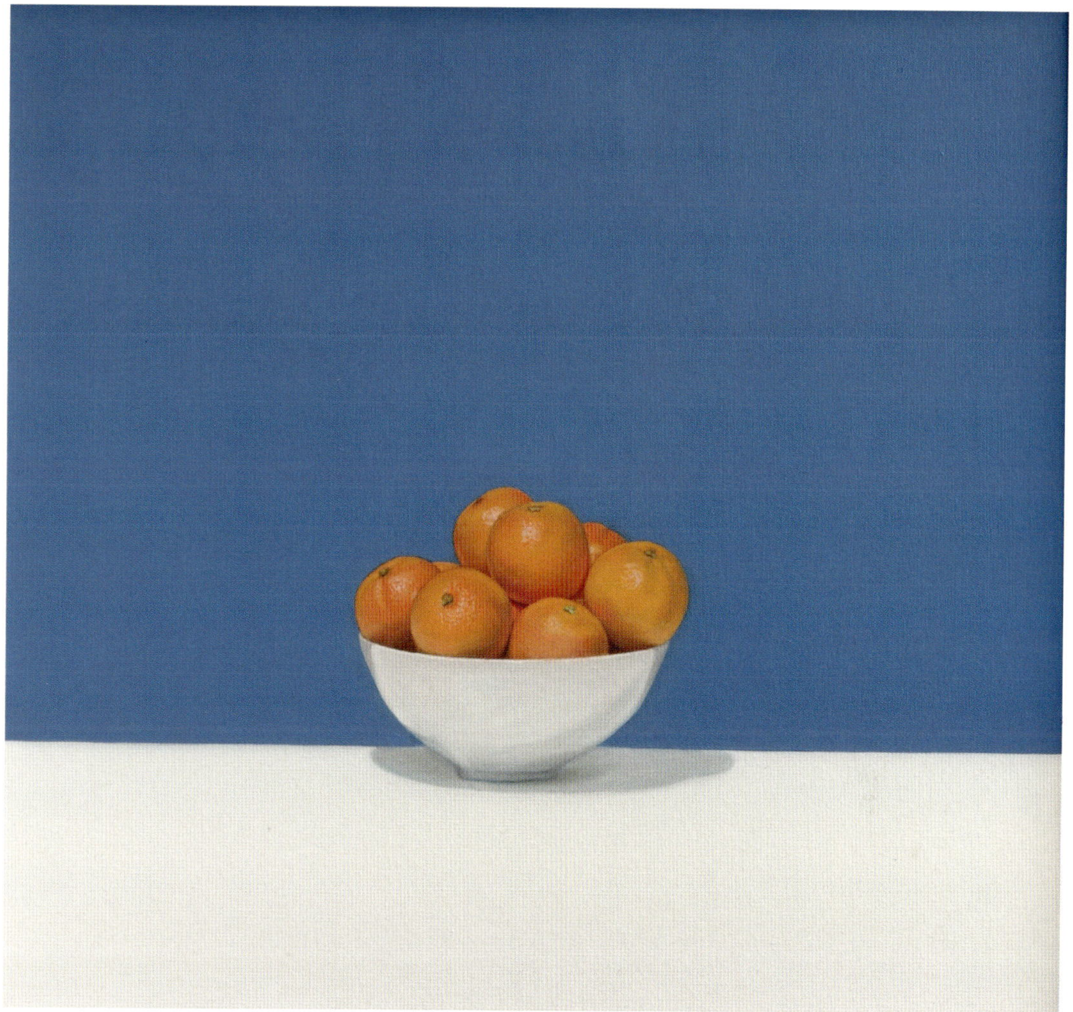

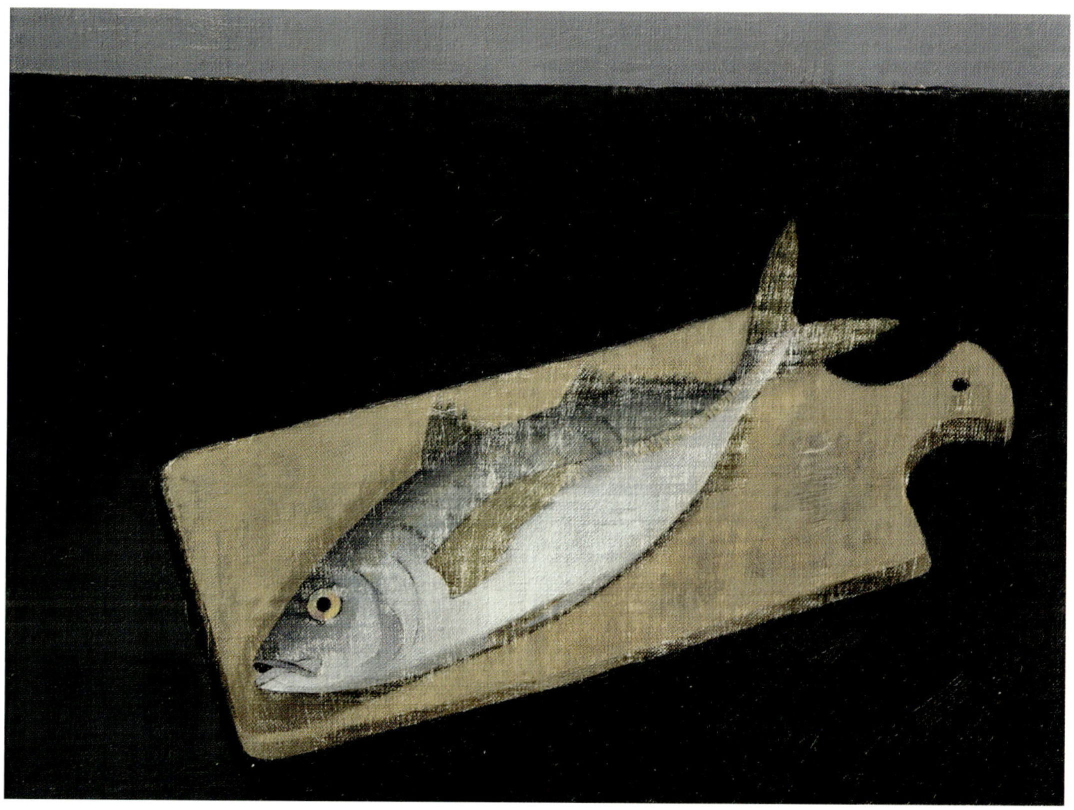

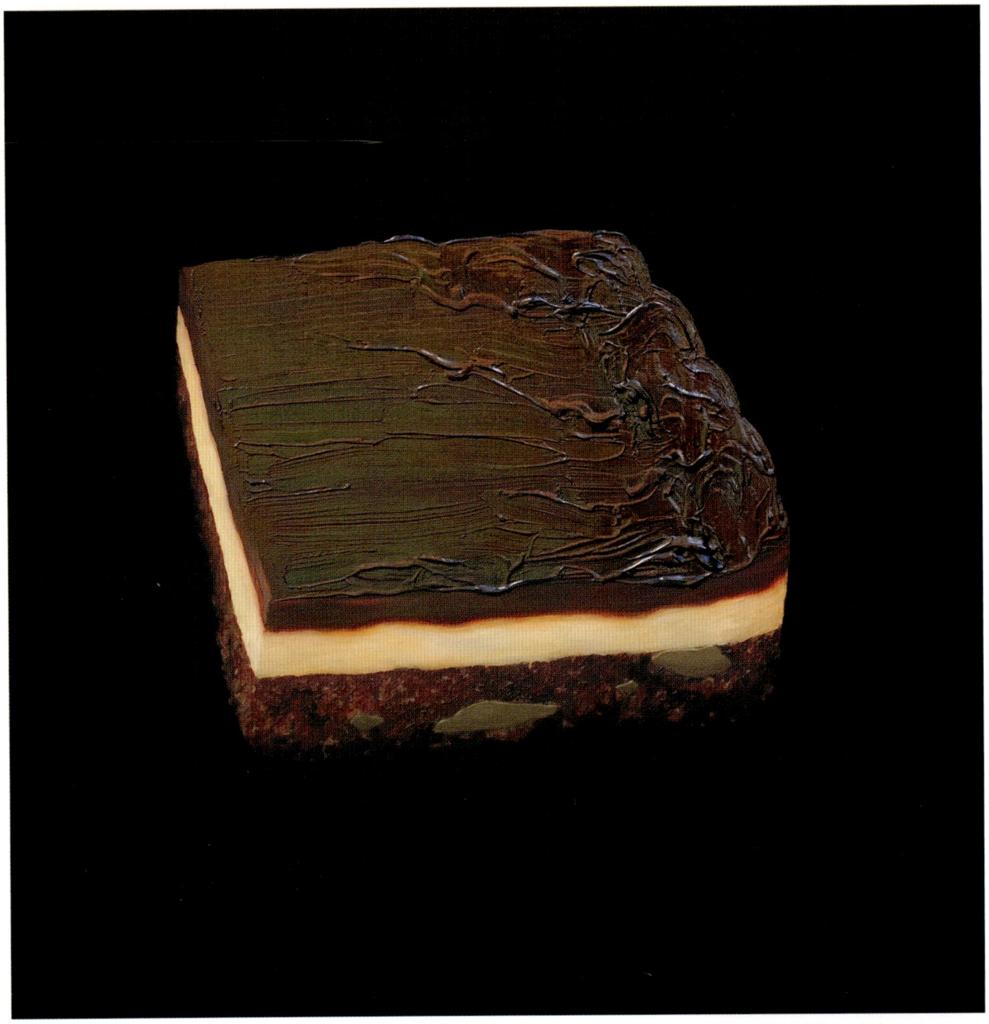

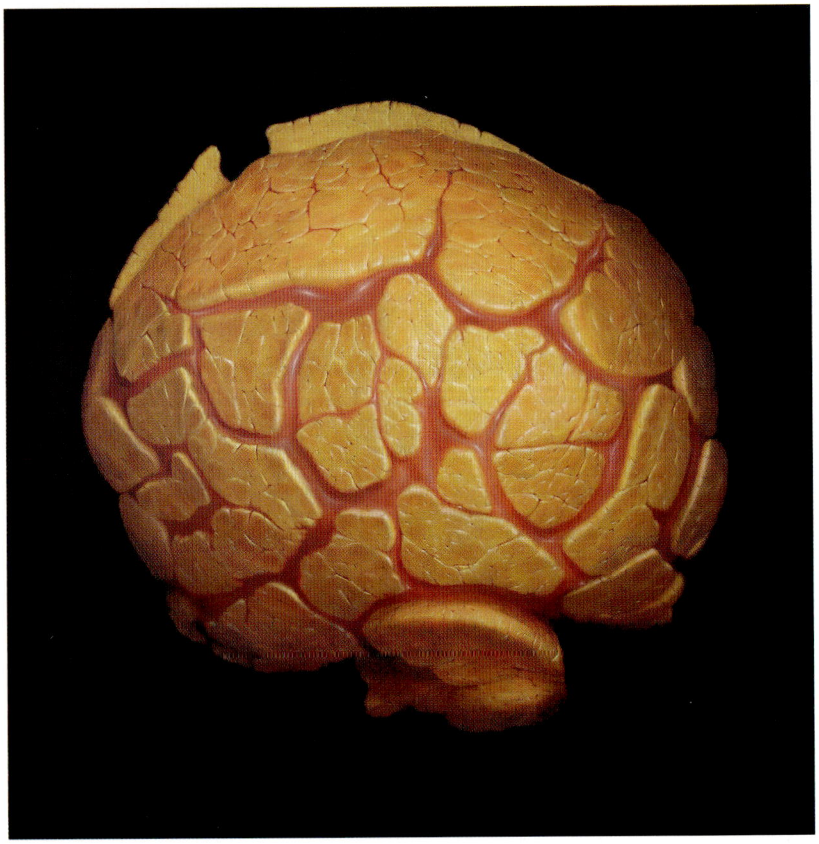

ABOVE

Andro Semeiko

Very Big Chocolate Cake, 2006

acrylic on canvas

RIGHT

Andro Semeiko

Very Big Toffee Popcorn, 2005

acrylic and oil on canvas

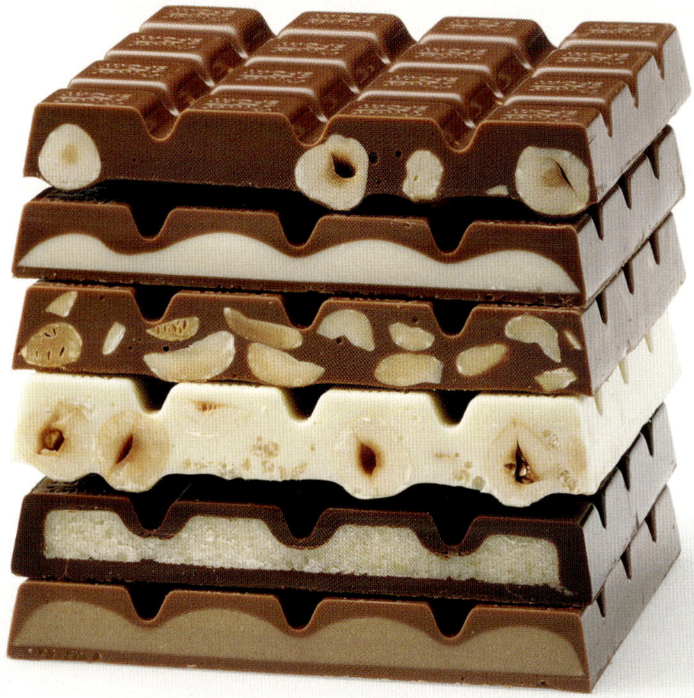

For his *The Order of Objects* series, **Andro Semeiko** painted close-ups of relatively small objects at a scale much larger than life. The square canvases of *Very Big Chocolate Cake* and *Very Big Toffee Popcorn* measure 152 by 152 cm in size and fill the viewers gaze with a surfeit of sugary unhealthiness. The works beg the question, 'How much of a good thing is a bad thing?' Semeiko hones in on patterns of consumption, but his lifelike representations of these foods aim at objectivity.

'I don't like to stand in front of the camera or behind the camera, I like to stand beside the camera,' says the conceptual artist **Christopher Williams**, who uses the services of professional commercial photographers to make images that deconstruct advertising, the mechanisms of communication and photography itself. His work looks at how images are classified and manipulated to construct meaning and desire. His polemical quest seeks to assist the viewer in recognizing the ways in which societal and industrial controls are made to look completely natural and obvious despite being artificial constructs.

ABOVE · Christopher Williams
RITTERSPORT Von oben nach unten/ from the top to the bottom 100 g Tafeln / 100 g Bars Offizieller Produktname / Official Product Name / EAN Code Bar / UPC Code for Case / Bars per Case Voll Nuss / Whole Hazelnuts / 4000417019004 / 050255013005 / 10 Joghurt / Yogurt / 40004170270 09 / 050255027000 / 12 Voll Erdnuss / 4000417262202 / 10 Weisse Voll Nuss / White Whole Hazelnuts / 4000417013002 / 050255013003 / ... / 10 Marzipan / Marzipan / 4000417025005 / 050255025006 / 12 Cappuccino / Cappuccino / 4000417230003 / 0550255230042 / 12 Fotostudio Axel Gnad, Düsseldorf, October 24th, 2008 [***No. 1***], 2009
archival pigment print

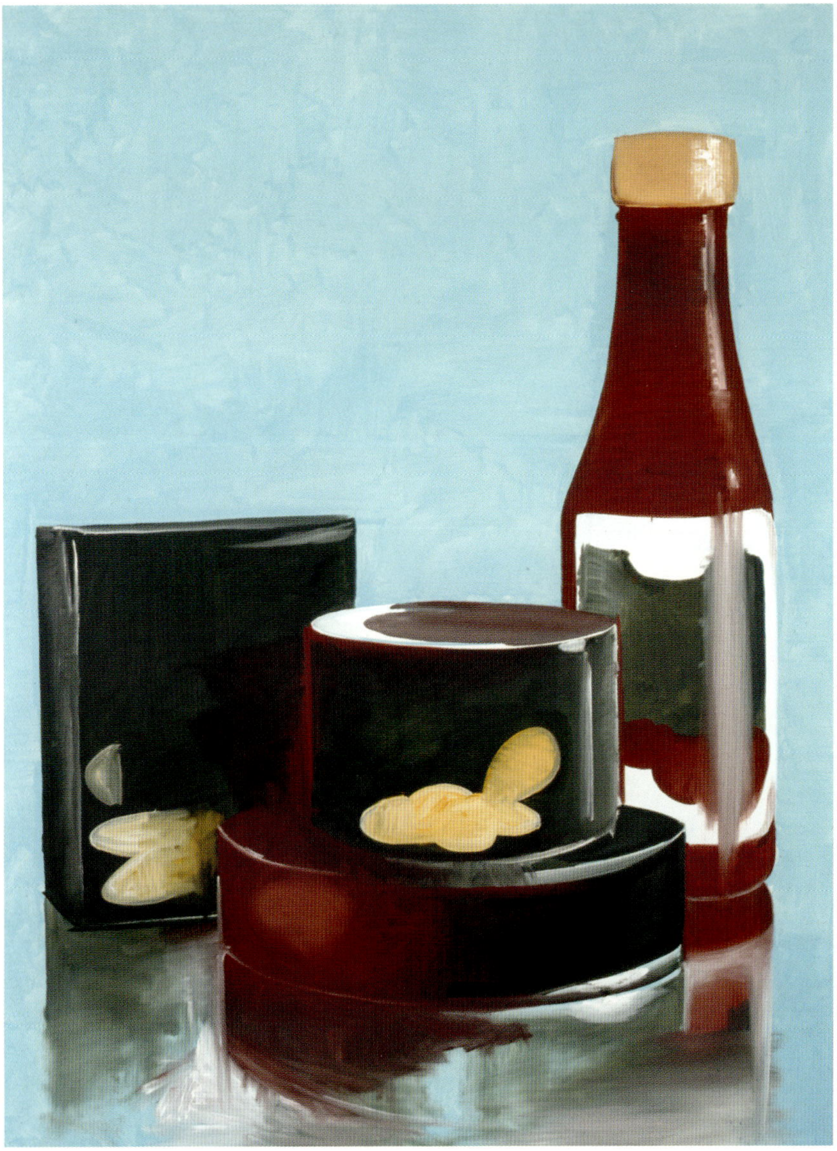

ABOVE
Wilhelm Sasnal
Food, 2008
oil on canvas

OPPOSITE
Michael Hilsman
Still Life with Thumb, 2011
oil and acrylic on canvas

Wilhelm Sasnal questions in his work the stability of the painting form in the modern age of image gathering. He often paints from found photographs, as well as from ones he has taken, and the resulting works can be abstract or figurative. His 2009 exhibition in London explored food and the politics of its packaging, global trade and effect on local agricultural economies.

Michael Hilsman's still lifes mix abstraction with elements of realism and surrealism. In his large painting *Still Life with Pears and Mango* (title page), he portrayed the fruits in a traditional style, yet they float in an undefined, abstract space surrounded by arches of paint. In *Still Life with Thumb*, a fairly realistic, detached thumb is served up alongside more typical offerings. The picture plane drifts out towards viewers as if the whole concoction is about to spill onto them, while a dizzy unsteadiness ensures that this still life looks anything but still.

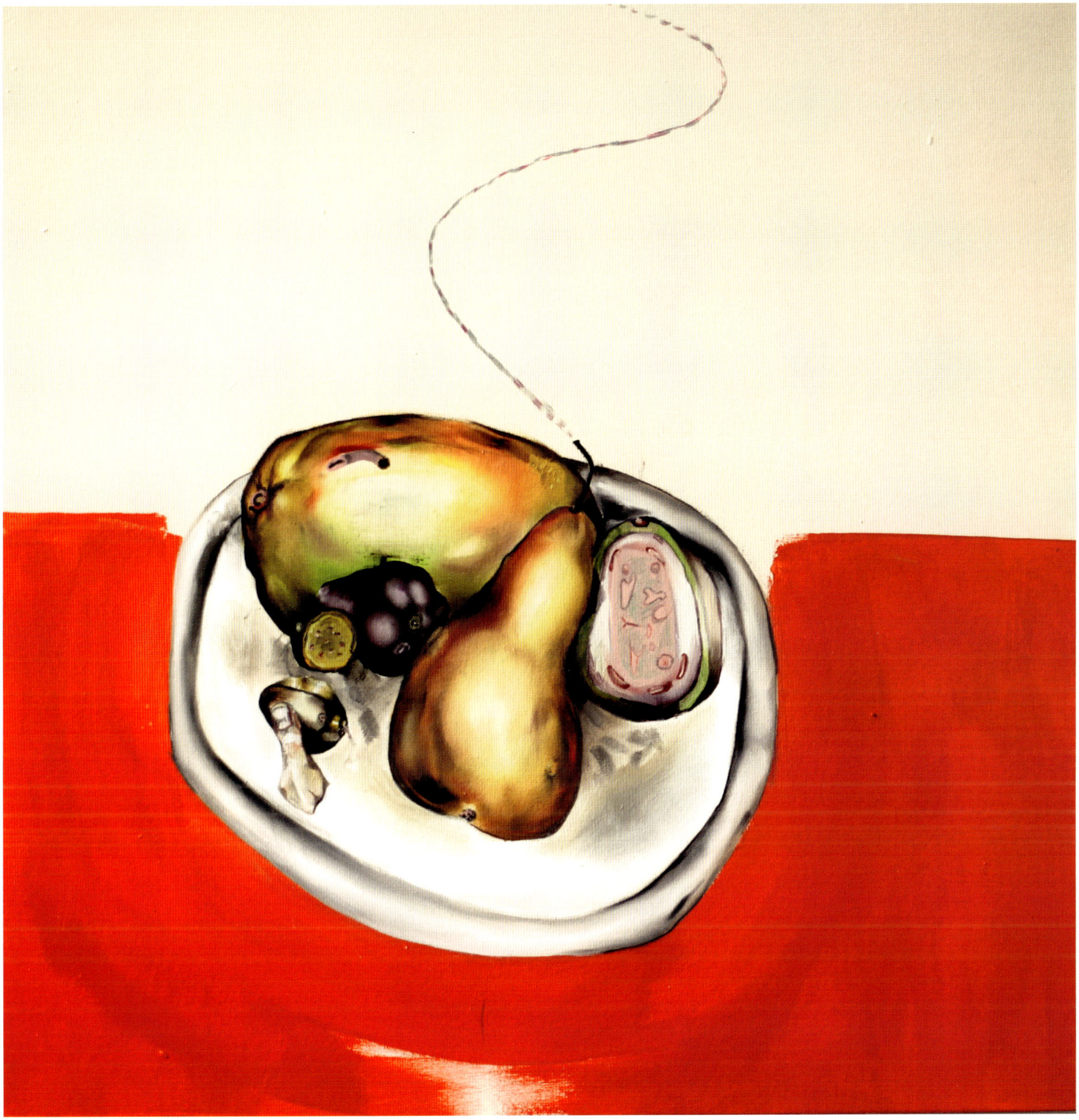

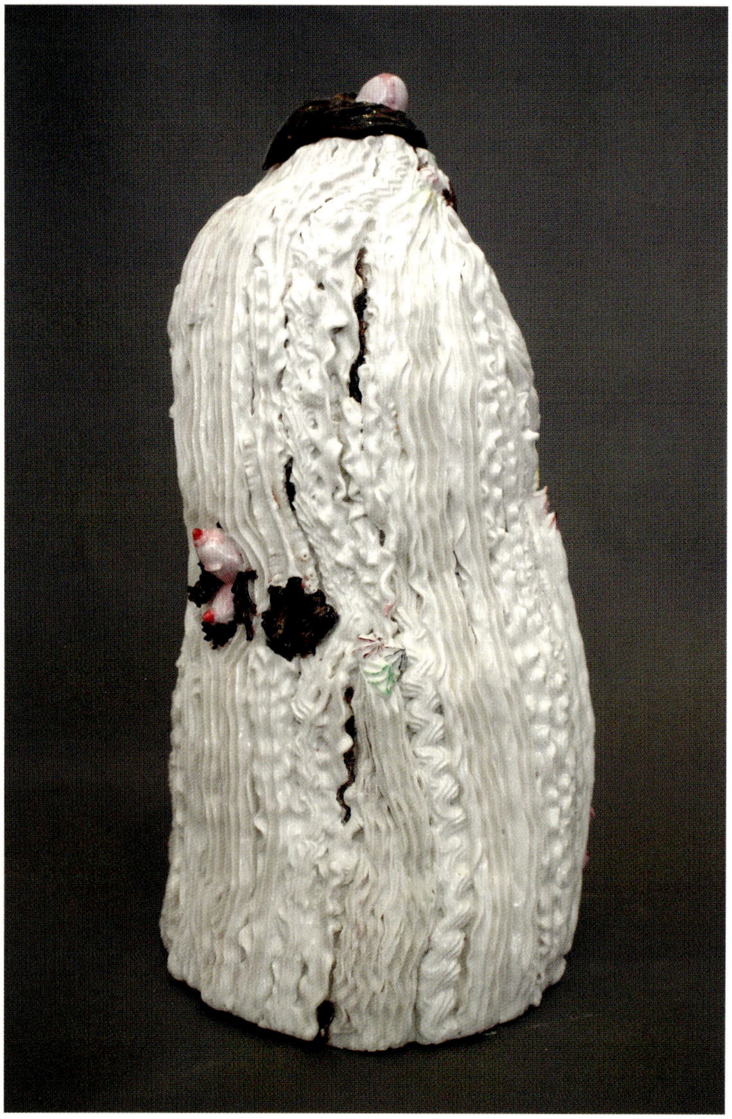

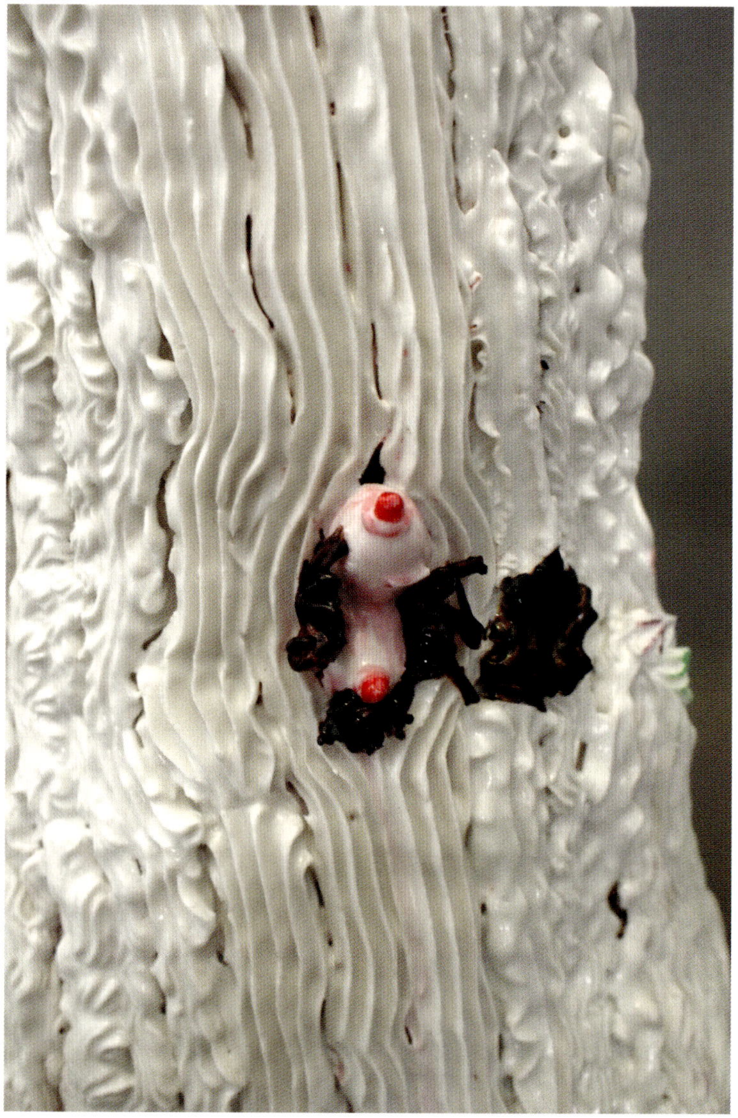

Annie Attridge's porcelain sculpture *Chocolate Chip Flirt* resembles a rather grotesque wedding cake, a sweet confection gone terribly wrong. Surrounded by what one hopes are splodges of chocolate, tiny pink breasts burst out from the disorderly seams of white icing, recalling the Sapphic frolicking of female nudes often depicted in Meissen porcelain figurines.

Michael Raedecker's *wrong* painting features a more typical wedding cake. Its title and muted, murky palette, however, hint that the associated occasion may not be all that celebratory. Though wedding scenes often feature in the paintings of the Dutch Old Masters, including those of Abraham Bloemaert, Jan Steen and both Brueghels, Elder and Younger, in their works people are always present and joyfully celebrate the union. Here the cake alone hints at the nuptials.

ABOVE
Annie Attridge
Chocolate Chip Flirt, 2012
(front and detail) porcelain, enamel and tin glaze

OPPOSITE
Michael Raedecker
wrong, 2009
acrylic and thread on canvas

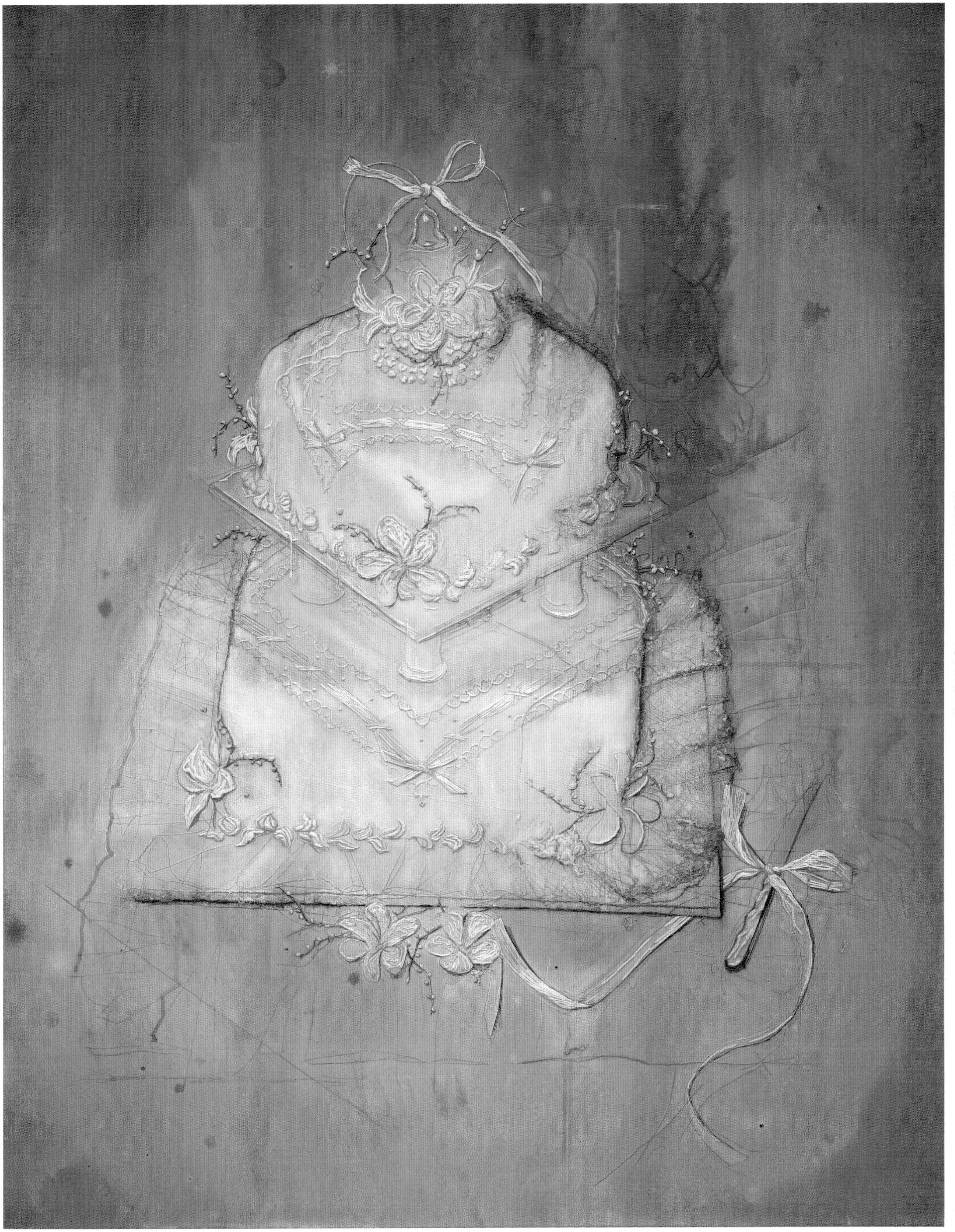

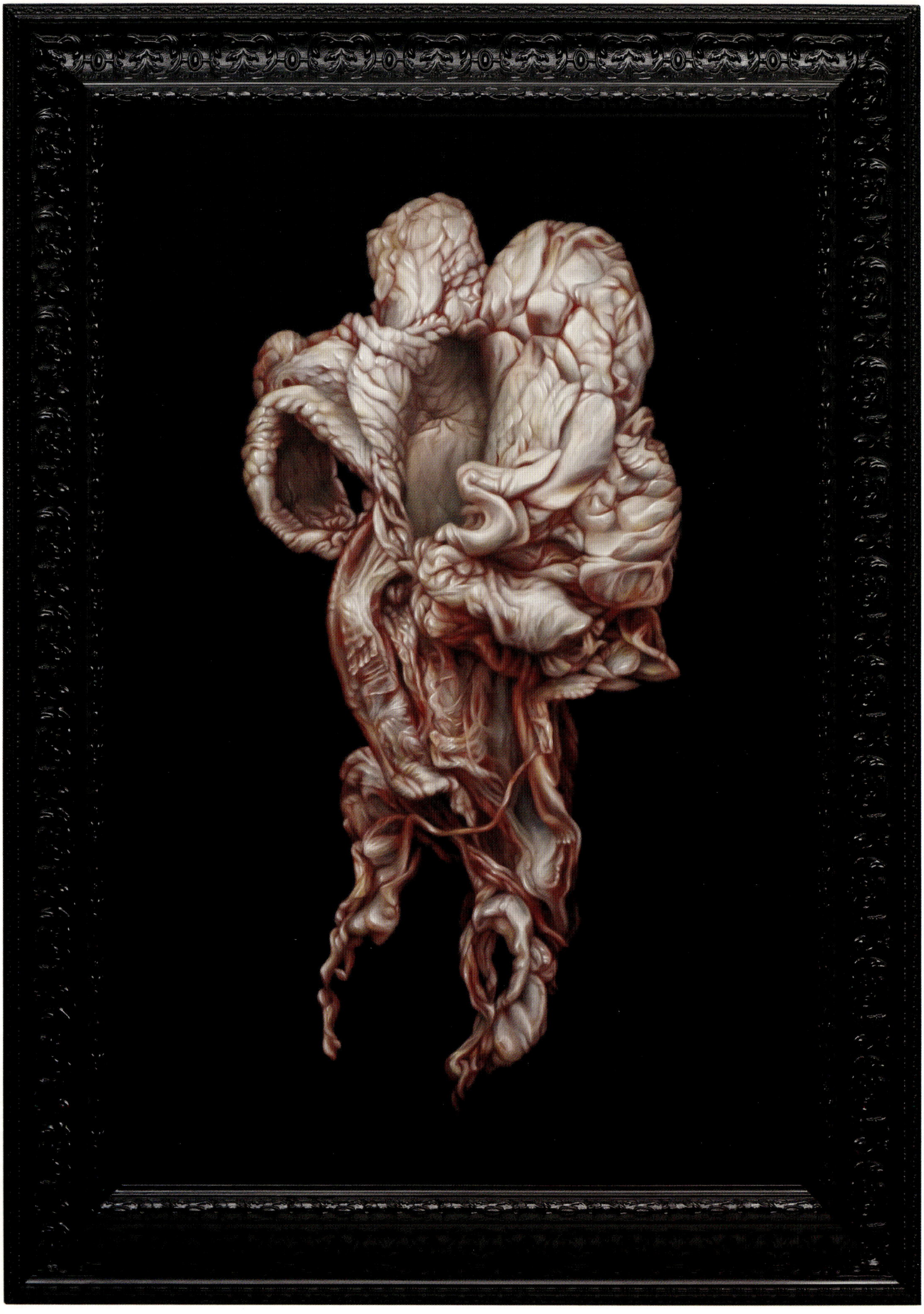

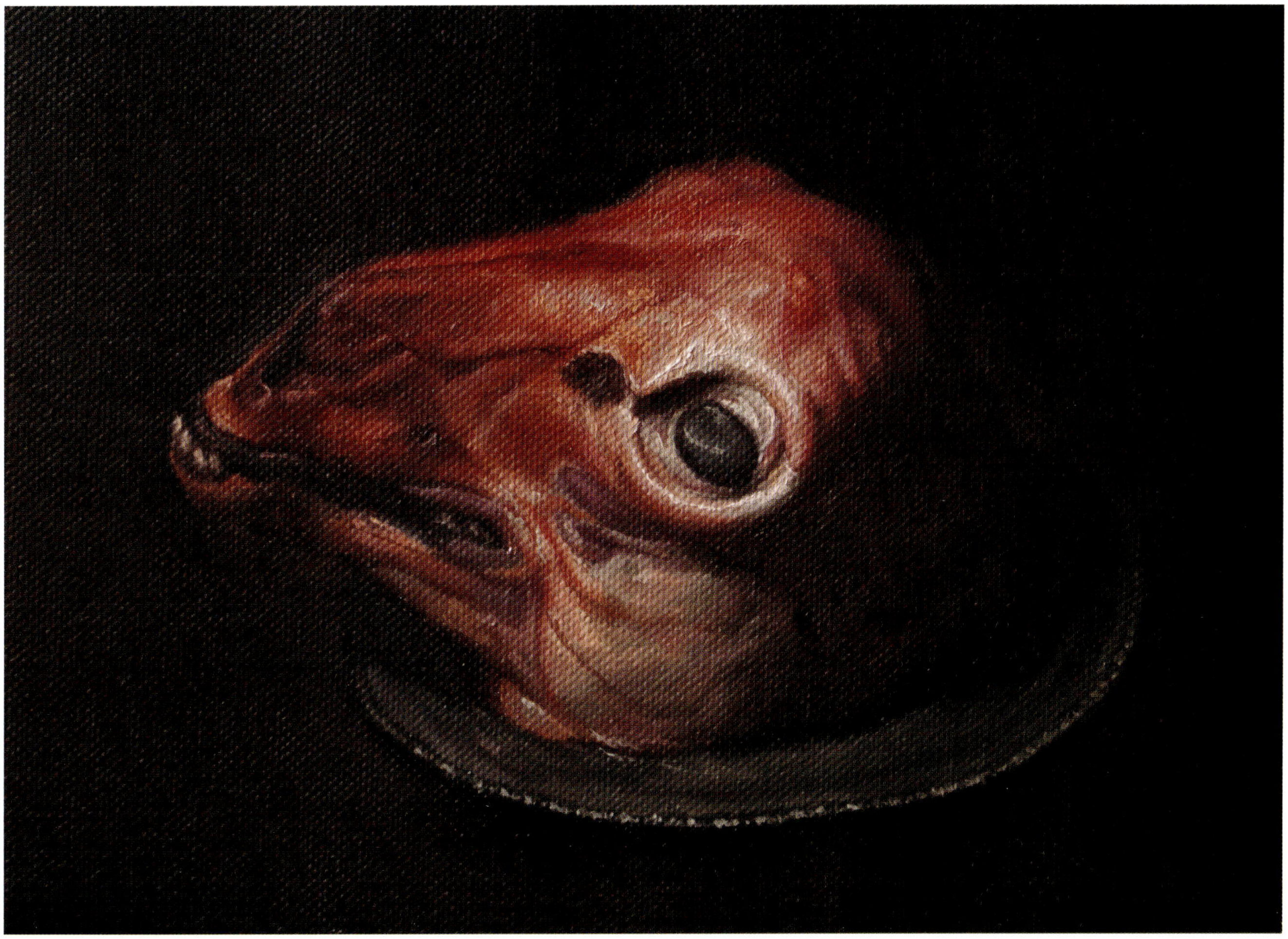

OPPOSITE
Victoria Reynolds
Reindeer Voluptuary, 2008
oil on panel and frame

ABOVE
Rigoberto A. Gonzalez
Cabrito Degollado (***Goat Head***), 2008 · oil on linen

Victoria Reynolds's *Reindeer Voluptuary* forms part of a series depicting raw flesh in ornate frames. These paintings recall scenes by Carracci, Chardin and Goya of freshly butchered animal flesh, as well as ritual animal sacrifice. Reynolds has said:

> *In Dutch Protestant paintings of the fifteenth and sixteenth centuries, meat is often referred to as 'the weak flesh'. In my paintings, the beauty of the flesh is shown, and the ornate frames emphasize the non-Puritanical content. People call the frames 'over the top' or excessive. They're often painted to match the meat. When viewing the paintings, some say they have a gag reflex while thinking at the same time they're beautiful.*

A similar gag reflex might be triggered by the work of **Rigoberto A. Gonzalez**, who has painted the decapitated victims of Mexico's drug wars. His *Cabrito Degollado* (*Goat Head*) recalls these works as much as the Mexican custom of celebrating significant events with a barbecued baby goat or pig. Gonzalez has said:

> *My students, when they find out I'm from Mexico, have asked me if I've ever slaughtered a pig. That's what they think goes on over there. And it does. I've never held the knife, but I remember seeing my father, my father's brothers, kill and butcher a pig...for big celebrations. Over here* [in the US], *meat is packaged, you don't see the process. All of that stuff is kept hidden. But it's brutal, and it's killing, and it's commonplace.... Thinking of the pigs, and other animals I've seen killed for food, I've wondered if that makes people less sensitive to violence in Mexico.*

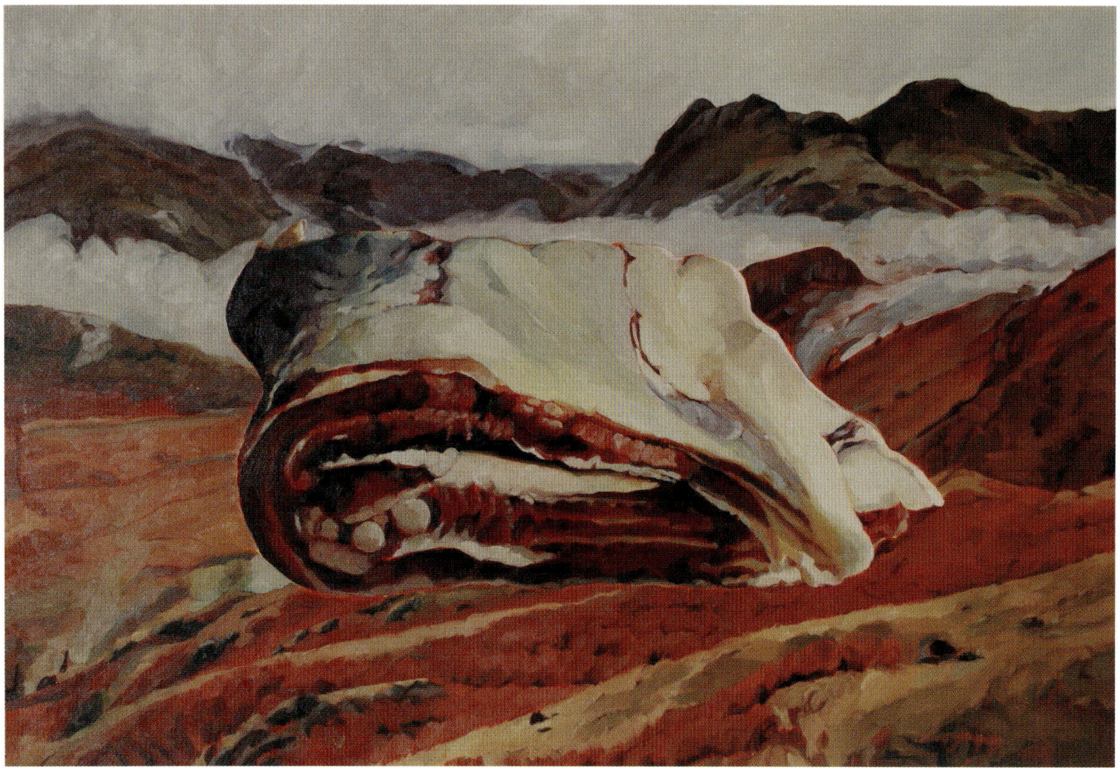

Rebecca Scott in her *Meat* series investigates notions of 'the romantic' and 'the real'. These paintings revisit illustrations of meat taken from traditional cookbooks aimed at urban dwellers, who are physically and emotionally disconnected from the raising and slaughtering of animals for food. Scott juxtaposes these slabs of meat with rural landscapes.

Cindy Wright's paintings of foodstuffs confront viewers with the reality that eating meat and fish comes at a real cost, the death of once living creatures. Her large painting *Baconsquare*, at over two by two metres in size, details the moist, uncooked flesh of the pig that provides this daily breakfast food. The bloody, gutted fish coiled within a goldfish bowl in *Nature Morte 2* stares out of the frame in an accusatory fashion. The fluted bowl sits atop a delicate doily, adding to the pathos of the image.

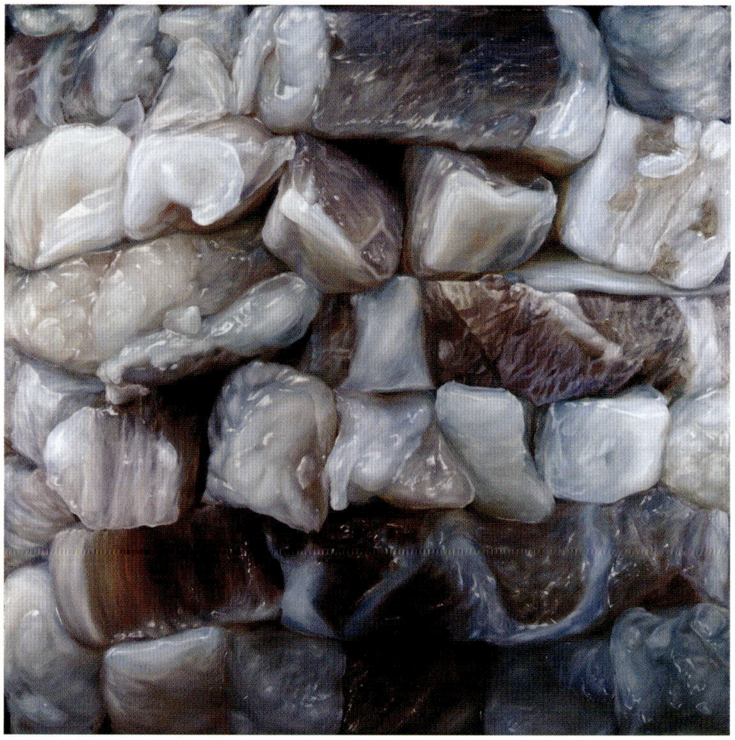

ABOVE · Rebecca Scott · *Red in Tooth and Claw*, 2008 · oil on canvas

RIGHT · Cindy Wright · *Baconsquare*, 2008 · oil on canvas

OPPOSITE · Cindy Wright *Nature Morte 2*, 2010 · oil on linen

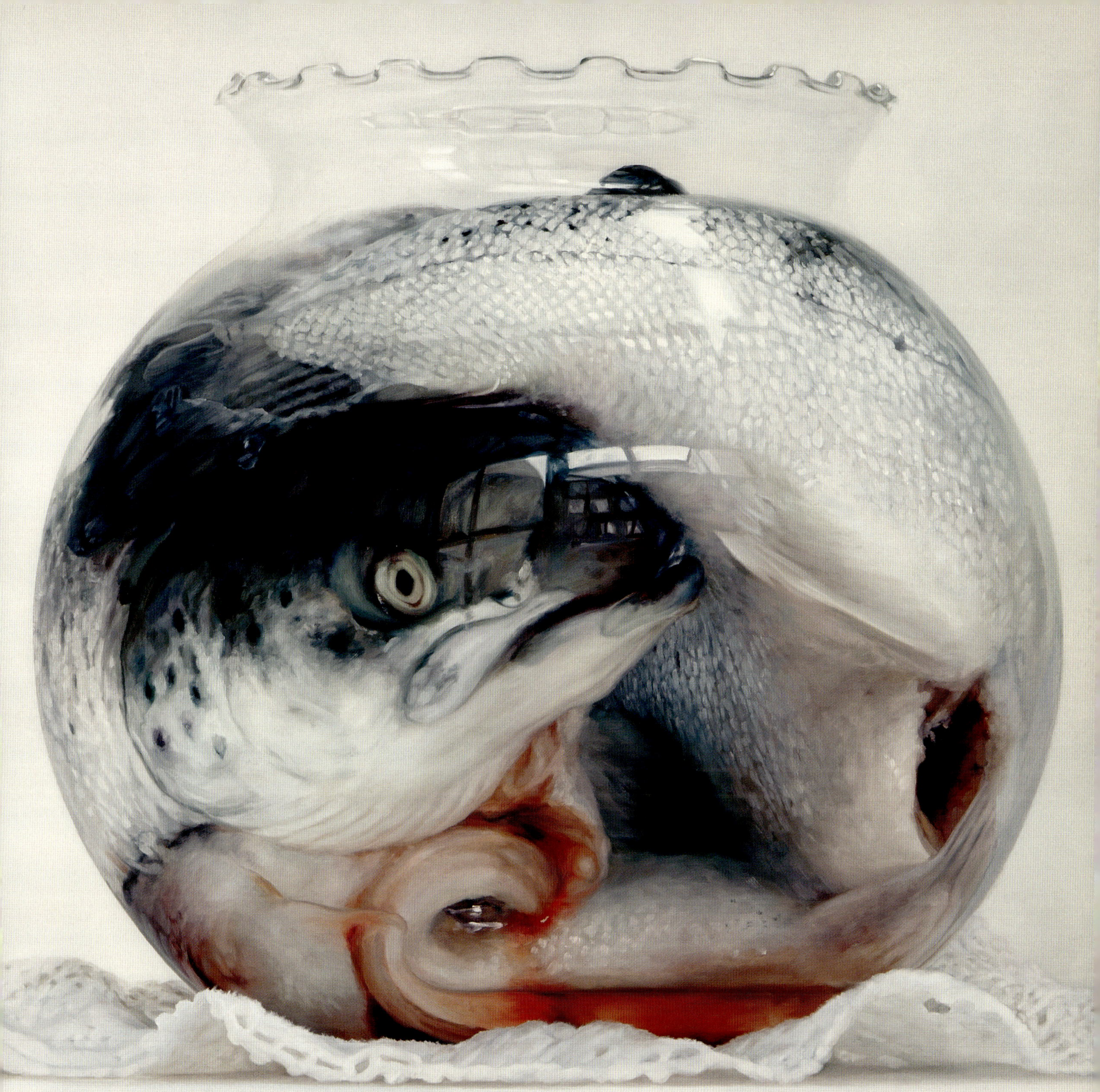

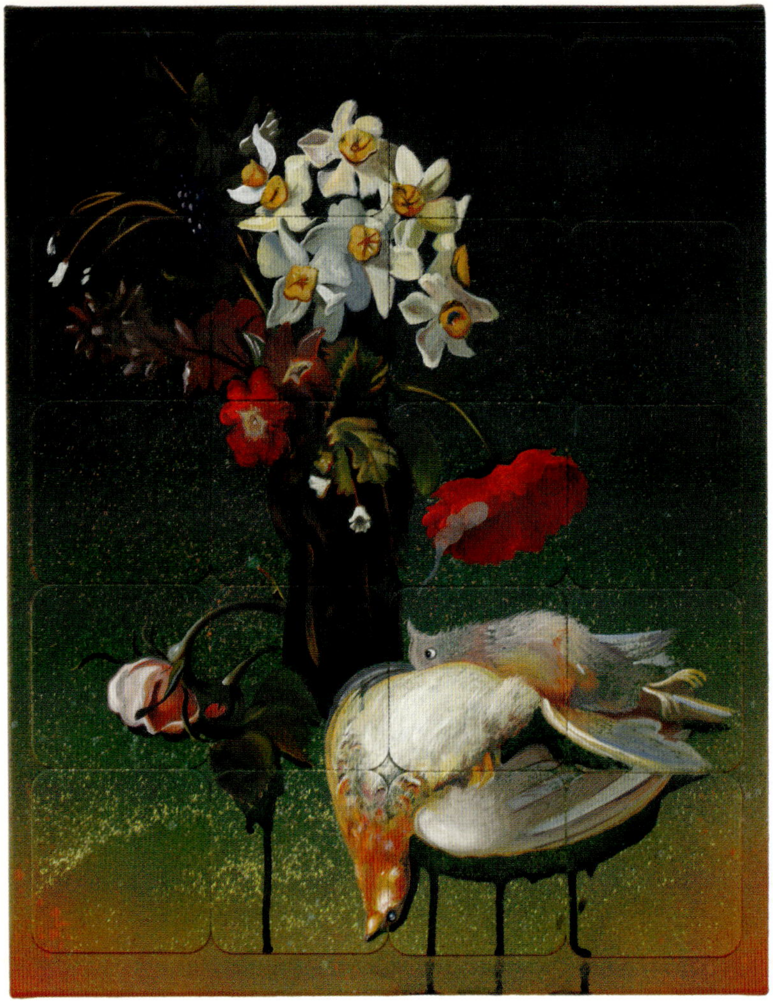

Paul McDevitt has made a series of still lifes that visually reference Joris van Son's *Still Life with Allegory of Human Life* (1658–60) while being made up of painted beer coasters, mounted together on canvas to form a whole. McDevitt's decision to paint on the small cardboard squares used to soak up an intoxicant (beer) ties together notions of human frailty and the quest for altered states of consciousness.

Simon English's *Forbidden Fruit* alludes not only to the apple that led to Adam and Eve's expulsion from the Garden of Eden, but also the derogative designation of gay men as *fruits*. The forbidden apple is thus tied to the traditionally forbidden love between two men. With its many different frames, the work offers up a complex visual and textual revisiting of the still-life tradition.

Many of **Julie Heffernan**'s self-portraits resemble anything but self-portraits. *Self Portrait as Root III* (page 118) features a fanciful pyramid of fruit (apples, pears, peaches, grapes), lush and ripe, that seems to have dropped into existence thanks to the bounty of the surrounding trees. Heffernan has explained that she titled her works self-portraits 'because they seemed to me to be portraits of the interior self – a much more apt reflection of myself than a mirror could afford.'

Thomas Woodruff's highly stylized and intricate paintings range in content from a series of 365 individual apples, *Apple Canon* (1996), painted to ward off his friends' deaths ('an apple a day keeps the doctor away'), and extravagantly costumed animals (tigers, bats, dolphins), but they are all rendered in a style he calls *neo-fabulist*. *(Still Life Variation) Sanguinic* (page 119), featuring elaborately carved watermelons and a massive bouquet, comes from his series *The Four Temperament Variations*, which aimed to queer the traditional still life and its components.

ABOVE
Paul McDevitt
We Must Heap Up a Great Pile of Doing, for a Small Diameter of Being, 2008
acrylic, gouache, colour pencil, ink and beer mats on canvas

OPPOSITE
Simon English
Forbidden Fruit, 2008
crayon, ink, acrylic, gouache and oil on paper

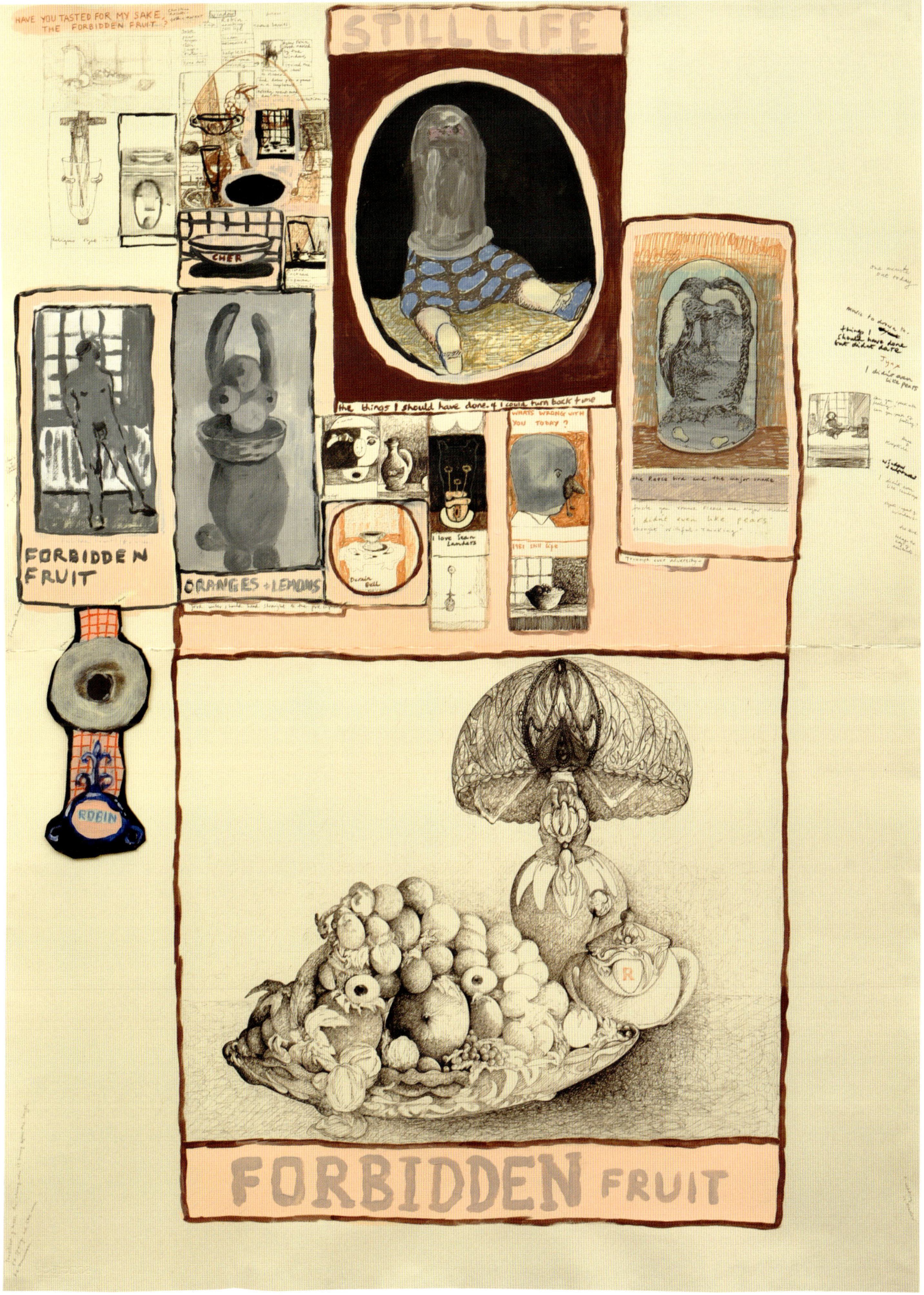

HAVE YOU TASTED FOR MY SAKE, THE FORBIDDEN FRUIT?
STILL LIFE
CHER
the things I should have done. if I could turn back time
FORBIDDEN FRUIT
ORANGES + LEMONS
WHATS WRONG WITH YOU TODAY?
I love Sean Landers
1981 Still Life
I didnt even like pears
Triumph over adversity
ROBIN
R
FORBIDDEN FRUIT

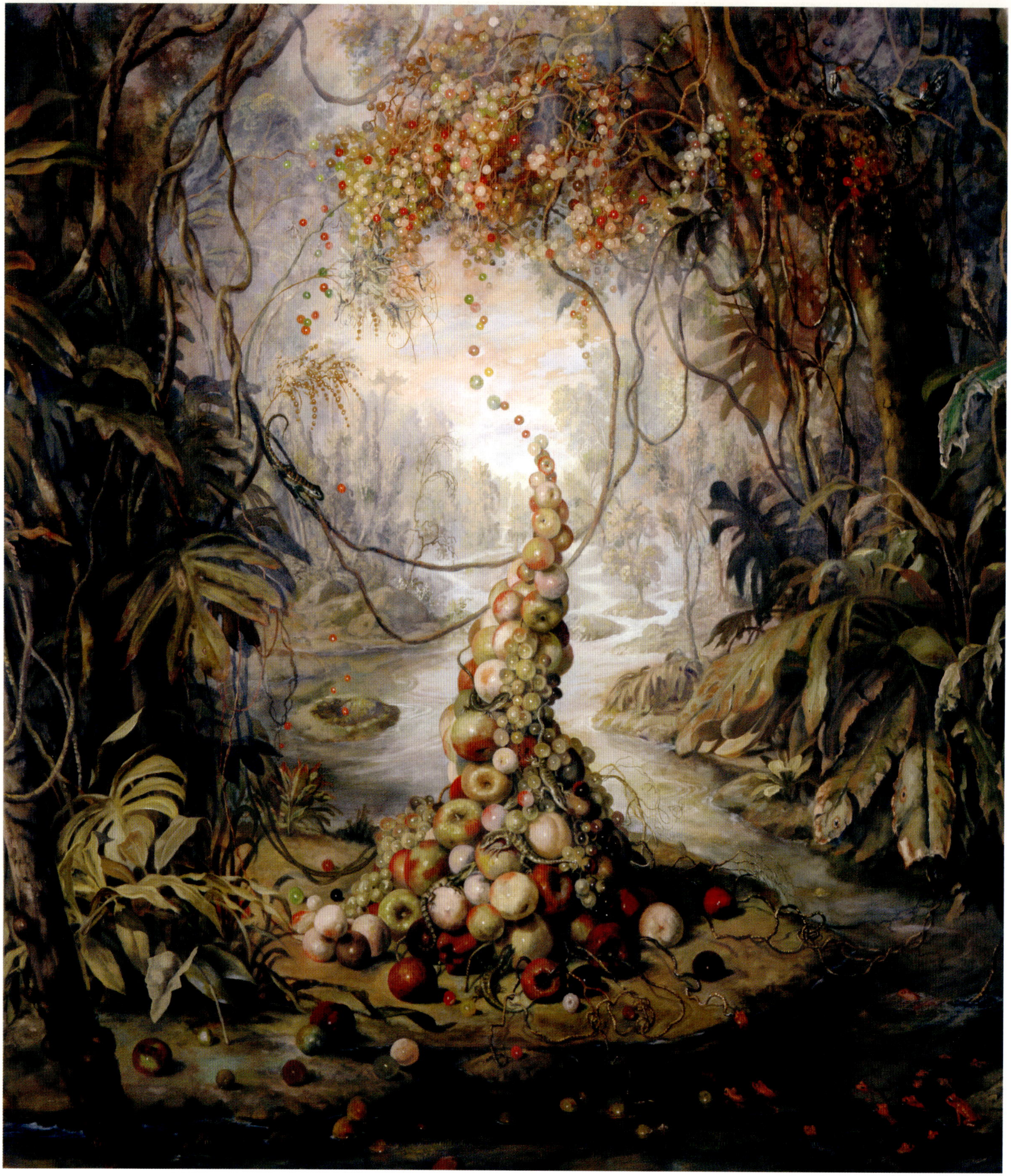

ABOVE
Julie Heffernan
Self Portrait as Root III, 2006
oil on canvas

OPPOSITE
Thomas Woodruff
(***Still Life Variation***) ***Sanguinic***, 2009–10
acrylic on linen

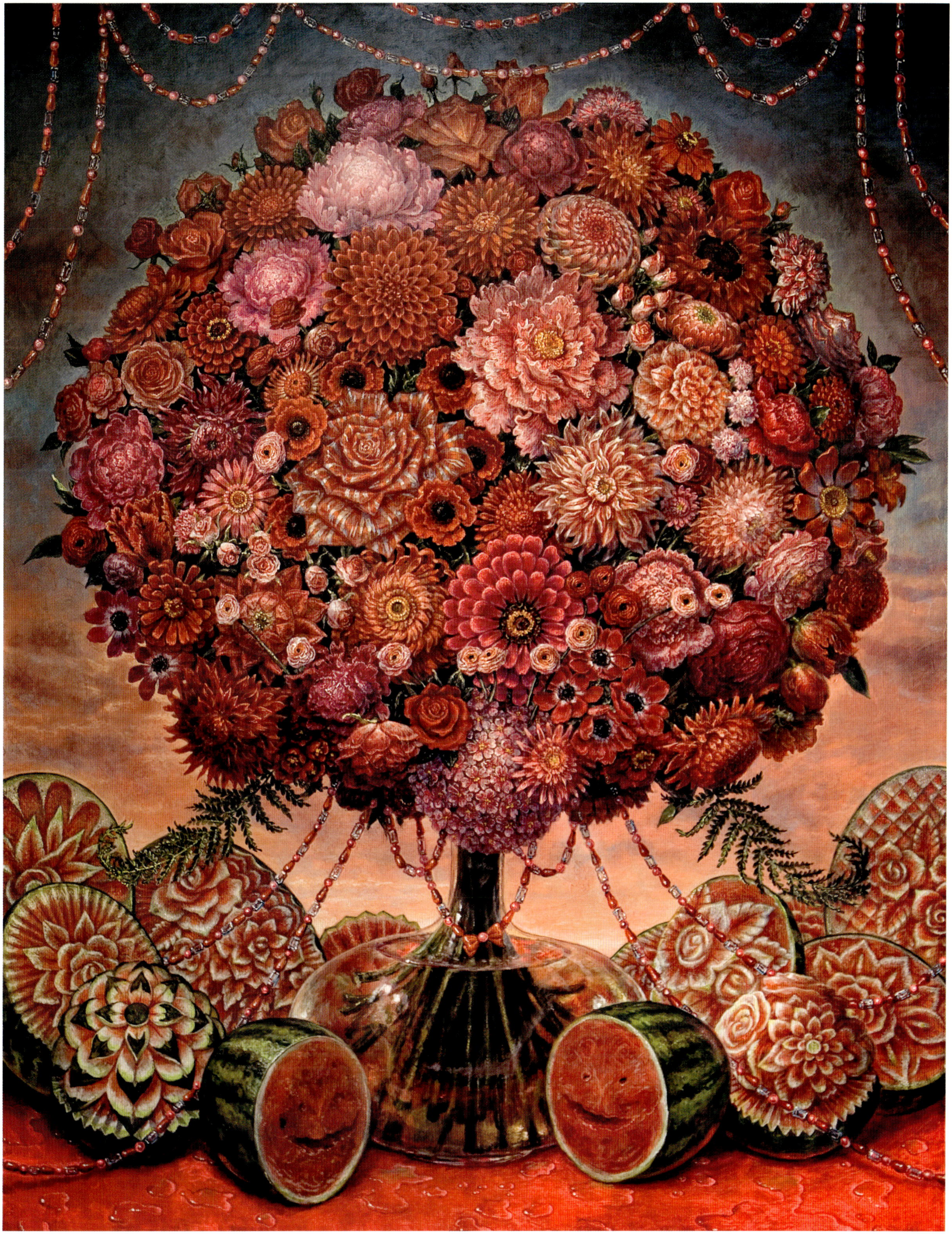

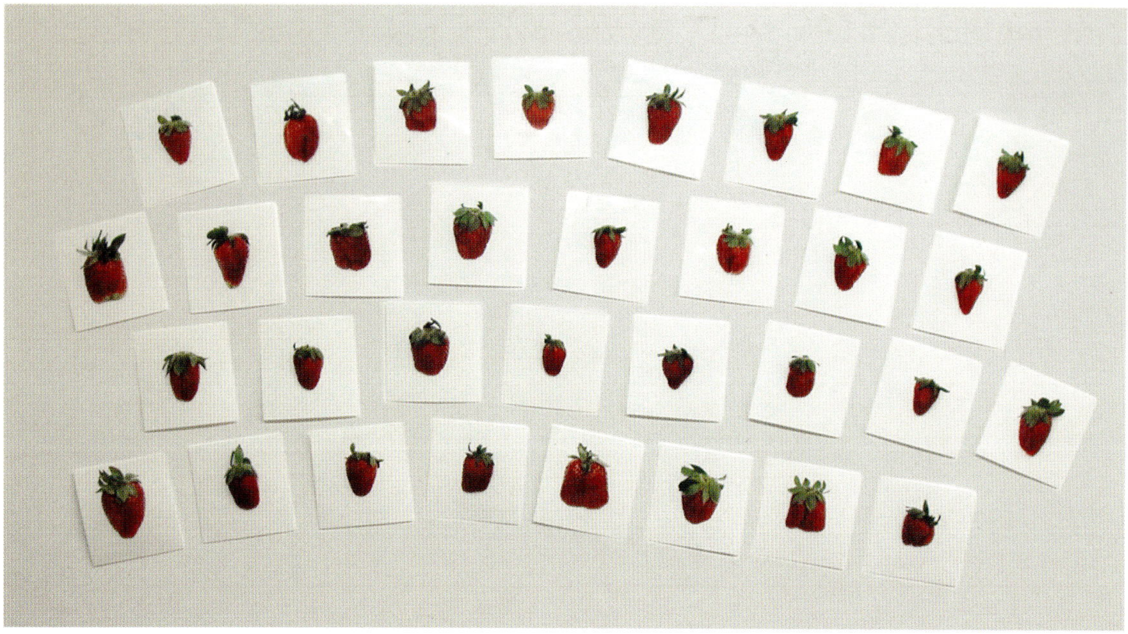

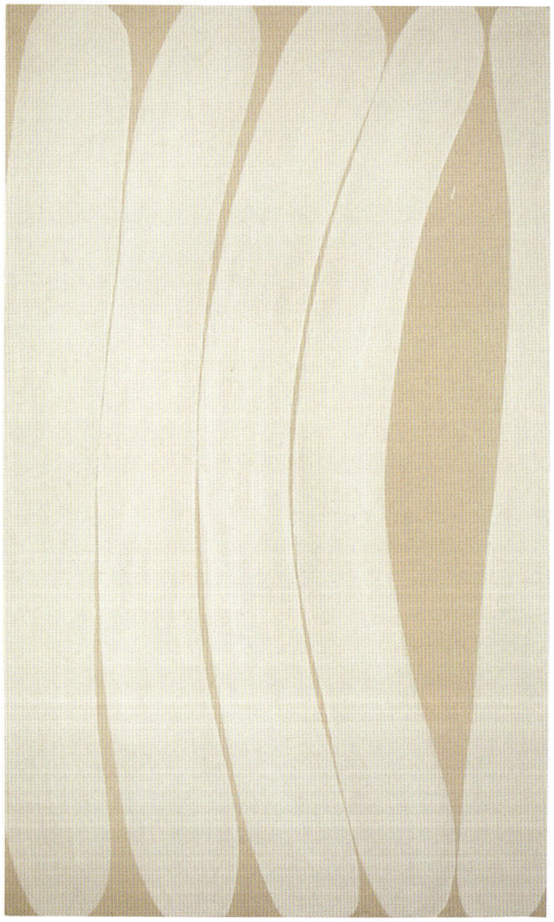

Hans-Peter Feldmann has said: 'I started cutting pictures from my parents' books at the age of five. I don't know why I did this...but it was 1946, the war was just over. We had lived our life in the bombings. It was traumatic. There was no toy, so I cut pictures of everything and put them together.' The artist has continued to cut up images and piece them together in highly conceptual ways. *One Pound Strawberries* features thirty-four photographs of strawberries, each berry similar to the others but also visibly different. In bringing together these disparate fruits to form a greater whole, Feldmann reminds viewers that they too belong to a greater humanity.

Andrew Guenther depicts hot dogs in many of his works. *Bite Me* (2008) features a sunglass-sporting, cigarette-smoking frankfurter belligerently addressing the viewer; *Tropical Hotdog* (2010) has one lounging on a bun in the sun; another takes a *Hotdog Nap* (2009) on a clean white pillow in an unmade bed. *Hotdogs* departs from its more representational predecessors; only its title alerts viewers to the nature of these five white, minimalist forms.

Anja Priska's *Dance, Dance, Dance* features an ape atop a cornucopia of foodstuffs. Food and apes recur throughout her works, reminding viewers of their own baser urges. Priska has said that her apes hint at our genetic memory, which lingers at cellular level. Monkeys feature in traditional still lifes by Albrecht Dürer, Jan Jansz. de Heem and Jean-Baptiste-Siméon Chardin. Their presence suggests a wildness – of nature and man at their most erotic and potentially destructive.

ABOVE
Hans-Peter Feldmann
One Pound Strawberries
34 photographs

LEFT
Andrew Guenther
Hotdogs, 2011 · acrylic on unprimed canvas

OPPOSITE
Anja Priska
Dance, Dance, Dance, 2009 · oil on canvas

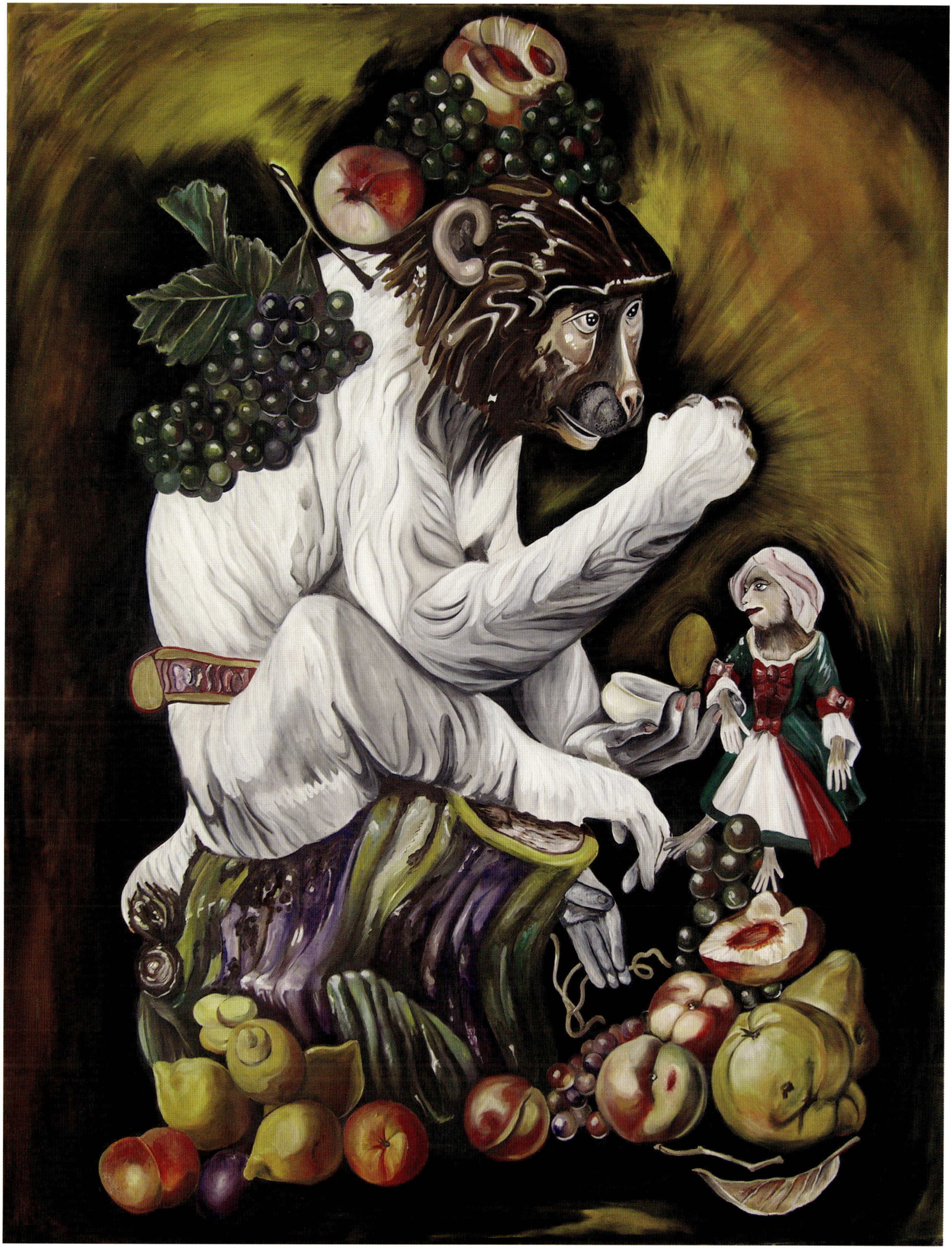

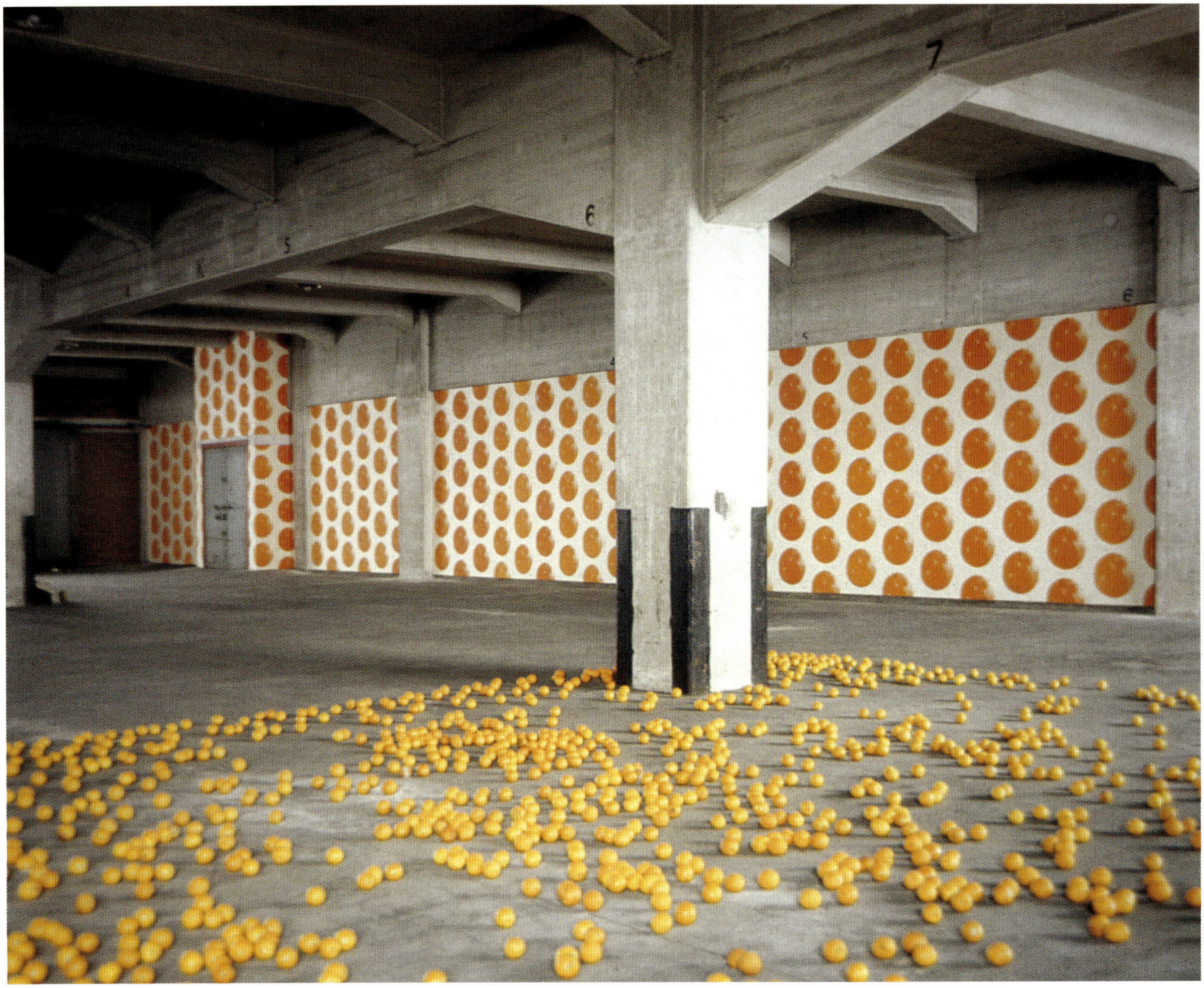

ABOVE
Anya Gallaccio
Tense, 1990
1 ton of oranges and
silkscreen on paper

OPPOSITE
Peter Coffin
Untitled (***Orange Pyramid***),
2007 · table and oranges

When oranges were first brought to Europe they were often given as exotic gifts to important dignitaries. Orangeries soon became a status symbol; many historians believe, for example, that the red balls on the Medici family's coat of arms are in fact oranges. Citrus fruits in turn became a symbol of power in still-life paintings. **Anya Gallaccio**'s installation *Tense* featured a ton of actual oranges scattered across the floor of a disused warehouse along with silkscreen versions of the fruit on the walls. While the real oranges decayed, their photographic counterparts remained larger and fresher than life. **Peter Coffin**'s *Untitled* (*Orange Pyramid*) recalls historical displays of abundance as well as the displays of modern supermarkets wherein all but the poorest members of society now have access to the fruit.

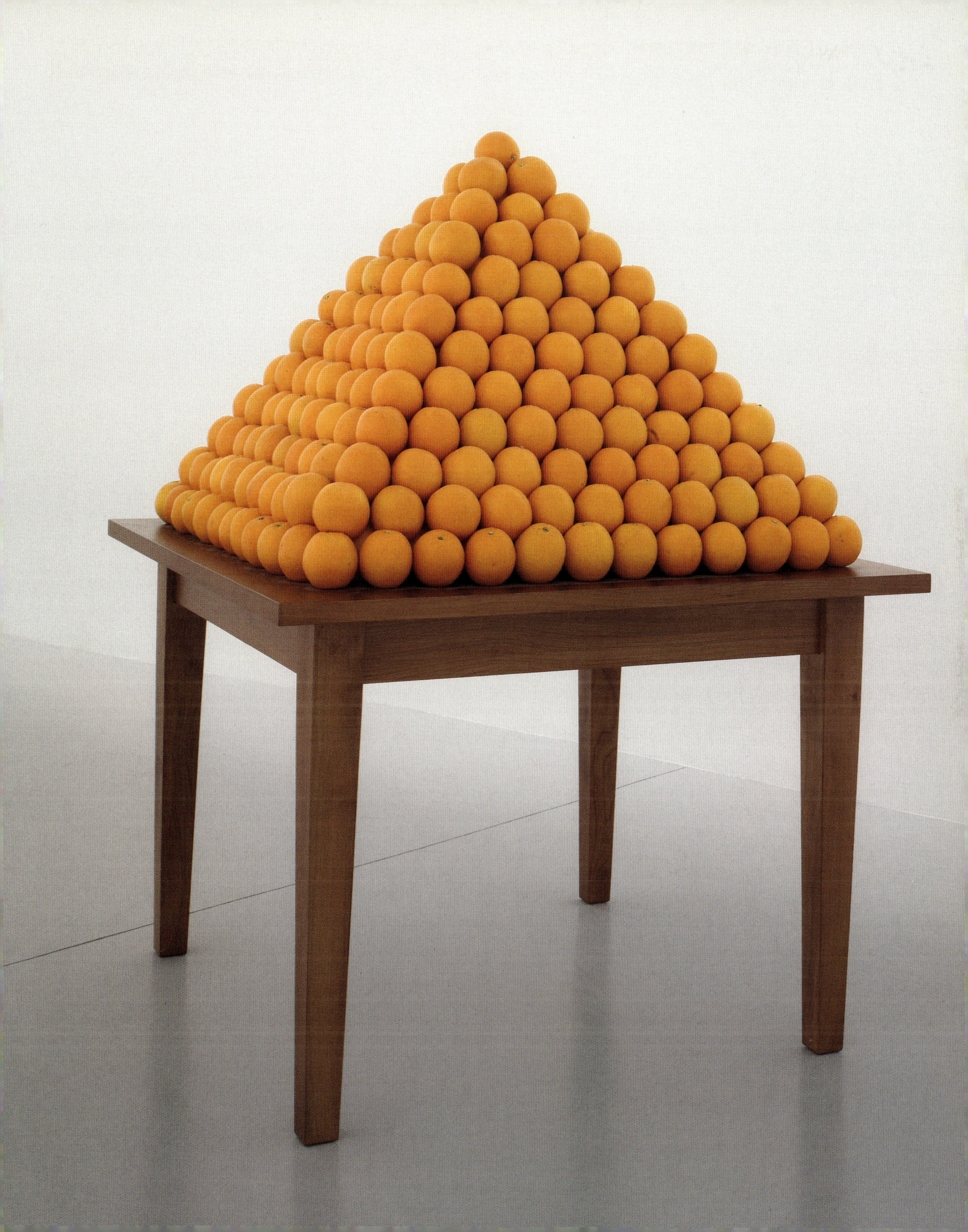

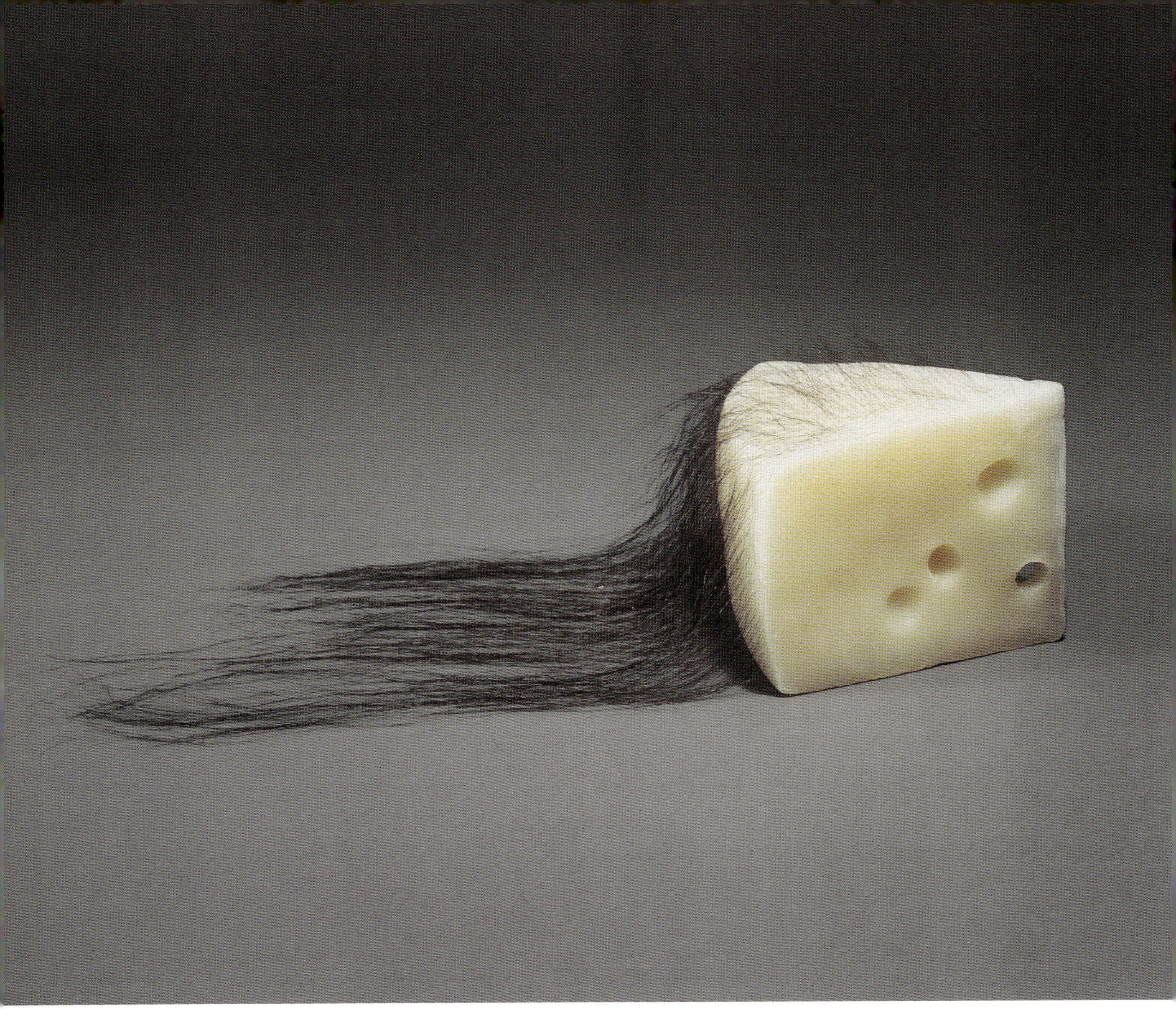

ABOVE
Robert Gober
Untitled, 2005
beeswax and human hair

OPPOSITE TOP
Robert Gober
Bag of Donuts, 1989
acid free hand-cut paper, graphite dough and synthetic resin

OPPOSITE BOTTOM
Yuken Teruya
Scarlet Birds, Crimson Sky, 2010 (detail)
KFC package (S)

Robert Gober selects many everyday objects as the basis for his disturbing, almost surreal works, which include sinks vastly enlarged in scale and drain holes in vertical walls. All of Gober's works are meticulously made in his studio to achieve highly realistic detail. As if emerged from one of his darker dreams, *Untitled* appears to be a wedge of cheese that has sprouted human hair. To create *Bag of Donuts*, the artist fried the graphite dough, drained it, then found a scientific way to stabilize it. So authentic did the the resulting pastries appear that a tipsy Ed Brzezinski, critic and curator, grabbed one from the handmade bag on display in a New York gallery and tried to eat it. He had to be hospitalized after ingesting the chemicals.

For his 2010 installation *Scarlet Birds, Crimson Sky*, **Yuken Teruya** employed the Okinawan hand-dyeing technique of *bingata*, originally used to dye kimono fabric. Stencils cut out from food packaging and tissue boxes were used to dye the motifs that dotted an over twelve-metre-long fabric length suspended from the gallery's ceiling. Below, Teruya positioned the altered packaging on an equally long table, including a fighter jet cut into a Kentucky Fried Chicken box (right). Traditional symbols of *bingata* mixed with contemporary images of power (President Obama, police cars, the American eagle seal) in a commentary on the continuing presence of the American military in Japan.

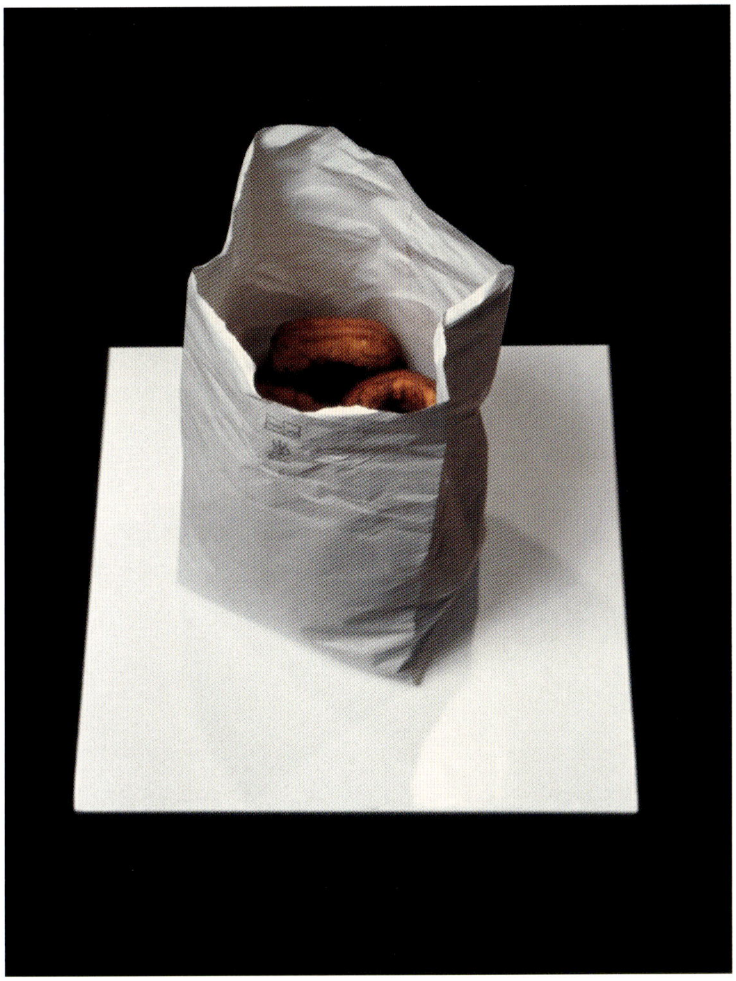

'Look, it was an honest mistake...I was hungry. I'd been drinking and I hadn't eaten anything all day. I noticed this bag of doughnuts sitting on a pedestal. Plain doughnuts with no sugar. I figured somebody had brought them and then gotten tired of them. So I grabbed one and bit it. It tasted stale.'

—ED BRZEZINSKI

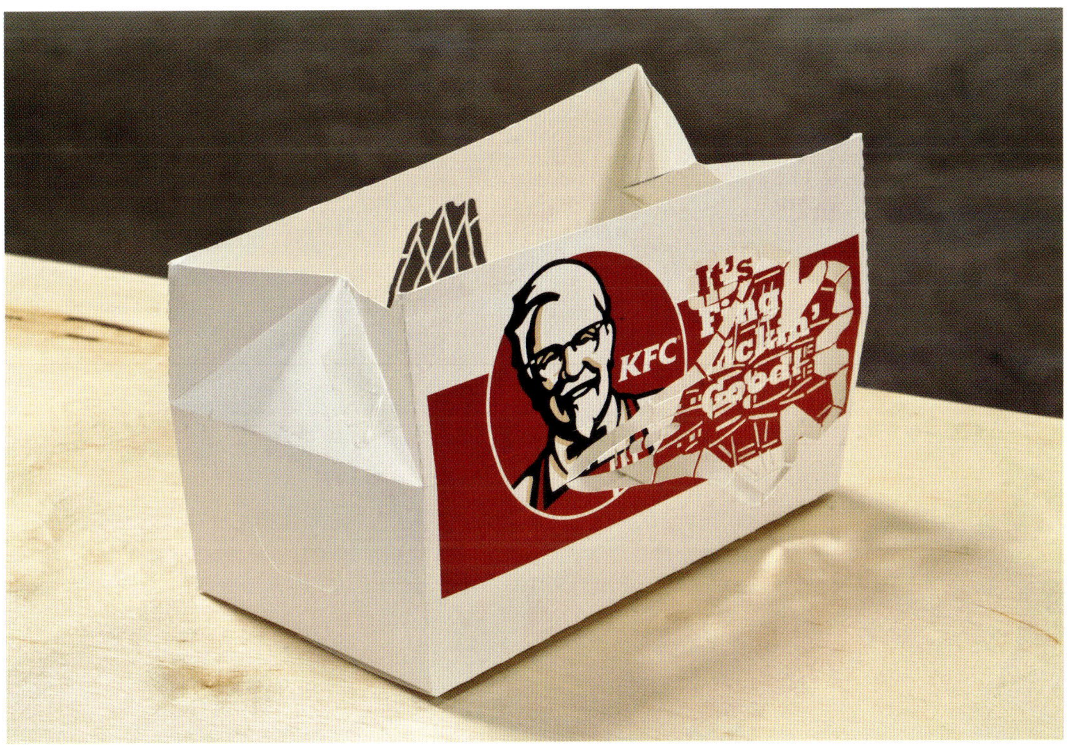

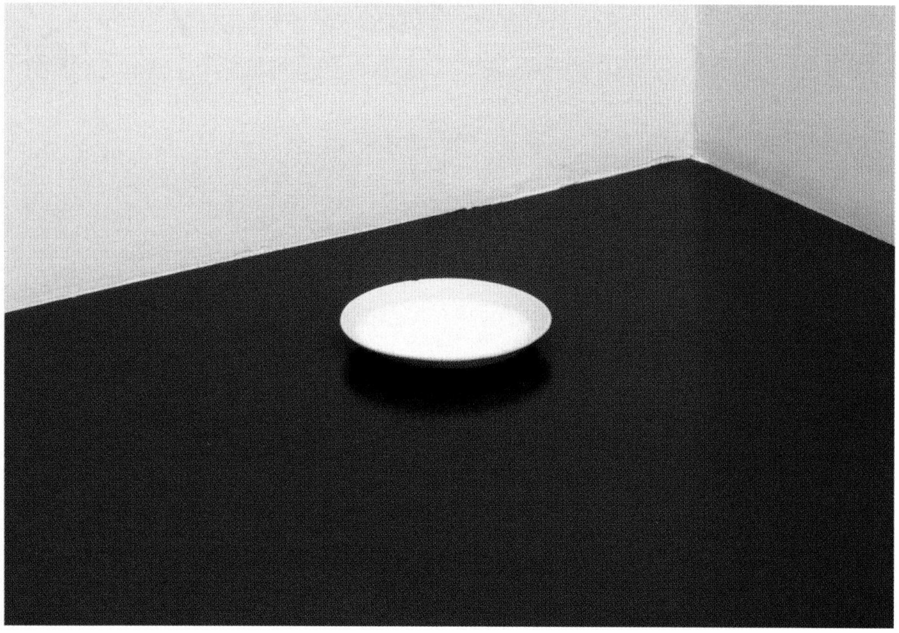

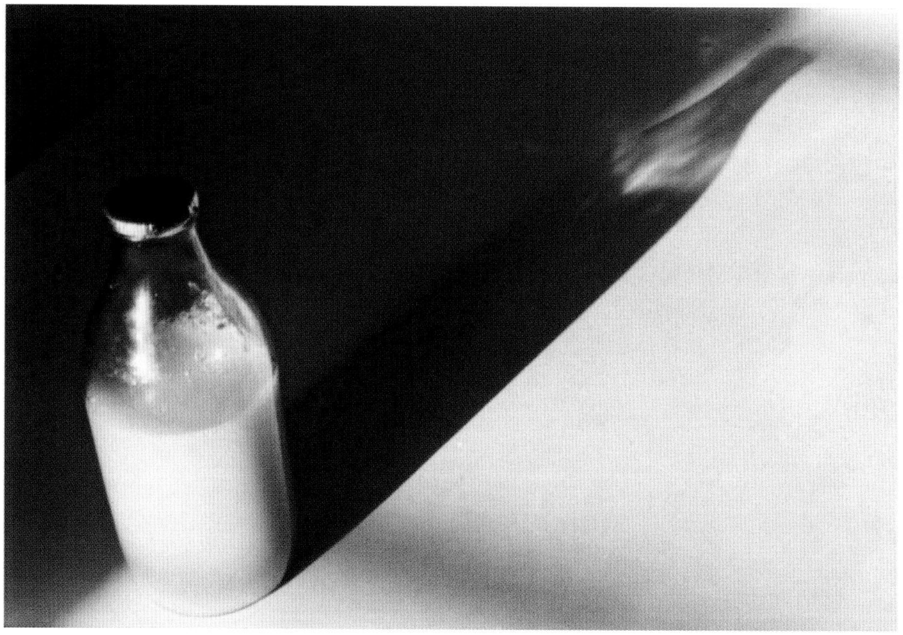

ABOVE
Kris Martin
***Plate with milk*, 2005**
plate and milk

RIGHT
Renata Hegyi
***Bottle and Shade*, 2003**
gelatin silver print

OPPOSITE
Peter Abrahams
***Milk and Earth*, 2009**
archival pigment print

Milk is often connected with purity, not only because it is white, but also because it is seen as a link between mother and child in mammalian species. **Kris Martin**'s *Plate with milk* sculpture presents a visual conundrum: is the work simply a meal for an absent cat or a sly, minimalist comment on the human need for meaning. **Renata Hegyi**'s *Bottle and Shade* from her *Waiting for time to pass* series features a bottle of milk with a long shadow stretching out behind it; the slow passage of time hangs heavy in the photograph. **Peter Abrahams**'s *Milk and Earth* is from his *vanitas* series of still-life photographs. Milk recurs as a fixture in a number of these images, sometimes in contrast to other fluids (*Milk and Ink*) or, as here, against soil. Abrahams stages objects in his studio to play on traditional tropes, yet in their simplicity and clarity the resulting photographs are almost cartoons of depiction. As with Martin's actual bowl of milk, it is simplicity itself that disturbs.

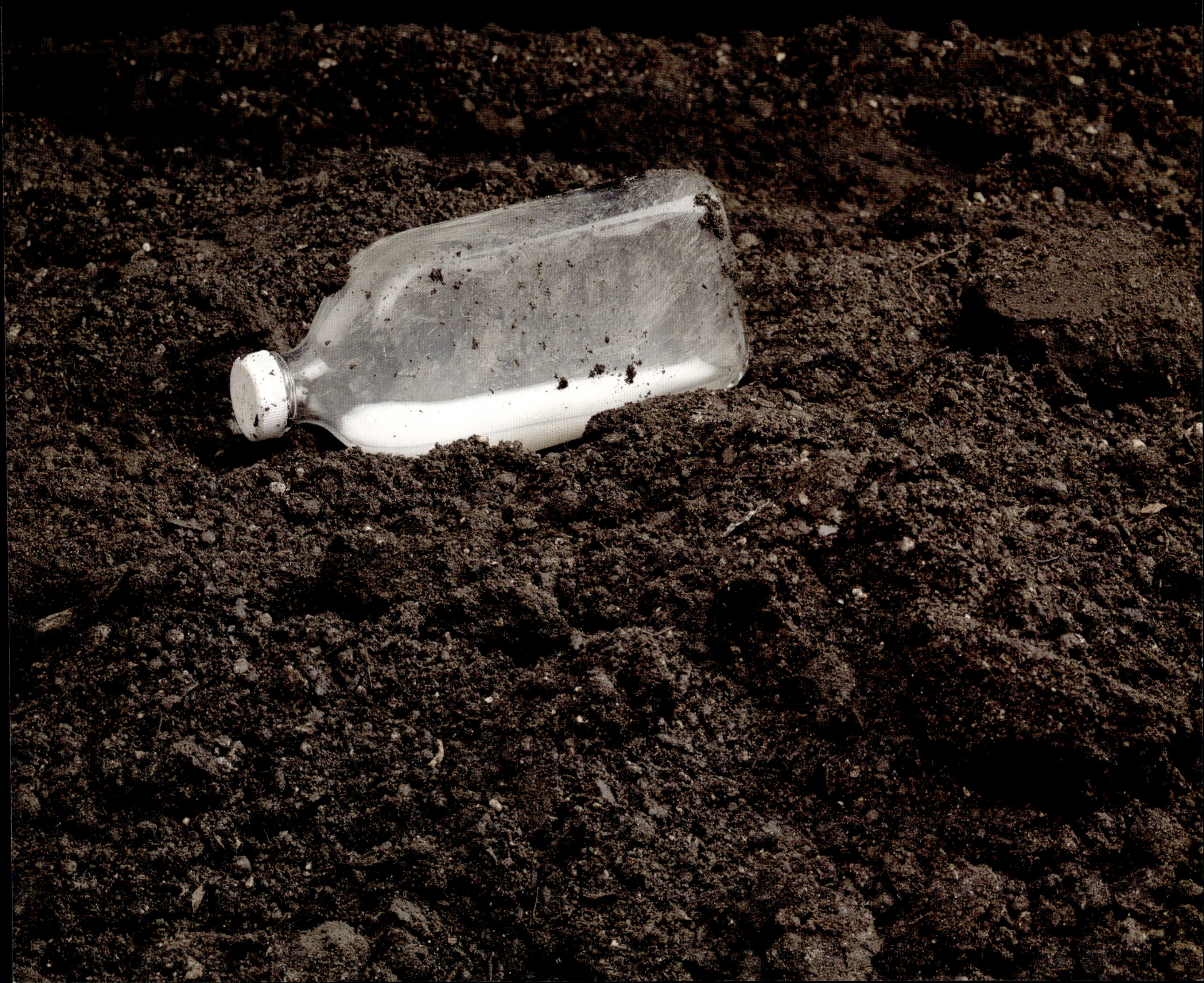

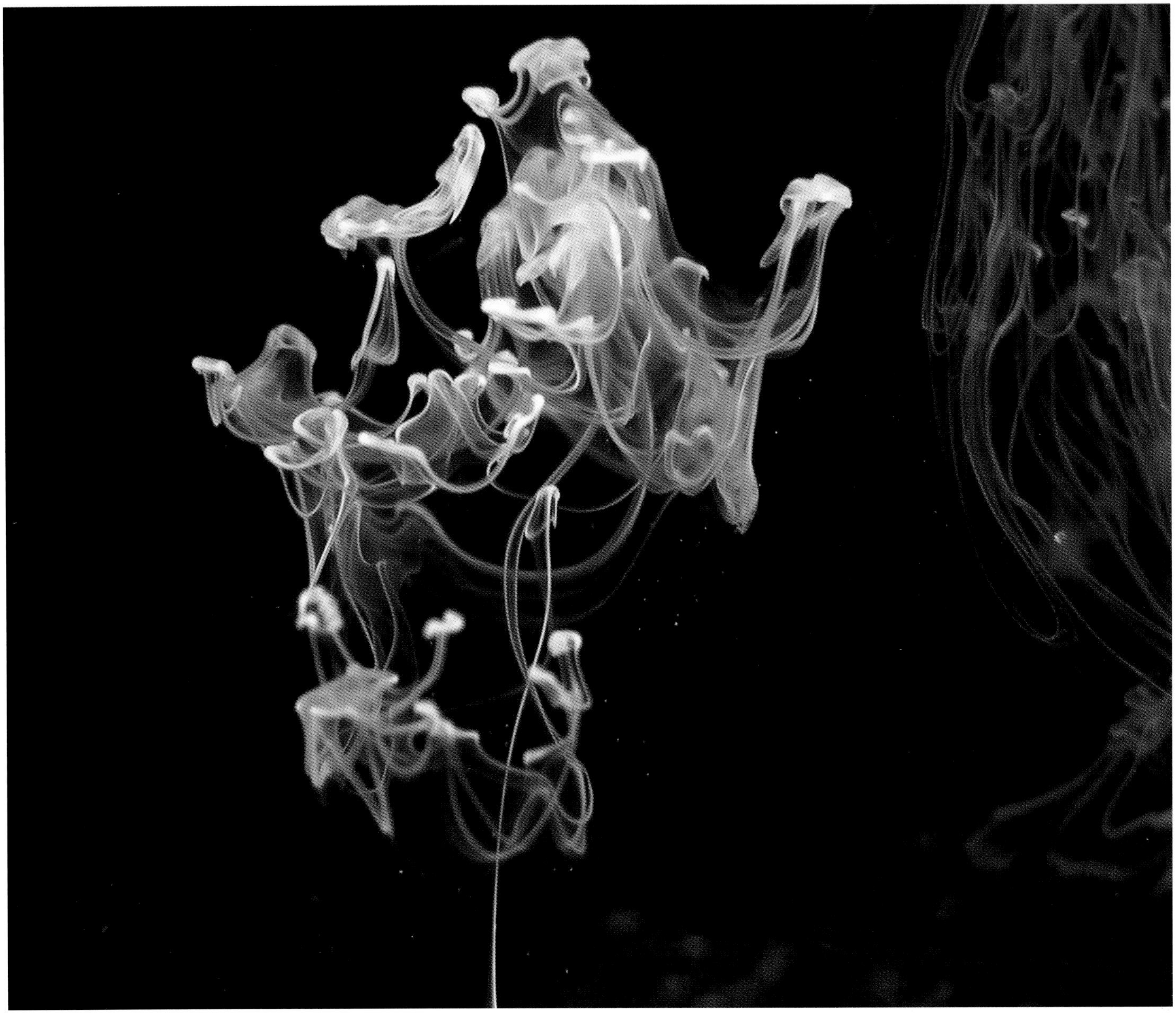

ABOVE
Saara Ekström · still from the installation *Grotesque & Arabesque (milk) I*, 2005
MiniDV transferred on DVD

OPPOSITE TOP AND CENTRE
Saara Ekström · stills from *Domestic Nature Morte*, 2004 · digital camera stop-frame animation transferred on DVD

OPPOSITE BOTTOM
Saara Ekström · *Carnation*, 1997 (detail) · digital print

In **Saara Ekström**'s *Grotesque & Arabesque (milk) I*, a drop of milk elegantly dissipates in a glass of water. Her *Domestic Nature Morte* consists of a large-scale video projection of a dish of ripe red tomatoes rotting over a period of a month. Played in a continuous loop, the stop-frame animation shows the tomatoes collapse and desiccate only to plump up and rejuvenate as quickly as they fade. These works followed *Cries and Whispers* (2002), in which viewers watched the dying movements of opened oysters. Ekström uses video to capture her subjects in real time, then edits or accelerates the footage to create artworks that convey the passage of time and the tissue-thin grasp that all living creatures have on their continued existence on earth. Her *Carnation* installation featured twelve pig haunches, each tattooed (after the animals were killed) with the eponymous flower or coiled thorns, and preserved in a freezer.

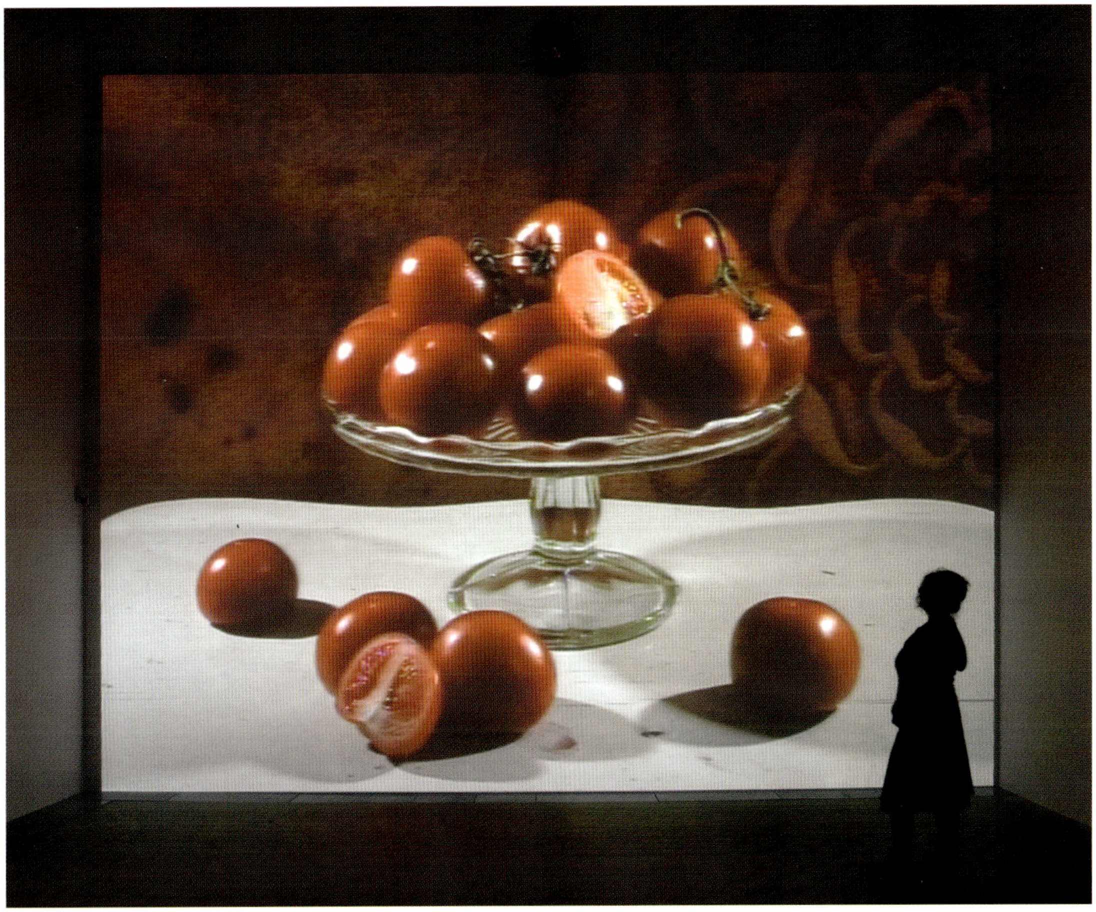

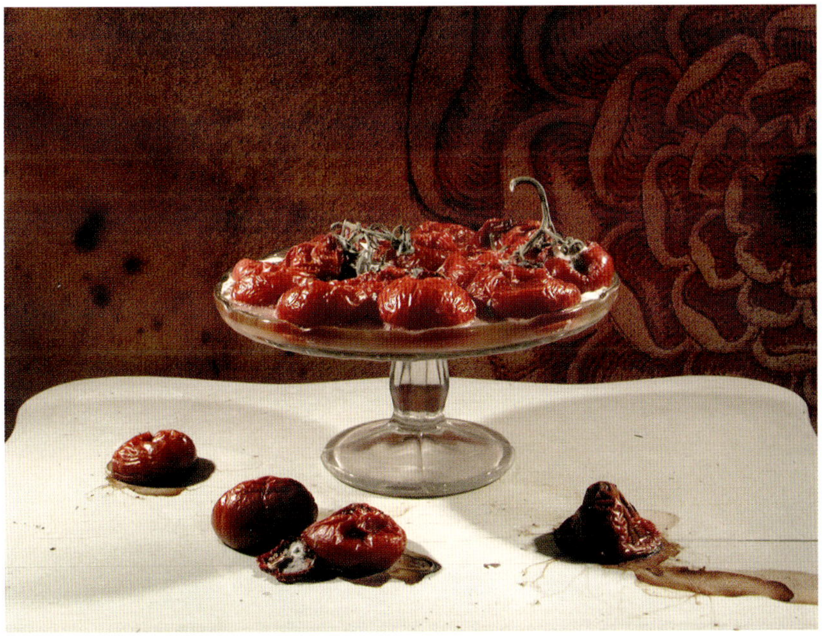

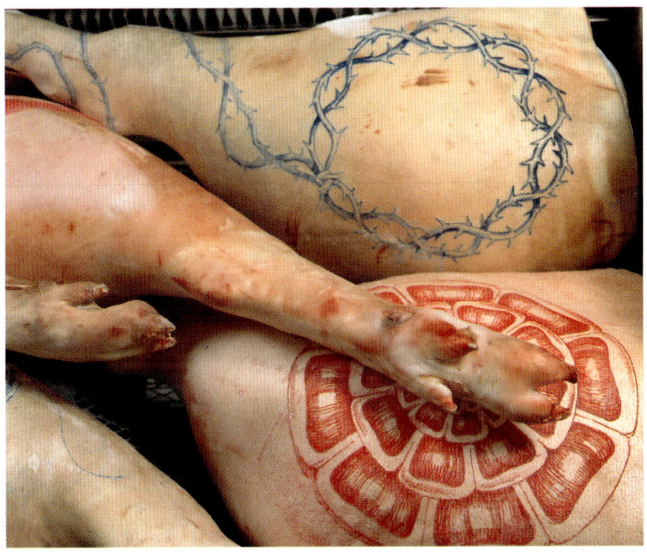

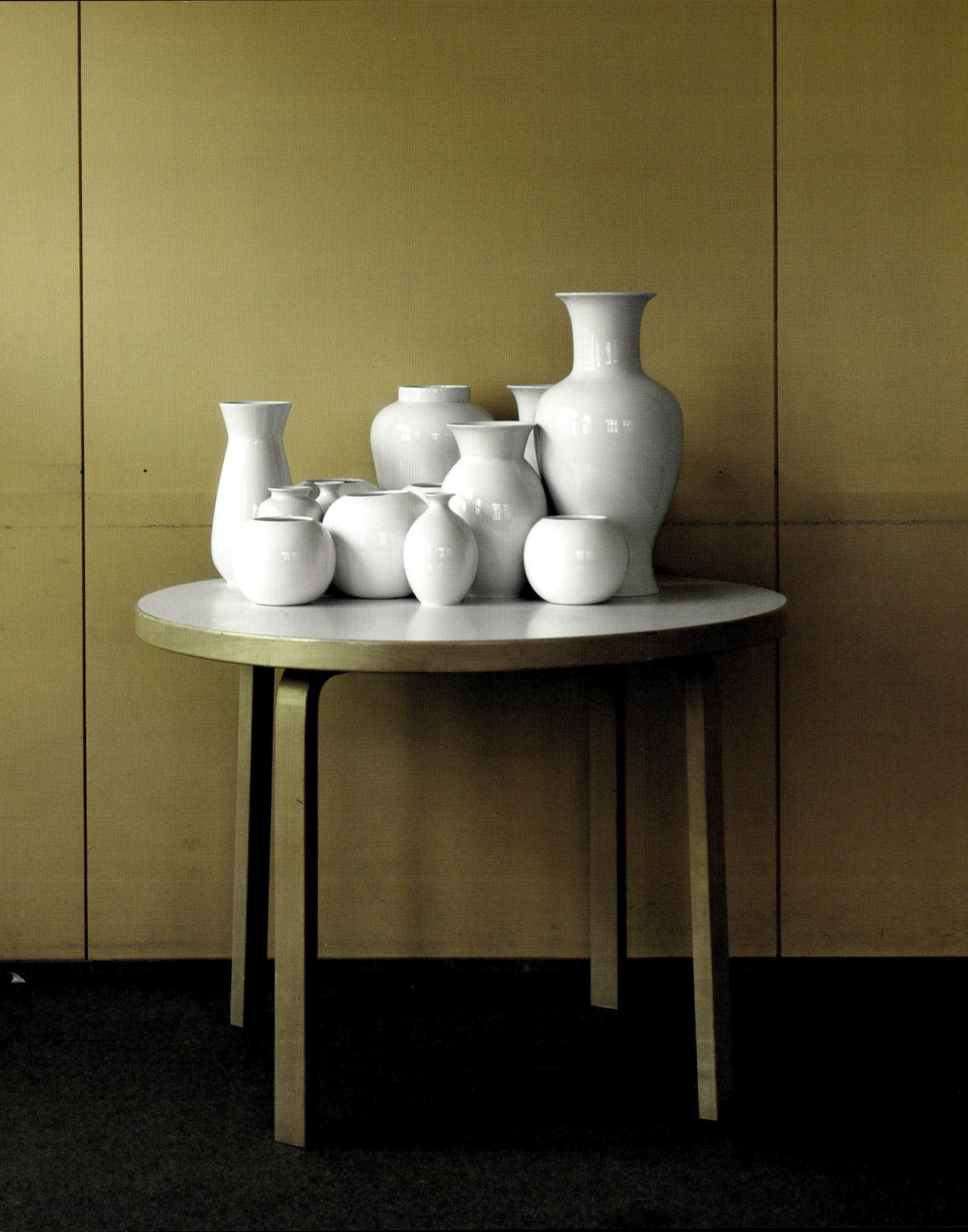

Section Three

House & Home

HOUSE & HOME

*As any object, the vase is a product of its time;
it not only speaks of its own cultural and
aesthetic construction but also reflects
back upon a pre-existing period.*

—MARK ALICE DURANT, on McDermott & McGough's *Eighteenth-Century Salon as Reflected in a Nineteenth-Century Vase, 1907*, 1988

All our possessions speak about us in silent ways, often revealing those things about us that are most secret – and that we would prefer to keep quiet. In traditional still-life paintings the meaning behind the objects on display was not so secretive. Almost all were selected for their symbolism or metaphorical significance and what they might reveal about the owner of that painting. Pewter drinking cups, fine china, hand-crafted silver and drinking horns (often fashioned from bull horns) were among the many household objects that indicated the high status of the owner. One of the outcomes of the Protestant Reformation of the sixteenth century was that a prosperous life came to be a sign of a pious life, rather than its antithesis. Calvinists in particular considered success and wealth to be evidence of a pious, hardworking life, which was to be pursued in the hope of increasing one's chances of salvation in the next.

Where the household items on display in traditional still lifes were often intended to indicate the class and rank of their owner, contemporary still lifes are often more nuanced. Artists look both back and forward in these works, drawing on the innovations of their predecessors while themselves innovating in both medium and message. Fine china, for example, was initially very much an indication of wealth upon its introduction to Europe from China, and only those who could afford to dine off the very best had it in their homes in place of standard earthenware. It was not until 1710, with the opening of the Meissen factory in Germany, that these blue-and-white dishes became available to the emerging mercantile class.

Contemporary artists such as Livia Marin, Stephanie Syjuco and Matt Smith have drawn on this heritage in works that examine these once prized possessions in the context of the museums to which many now belong (pages 164, 165 and 169). These works interrogate the validity that being part of a collection, particularly one in a museum, confers on objects and at the same time seek to understand the collector's passion for ownership. Their disparate approaches often call for feminist or queer readings. Patrick Jackson, John Mitchell and Paul Wood put the found but unvalued object at the heart of their works, carefully selecting discarded ceramic goods and exhibiting them as collections in their own right (pages 170 and 171). This interest in presenting household objects outside of their original domestic domain provokes viewers to contemplate the objects that they themselves own or collect. They may even come to consider what will happen to these inanimate goods after their own death. Other contemporary artists use the imagery or form of historical objects as their template to create fanciful works that only reveal anachronistic qualities on closer inspection. At a glance, for example, Joan Bankemper's Baroque-inspired vases would not look out of place in an eighteenth-century palace collection (page 171). Upon looking closer, one discovers they are topsy-turvy modern ceramic collages, where old-fashioned elements mix incongruously with pieces of contemporary china.

Some objects that we now take for granted, including knives and forks, were once rarities and their appearance in still lifes thus indicative of status. The idea of cutlery as a luxury item may seem unlikely today, but because these implements first came into use among the higher levels of society they were originally very much symbols of cultivation. The book or writing device was another household object that denoted wealth and education during the time when the still life was at its height. Feather quills and ink wells can be found in countless historical works where their presence implied the sophistication of their owner. Contemporary artists incorporate the book and all its connotations – many of which remain the same – in works that question its status in the digital age.

As in the past when new objects of interest, such as shells from the Pacific, were included for their novelty, contemporary artists have introduced newly invented and manufactured objects to the still life, including plastic Tupperware (Jane Simpson, page 142) and headphones (Jan Merta, page 149). Clocks, watches and hourglasses continue to operate as unambiguous metaphors for time and its inevitable forward flow, and contemporary artists are keen to explore these motifs. Clothing has also become a subject of fascination. The clothes we wear tell stories of our personal taste, gender and, as always, class and position in society: a Chanel jacket shows the wealth of the wearer, while denim overalls might suggest not only a farm hand, but also masculinity. Only recently have grieving families stopped wearing mourning black for extended periods; now it is generally worn only on the day of the funeral. Unworn, a limp overcoat or dressing gown invokes absence, even death, and begs the question of whether its owner will ever wear it again.

The temporary usage of things, the fact that ultimately death will part all of us from our worldly possessions, whatever implicit myths consumerism may perpetrate, is a theme that runs throughout these contemporary still lifes though without the moral judgment one might have expected in the past. Instead, there is a sense that these objects may well outlive their original owner and so their value will inevitably shift; one ceramic dish could end up in a museum, another may slowly break into pieces in a landfill. An increasing emphasis on sustainability also suggests that the objects that fill our homes and our lives are only on loan until passed on to future generations. As the 2013 advertising campaign for luxury Swiss watch manufacturer Patek Philippe puts it: 'You merely look after it for the next generation.'

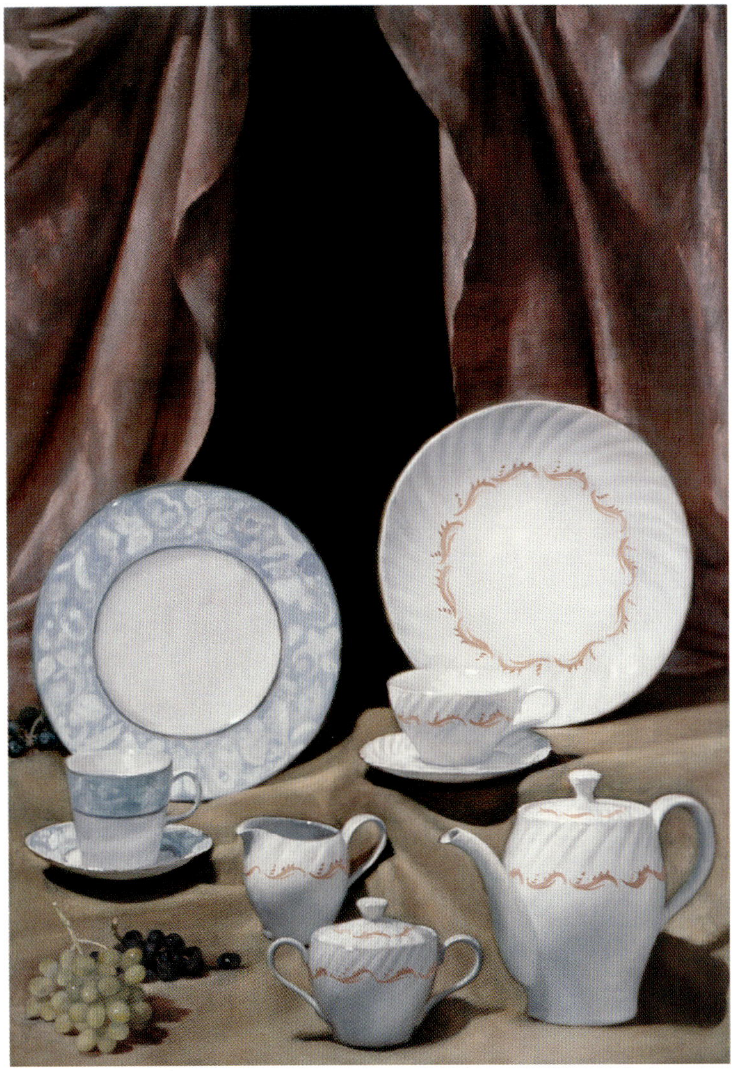

'I saw a lot of ceramic art in Seattle in the sixties and seventies. Nothing is more immediate or primal than clay.... All my work is the actual size it needs to be.'

—CHARLES LEDRAY

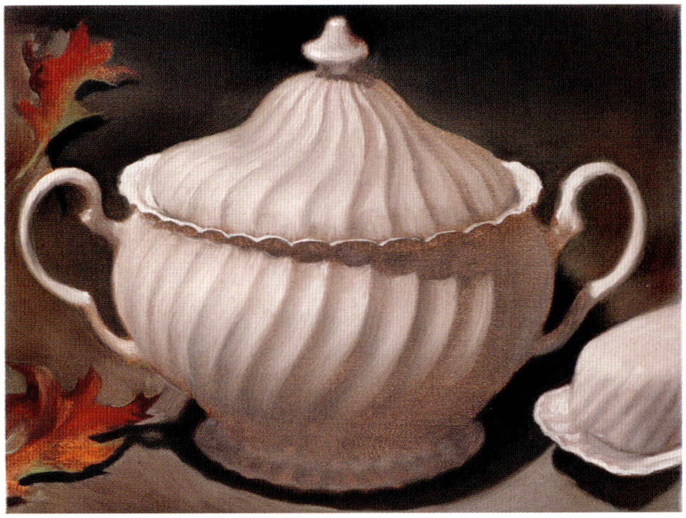

John Currin is well known for applying his skill in historical painting techniques to the examination of contemporary middle-class life. He has painted nudes of his wife (à la Cranach), gay men, flowers (see page 24), pornography and, as in *Monroeville* and *Urn*, china dishes. The resulting works are held as beautiful, or at least collectable, by his many patrons. These particular still-life paintings question what is beautiful, as well as who should be allowed to answer that question.

Charles LeDray's *Milk and Honey* features two thousand doll-sized, hand-thrown porcelain pots, arranged over six glass shelves in a cabinet. Whether a coffee pot or a vase, with or without a handle, each object is unique, having been formed by the artist on a miniature potter's wheel. Other works demonstrate LeDray's fine sewing skills, acquired from his mother at a young age. Whether hand-stitching minute pieces of clothing or throwing together tiny china vessels, LeDray creates works that confound gender expectations.

PAGE 130
Saara Ekström · ***A Single Charm is Doubtful (liquids)***, 2010 (detail)
C-print

ABOVE LEFT
John Currin · ***Monroeville***, 2008
oil on canvas

ABOVE RIGHT
John Currin · ***Urn***, 2003
oil on canvas

OPPOSITE
Charles LeDray · ***Milk and Honey***, 1994–96 · porcelain objects, glass and wood

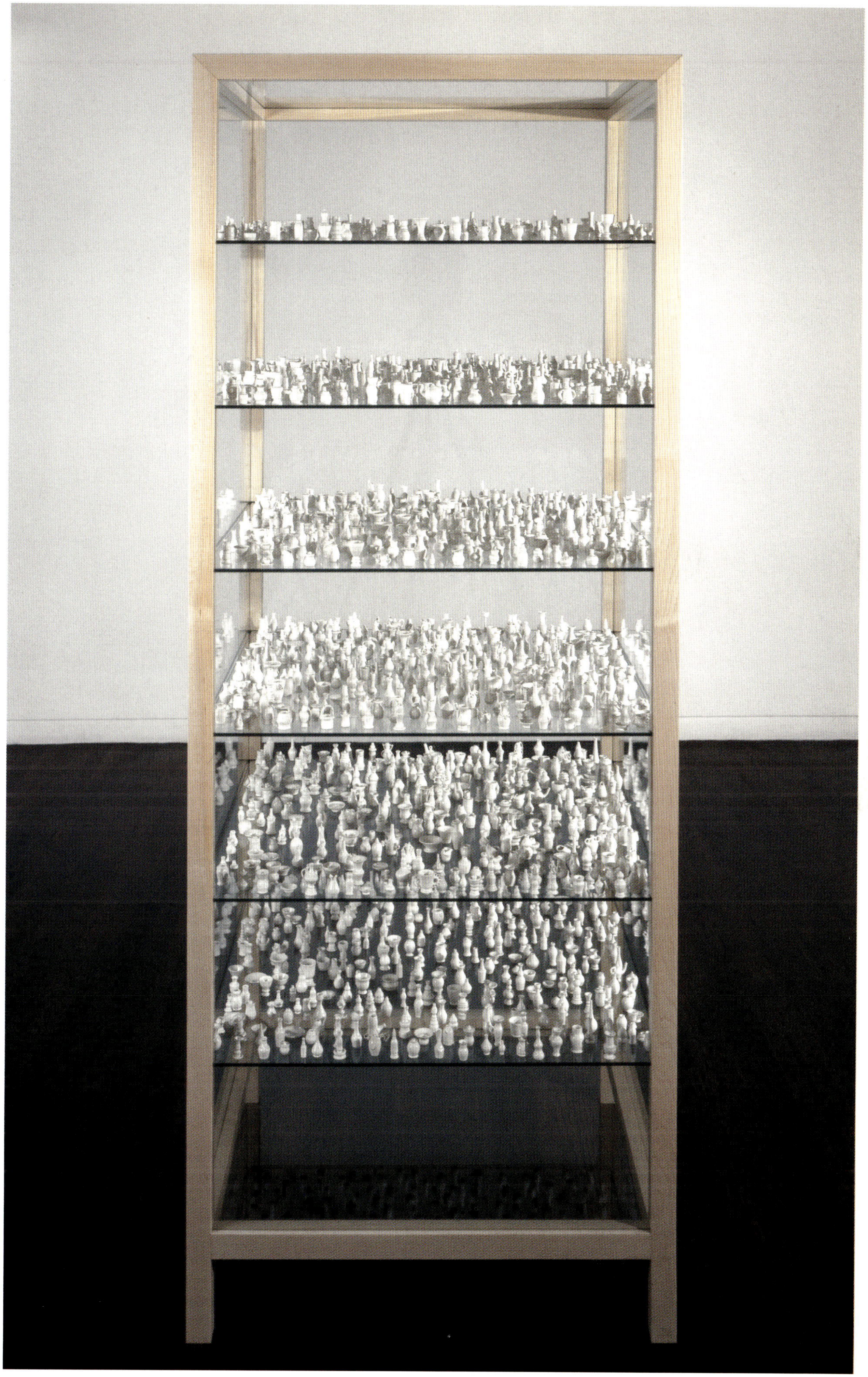

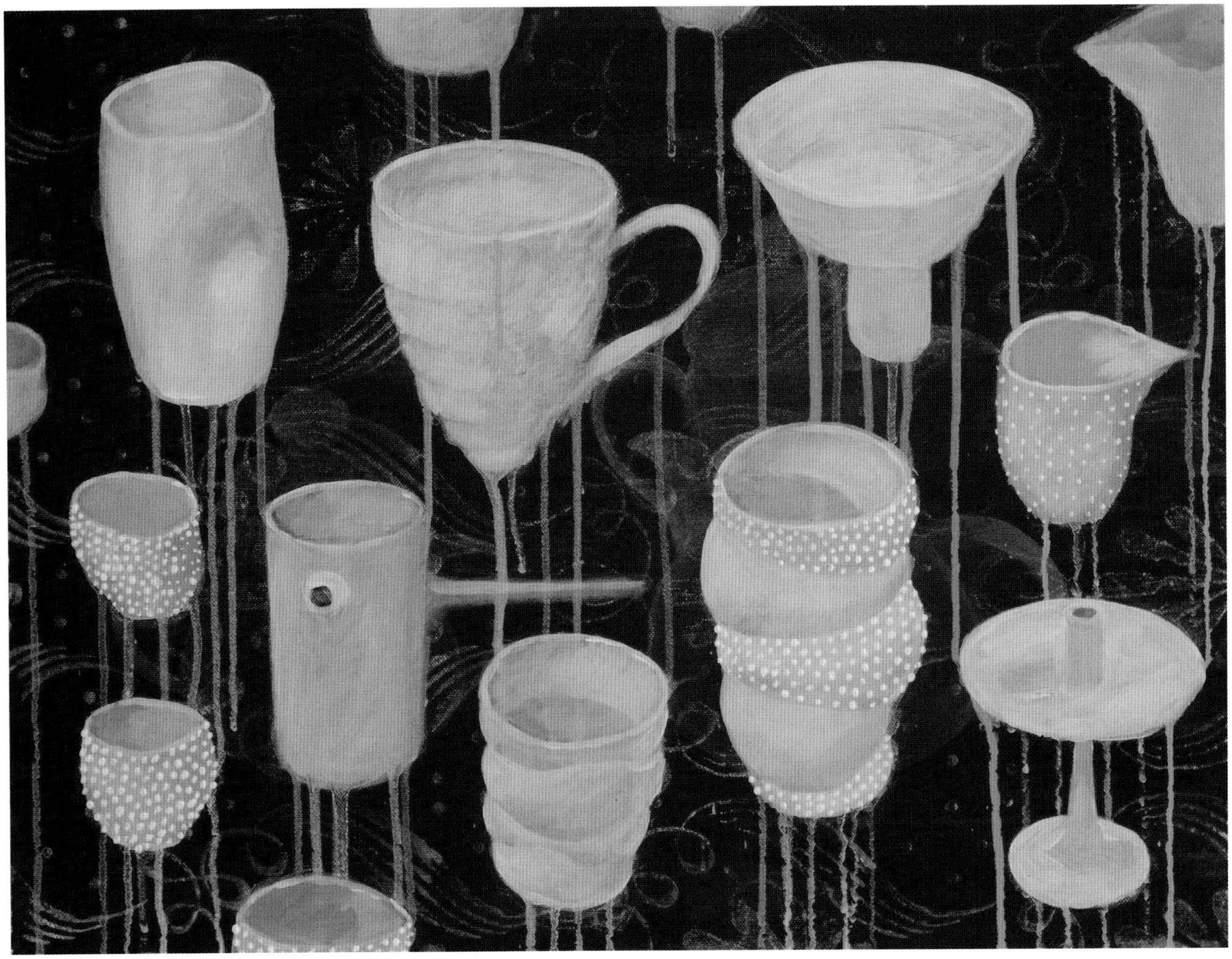

ABOVE
Jane Telford
***Porcelain Black*, 2012**
acrylic on canvas

OPPOSITE
Clare Twomey
***Monument*, 2009**
ceramic waste

Jane Telford's painting *Porcelain Black* offers a personal, almost private, investigation of the domestic. Her works often feature familiar household dishes rendered strange through the repetition of muted colours, whether slate, coral or honey. Floating against an abstract background, the vessels of *Porcelain Black* seem set to melt away.

While also a depiction of domestic tableware, **Clare Twomey**'s *Monument* differs greatly from Telford's *Porcelain Black*. This massive work is composed of thirty cubic metres of ceramic waste (dishes broken during manufacture or discarded as seconds), which, in this particular version, is piled into the Middlesbrough Institute of Modern Art up to a height of almost eight metres (each version of the installation is unique). At any moment, it feels as if the precarious heap could avalanche down onto the unsuspecting visitors below. The visual weight of the piece matches its physical mass, recalling the domestic devastation caused by earthquakes or man-made destruction.

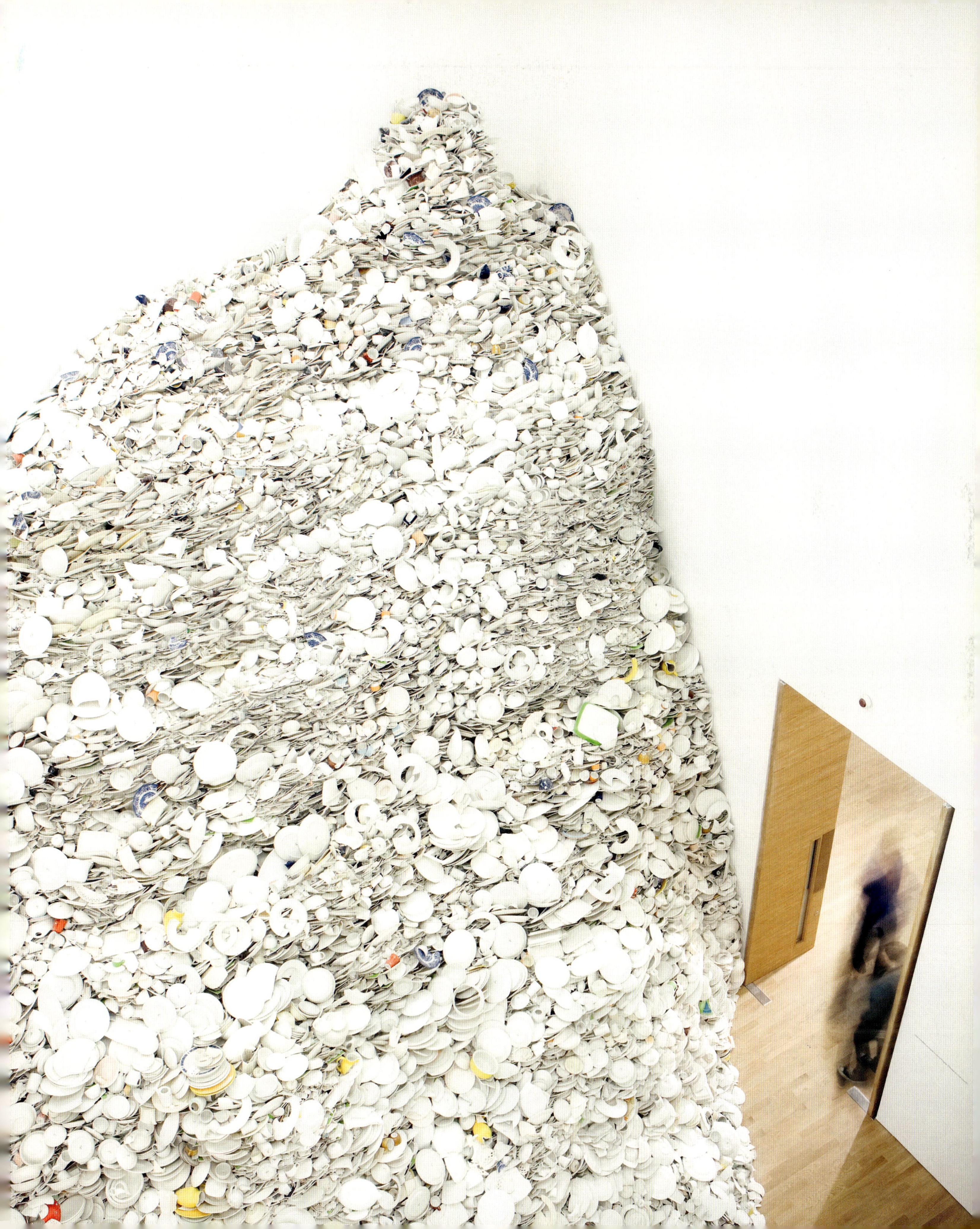

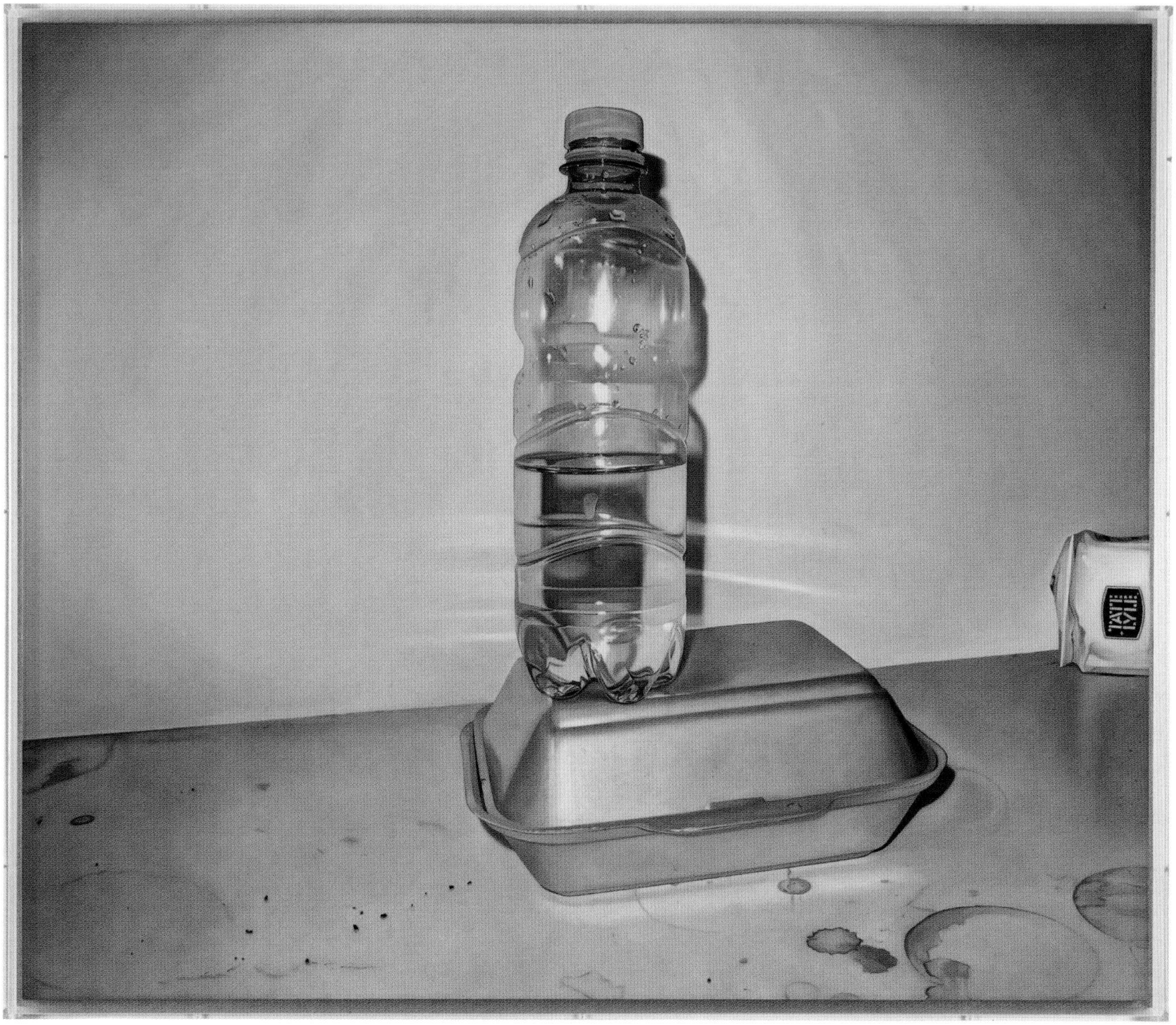

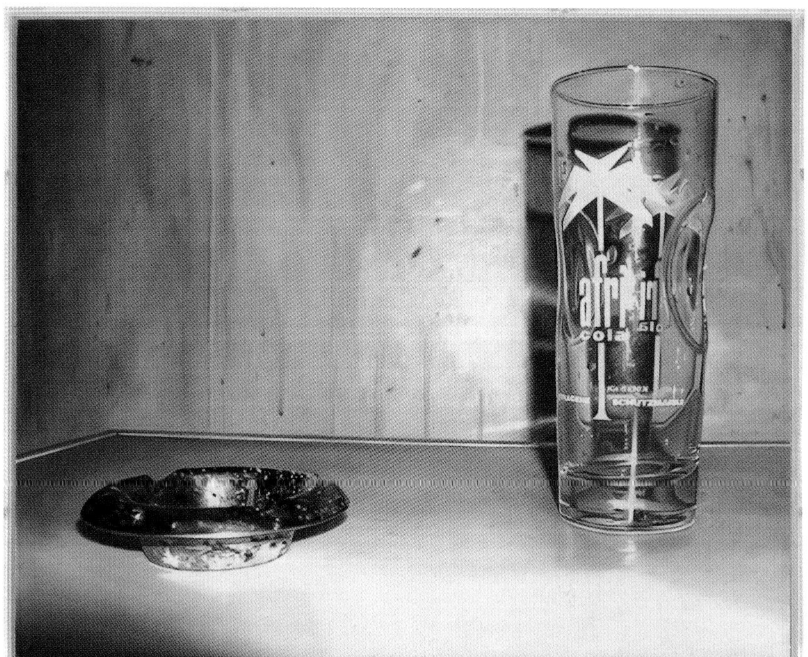
afri
cola

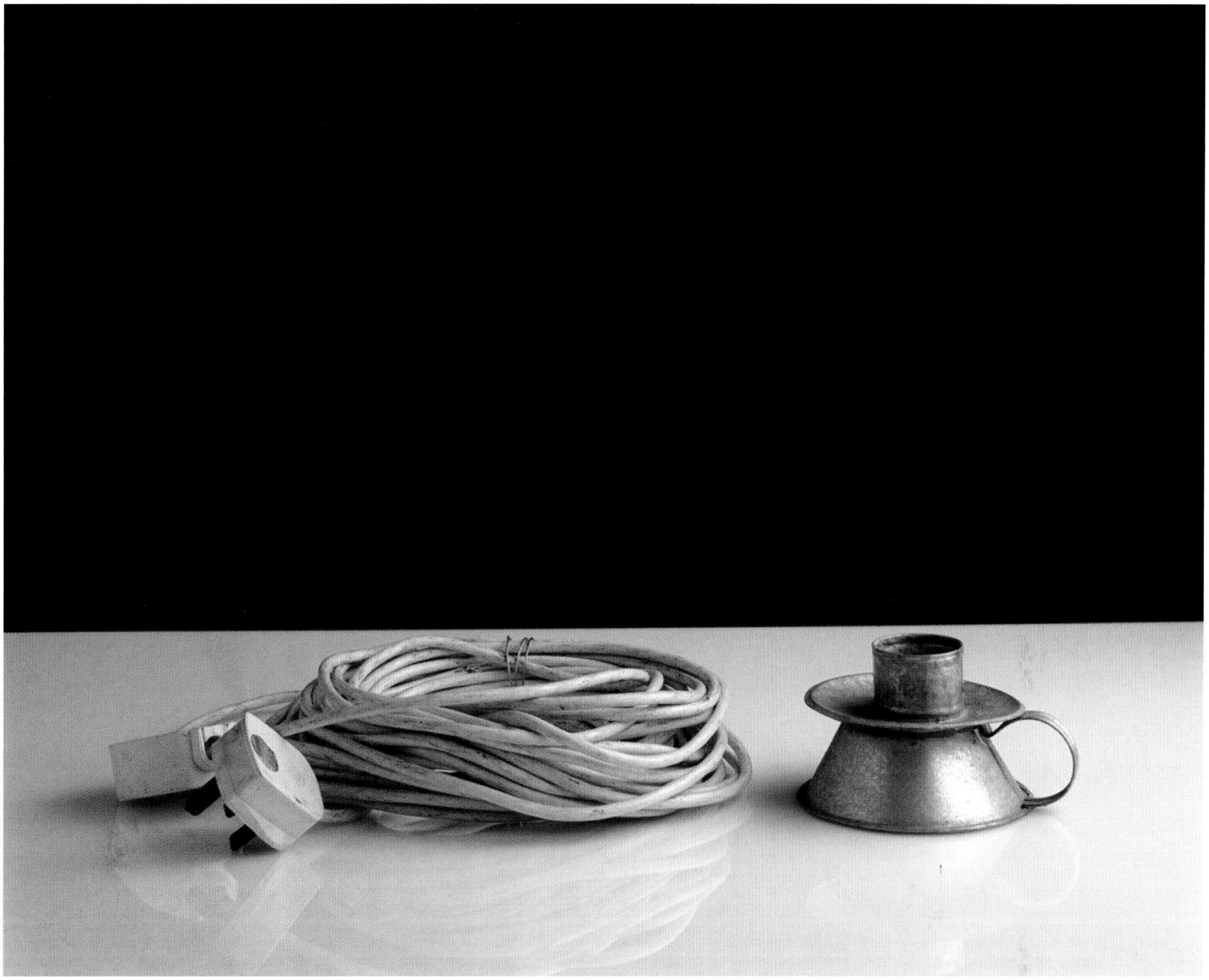

OPPOSITE TOP
James White
Burger Box, 2010
oil and varnish on birch-ply
in Perspex box frame

OPPOSITE BOTTOM
James White
Afri Cola, 2007
oil and varnish on birch-ply
in Perspex box frame

ABOVE
Peter Abrahams
Illuminations; Coiled, 2007
archival pigment print

James White's paintings in black, grey and white originate as photographs that he then reproduces as exactly as possible in paint. *Burger Box* and *Afri Cola* lifelessly depict the artist's day-to-day existence, hinting at an unseen human presence that may remain just outside the frame. Each painting is enclosed in a clear Perspex box, sealing out the viewer even as the painting seals out its creator.

Peter Abrahams carefully constructed the still-life tableaux that he photographed for his *Illuminations* series so that household items, bought by the artist either in charity shops or inexpensive pound stores, took on the same gravitas as the more luxurious objects of Old Master paintings. The artist is interested in the anonymous histories of these mean objects, which are either second-hand or have been manufactured in foreign countries using inexpensive human labour, before being sold in the West for a pittance.

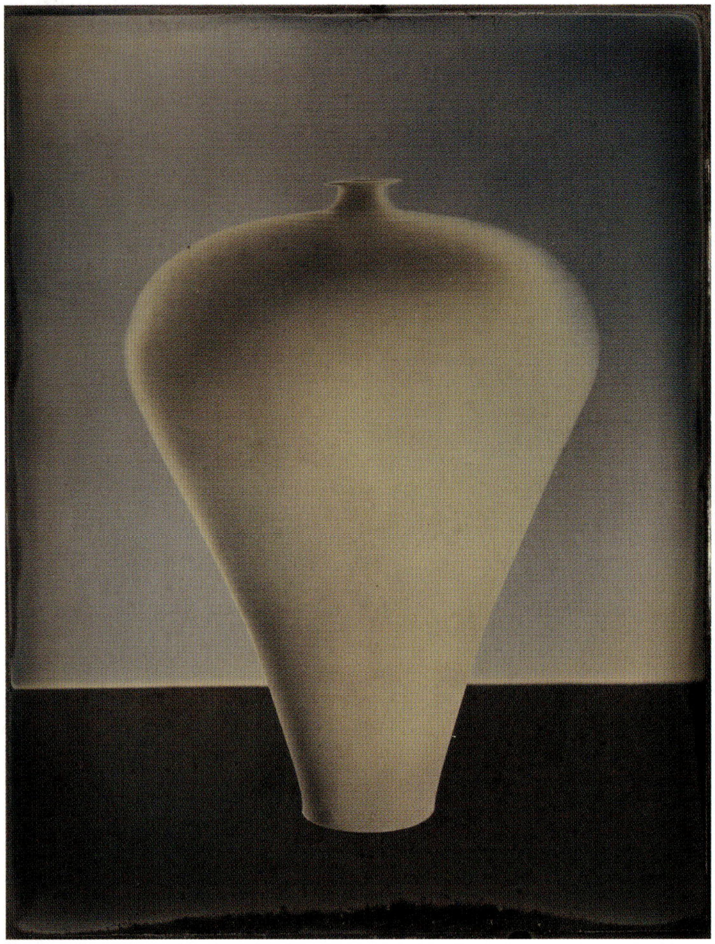

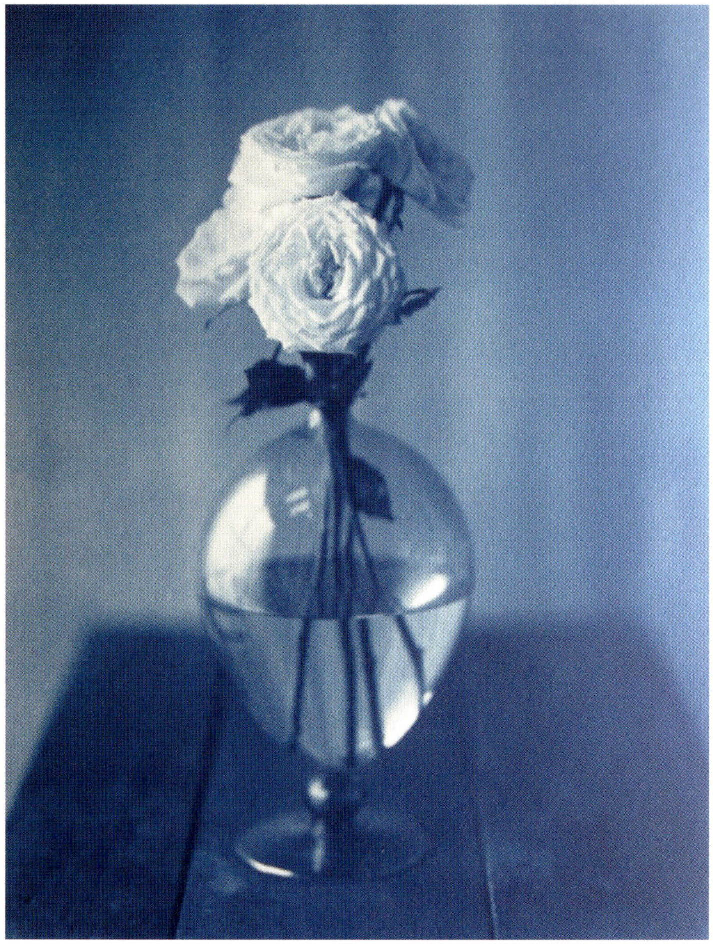

Adam Fuss uses a variety of photographic techniques in his attempts to capture the ephemeral (birds in flight, water disturbed by droplets, smoke rising) and notions of death, life and transcendence. Of his softly blue daguerreotypes Fuss has said: 'blue is not only a very beautiful hue, but blueness also conveys a sadness, a sense of loss....Yes, I do deal with death, but to me death isn't necessarily morbid or taboo. It's part of life.'

John Dugdale and **McDermott & McGough** also use historical camera techniques, particularly the cyanotype. *Petals* depicts what seems to be a traditional still life yet in its creation the work is truly unique for Dugdale is almost completely blind, the consequence of a HIV-related illness. To create his photographs, he describes to an assistant what the image should look like. He has said: 'The quietude that people respond to in my pictures is, in part, because of the way the pictures are made: no flash; no harsh electric light; not even the sound of the shutter – just a lens cap removed, and then gently replaced. This encounter provides, for me, a metaphor for looking.'

McDermott & McGough put an empty vase at the centre of their cyanotype but, in naming it *18th-Century Salon as Reflected in a 19th-Century Vase, 1907*, the artists invite viewers to look closer at the glass reflection, in which one can faintly make out a domestic interior. Dating the work to 1907, despite it being created in 1988, is typical of the artists' playful approach to time (see page 100).

ABOVE LEFT
Adam Fuss
Untitled, 2008
daguerreotype

ABOVE RIGHT
John Dugdale
Petals, 1998
cyanotype

OPPOSITE
McDermott & McGough
18th-Century Salon as Reflected in a 19th-Century Vase, 1907, 1988
cyanotype

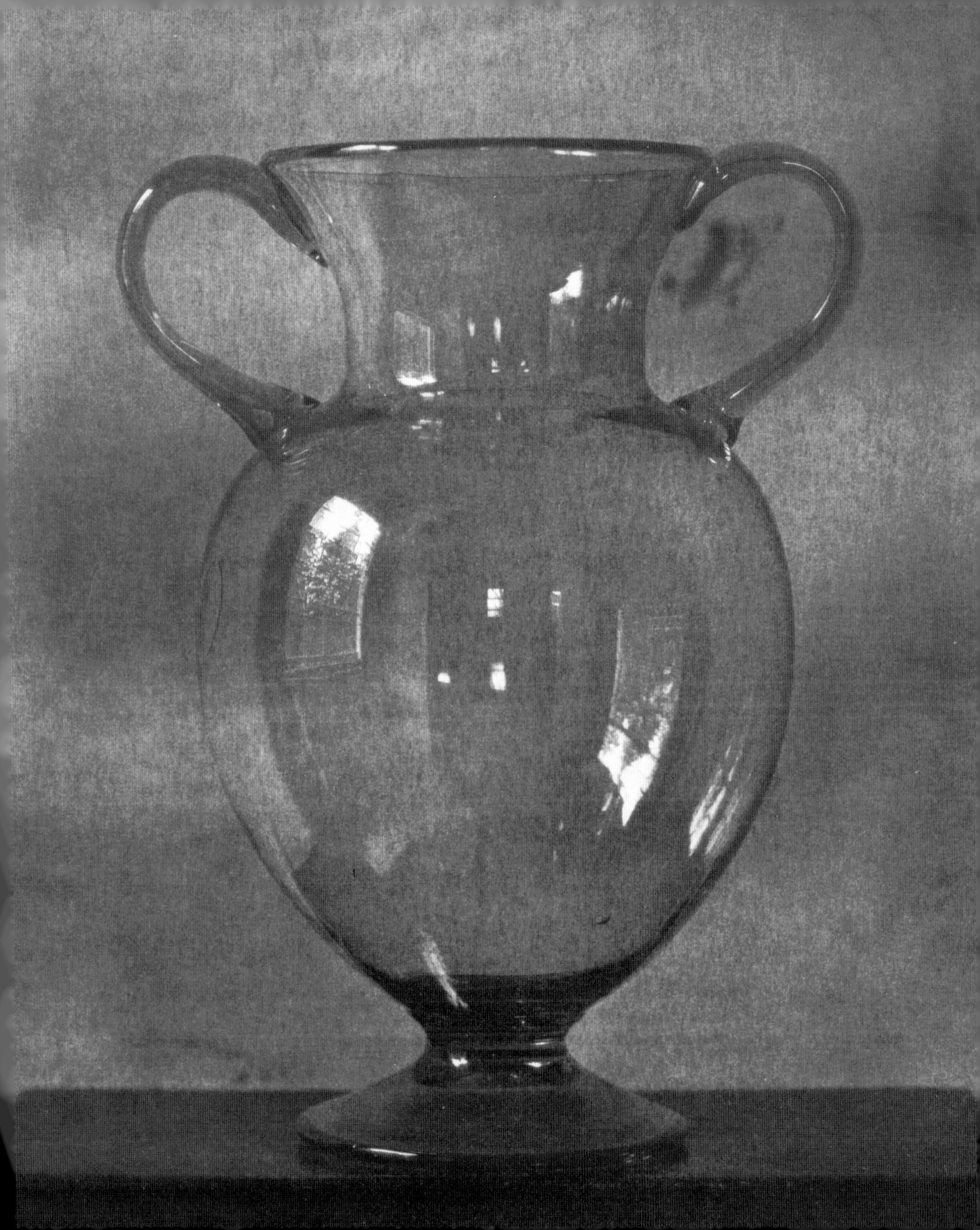

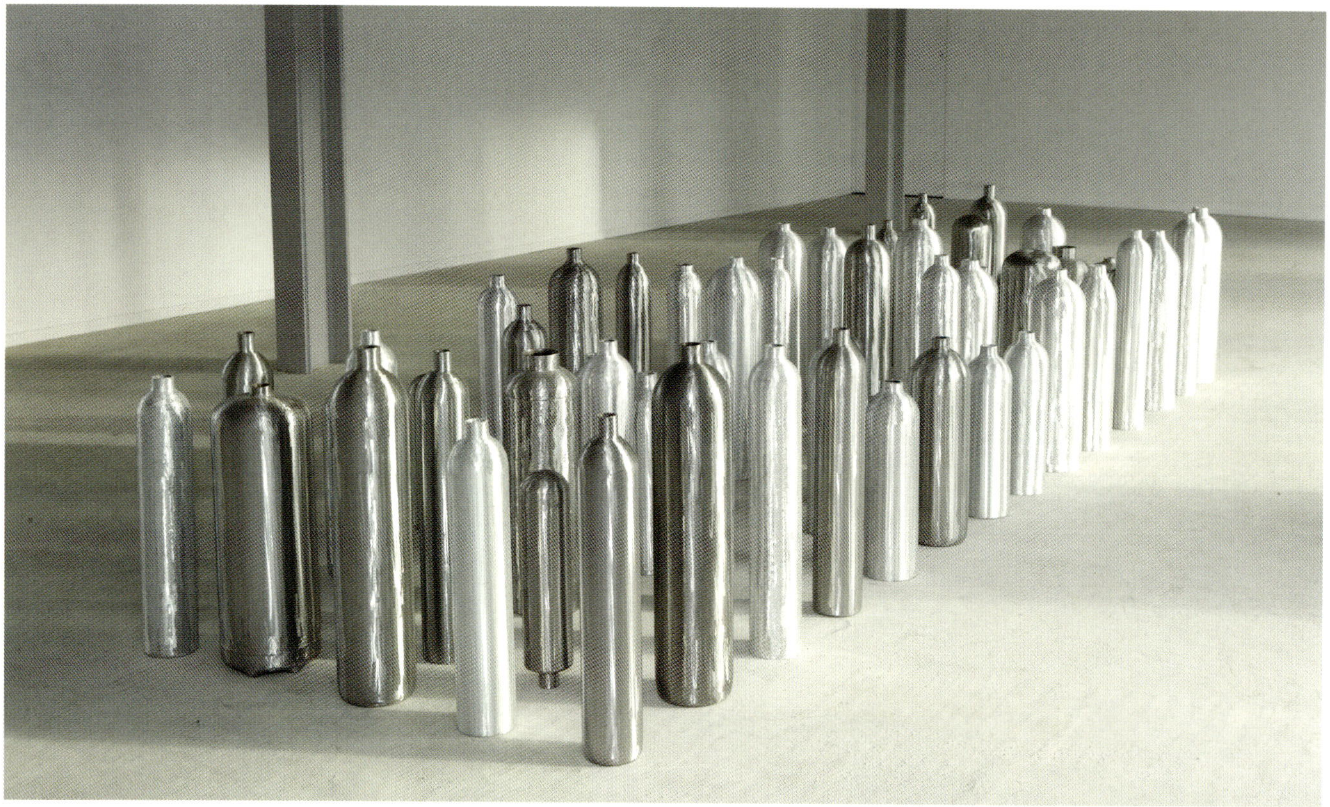

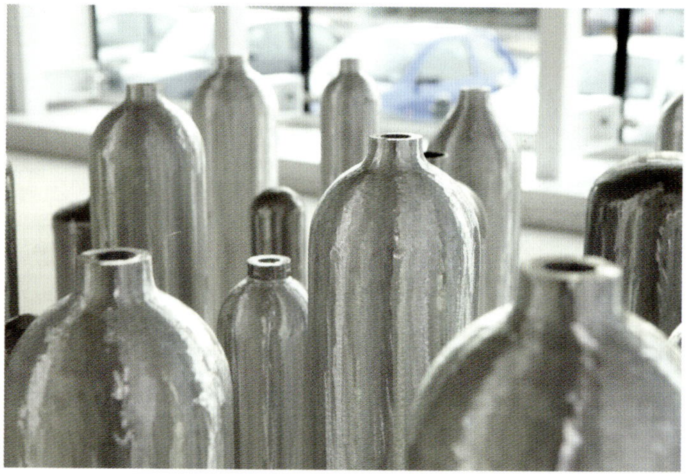

Tony Charles's *Still Life Unpainted* features ordinary metal gas containers of the kind that usually comes brightly painted in a colour that identifies the type of gas inside: orange for helium, blue for argon, red for hydrogen and black for oxygen. Charles used a simple grinder to remove all traces of this paint, while at the same time creating new marks on the empty containers. His minimalist installation calls to mind the still lifes of the early twentieth-century Italian artist Giorgio Morandi, in which the muted tones and shading of colours vary subtly between one painted bottle and the next.

Jane Simpson has experimented with the domestic still life in various media, from photographs to silicone rubber casts. Like Charles, she takes inspiration from Morandi. Her photograph *Radioactive Tupperware (revisited)* catches the moment when a soft ray of sunshine has set the modest vessels aglow. Her more robust, colourful and often comical rubber tableaux (many of the larger pieces are floppy and limp), for example *Baroque Bouquet*, look further back in art history for their genesis.

Lisa Milroy has been documenting the everyday object since the early years of her career, initially painting women's shoes in pairs that, while lined up in rows and columns recalling the classical grid, are somehow askew, a bit off kilter, disrupted and disturbing. Other series have seen her depict light bulbs, shirts and vases, usually from memory, in an effort to capture their essence. Her curatorial interest in objects, in ordering them and in finding their underlying systems of being, can be seen in the way she reduces them to almost abstract memories.

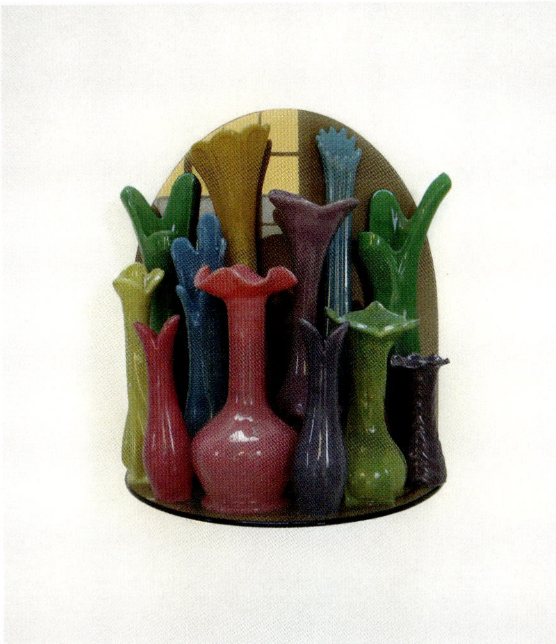

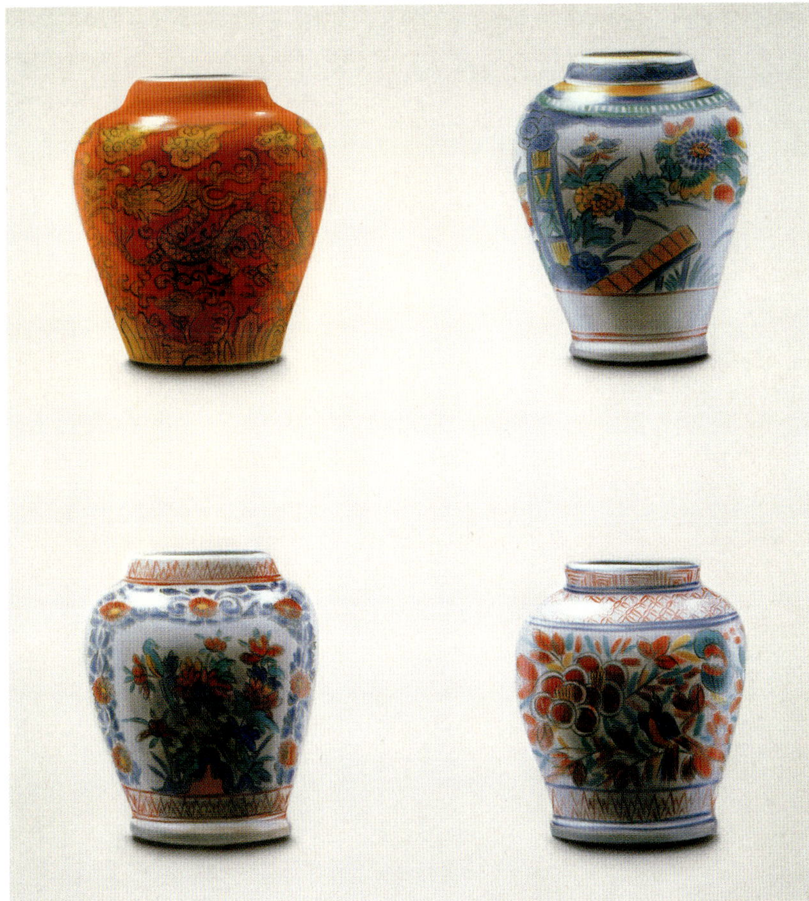

OPPOSITE
Tony Charles
Still Life Unpainted, 2012
(installation view and detail)
steel and aluminium

ABOVE LEFT
Jane Simpson
Baroque Bouquet, 2006
platinum-based silicone
and Perspex

ABOVE RIGHT
Lisa Milroy
Four Vases, 2006
oil on canvas

RIGHT
Jane Simpson
Radioactive Tupperware
(***revisited***), 2012
archival digital giclée print

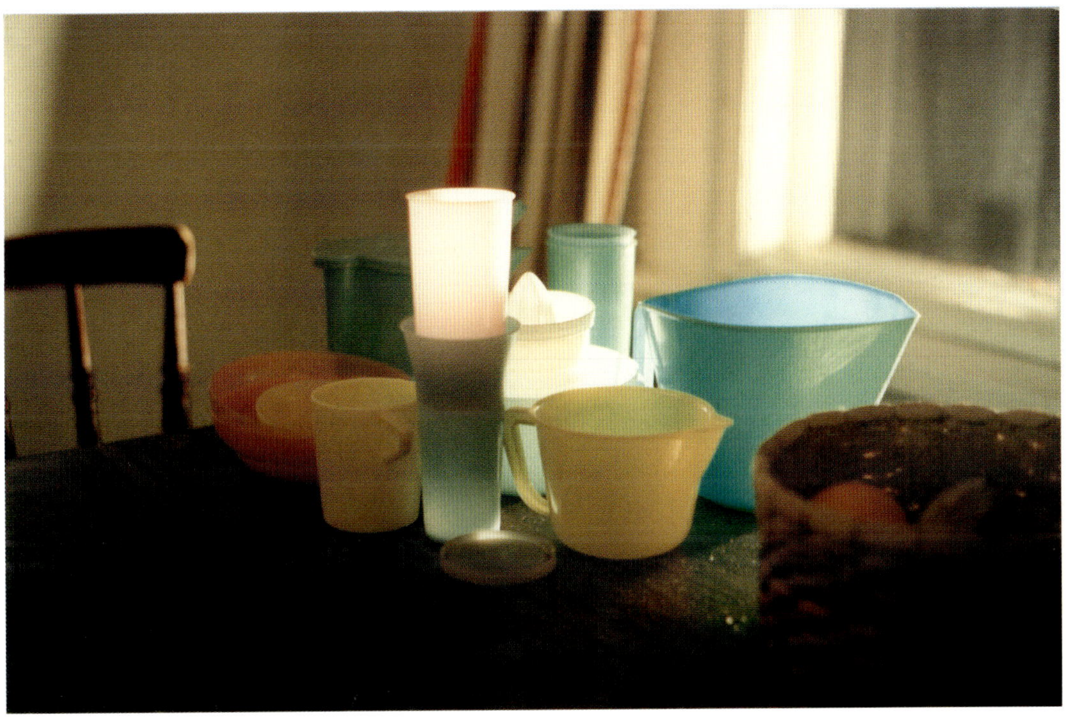

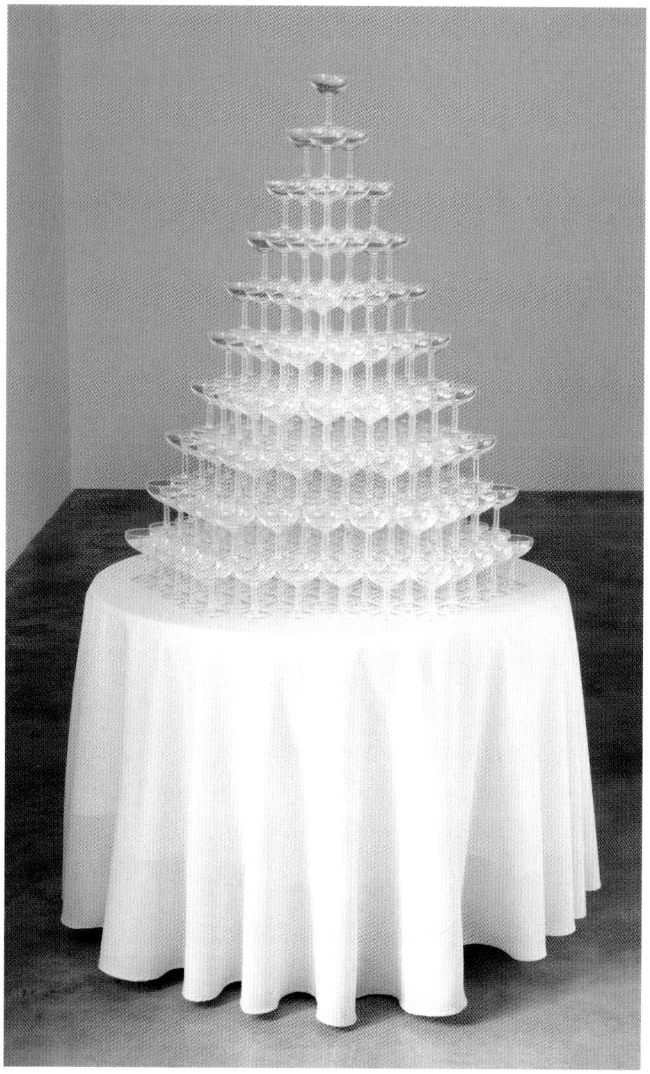

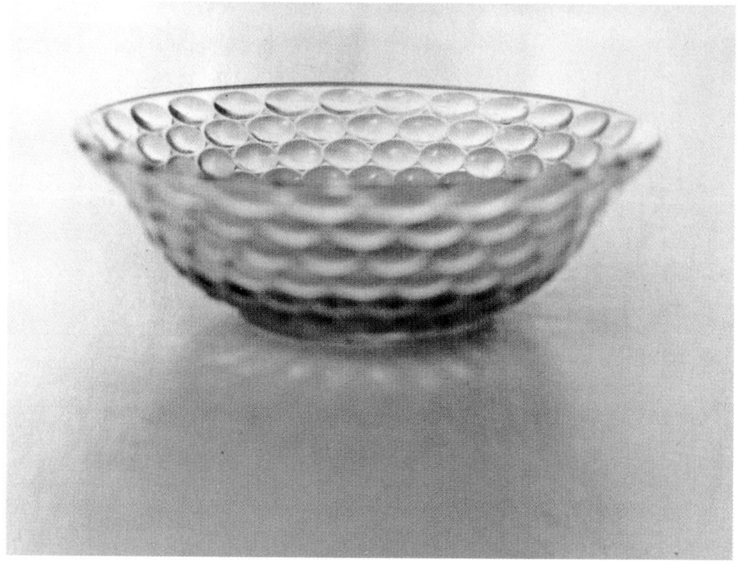

ABOVE LEFT
Peter Coffin
***Untitled (Champagne Pyramid)*, 2010**
table on wheels with motor, champagne glasses

ABOVE RIGHT
Renata Hegyi
***For Cherries*, 2003**
gelatin silver print

OPPOSITE
Matthew Darbyshire
***Untitled: Shelves No. 8*, 2011**
various glass and plastic components, shelving units and Perspex cases

Peter Coffin's sculpture *Untitled (Champagne Pyramid)* and **Renata Hegyi**'s photograph *For Cherries* both celebrate empty glass vessels that seem to await an expected visitor. These works are empty of all human presence and yet their subjects hint at past, present and possible narratives of human engagement. Of the viewer's ability to locate meaning in his works, Coffin has said: 'The truth is that man's capacity for symbol-mongering in general and language in particular is so intimately part and parcel of his human being, of his perceiving and knowing, of his very consciousness itself, that it is all but impossible for him to focus on the magic prism through which he sees everything else.'

Matthew Darbyshire's works also hint at an absent human participant. His collection of objects placed in vitrines recall the works of Marcel Duchamp, Jeff Koons and Damien Hirst, as much as personal collectors or hoarders. Contemporary and retro goods occupy the same space, as if chosen by a very odd decorator. The objects of *Untitled: Shelves No. 8* all seem to have been chosen for their colour, while those included in other works (*Stool Series*, 2010) were selected for their shape. Darbyshire explains his motivations as an artist: 'I'm wary of consumerism – particularly the agendas of those who abuse it....I don't set out to make work that is "anti-consumerist". I make work in response to that which surrounds me – that which most interests me and that which I am drawn to. It's probably a combination of formal attribute, social and political implication, personal association and whim....'

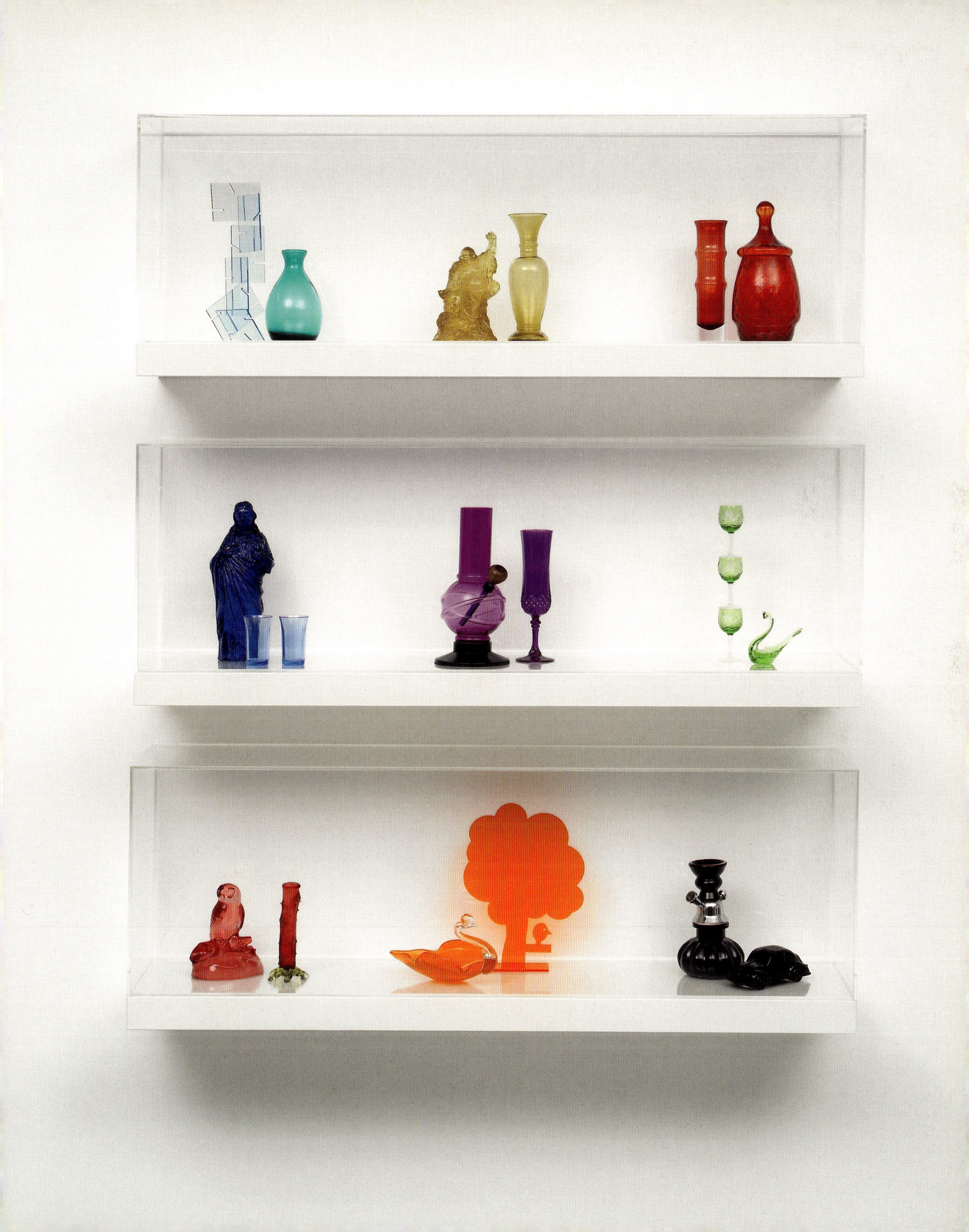

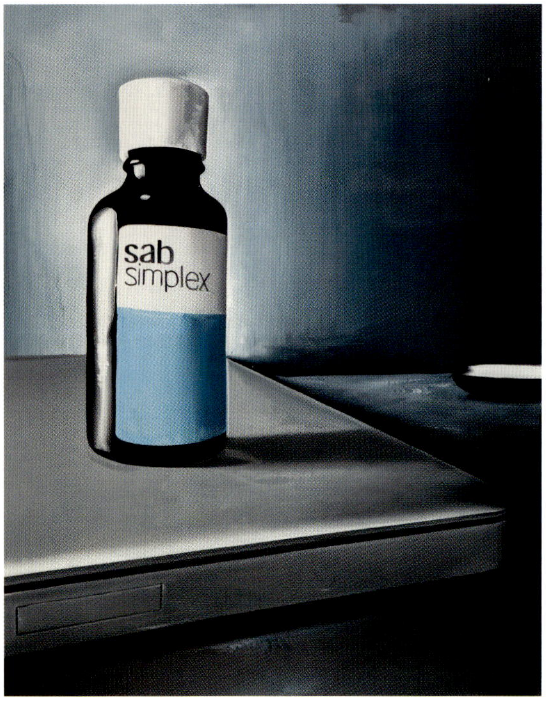

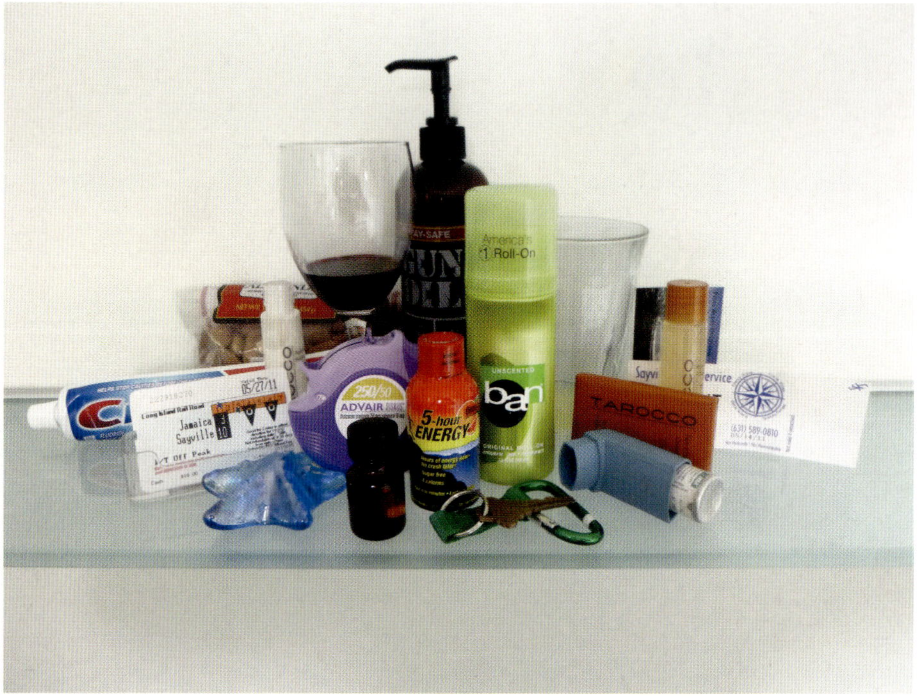

Wilhelm Sasnal, **Darren Jones** and **Michael Craig-Martin** all use the everyday object to achieve a certain effect in their works. Whether executed in a stylized, almost graphic manner (Craig-Martin), a more painterly fashion (Sasnal) or as sculptural objects (Jones), their shared fascination with the everyday allows the viewer to contemplate the often overlooked objects littered throughout our homes.

In his paintings Sasnal attempts to hone in on the essence of things: flowers, books, people, landscapes or even, in *Untitled*, a small bottle of Sab Simplex, a baby remedy for bad tummies (the artist has small children), which sits atop a closed laptop. Jones's *A Time and a Place* displays the cluster of 'personal objects which one accumulates on short trips away from home', according to the artist. 'They exist together only momentarily in the hotel room or friend's apartment, dispersed, discarded or left behind when we leave,' yet they speak volumes about their invisible owner, as they include an inhaler, poppers, an energy drink, deodorant and silicon-based 'Gun Oil' lubricant. In Craig-Martin's *Eye of the Storm* objects overlap and merge, and viewers are left to construct meaning on their own. Craig-Martin prefers these household goods 'because they're so familiar, they're like a universal language, anybody can see them'.

ABOVE LEFT
Wilhelm Sasnal
Untitled, 2011
oil on canvas

ABOVE RIGHT
Darren Jones
A Time and a Place, 2011
various elements

OPPOSITE
Michael Craig-Martin
Eye of the Storm, 2002
acrylic on canvas

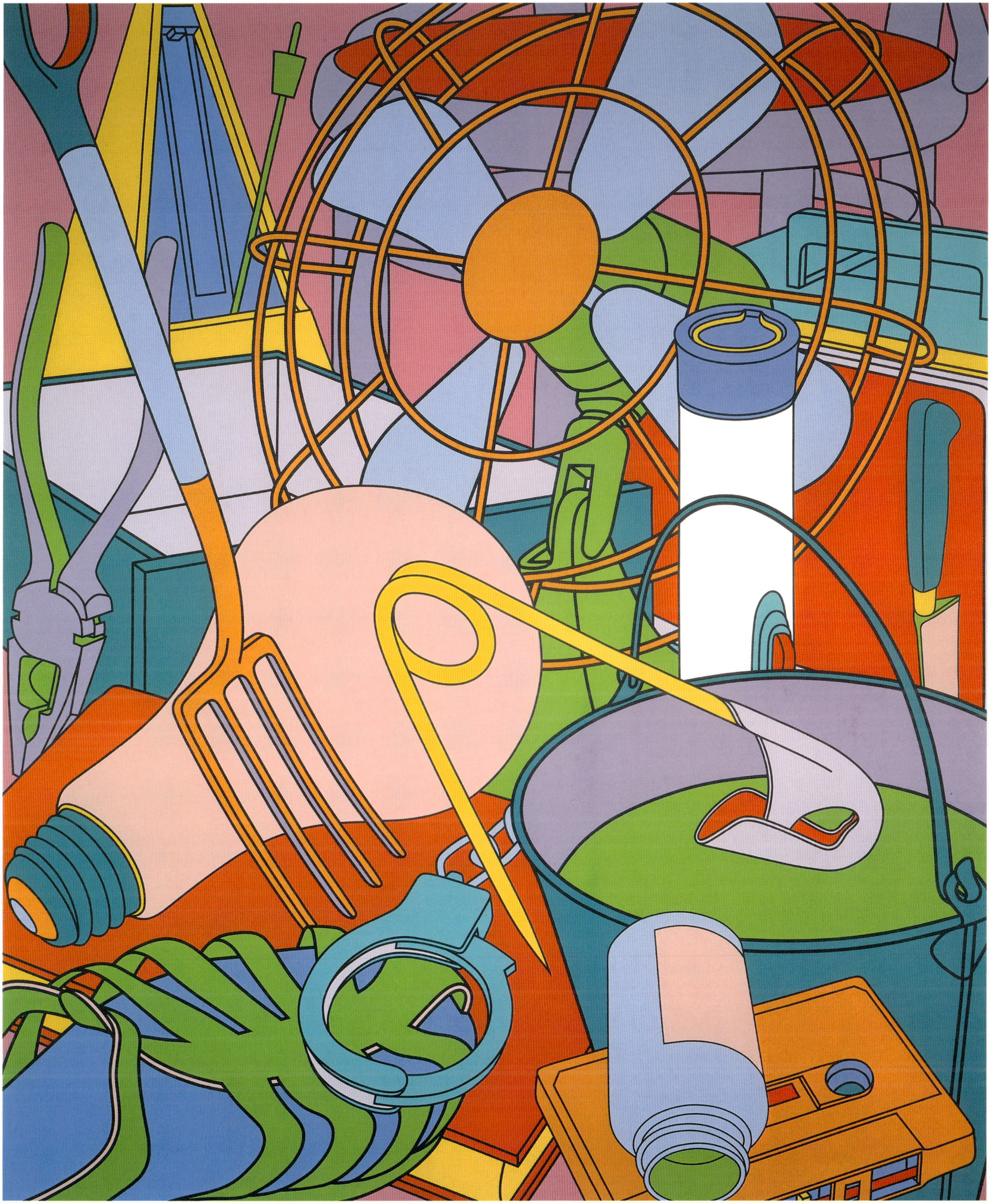

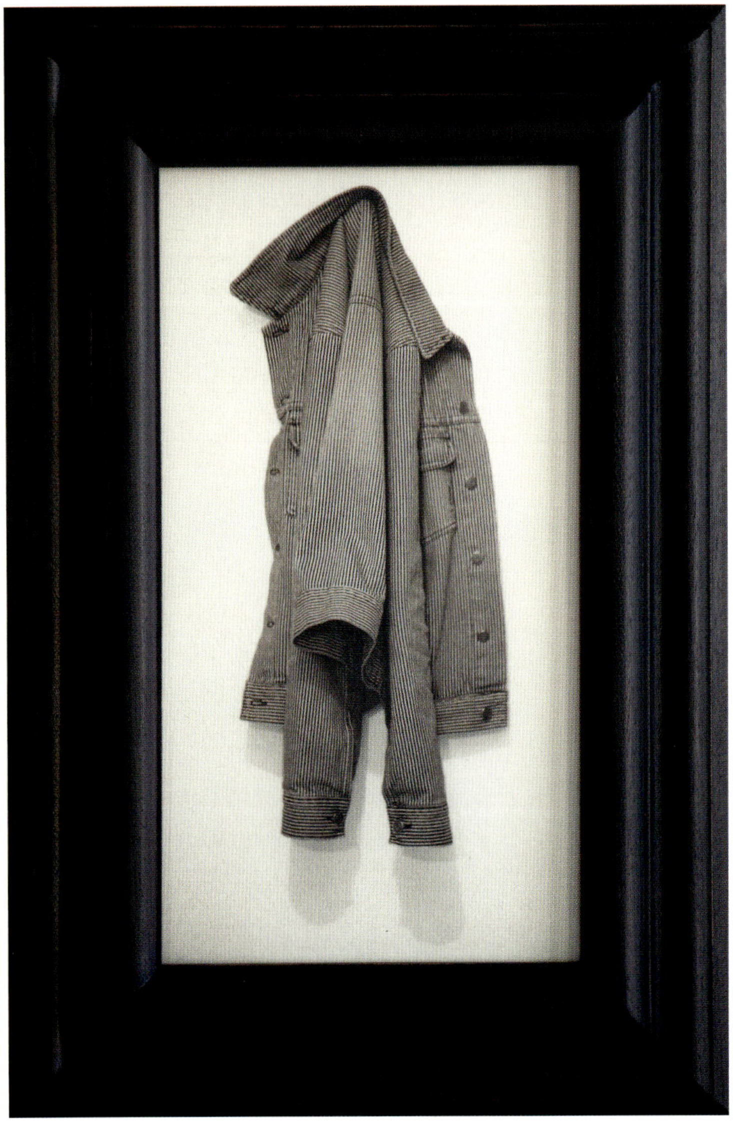

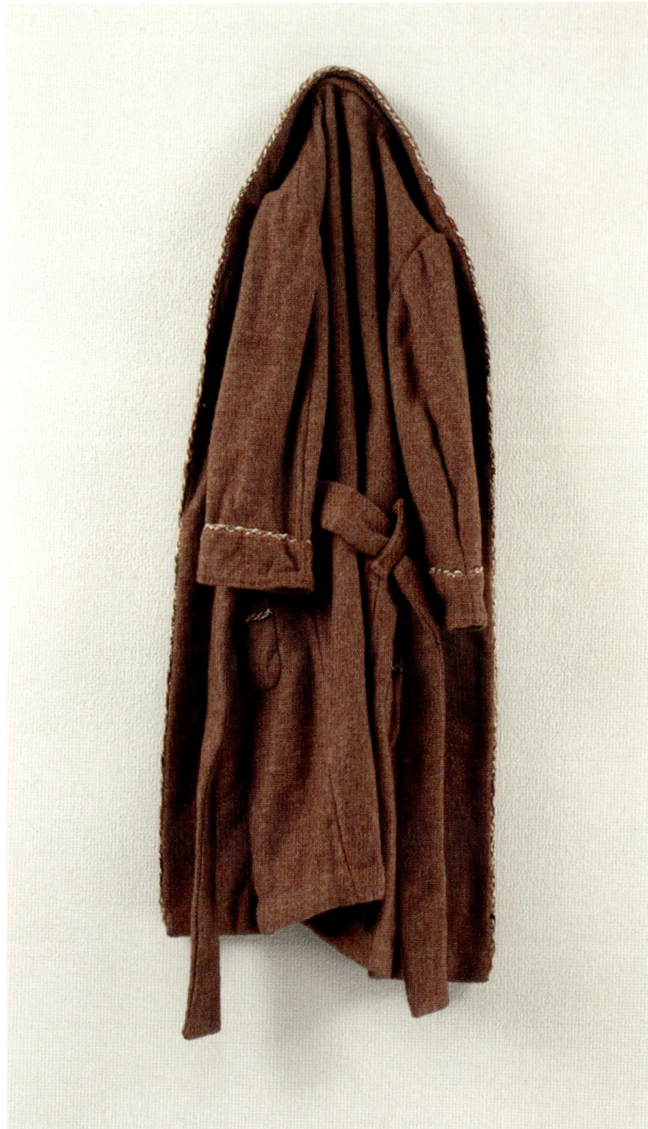

Jefferson Hayman's framed photograph *My Jacket*, **Charles LeDray**'s sculpture *Becoming/FIGHT* and **Colin Smith**'s oil painting *Overcoat 1* all feature an item of male clothing that, hanging limply from a wall or in an indeterminate space, has taken on the quality of shed skin. While Hayman photographed his jacket and Smith painted his overcoat, LeDray made an actual bathrobe, though at a tiny scale (it measures only fifty-three cm top to bottom).

Andro Semeiko investigates in his works how objective it is possible to be when depicting everyday objects. Whether painting foodstuffs, homewares, clothes, watches or other consumer items, Semeiko aims for an almost scientific presentation. Each object is surrounded only by darkness, as if resting upon a lab slide.

ABOVE LEFT
Jefferson Hayman
My Jacket, 2010
platinum print and
artist-made frame

ABOVE RIGHT
Charles LeDray
Becoming/FIGHT, 1992
flannel, thread, silk and
cotton

OPPOSITE LEFT
Colin Smith
Overcoat 1, 2005
oil on canvas

OPPOSITE TOP RIGHT
Andro Semeiko
Black Shoe, 2005
acrylic on canvas

OPPOSITE BOTTOM RIGHT
Jan Merta
Ambiciózní fuga /
Ambitious Fugue, 2008–9
oil on canvas

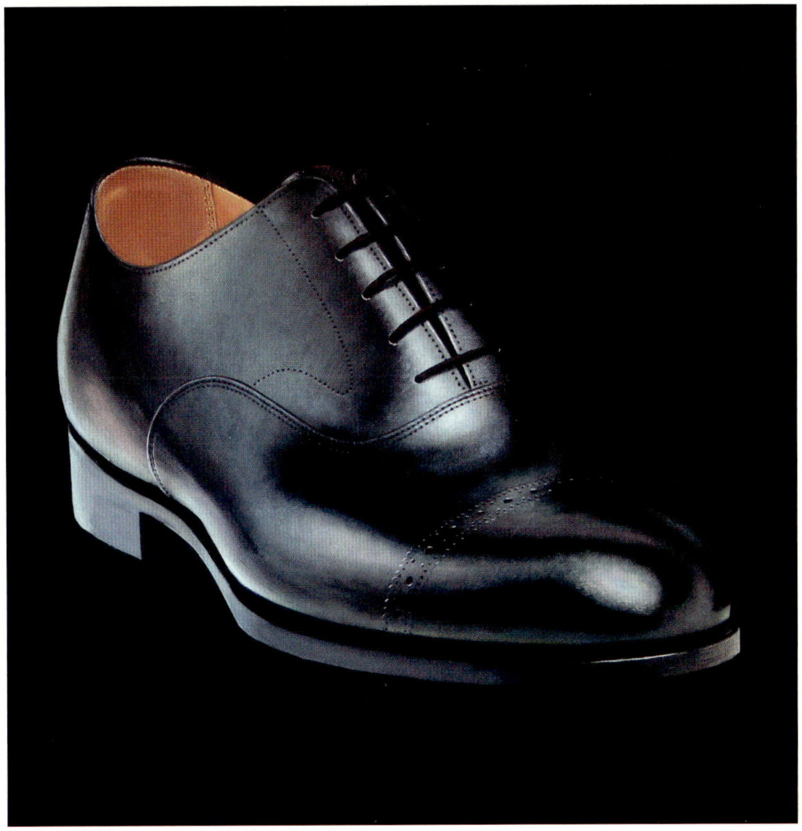

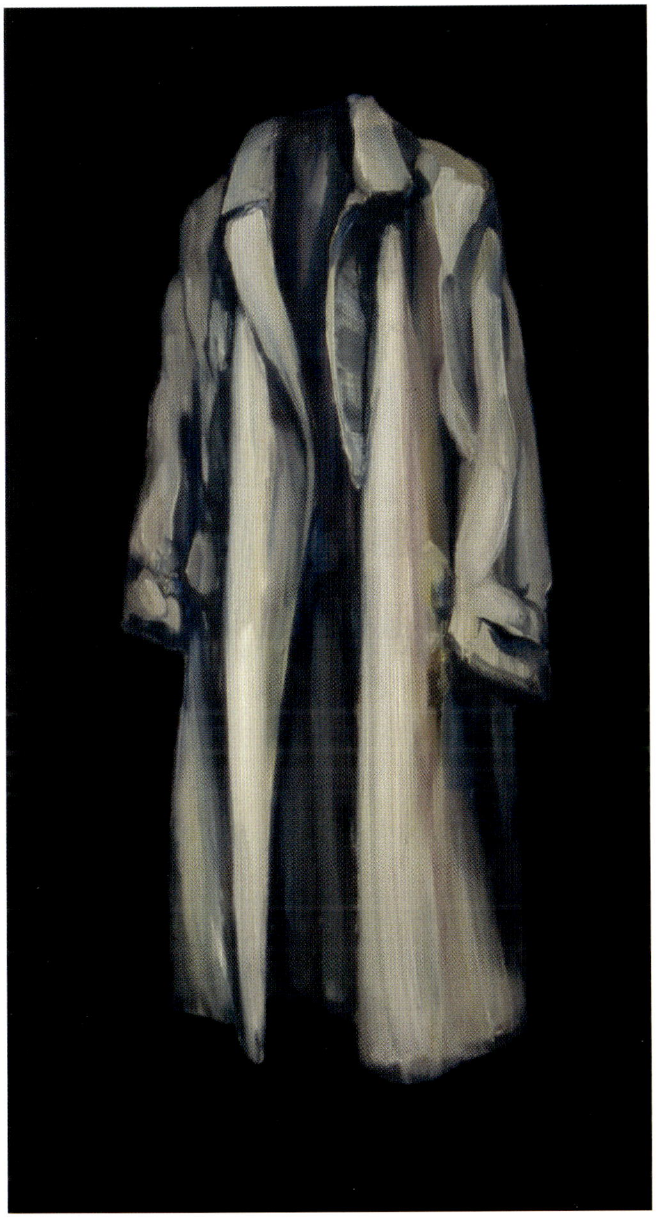

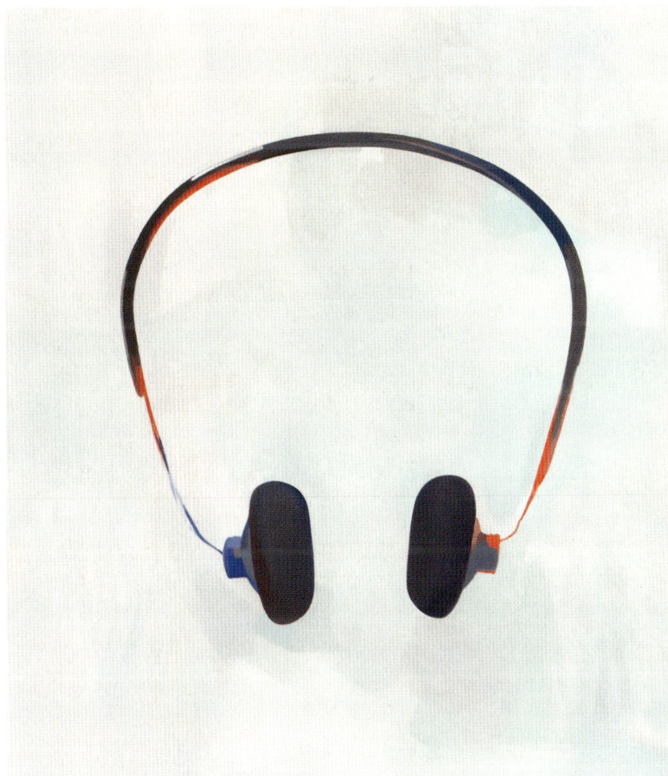

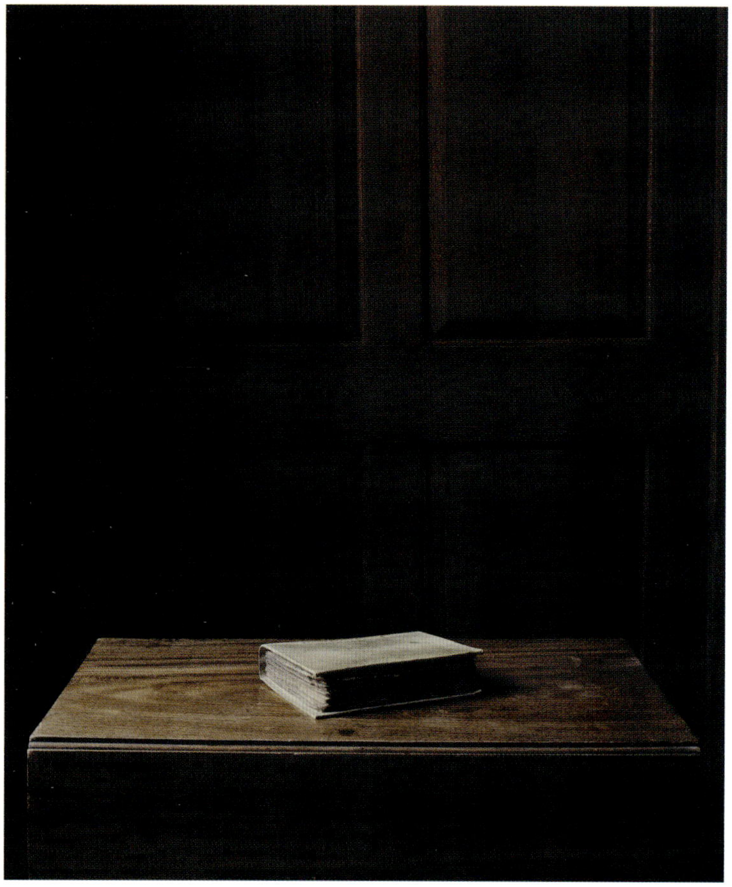

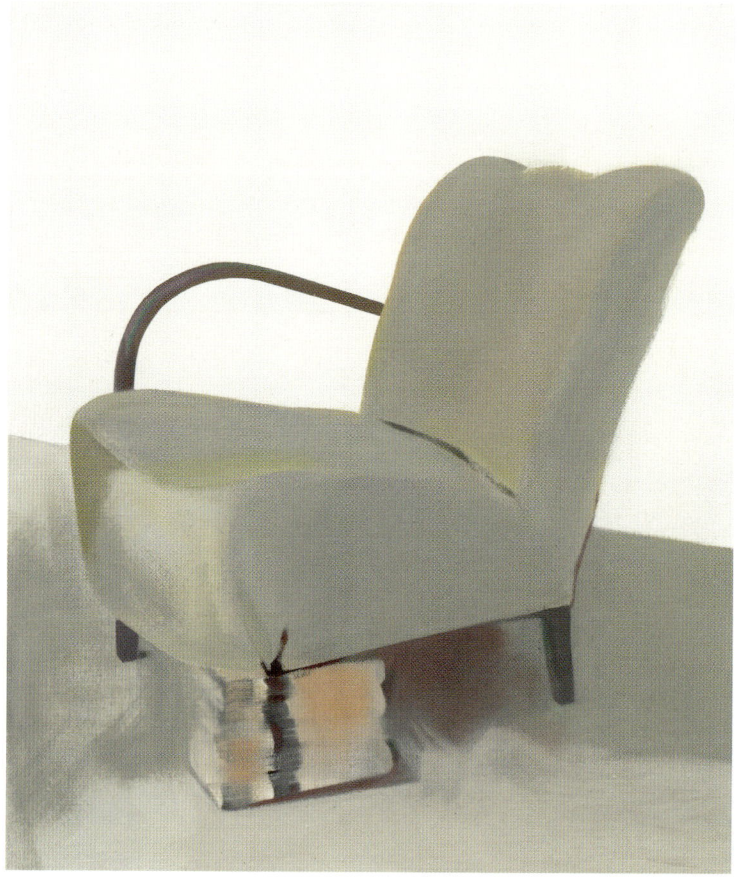

ABOVE LEFT
Daniel Gustav Cramer
Untitled (*Eusebius – Jerome*), 2009 · C-print

ABOVE RIGHT
Jan Merta · *Solidarita* (*Polovina sebraných spisů J. W. Goetha*) / *Solidarity* (*Half of the Collected Writings of J. W. Goethe*), 2008–9 oil on canvas

To create *Untitled* (*Eusebius – Jerome*) **Daniel Gustav Cramer** photographed the Eusebius–Jerome manuscript, the oldest book (dating from 378 AD) in the Bodleian Library, Oxford. It contains detailed accounts of all the then known histories of mankind's origins, from Adam and Eve to ancient Greek and Roman mythology. Cramer photographed the book shut, as if history itself is a closed book, inaccessible to all.

Jan Merta selects everyday objects as the basis for his paintings and at first they might seem simple representations. But there is always a twist. In *Solidarita* the books stacked together to hold up the three-legged chair are identified in the work's full title as those of the German poet Goethe, which alters how a viewer *reads* and understands the painting. The odd, subdued colour palette and flatness of Merta's works underscore these enigmatic qualities. Is it a classical fugue that can be heard playing in the headphones of *Ambiciózní fuga / Ambitious Fugue* (page 149) or something more contemporary? Merta's works update traditional still-life tropes by reinterpreting them with modern pictorial equivalents.

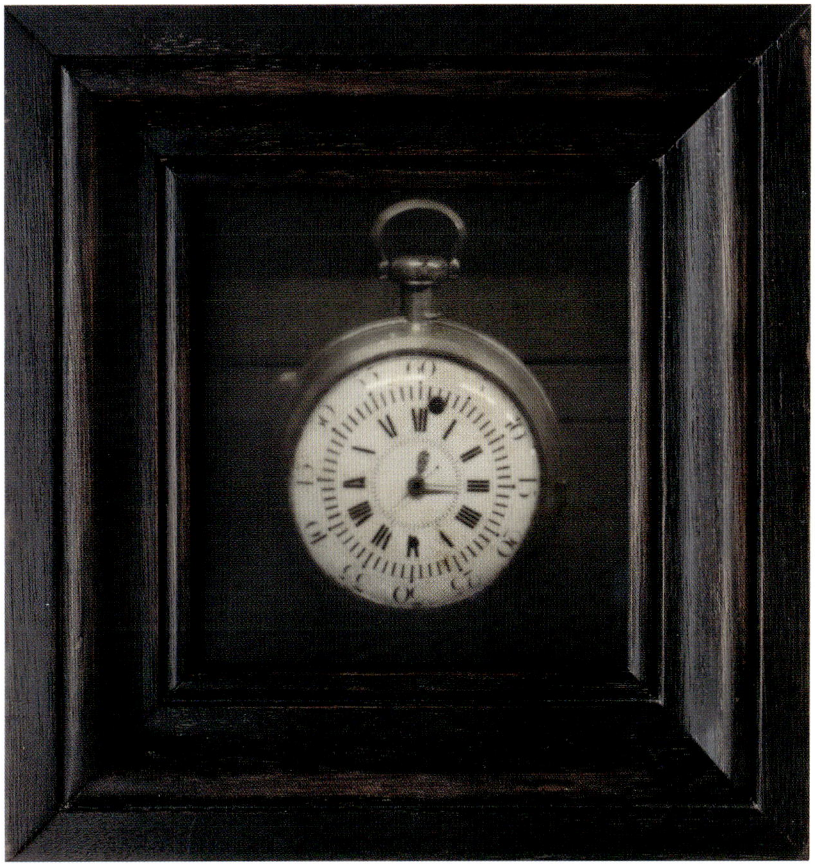

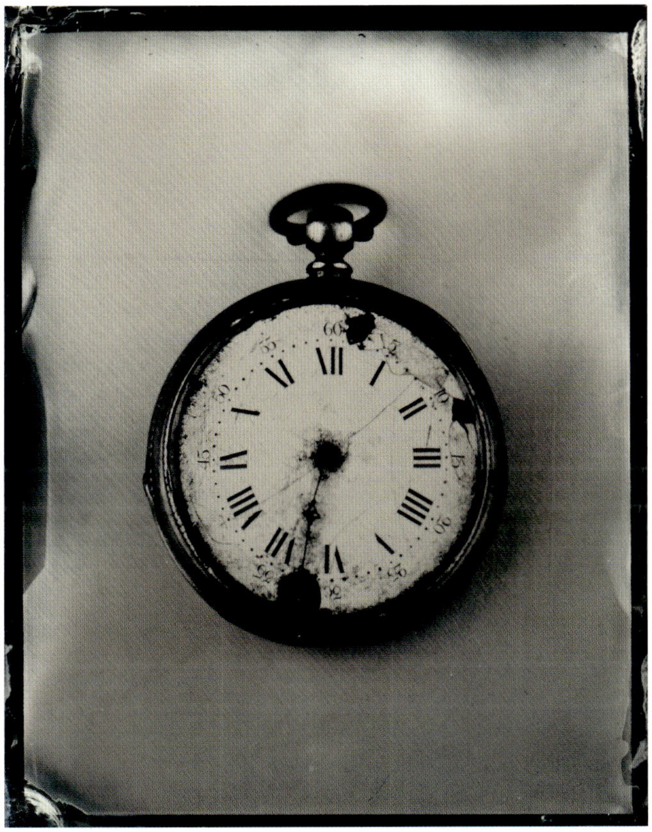

LEFT
Susan Seubert
Pocket Watch, 2011
ambrotype

ABOVE
Jefferson Hayman
Pocket Watch, 2007
toned silver gelatin print,
artist-made frame

Time-telling technologies (a sundial, an hourglass, a clock) can operate as metaphorical reminders of the unceasing passage of time. A broken watch or clock has additional poignancy for it alludes to death when time does stop, at least for that individual. **Susan Seubert** and **Jefferson Hayman**'s photographs of stopped pocket watches compound this symbolism with the intentionally antique appearances of their prints.

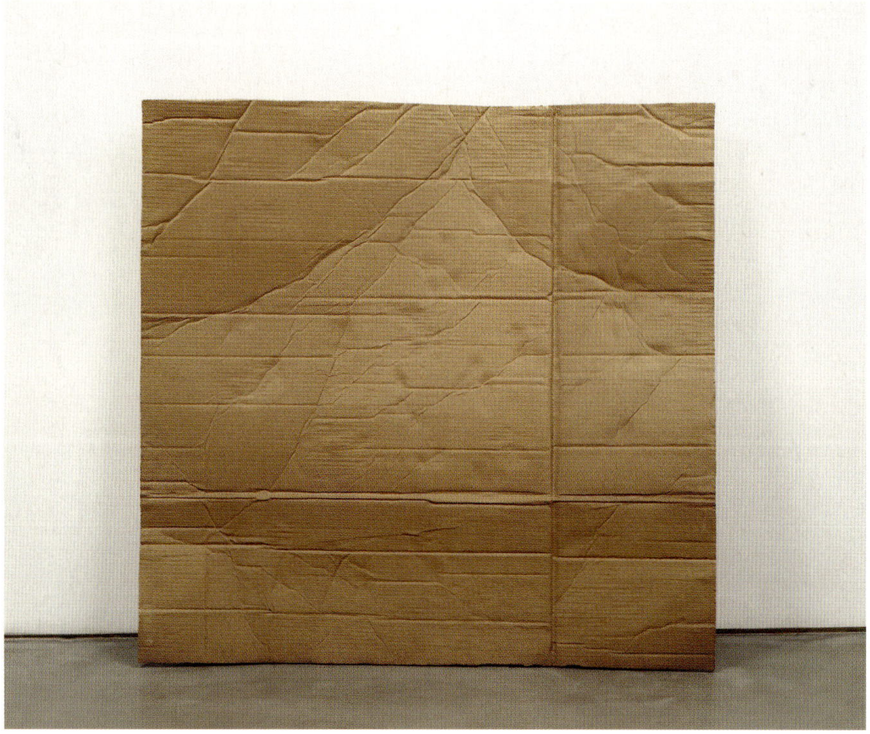

Ugo Rondinone's *still.life. (cardboard leaning on the wall)* is another work in his ongoing *still.life.* series (see page 61); here, a flattened cardboard box has been cast in bronze then painted to resemble the real thing. As with the other works presented in the artist's 2009 'Nude' exhibition, the cardboard box is shown raw and exposed, yet this apparent vulnerability is a fiction. These painted metal *trompe-l'œil* objects ape the traditional still life, which also purports to present something in its unaltered natural state despite the artifice behind its composition and creation.

Bill Jacobson's *Place* series consists only of photographs of rectanglular shapes. Of his motivations, Jacobson has commented: 'I realized what interested me most was humanly constructed space. I became drawn to the rectangle as something which really doesn't exist in nature, but which also represents an archetype of our visual journey through the world. So much of what we make is consistently rectangular.' In *Place (Series) #58* a simple cardboard box becomes the focus for a still life, mysterious and hinting at an unknown narrative.

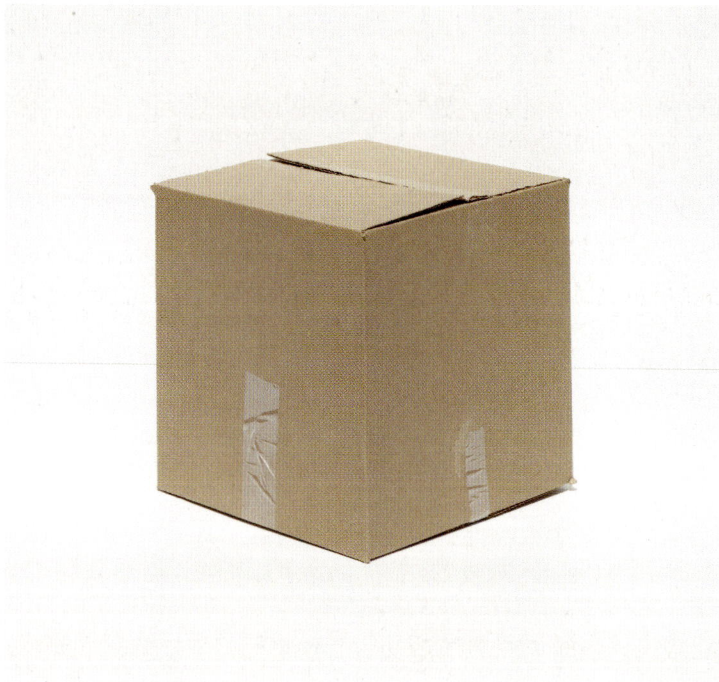

ABOVE
Ugo Rondinone
***still.life. (cardboard leaning on the wall)*, 2009**
bronze cast, lead and paint

RIGHT
Bill Jacobson
***Place (Series) #58*, 2009**
pigment print

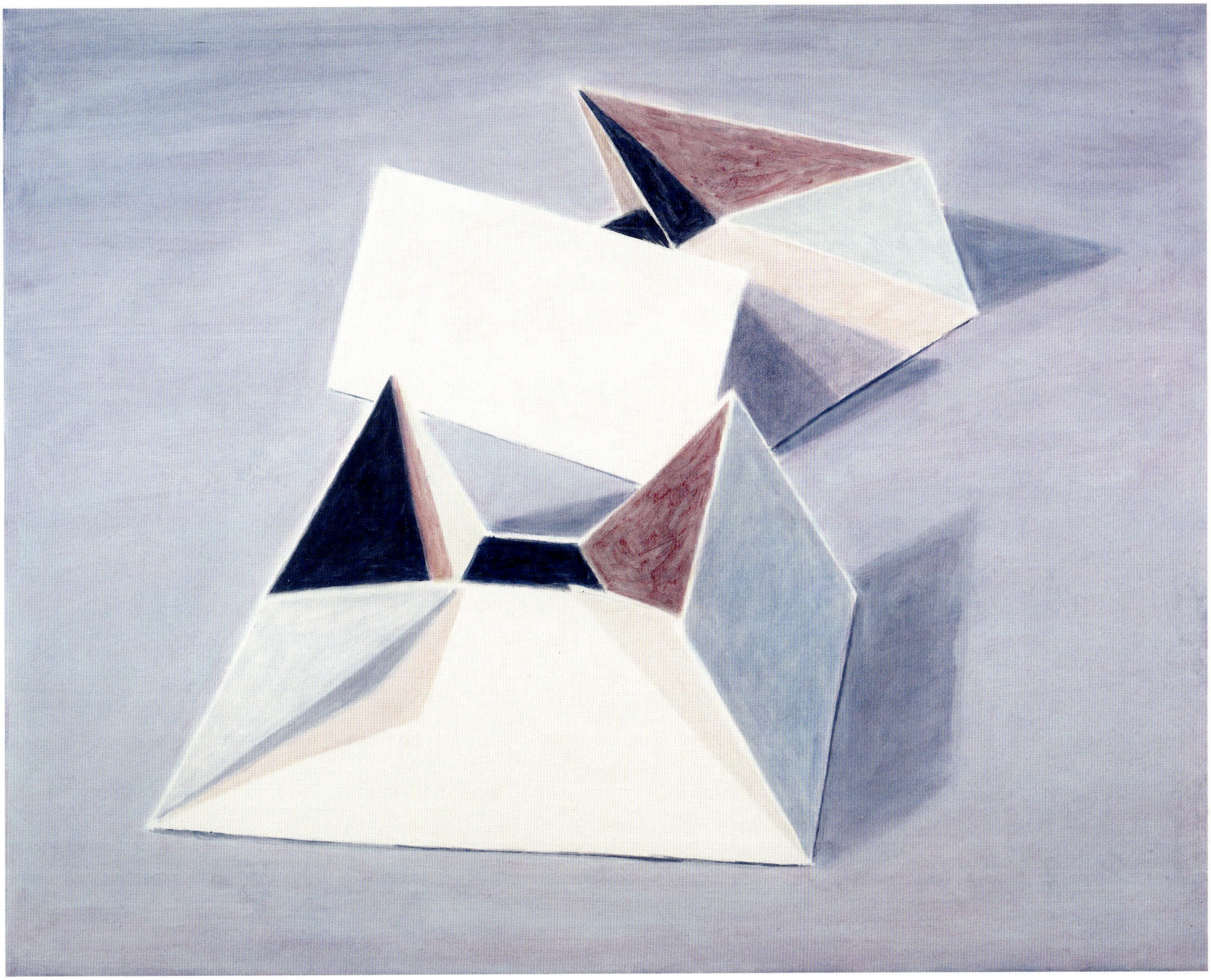

ABOVE
Bruno Pacheco
Folding Box, 2010
oil on canvas

Bruno Pacheco documents the world as he sees it. Like a diarist, he keeps a photographic record of all those things he has encountered that catch his eye, including landscapes, beached whales, a woollen cap or empty cardboard boxes. Photographs of photographs are transformed into large-scale oil paintings or smaller watercolours. In recording much of what he sees, Pacheco seeks to maintain a distance between himself and the world.

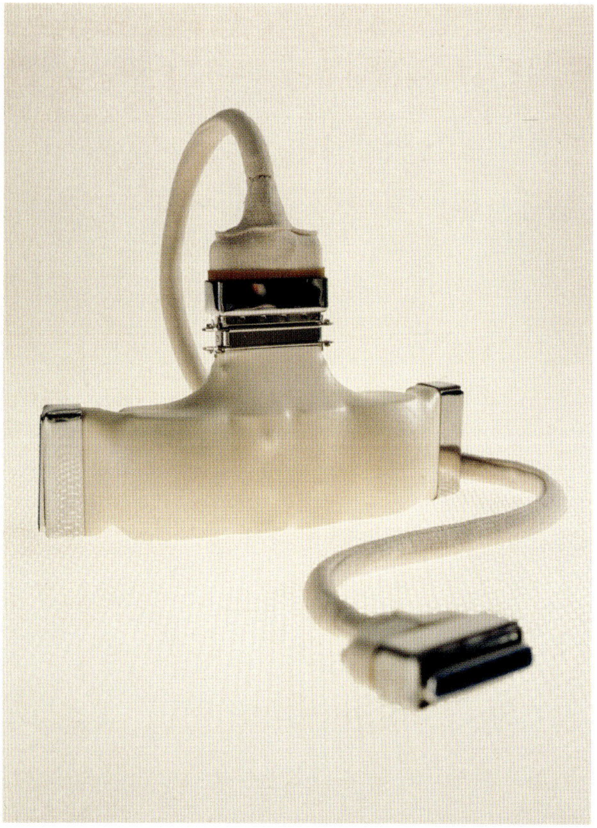

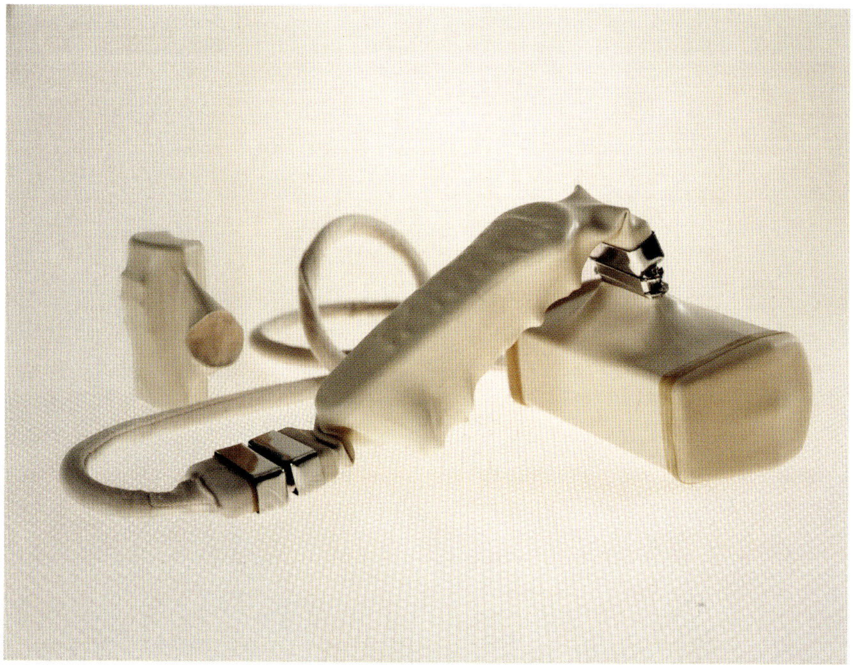

Aziz + Cucher have been at the forefront of digital art, whether airbrushing away sexual body parts for their 'Faith, Honor, and Beauty' exhibition (1992) or designing still lifes of gadgets imagined for the new millennium in 'PLASMORPHICA' (1997). The abject objects created for that exhibition, disturbing mixtures of artificial skin and computer plug-ins, were wrapped around floor-to-ceiling poles like futuristic strippers reduced to nothing but their genitalia. The accompanying photographs captured these creations, part prosthetics, part sex toys with a hint of sweat, to give new definition to the domestic still life.

Shirana Shahbazi not only photographs obvious still-life subjects (flowers, fruit, butterflies, skulls), but also complex, abstract compositions, such as [*Komposition-01-2011*]. She makes no recourse to digital means in constructing these tableaux but selects and positions physical objects in her studio, which she then photographs.

ABOVE LEFT
Aziz + Cucher
Plasmorphica
Still-Life #7, 1996
C-print

ABOVE RIGHT
Aziz + Cucher
Plasmorphica
Still-Life #2, 1996
C-print

OPPOSITE
Shirana Shahbazi
[***Komposition-01-2011***]
C-print on aluminium

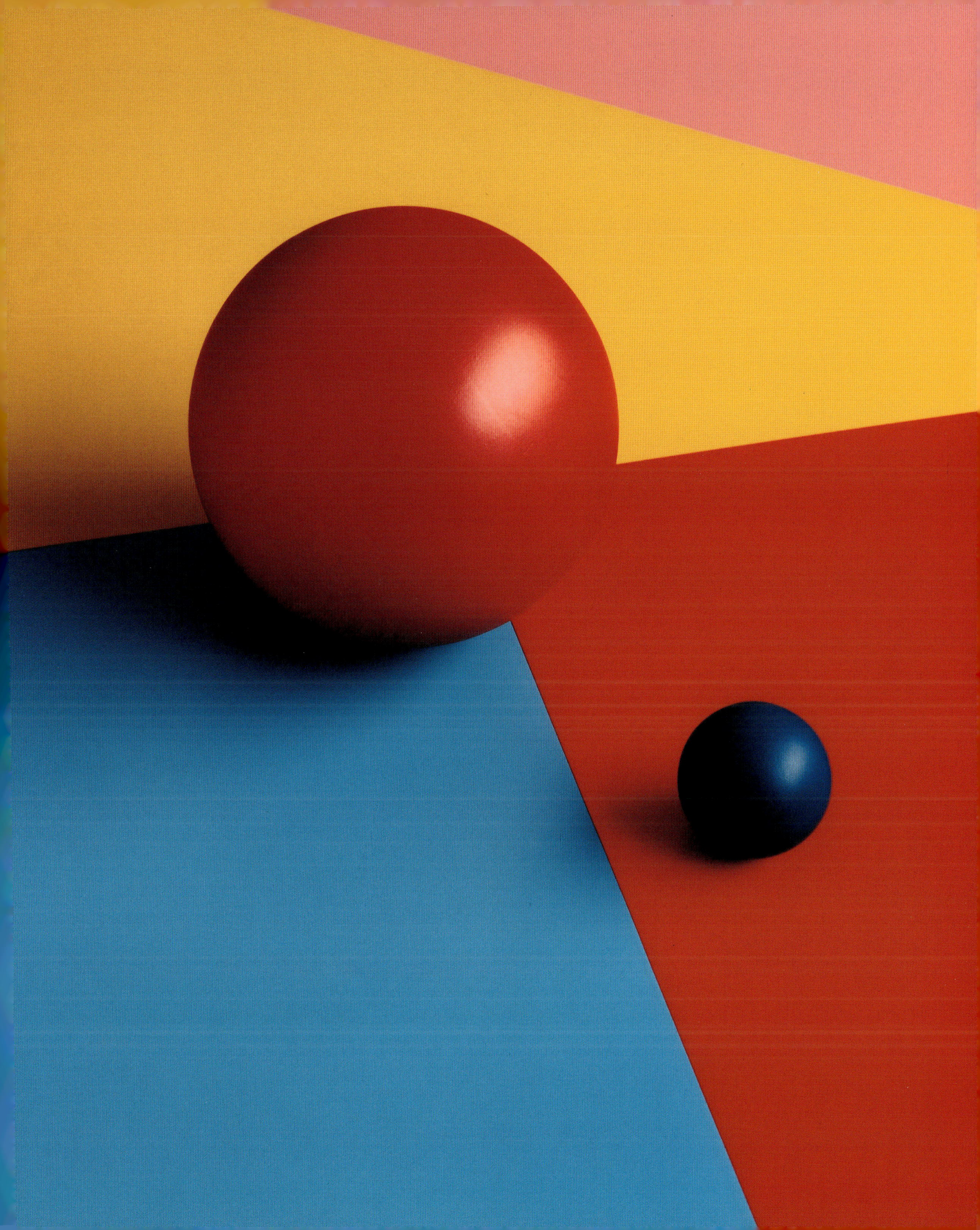

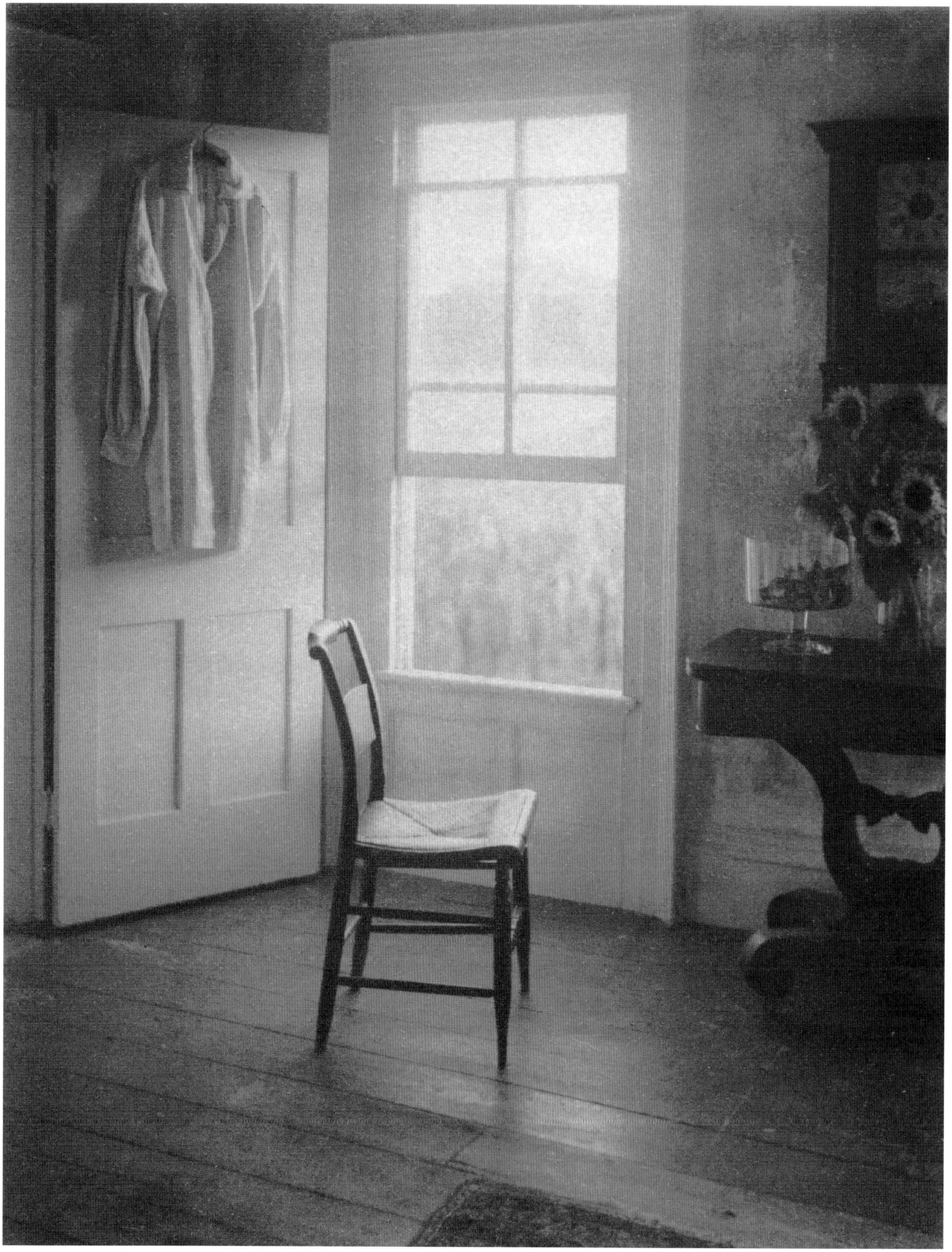

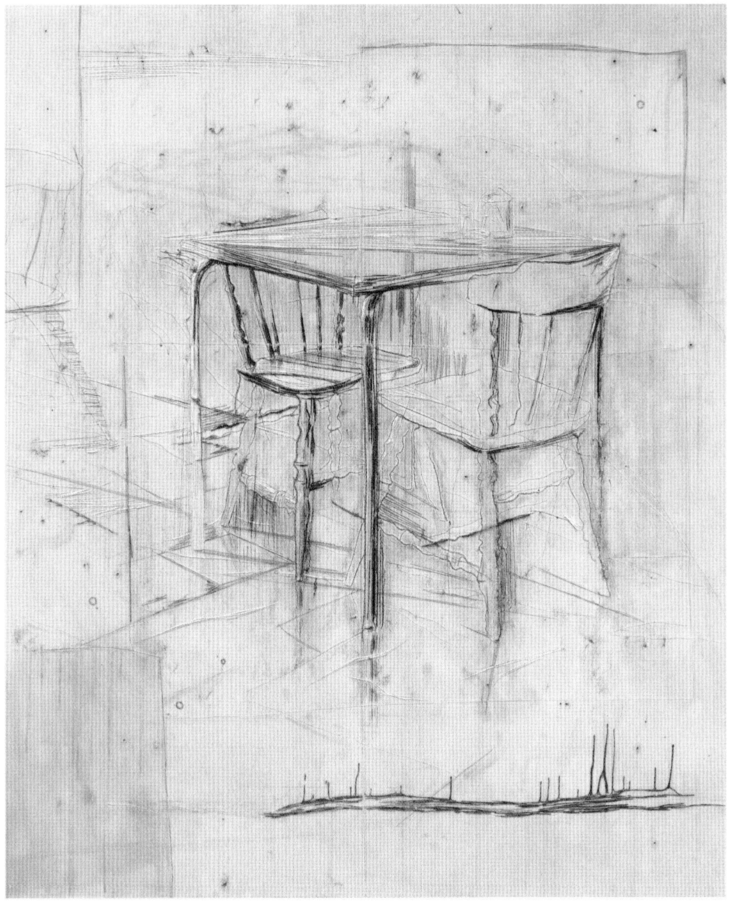

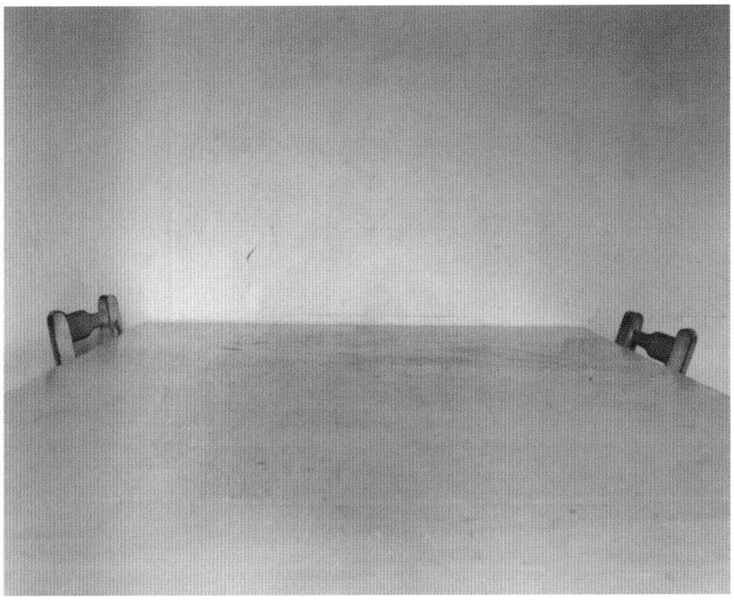

The absent individual is at the heart of **John Dugdale**'s *Empire Chair in the Gloaming*, **Renata Hegyi**'s *Dialog* and **Michael Raedecker**'s *frame*. Hegyi's photograph with its two facing chairs implies the potential for dialogue even as the divisive expanse of the table top edges out the possibility of a successful resolution. Raedecker's painting includes the same motif, his chairs pushed in tight to the table evoking an empty arena of lost conversation. Dugdale's cyanotype resembles a long-lost photograph, its gloaming, or twilight, the result of the medium's blue overcast. This moodiness and the vacant chair that sits unoccupied in the well-appointed living space recall viewers to the passage of time, from day to night, from life to death, an inevitability alluded to in all three works.

OPPOSITE
John Dugdale
Empire Chair in the Gloaming, 1994
cyanotype

ABOVE LEFT
Renata Hegyi
Dialog, 2003
gelatin silver print

ABOVE RIGHT
Michael Raedecker
frame, 2008
acrylic and thread
on canvas

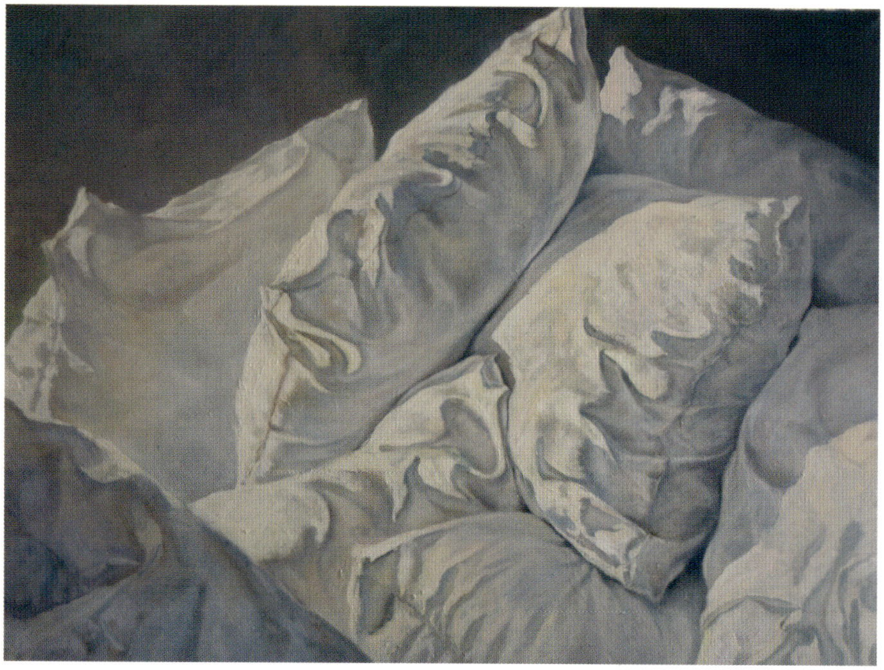

In **Derek Buckner**'s *White Series* the artist closely observes the billowing or crumpled folds of white textiles, be they hanging sheets or stuffed pillows, as in *Assemblage #2*. His interest in how light falls on fabric, creating intricate and subtle shadows, is conveyed through the fusing of abstract and representational renderings. This pile of pillows seems both inviting yet altogether full, while the dark shadows at the pillows' edges introduce an air of loss.

Jan Merta puts loss front and centre (even if the knife is slightly to the right) in *Zátiší s nožem* (*Hranice spasitelnosti*) / *Still Life with a Knife* (*The Limits of Salvationability*). The muted brown handle of the knife adds colour to an otherwise grey palette, though the possibility of bright red blood looms large. Anton Chekhov famously said a gun must only appear onstage if in a later act it is used; the title of this work and the dynamic positioning of the knife on the edge of the table suggests a similarly violent conclusion.

For her *Perfect Life* series, **Rebecca Scott** painted works that offer a harsh critique of the 'perfect' lives found in women's lifestyle magazines and catalogues. Scott takes her inspiration from images that dictate the ways in which she should make her home perfect. She recognizes that these illustrations of domestic bliss are aimed at her, not her male partner, and that it is *her* job as a woman to be the ideal wife and hostess. It is this narrative that reflects off the shining crystal in her paintings and which disrupts what would otherwise be traditional still lifes.

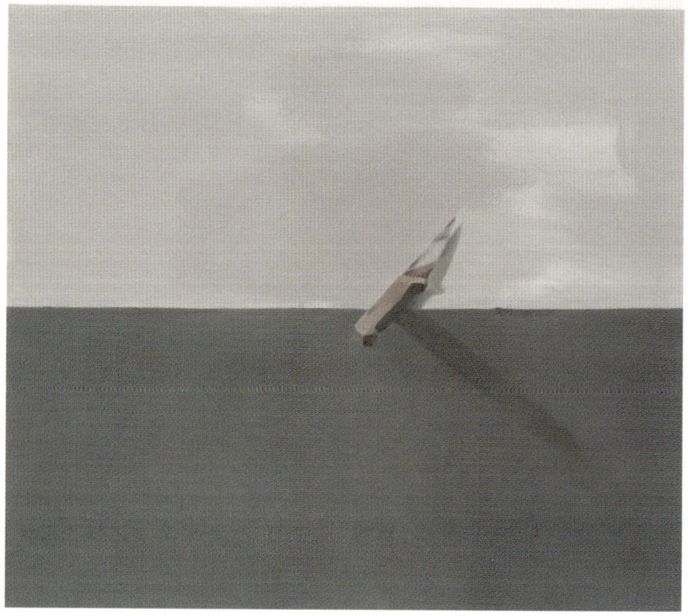

ABOVE
Derek Buckner
Assemblage #2, 2010
oil on linen

RIGHT
Jan Merta · *Zátiší s nožem* (*Hranice spasitelnosti*) / *Still Life with a Knife* (*The Limits of Salvationability*)
2009 · oil on canvas

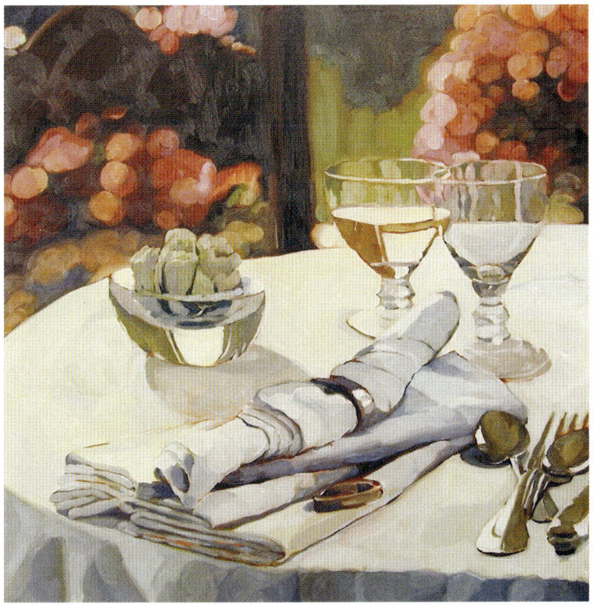

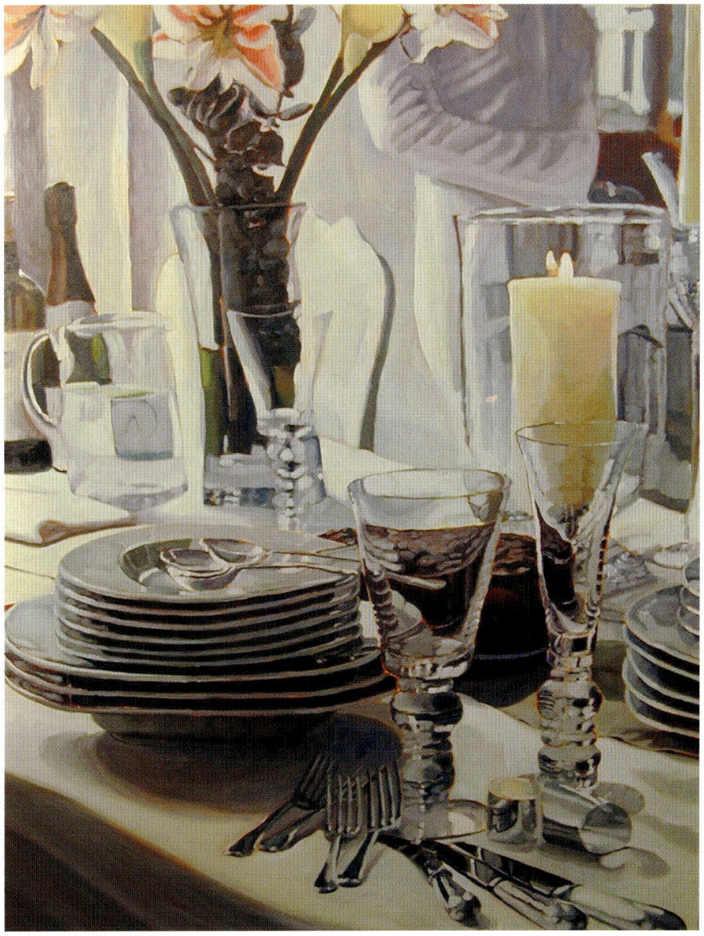

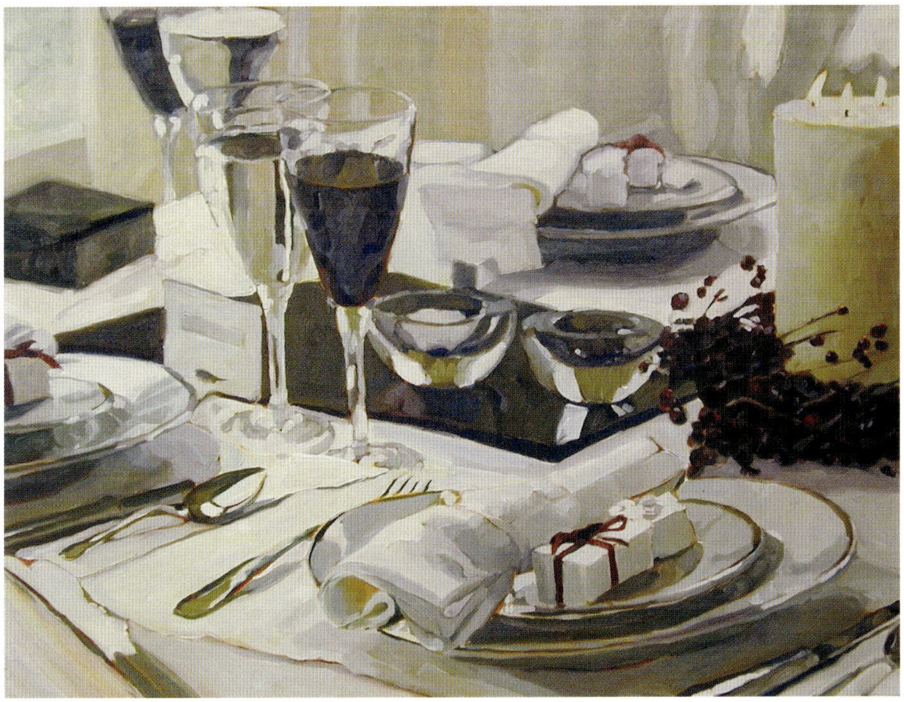

ABOVE LEFT
Rebecca Scott
***Oh, it's a perfect day*, 2005**
oil on canvas

ABOVE RIGHT
Rebecca Scott
***The Perfect Hostess*, 2006**
oil on canvas

LEFT
Rebecca Scott
***The Perfect Christmas Dinner*, 2006**
oil on canvas

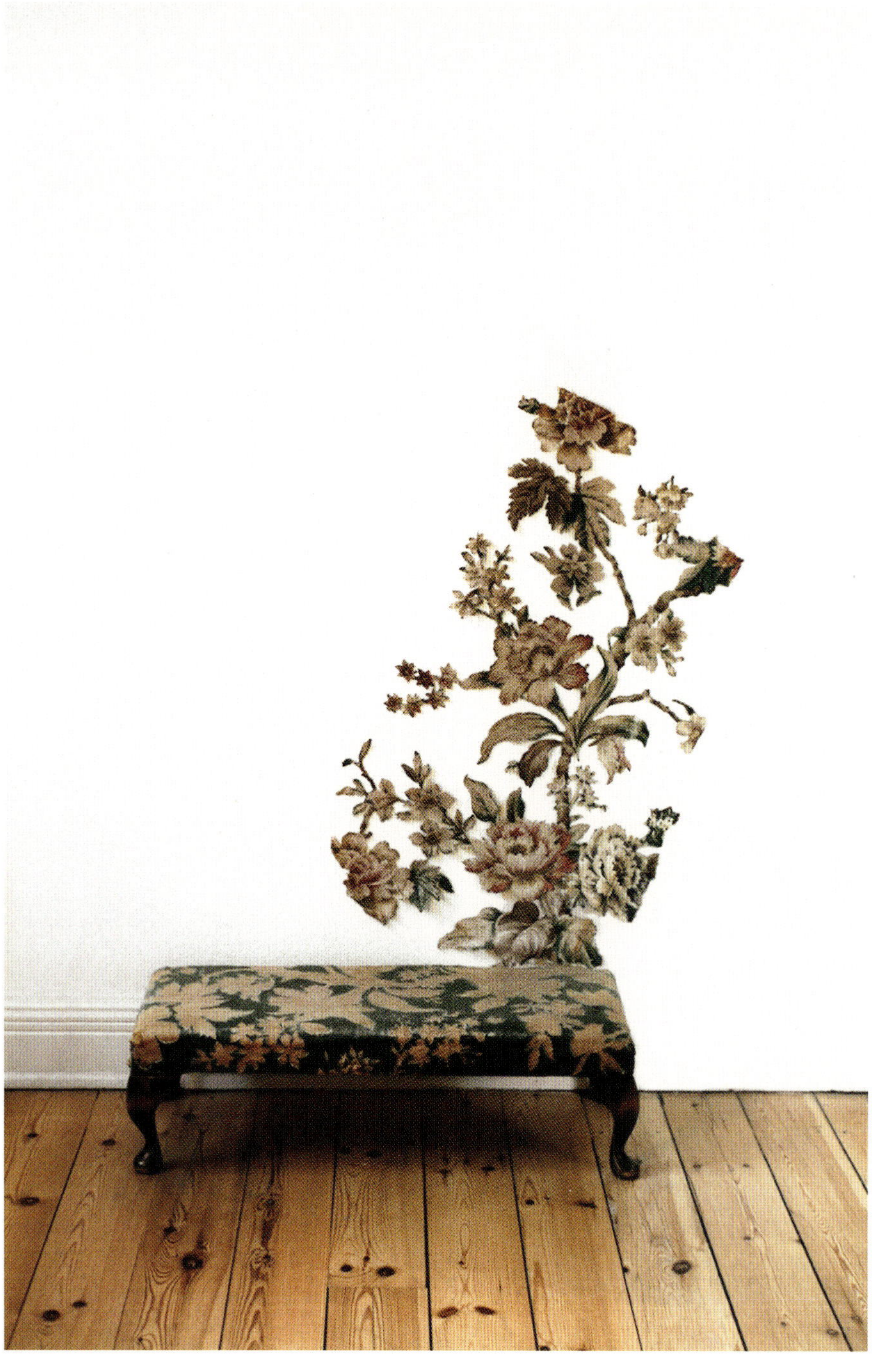

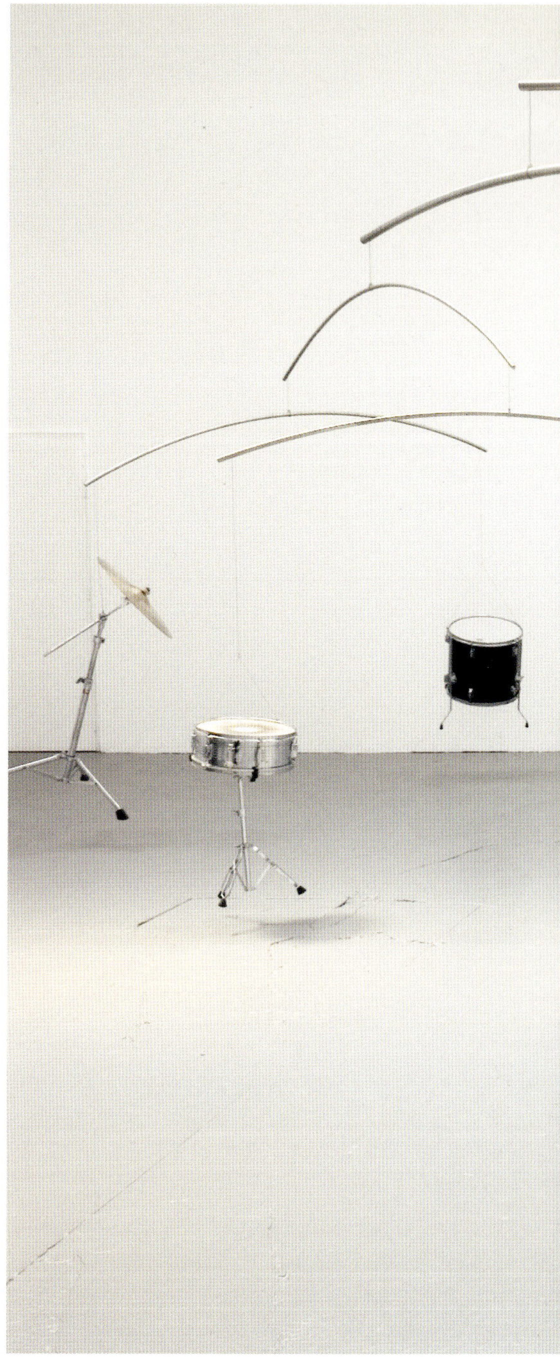

Janne Malmros has made a series of installations and sculptures by cutting out the patterns on existing objects to form new creations. In *Outfit* (2010), the flowers on a dress, once removed from the original, came to form a large sculptural work. To create *Unfold*, Malmros cut the traditional floral pattern from the upholstery of an antique footstool and mounted it onto the wall behind.

ABOVE
Janne Malmros
Unfold, 2007
period English footstool
with cut floral covering

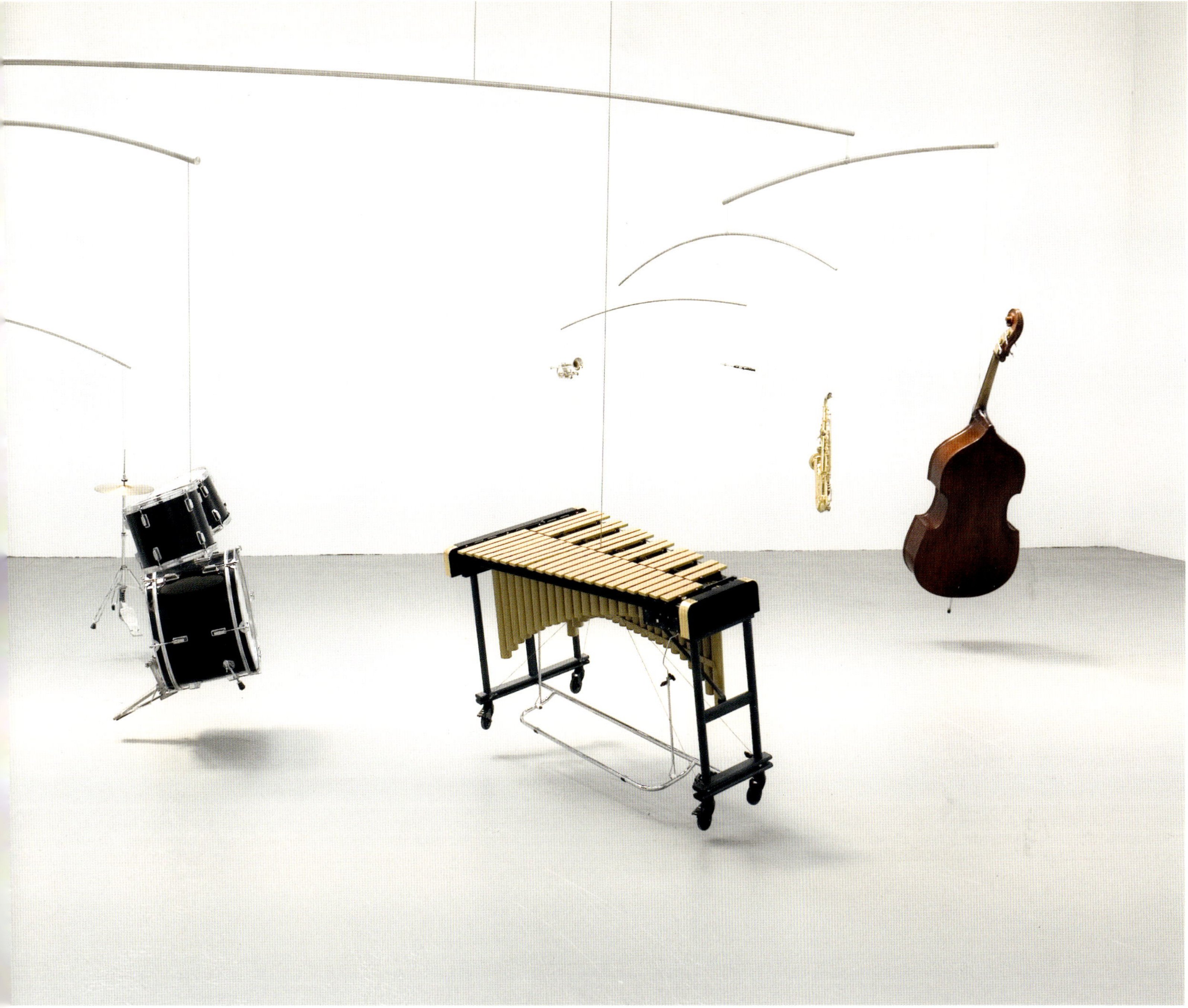

ABOVE
Peter Coffin
Untitled **(*Free Jazz Mobile*)**, 2007
mobile structure and musical instruments

Peter Coffin is a conceptual artist whose subjects differ from work to work (see page 144), even as one element remains consistent: his commitment to intellectual fun. For him, 'Play is not ordinary life. It is a way of stepping...into a temporary sphere of activity with a disposition all its own.' His *Untitled* (*Free Jazz Mobile*) allows even the most unmusical of individuals the chance to *play* the instruments. As the oversized mobile rotates slowly, an ever-changing still life comes into focus.

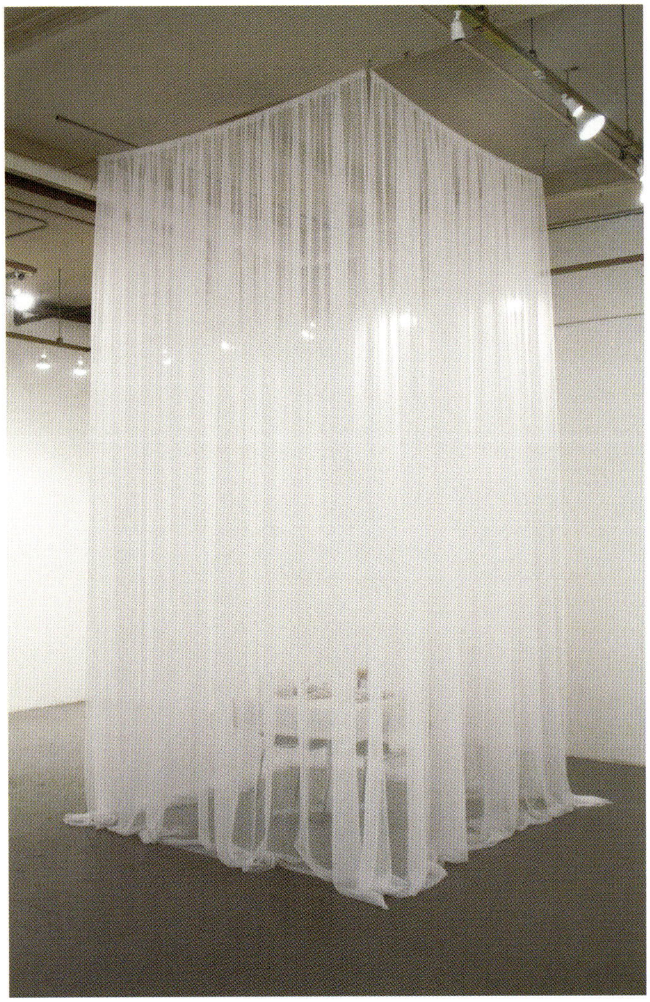

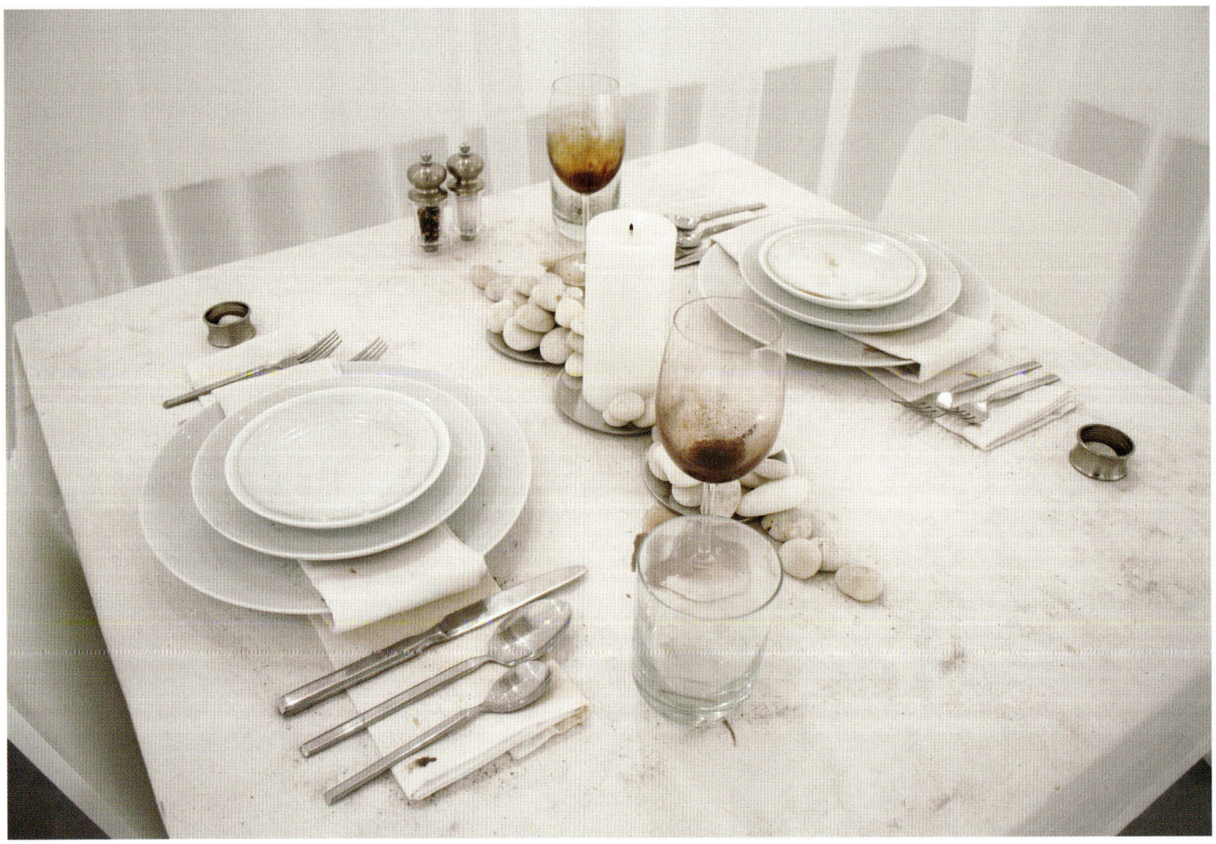

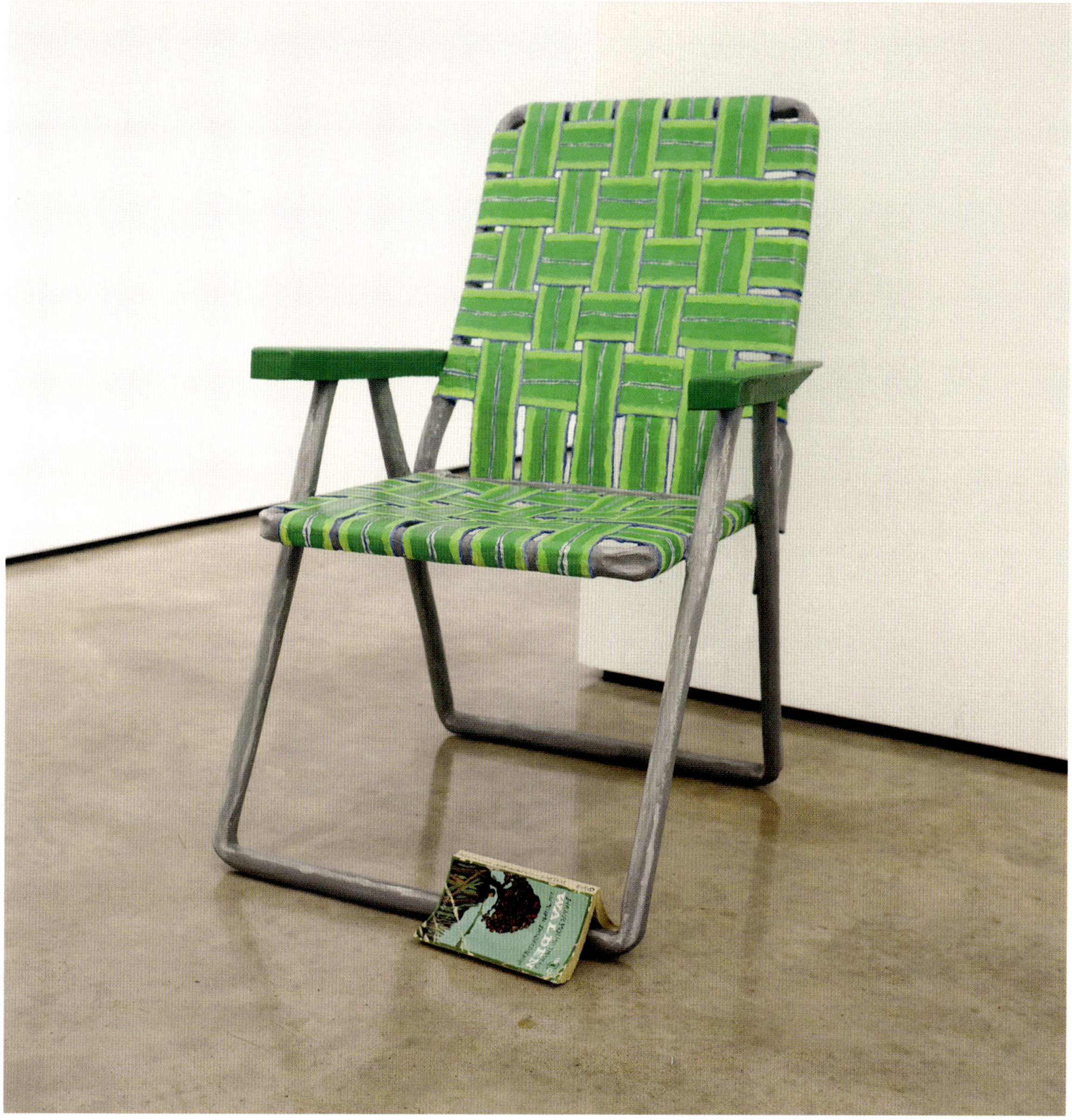

Darren Jones set up his *Reservation* installation six months prior to its actual exhibition, enough time for the wine to evaporate from its glasses and dust to gather over the table set for two. Like Miss Havisham's wedding feast, the ghostly table setting is shrouded physically as well as in its underlying narrative. Who was to have this tête-à-tête? Why did they not? The extinguished candle, a traditional still-life motif (see Chapter 5), hints at a dark backstory.

Conrad Bakker's 2010 exhibition 'Relax and Take Your Fucking Time' took its name from a spam email promoting a type of Viagra. Bakker took that imperative not only as inspiration for his sculptures' subject matter, but also as the rationale behind their creation; each work was painstakingly carved from wood and then painted so as to duplicate the object it represents. His interest is not in creating *trompe-l'œil* effects – though the sculptures look real from a distance, they are easily decoded close up – but in making works that 'critically comment upon and make tangible the everyday economies between persons and things and spaces'.

OPPOSITE
Darren Jones
Reservation, 2007
(external and internal views) · muslin, table settings and wine

ABOVE
Conrad Bakker
Untitled Project: LAWNCHAIR (Walden), 2010 · oil on carved wood

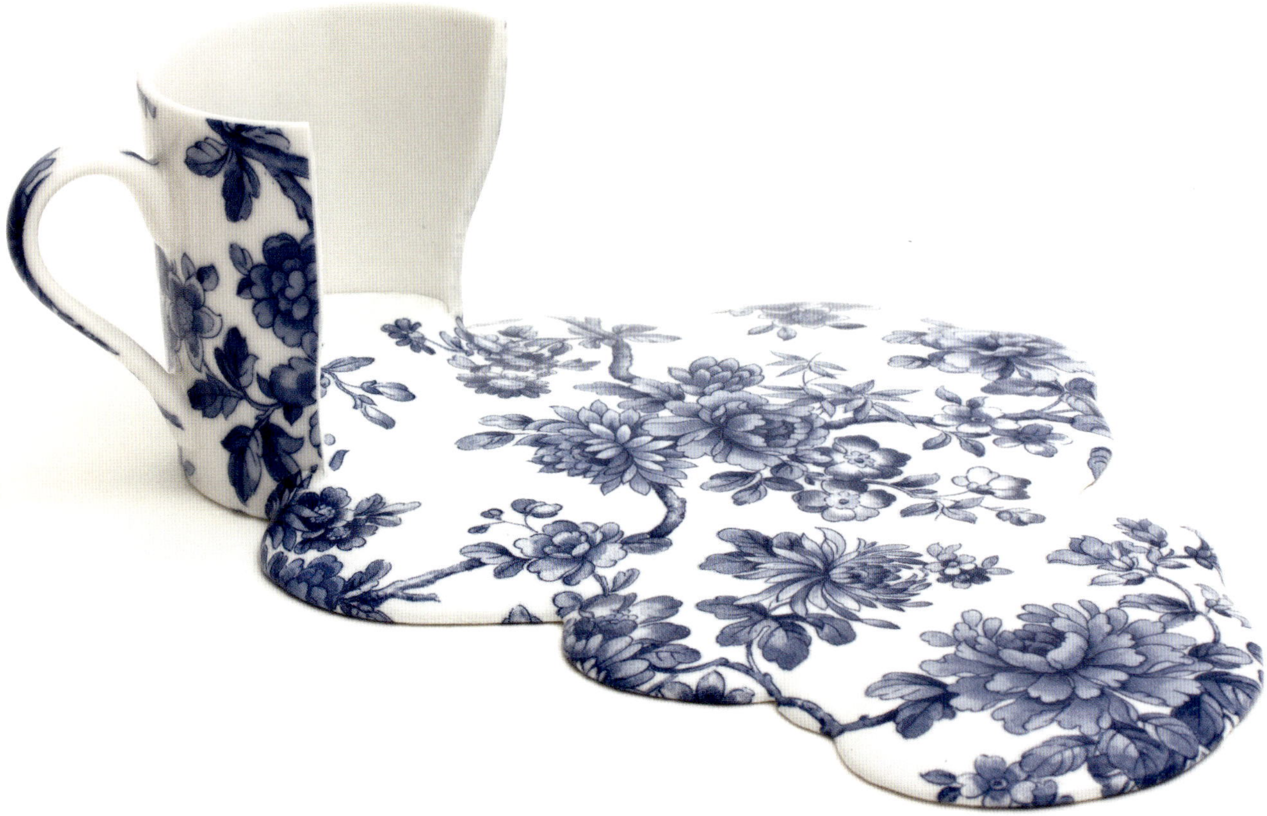

ABOVE
Livia Marin · from the series ***Broken Things***, 2011 · crockery, plaster, varnish, transfer-print

OPPOSITE TOP
Stephanie Syjuco
Blue Selection from 'Raiders: International Booty, Bountiful Harvest (Selections from the A____ A__ M_____)', 2011 · archival Epson photo prints mounted on laser-cut wood, hardware and crates

OPPOSITE BOTTOM
Stephanie Syjuco
'Raiders: International Booty, Bountiful Harvest (Selections from the A____ A__ M_____)', 2011 (installation view) archival Epson photo prints mounted on laser-cut wood, hardware and crates

Livia Marin's *Broken Things* installation saw her take everyday broken ceramic objects and transform them into something new and whole. She has said: 'What fascinates me about everyday objects are the traces of humanity that are lodged in them and which it is possible to bring to the fore in art.' In rehabilitating damaged household goods, Marin rehabilitates the humanity associated with these objects and creates works that hint at both death and rebirth.

Stephanie Syjuco's exhibition 'RAIDERS: International Booty, Bountiful Harvest (Selections from the Collection of the A____ A__ M_____)' featured 135 photographs of antique vessels cut to scale and mounted on board. These were then arranged into attractive groupings, such as *Blue Selection*. Syjuco had downloaded the freely available images from the website of the San Francisco Asian Arts Museum. Her flattening of priceless three-dimensional antiquities offered a critique on the practice of collecting (cultures, as much as objects) that extended to the virtual world, where online museum databases further reinforce false notions of institutional objectivity.

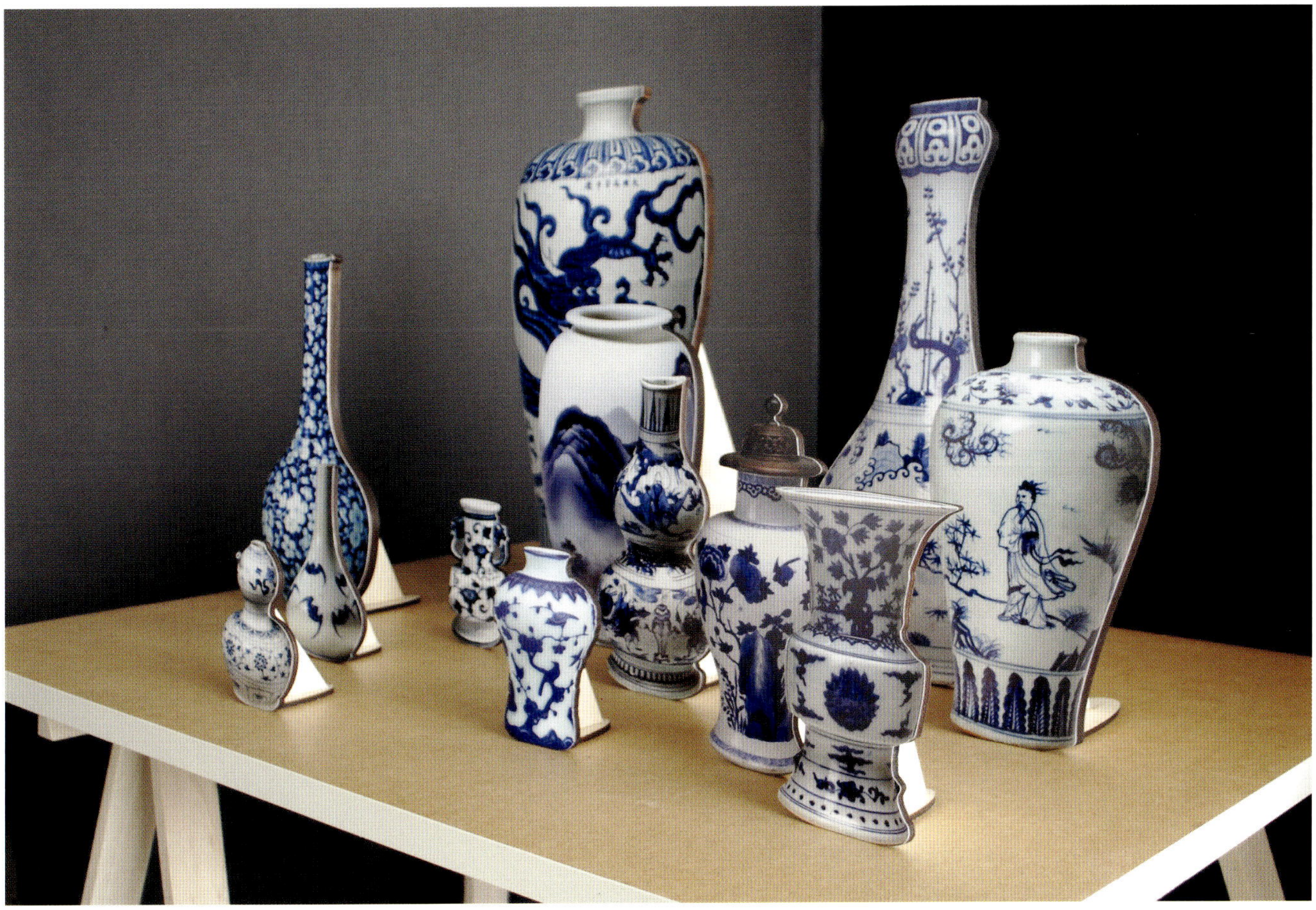

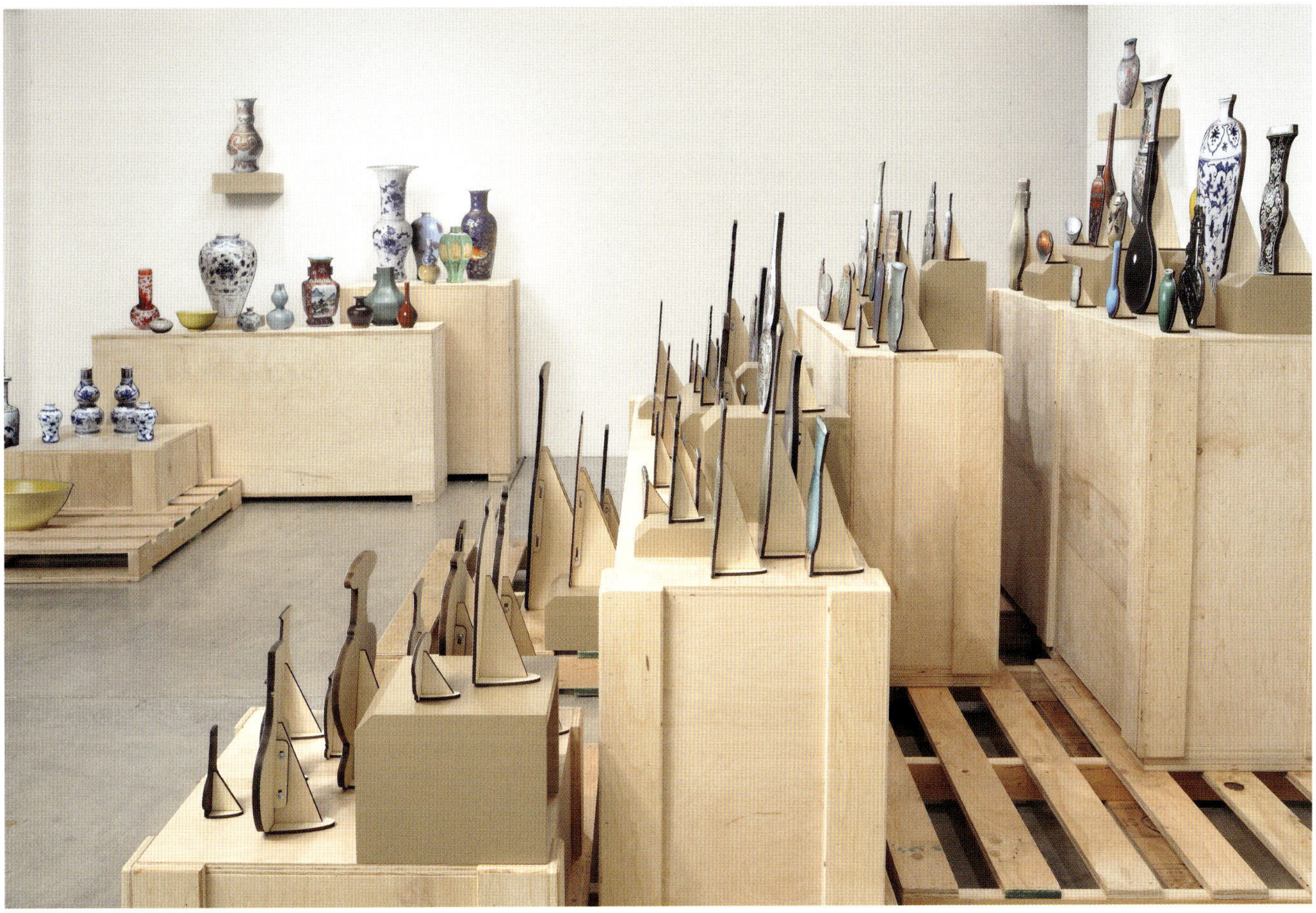

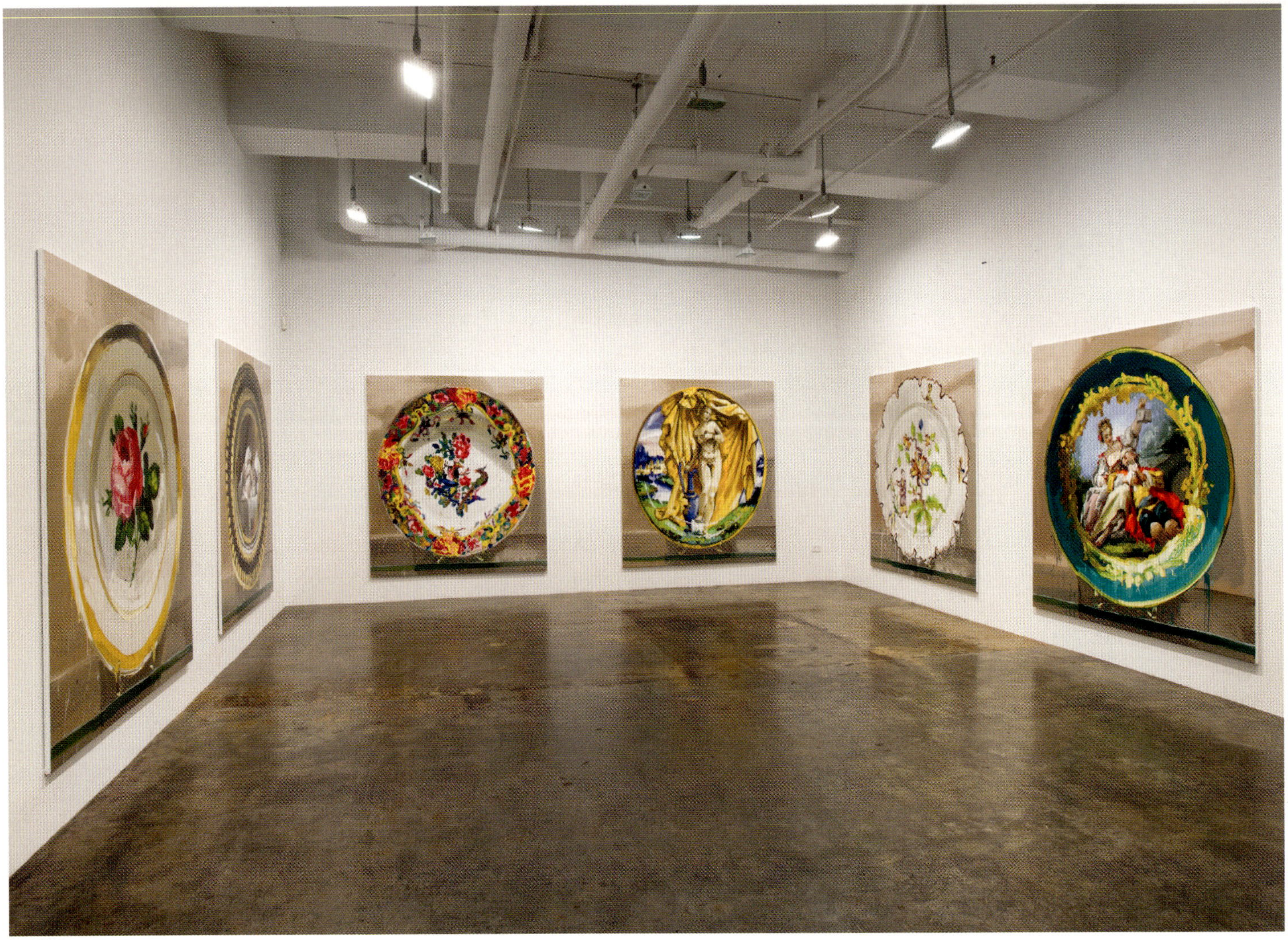

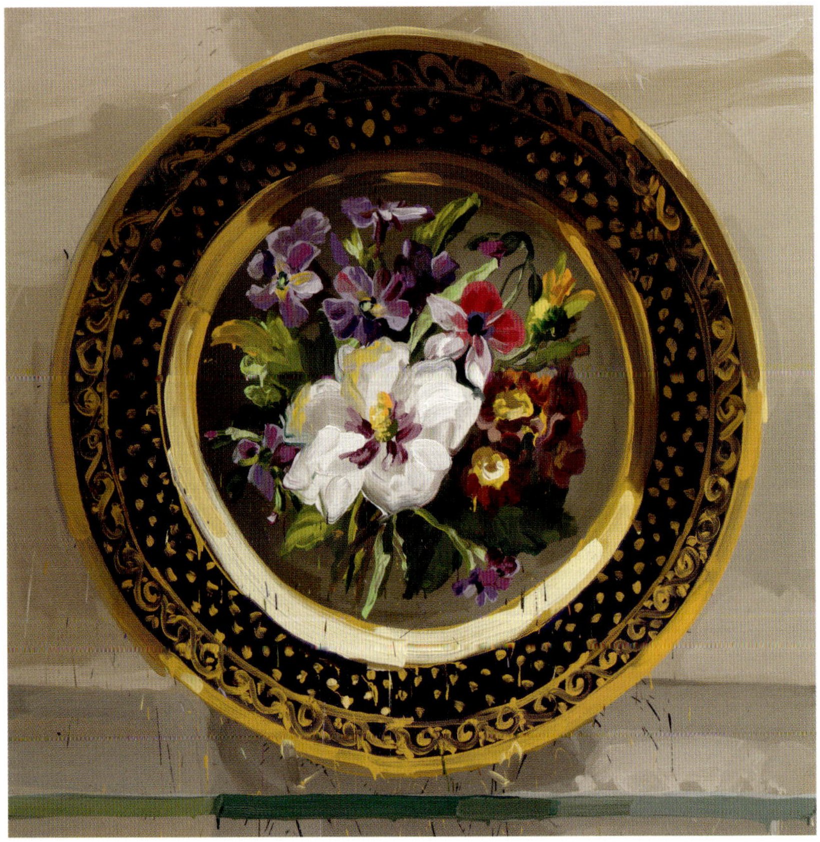

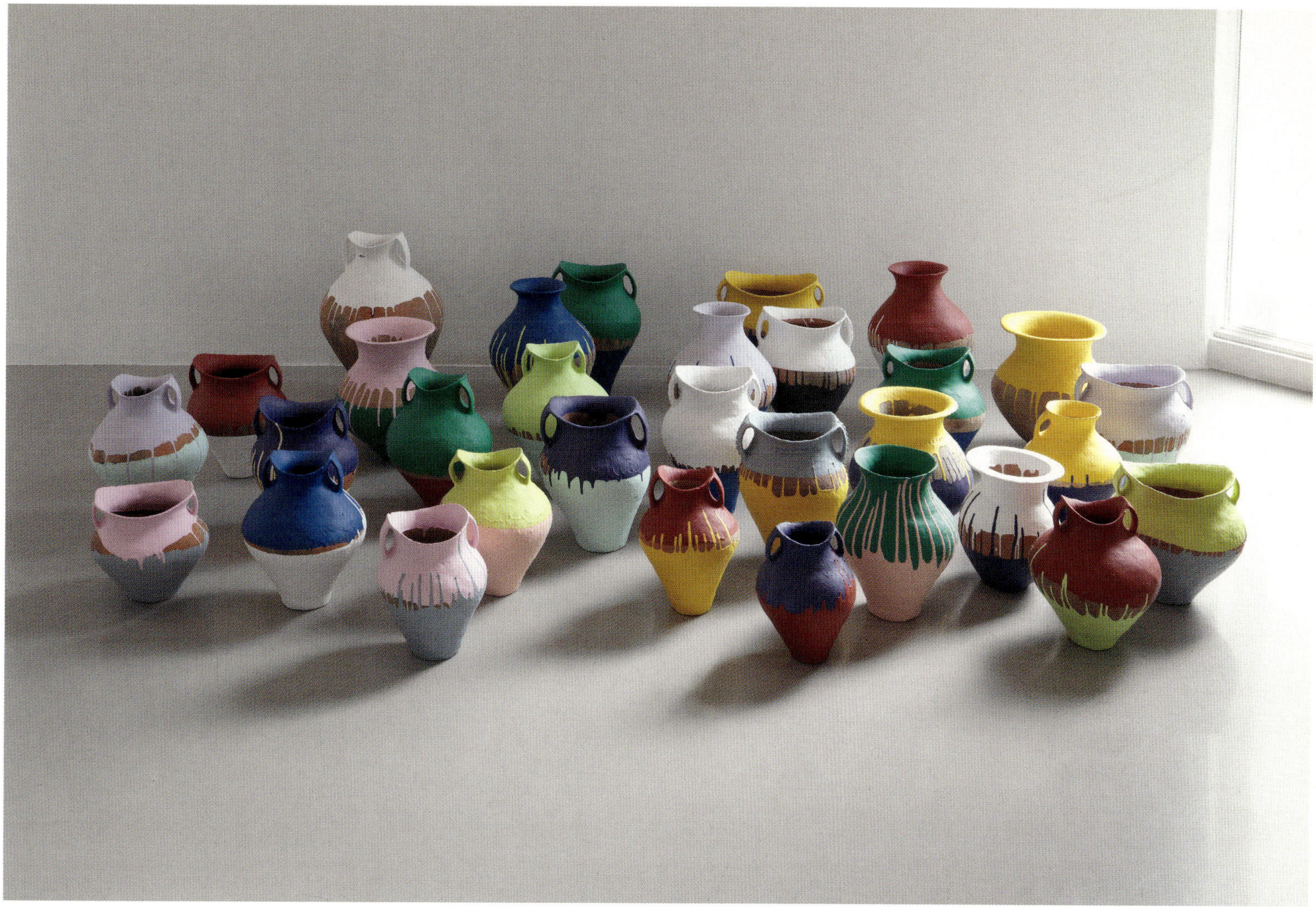

OPPOSITE TOP
Jan De Vliegher
'Treasury', 2012
(installation view)
oil on canvas

OPPOSITE BOTTOM
Jan De Vliegher
Sèvres, White Flower, 2012
oil on canvas

ABOVE
Ai Weiwei
Coloured Vases, 2010
31 Han Dynasty vessels
and industrial paint

Jan De Vliegher's 'Treasury' exhibition presented a series of large, robust paintings of small, delicate objects. Each painting details a single porcelain plate, such as *Sèvres, White Flower*, which might come from any number of sources (France, China, England) and any point in history. All are painted in an almost realistic style that at the same time flirts with abstraction since drips and brush strokes are left obvious. The paintings all measure two metres by two metres and visually overpower viewers, as if to place them inside a cabinet of wonder.

Ai Weiwei is well known for works that revisit Chinese traditions and objects in order to criticize the limitations imposed on artistic experimentation and freedom. To create *Coloured Vases*, Ai dipped thirty-one precious earthenware urns from the Han Dynasty (206 BC to AD 220) into brightly coloured paints. Or did he? Whether or not they *are* real Han vessels or replicas like those sold to tourists (there is a thriving market for Han urns, which are mostly counterfeit reproductions), the artist presents them as real. Such intervention calls into question the high status and value attributed to the antique or ancient object – for *Dropping a Han Dynasty Urn* (1995), Ai photographed himself doing just that – and suggests that an object seemingly at the end of its existence might be better off transformed and reborn as something else.

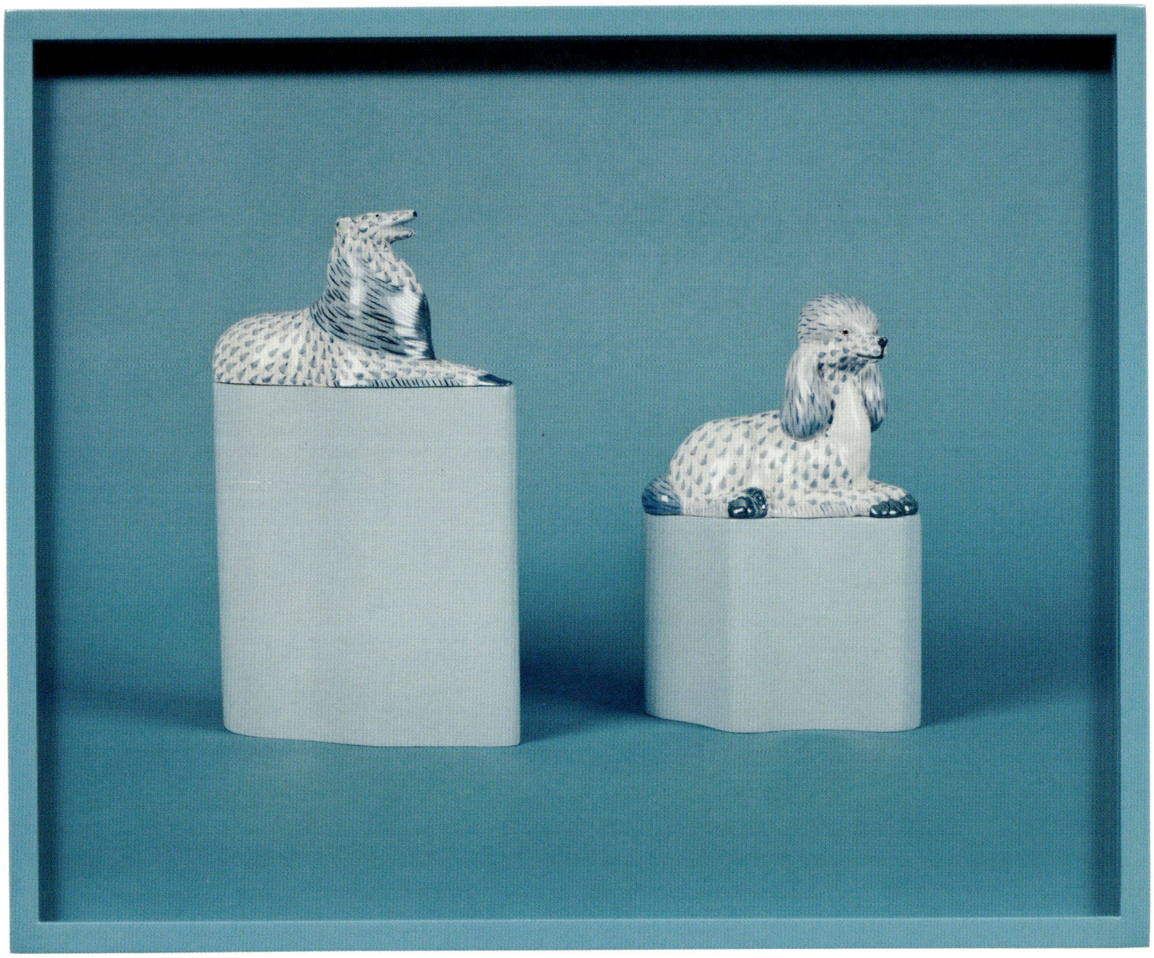

ABOVE
Elad Lassry
Collie, Poodle, 2011
C-print, painted frame

OPPOSITE TOP
Barnaby Barford
Do it again, I didn't press record, 2009
porcelain, ceramic, enamel paint, wood and other media

OPPOSITE BOTTOM
Matt Smith
Looking for a Chicken Hawk, 2010
cast earthenware, underglaze and decals

Elad Lassry knowingly plays with the still-life tradition in his photographs, whether shot in landscape format, as in *Collie, Poodle*, or in portrait format. Lassry views the frame as an extension of the photograph and often paints it one of the dominant colours found in the image, turning two-dimensional photographs into three-dimensional objects.

Barnaby Barford uses found ceramic figurines to construct works with complex and often adult themes. In *Do it again, I didn't press record*, part of a series called *The Good The Bad The Belle*, a hooded child uses his camera phone to document a friend violently kicking another child, an all too familiar news item. The inherent cuteness of the small figurines makes for an ironic comparison of idealized innocence and actual behaviour.

Matt Smith's diminutive porcelain still life *Looking for a Chicken Hawk* shows the meeting of two gay characters, one human and one a chicken dressed in a rakish suit. In gay parlance, an innocent or naïve young man is often called a *chicken* and an older man who is sexually attracted to such youth is called a *chicken hawk*. The work was part of *Queering the Museum*, Smith's series of ceramic interventions at the Birmingham Museum and Art Gallery, which explored the queer histories behind collections of porcelain and the possibilities for queer display within contemporary culture.

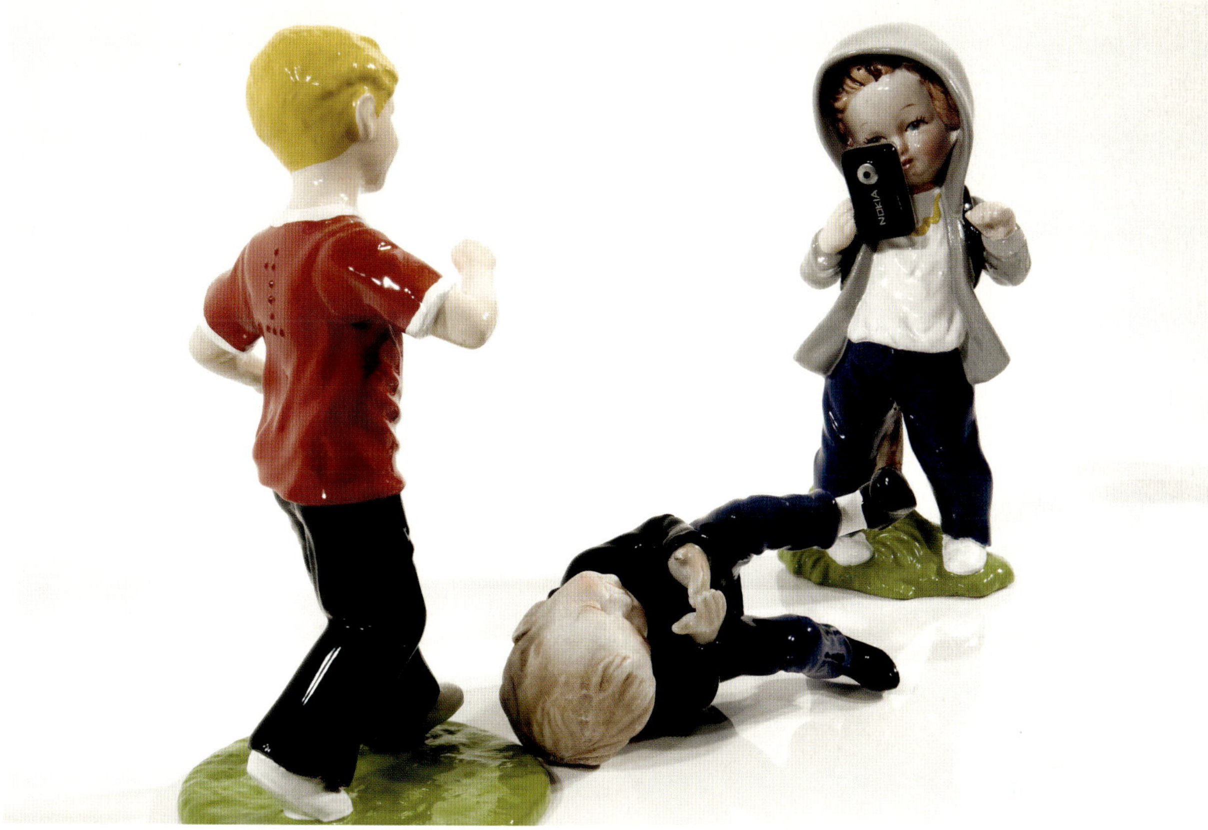

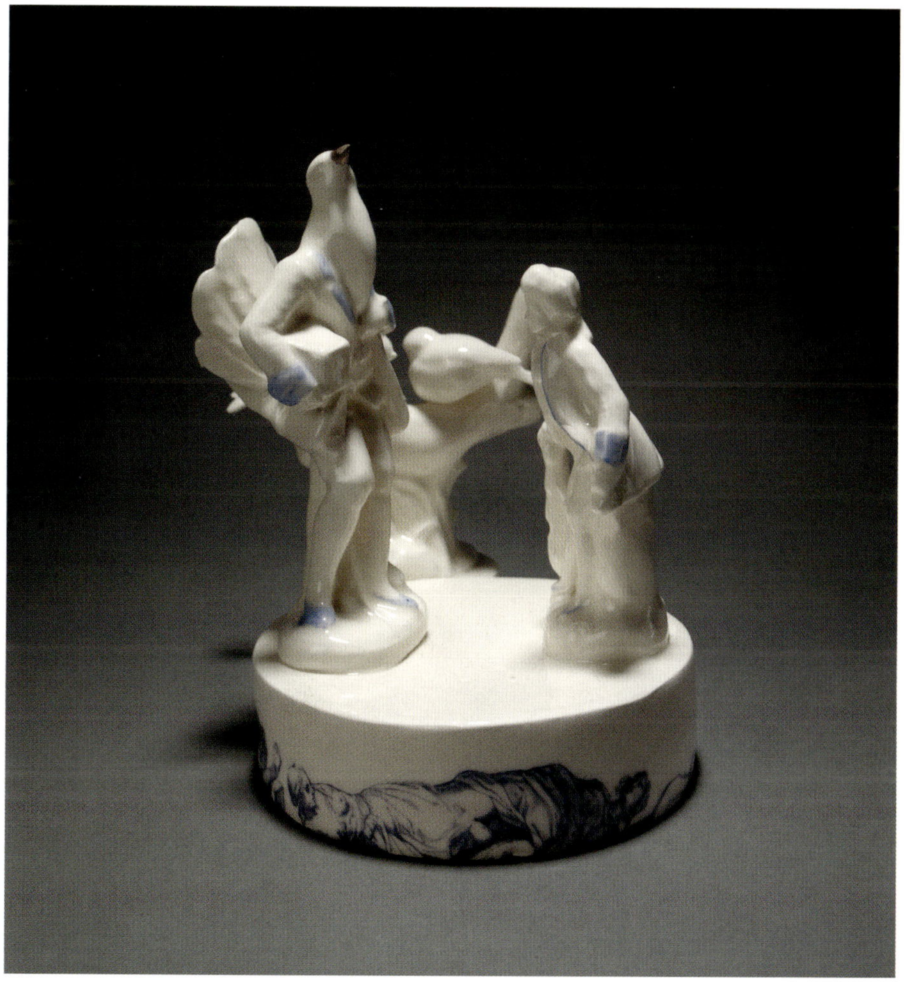

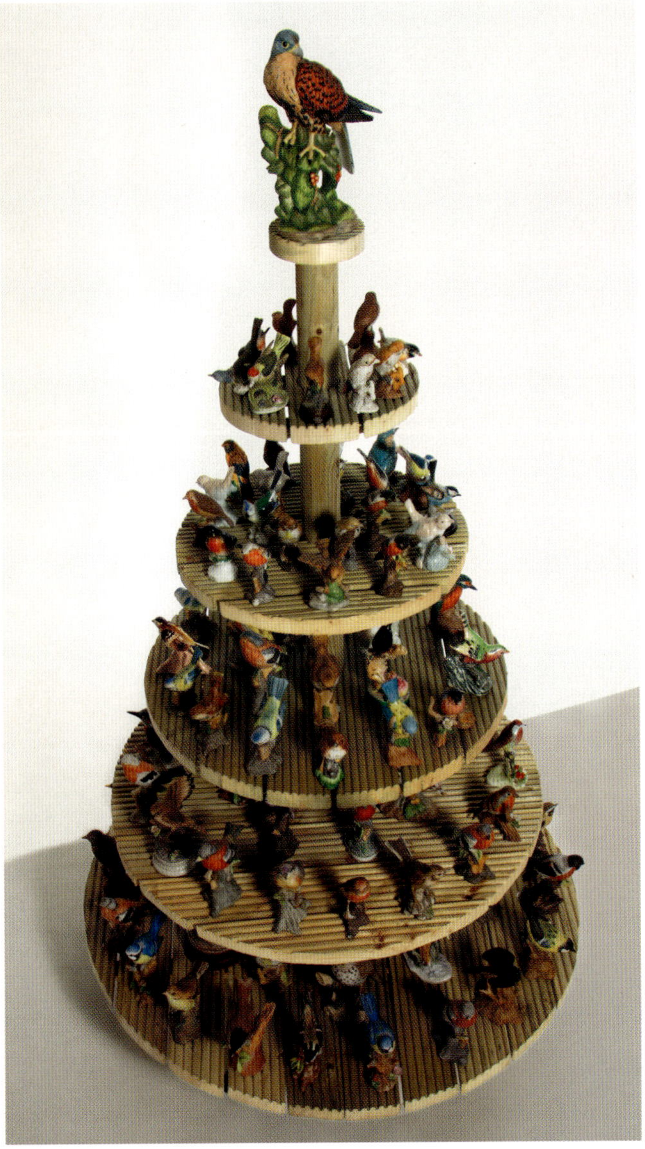

John Mitchell often pairs found ceramics with other media and then places them in odd settings (an actual mouse hole, outdoor objects used inside, museum collections). For the artist's 2009 installation *Dawn Chorus* birdsong twittered throughout the gallery as if the colourful ceramic birds that he had collected and positioned around the room, as well as on a tiered shelf, had all united in song.

For his series *Tchotchke Stacks* (2010), **Patrick Jackson** combed second-hand stores for kitsch objects that were then chosen for their structural integrity regardless of their subject matter. Small mirrored plinths made sure that each object reached the same height so that it could fulfil its new-found function as a caryatid, or architectural support. The objects that could support the most weight were placed at the bottom of his stacks (an intentional allusion to the minimalist 'stacks' of Richard Serra and Donald Judd), and the more fragile pieces further up.

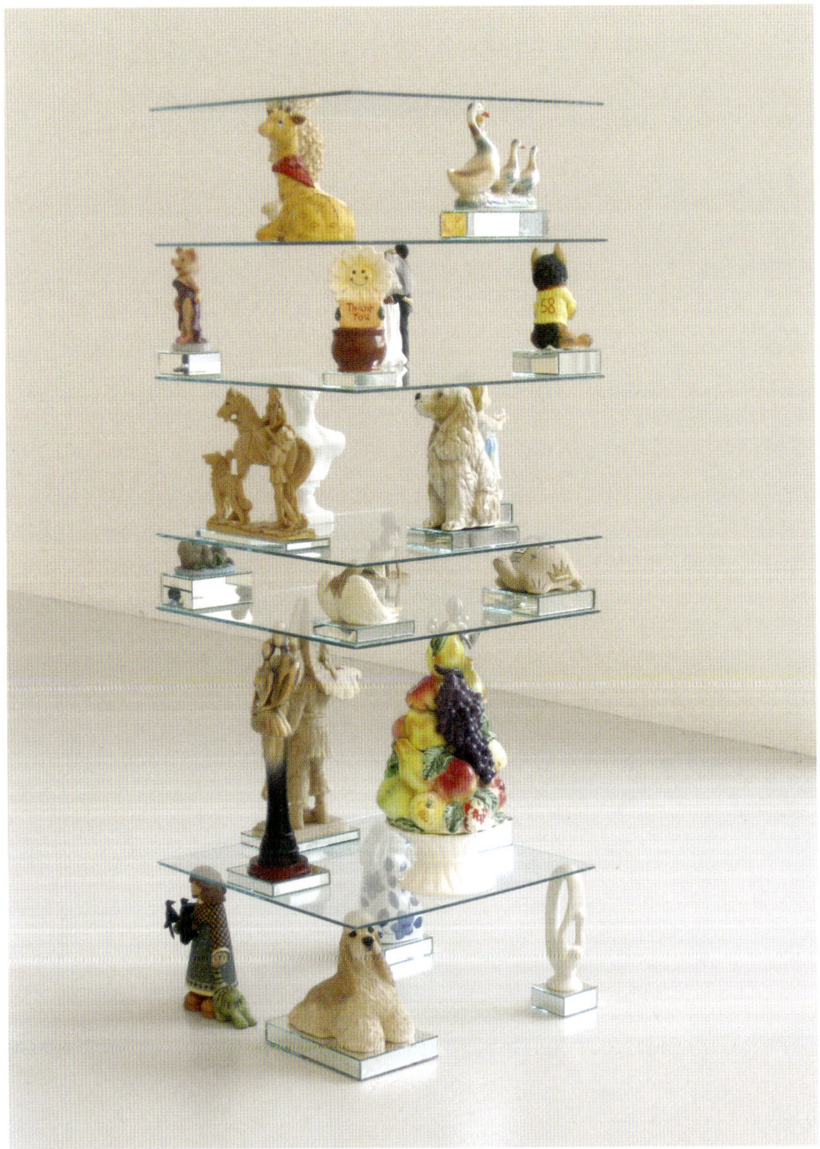

ABOVE
John Mitchell
Dawn Chorus, 2009
ceramic and china birds, garden decking and audio birdsong

RIGHT
Patrick Jackson
Tchotchke Stack 17, 2010
tchotchkes, glass, mirrors, wood and coins

OPPOSITE LEFT
Paul Wood
Domestic Slump I, 2005
refired found ceramic objects

OPPOSITE RIGHT
Joan Bankemper
Suzanna's Garden of Earthly Delights, 2009/10 · ceramic and mixed media

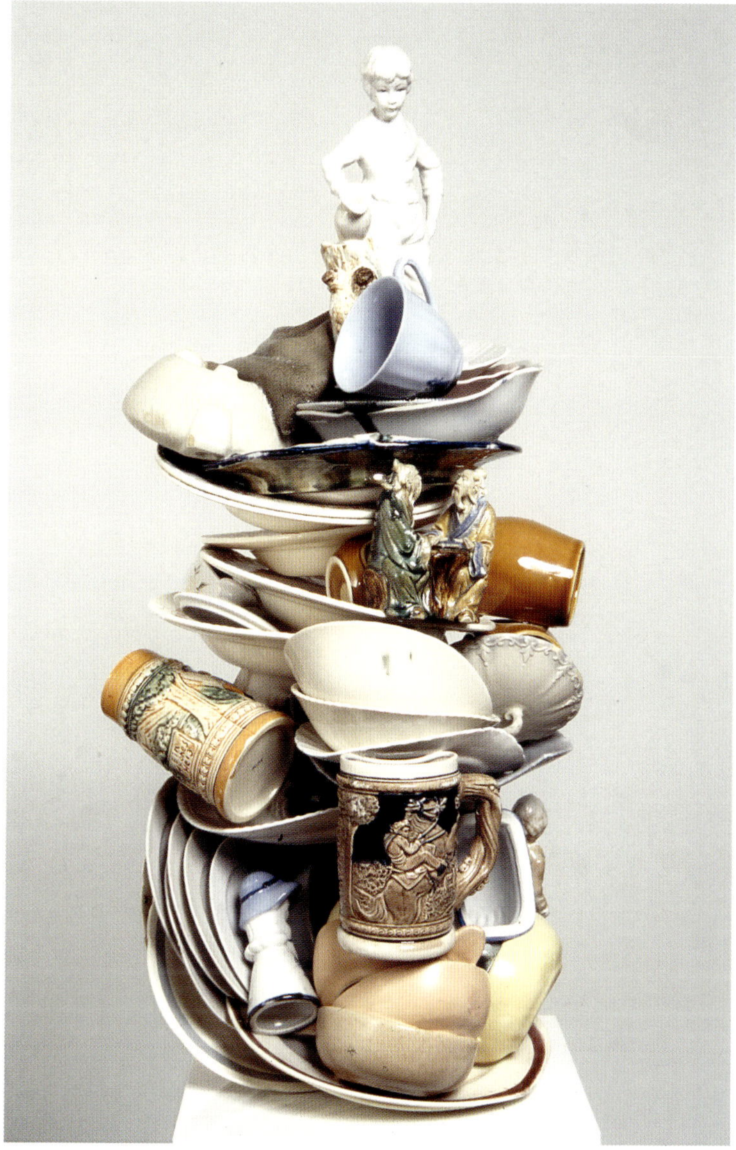

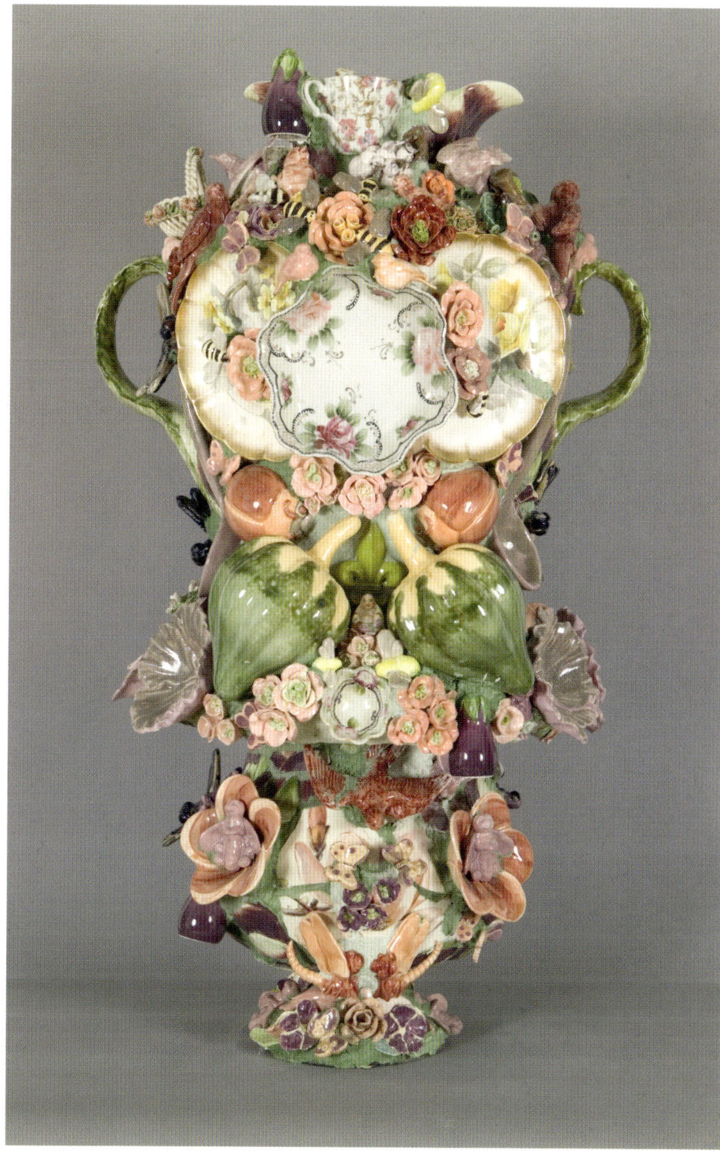

Paul Wood creates his sculptures by gathering ceramic homewares from second-hand and charity shops then refiring them into a warped whole. He has also subjected the homeware of the deceased to this process, creating poignant memorials to the dead, such as *L.N. Fowler* (2010). The artist has said: 'The rejected ceramics are thus transformed from unfashionable clutter and resurrected into small monuments to their past existence.'

Joan Bankemper is a gardener as well as an artist, and for over fifteen years she has been bringing together the two disciplines to create site-specific, organic interventions in urban landscapes, from Sicily to Texas. A recent turn to ceramics has resulted in unique vessels encrusted with any number of details, each cast from one of 1,500 moulds she has collected. The resulting works incorporate many traditional *nature morte* motifs, including bees, birds, flowers and vegetables.

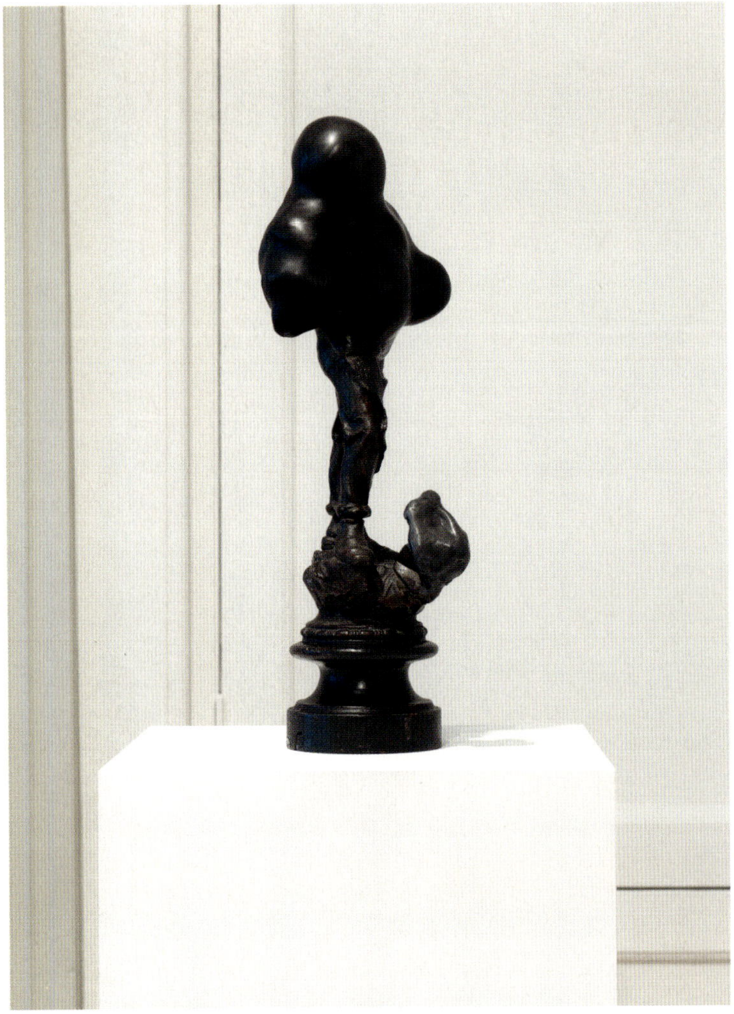

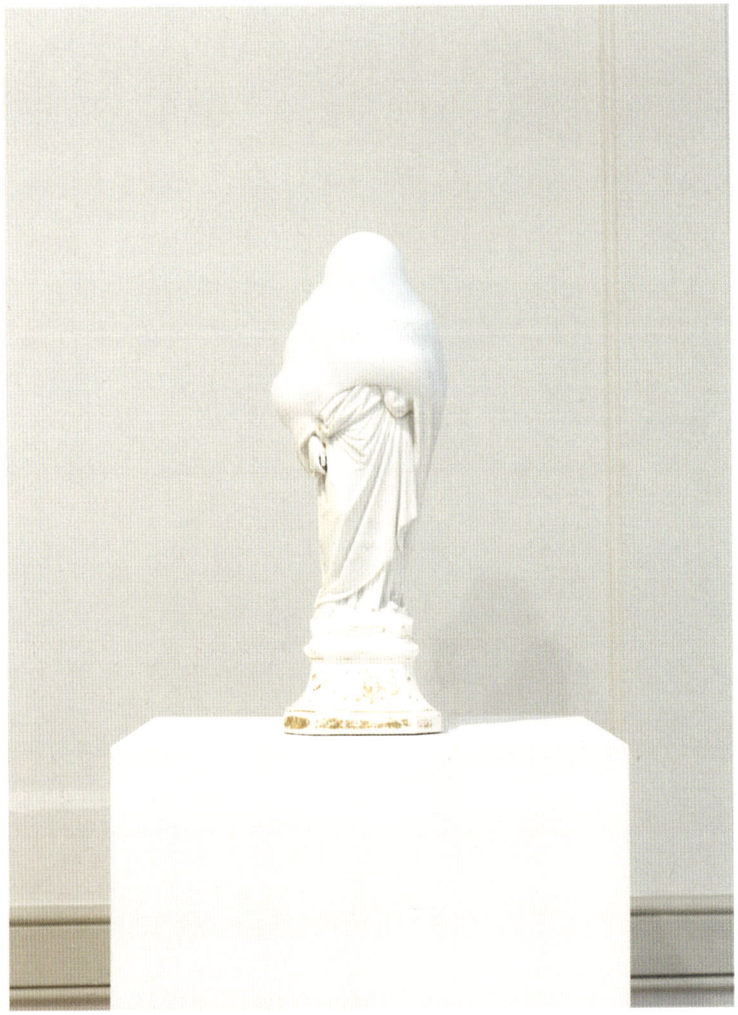

Richard Stone dips found metal and porcelain Victorian figurines in wax until their features and heroic gestures are lost, smoothed into abstract forms. This artistic cannibalism evokes the modern debasement of nineteenth-century Romanticism as well as the eventual demise of man *and* art. Stone's painted works differ in that it is the process of subtraction that obliterates the old. He creates his 'erased paintings' by sanding away the surface of antique oil paintings so that only ghosts of the originals remain.

ABOVE LEFT
Richard Stone
narcissus and
the ground, 2011
antique spelter, wood
and wax

ABOVE RIGHT
Richard Stone
the day will come, 2011
antique parian porcelain
and wax

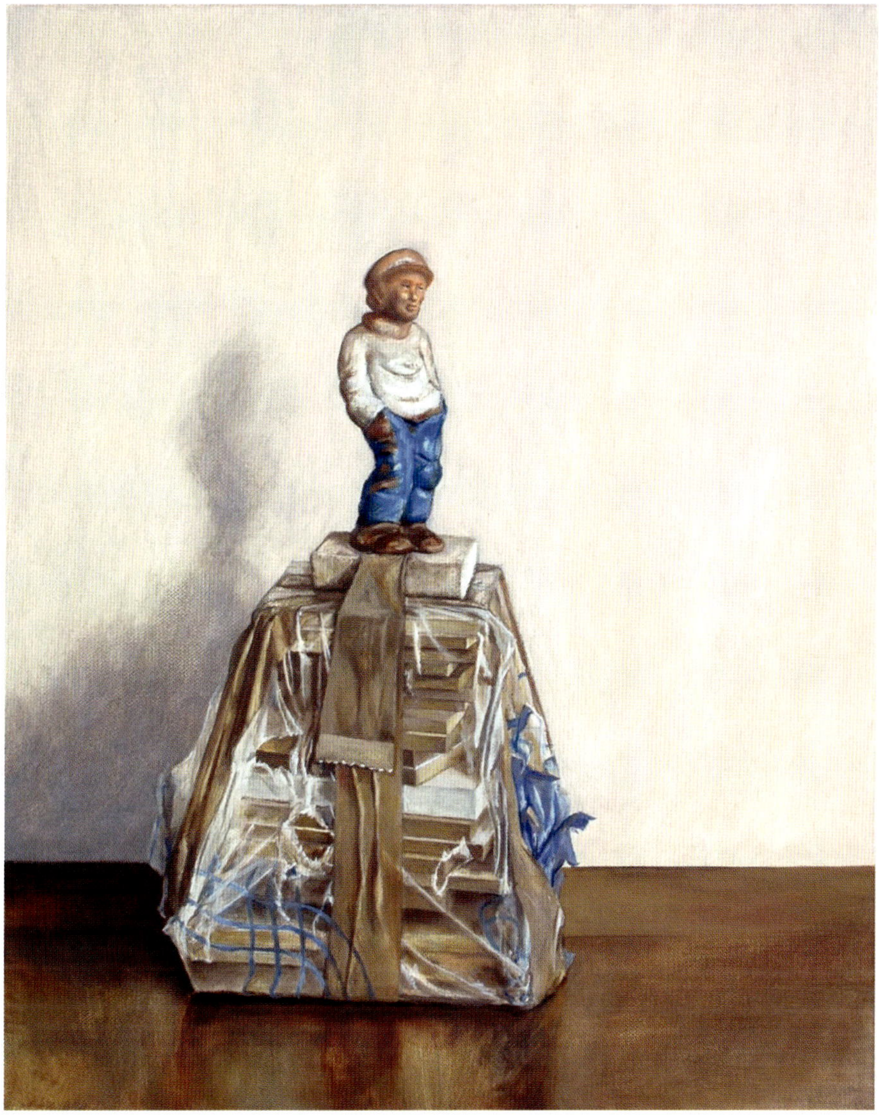

David Edmond has painted a number of formally arranged tableaux featuring kitsch ceramic figurines. In *The Collector*, a slouching figure stands atop a plastic-wrapped pile of what appear to be frames and canvases, roughly bound by brown packing tape. Like Barnaby Barford, Edmond disrupts the 'cutesy' qualities of his featured objects in order to ask what it is we collect and why, and whether, as in Old Master *vanitas* paintings, these are objects that we should hold dear.

ABOVE
David Edmond
The Collector, 2011
oil on canvas

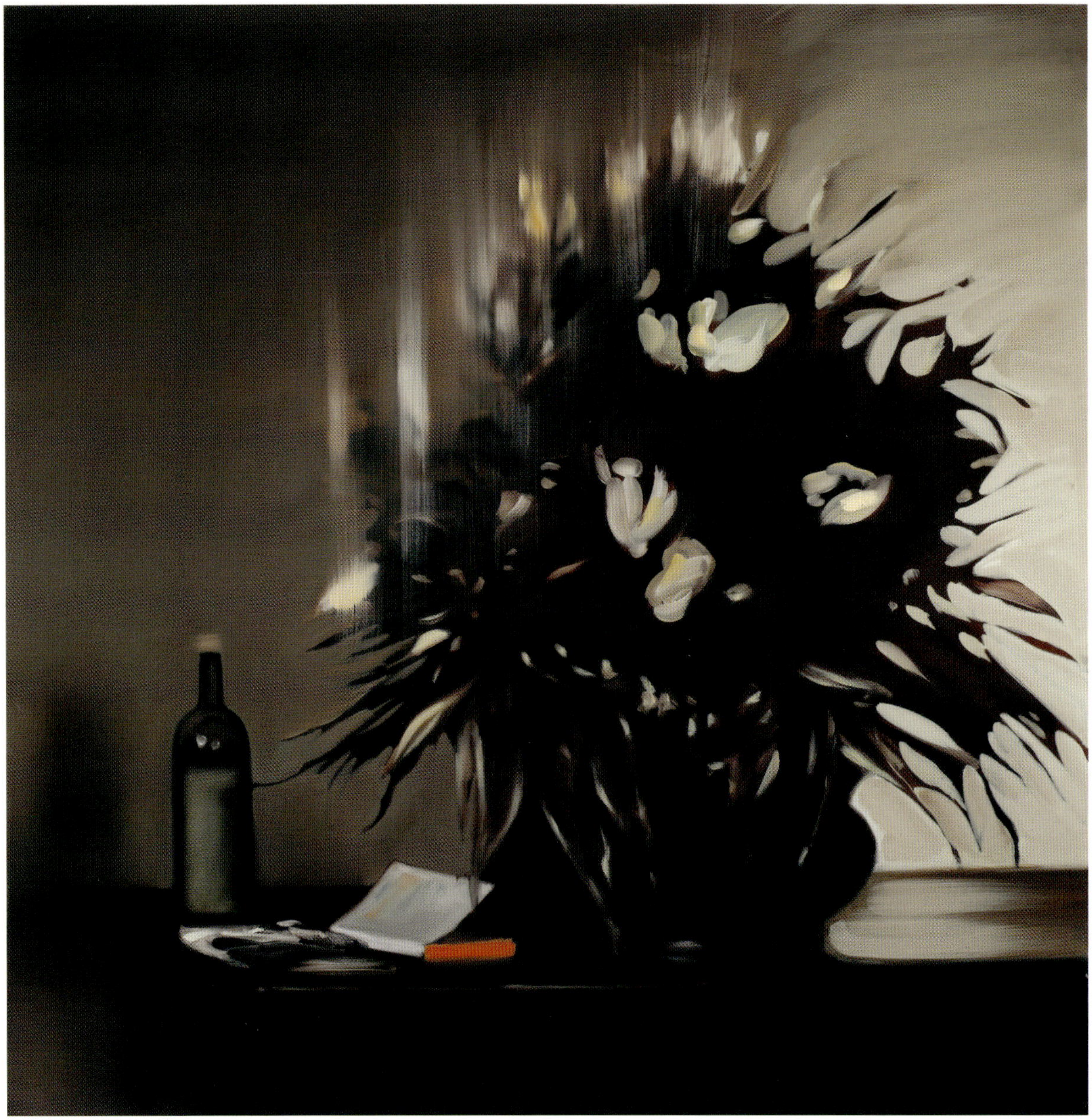

ABOVE
Theodora Allen
***A Song For You*, 2011**
oil on canvas

OPPOSITE
Ernst Billgren
***Mermaid's View*, 2011**
Murano glass, sand and wood

Theodora Allen makes what appear to be simple, almost casual still lifes of domestic interiors, yet her source material actually comes from old record album covers. Focusing on a small detail of the whole, she then paints something that is doubly familiar but still distant. As less and less music-related packaging is now being produced, her paintings also act as records or memorials of past technologies, such as *A Song For You*, which is based on a Gram Parsons album cover from 1973.

Ernst Billgren's series *Mermaid's View* comprises five separate works that at first glance seem to be standard two-dimensional paintings. Upon looking closer, viewers are taken aback by a three-dimensional illusion of endlessness; for mounted into the wall behind each frame is a hidden box containing blown glass shells and plants – made in Venice at the Berengo Studios – resting on actual sand. The views, while reminiscent of traditional still-life paintings, are in fact sculptures, which seen through the mechanism of the picture frame (also Murano glass), and amplified by the mirrored insides of the box, take on a heightened artificiality.

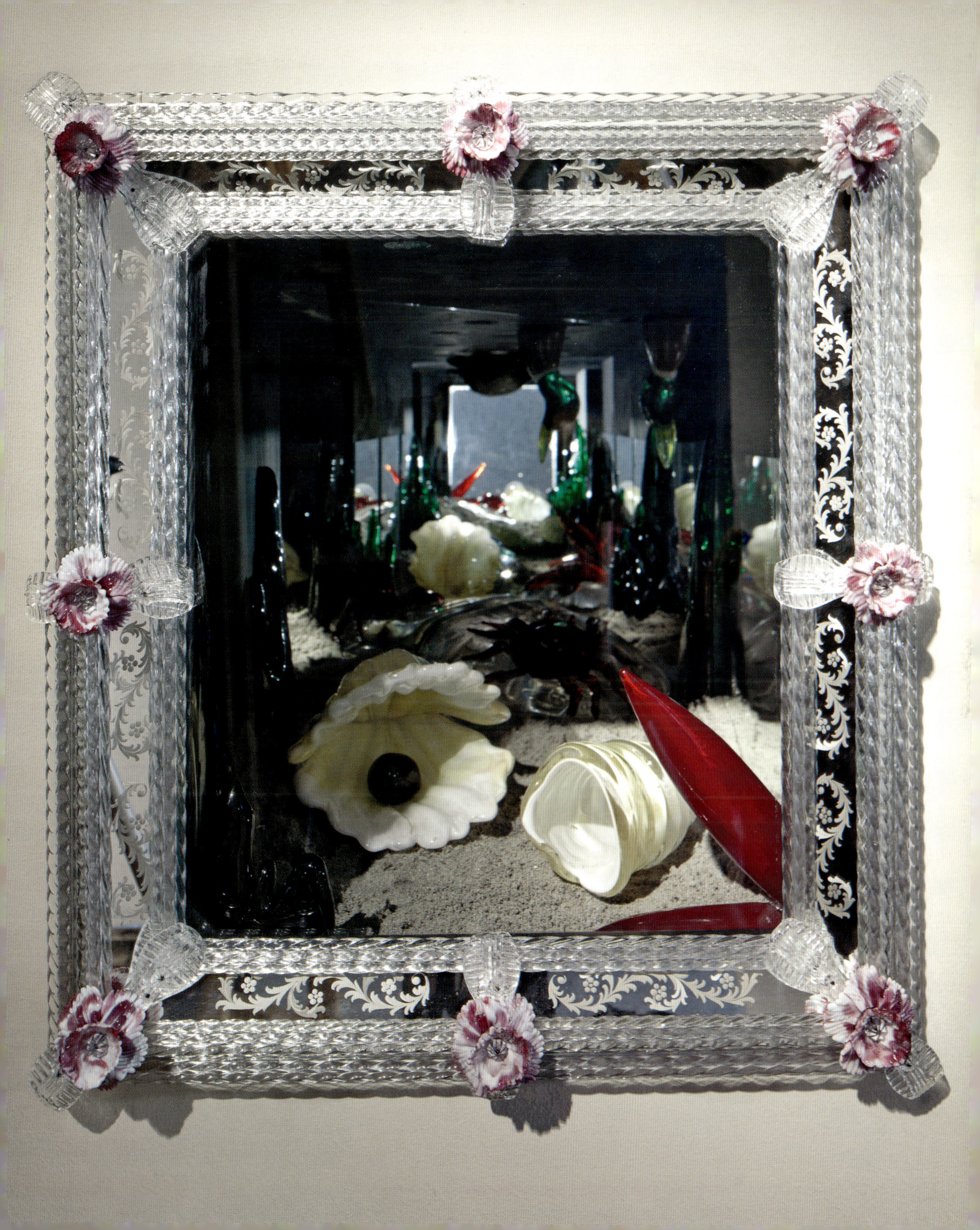

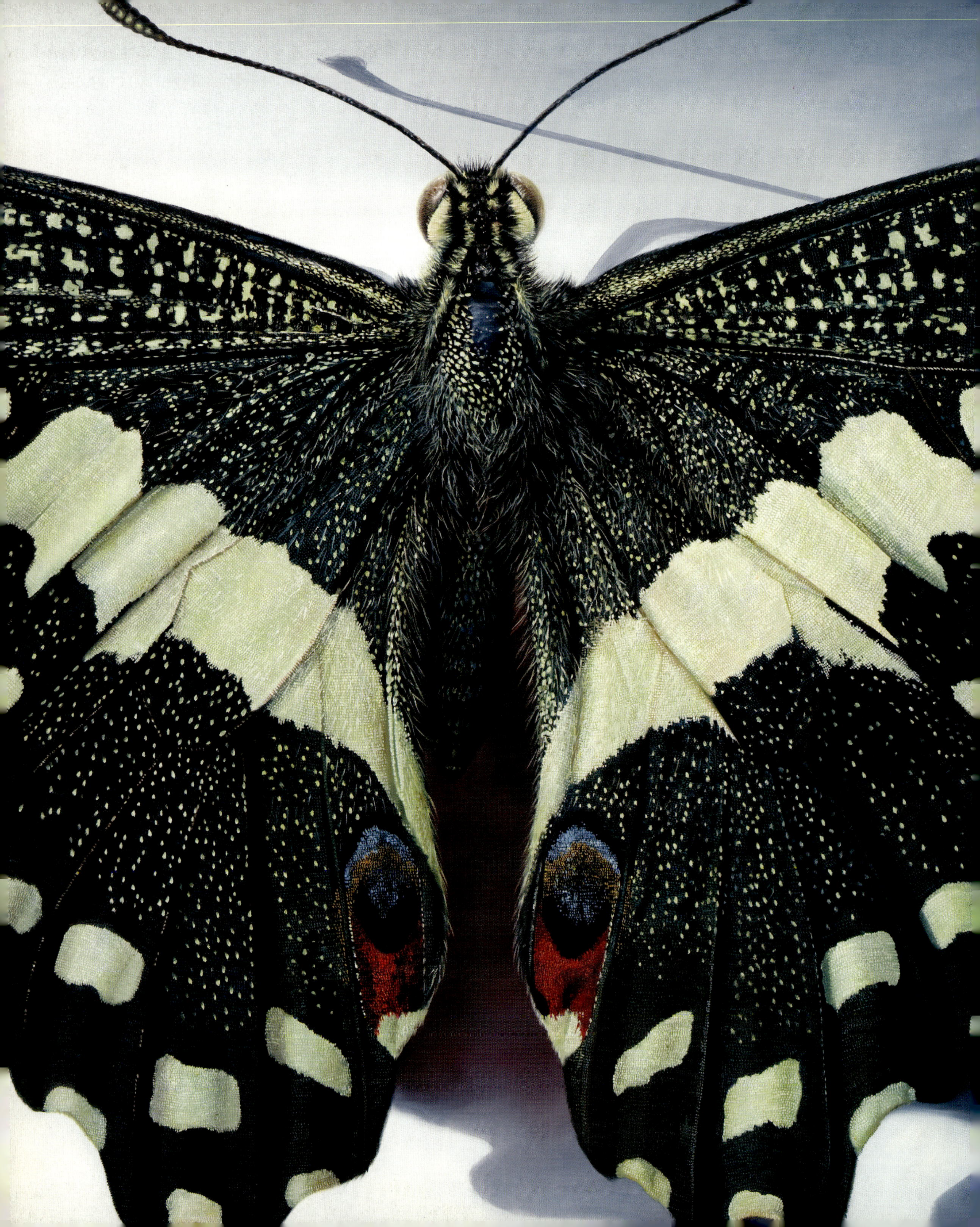

Section Four

FAUNA

FAUNA

Each animal is an end in itself...
We conceive of the individual animal as a small world,
existing for its own sake, by its own means.
Every creature is its own reason to be.

—JOHANN WOLFGANG VON GOETHE, 1795

As the subject of the earliest human artworks, painted onto the walls of prehistoric caves, animals held special significance, not only to their painters, but also to their immediate society. Human relations with other sentient beings have always been complex. Animals, as well as being food, were also seen in traditional societies (somewhat counterintuitively) as earthly incarnations of religious deities or valued spirits that guided humans in this world and the next. Such complex beliefs can be found in most cultures across the world and over time. The animal still life is one of the more thought-provoking strands of the tradition for another reason: the lifeless form of a once living and breathing creature demands our empathy in a way that flora, foodstuffs and inanimate objects do not. We are merely animals after all (*homo sapiens*), and though at the top of the food chain we too could find our life snuffed out in the blink of an eye (most likely by another human).

In the painting traditions of the sixteenth century, living animals appeared primarily because they were then recognizable status symbols: a well-groomed horse or a fine hound were expensive and owned only by the affluent. Dead animals heaped high in a well-stocked kitchen, perhaps recently taken in a successful hunt, also indicated wealth but with the added reminder of impending death for all. Individual animals might also appear because of their historical associations with different human qualities or attributes – the fox is considered cunning, the tortoise steadfast – and even today these interpretations still influence our readings of works of art. In much of Western religious painting the lamb was a stand-in for Christ, white, fluffy and innocent (and often bound). In contrast, the snake and goat are incarnations or servants of Satan; in the Garden of Eden it was the serpent who convinced Eve to eat of the forbidden fruit, the apple, and to share it with Adam, while goats are said to be randy and sexually promiscuous. Satan is often depicted as half man, half goat.

Many other animals are still considered inherently good or evil, though which of the two is often determined by culture and religion. Dogs are known as man's best friend in the West, but in Islamic societies they are often viewed as unclean, even evil, particularly black dogs. Native Americans have their own different readings of animals and their qualities. Among some communities, the snake is a symbol of transmutation, not of evil, and speaks of life, death and rebirth, as manifested in the shedding of the snake's skin. The wolf is considered a pathfinder and embodiment of loyalty and family, while its relative the coyote is known as a trickster.

The contemporary animal still life recalls these historical meanings and its artistic predecessors but its updated imagery makes it relevant for the twenty-first century. Insects such as the common fly, mosquito and moth have been revisited as symbols of decay or death but with a twist, such as their contribution to ecological renewal. Damien Hirst's use of living and dead butterflies as metaphors for transformation and rebirth is well known, but other artists, including Cindy Wright (page 176) and Adam Fuss (page 225), have used them too in unexpected ways. Bees and ants were historically depicted to suggest industry and hard work, yet Kris Martin (page 220) and Tomáš Libertíny (page 221) use them in ways that do not repeat this formula. The visual trope of the dead hare or game bird hanging limply from a kitchen peg, common in traditional still lifes, has been reincarnated and disturbed – as in the glass sculptures of Marta Klonowska, the video works of Sam Taylor-Johnson and the photographs of Shirana Shahbazi (pages 185, 186 and 187).

The increasing incorporation of taxidermy into art in recent years has brought new meaning to the idea of 'stilled life'. Some artists use long-dead taxidermy animals from the nineteenth century, while others have mastered the art of taxidermy themselves to create still-life sculptures made to their own design. In *Head On* Chinese artist Cai Guo-Qiang positioned a long stream of wolves frozen in motion: some are poised mid-leap about to crash headlong into a wall of glass; others already have, their bodies pressed against it or falling; still others have turned back the way they came as if to begin the cycle all over again (pages 194–95).

Of all the contemporary artists working with the preserved remains of animals, Shane Mecklenburger has taken this practice to the most extreme in transforming the roadkill carcass of an armadillo into a diamond via a method intended for human remains (popularly marketed as Life Gems) while documenting the entire process (page 201). But whether alive or dead or in a transformed state (taxidermy, carbonized, mechanized), and whatever their symbolism, the animals and creatures featured in the works included in this chapter are all contemporary still lifes. As such, each work places a lingering emphasis on mortality and the imminent death of all living creatures, reminding us that we too are only *homo sapiens* and but a few genes away from our closest relations, the great apes. Death stalks us all.

Gabriel Orozco considers his work *Dark Wave* to be essentially 'a drawing'. To create the massive sculpture, a twenty-strong team at the Factum Arte studio in Madrid first made casts of the bones of a real whale found on the south-west coast of Spain and then reassembled these into a life-size duplicate. A grid-like pattern was then drawn onto the casts, marking out the topographical detail of this substituted version of a fourteen-metre-long Fin whale (common rorqual). A creature of awe and fear due to its imposing size, the whale has appeared in many guises, from the story of Jonah being swallowed by a whale in the Bible (a scene replayed by Disney and Hollywood) to Herman Melville's murderous sperm whale in *Moby Dick*. In Renaissance paintings, whales are often depicted as monsters of the deep and symbols of the devil, their huge mouths acting as the entrance to hell.

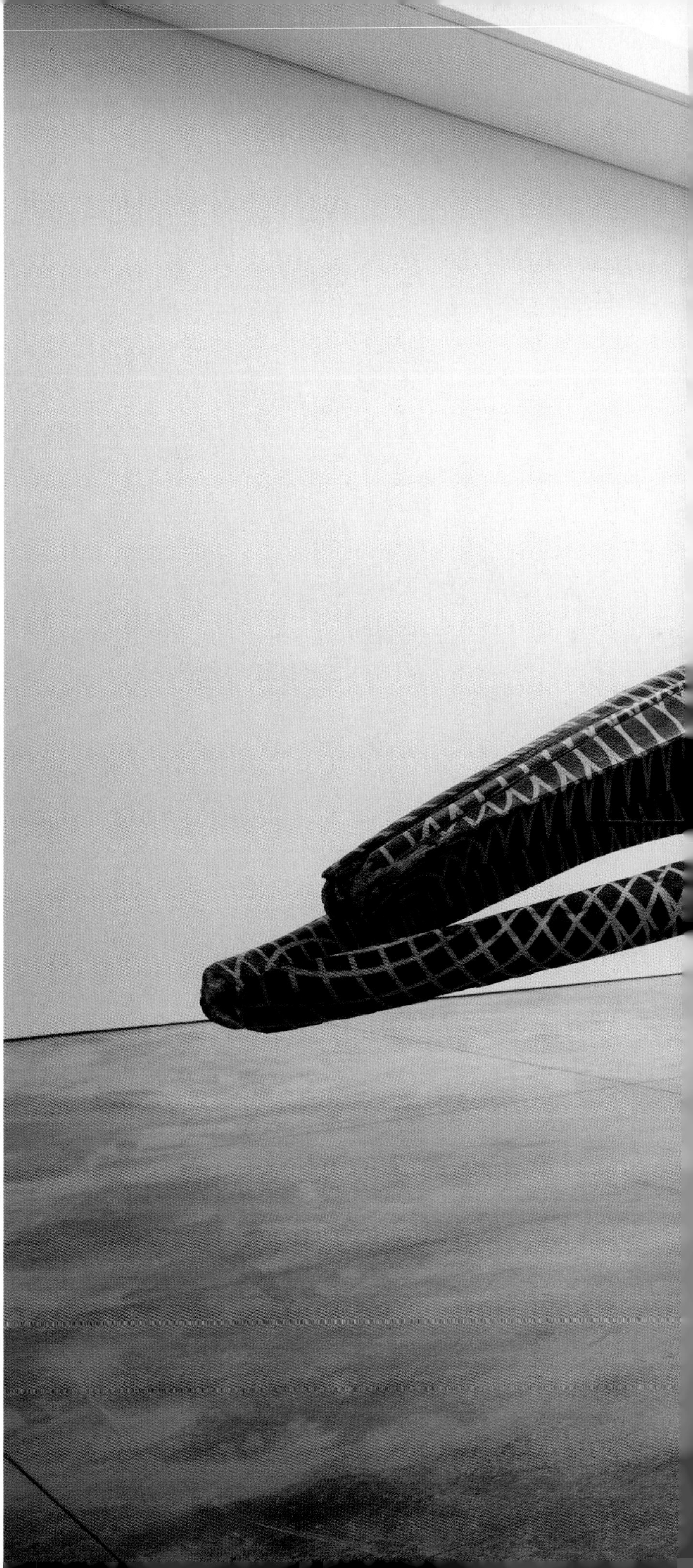

PAGE 176
Cindy Wright
Poisonous wave, 2007
(detail) · oil on canvas

RIGHT
Gabriel Orozco
Dark Wave, 2006
calcium carbonate and
resin with graphite

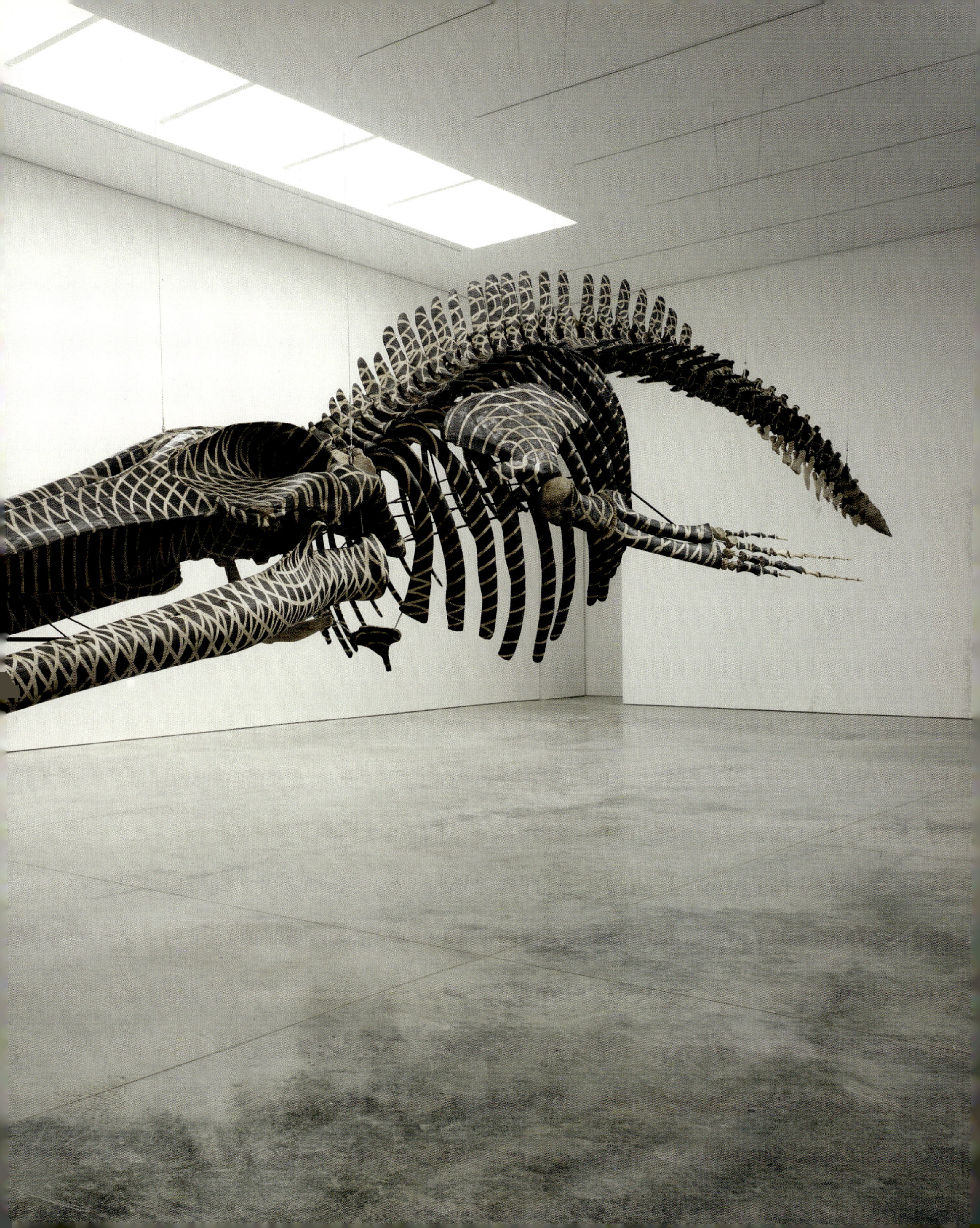

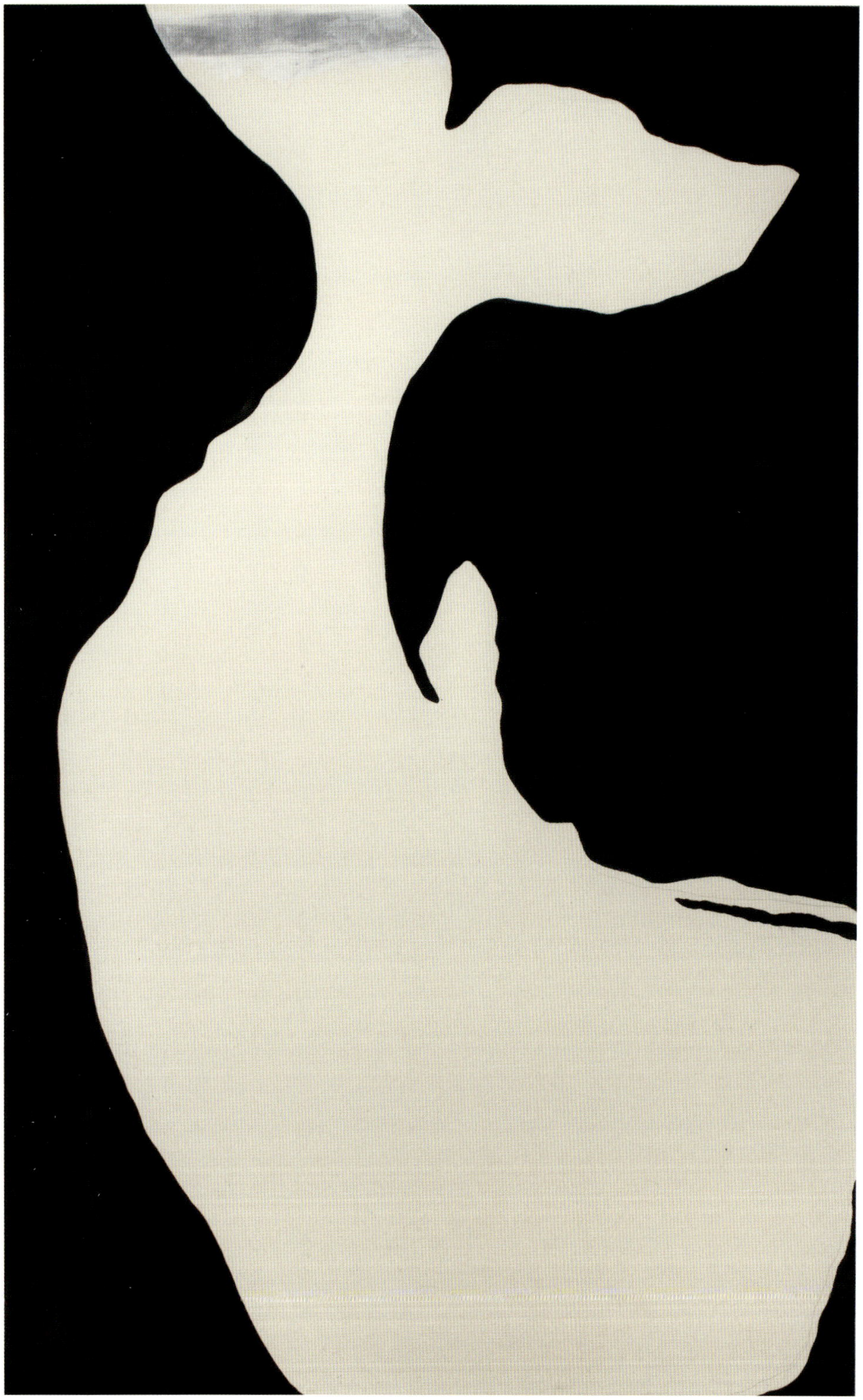

'I make negative things look pretty. Moreover, I try to make sense of destructive energies and those that we have termed negative. I try to present a case and let the viewer decide if they would like to participate or not.'

—ANDREW GUENTHER

Andrew Guenther's black-and-white painting of a sick whale, seemingly drifting uneasily towards the sea floor, was followed by a number of paintings of sick dolphins the subsequent year (these with white outlines against brightly coloured or black backgrounds). The poignant descent of these creatures into the depths contrasts with the dark humour found in Guenther's colourful depictions of plants and foodstuffs. Guenther has said that his approach to art is as 'an enthusiastic scientist rediscovering the complexities of modern life'.

ABOVE · Andrew Guenther · *Sick Whale*, 2011
acrylic on unprimed canvas

OPPOSITE TOP · Elaine Bradford · *Pushmi-Pullyu* (*Tragus januali*), 2009 · taxidermy aoudad sheep, crocheted yarn and mixed media

OPPOSITE BOTTOM · Miho Sato · *Monster*, 2007
acrylic on board

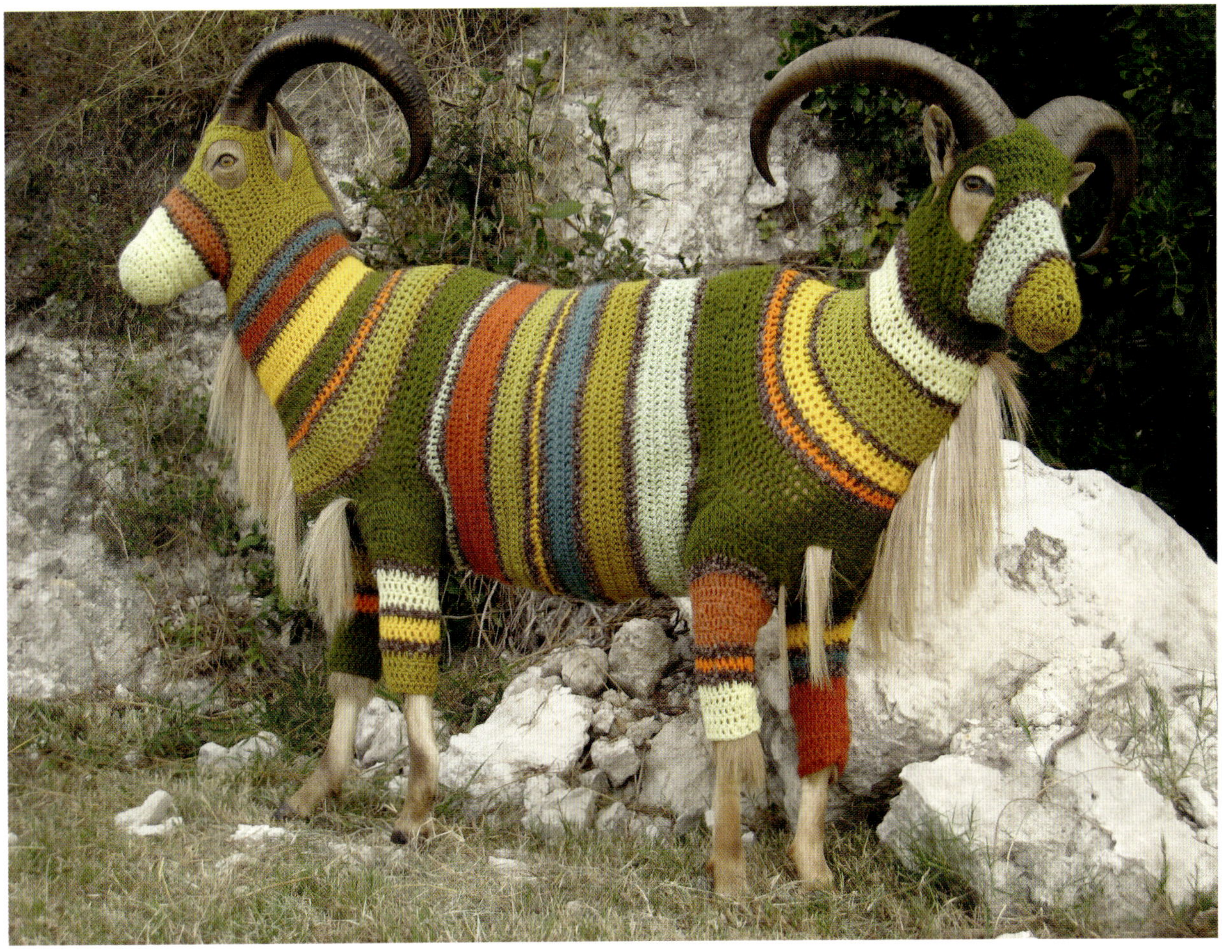

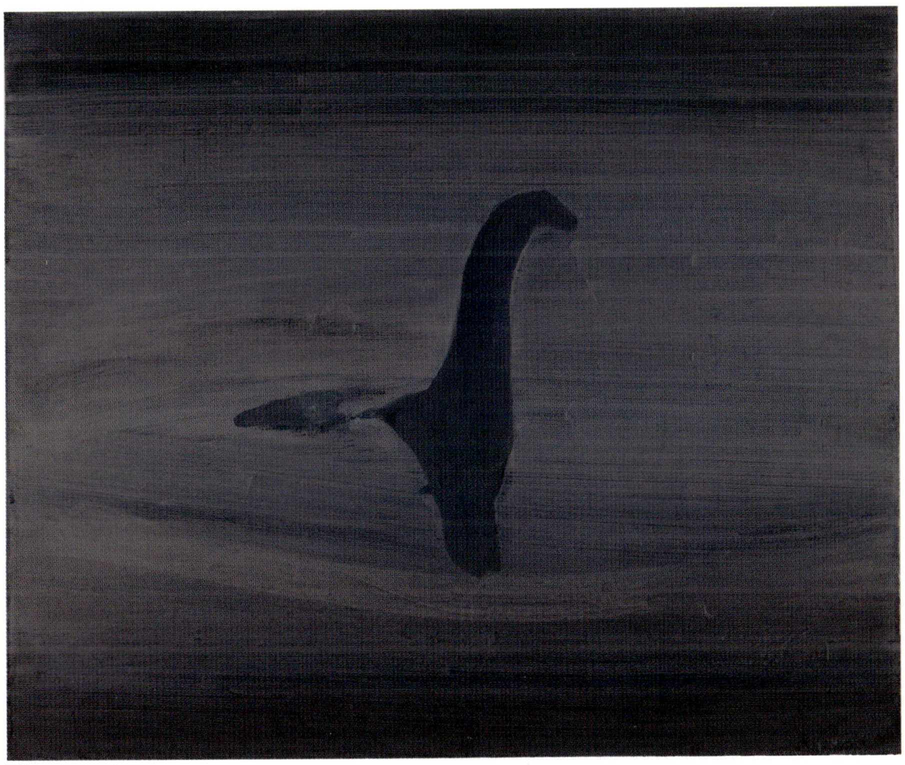

Both **Elaine Bradford** and **Miho Sato** are interested in the depiction of mythical beings. Bradford has gone so far as to found the Museum of Unnatural History where she displays her imaginary constructions as if they were only recently discovered species. Her *Pushmi-Pullyu* (*Tragus januali*) features a taxidermy double-headed sheep in a colourful knitted jumper; her *Longcat* (*Lynx metamorpha*) and *Pair-bears* (*Procyon besheret*) are similarly kitted out. All of these fabrications are given an extended backstory (of the artist's making) as to how they live in the wild. Sato's *Monster* features possibly the most famous of all reptiles, the Loch Ness Monster, said to be a dinosaur still living in a Scottish lake. For her painting, Sato copied an image that has been shown over and over in newspapers, on television and on the internet to *prove* its existence. Yet this monster remains as elusive as any of Bradford's creatures.

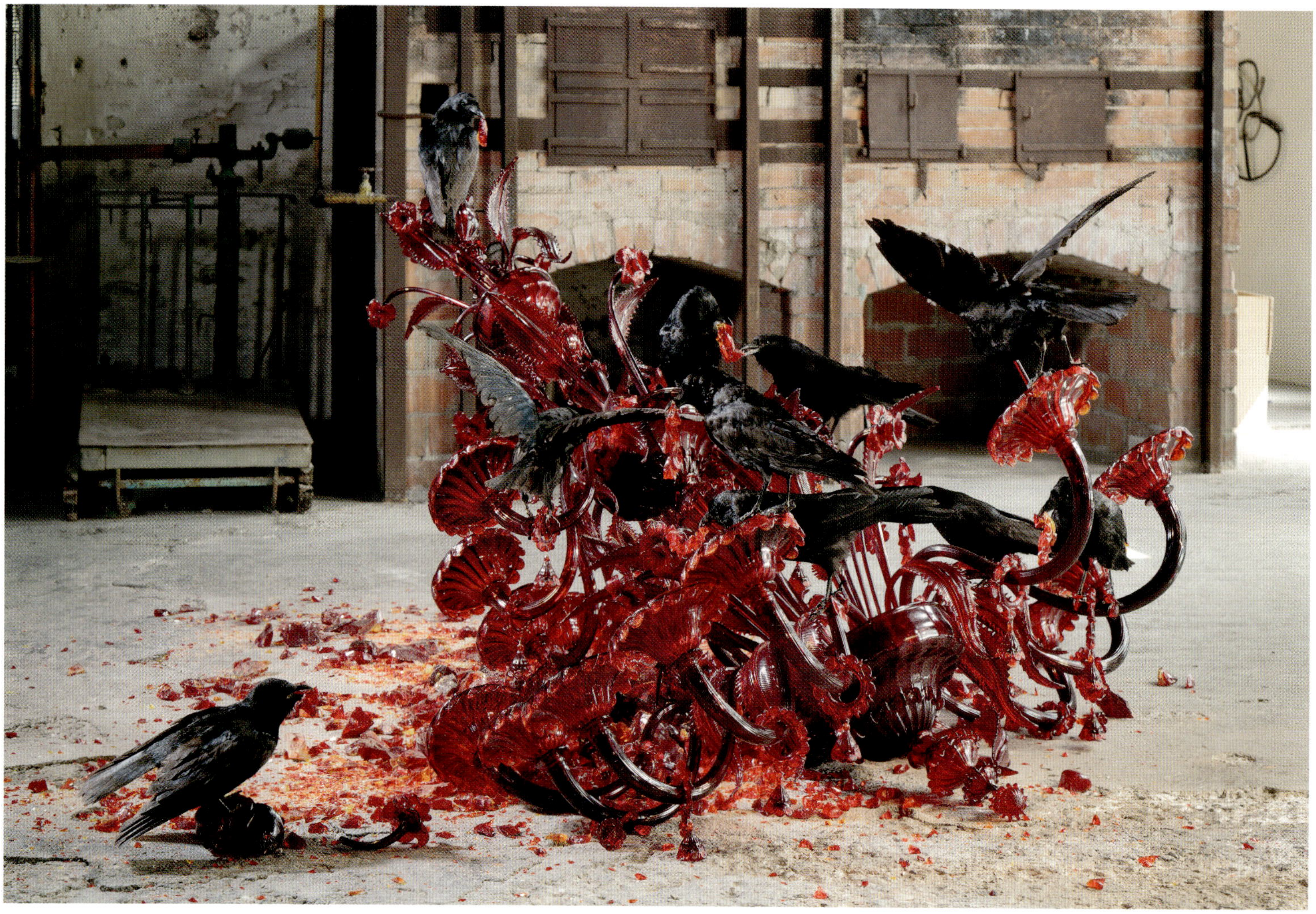

ABOVE
Javier Pérez
Carroña, 2011
Murano glass chandelier
and stuffed crows

OPPOSITE
Marta Klonowska
Large Kitchen Still Life after Michel de Bouillon, 2009
glass and metal

Javier Pérez often uses dissonant materials (silkworm cocoons and ceramics; cattle intestines and blown glass) to confront the viewer with death, mortality and impermanence. In his work *Carroña* (Carrion), black crows seem to be disembowelling a smashed, red chandelier. Pérez notes that he likes to transform ready-made objects so as to provoke multiple interpretations: 'Here there are two different levels of opposed meaning: luxury, brightness, this aspect that characterizes glass, Murano glass in particular, [here] transformed into something desolate.'

Marta Klonowska's *Large Kitchen Still Life after Michel de Bouillon* consists of a glass hare modelled after a similarly positioned hare in a traditional still-life painting by Michel de Bouillon, a seventeenth-century French painter. Klonowska often bases her delicate sculptures of wild animals and pets (mainly dogs) on those depicted in historical paintings; there the animal in question, dead or alive, was often included as a symbol of status and wealth. Klonowska's creatures are usually the same size as their counterparts in the source images.

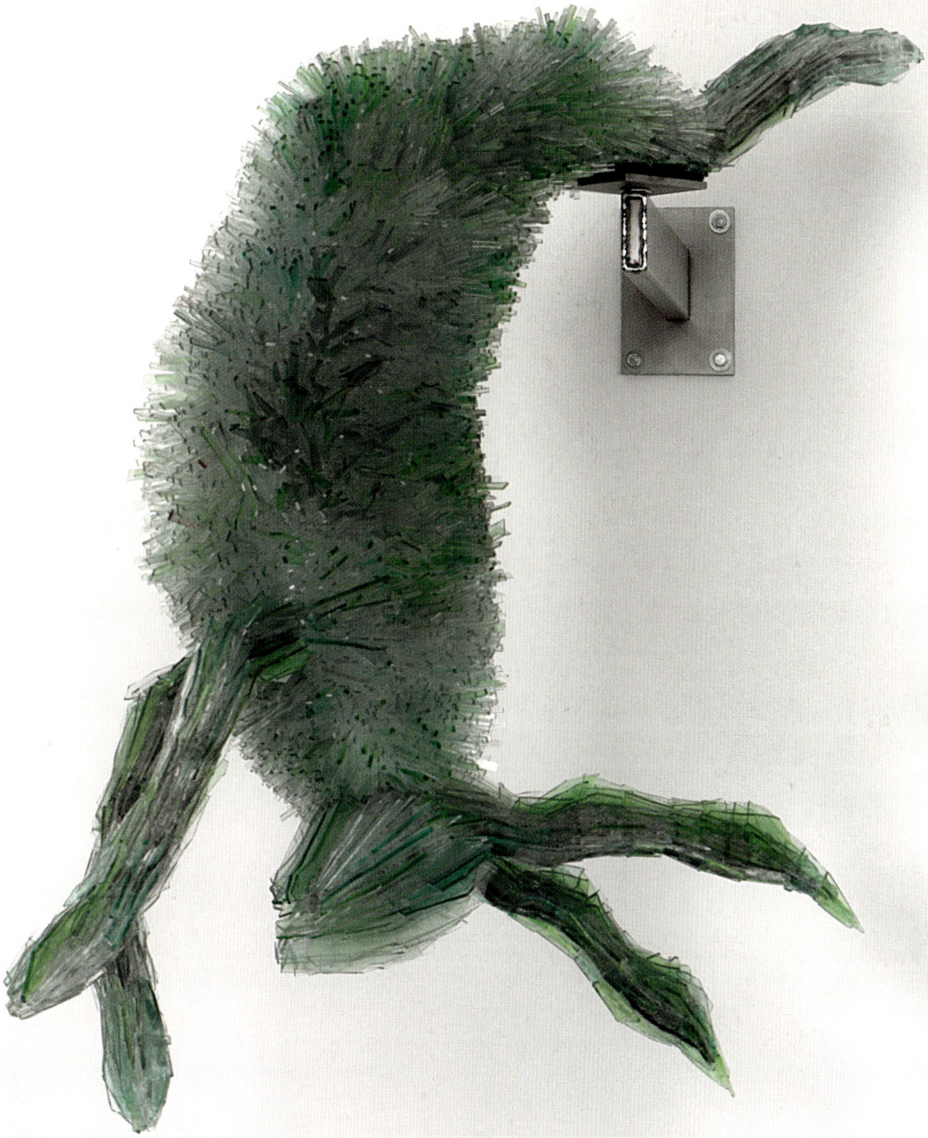

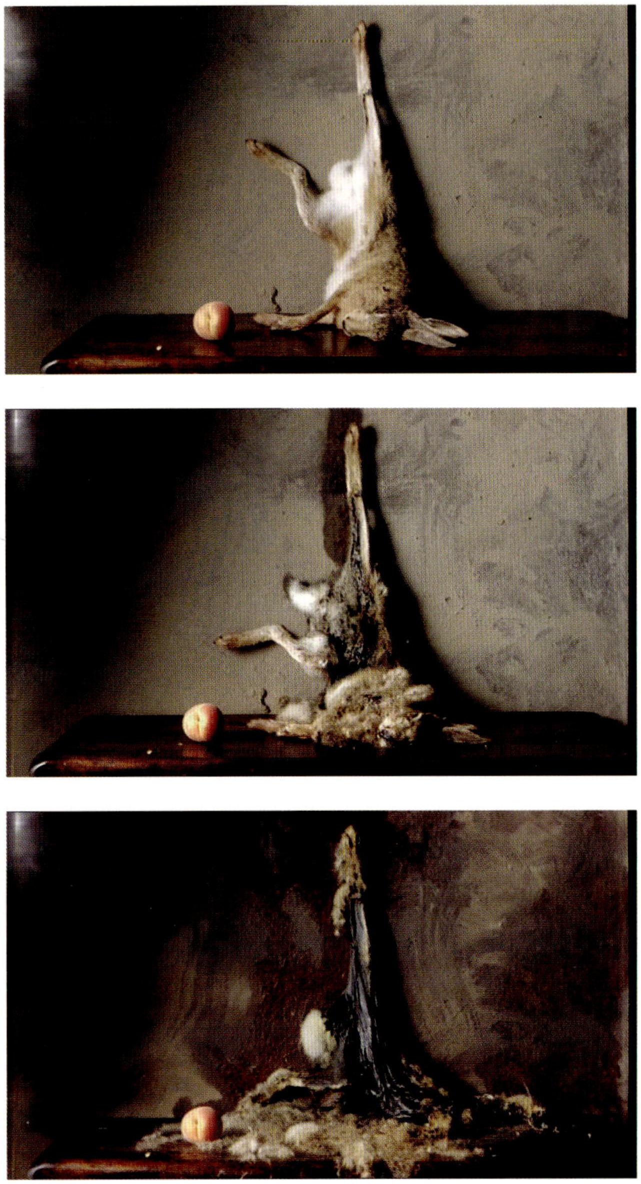

ABOVE
Sam Taylor-Johnson
A Little Death, 2002
35 mm film/DVD

OPPOSITE
Shirana Shahbazi
[*Voegel-02-2007*]
C-print on aluminium

Sam Taylor-Johnson's video *A Little Death* features a dead hare with its leg pegged to a wall (a familiar motif in many seventeenth-century animal still lifes). Time-lapse photography documents the decay of the hare, as maggots cover the table and the animal's fur slides away from its body. The insects disappear when there is no more flesh to consume, yet a plump peach next to the rabbit remains incongruously firm and ripe throughout. Taylor-Johnson's video recalls historical Flemish still lifes, which invited viewers to contemplate the passing of time. Here, viewers see time rush past their eyes.

Shirana Shahbazi often places the subjects of her still-life compositions against black backgrounds, which while looking back to the traditional still life of the seventeenth century also nods to current advertising photography. Her [*Voegel-02-2007*] could as easily be an image for a sales campaign to encourage the public to eat more game as a meditation on death and transience. A lack of context leads viewers to speculate on what that context could be, or should be, and speaks of greater philosophical and artistic depth.

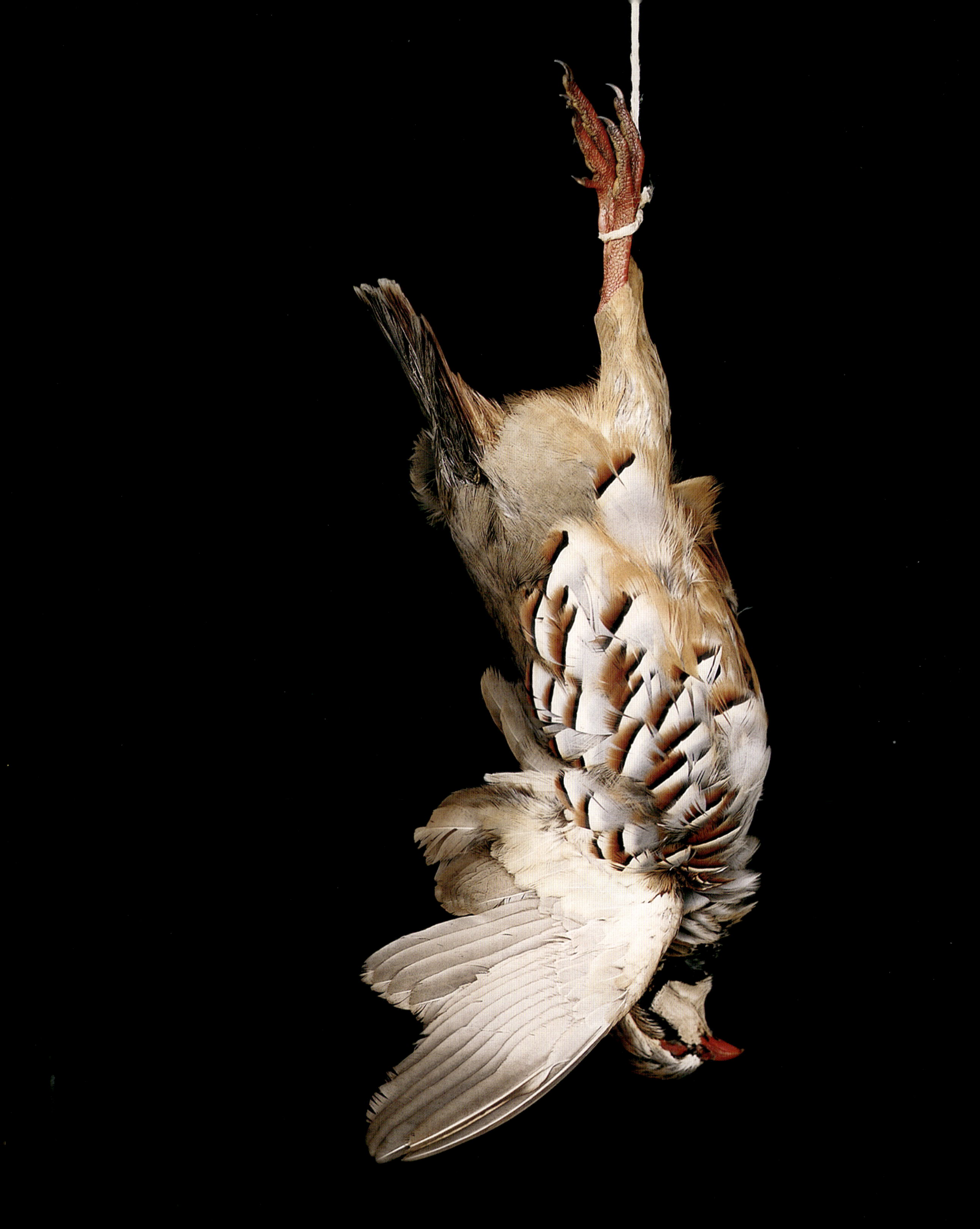

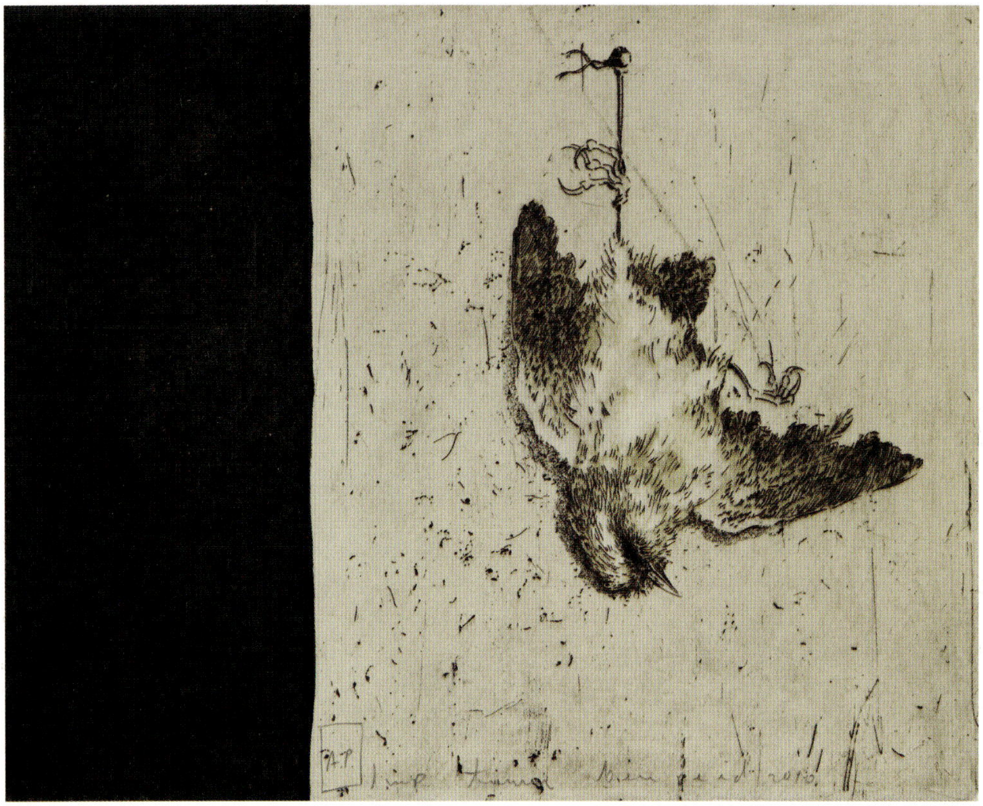

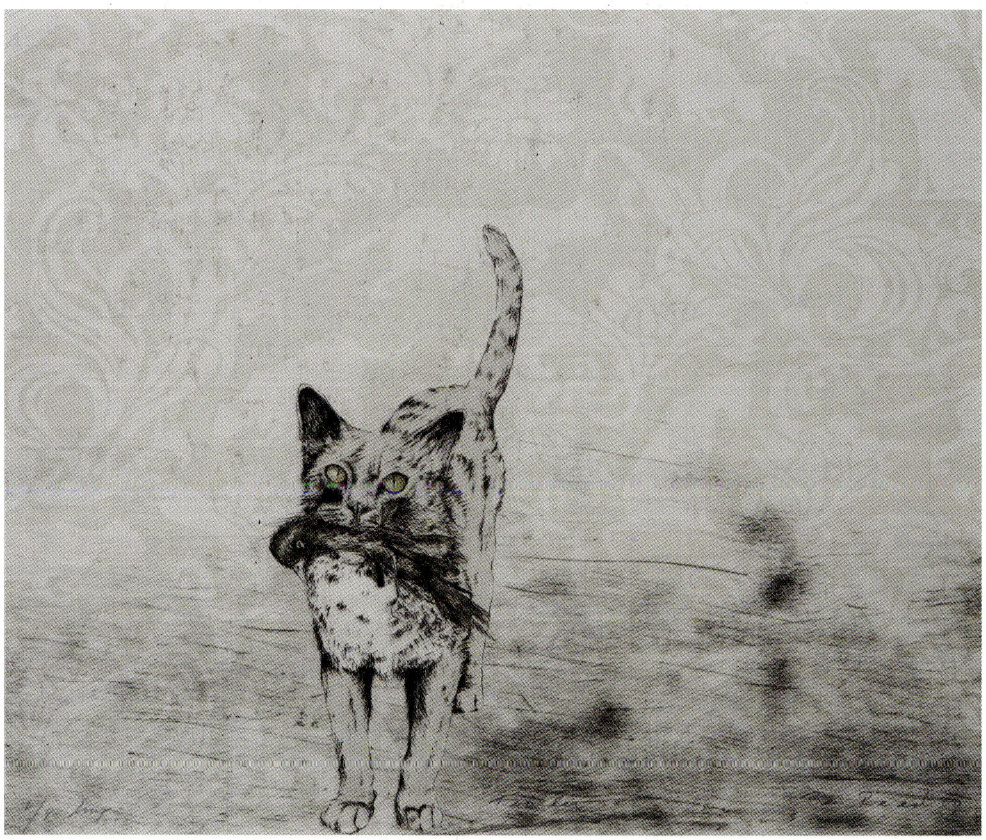

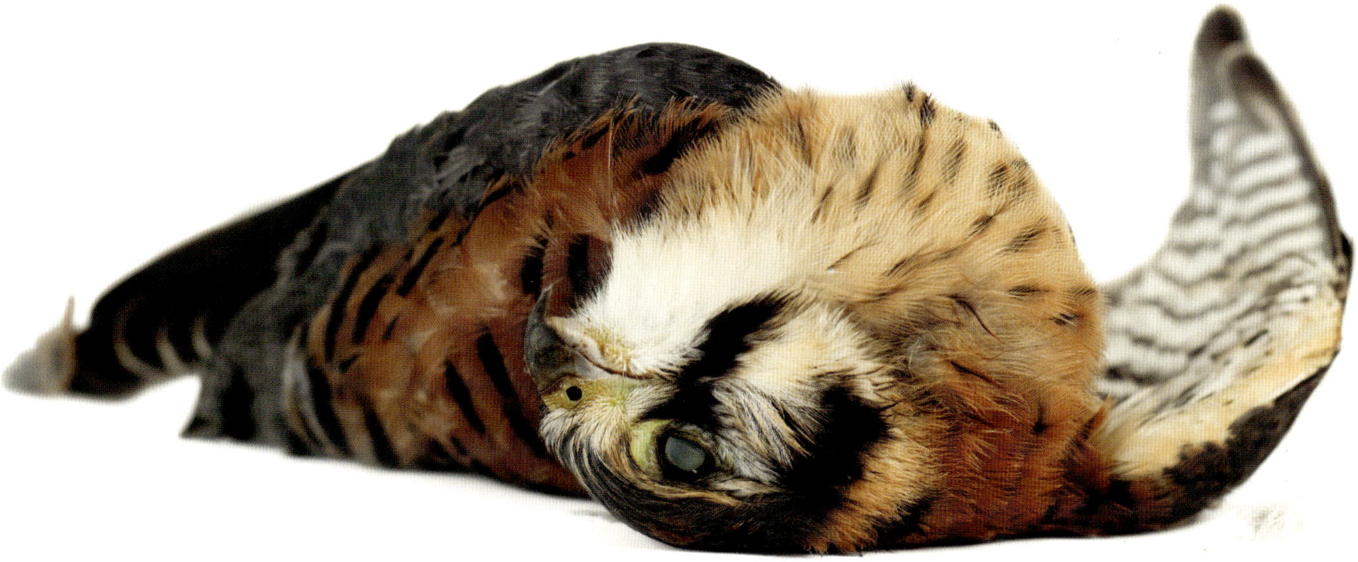

OPPOSITE TOP
Ben Reid
***tumu*, 2010**
drypoint, intaglio and relief print

OPPOSITE BOTTOM
Ben Reid
***Tibbles*, 2008**
drypoint, relief and woodblock print

ABOVE
Susan Silas
***eyes wide shut*, 2010**
giclée print on Hahnemühle photo rag

Ben Reid's *Paradise Lost* series of prints explores the impact of humans on the fragile ecosystems of his native New Zealand, whether caused by European settlers or local Maori peoples. *Tibbles* features a proud house cat holding in its mouth an indigenous bird, one which prior to the introduction of cats faced no such natural predators, while *tumu* shows the effective bird trap of the Maori in action. Reid refers to these works as 'small stories for those prepared to listen'.

Susan Silas photographed dead and decaying birds (hawks, doves) for her series *found birds, 2000 – the present.* Shot against a simple white or black background, the stilled life on display forces the viewer to contemplate their own mortality. Silas is interested in the history of images that aestheticize death and the way in which photography functions as a marker of absence.

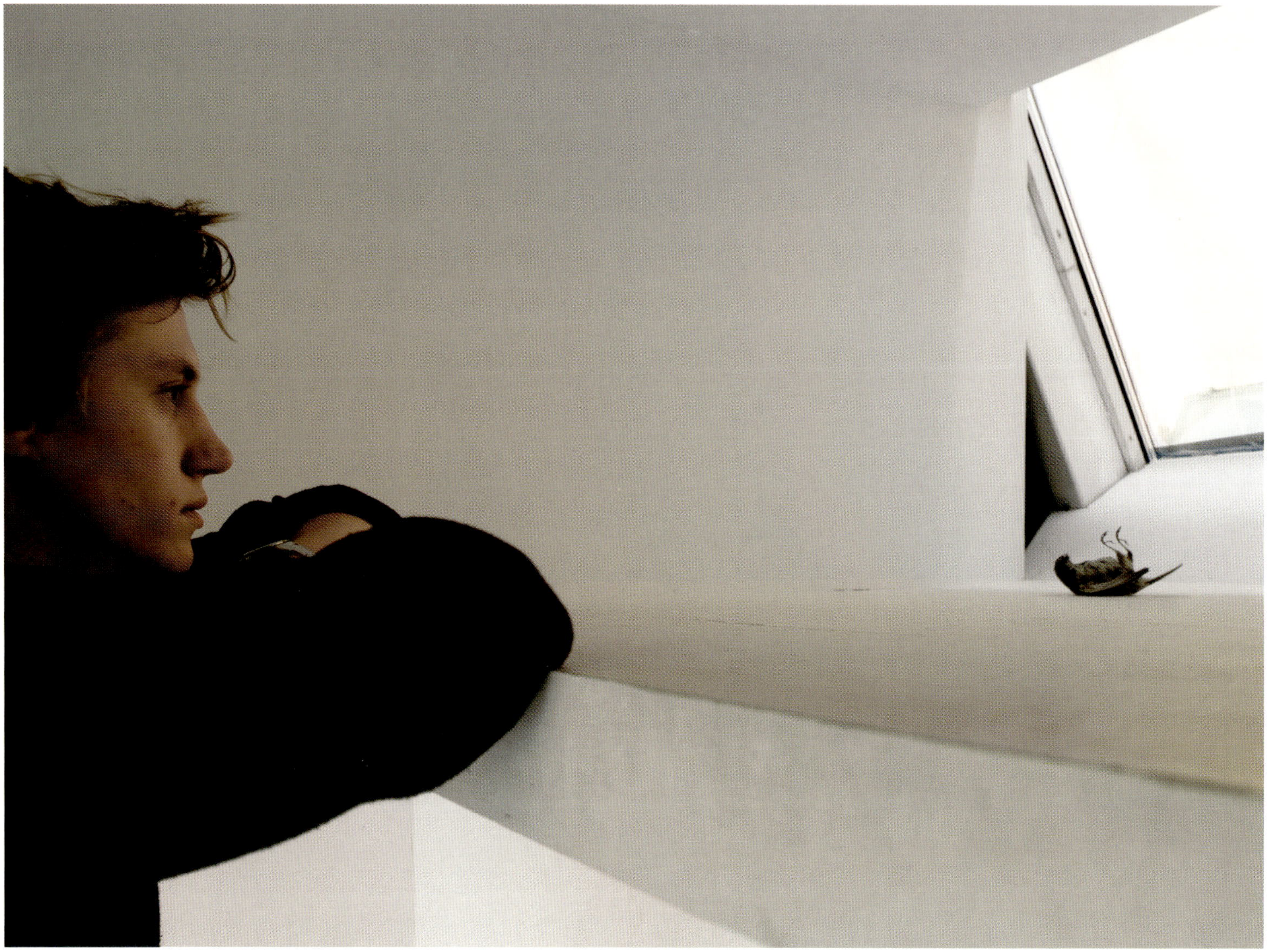

ABOVE
Elmgreen & Dragset
Somewhere in the World it's 4 o'clock – Blocking the View – Just a Single Wrong Move, 2004
animatronic twitching sparrow

OPPOSITE TOP
Taryn Simon · ***Contraband***,
installation image, Gagosian Gallery, 2010

OPPOSITE BOTTOM
Taryn Simon · ***Bird corpse, labeled as home décor, Indonesia to Miami, Florida (prohibited)*** [detail], 2010

Elmgreen & Dragset's animatronic sparrow looks amazingly lifelike as it shudders in a series of death throes. The fluttering of its tiny mechanical heartbeat purposely tears at viewers' own heart strings as the small bird endlessly dies in front of our eyes. The artists say the work draws attention to the increasing disappearance of sparrows within the UK, as well as the decline of English working-class identity ('Cockney Sparrows'). The work is intended to contrast our individual feelings of powerlessness in the face of a rapidly changing world with how easily each of us can be affected by small events, even the death of a bird.

Taryn Simon created her *Contraband* series at the US Postal Service International Mail Facility and the US Customs inspection site, both at New York's JFK Airport. Over four days, she shot 1,075 photographs of items being smuggled into America and deemed illegal or prohibited: contraband cigarettes, foodstuffs (beans, pork fat), drugs (steroids, Viagra, heroin), fake perfumes and luxury items, or animals and their parts (deer penis, cow hoof, dried guinea pig, chicken feet). One small, dead bird, en route from Indonesia to Miami, was labelled disingenuously as 'home décor'. Shown together, Simon's photographs form a strong narrative of desire.

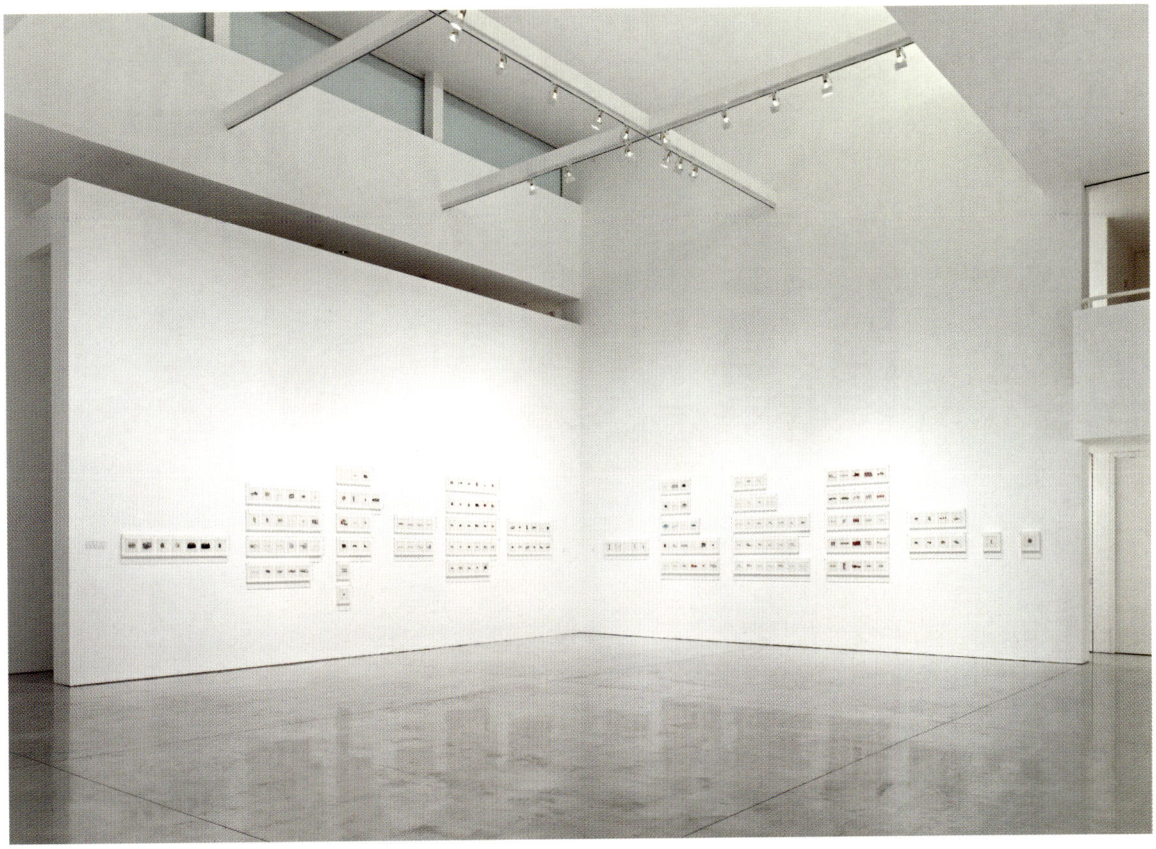

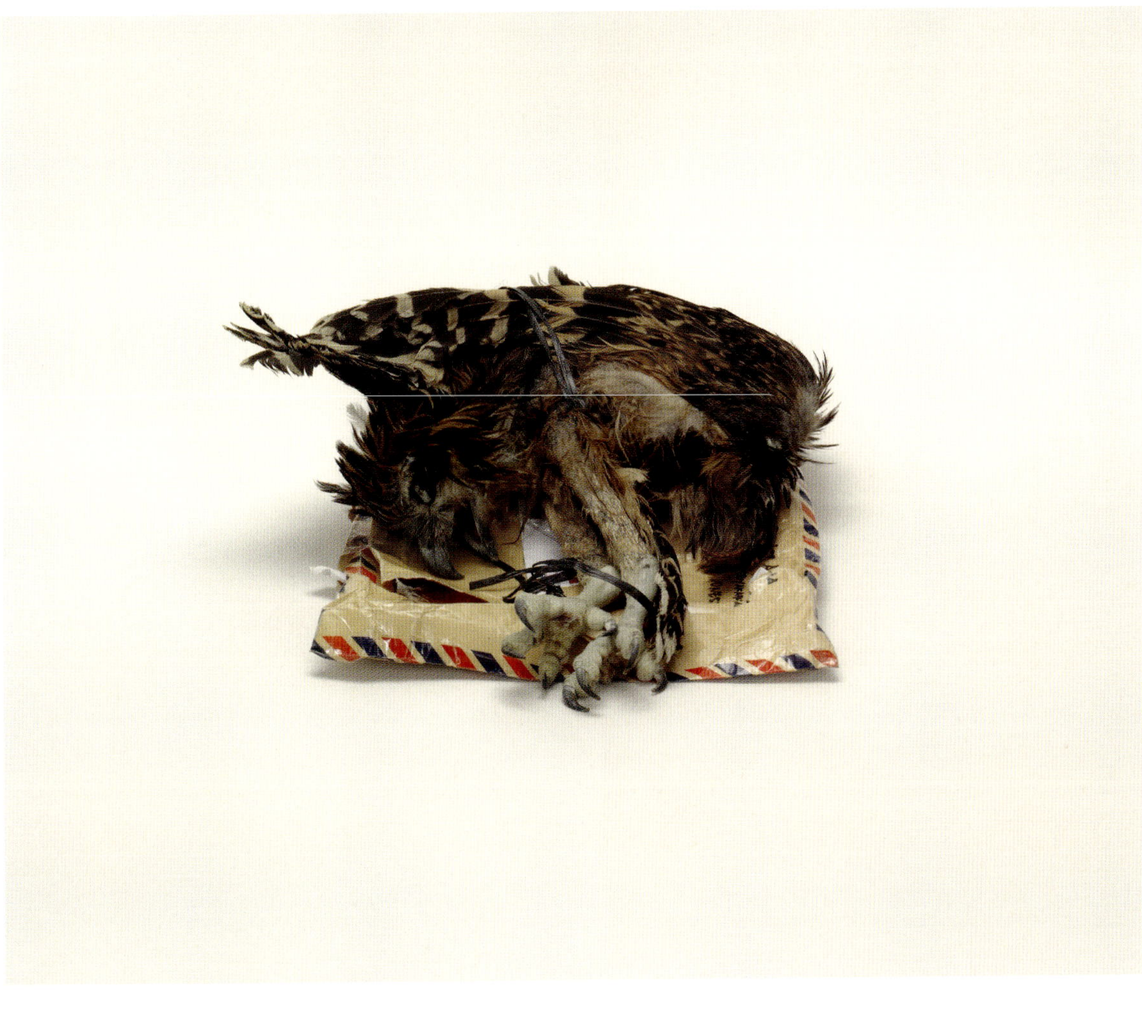

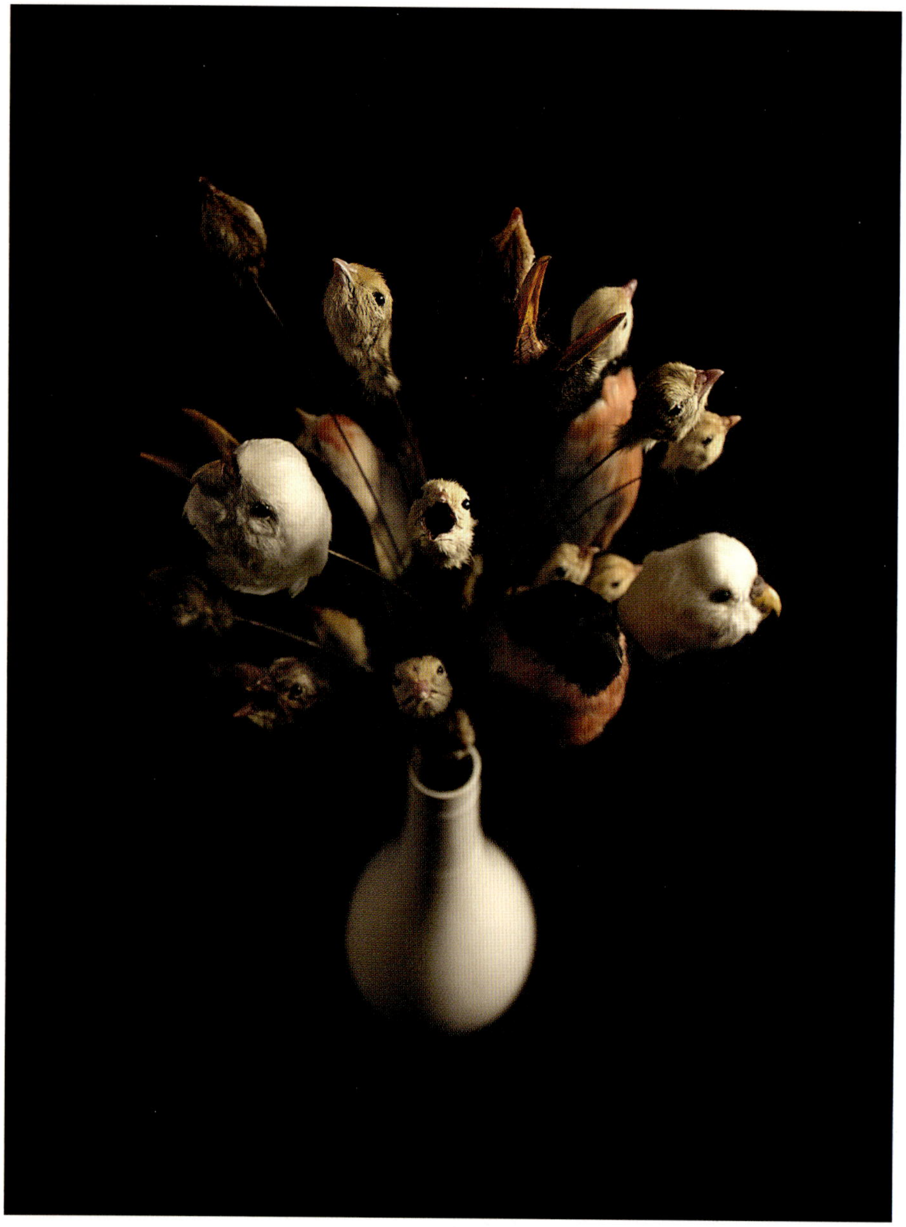

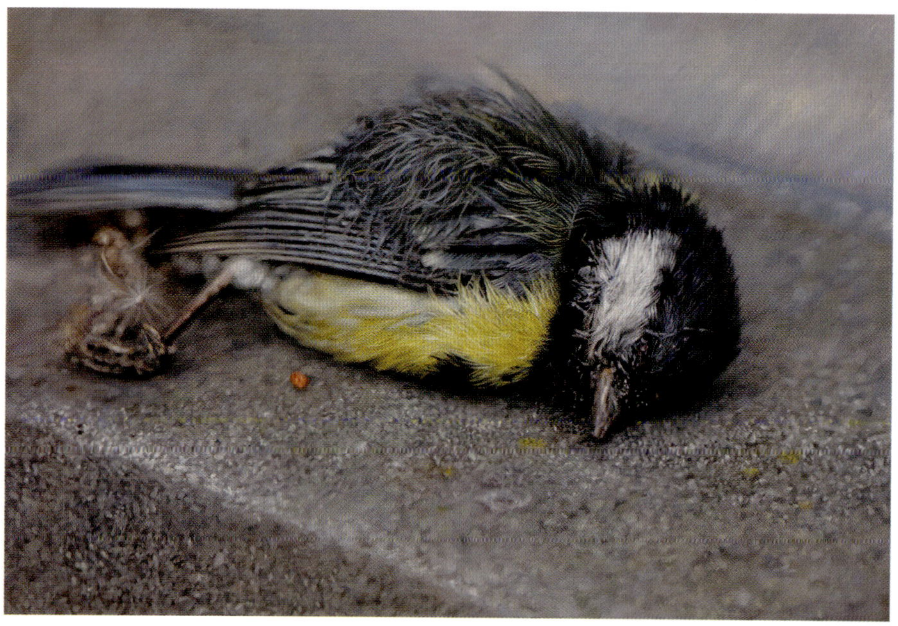

Polly Morgan uses taxidermy animals as the source material for her sculptures. The swarm of dismembered bird heads that makes up *Feed Me* seems to pour up and out of a vase barely able to contain its occupants desire for sustenance and life. Morgan named her 2010 'Psychopomps' exhibition, and its four suspended taxidermy sculptures, after the mythical beings said to guide the human soul to the underworld after death. In Classical mythology these guides were often represented as domesticated animals (dogs, horses) or wild birds.

Cindy Wright's painting of a dead *Koolmeesje*, or Great Tit, is a delicate and touching work. These small, non-migratory birds have successfully adapted to urban settings and are well known to gardeners throughout Europe. While birds have appeared in art as messengers for the gods, or as one aspect of a god's physical form (Ra, the Egyptian sun god, had the head of a falcon and the body of a man), Wright's bird, dead on the unforgiving pavement, serves as a poignant reminder of mortality.

While out walking, **Daniel Gustav Cramer** found a dead cat frozen in rigor mortis but looking like it was still alive and playful. He photographed the animal; by chance, on his return to the spot the next day, the cat was covered in snow, so he photographed it again. The resulting work, *Cat*, consists of both photographs and a short description of the incident. It highlights how in the digital age an image can easily deceive us, asking us to question at all times what it is we are looking at and to investigate our response to nature, the 'natural' and to death.

Cai Guo-Qiang's *Head On* evokes not only the infamous Berlin Wall (the work was first exhibited in Berlin) and society's collective ability to hurl itself towards disaster – be it through ideology (Communism, Nazism) or mass hysteria – but also man's ability to recover from such destructive acts of hubris. Cai's installation of ninety-nine wolves charging headlong into a glass wall reminds us that, like wolves, humans are very much pack animals and can work together, for better or for worse.

OPPOSITE TOP
Polly Morgan · ***Feed Me***, 2010
taxidermy, steel, metal vase, clay and glass

OPPOSITE BOTTOM
Cindy Wright · ***Koolmeesje***, 2010 · oil on linen

RIGHT AND BELOW
Daniel Gustav Cramer
Cat, 2002/11 · 2 C-prints, 1 framed text

NEXT PAGE
Cai Guo-Qiang · ***Head On***, 2006 · 99 life-sized replicas of wolves (gauze, resin and painted hide) and glass wall

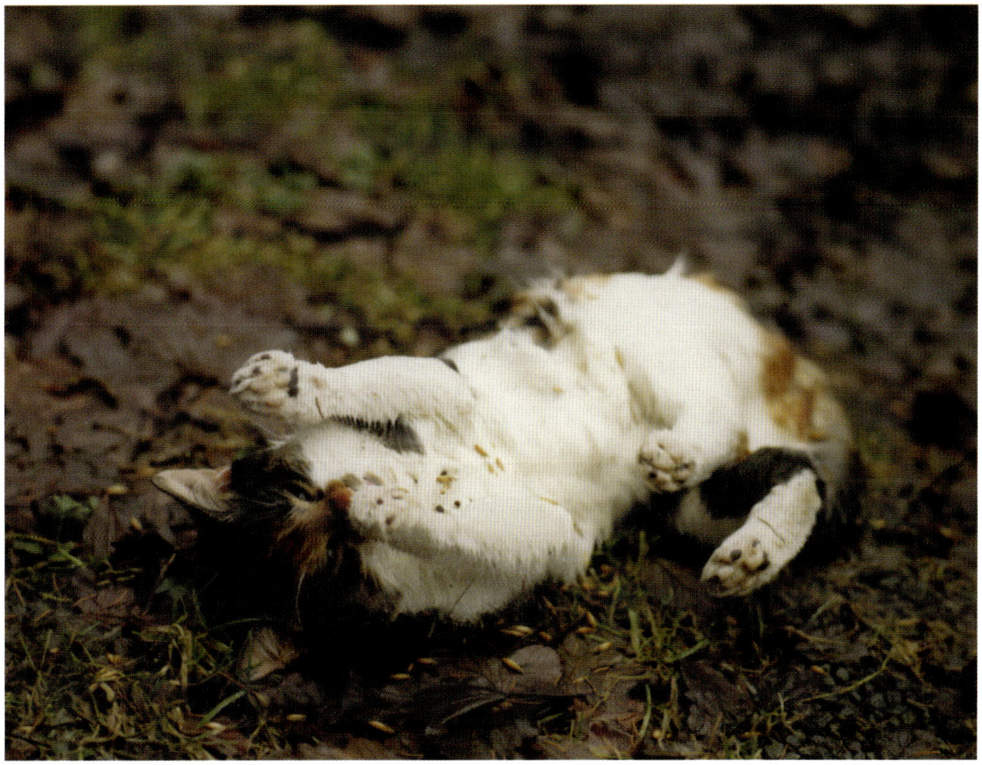

On December 31, I walked up a hill with three friends in Tühringen, near Ilmenau. We found a dead cat lying on its back. Her position seemed as if death caught her by surprise in a moment of joy and play. In the night, we lightened firecrackers. It started snowing. The following morning we decided to walk up the hill again.

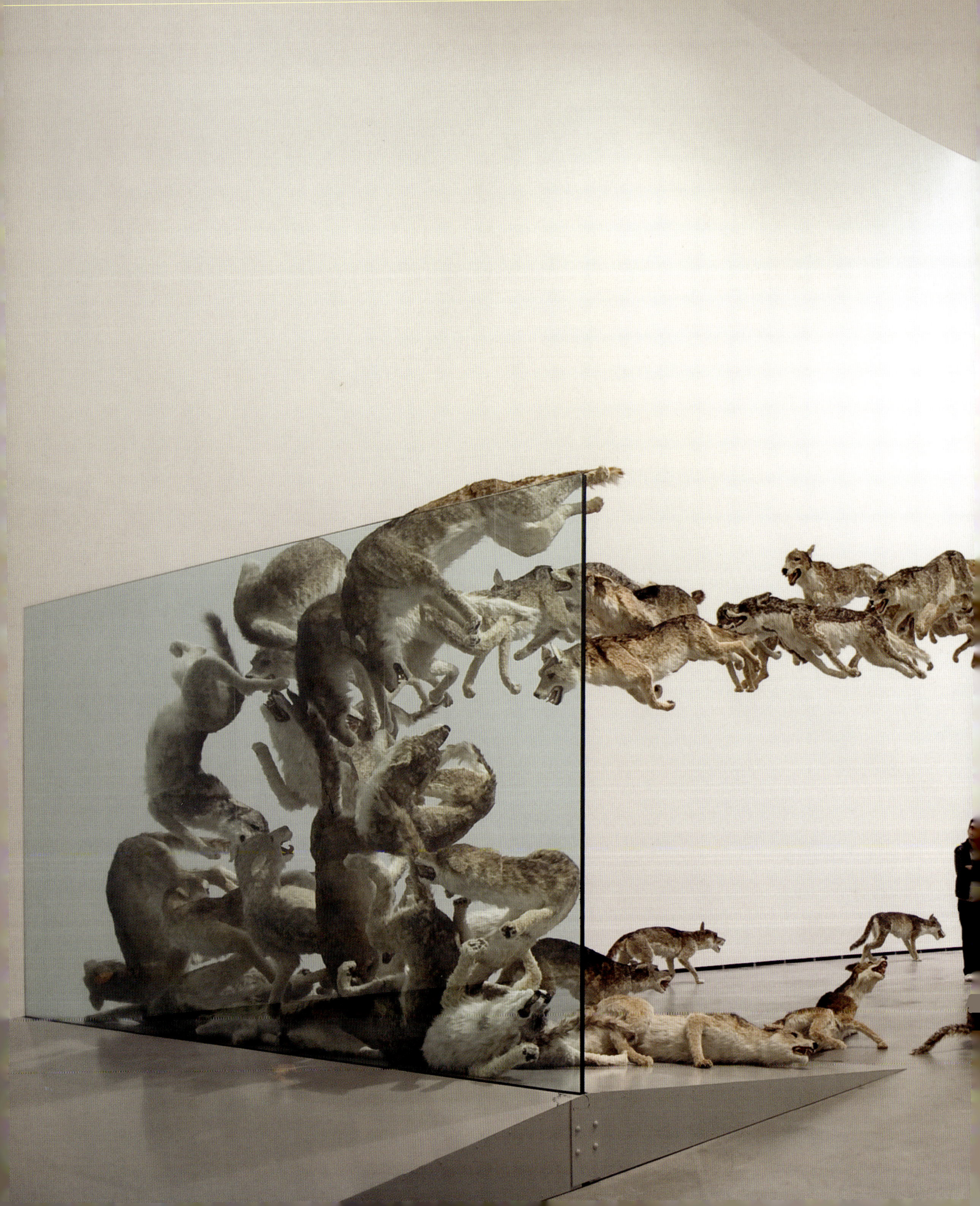

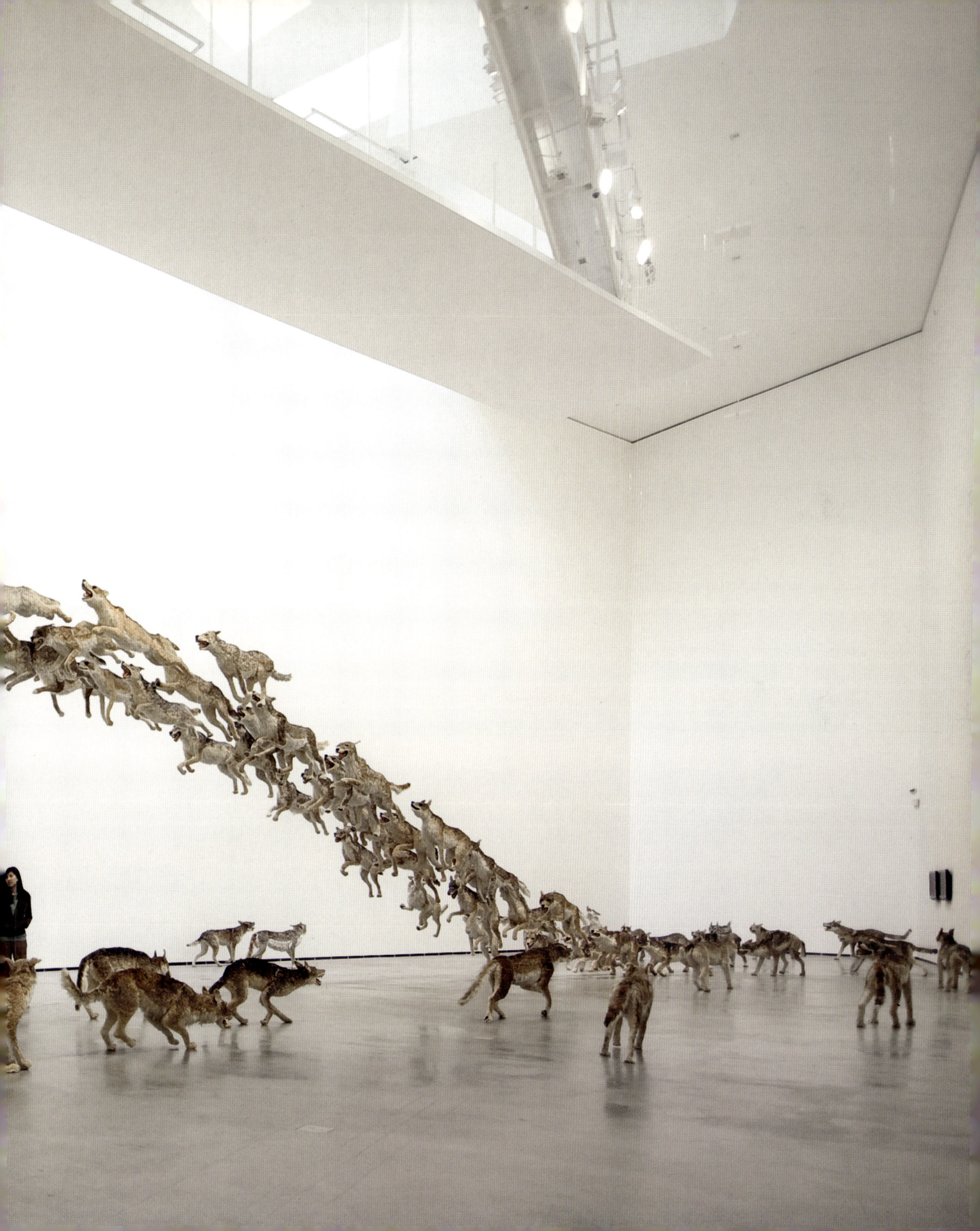

Nancy Fouts often incorporates taxidermy animals into her surreal works, be it a snail crawling along the edge of a razor blade, a budgerigar breaking out of a glass bell jar, a ladybird taking the place of a spot on a domino or a *Rabbit with Curlers*. Her quirky alterations to these ready-made and inherently sad husks of animals – they are dead and stuffed after all – somehow manage to bring the creatures back to life.

Sherrie Levine uses appropriation in her art, re-photographing or making sculptures based on the works of artists such as Man Ray, Marcel Duchamp and Walker Evans. For her 2011 exhibition 'The Desert' Levine made bronze casts of bobcat and javelina skulls, referencing the animal skulls that appear in Georgia O'Keeffe's still-life paintings. Levine showed the editions of each skull together, as multiples, thereby referencing her own practice through repetition, as well as that of O'Keeffe. Levine had previously cast cattle skulls for a show at the Georgia O'Keeffe Museum in Santa Fe, where she now lives.

Klaus Pichler's series of photographs called *Skeletons in the Closet* captures taxidermy animals that appear surprised, as if caught unaware by the flash of the camera. Each one looks baffled by its current situation, whether stranded in an elevator (*Elevator Bear*, 2011), stuck in a basement (*Basement Shark*, 2011) or placed in storage, as in *Plastic Deers*. These works offer insight into the casual disregard we have for the lifeless bodies of our fellow creatures.

Matt Smith is often invited to add his works to historical collections of ceramics or taxidermy animals. For *Otters and Bears*, Smith positioned ceramic bears of his own making alongside a found stuffed otter. The work is a clever reference to the parlance of contemporary gay culture, in which large, hairy men are often called *bears*, and the younger, slimmer men who find them attractive are called *otters*.

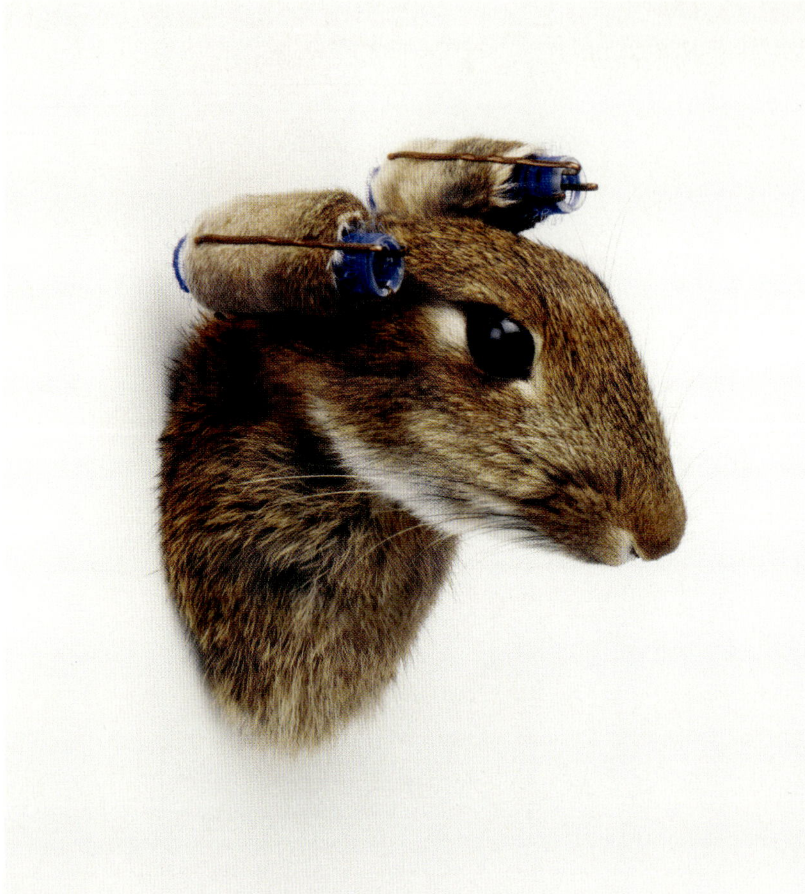

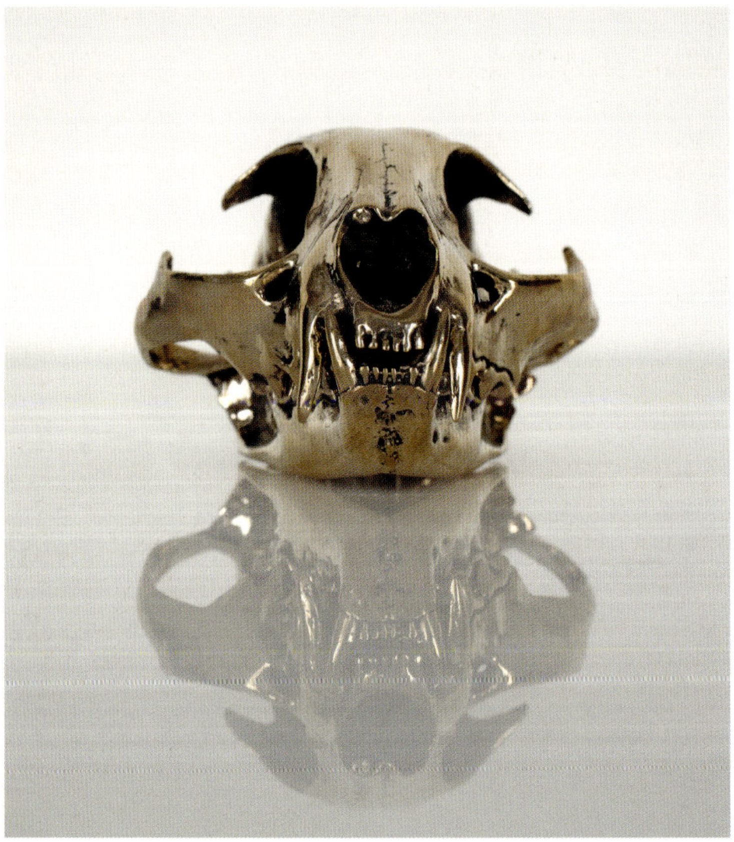

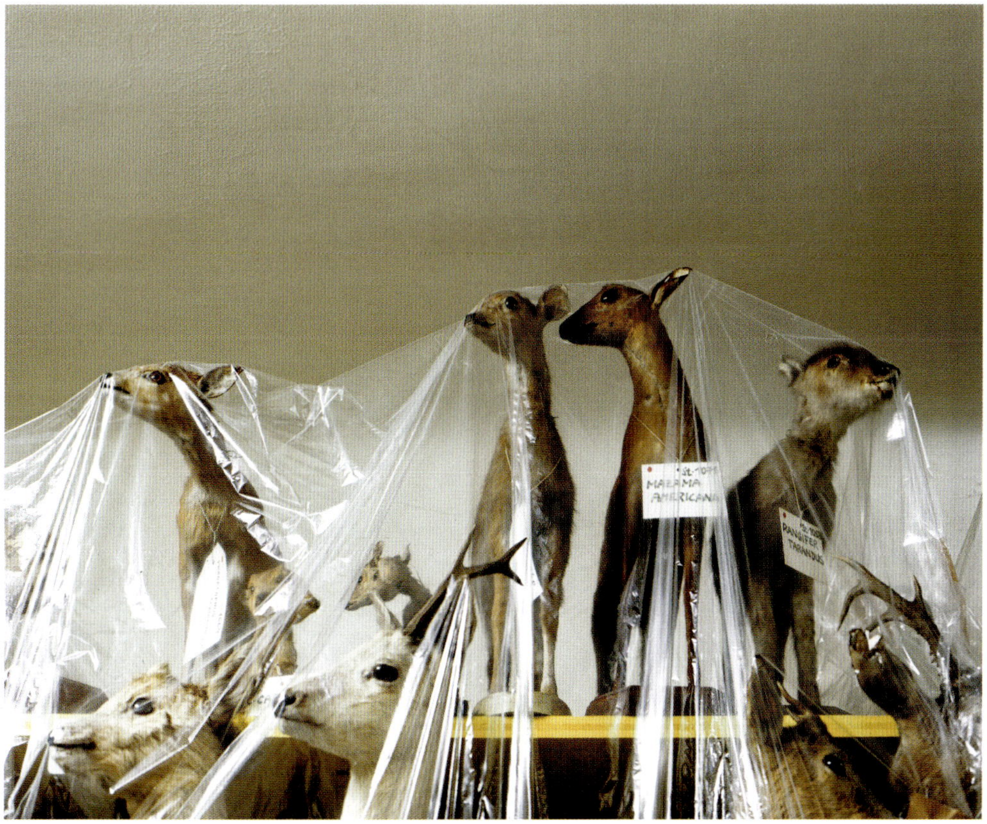

OPPOSITE TOP
Nancy Fouts
Rabbit with Curlers, 2010
taxidermy rabbit, curlers and kirby grips

OPPOSITE BOTTOM
Sherrie Levine
Bobcat Skull, 2010
cast bronze

LEFT
Klaus Pichler
Plastic Deers, 2010
digital C-Print

BELOW
Matt Smith
Otters and Bears, 2010
taxidermy otter and salt-glazed ceramic bears

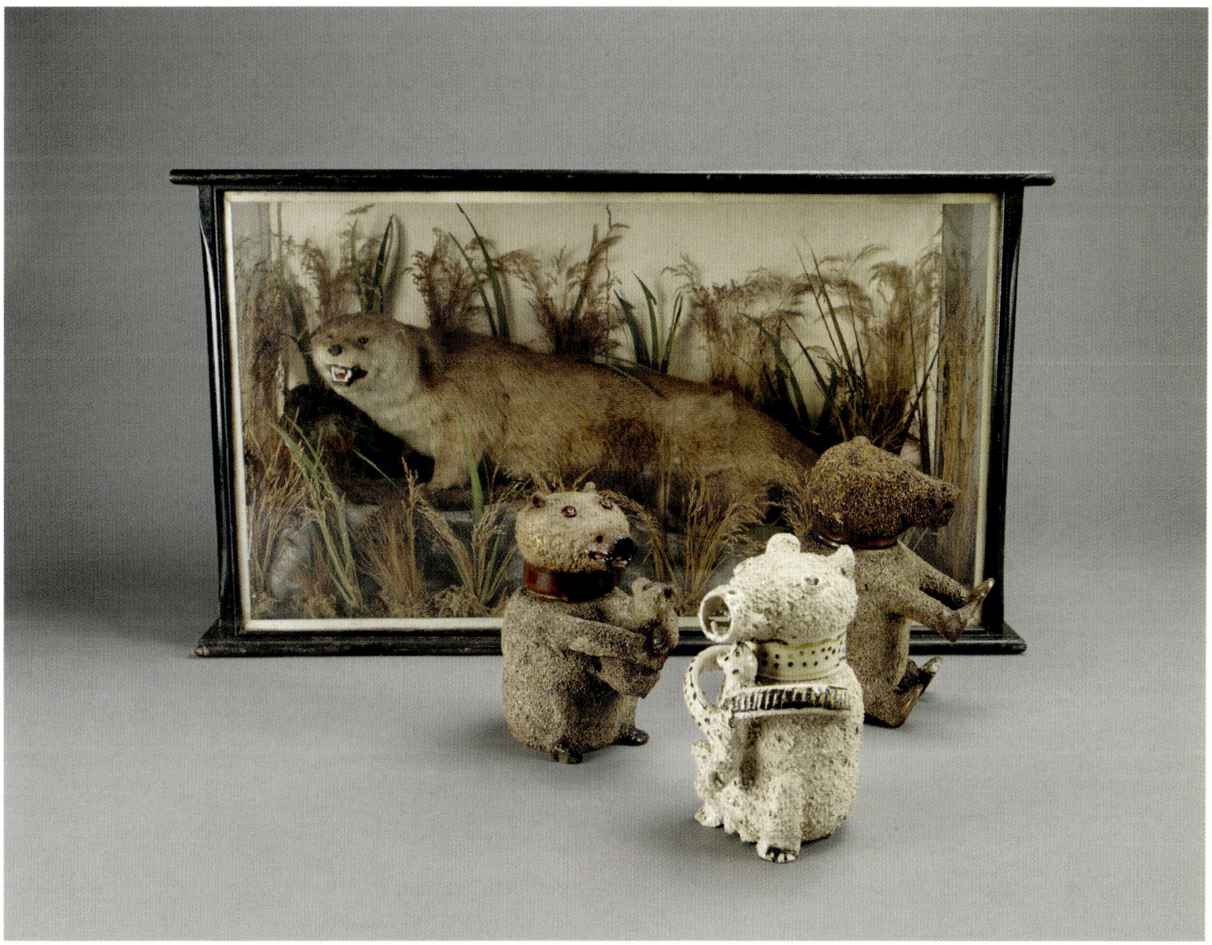

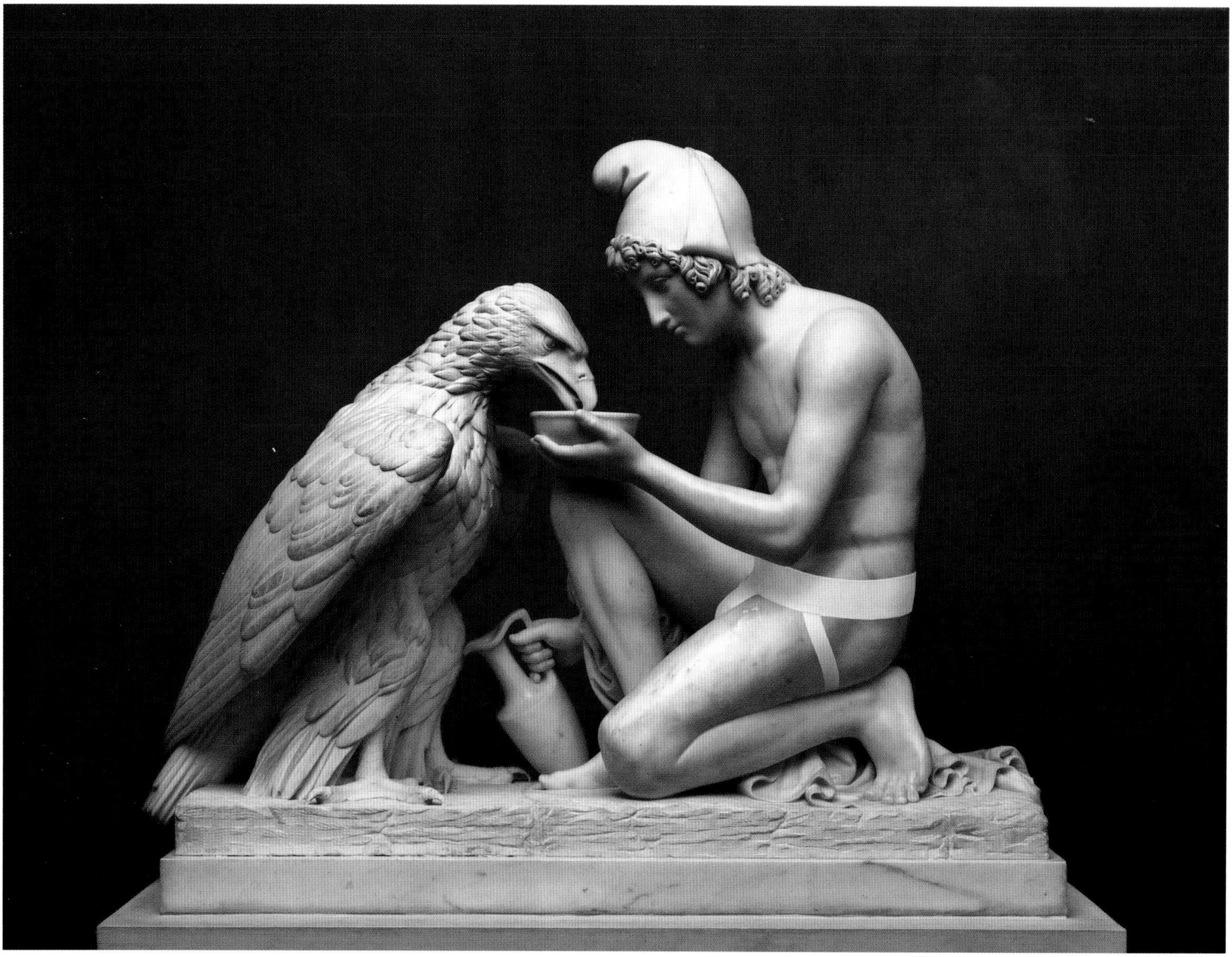

ABOVE
Elmgreen & Dragset
Ganymede (Jockstrap), 2009
laserchrome colour print mounted on aluminium with Plexiglas

Elmgreen & Dragset adapted pre-existing classical marble sculptures to create such photographs as *Ganymede (Jockstrap)*. This work features Zeus, in the form an eagle, drinking from a libation offered by the youthful Ganymede, who wears a contemporary athletic supporter added by the artists. In ancient Greek creation myth, Zeus takes Ganymede to be his cup-bearer, and male lover, on Mount Olympus. Upon the mortal's death, he transforms him into a constellation so that he can live forever. In the Classical Greek world, older men were expected to take young male lovers. Elmgreen & Dragset are committed to queering the historical view of human nature by examining the fictions that underpin social norms and expectations.

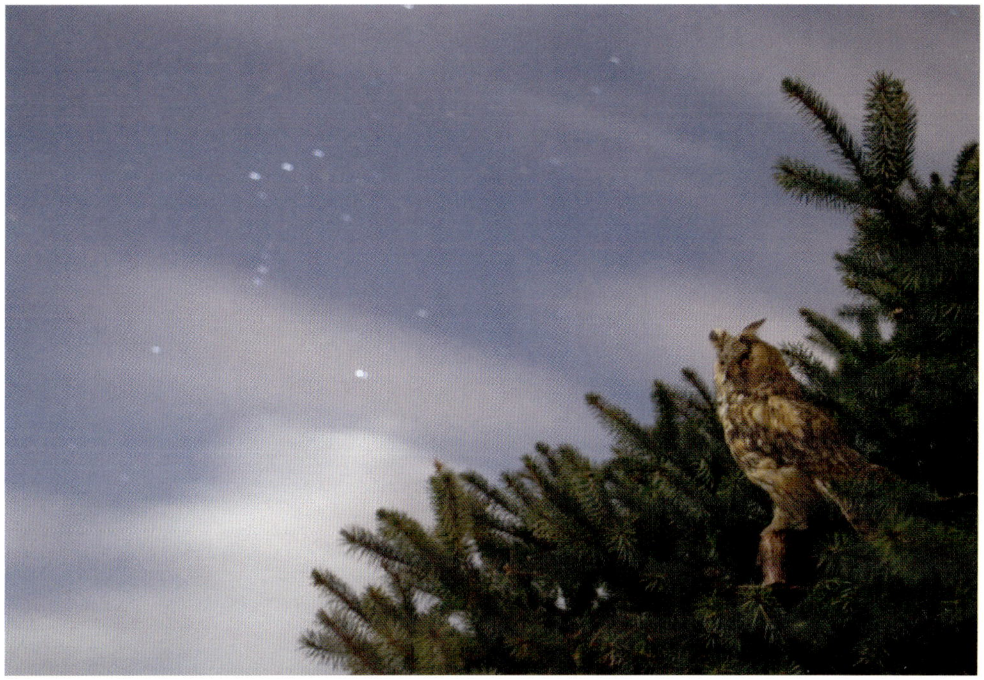

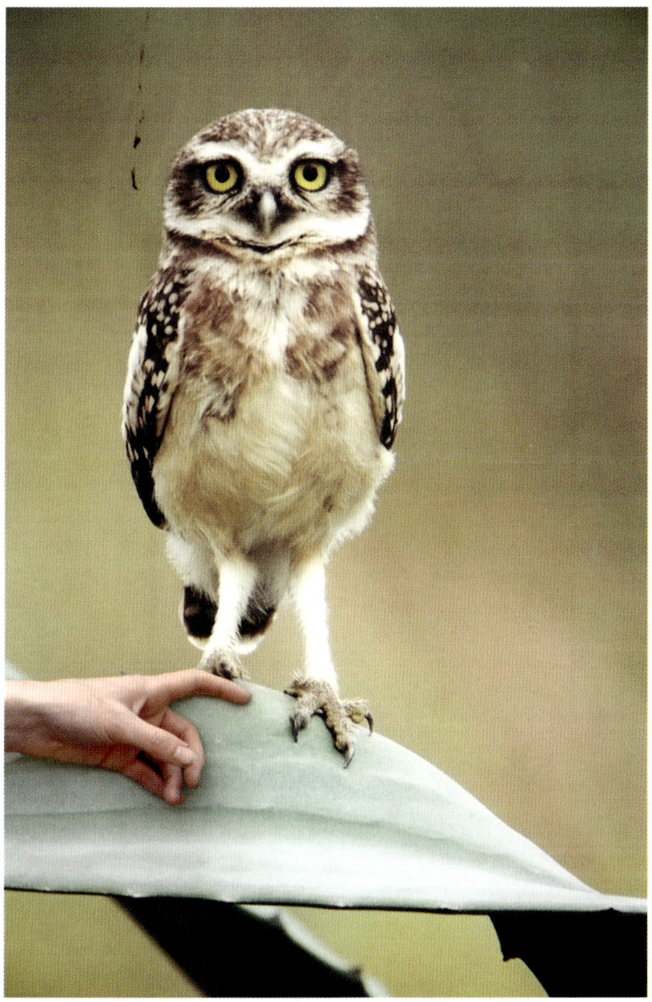

Jan Kjetil Bjørheim used a large collection of taxidermy animals stuffed by a neighbour to create his series of still-life photographs that *return* these creatures to the wild. For *Still Life, Nocturn– Owl in Pine*, Bjørheim placed an owl in a real tree against the Norwegian night sky. The resulting photograph is almost as surreal and constructed as if it were painted. Other works from his *Still Life* series verge on the tragi-comic: a Bambi-esque *Deer* (2006) returns to the forest and *Goats* (2006) scavenge in a scrap yard.

Alana Lake used a pre-existing image of an owl to create her clever photograph, *The Closer you are the Further you Become, ii (creepy)*. At a zoo with large photographs of birds mounted outside their enclosures, she had fellow artist Kraig Wilson extend his hand beneath the illustrated owl so as to make it appear that the bird was perched on his finger. Her photograph (of a photograph) distances the viewer from the artificiality of the zoo (these animals would not naturally be found there) yet places them within its frame. In Christian iconography, the owl has occupied a contradictory position as both a symbol for the devil, due to its nocturnal nature, and a symbol for Christ. In the twenty-first century, the owl is associated primarily with wisdom or knowledge.

LEFT
Alana Lake · *The Closer you are the Further you become, ii (creepy)*, 2010
archival digital print

ABOVE
Jan Kjetil Bjørheim
Still Life, Nocturn– Owl in Pine, 2007 · C-print

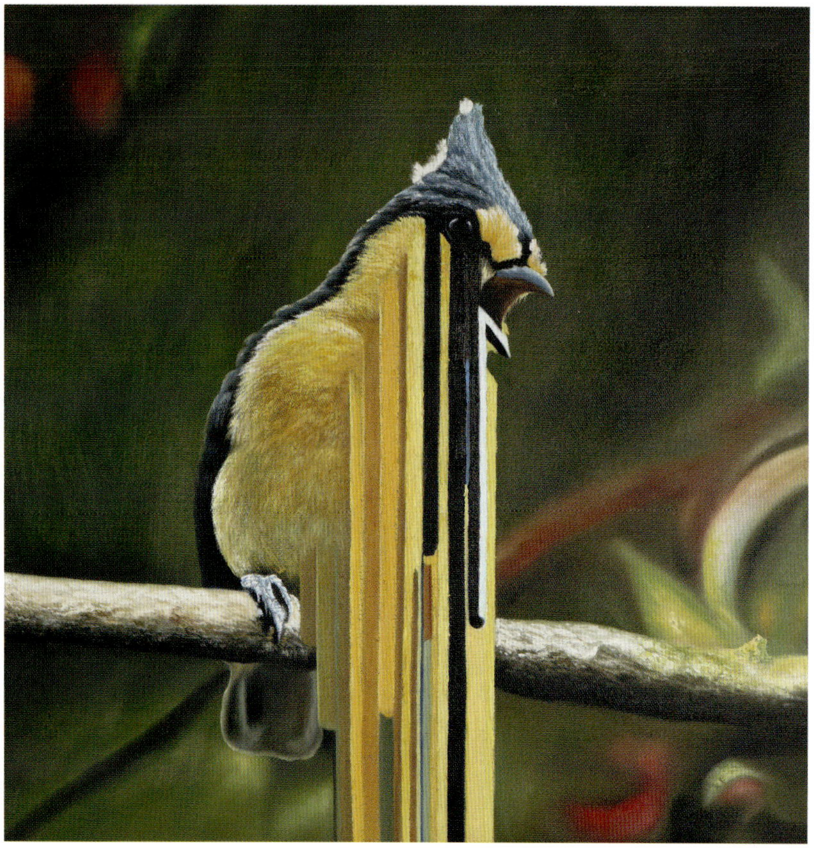

Maurizio Bongiovanni takes realism for a ride in his *Bird rib* oil paintings, forcing the viewer to recalibrate their ideas of what they are seeing. Otherwise straightforward paintings of wild birds are interrupted by what looks like fax machine bleeding, when parts of the image become dragged out, or computer pixellation gone wrong, Matrix-style. The paintings question visual representations of nature in the digital age. Bongiovanni sends his initial drawings to China, where paintings are produced to his specifications. When they arrive back in Italy, he fine tunes the images by making his own additions.

Shane Mecklenburger created his *Roadkill Diamond* by cremating the body of an armadillo found dead on a road in Palestine, Texas, and having its carbon ash compressed into a diamond. In Native American creation myths, the armadillo is viewed as a slow animal that while unhurried always gets it right. In modern times that admirable trait makes the animal a frequent victim of hit-and-runs, demonstrating how so often ancient and modern worlds collide.

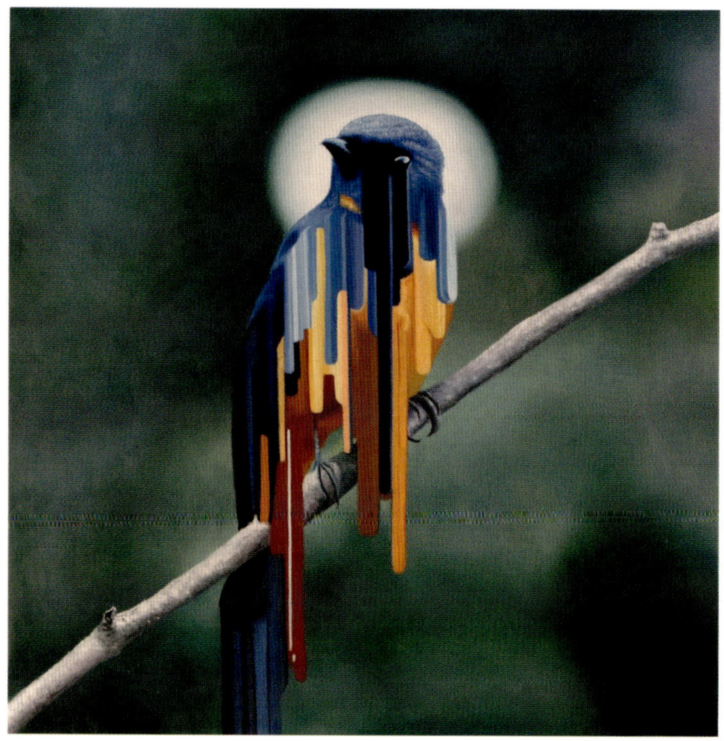

ABOVE
Maurizio Bongiovanni
Bird rib, (***yellow bird***), 2011
oil on canvas

RIGHT
Maurizio Bongiovanni
Bird rib, (***blue bird***), 2010
oil on canvas

RIGHT
Shane Mecklenburger
Treasure in Palestine, 2011
archival photographic print

BELOW LEFT AND RIGHT
Shane Mecklenburger
Roadkill Diamond, 2012
(installation view and detail)
diamond made from
armadillo remains and glass

BOTTOM
Shane Mecklenburger
laser inscription on ***Roadkill Diamond***, 2012 (detail)

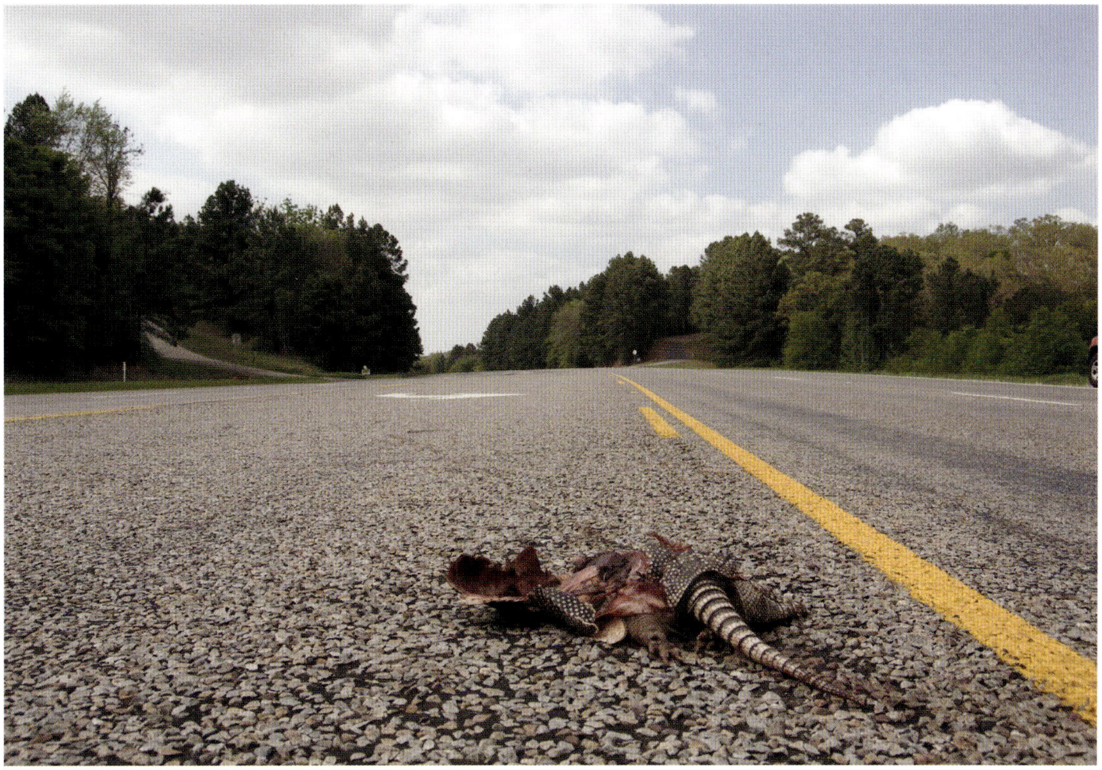

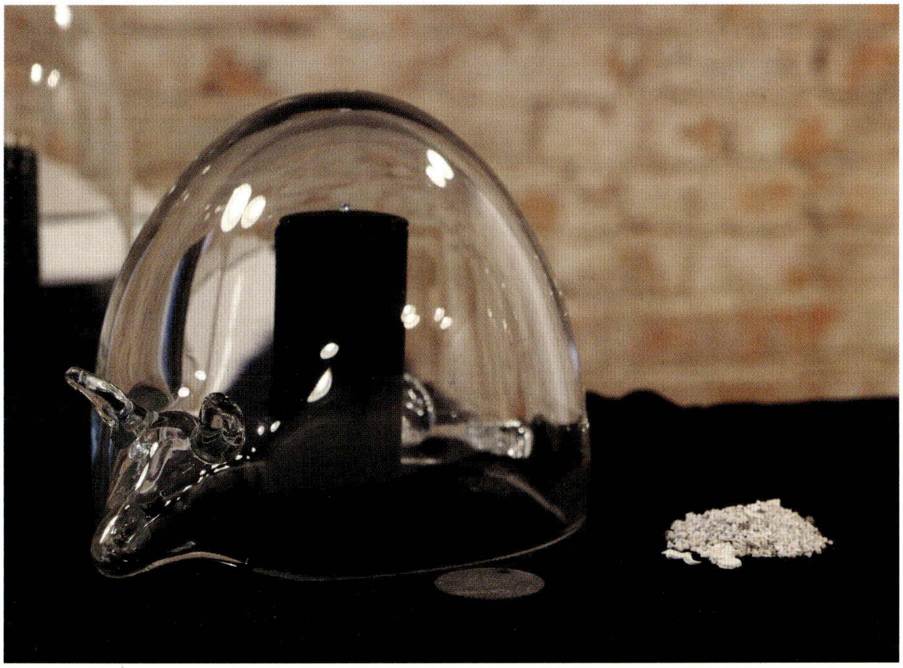

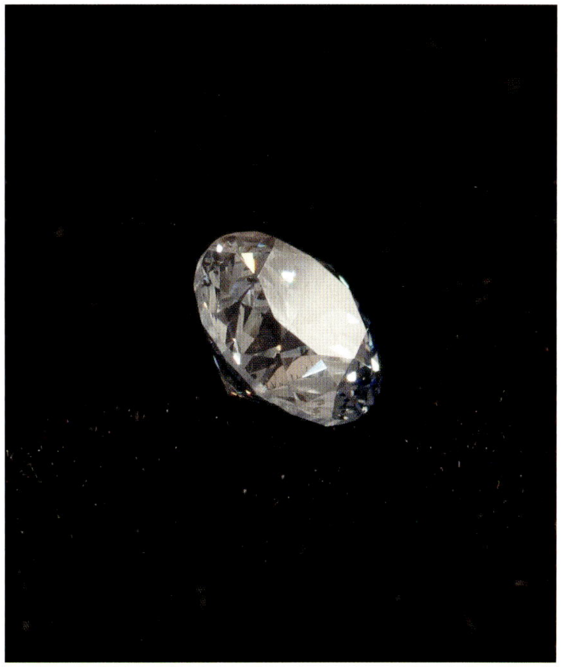

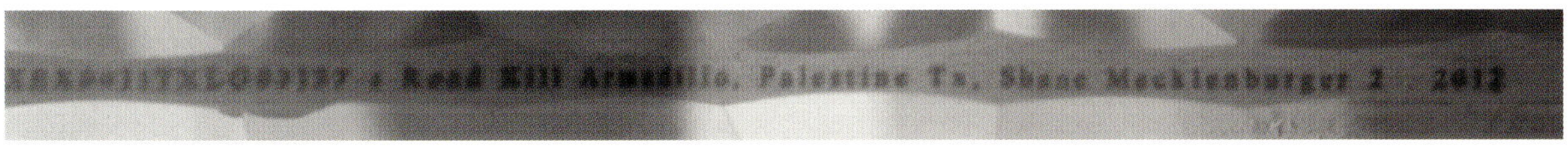

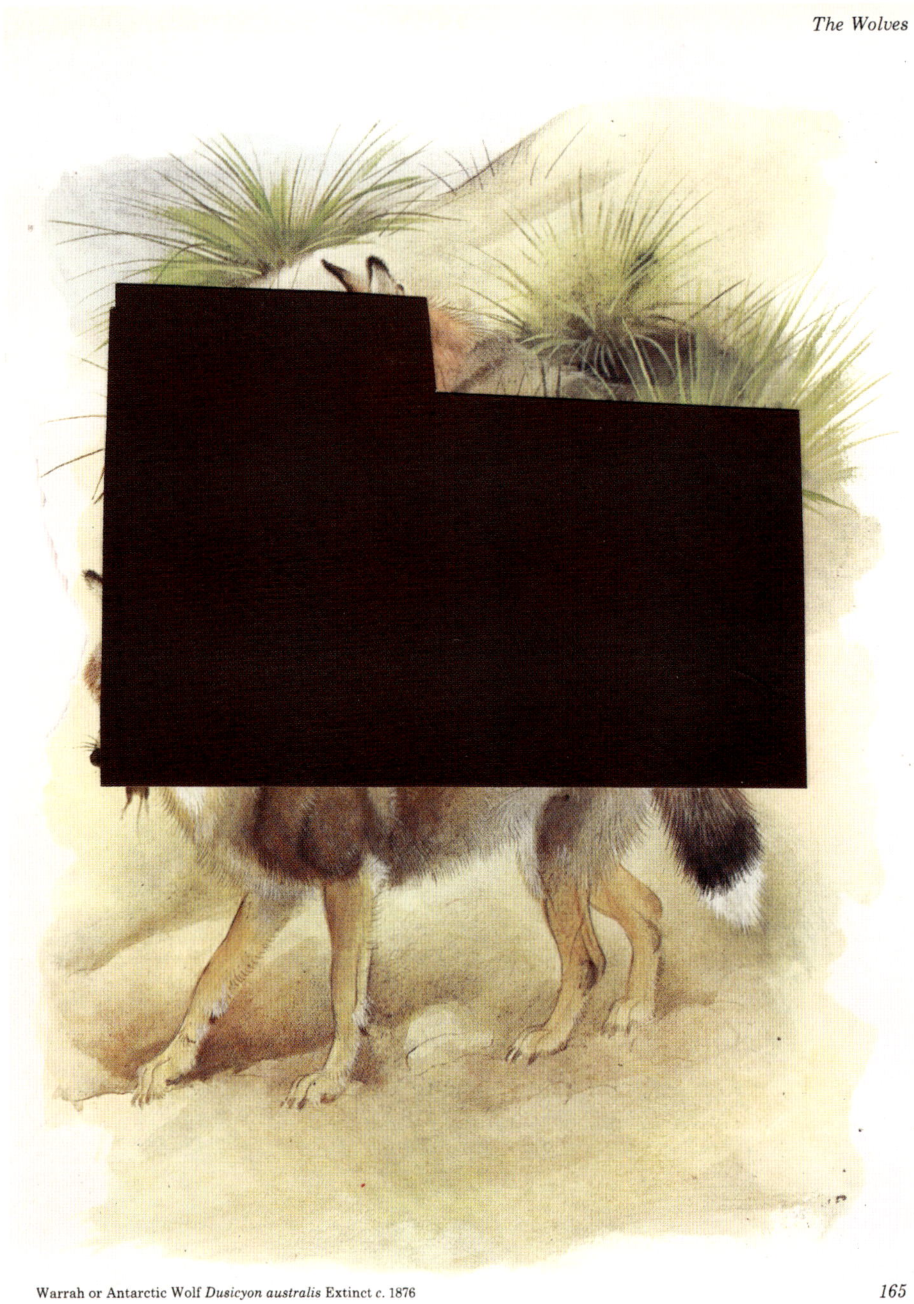

ABOVE
Brion Nuda Rosch
Warrah or Antarctic Wolf Dusicyon australis, 2011
acrylic on found book page

Brion Nuda Rosch covered found book illustrations of wolves hunted to extinction with brown paint for his series *Vanished 1700 through 1900*. His violent imposition of paint creates a void that underscores extinction as the ultimate in 'stilled' animal life, the whole line of a species eradicated forever from the planet. This simple yet powerful action recalls Robert Rauschenberg's *Erased de Kooning Drawing* (1953) and acts as a reminder that human insensitivity and arrogance might likewise lead to our own demise as a species.

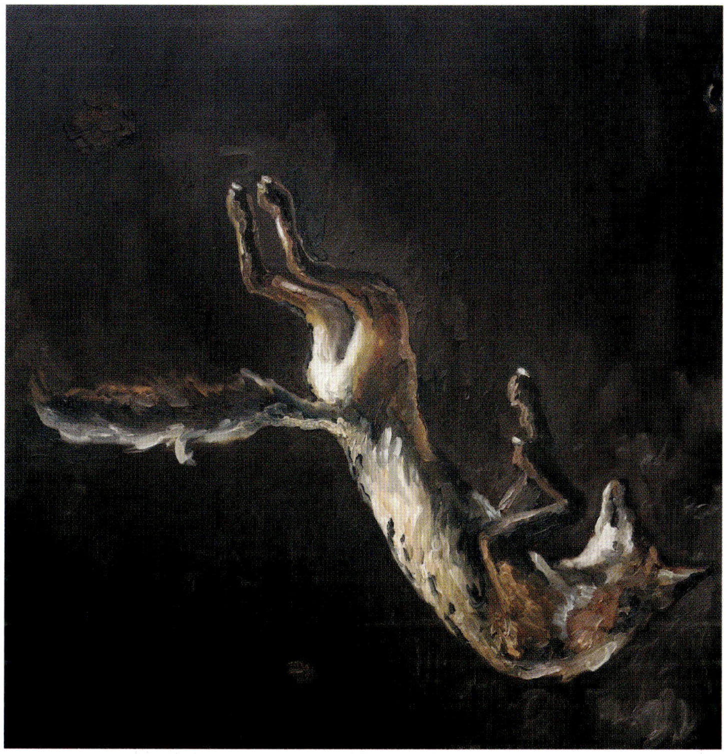

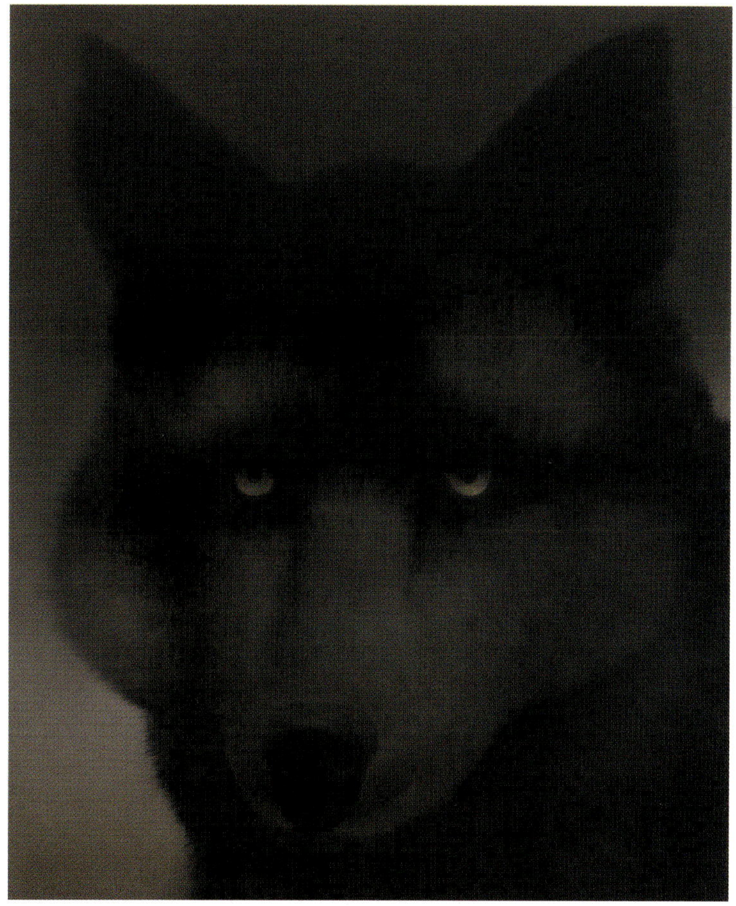

ABOVE LEFT
Karl de Vroomen
Falling fox, 2011
oil on canvas

ABOVE RIGHT
Peter Vos
Untitled (canis), 2008
oil on canvas

Karl de Vroomen features animals in his paintings (as well as objects and interiors) that all evoke a sense of unease, distrust or disturbance of the norm. An unknown, untold narrative is always hinted at in these works, leading us to re-examine the everyday, not for a moral purpose, as in historical still lifes, but so that we might see the familiar through fresh eyes and reconsider our preconceptions about nature and the natural.

Peter Vos has made a series of still lifes of fruit and flowers, as well as close-up views of nocturnal wild animals, all painted from life. His interest in Romanticism (drawing on the mountain scapes of the nineteenth-century artist Caspar David Friedrich) has a dark side, and in such works as *Untitled (canis)* the inherent danger found in nature and the ever-present threat it poses acts to remind viewers of their mortality. Both the wolf and the fox have traditionally held symbolic meaning for Christians, the former as a symbol of reform, the latter as the devil.

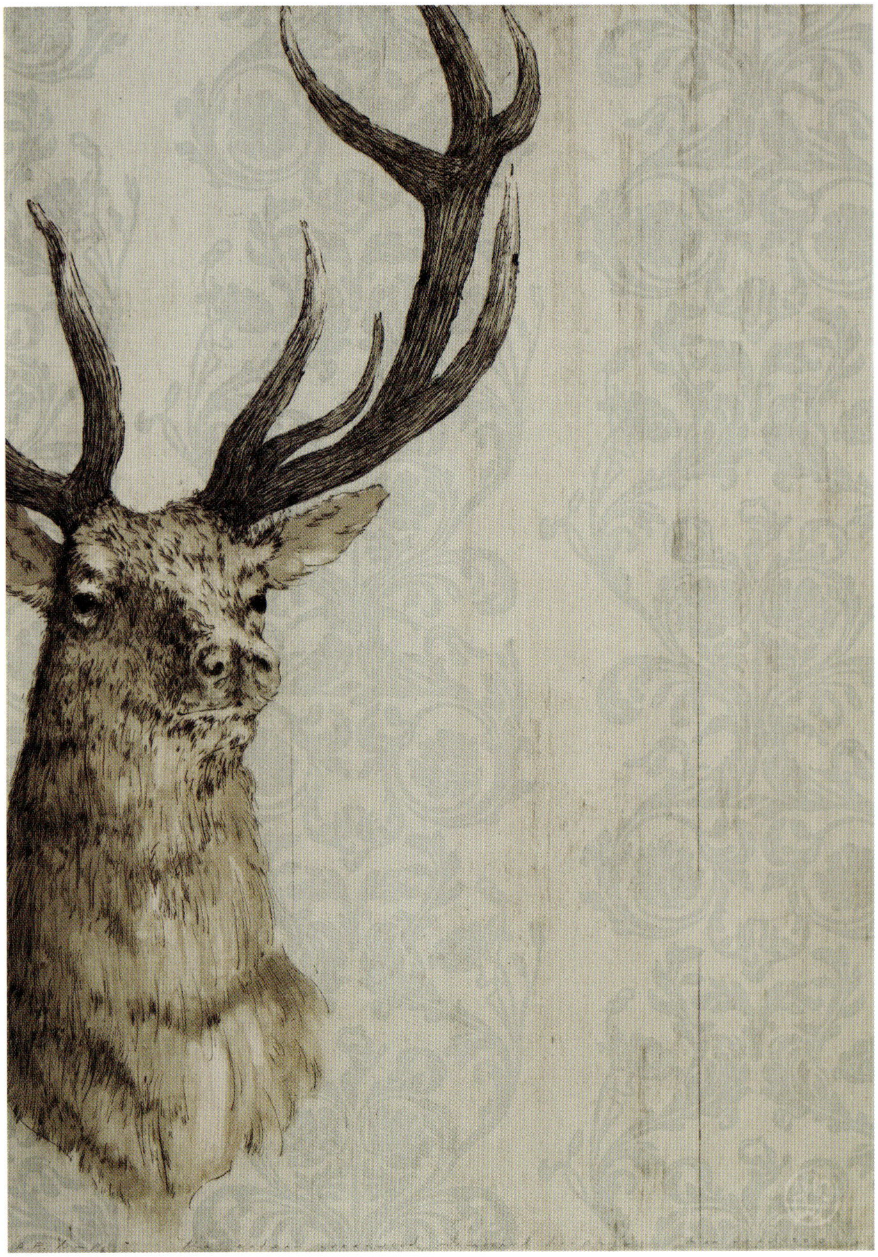

ABOVE
Ben Reid
the eileen greenwood memorial trophy, 2010
drypoint, relief and woodblock print

Ben Reid's *the eileen greenwood memorial trophy* addresses the fact that deer are not native to New Zealand but were imported by the British in the mid-nineteenth century. When the deer quickly overran the island nation's forests because they were without native predators, they became the cause of much natural destruction and the extinction of many indigenous plants. Their prevalence almost destroyed one of the country's best-known flowers, the Mount Cook lily, which forms the background pattern of this work. Conservationists and sport hunters have worked together to diminish this damage in an unlikely alliance.

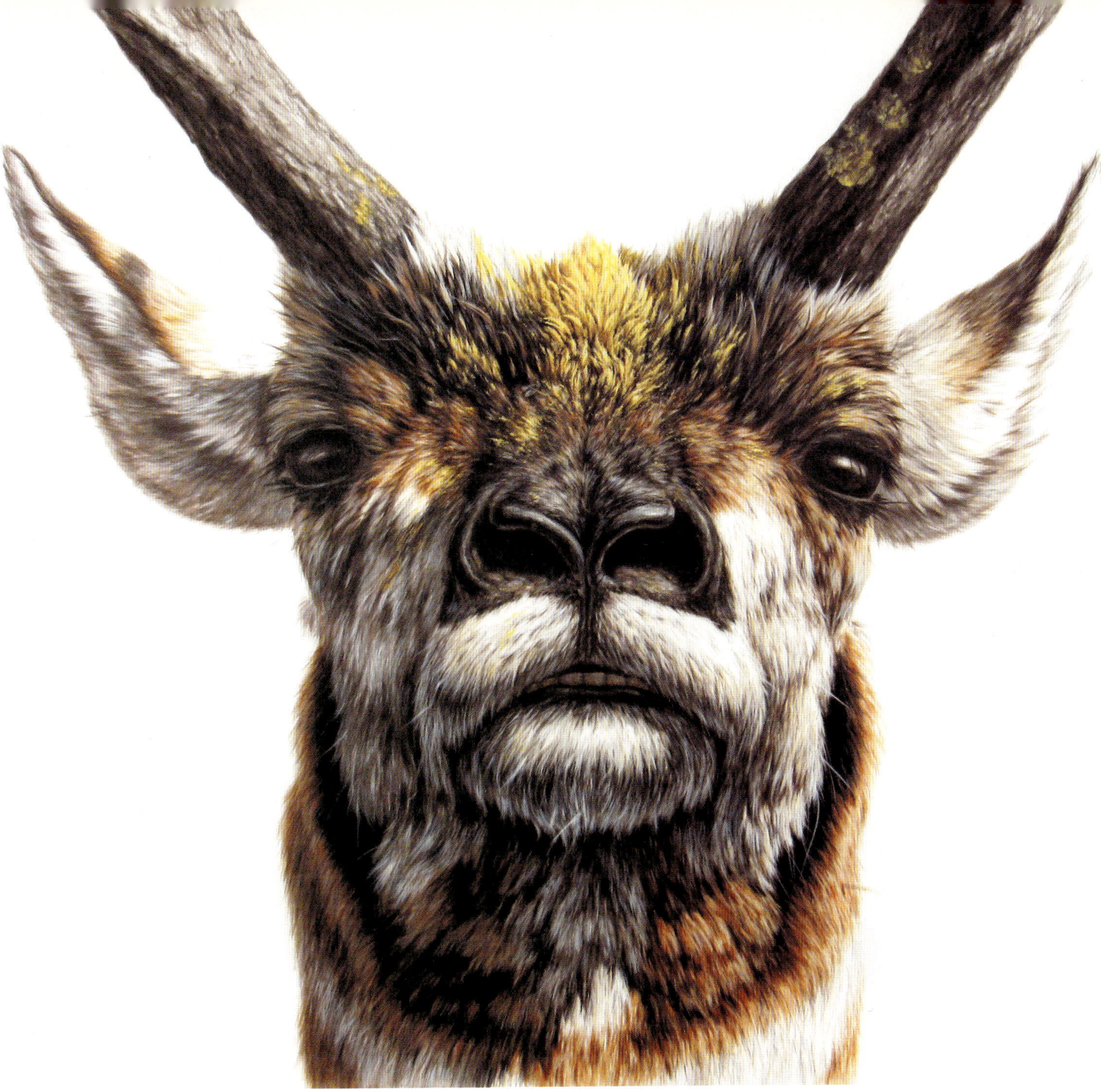

George Boorujy's *Fugue* presents a stag's head staring out at the viewer, its eyes cold and hard like the glass ones that adorn stuffed trophy heads. Boorujy has drawn his stag with the same level of technical skill displayed in Frans Snyders's *Still Life with a Dead Stag* (*c.* 1600–50) and Jan Weenix's *A Dog and a Cat near a Partially Disembowelled Deer* (*c.* 1647–60). He says: 'I want the viewer to confront the subject.... We use animals for so much – for stand-ins, symbols, labour, companionship, food. I want people to think about what they are, how they've been formed to do what they do.'

ABOVE
George Boorujy
Fugue, 2010
ink on paper

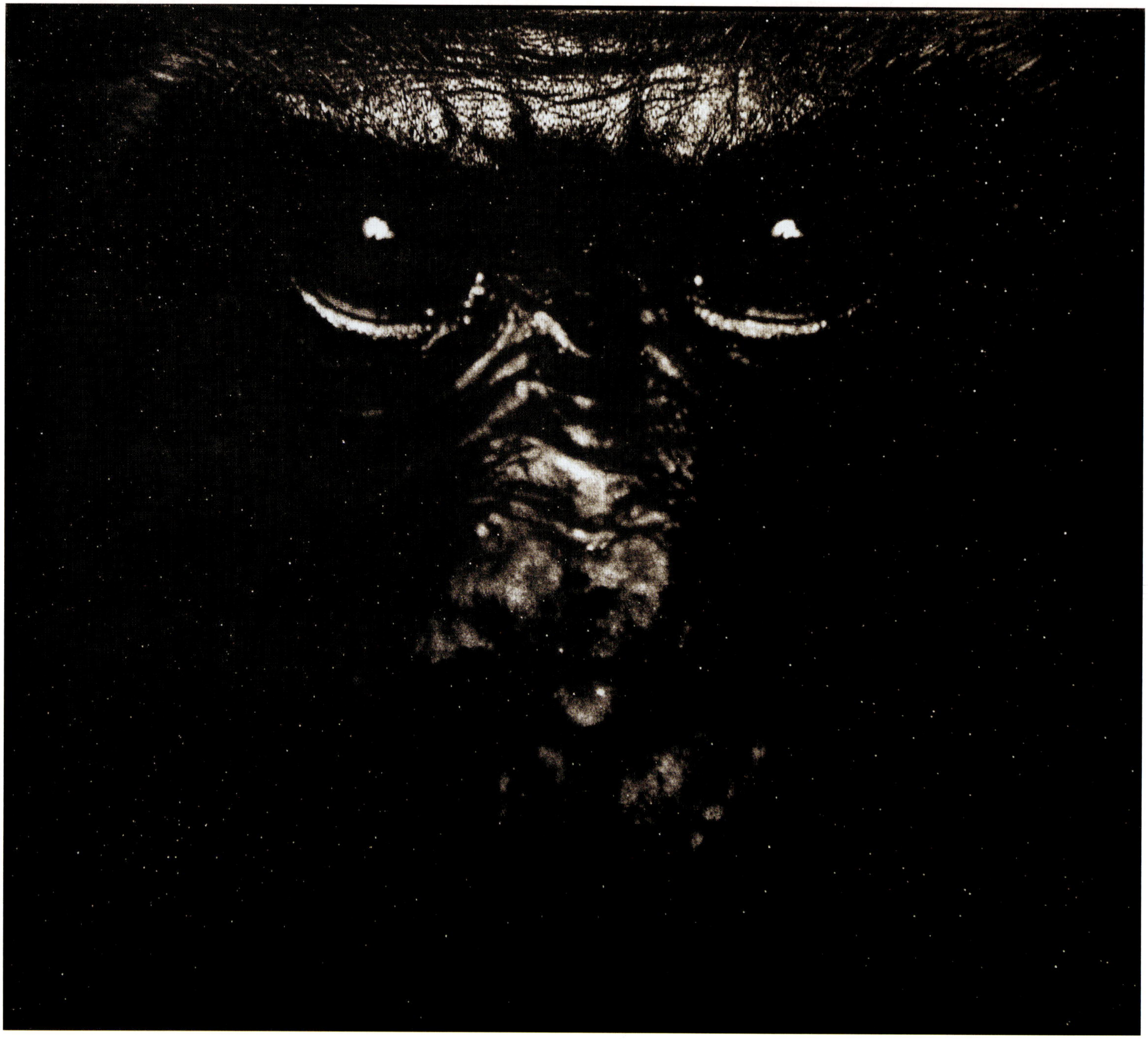

ABOVE
Madeleine Farley
Tiya, 2010
silkscreen print on canvas
with diamond dust

Madeleine Farley's *Endangered* series of prints developed out of her film about the return of three orphaned gorillas from Kent, England, to Gabon in Central Africa. Living apes appear in many traditional still lifes as symbols of humans at their worst or most primitive, from Dürer's fifteenth-century work *The Virgin and Child with the Monkey* to Chardin's eighteenth-century *The Monkey Antiquarian* and *The Monkey Painter*. Only after nineteenth-century developments in science began to link humans and apes did our artistic depictions of these primates become less about us and more about them.

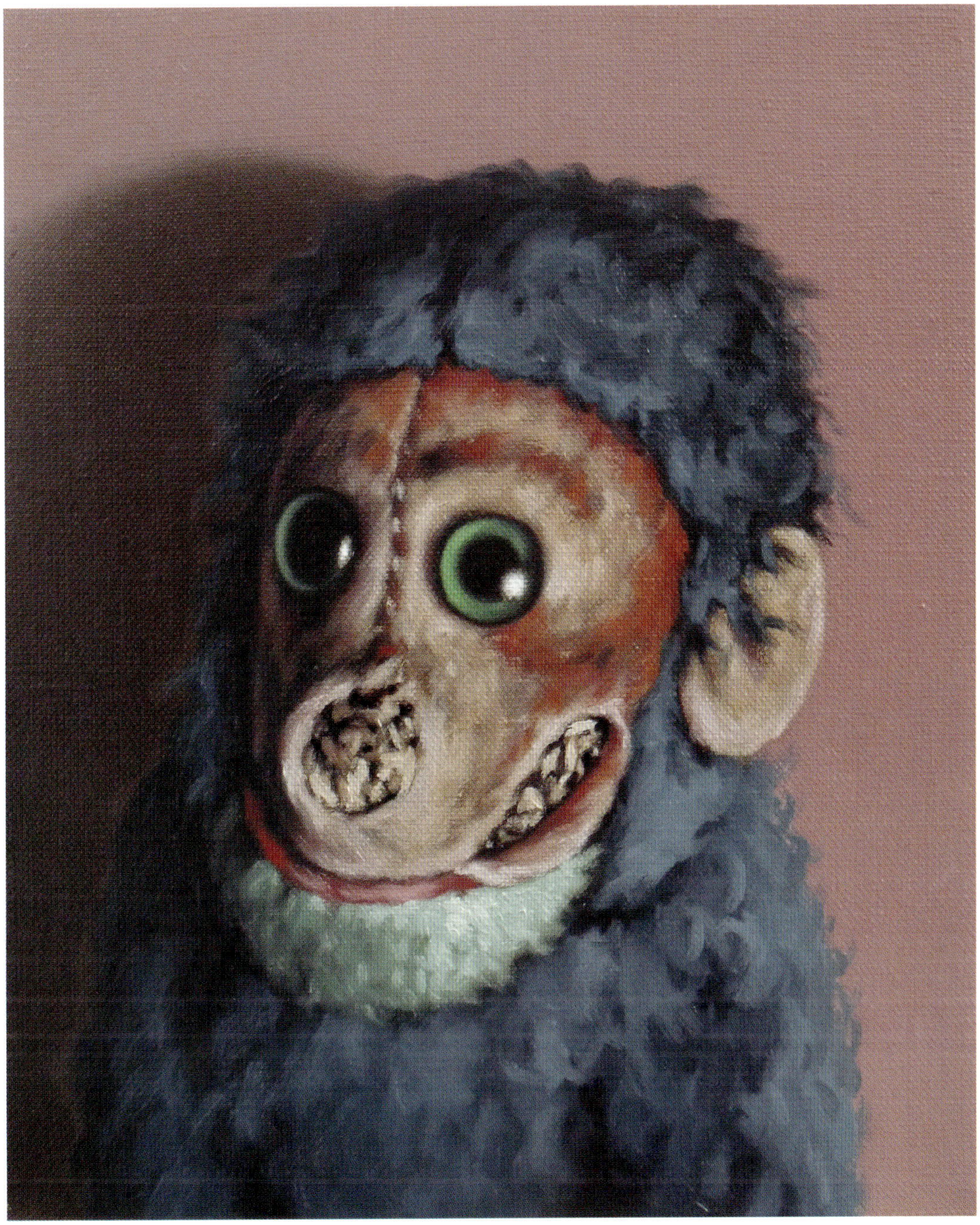

ABOVE
Peter Jones
Ollie Monkey, 2007
oil on linen

Lambs, bunnies and fish are the subjects of many works by **Peter Jones** but his real fascination lies with monkeys; not real monkeys but vintage stuffed toys on the verge of falling apart. Each one is nearing the end of its lifespan and possesses an inherent vulnerability that is doubled because, as a still-life subject, it is ready for inspection. Worn out from either love or neglect, this cheeky monkey relentlessly returns the viewer's gaze.

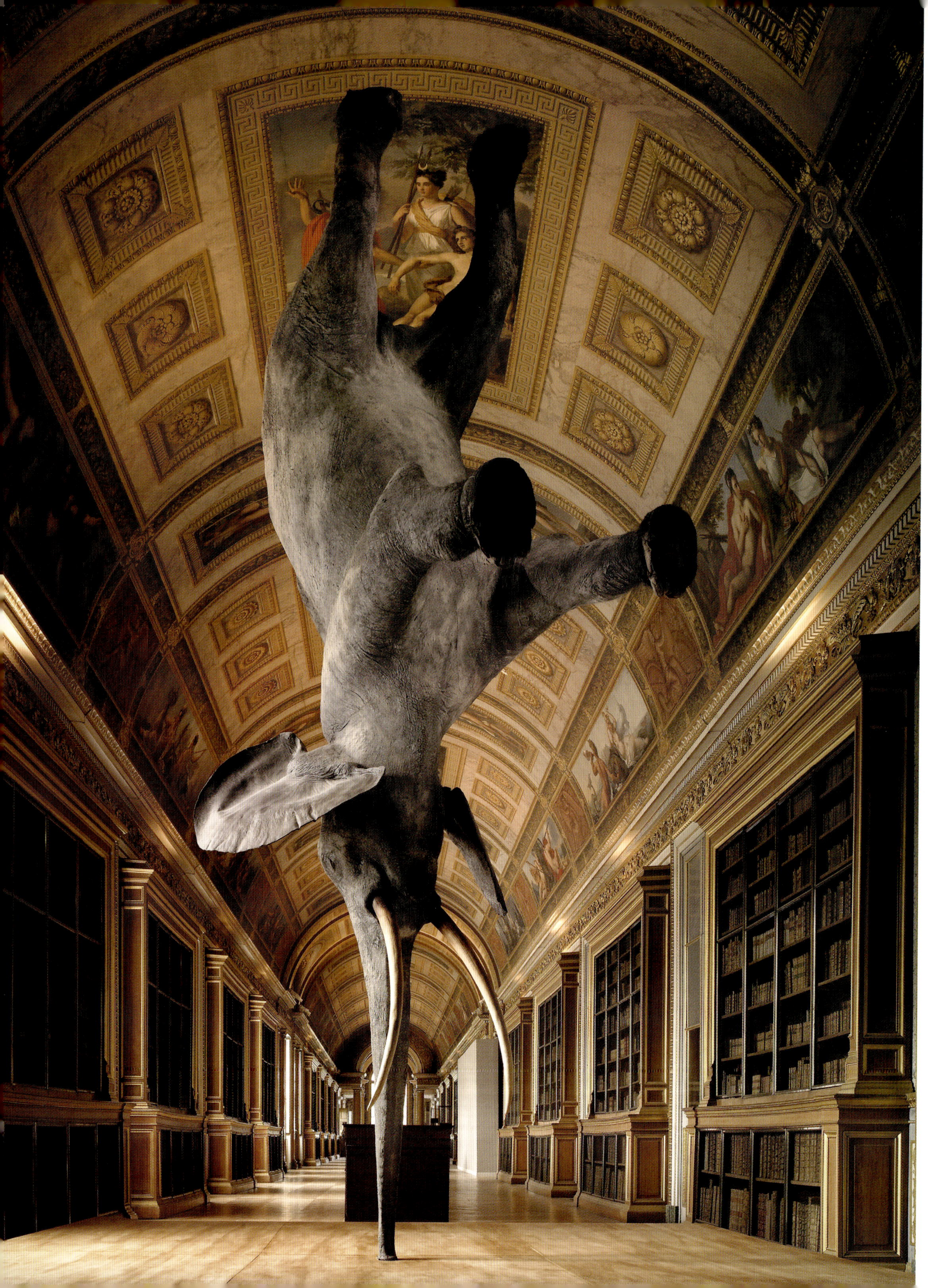

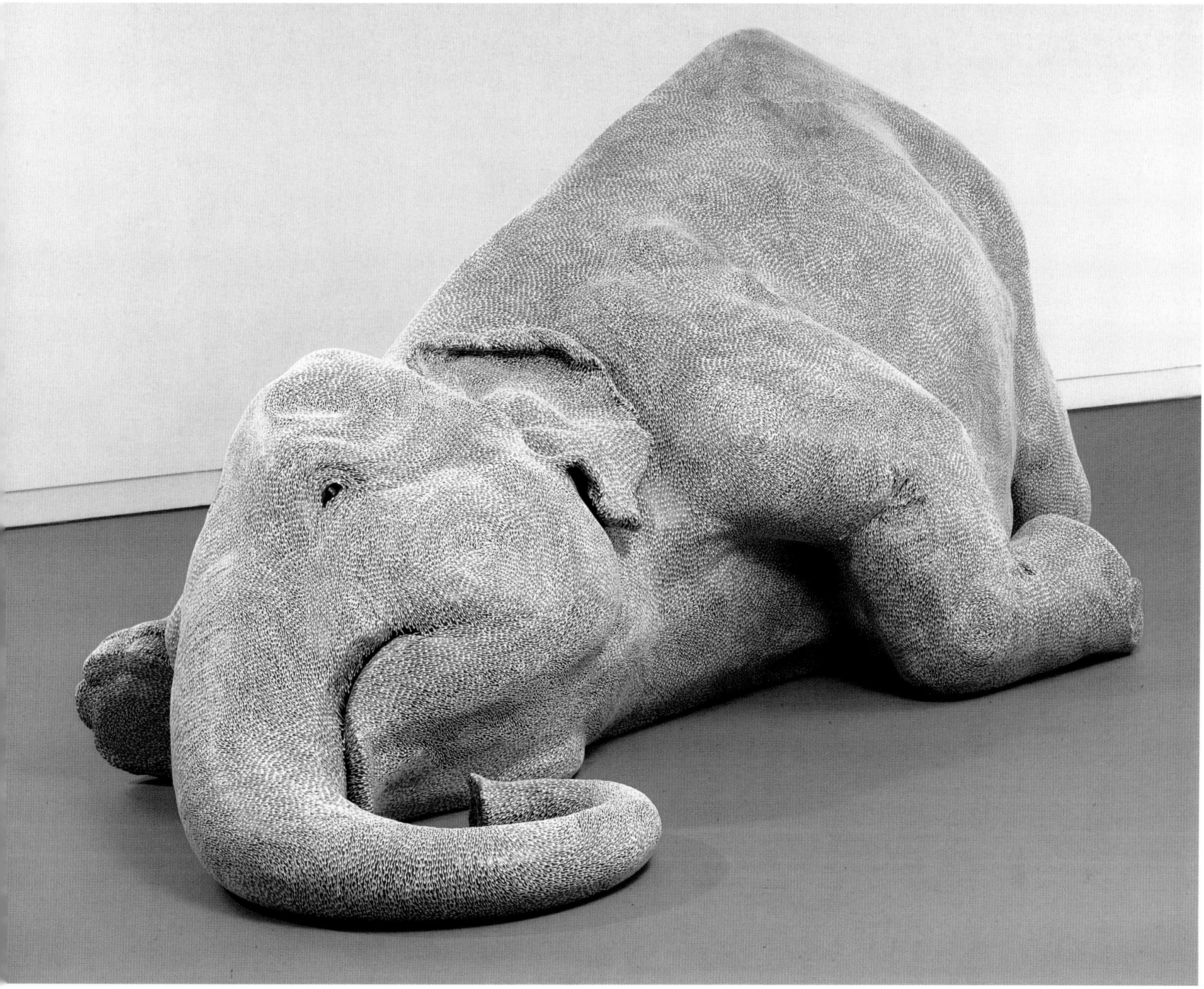

OPPOSITE
Daniel Firman
Würsa (à 18 000 km de la Terre), 2006–8
taxidermy, fibreglass and polyester resin

ABOVE
Bharti Kher
The Skin Speaks a Language Not Its Own, 2006
bindis on fibreglass

Daniel Firman's taxidermy elephant *Würsa (à 18 000 km de la Terre)* has been installed in several locations but always standing on its trunk. The enormous pachyderm floats in the air in a playful, comic fashion that is intended to show what an elephant could do were it freed from gravity and floating 18,000 kilometres above the earth. Firman had the elephant professionally preserved by Belgian taxidermist Jean-Pierre Gérard-Simon. For the first installation of *Nasutamanus* (2012), Firman affixed the trunk of a man-made elephant to the Galerie Perrotin wall so that it lay horizontally, upside down, feet in the air.

Bharti Kher explores her cultural roots as a British-born woman of Indian descent and her works often feature the bindi. The 'third eye' (of wisdom) in Hindu creation myths, the bindi is worn by humans as a red dot on the forehead. Commercial bindis of all manner of decoration and materials can now also be bought and it is these that Kher uses. In *The Skin Speaks a Language Not Its Own*, a fibreglass elephant has been covered in white, sperm-shaped bindis, lending its 'skin' a vulnerability that matches its dead or dying pose.

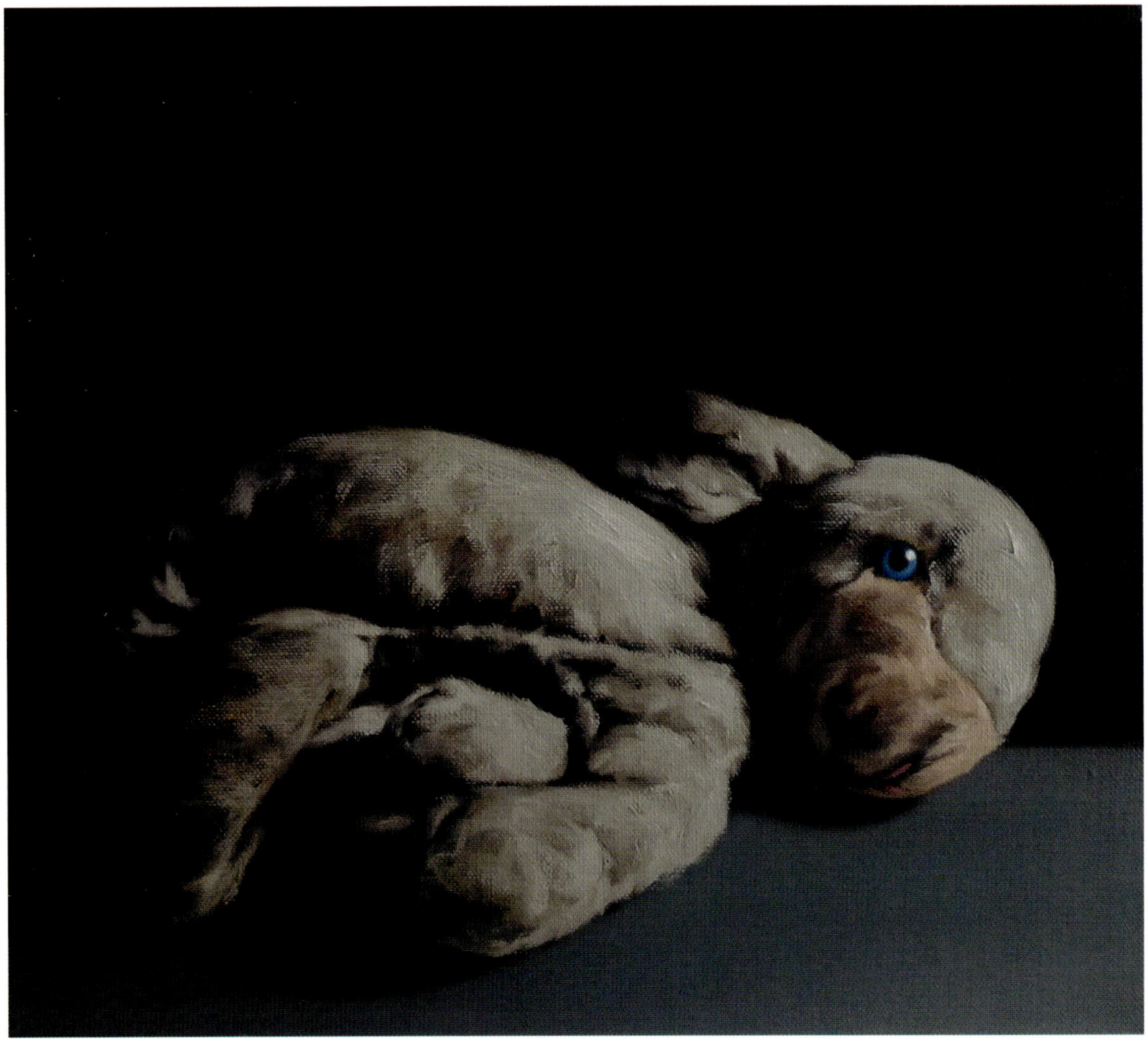

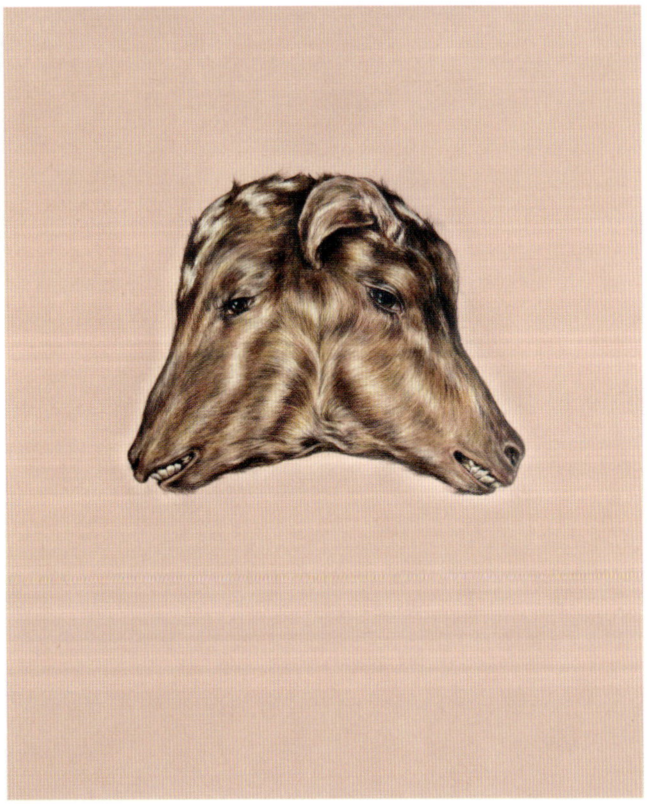

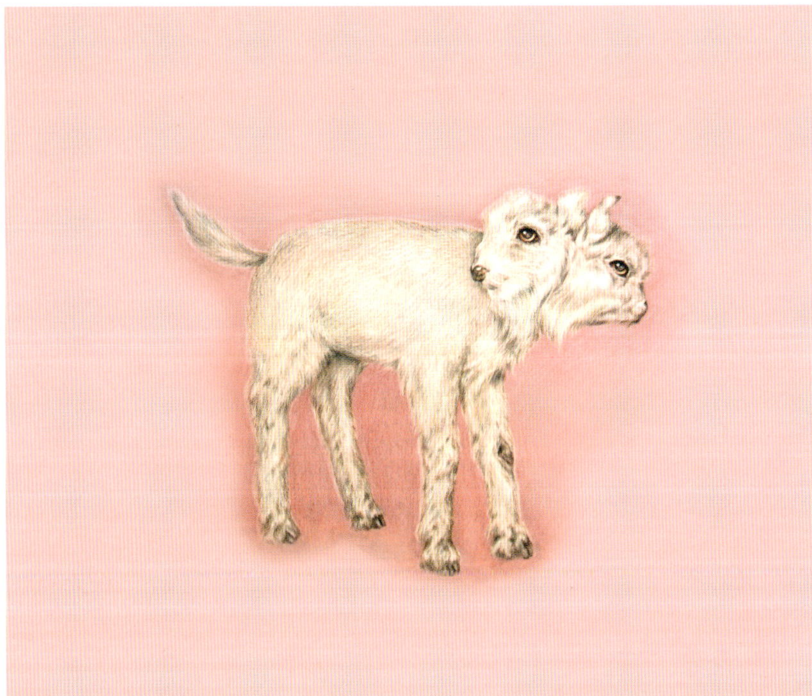

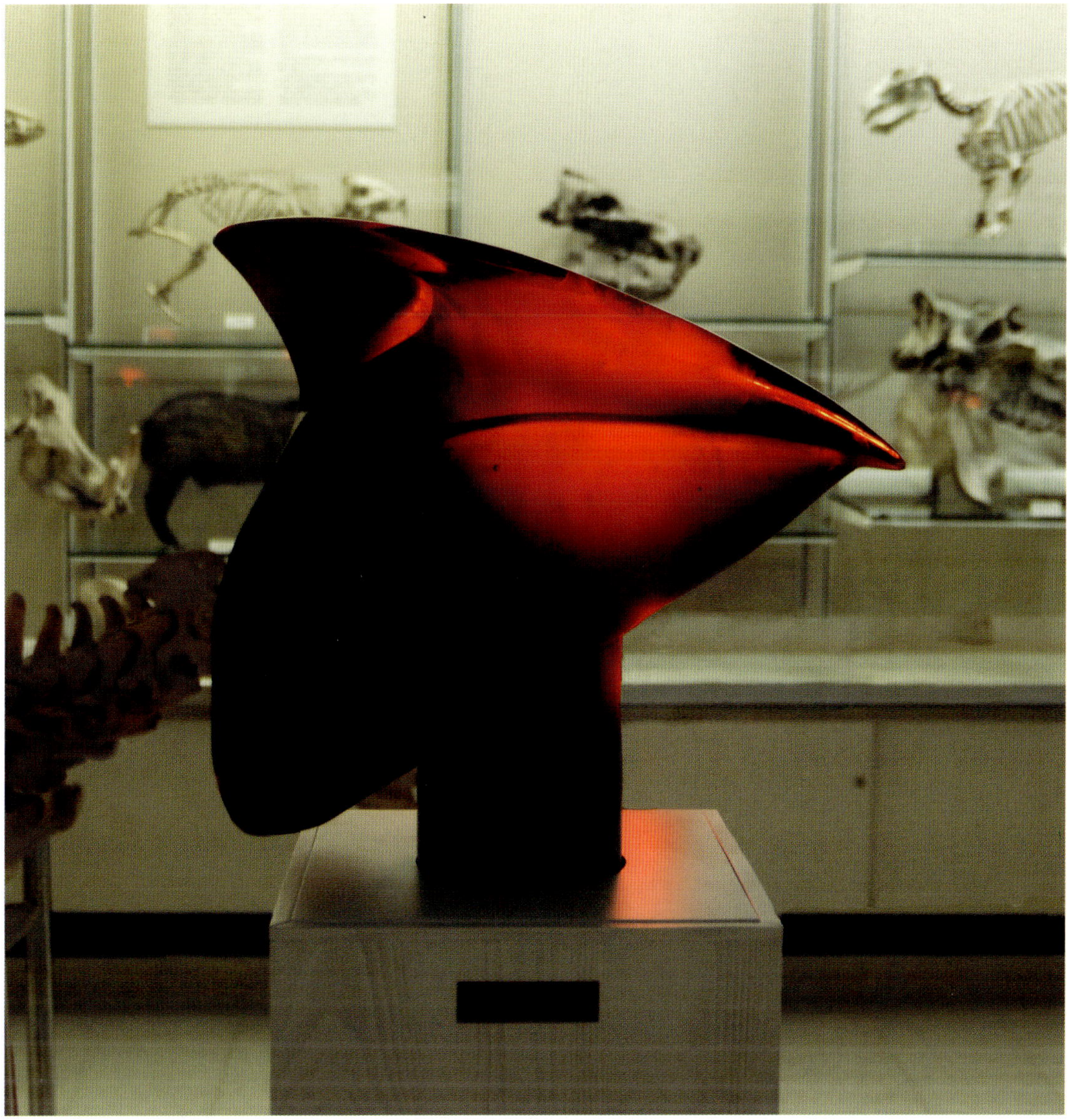

OPPOSITE TOP
Peter Jones
Lamb, 2009
oil on linen

OPPOSITE BOTTOM LEFT
Filippa Barkman
Disagreement, 2008
colour pencil on paper

OPPOSITE BOTTOM RIGHT
Filippa Barkman
Still, 2008
colour pencil on paper

ABOVE
Tolly Nason
Large Cactus Finch
Geospiza conirostris, 2009
kiln cast glass

Peter Jones leaves the histories of the discarded soft toys featured in his works ambiguous so that viewers will revisit their own childhood memories. He notes: 'I don't deny the inherent symbolism of the subject or the possibility of metaphor or even *memento mori*. Although I usually describe my paintings as portraits, they often seem closer to the tradition of still life.'

Filippa Barkman's series of drawings *In Limbo* includes a number of picturesque sketches of mutated animals, specimens from an alternative Garden of Eden. In *Disagreement*, the disembodied heads of a Siamese goat-like animal grimace in opposite directions; in *Still*, a baby goat with two heads stands placidly against a light pink background. These delicate drawings on candy-coloured paper are in sharp contrast to their difficult subject matter. Goats have traditionally represented the damned in historical artworks, as opposed to sheep, which represent the followers of Christ.

Tolly Nason developed her 2009 installation *Seeing the Light: Finch by Finch* as part of the 800th anniversary celebrations of Cambridge University and the 150th anniversary of Charles Darwin's *On the Origin of Species*. The installation consisted of fourteen large, glass replicas of finch beaks, Darwin's evidence for how finches evolved over time in order to obtain food on the Galápagos Islands. Lit from behind and twenty times the size of the originals, Nason's beaks glowed while resting on their individual plinths inside the university museum's skeleton room.

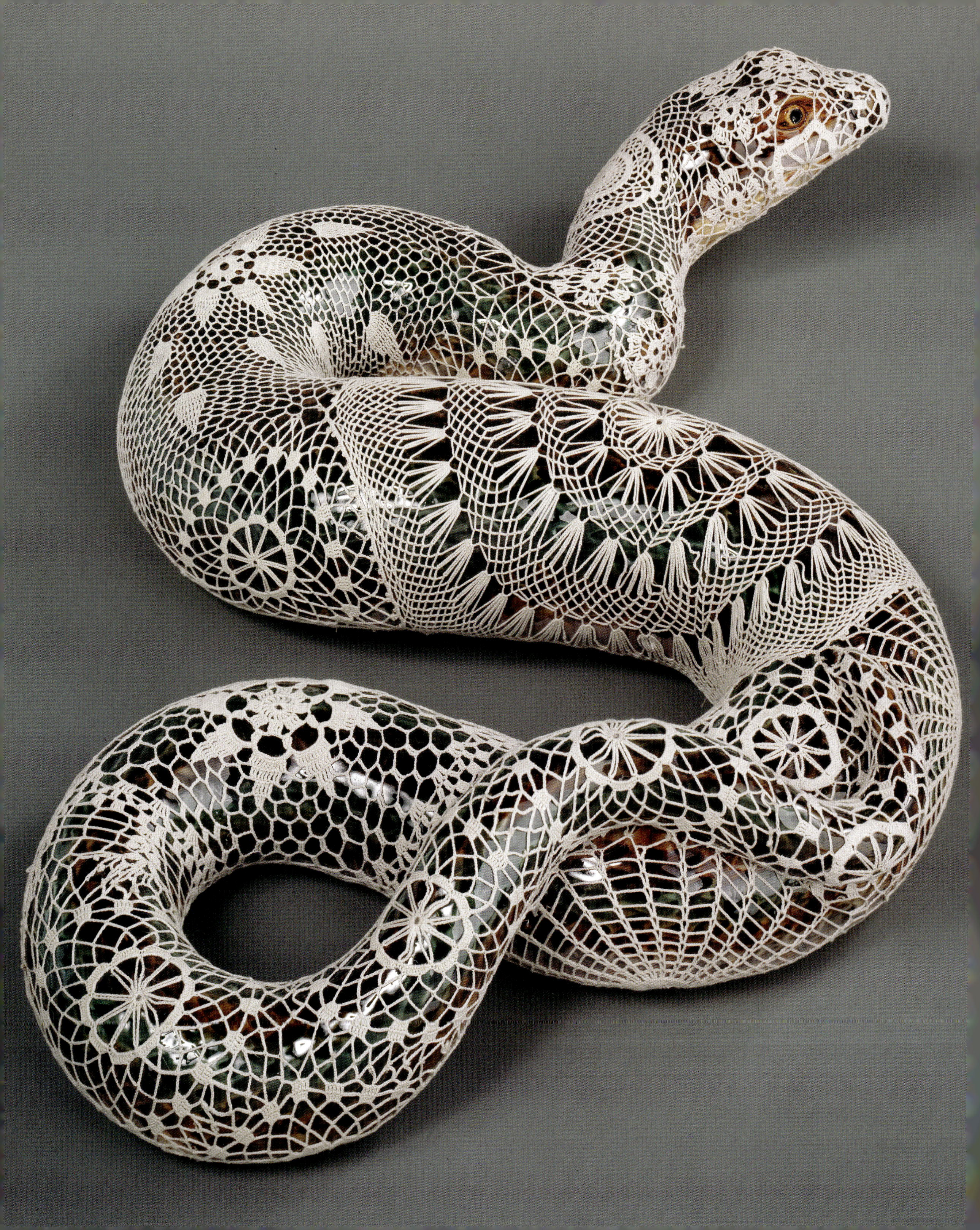

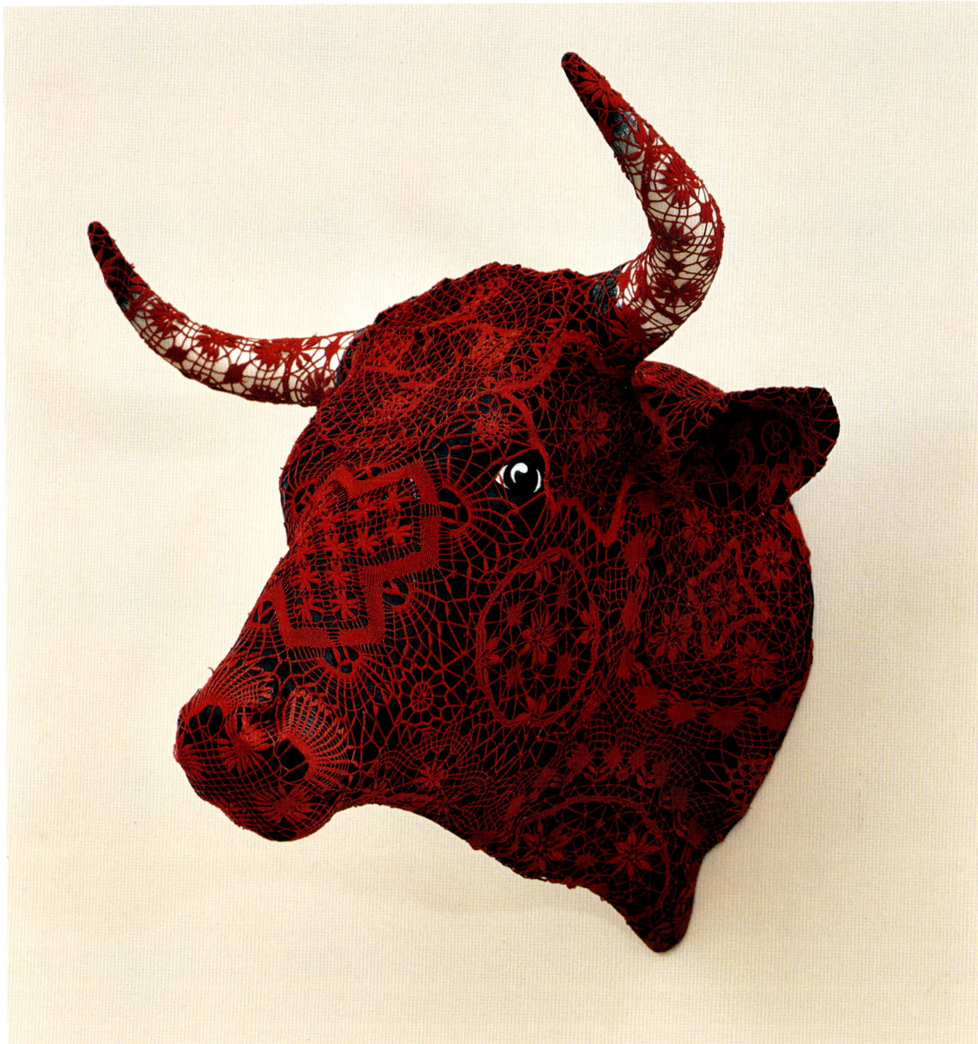

OPPOSITE
Joana Vasconcelos
Giallina, 2008 · Rafael Bordalo Pinheiro faience painted with ceramic glaze, handmade cotton crochet

ABOVE
Joana Vasconcelos
Capote, 2009 · Rafael Bordalo Pinheiro acrylic-painted faience, bobbin lace and handmade cotton crochet

Joana Vasconcelos looks to her Portuguese roots in the construction of her sculptural works, which incorporate national handicraft traditions (ceramics, crochet, embroidery) in new and unexpected ways. To create such works as *Giallina* and *Capote* she selects a number of cotton doilies (bought from local craftswomen) from her collection and dismantles them. The doilies are then reassembled over the surface of a glazed ceramic animal from the traditional Rafael Bordalo Pinheiro factory, and this 'second skin' is sewn together by Vasconcelos's team. Her practice conflates Duchamp's mode of not making with a custom of making by hand in order to question what we conceive of as natural.

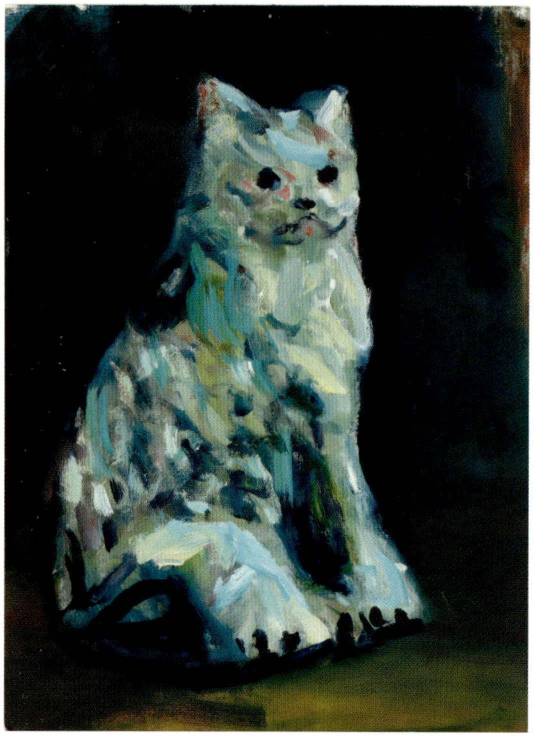

Paul Housley is intensely interested in the act of painting and his works often reference other paintings. He has happily appropriated from such artists as Rembrandt and Picasso to paint still lifes that he suggests are all in some way self-portraits. Housley states: 'As always there is no ironic distance in the work, the artist "believes" in paint and is enthralled with the myriad of nuances and possibilities brought about by the simple but ultimately unknowable act of painting.'

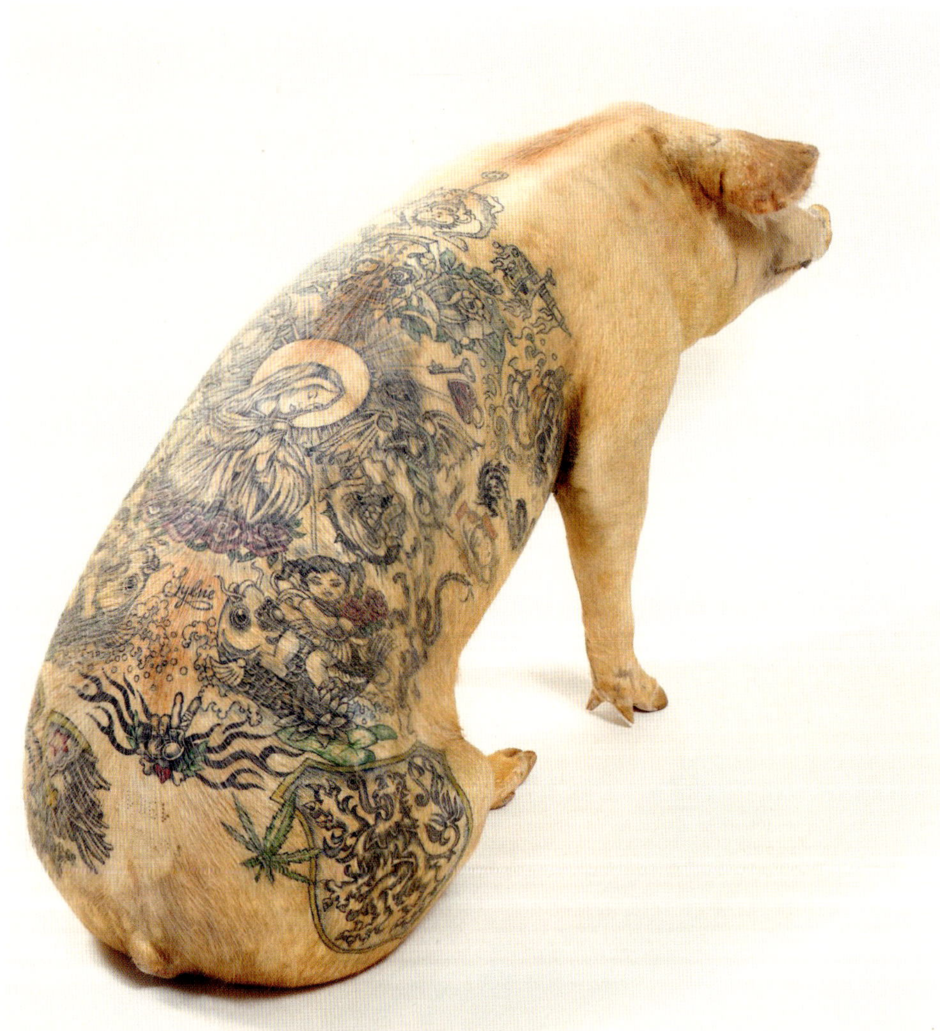

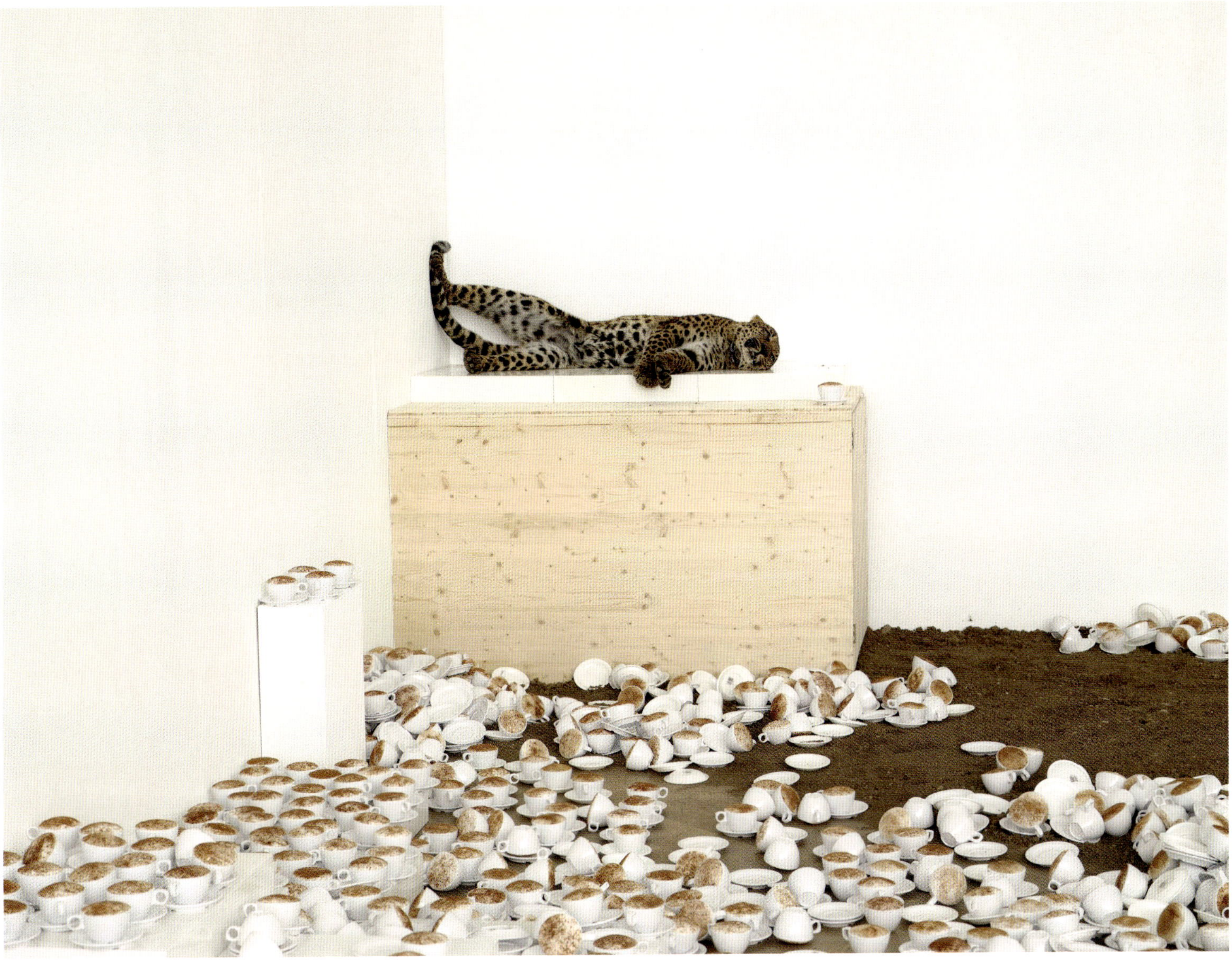

OPPOSITE TOP
Paul Housley
Velazquez, 2010
oil on paper

OPPOSITE BOTTOM
Wim Delvoye
Sylvie, 2006
stuffed tattooed pig

ABOVE
Paola Pivi
Don't disturb me, 2007
photographic print, aluminium, glass and frame

Wim Delvoye is the vegetarian Belgian artist behind the contentious tattooing of live pigs into works of art. At a pig farm in Beijing owned by the artist, Delvoye and his assistants sedate pigs before inking them with intricate and permanent tattoos. Over time, as the pigs grow, the tattoos stretch and increase in size and, in the artist's mind, in value. Delvoye displays the pigs alive in galleries, as well as stuffed, in order to question the notion of animal rights, as well as art-world values and valuations.

In **Paola Pivi**'s photograph *Don't disturb me*, a leopard (a historical symbol for the Antichrist) lies atop a crate in a room filled with three thousand cappuccinos. As a multimedia artist predominantly making installations, Pivi commissions Hugo Glendinning or Attilio Maranzano to create her photographs. She explains: 'The collaboration I have with the photographer is very important. I rarely take my own pictures.... We don't even have to talk to each other. That is the most wonderful form of collaboration that has happened to me. He's doing his job, I'm doing my job, and we don't need to talk.' Pivi's use of animals adds a third party to her collaborations, whether they are living, dead and stuffed, or artificial.

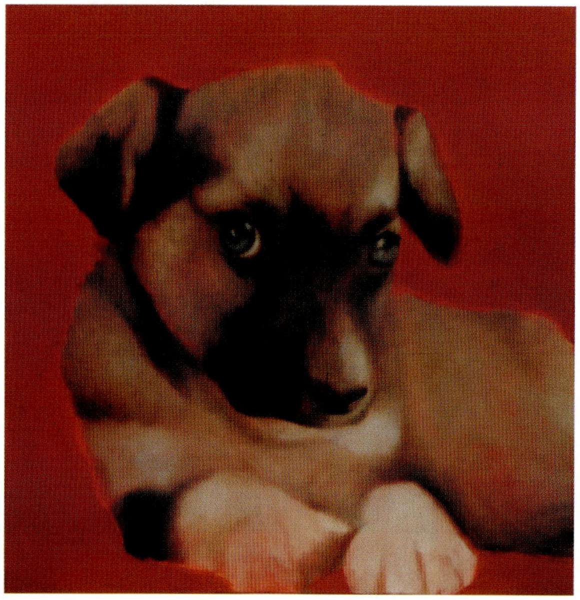
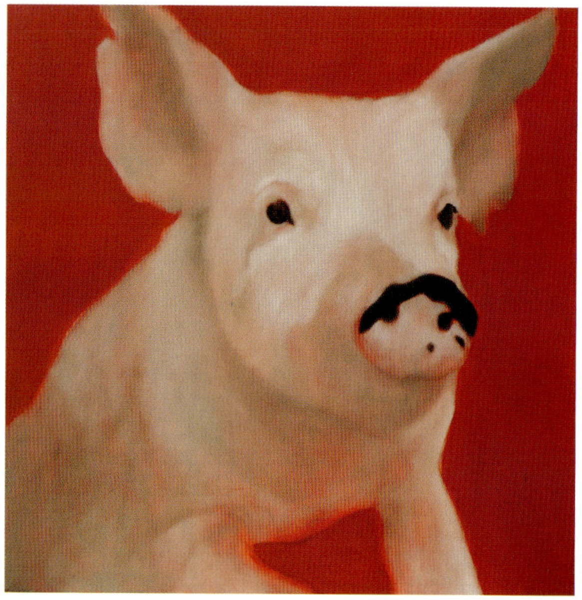
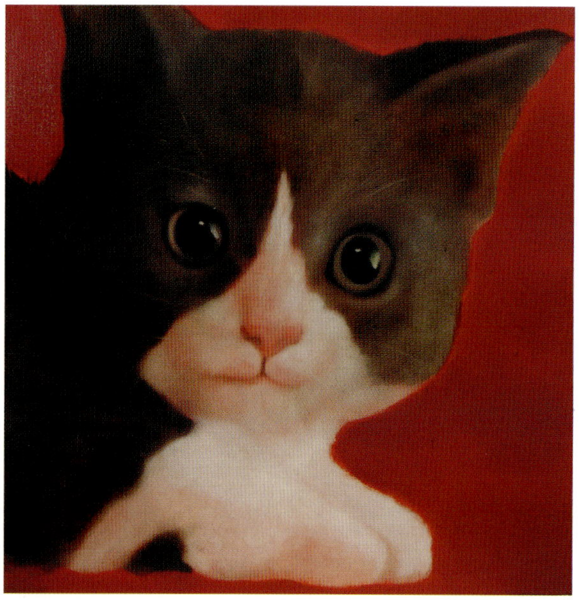
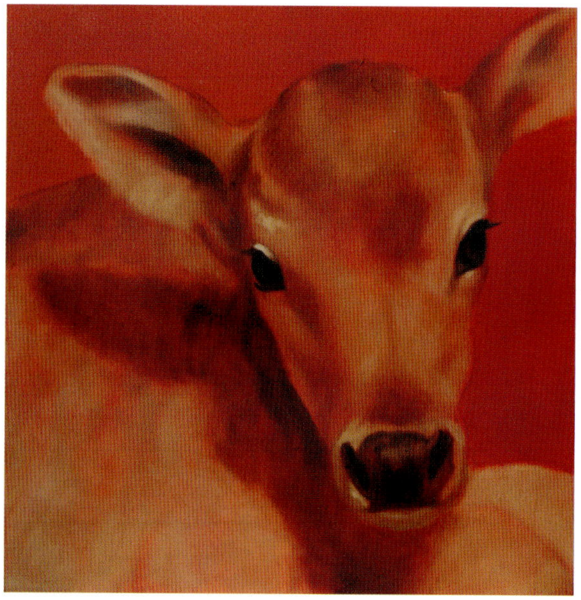
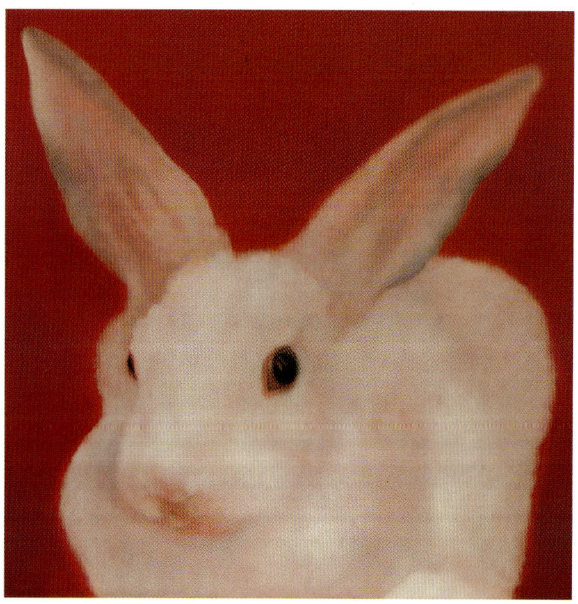
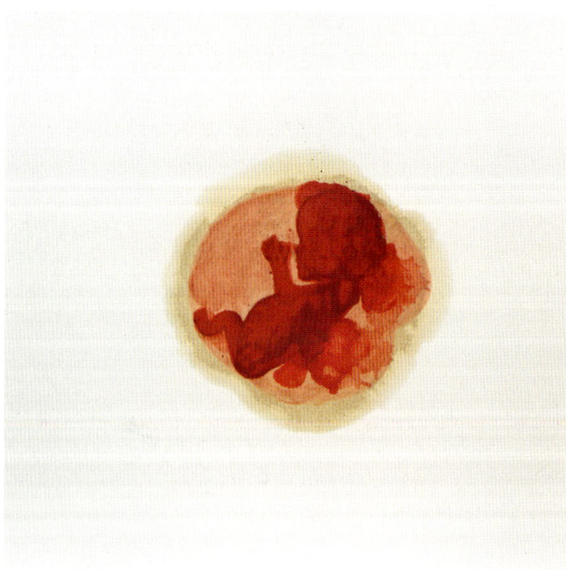

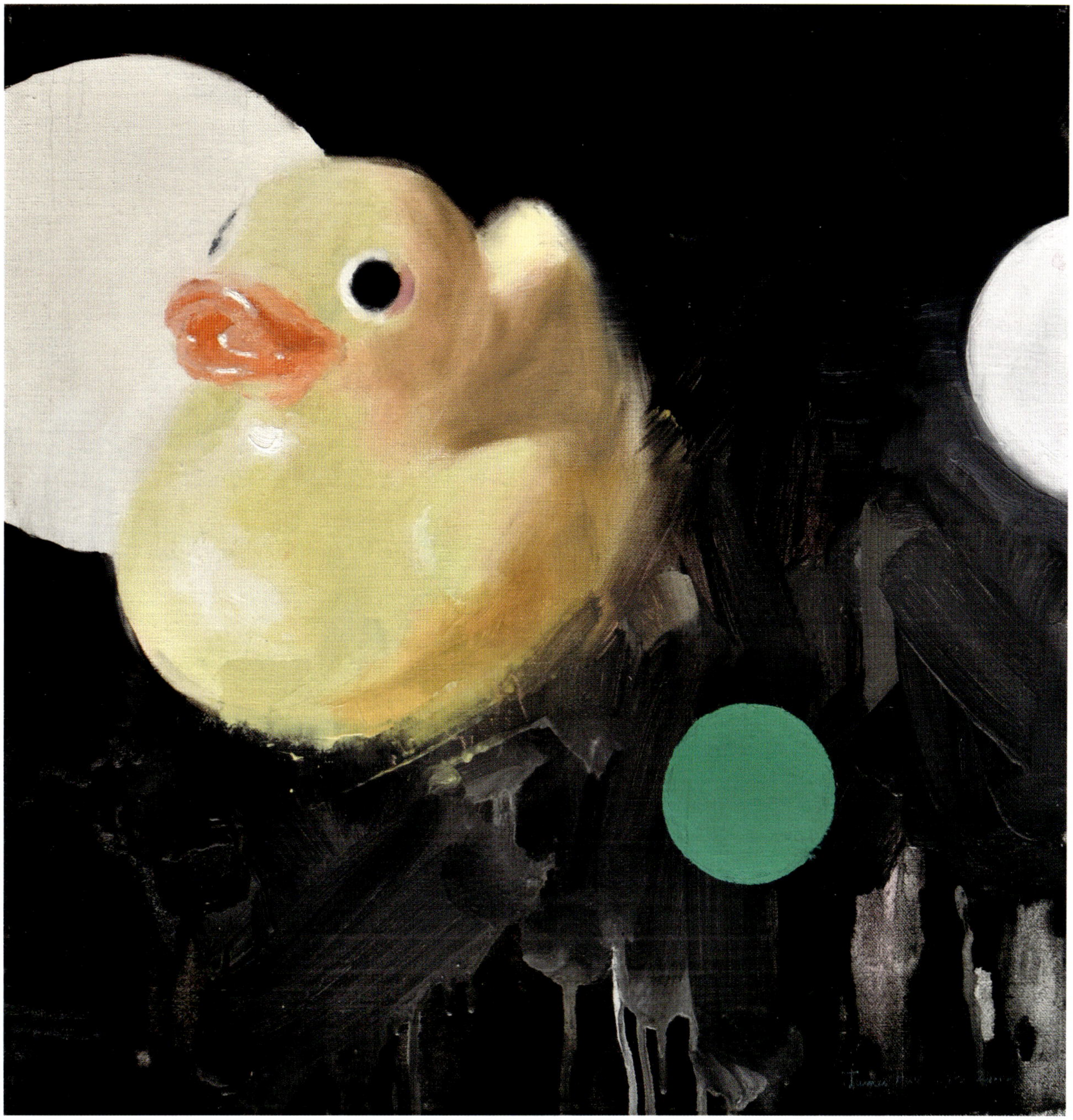

Pradeep L. Mishra's 2010 exhibition 'lovetolive' at the Palette Art Gallery in New Delhi featured paintings of cuddly puppies, kittens and bunnies. These highly anthropomorphized animals were painted realistically on a red background. On the opposite side of the gallery, the same animals were again rendered, this time in red paint on white paper. Here the paint was loose, dripping and running down the canvas as if to recall the abattoir rather than the greeting card. On this wall, a painting of a human foetus also appeared.

James Hart Dyke was the first artist-in-residence with the British Secret Intelligence Service (MI6) and his exhibition 'A Year with MI6' marked the organization's centenary in 2011. Hart Dyke had been a war artist with the Grenadier Guards in Iraq and Afghanistan but still had to undergo extensive vetting. *Waiting in the Hotel Room*, *Dog in the round* and *Toy Duck* (all 2010) explore hidden aspects of surveillance. The duck in question had been used in an undercover operation, a secret camera hidden in its eye; the green dot in the same work alludes to the custom that the chief of MI6 writes only in green ink.

OPPOSITE RED IMAGES
Pradeep L. Mishra
paintings from 'lovetolive', 2010 · oil on canvas

OPPOSITE WHITE IMAGE
Pradeep L. Mishra
painting from 'lovetolive', 2010 · oil on paper

ABOVE
James Hart Dyke
Toy Duck, 2010
oil on canvas

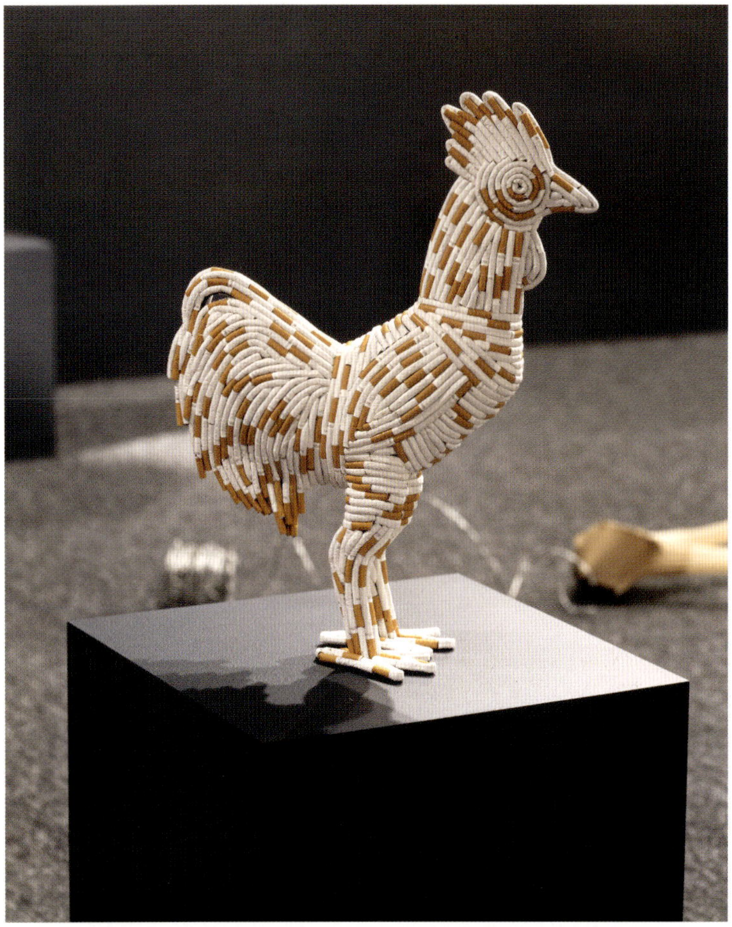

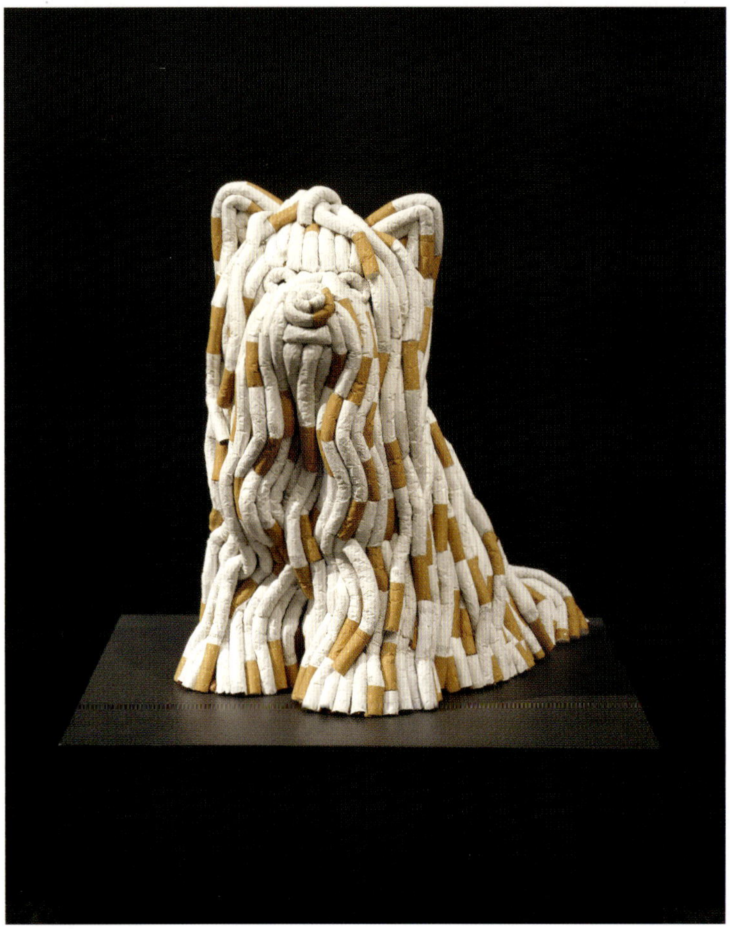

Sarah Lucas shot to fame in the 1990s as part of the Young British Artists (YBAs), but unlike her cohorts she has shied away from publicity, even declining to be nominated for the prestigious Turner Prize, awarded annually by the Tate Gallery, London. Lucas has made a number of sculptures covered in unused cigarettes, including *Cock* and *Coco*. The cockerel was traditionally a symbol of vigilance and represented St Peter's repentance after his betrayal of Christ. While a dog is typically an indicator of fidelity or loyalty in the West, in Islamic culture it is an incarnation of the devil; here, it recalls Jeff Koons's giant topiary *Puppy* (1992).

Edward Kay has made several bodies of work that take inspiration from the Rococo style and specific artists or paintings of this period. The artist often takes a satirical look at the history of painting in works that also reference animated cartoons. His *Illustration from 'A Child's Guide to Rejection'* features a perfect hybrid rooster and alludes to the breeding process for these animals, during which any bird deemed imperfect is immediately killed.

ABOVE · Sarah Lucas · *Cock*, 2005
metal cockerel, cigarettes and glue

LEFT · Sarah Lucas · *Coco*, 2005
china cast dog, cigarettes and glue

OPPOSITE · Edward Kay · *Illustration from 'A Child's Guide to Rejection'*, 2005 · oil on canvas laid on panel

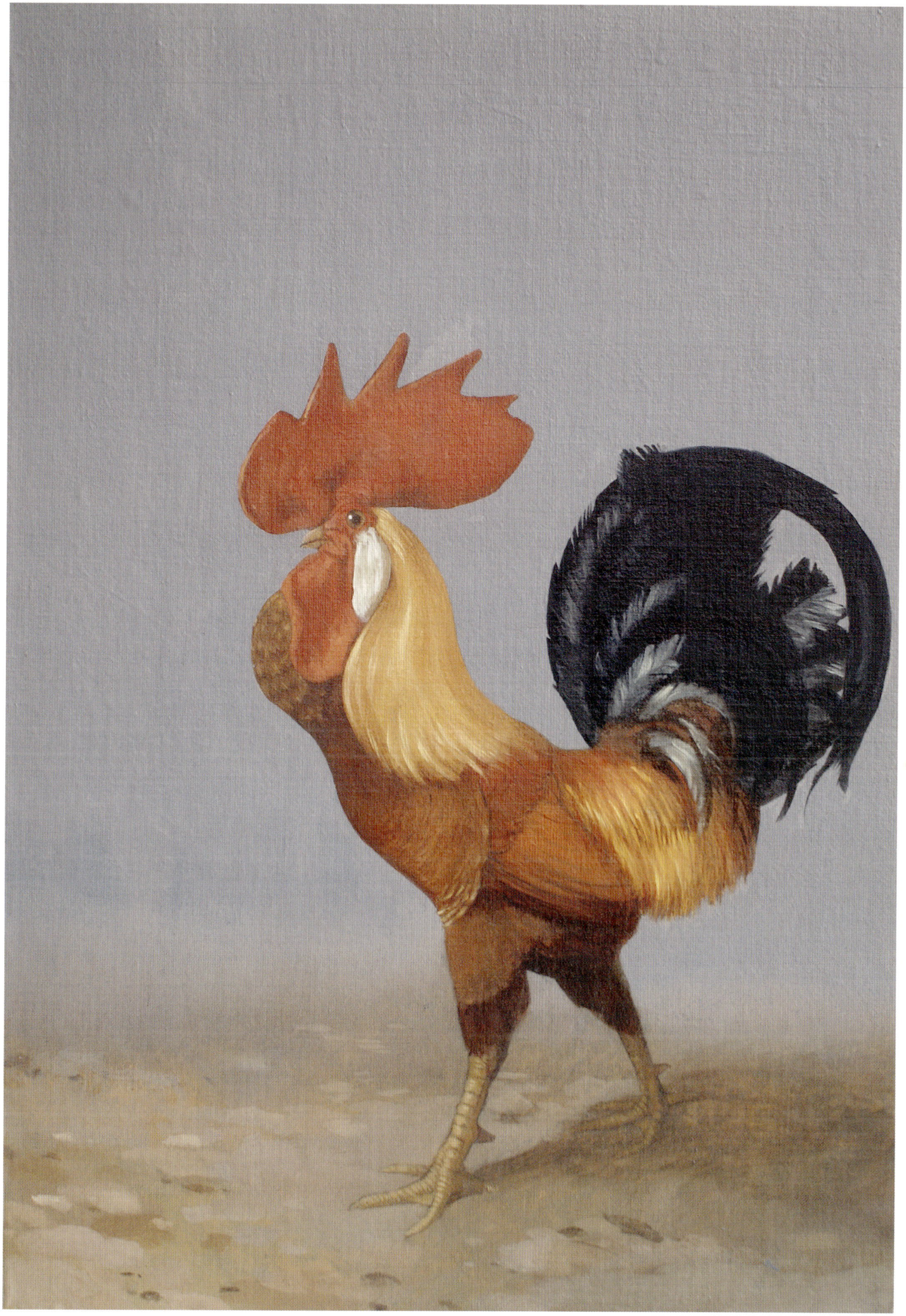

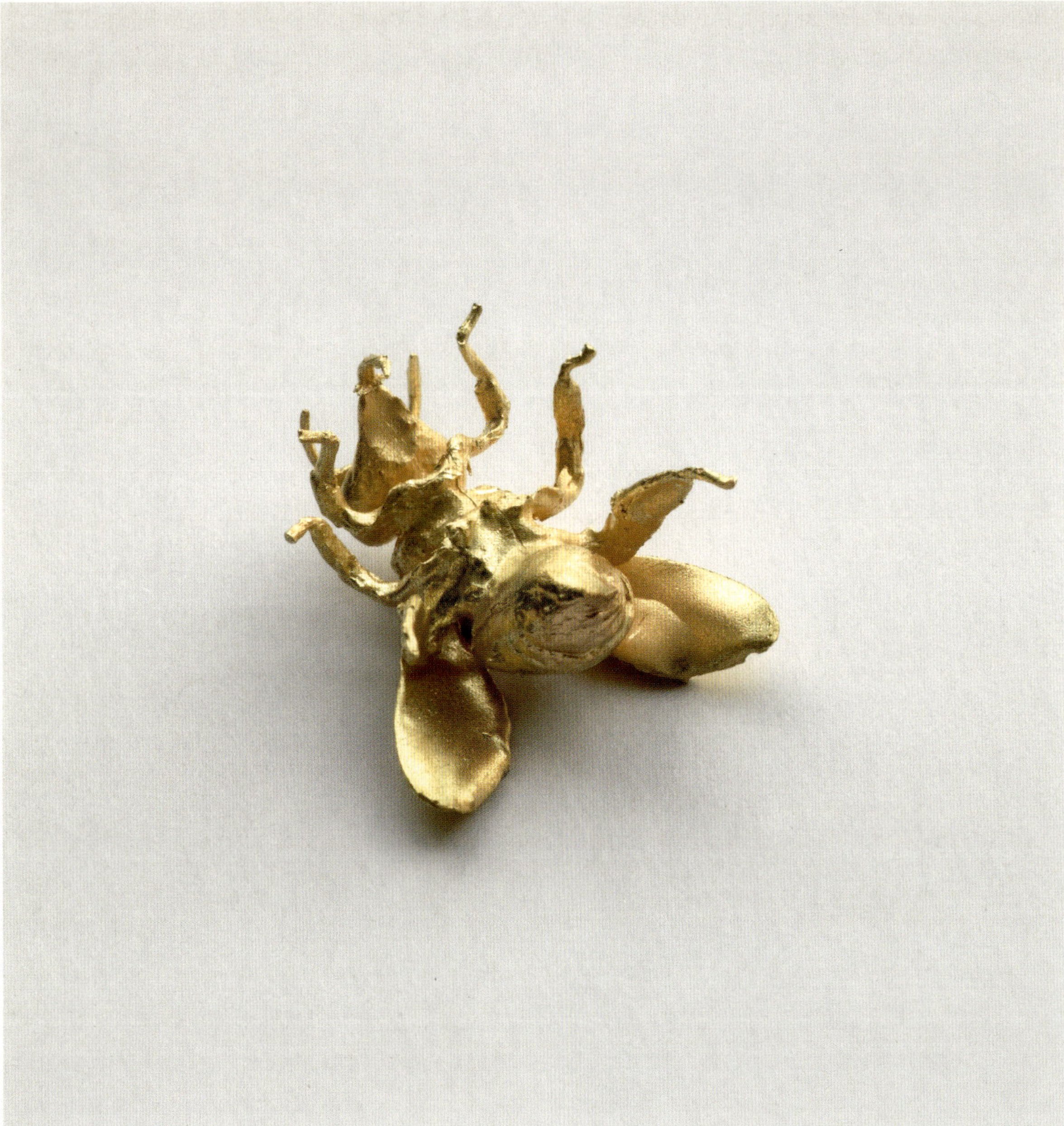

ABOVE
Kris Martin
Bee, 2009
solid gold

OPPOSITE
Tomáš Libertíny
The Seed of Narcissus, 2011
mirrored glass
and beeswax

Kris Martin employs a variety of strategies in his works, which range from installations to small sculptures, that question cultural norms or investigate religious symbols and spirituality. His tiny, solid gold *Bee* lies forlorn on its back, dead probably after unleashing its sting in self-defence. Bees have long been depicted as models of efficiency, stable social order and industry.

Tomáš Libertíny created his *The Seed of Narcissus* by encouraging bees to build a hive to surround a large, mirrored object of his design. Libertíny has made many works with the help of bees, a process that he calls 'slow prototyping'. Here, 'connecting the beeswax with the glass seemed a very logical combination even though one is natural and the other is completely industrial: merging them together in some kind of poetic manifestation that claims the space but it also has its own story.' The seed-shaped glass reflects viewers as well as the industry of the bees, which is shown in a separate video.

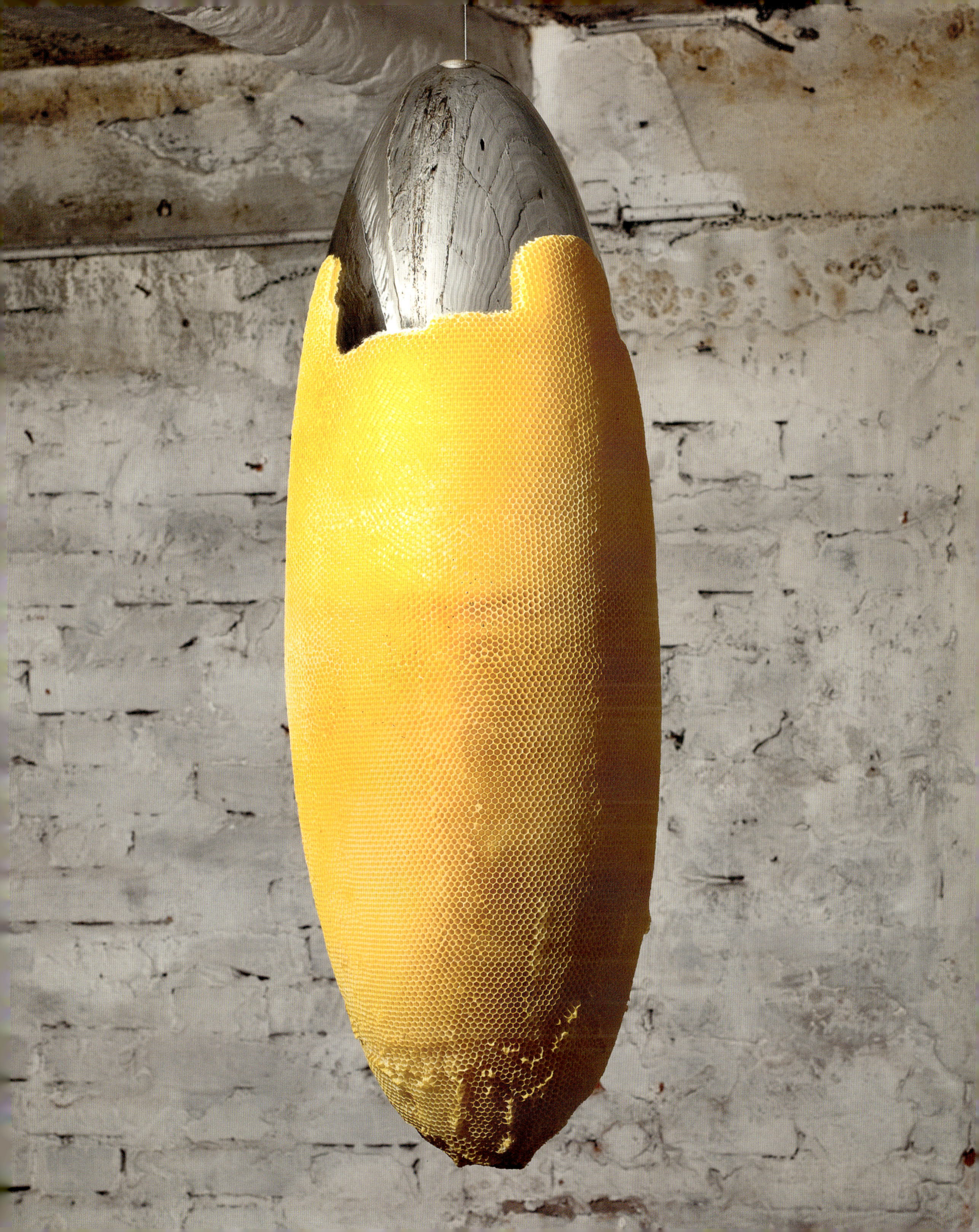

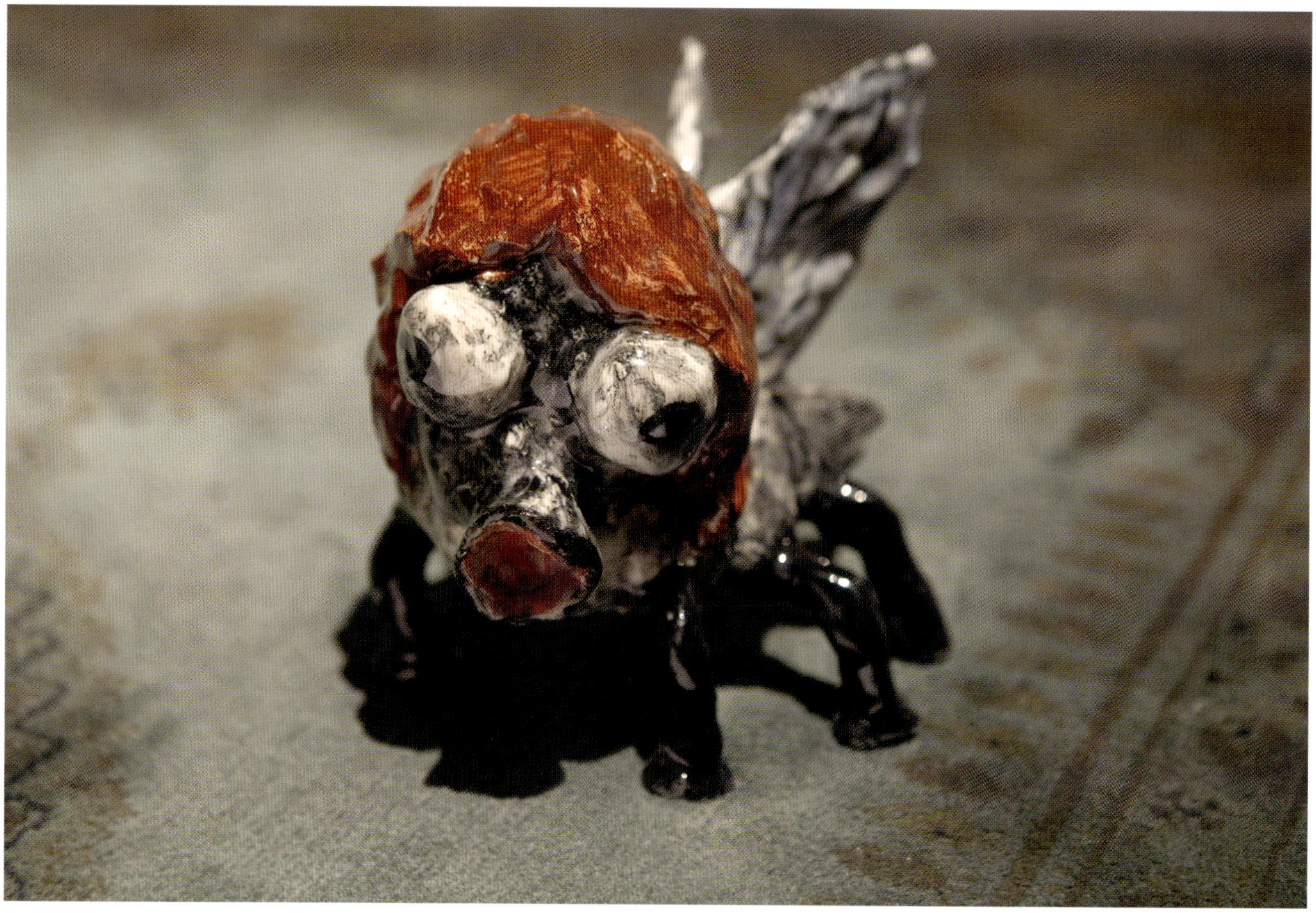

ABOVE
Klara Kristalova
A fly on your floor, 2010
glazed stoneware

OPPOSITE TOP LEFT
Lisa Sweeney
Fly, 2009
pencil on gesso board

OPPOSITE TOP RIGHT
Cindy Wright
Spaceinvaders, 2008
oil on canvas

OPPOSITE BOTTOM
Maryam Amiryani
Fly, White Plate, 2008
oil on linen

Klara Kristalova's *A fly on your floor* recalls the 1958 film *The Fly* (and its 1986 remake) in which a mad scientist accidentally turns himself into a human fly and proceeds to cause terror and havoc. Kristalova uses traditional Meissen porcelain techniques to create intimate sculptures that speak of death and possible destruction. Flies have long appeared in art as carriers of disease and their inclusion in traditional still lifes was intended to remind viewers of their mortality.

Lisa Sweeney's sketch of a single dead fly, **Cindy Wright**'s oil painting of many dead flies and **Maryam Amiryani**'s painting of a living fly all figure this insect as an example of nature invading the domestic environment. Sweeney explains that her work 'is concerned with the banal and everyday stuff that is sometimes overlooked and undervalued. Seeing the fragile beauty in something like a dead fly may make us realize that everything, no matter how small and seemingly insignificant, has a value.' Amiryani is interested in the everyday and homes in on the quiet moments of life to create what she calls 'minimalist theatre'. Wright's collection of dead flies on graph paper implicates the viewer as a collector, or scientist, and most likely the cause of the insects' shortened lives. In all these works, the fragility of life comes under observation.

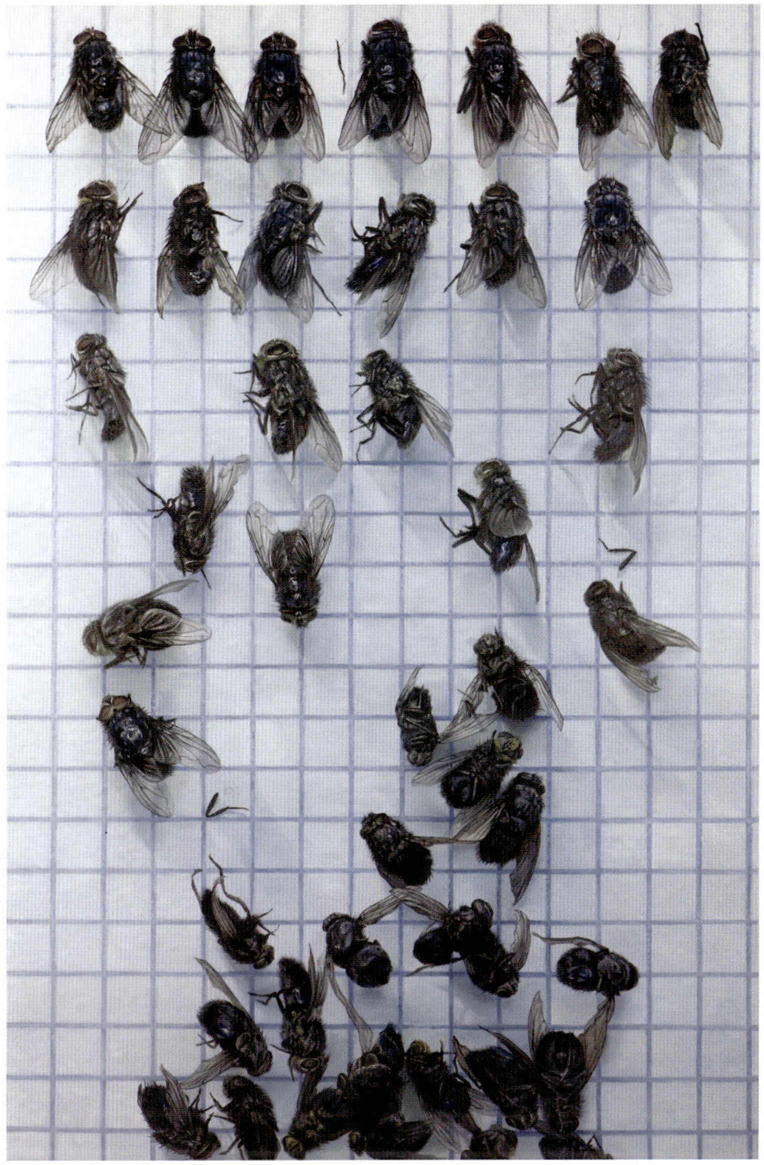
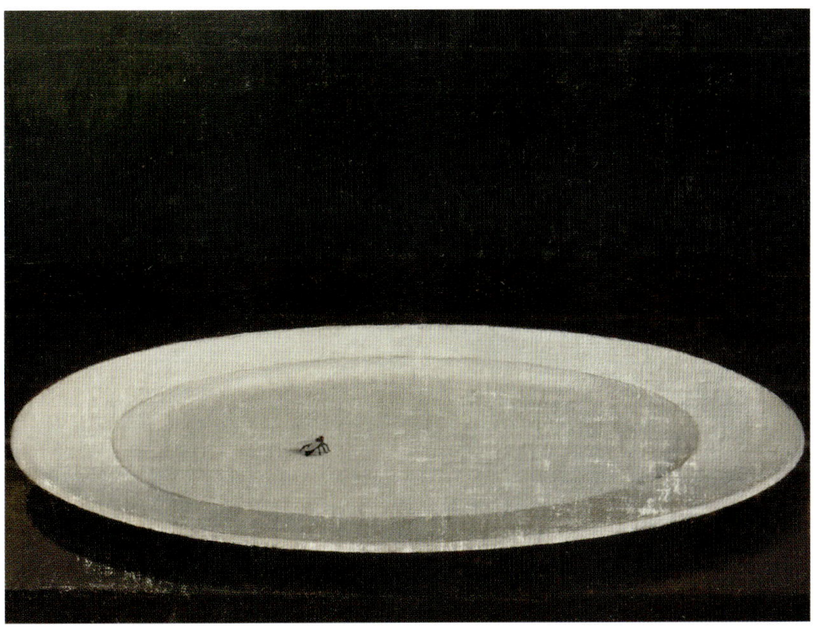

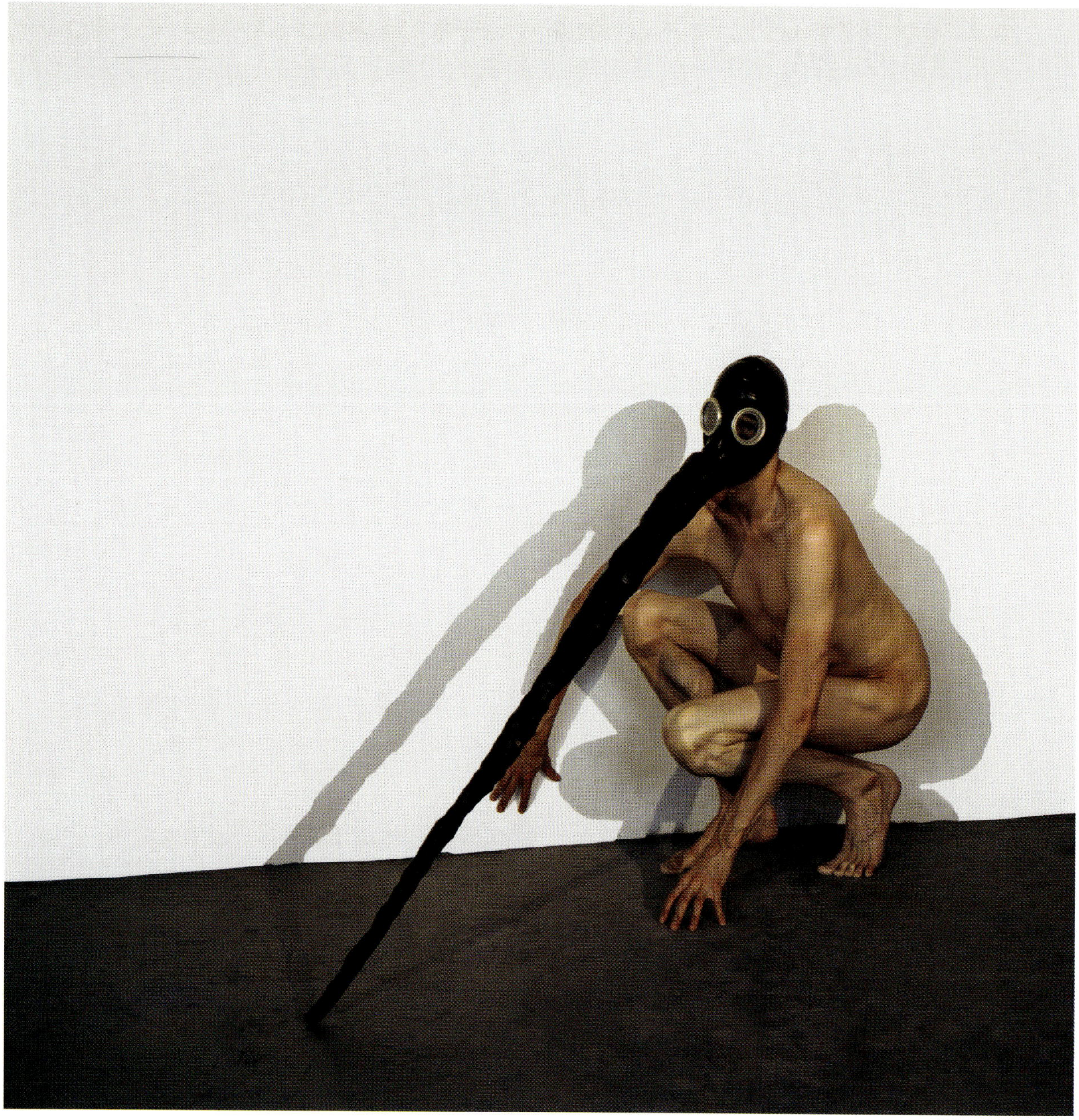

ABOVE
Roberto Ekholm
Mosquito Man #1
(*congress*), 2009
archival print

OPPOSITE
Adam Fuss
Untitled, 2003
pigment print

Roberto Ekholm's performance series *Mr Mosquito* sees the artist naked, save for a World War II gas mask altered to resemble the stinger of the insect. As an agent in the transmission of disease, the mosquito has become a symbol with which to explore gay male sexuality, the spread of HIV, and the fears and misconceptions that surround both. The series includes anatomical drawings of mosquitos and photographs of the performance. Together, the works allude to the mythical status of blood while also interrogating the issues involved in the HIV pandemic.

In his photographs, **Adam Fuss** often catches the moment of change from one state of being to another. His *Untitled* images of butterfly chrysalids are printed very large and thus resemble sarcophagi as much as the protective casings of fragile insects. Notions of death and rebirth surface, echoing the traditional use of caterpillars and butterflies in the still-life tradition, which signalled the possibility of an afterlife for the deserving.

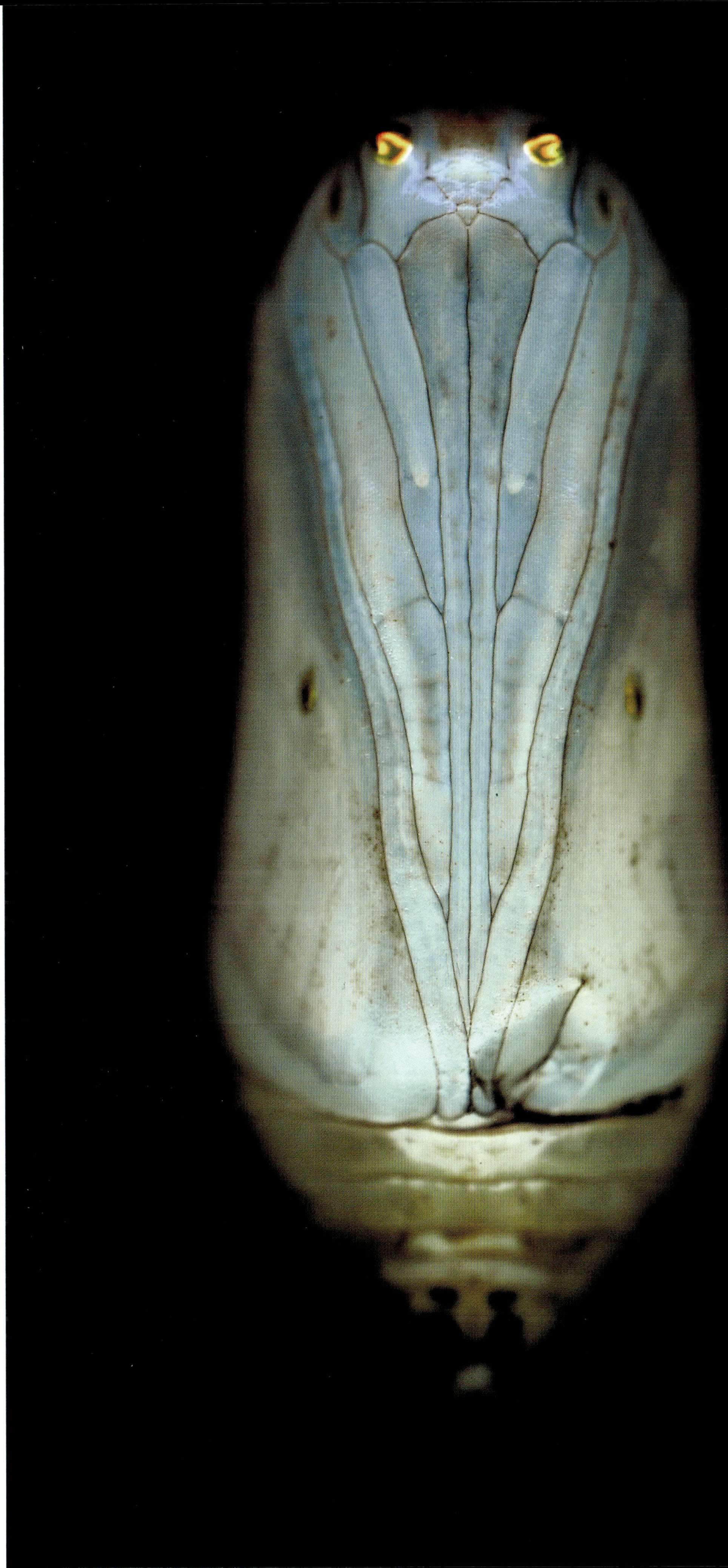

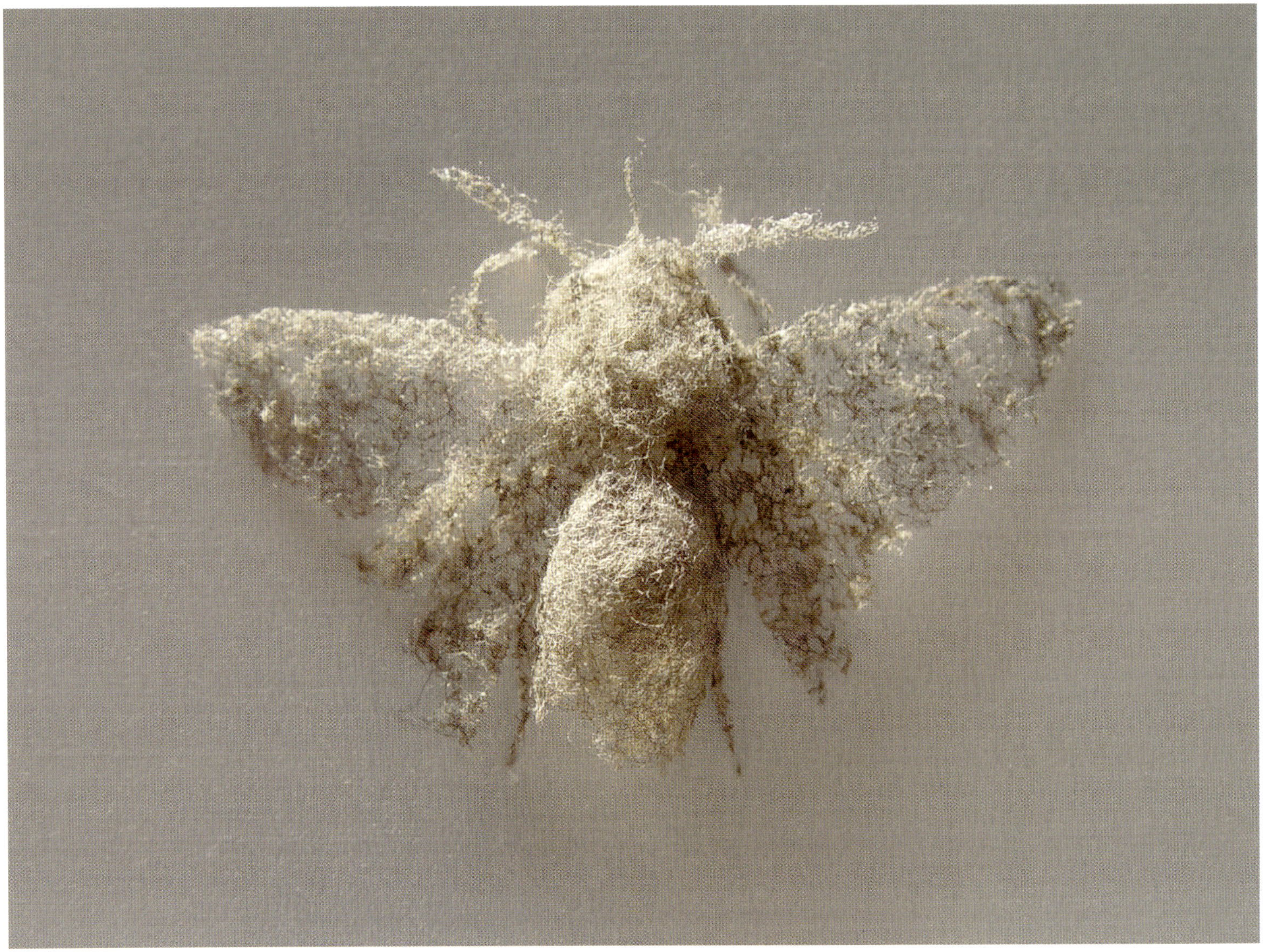

ABOVE
Paul Hazelton
Moth-er, 2006
household dust

OPPOSITE
Janne Malmros
Black-veined Whites 1906–1947, 2010
plywood, brown wrapping paper, nails and entomologist foam; pencil, Indian and acrylic ink on *The Butterflies of the British Isles* (Richard South, F.E.S. London Editions 1906–1947)

Paul Hazelton collects dust from surrounding interiors (but never from a vacuum cleaner), which he then wets and forms into sculptures. These are then allowed to slowly dry into permanent, though fragile, works of art. Hazelton has linked his sculptures to 'an impossible desire to come clean'. He says: 'When I was growing up, creating dust and getting dirty were taboo, but even clean living creates dust and dirt. Like expulsions from the immaculate environment of my youth, I now create "immaculate conceptions" – concepts involving the control of dirt and the subversion of cleanliness.'

Janne Malmros hunted down all eight editions of *The Butterflies of the British Isles* by Richard South to create her work, *Black-veined Whites 1906–1947*. She then affixed the books onto a board just as the English entomologist would have pinned down his butterfly specimens. Each edition of the book is slightly different as publishers adapted to the differing social and economic situations of the times; after the first printing of 1906, every book was either larger or smaller, and, in the case of the edition printed during wartime, the paper was thinner and speckled.

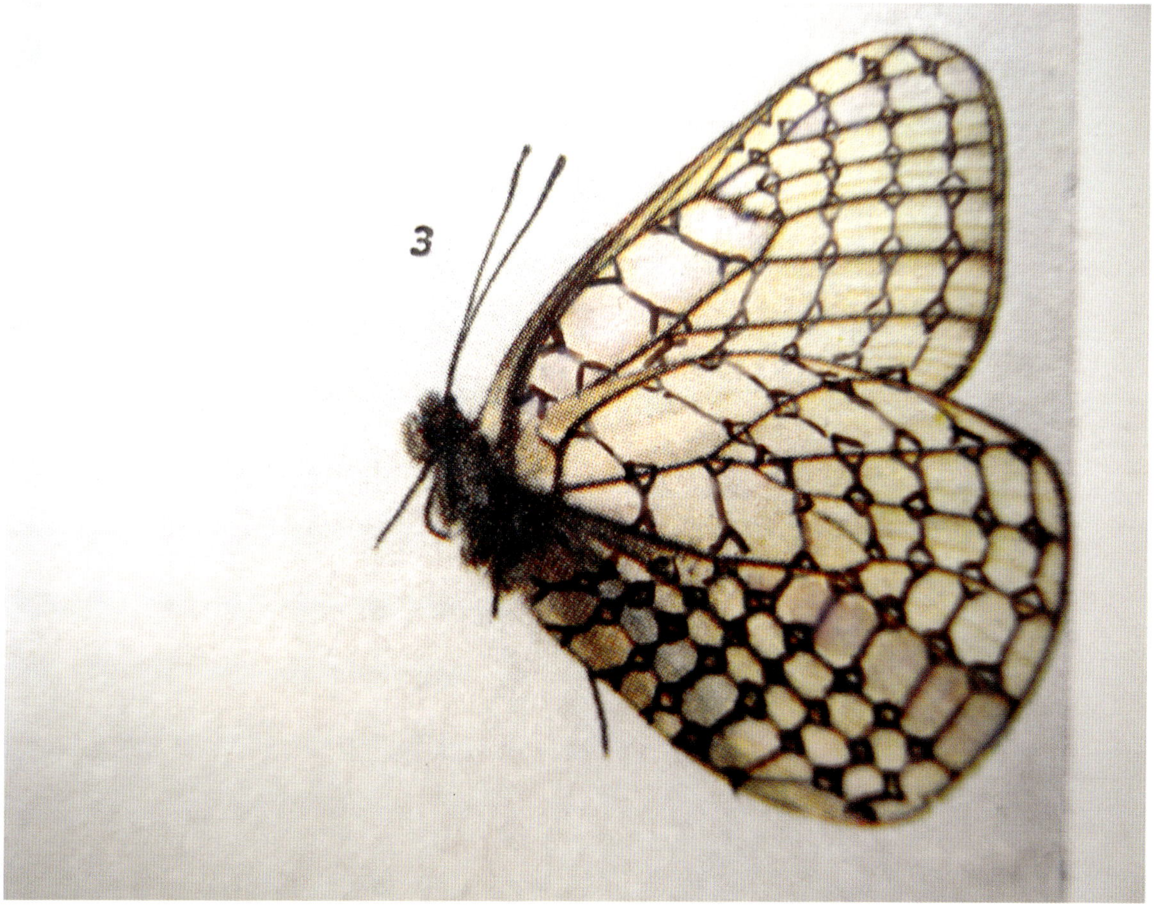
3

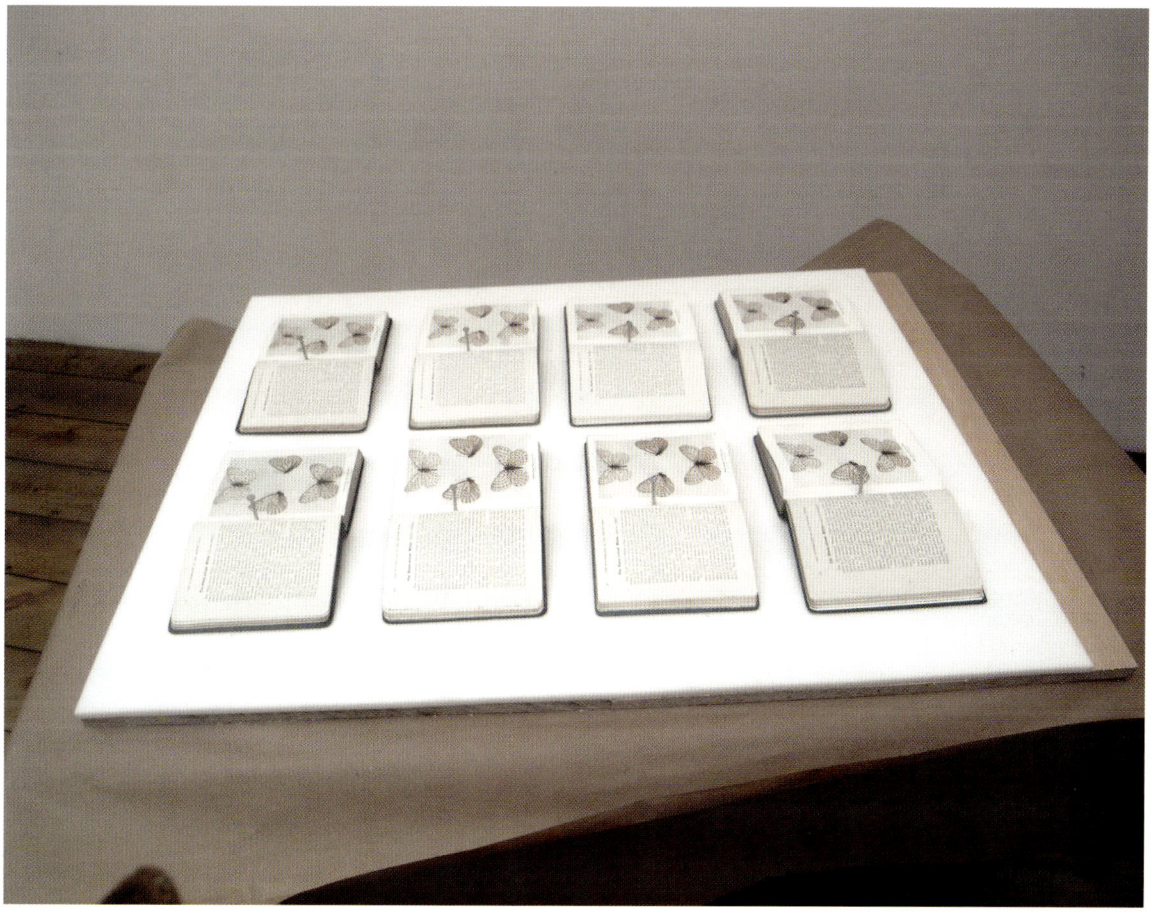

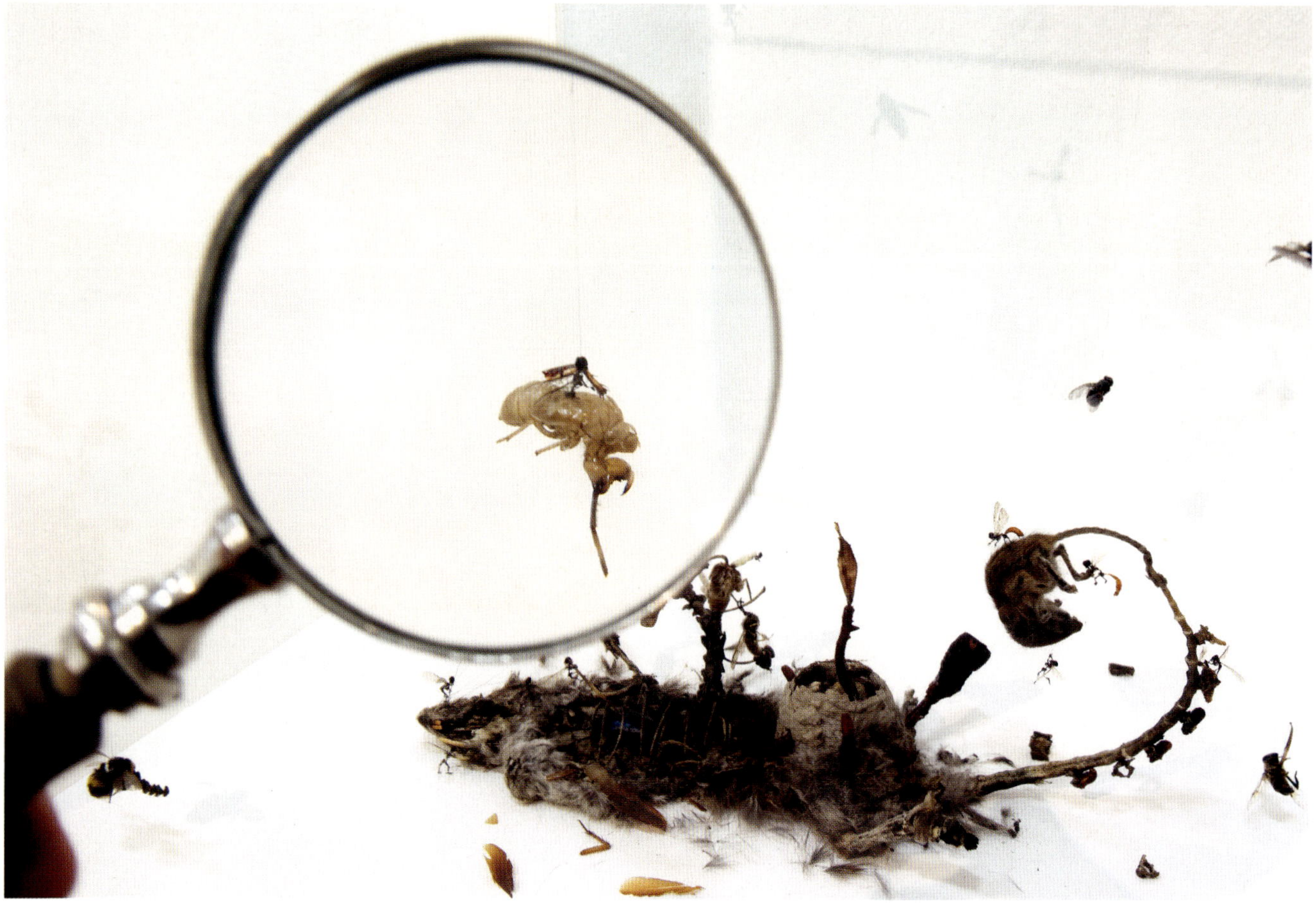

ABOVE
Tessa Farmer
The Resurrection of the Rat, 2008
dried rat, mummified mouse, dried insects, hedgehog spines, wasp nest and plant roots

Tessa Farmer uses the dead bodies of animals and insects in her works. Tiny flies become flying skeletons, ants work away like small devils, parasitoid wasps transform into fairies that strip a dead fox, and bees and other bugs eat away at a decaying rat. These small tableaux usually develop from artist residencies (at the Natural History Museum, London; the Arboretum Kalmthout, Belgium) that allow her to look not only at natural processes, but also at the fiction of their depiction in museum settings.

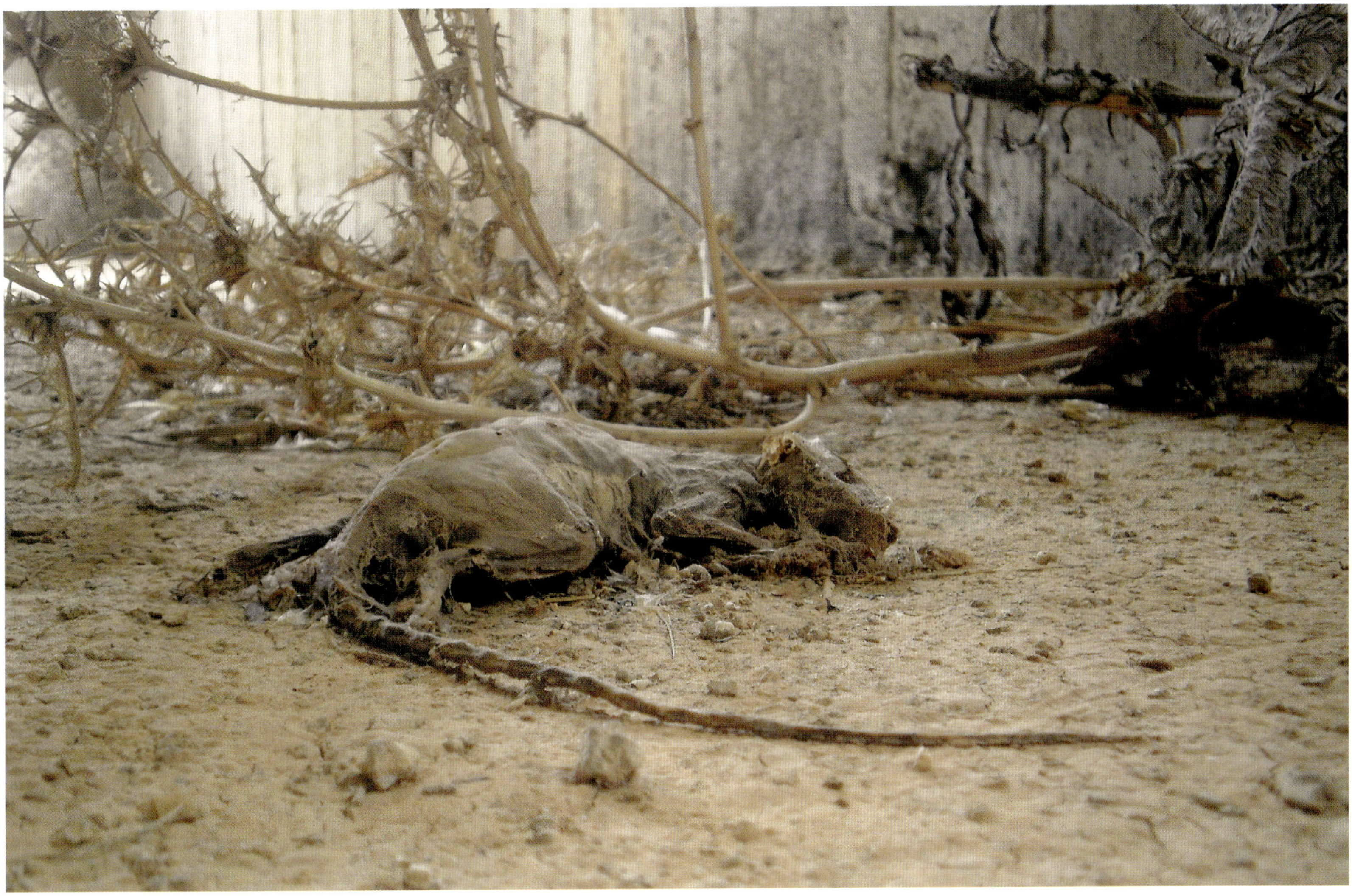

ABOVE
Berthold Bell
Still Life In Plato's Cave, 22 March 2011
digital photograph

Berthold Bell's *Still Life In Plato's Cave* belongs to a series of photographs that documents contemporary Greece, a nation haunted by an agonizing political and monetary crisis. Bell found this scene of a desiccated rat surrounded by dried weeds inside a partially built, concrete building on the Greek island of Paros. Here not only has natural life 'stilled' but so too has economic life; the skeletal building has been unfinished for many years and it is unlikely it will ever be completed.

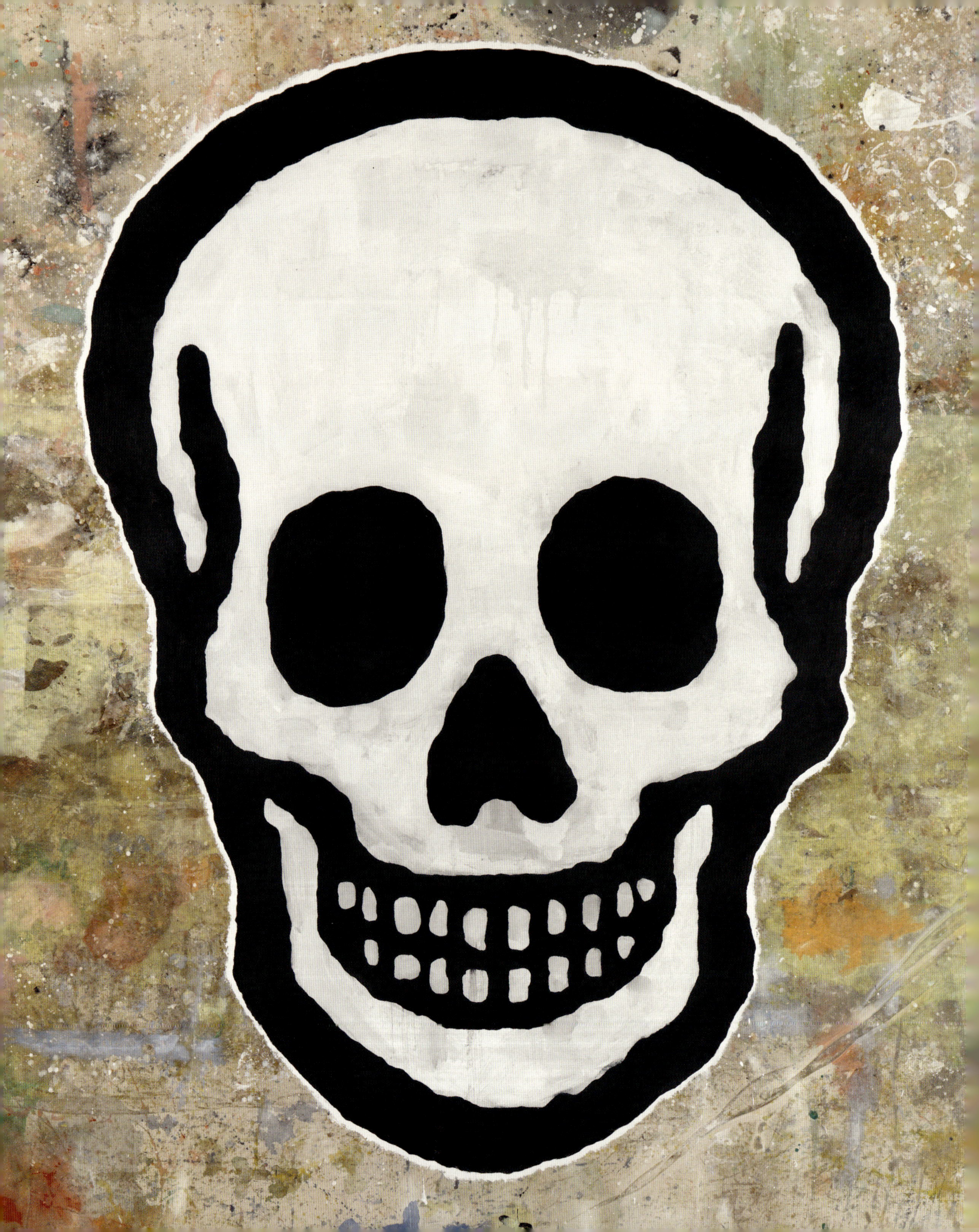

Section Five

DEATH

DEATH

Yes, Death. Death must be so beautiful. To lie in the soft brown earth, with the grasses waving above one's head, and listen to silence. To have no yesterday, and no tomorrow. To forget time, to forgive life, to be at peace. You can help me. You can open for me the portals of Death's house, for Love is always with you, and Love is stronger than Death is.

—OSCAR WILDE, *The Canterville Ghost*, 1887

At some point during the long evolutionary process from amoeba to human we developed our own unique take on what it means to die. Though it is certainly an innate fear of death that causes other animals to flee their untimely end – as the deer flees the wolf, the zebra the lion, the frog the bird, the insect the snake – none of these creatures fears the fires of hell or the never-ending darkness of Hades; they simply do not want to end up as prey. For death is a particularly human preoccupation, an anxiety and inevitability from the moment we are born, and for anti-abortionists, from the moment of conception.

Religious doctrines the world over instruct followers to worry less about life after birth and more about life after death. Death is something to be overcome, a hurdle rather than an irrevocable finality. They teach that death may be defeated and of a life after it. The democratic extension of the afterlife to all belongs very much to the Judeo-Christian tradition. In the ancient world it was only the souls of kings that warranted real consideration, so much so that of the art and artefacts that remain from these eras a surprising proportion relate to the lavish preparations for their rulers' afterlives – just think of the pyramids in Egypt or the tombs of Roman emperors. The lives and deaths of ordinary men and women, the stonecutters, weavers and cleaners of the day, remained unheralded. The modest gravestone would later ensure some recognition for those whose deaths passed otherwise unremarked by history, although certainly their passing may have been mourned by loved ones.

Love, of course, is the other anxiety we carry with us. We fear the prospect of never finding it, almost as much as we fear losing it to death, whether our own or that of our loved one. Surely our attachment to an afterlife is in part linked to one unanswerable question: does true love end in the grave? For to believe in an afterlife is to believe that we will at some point be reunited with our loved ones and so achieve eternal happiness. It is the hope that Romeo and Juliet both clung to in their last moments. But the promise of eternal life belongs only to believers; for the atheist there is only death, then nothing. And even the believer knows that salvation comes to only the chosen few and that while they may worship their chosen deity there is no guarantee that such devotion will be rewarded.

Reminders of death, ever approaching and unavoidable, thus historically acted as an incitement to believers to live out their lives according to the doctrines of their faith. For example, the Latin phrase *memento mori* – remember you will die – resonated with Christians throughout the Middle Ages. In religious art, Death and his associates – the skull, the Grim Reaper, the skeleton, among others – appeared frequently as prompts to reflect on one's own mortality and, in turn, on one's earthly sins. The *vanitas* paintings that first emerged in the early seventeenth century were intended to have a similar effect. These still lifes usually depict an assortment of personal or domestic objects from around the home, some attractive, others less so, but the constant is at least one allusion to death. Burning candles represented the eventual extinguishing of a man's life, an hourglass the ever-onward ticking of time. The most widely recognized symbol of all *vanitas* paintings is the human skull. Tucked among the material possessions of a wealthy merchant or landowner, the skull throws into sharp relief the transience of earthly pleasures. The term *vanitas* comes from a longer biblical Latin aphorism from the Book of Ecclesiastes: *Vanitas vanitatum omnia vanitas*, or 'vanity of vanities, all is vanity'. Translating the same phrase from the Hebrew results in the slightly altered version, 'vapour of vapours'. Despite their differences, both translations evoke the futility of worldly possessions and the fragility of human life.

Many contemporary artists have found inspiration in the *vanitas* still life, and the skull in particular has become a regular fixture in the current visual vocabulary. Donald Baechler's *SKULL* (page 230), part of a series of works with Wes Lang called *Skulls and Shit*, takes the simple skull as its starting point in order to make a comic, though still apocalyptic, reminder of the impending death of the viewer (and artist). Other artists have made works with actual human skulls. To create his *For the Love of God* Damien Hirst took a real human skull (from the eighteenth century) and had it cast in platinum and set with 8,601 diamonds (page 234). The work is said to represent a victory over death, but one that might also prove in vain, for any attempt to conquer death only ever reveals its ultimate destructive power. A quieter, and perhaps more potent, work is Gabriel Orozco's *Black Kites*, an actual skull upon which the artist used a graphite pencil to mark out a map of a lost life (page 235). Oddly, both artists left the teeth alone. The other similarities belong to the artefact itself – the empty eye sockets, the scale – and remind all viewers that beneath flesh and blood, our own skull lies hidden – for now.

Unlike their artistic forebears, contemporary artists, on the whole, choose not to impart any moral lessons in their works, perhaps saying instead that death is certain, our lives are short, and we should enjoy ourselves while we can. Like Oscar Wilde, they remind us that though life offers the possibility for beauty and love, the only certainty that death offers is the corruption of the flesh.

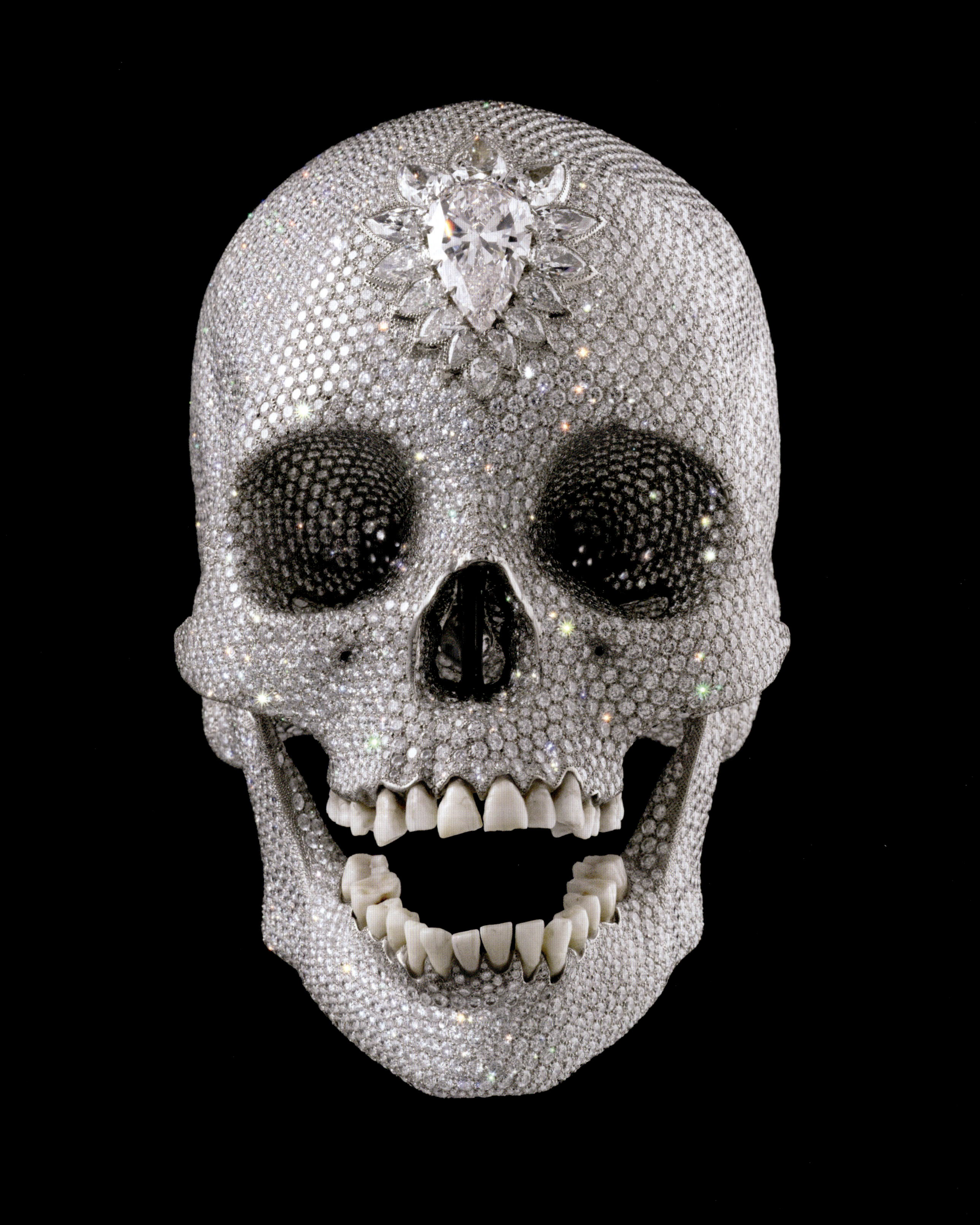

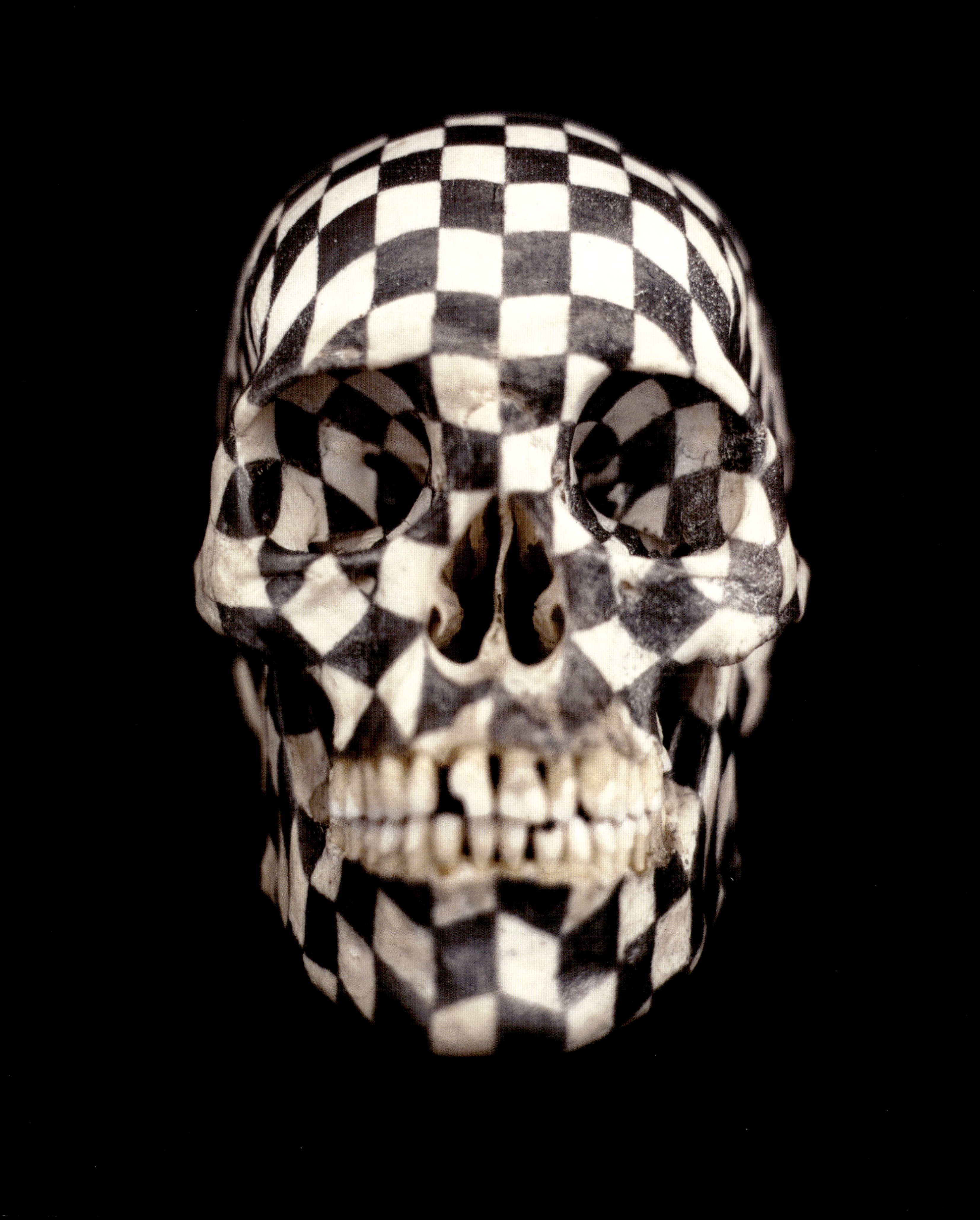

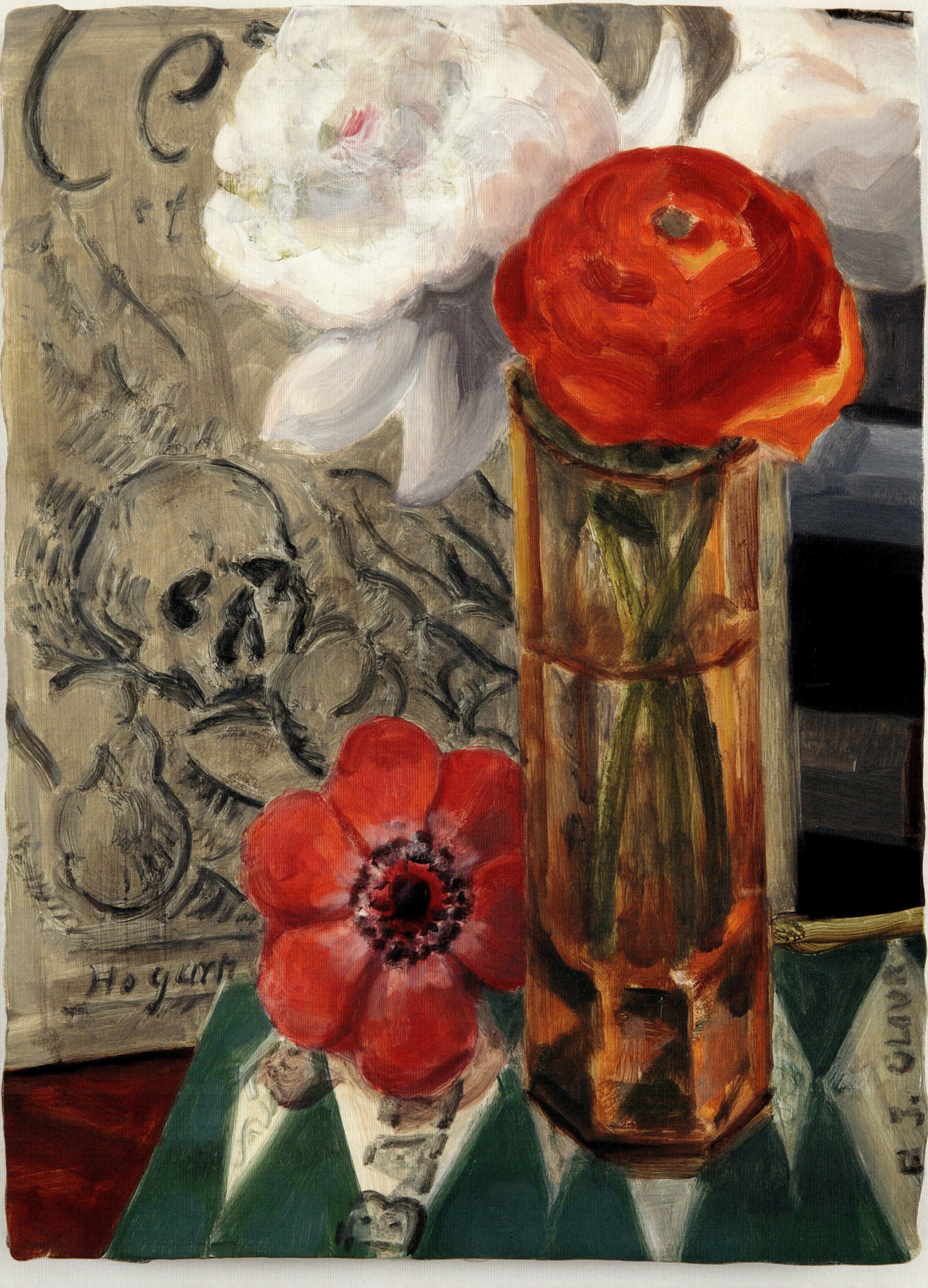

PAGE 230
Donald Baechler · ***SKULL***, 2009 (detail)
acrylic on canvas dropcloth

PREVIOUS PAGES LEFT
Damien Hirst · ***For the Love of God***, 2007
platinum, diamonds and human teeth

PREVIOUS PAGES RIGHT
Gabriel Orozco · ***Black Kites***, 1997
graphite on skull

OPPOSITE
Elizabeth Peyton · ***Cezanne + Balzac***, 2009
oil on linen on board

RIGHT
Alexander James, Distil Ennui Studio
Vanitas, 'The Great Leveler', 2011
C-print mounted on polished aluminium

BELOW
Shirana Shahbazi · [***Stilleben-33-2009***]
C-print on aluminium

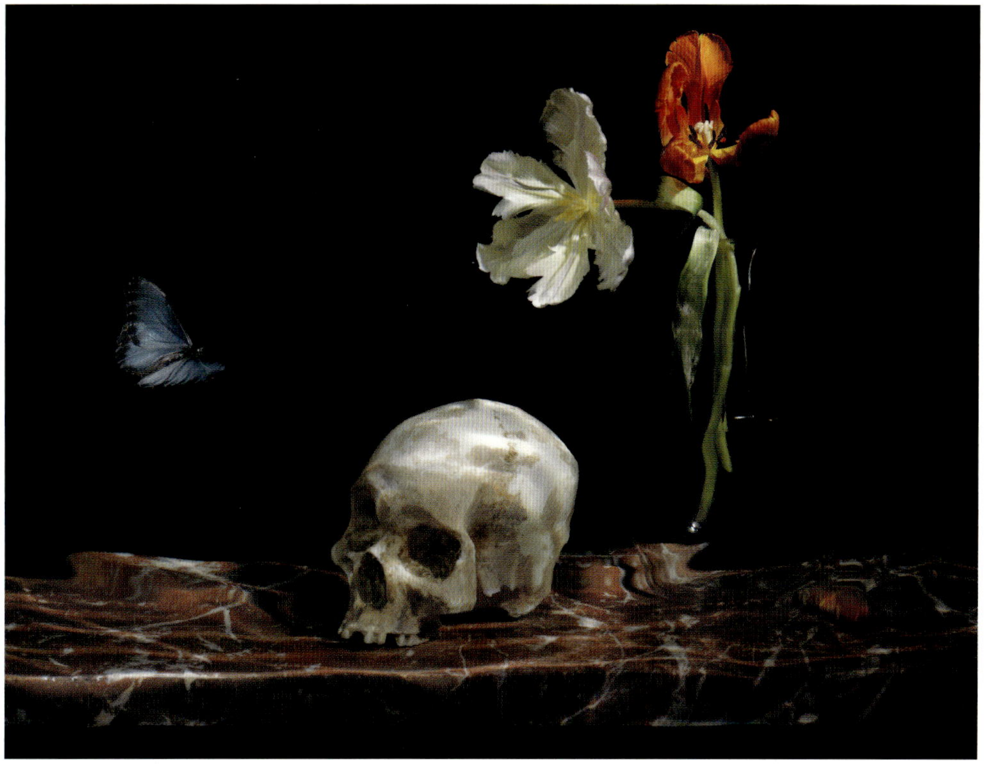

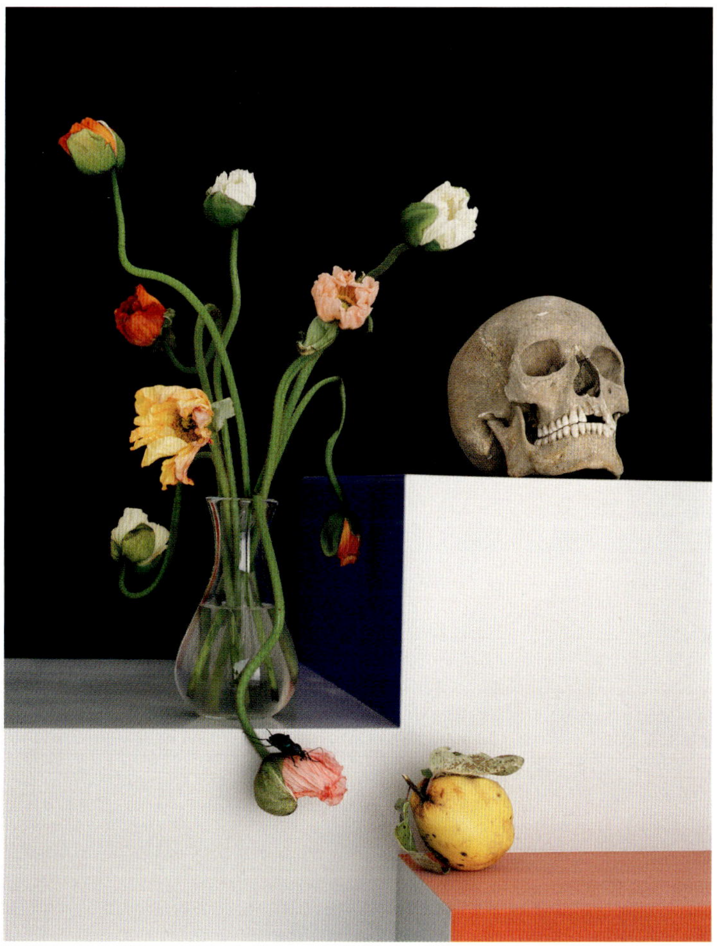

Elizabeth Peyton's ongoing interest in the famous and influential (see page 26) continues in *Cezanne + Balzac*, a homage to Honoré de Balzac and his contribution to the birth of modern fiction, and to Paul Cézanne and his groundbreaking style of painting. Her composition includes a drawing of a skull by Cézanne while a red poppy (another symbol of death) sits on top of a Balzac novel. The work brings together two very different artists (and art forms), who nonetheless both address memory, visual symbolism and loss.

Alexander James and **Shirana Shahbazi** have both constructed photographs that recall Dutch still lifes of the seventeenth century, but their methods differ. The flowers, skull and butterfly in James's *Vanitas, 'The Great Leveler'* were shot underwater; submerged in a large tank, they rest on a marble shelf and shimmer in their watery tomb. Shahbazi's [*Stilleben-33-2009*] presents a similar group of objects but the crispness of her photograph is at odds with James's mottled tones. One may feel like a stark warning of mortality, the other a half-remembered image from a dream, yet both successfully move the tradition of the still life forward.

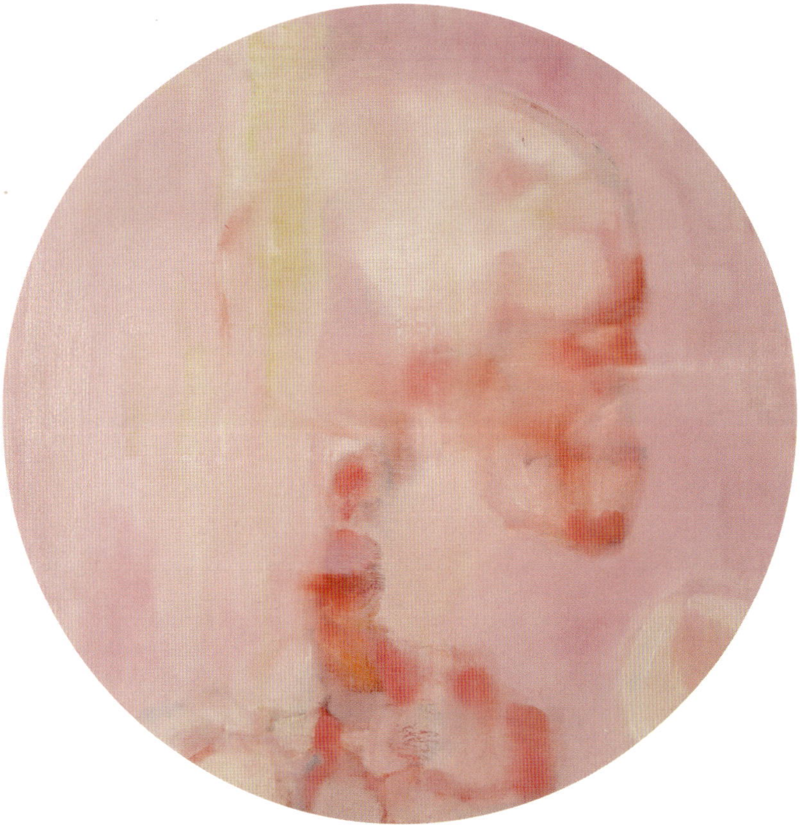

Sarah Elise Hall's *Temporal* is from a series of paintings based on three-dimensional PET (positron emission tomography) scans. Hall writes: 'I use medical imagery as my point of departure for a contemporary meditation on the nature of mortality. The idea of medical imagery, something that images the skeleton while we are still alive, seems somehow impossible for our minds to fully grasp. The body, presented in a form of stasis, is frozen between life and death.'

Paul McDevitt's *Mountain Flowers A* is an ink drawing on paper made using standard disposable pens. Its intricate rendering of a skull hidden in flowers is graphic yet subtle, evoking a Manga comic strip while pairing two common symbols of human mortality: a skull and flowers. The cool blue is offset by the hot red, which at a glance could be mistaken for flowing blood. Both colours are used in *Gray's Anatomy* to depict oxygenated blood (red) and unoxygenated blood (blue) within the human circulatory system.

Mathew Weir paints ceramic figurines into art-historical settings that also contain elements of Dutch still lifes. His paintings offer much beyond that traditional imagery, however, and address 'mental illness, slavery, death and racism'. Weir believes that 'figurines can be seen as a metaphor for the dead.... They are representations of people but they are also still, inanimate objects.'

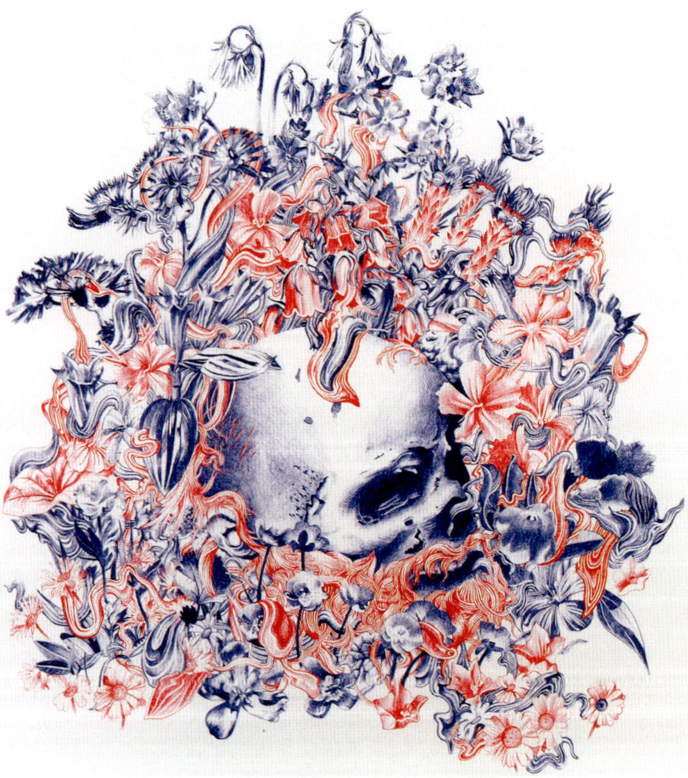

ABOVE · Sarah Elise Hall · *Temporal*, 2010 oil on panel

LEFT · Paul McDevitt · ***Mountain Flowers A***, 2005 · biro on paper

OPPOSITE · Mathew Weir · ***A Fool's Life***, 2010 · oil on canvas mounted on board

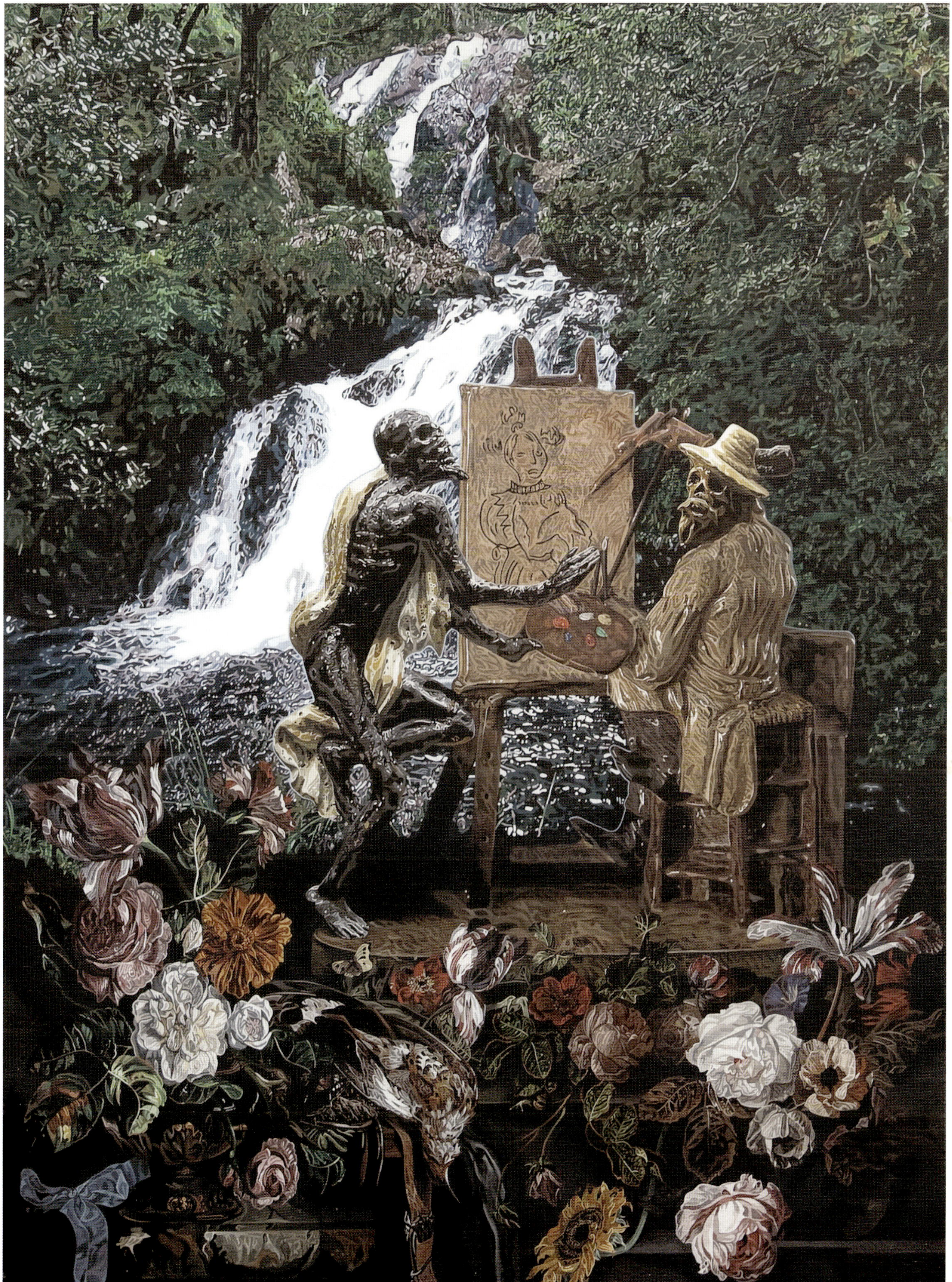

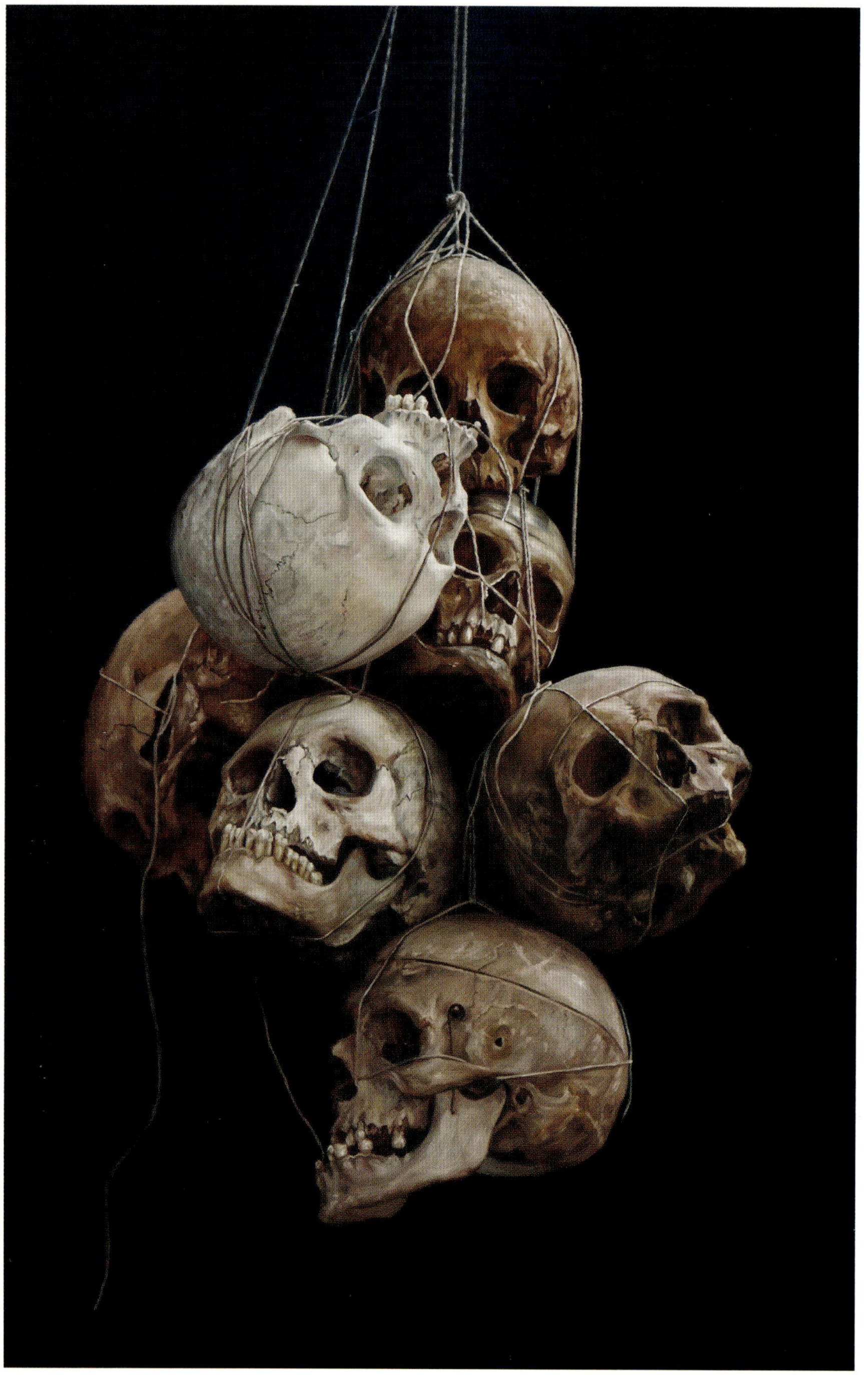

Cindy Wright's painting *Collector's Item* depicts a cache of human skulls suspended in string. That the skulls are strung together almost like fish on a line adds to the discomfort of the image. Who is the collector who would wish to display such a macabre hoard? They certainly look more like the bounty of some bloodthirsty warlord than specimens in a natural history museum – though with historical collecting practices of Western museums now under scrutiny, that distinction is no longer so clear.

Piotr Uklański was commissioned to create a portrait of a man using X-rays of his subject. The resulting work *Untitled* (*Monsieur François Pinault, President of Artemis*) transforms these medical images into a psychedelic skull and crossbones – a pirate emblem that stands in for the well-known billionaire and art patron.

Guillaume Paris's animation *Out of the Whale* is a complex digital work forever evolving in front of the viewer, from one minute to the next, from one exhibition to another. The still reproduced here is thus unique but it provides a sense of the overall work. A digitally rendered Pinocchio floats face down in a pool of water, a scene reminiscent of the original in the hand-drawn 1940 Disney film. Paris's work exists 'eternally', cheating death in a virtual domain.

'In this metaphysical desert, the "universe" is recalculated in real time at every instant: there will never be the same image twice, for all eternity....'

—GUILLAUME PARIS

ABOVE
Cindy Wright · ***Collector's Item***, 2010
oil on linen

OPPOSITE TOP
Piotr Uklański · ***Untitled*** **(*Monsieur François Pinault, President of Artemis*)**, 2003 · colour photograph

OPPOSITE BOTTOM
Guillaume Paris · ***Out of the Whale***, 2008 (film still)
real-time evolving permanent video, HD plasma screen, computer; colour, silent

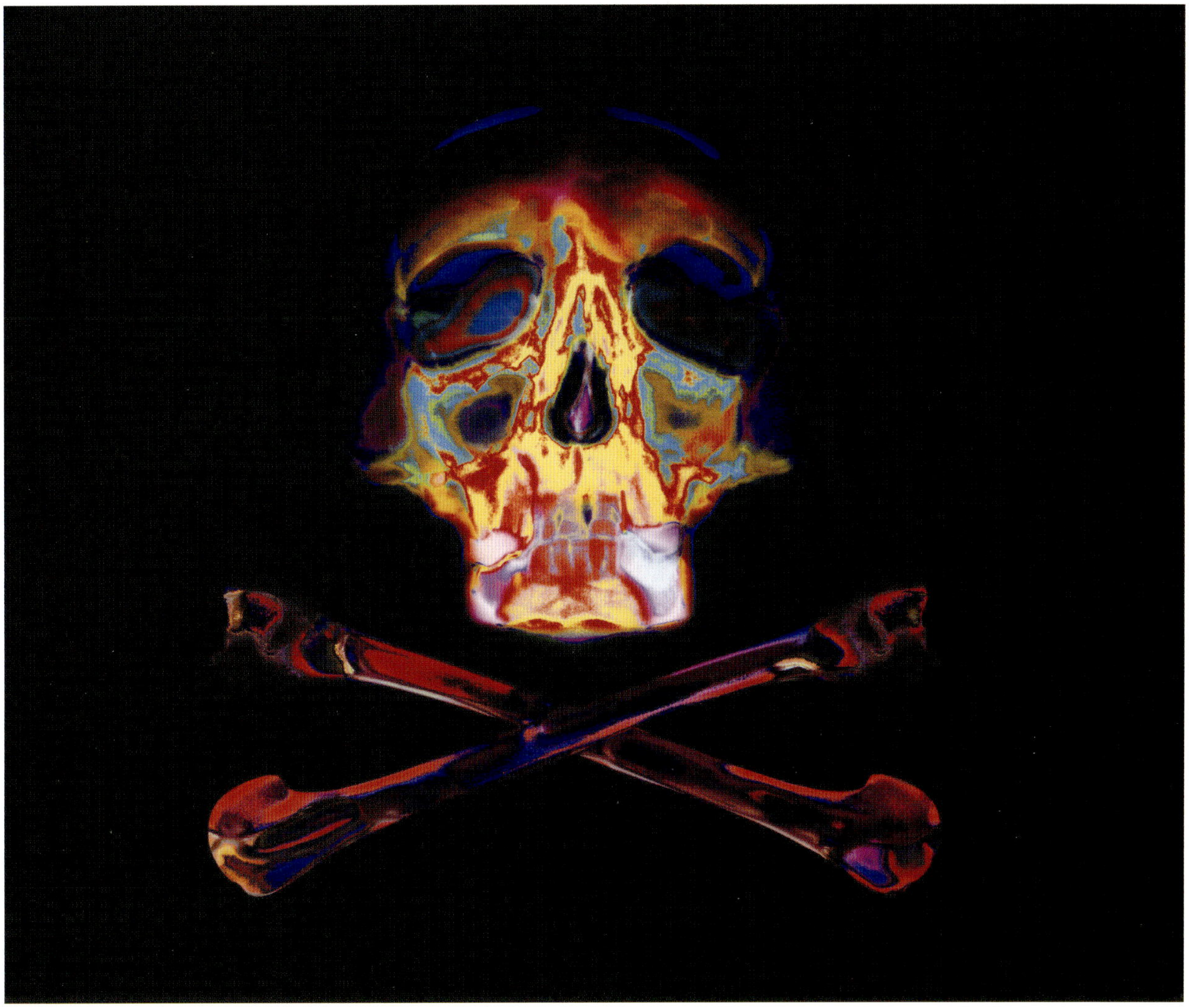

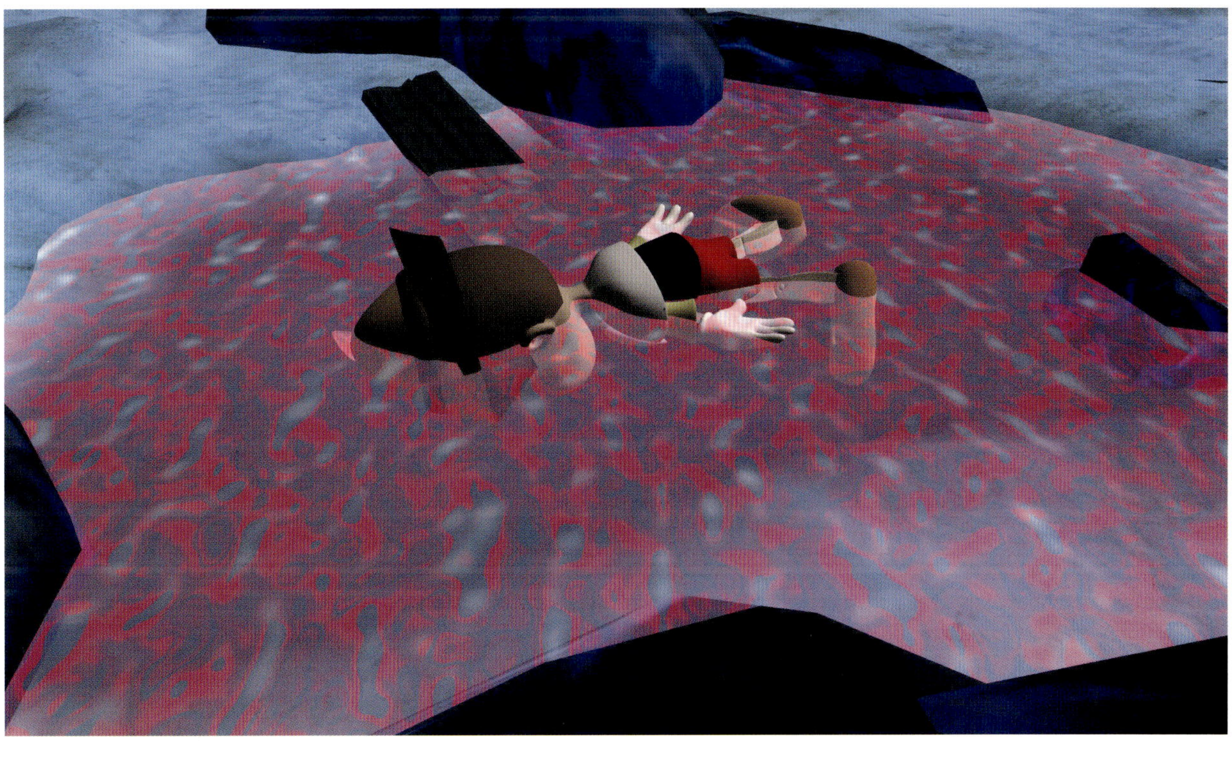

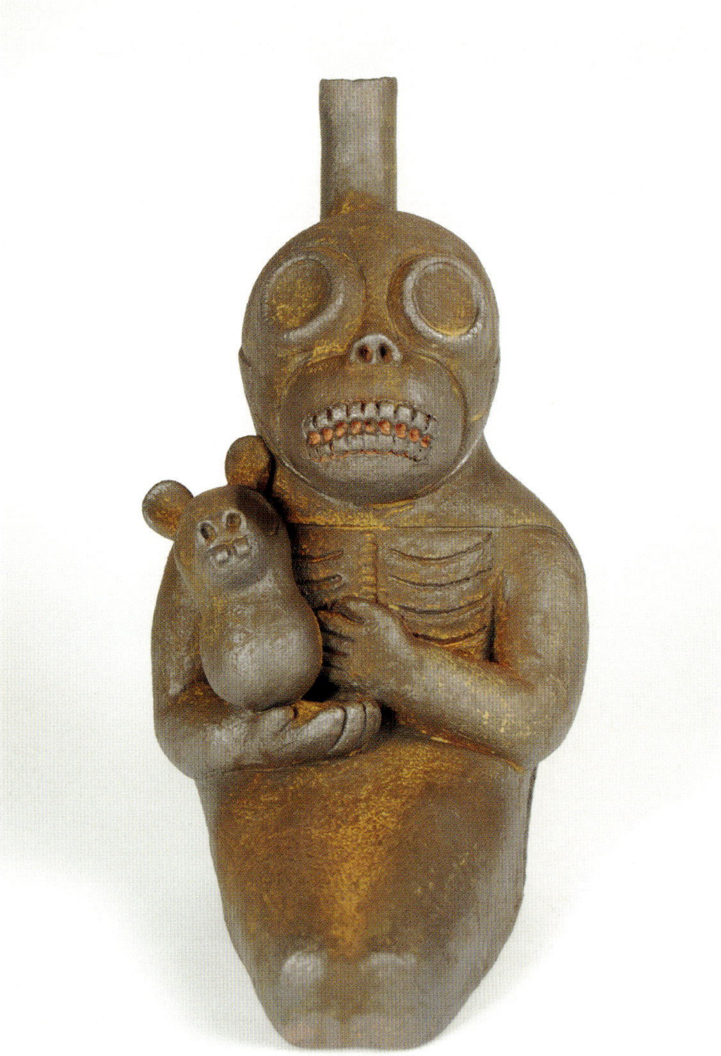

ABOVE
Nobuhito Nishigawara
Skeletal Bottle, 2009
clay, iron, bronze
and acrylic

OPPOSITE LEFT
Pharrell Williams
Inside Out, 2011
(detail) glass

OPPOSITE RIGHT
Marc Quinn
Waiting for Godot, 2006
patinated bronze

Nobuhito Nishigawara's *Skeletal Bottle* was moulded from clay then coated in iron, bronze and acrylic so as to resemble an artefact found on an archaeological dig. The pieces reference the Japanese *haniwa* funeral offerings of the Kofun Period (200–599 AD) that took many forms and were buried with the dead. His works also reference similar objects from pre-Colombian peoples. Nishigawara is interested in how these objects function beyond their original context; many now have new lives in museum collections.

'Contemporary popular culture not only reflects the attitudes and concerns of the present but also provides a link to the past.'

—NOBUHITO NISHIGAWARA

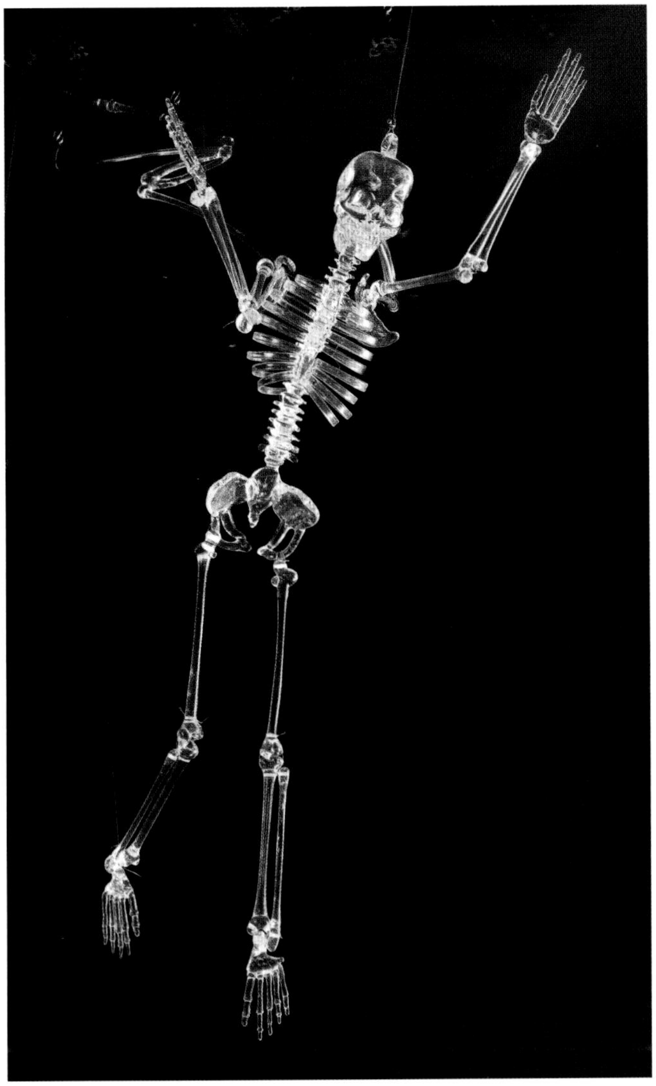

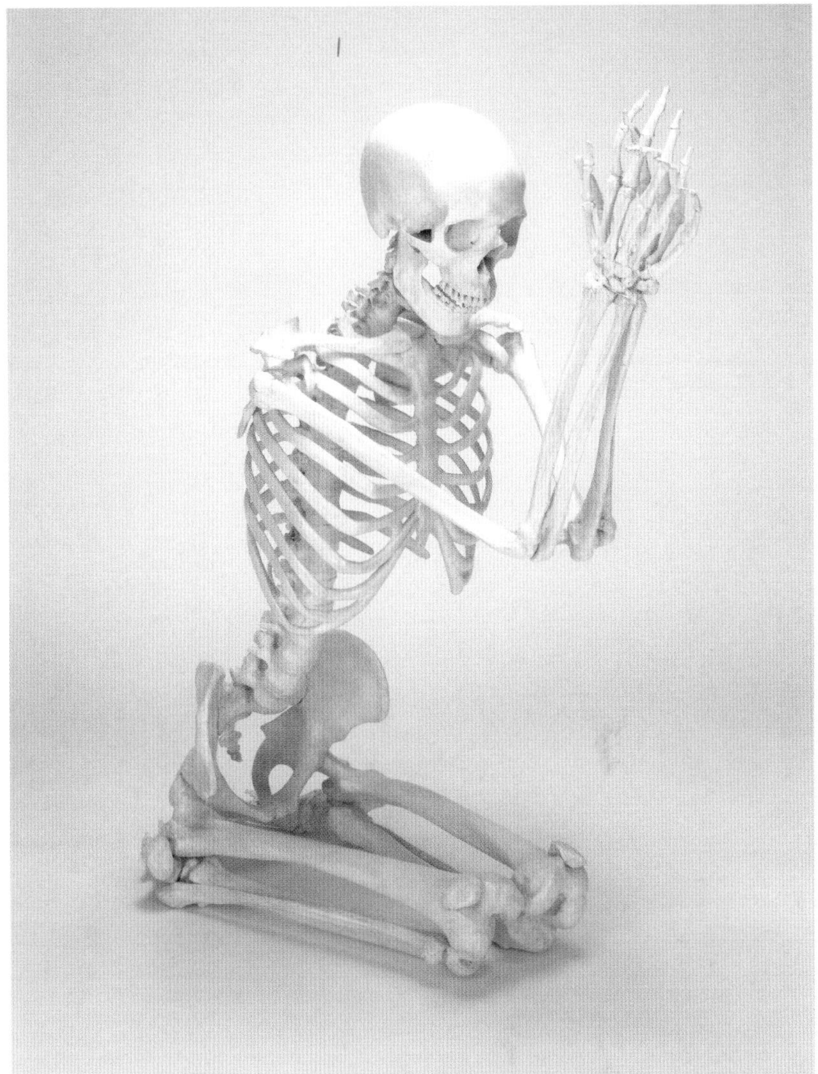

Pharrell Williams is a well-known singer, songwriter and fashion designer who participated in Glasstress 2011, which involved artists from different fields working with Venetian glassblowers to realize an artwork. Williams's installation *Inside Out* featured a large human-sized glass skeleton with feathered wings hovering over broken rocks on green Astroturf. Behind it, a smaller, wingless glass skeleton floated in the air. Williams has explained that 'It was important for [the work] to represent what the inside body of an angel (Greek for the word "messenger") looked like.'

Marc Quinn's sculpture *Waiting for Godot* consists of a bronze skeleton at prayer. Its title refers to the Samuel Beckett play in which two characters await the arrival of Godot to no avail. The play's existential questioning of the human need to believe in a greater power is paralleled in Quinn's sculpture. The work has been exhibited at the Casa di Giulietta, the mythical home of Shakespeare's Juliet in Verona, and Gloucester Cathedral, where it knelt before an altar. In both locations the setting reinforced the posing skeleton's faith in something beyond the tangible.

BELOW
Jan Fabre
***Untitled*, 2009**
glass and Bic ink

OPPOSITE
Yang Jiechang
***Underground Flowers*,**
1989–2009 (installation view and detail)
wooden cases with human bones from porcelain, hand-painted; silkscreen prints on silk

Jan Fabre's glass skull and literally crossed bones featured in Glasstress 2011, part of the 2011 Venice Biennale at the Palazzo Cavalli Franchetti. Fabre worked with the master artisans of the Berengo Studio in Murano to produce the work and then had his own team of assistants hand-colour the glass bones in his signature Bic pen ink.

Yang Jiechang was one of the first contemporary Chinese artists to gain international recognition. He works in many media: performance, calligraphy, ink painting, installation and sculpture. The installation *Underground Flowers* consists of hand-painted porcelain skulls and bones arranged and stacked in wooden trays as if in an archaeological museum. The work recalls China's troubled history, including the 1989 massacre in Tiananmen Square and the many millions lost in Mao's Great Leap Forward (1958–62) and Cultural Revolution (1966–76).

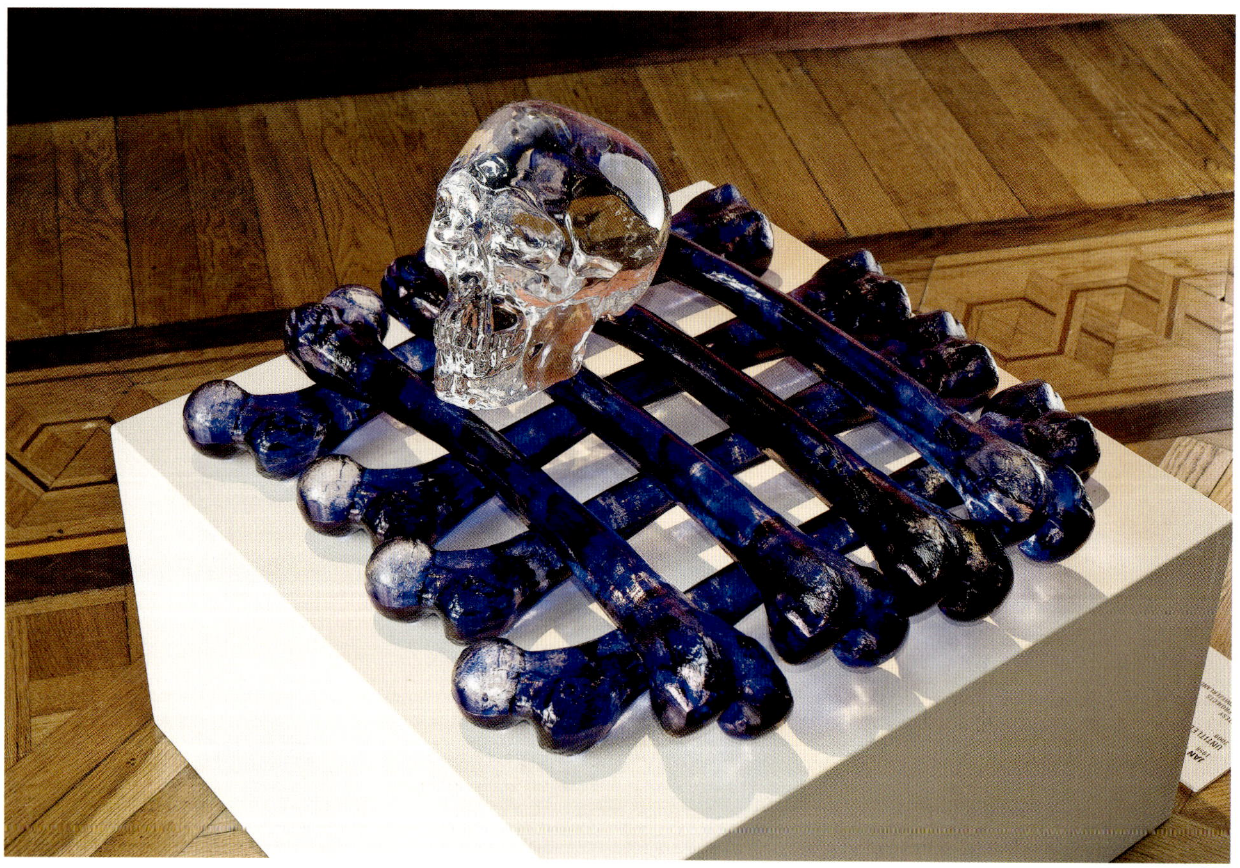

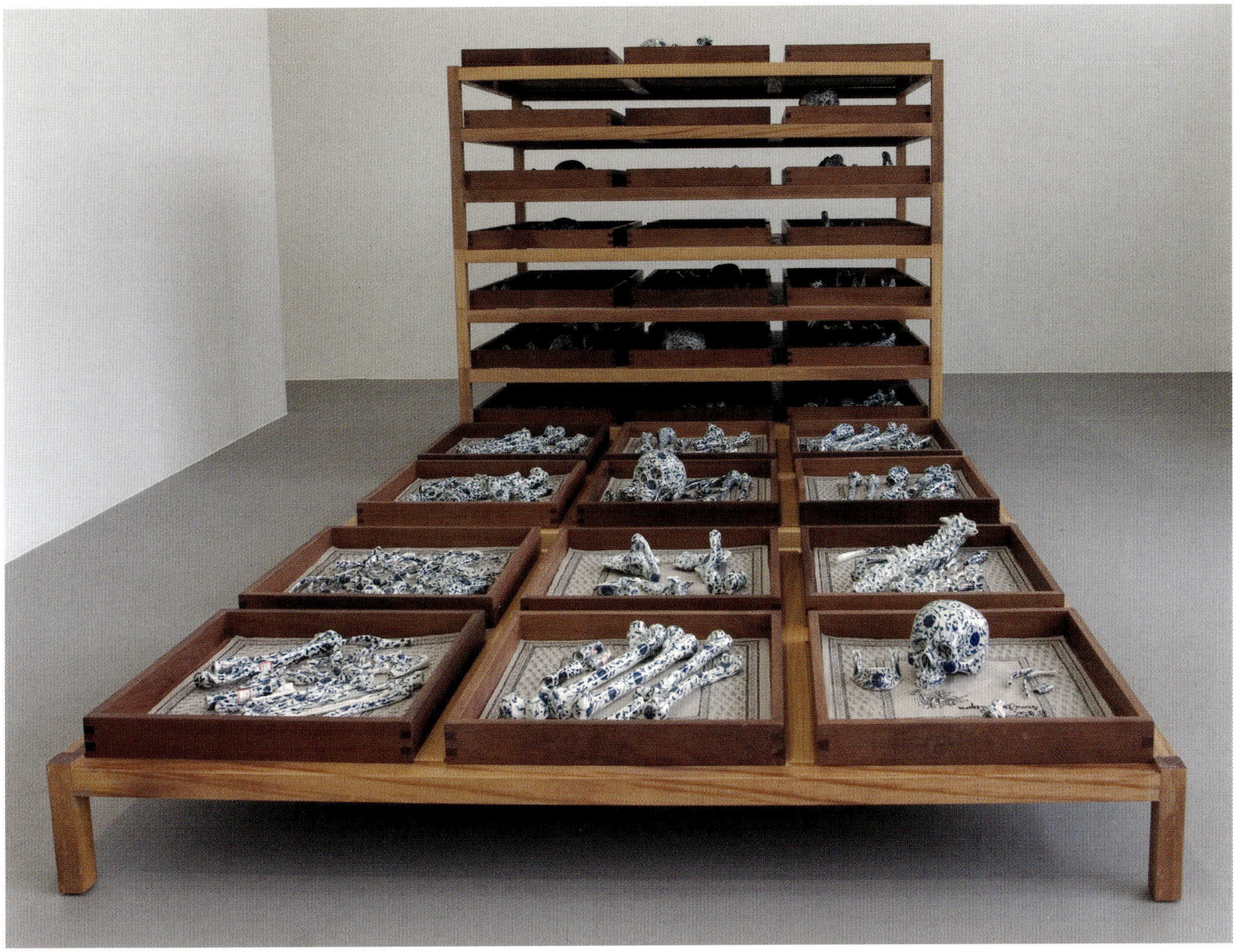

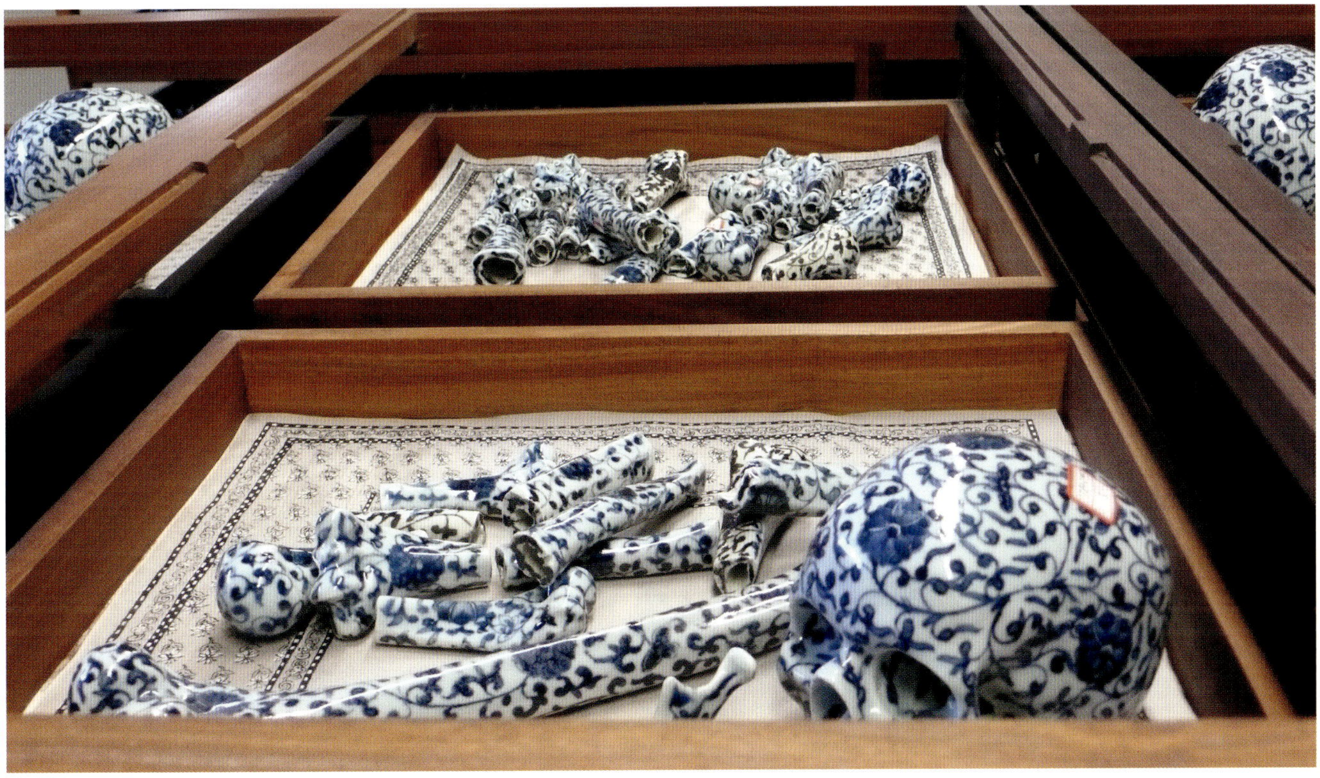

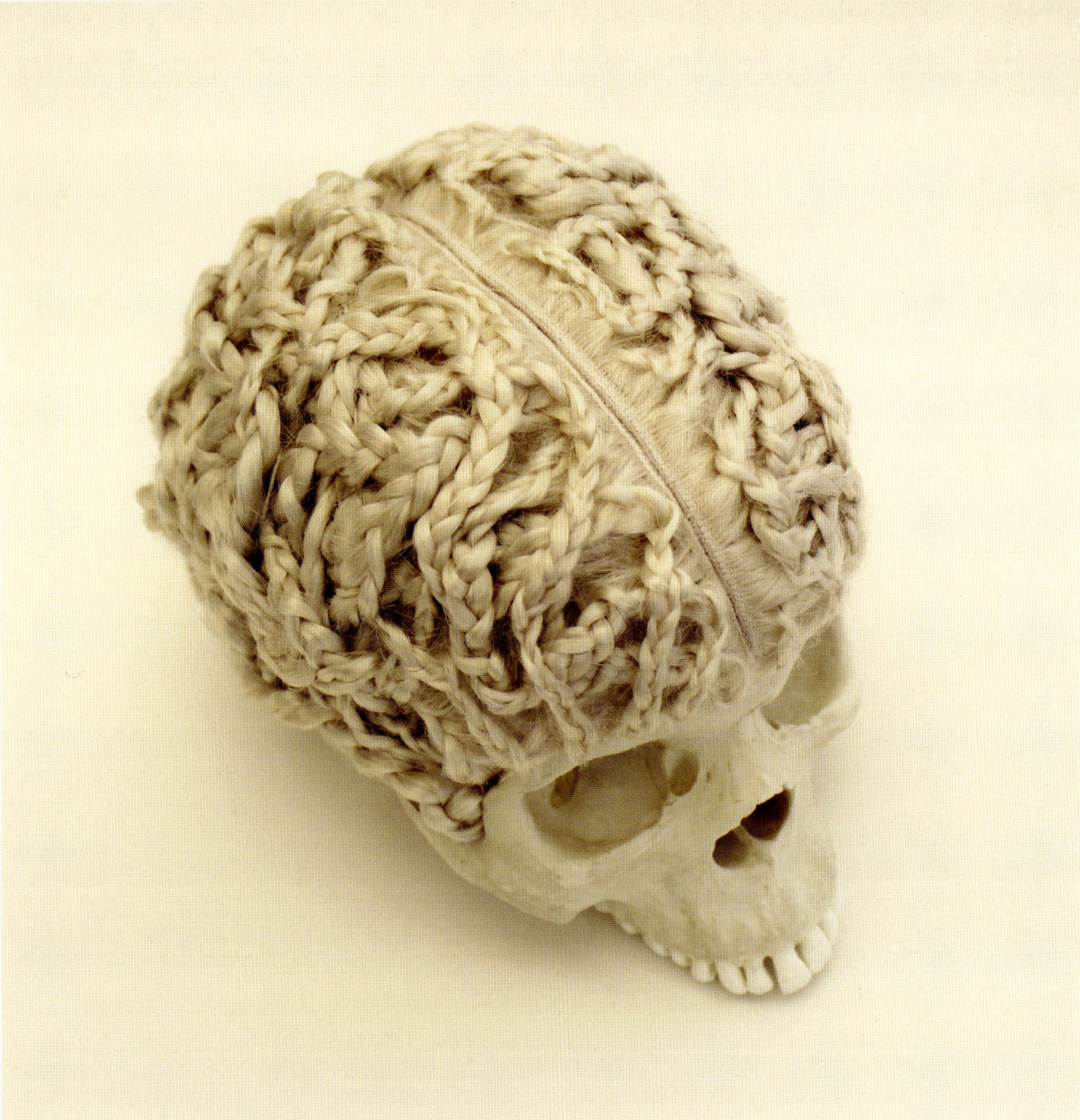

Hugh Hayden used new biomedical imaging technologies to create his work shown in the 2012 'Seeing Ourselves' exhibition in New York. His *Untitled* skull disrupts and challenges stereotypes and preconceived ideas about identity and its rooting in the physical body by intermingling art, science and medical developments. This *blurring* of visual languages and disciplines encouraged viewers to reflect on how politics, culture, ethnicity and sexuality all play out on the contested site of the human body. Curator Koan Jeff Baysa has said: 'Historically, the partial or fragmented image suggested grief and nostalgia for the loss of a vanished totality and a utopian wholeness. In diagnostic imaging, the body is examined in detail, piecemeal and irreconciled, described in terms of "cuts" and "slices".'

Museum Clausum (Klaus Wehner) selected the mass of swirling bodies that form *Head* from pornographic images found online. Their individual positioning suggests the act alluded to by the work's title as much as their overall positioning suggests the outline of that body part. This skull-shaped work is from the artist's *Hierophilia* (a sexual fetish for religious objects) series, which included works in the shape of Christian shrines, reliquaries or monstrances.

ABOVE
Hugh Hayden
Untitled, 2012
reproduction of African American male skull, human hair and adhesive

OPPOSITE
Museum Clausum
Head, 2012
C-print

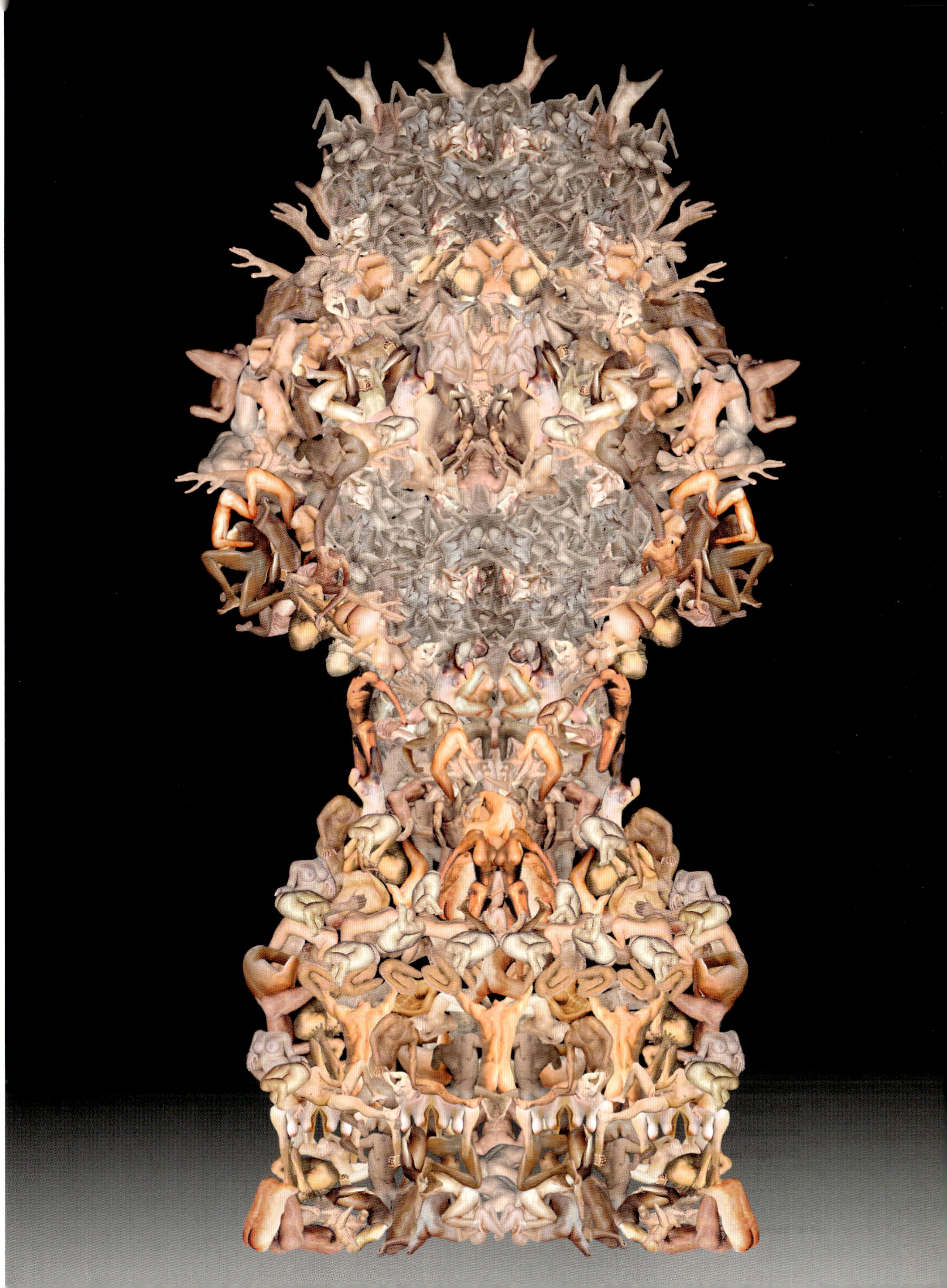

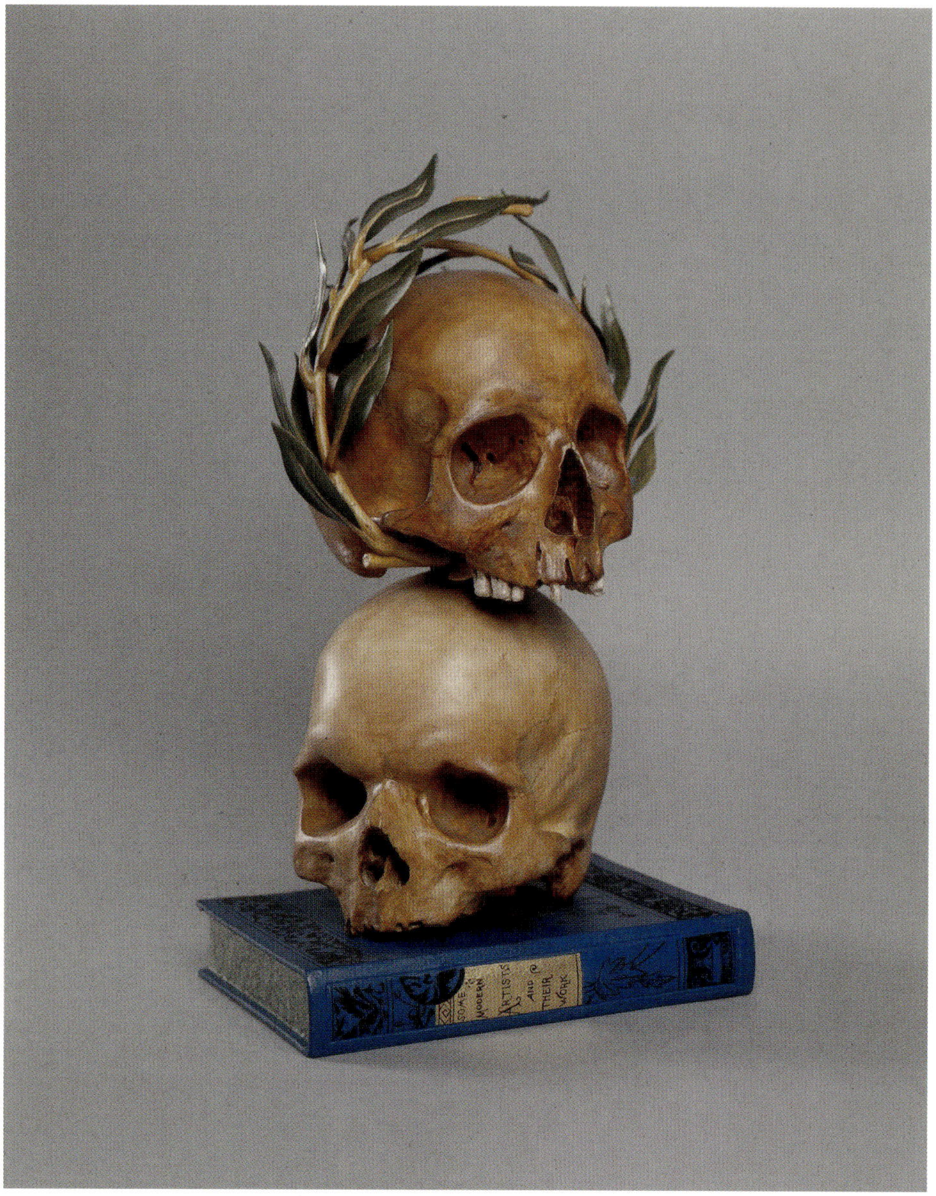

McDermott & McGough and **Roberto Ekholm** both present skulls on top of books in their respective works *Their Distant Voices, 1883* and *Untitled (The Healer)*. But there the similarities end. Ekholm's single skull sits on the *Encyclopedia of Aberrations*, though to what aberrations does the title refer – human, natural, moral? In one eye socket of the black plaster and resin skull, iron filings blossom out like a starburst. Decay and mortality are at the core of this work while McDermott & McGough allude to an afterlife, if only an artistic one. Their two skulls sit on Wilfrid Meynell's *Some Modern Artists and Their Work* and one skull wears a crown of laurel leaves (the symbol of the victor in ancient Greece). The message is clear: the artist may triumph over death through his or her art.

ABOVE
McDermott & McGough
Their Distant Voices, 1883, 2001
painted wooden sculpture

OPPOSITE
Roberto Ekholm
Untitled (The Healer), 2012
plaster, resin, neodymium magnets, iron filings, printed ink on paper

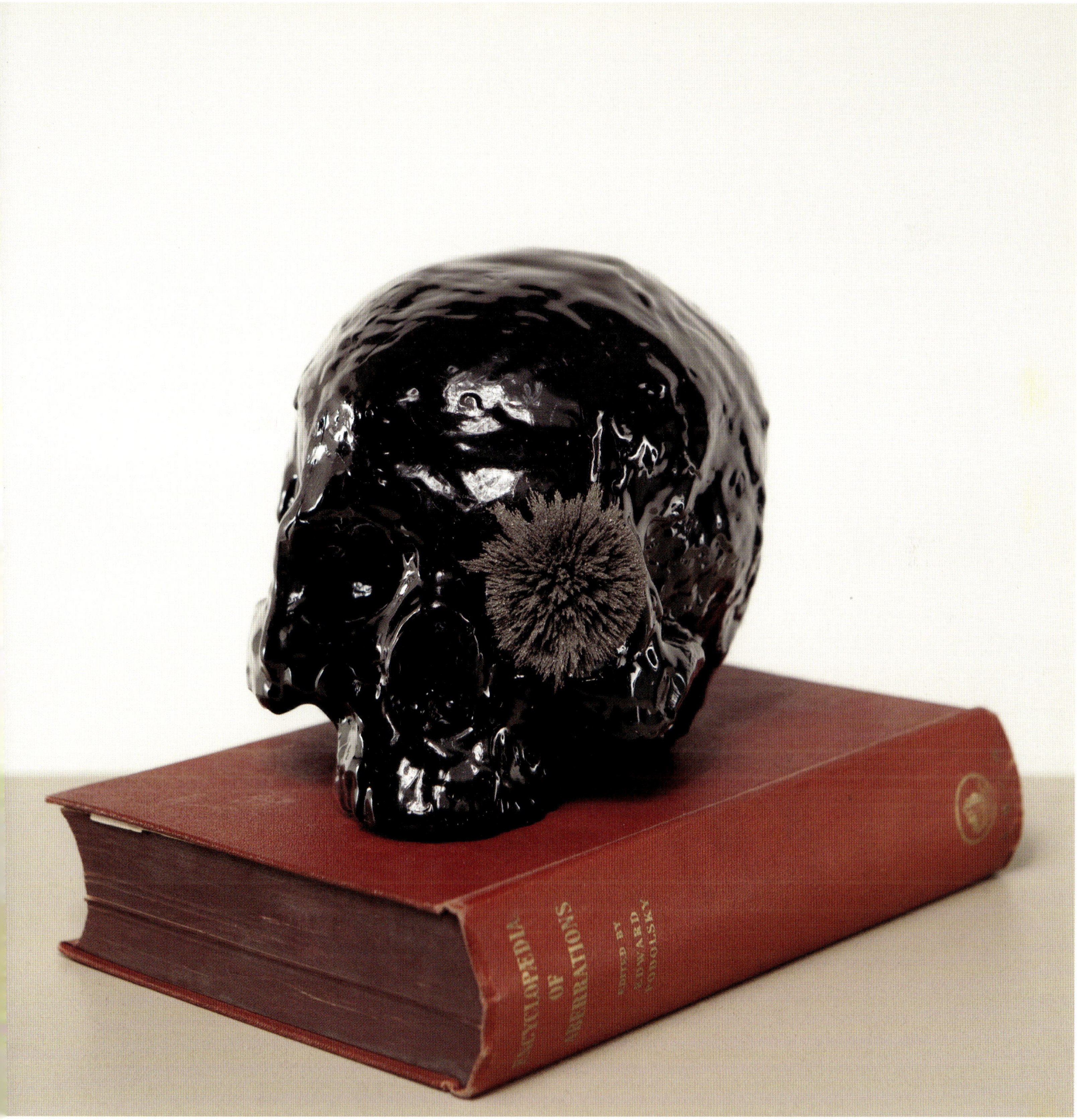
ENCYCLOPÆDIA
OF
ABERRATIONS
EDITED BY
EDWARD
PODOLSKY

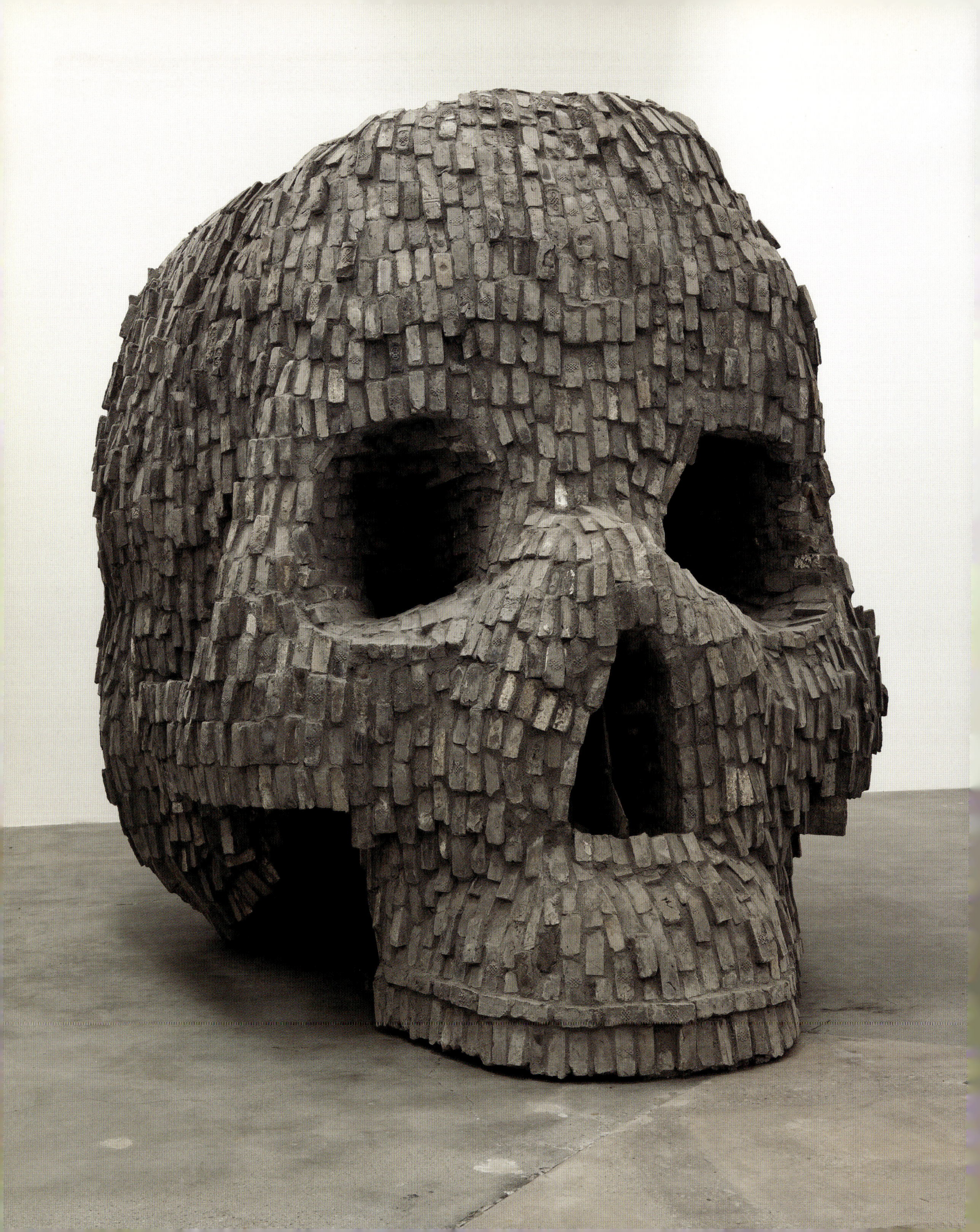

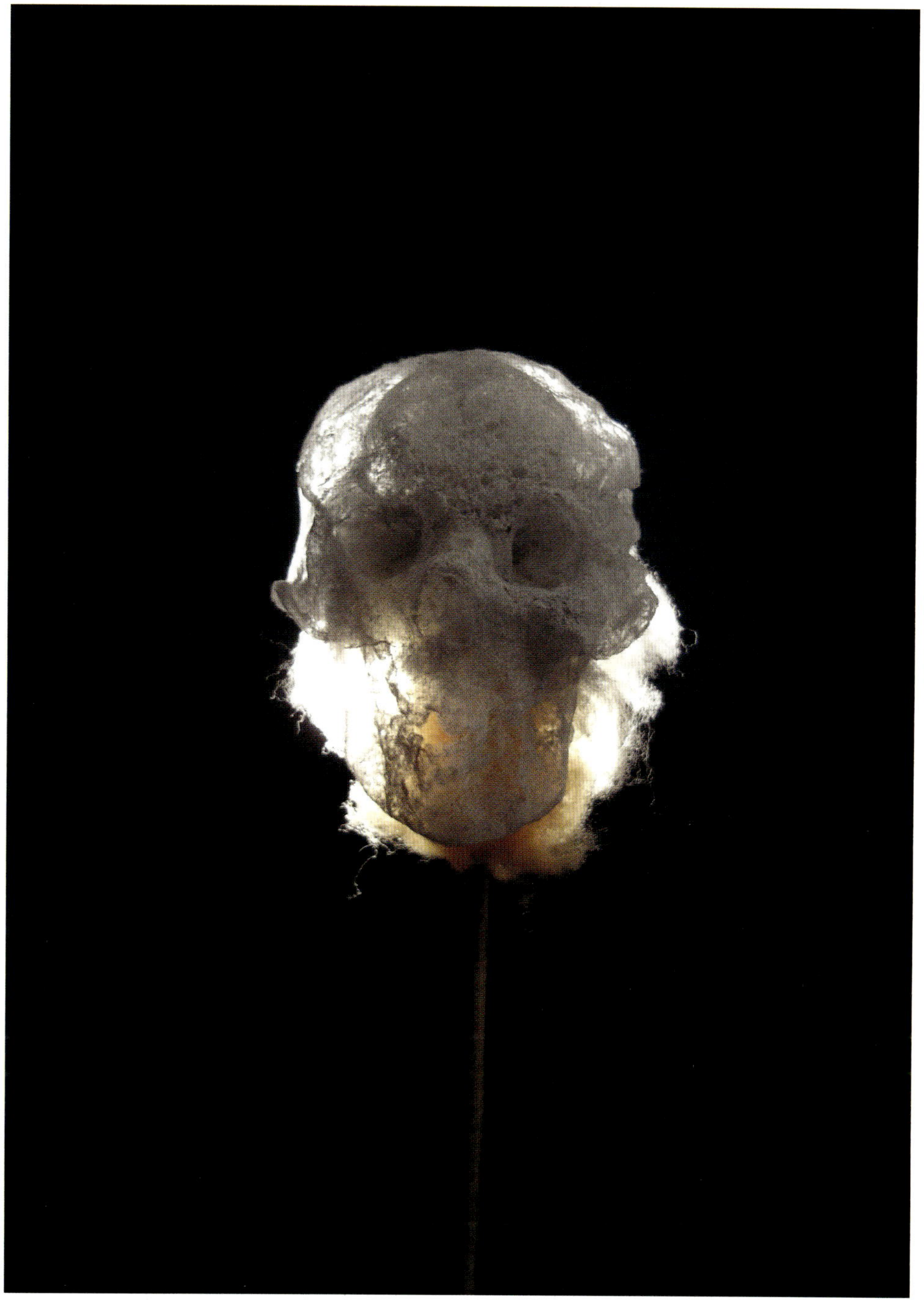

OPPOSITE
Zhang Huan
49 Days No.6, 2011
grey brick and steel

ABOVE
Paul Hazelton
Death Duster, 2011/12
synthetic wool duster
and household dust

Zhang Huan is one of China's most important performance artists (wearing suits of meat long before Lady Gaga) and is known for his ash paintings and sculptures. His 2011 exhibition '49 Days' featured two- and three-dimensional skulls made from bricks reclaimed from Shanghai building sites, where historical buildings were being swept away for modern glass structures. The bricks recall the workers who made them, the lost buildings and the impermanence of the work of humans. In the Buddhist belief system, after death a human soul remains on the earth for forty-nine days before being reincarnated.

In the Anglican Book of Common Prayer, the funeral service ends: *Ashes to ashes, dust to dust*. **Paul Hazelton** makes his fragile sculptures from the very dust of life, gathering it from the surfaces of his home. House dust is said to be up to seventy-five per cent sloughed off human skin and is a most apt material for *Death Duster*.

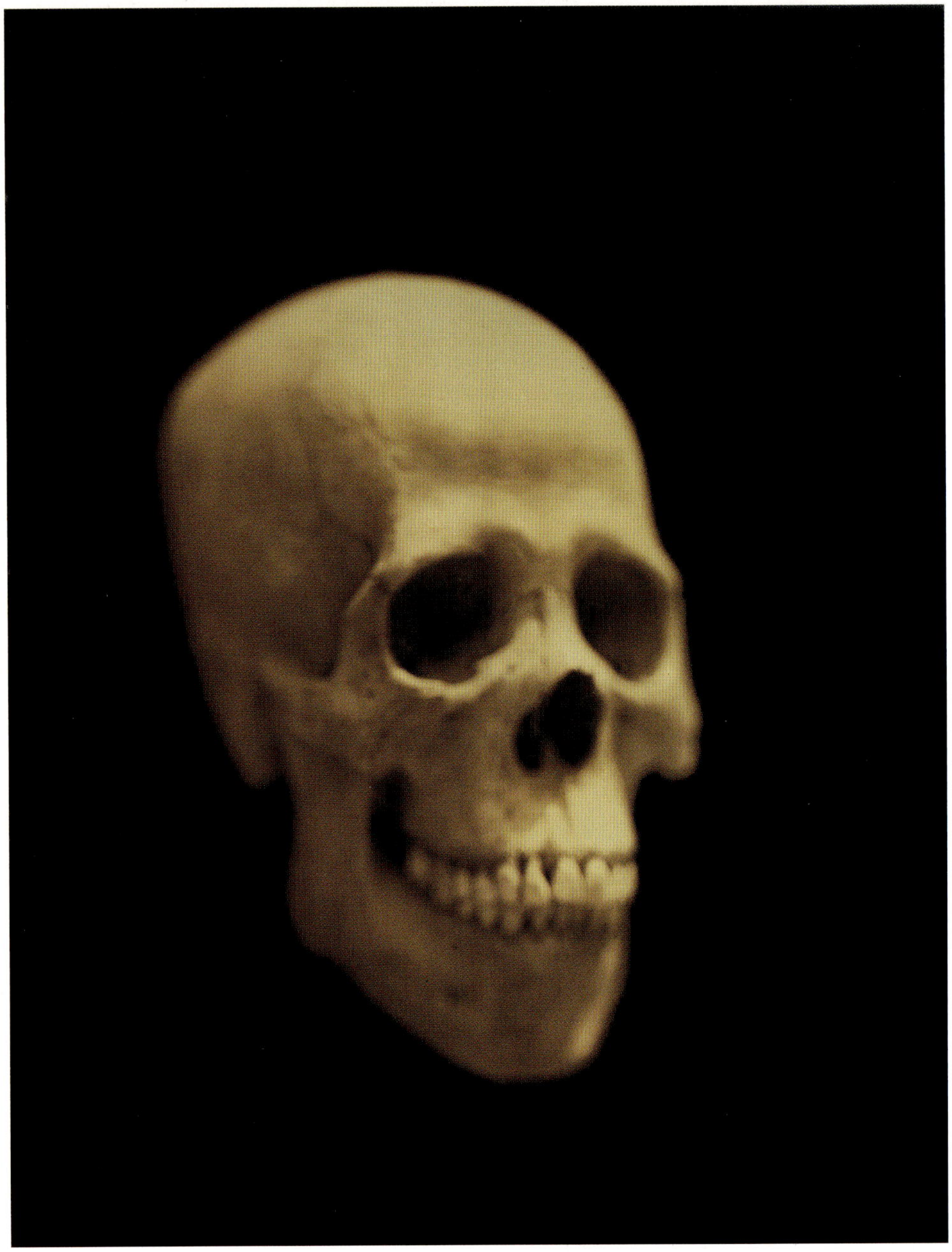

Adam Fuss's mirrored daguerreotypes of human skulls position the viewer directly in the gaze of death, as the depicted skull and reflection of the viewer merge into one. Fuss's interest in 'the dual role of photos as image and mirror' recalls Roland Barthes's observation in his book *Camera Lucida* that death is the essence of photography.

The artist who goes by the moniker **Jim Skull** makes skulls from papier mâché before gluing string onto them in intricate patterns. Left to dangle from the skull, the string contributes to the overall effect that these are the artefacts of some ancient tribal rite. His other skulls include portraits of individuals and some covered in strands of beads.

ABOVE
Adam Fuss
Untitled, 2002
daguerreotype

OPPOSITE
Jim Skull
Mister Smith, 2009
papier maché and
polyester rope

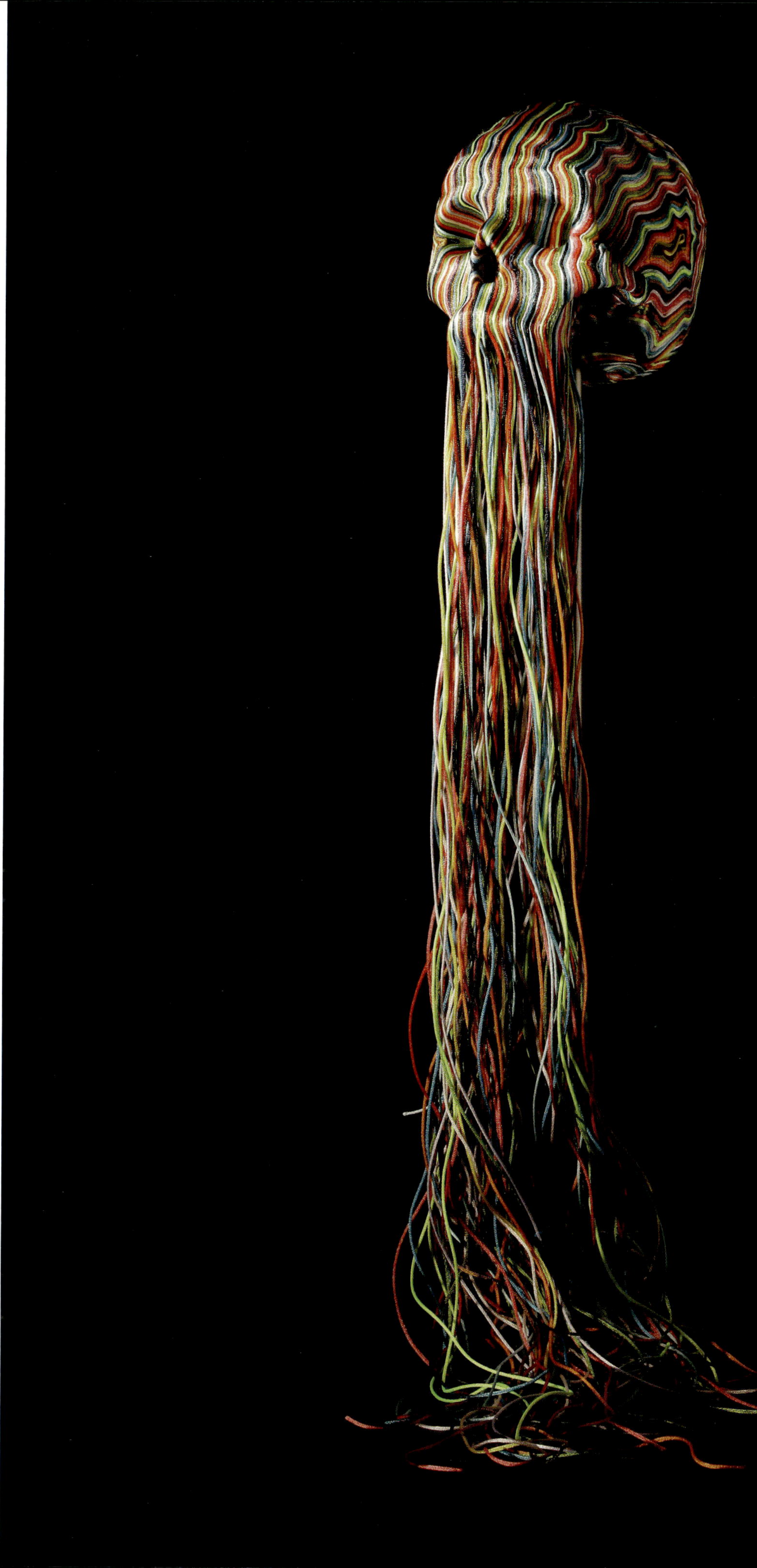

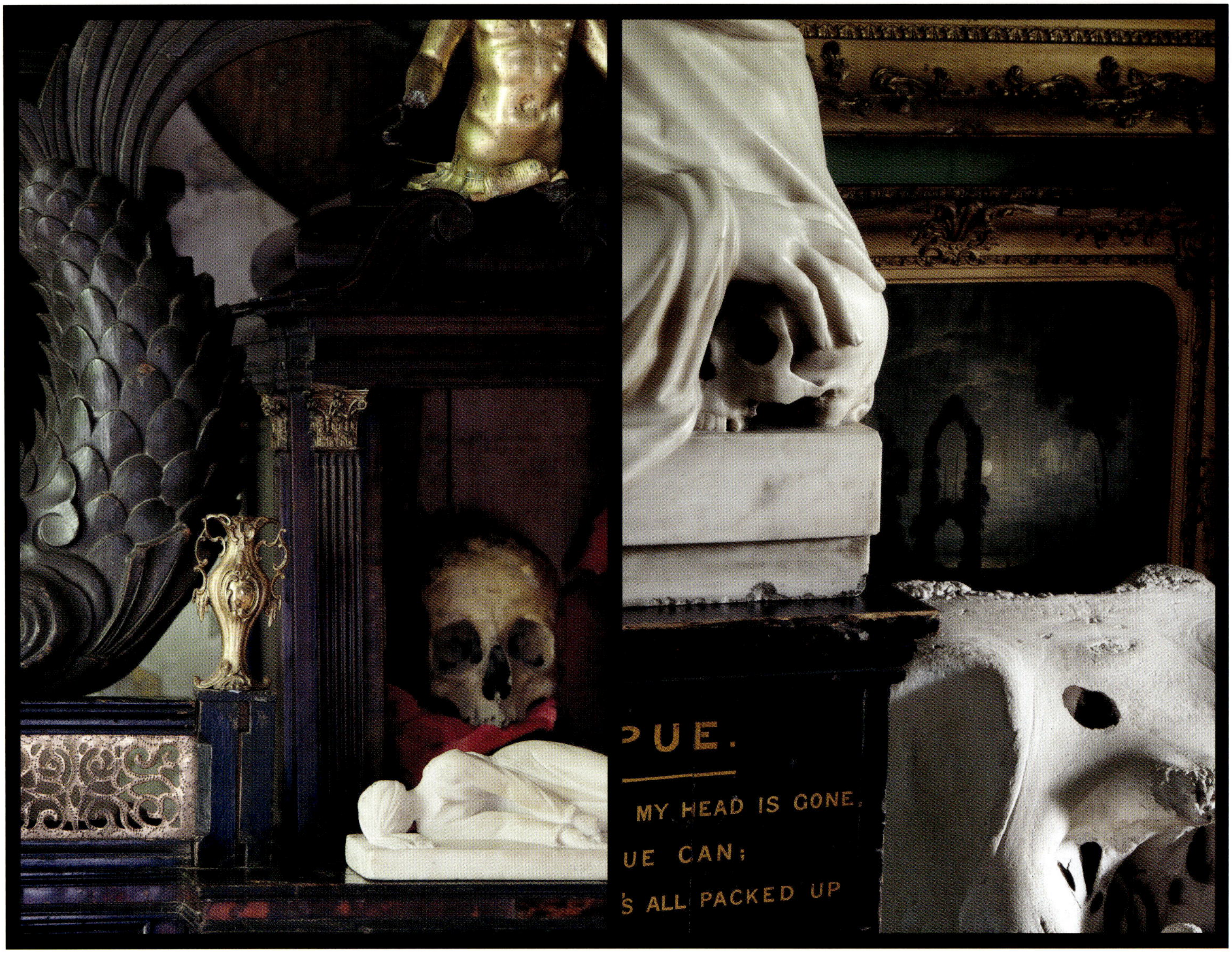

ABOVE
Museum Clausum
Museum Clausum, Wundercamera: Malplaquet House, Diptych # 23, London, 10 August 2010
C-prints

OPPOSITE TOP
Sherrie Levine
***Crystal Skulls: 1–12*, 2010**
cast glass, 12 parts and 12 vitrines

OPPOSITE BOTTOM
Angela Freiberger
***B* (*Brain*), 2009**
Carrara marble

Museum Clausum is the pseudonym employed by Klaus Wehner whose interest in the function of museums in society led to the photographic series *Wundercamera*, which subjectively documents museum collections, including those of the British Museum in London, the Museum Schnütgen in Cologne and the Bargello Museum in Florence. *Malplaquet House, Diptych # 23, London, 10 August 2010* features the skulls and sculptures of a private collection housed in East London.

Sherrie Levine installed *Crystal Skulls: 1–12* in Böhm Chapel, now an art gallery, on the outskirts of Cologne. Built after extensive Allied bombing of the city during World War II, the chapel offered a circular space for the artist to position her twelve wooden vitrines, inside of which she placed glass casts of a human skull. Her installation referenced the structure's architecture and its original use as a place of worship, reminding viewers that even buildings have lives and, indeed, afterlives.

Angela Freiberger experiments with her body in her performance art and with marble in her sculptures, which often become extensions of her own body. She has cast her back, feet and hands for use in some works and for others has had to imagine how her unreachable body parts might look, as with *B* (*Brain*).

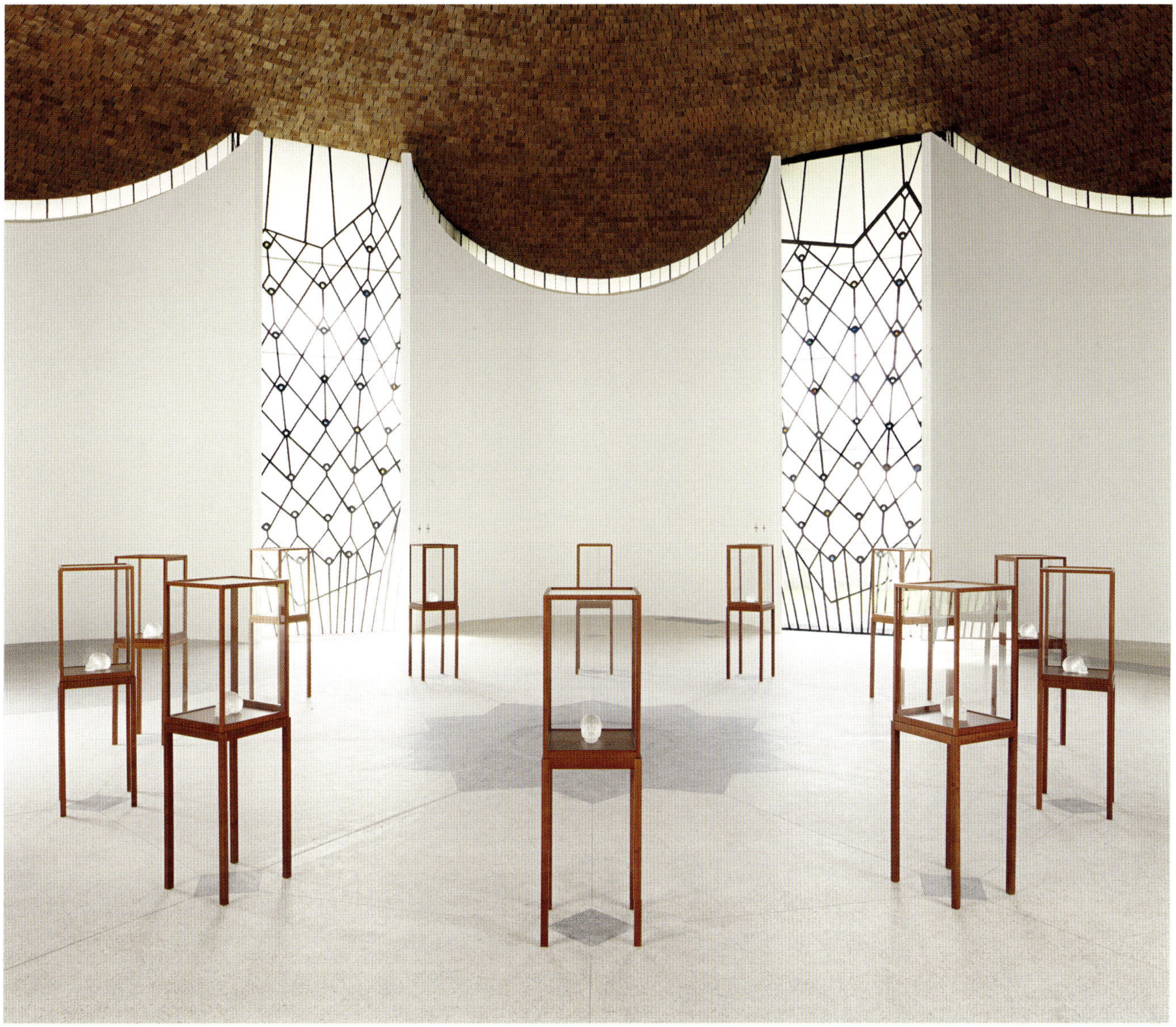

'The sculptures represent and contrast the finitude of the human body.'

—ANGELA FREIBERGER

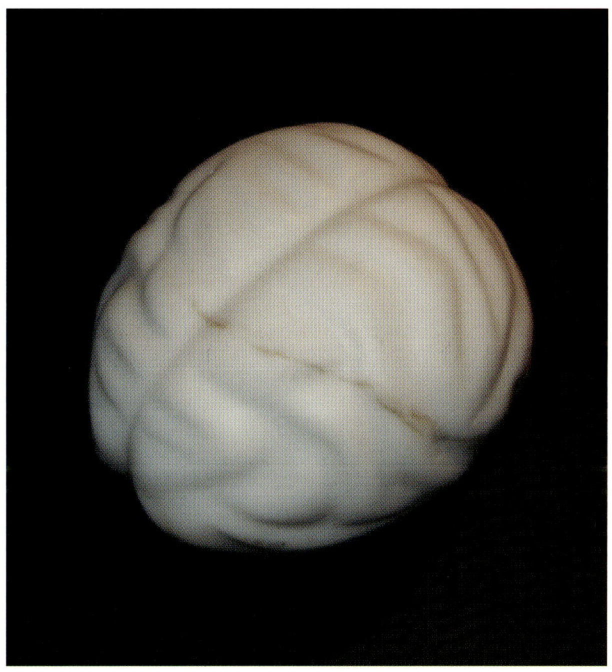

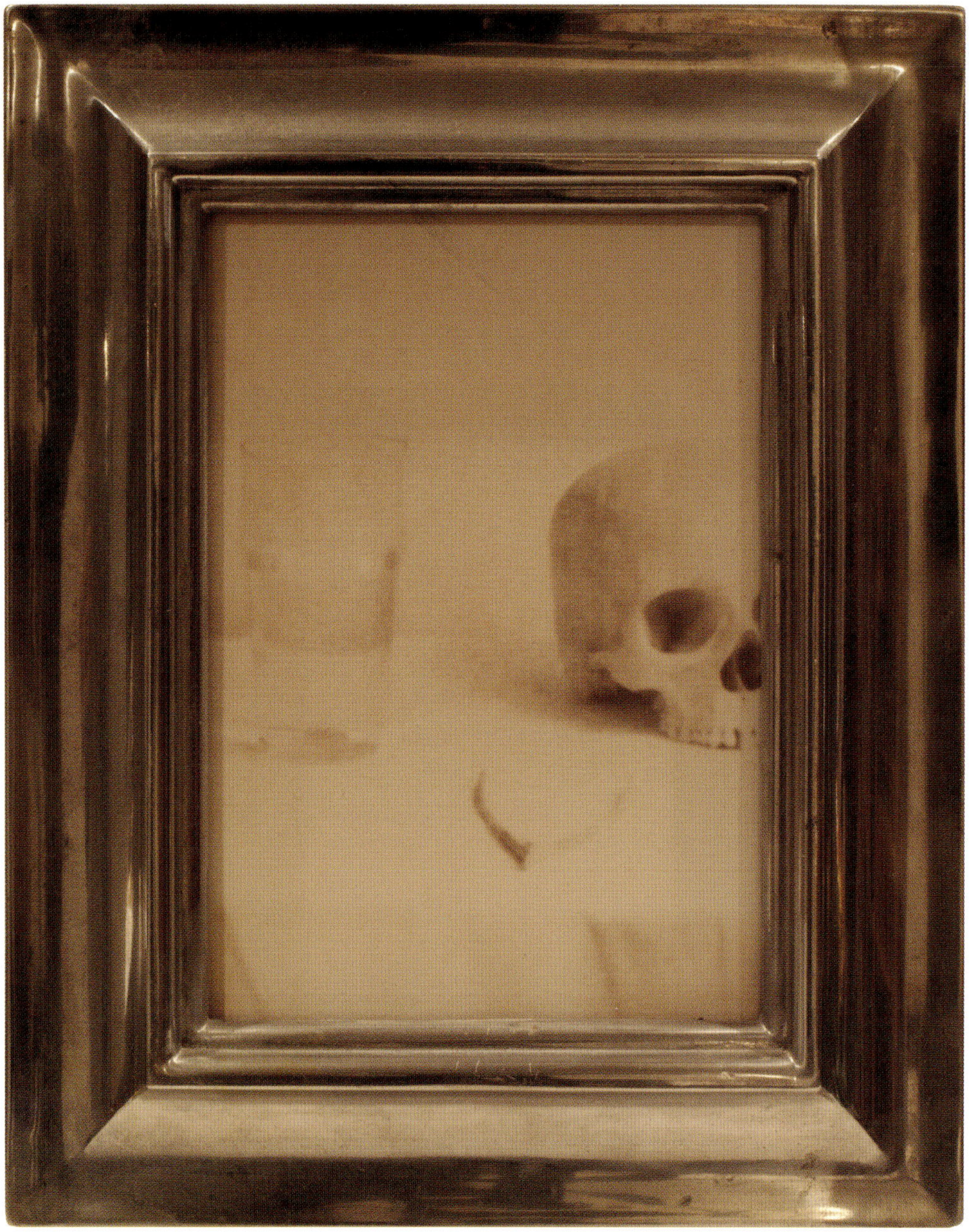

A glass half empty (or full), a jawless human skull and an unbroken wishbone rest on crisp white cloth in **Jefferson Hayman**'s *The Wishbone Table*. As with most of Hayman's work, the large, antique gilt frame is almost as important as the illustrated objects in projecting the illusion that the photograph is from well before 2010, its actual date of creation.

Caroline McCarthy used the same technique behind her *Floral Still Life* (see page 70) to compose her installation *Vanitas.* The resulting pixellated picture of a skull sitting next to an extinguished candle alludes to death and the passage of time. The fact that the picture has been made from a plastic bag intended for waste hints also at the possibility of a wasted life, thereby functioning along the lines of the classical *vanitas* trope yet in a very modern guise.

ABOVE
Jefferson Hayman
The Wishbone Table, 2010
salt print, antique frame

OPPOSITE
Caroline McCarthy
Vanitas, 2007 (installation view and details)
bin bag, canvas and MDF support, metal bracket

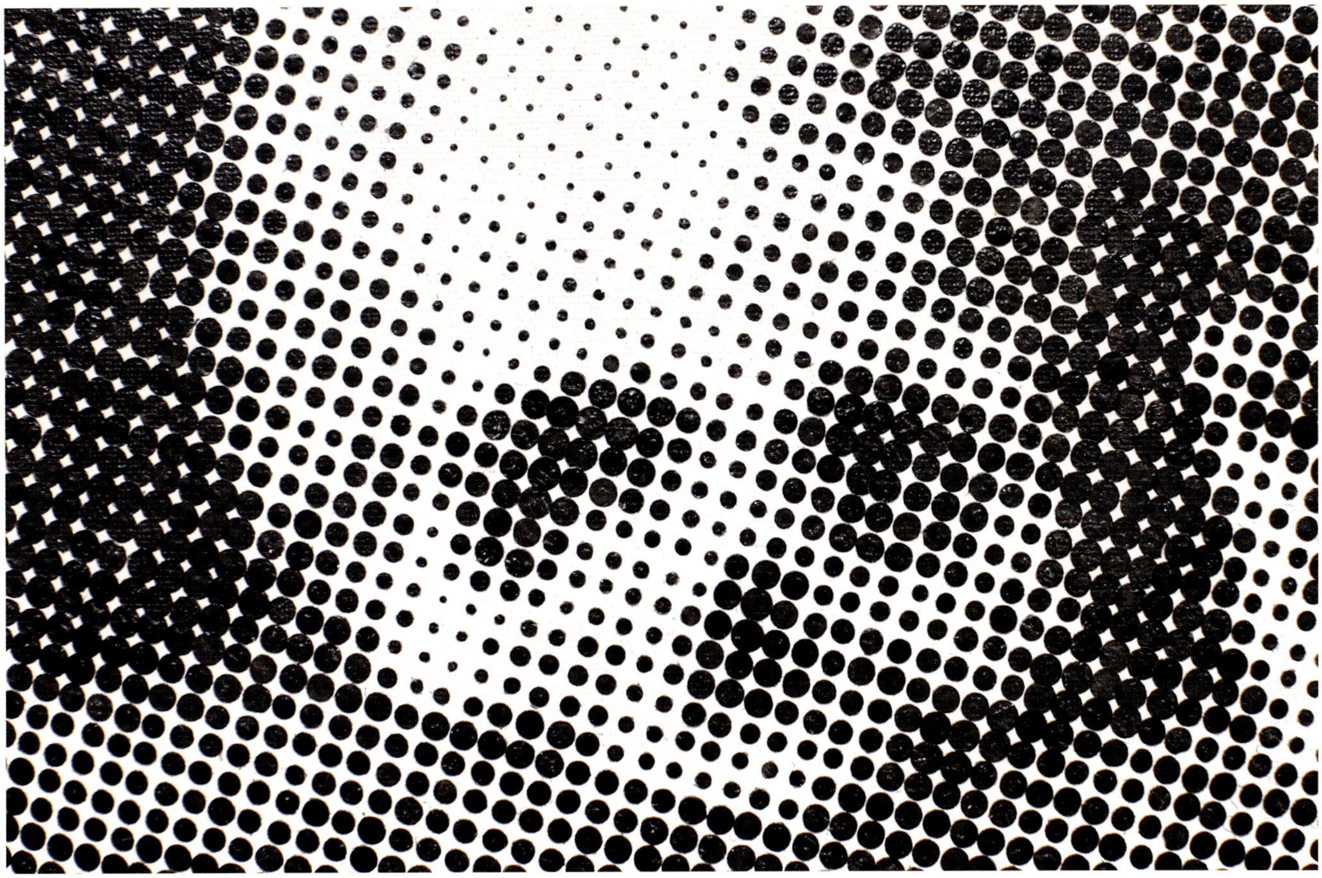

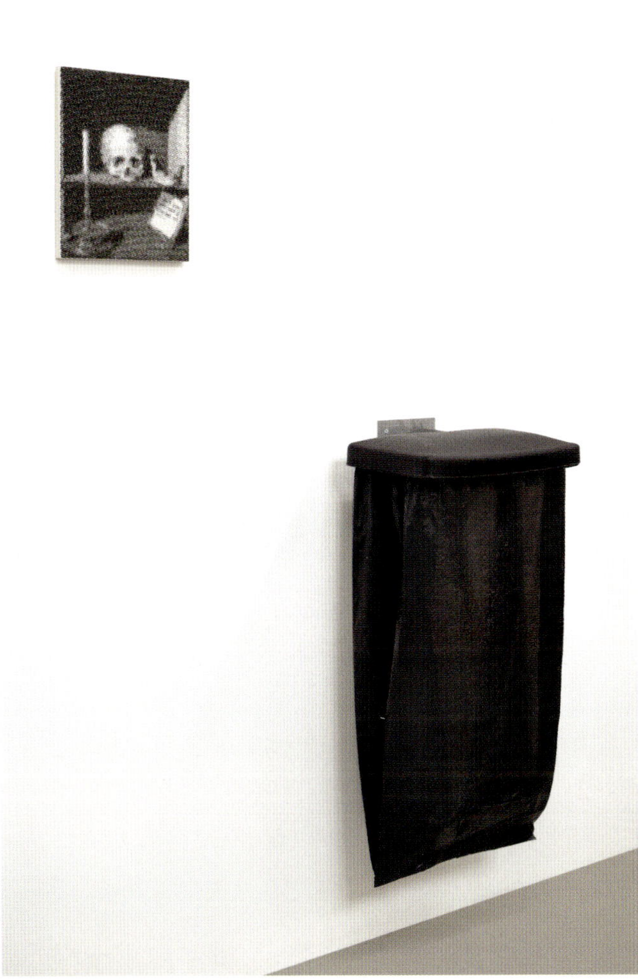

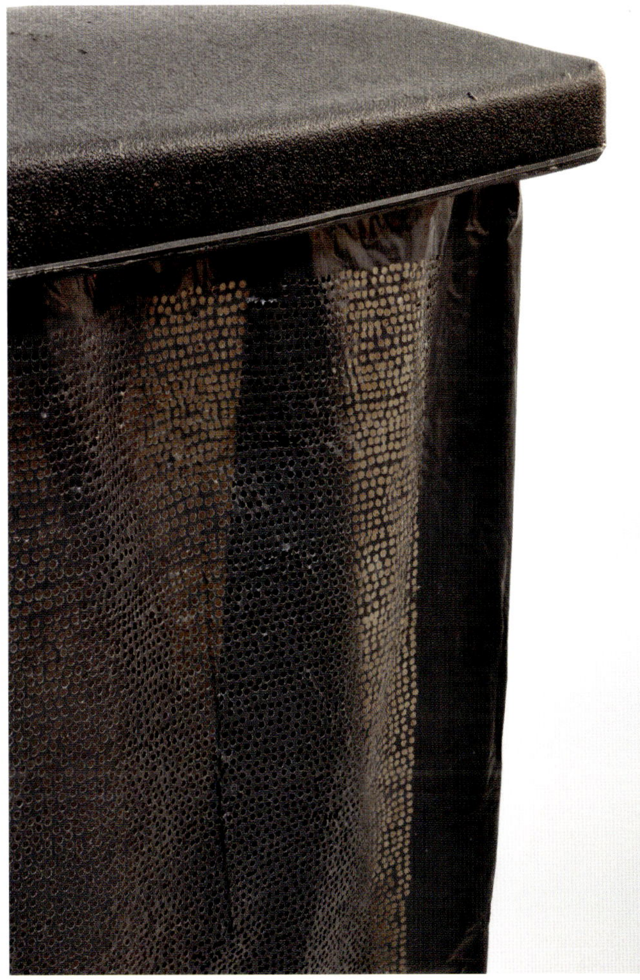

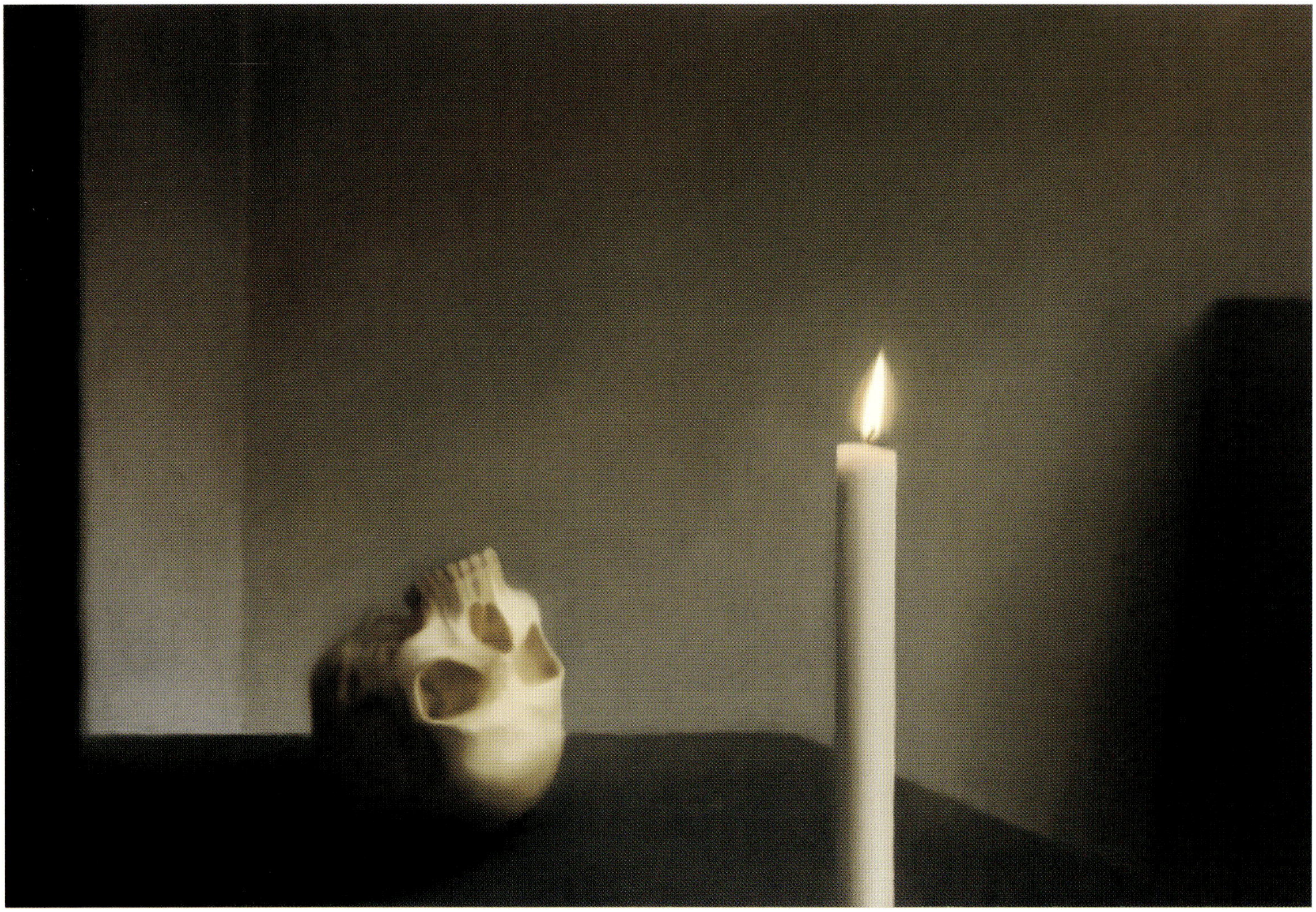

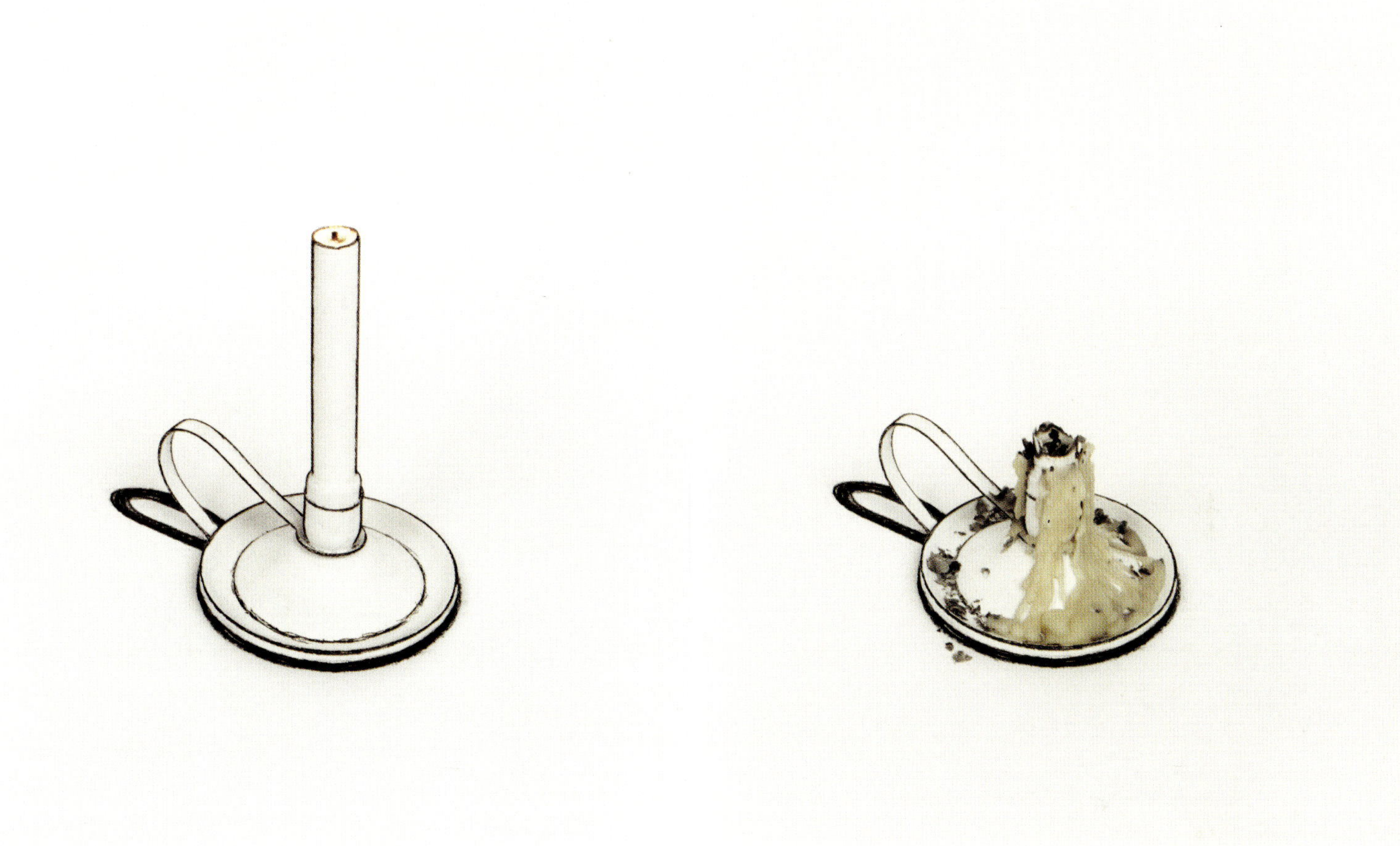

OPPOSITE
Gerhard Richter
Skull with Candle, 1983
oil on canvas

ABOVE
Cynthia Greig
Nature Morte no. 11
(***Burned at Both Ends***), 2010
chromogenic prints

The slowly burning candle and the remnants of a burnt candle have long been used to depict the imminence and ever-present threat of death. In Christian traditions the candle is used during Mass to remind the flock that their lives are burning out, that they too will soon die and they had best behave in the hope of redemption and an afterlife. The light candles give off is also said to be a reminder of Christ and his goodness. The modern candlelight vigil is seen as a rite of hope thoughout global communities, while Buddhists consider the burning candle a marker of enlightenment. **Gerhard Richter**'s *Skull with Candle* clearly fixes the relationship between the candle and death with the inclusion of an upturned skull. **Cynthia Greig**'s *Nature Morte no. 11 (Burned at Both Ends)* offers a more modern take on the historical warning about the fleetingness of time.

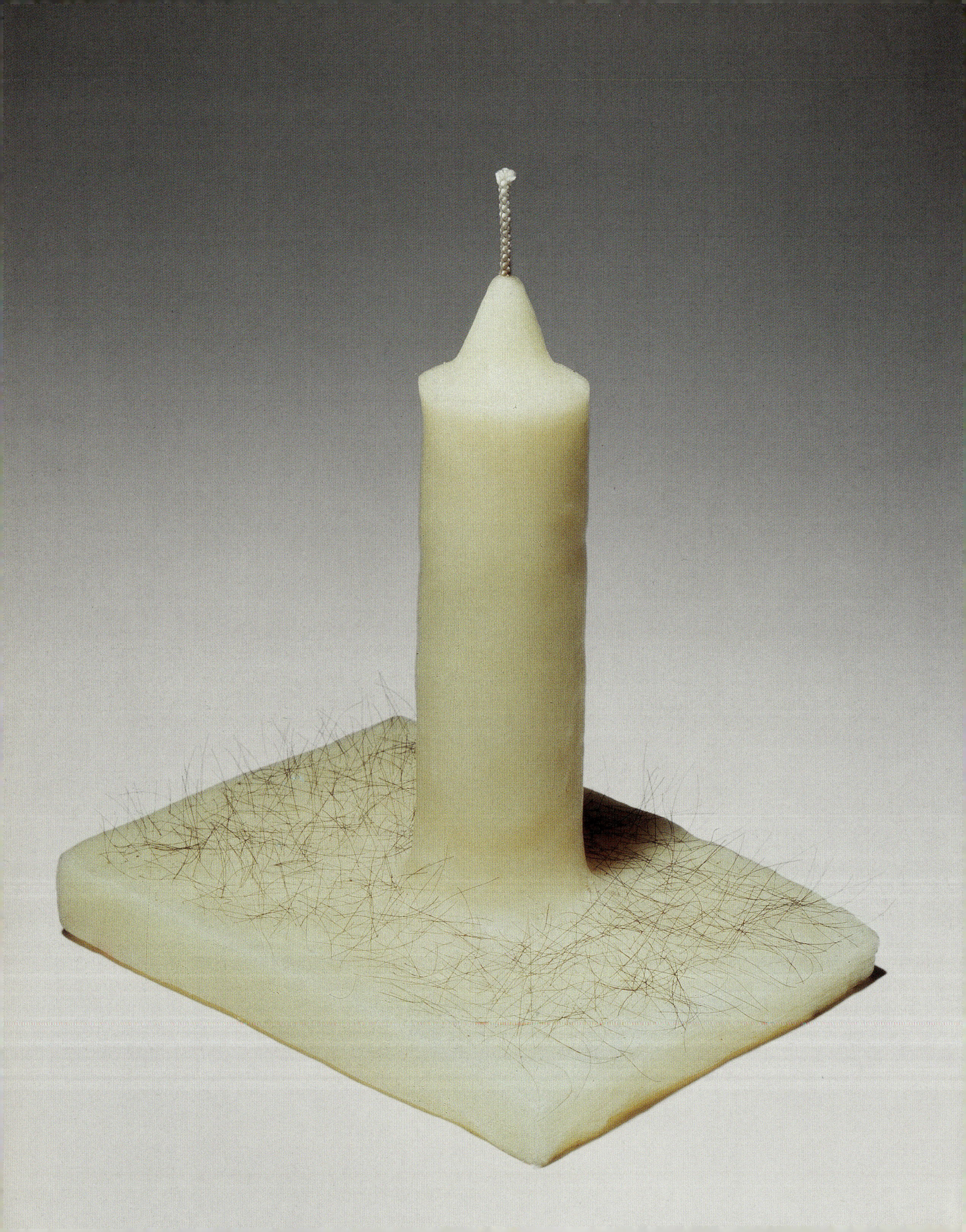

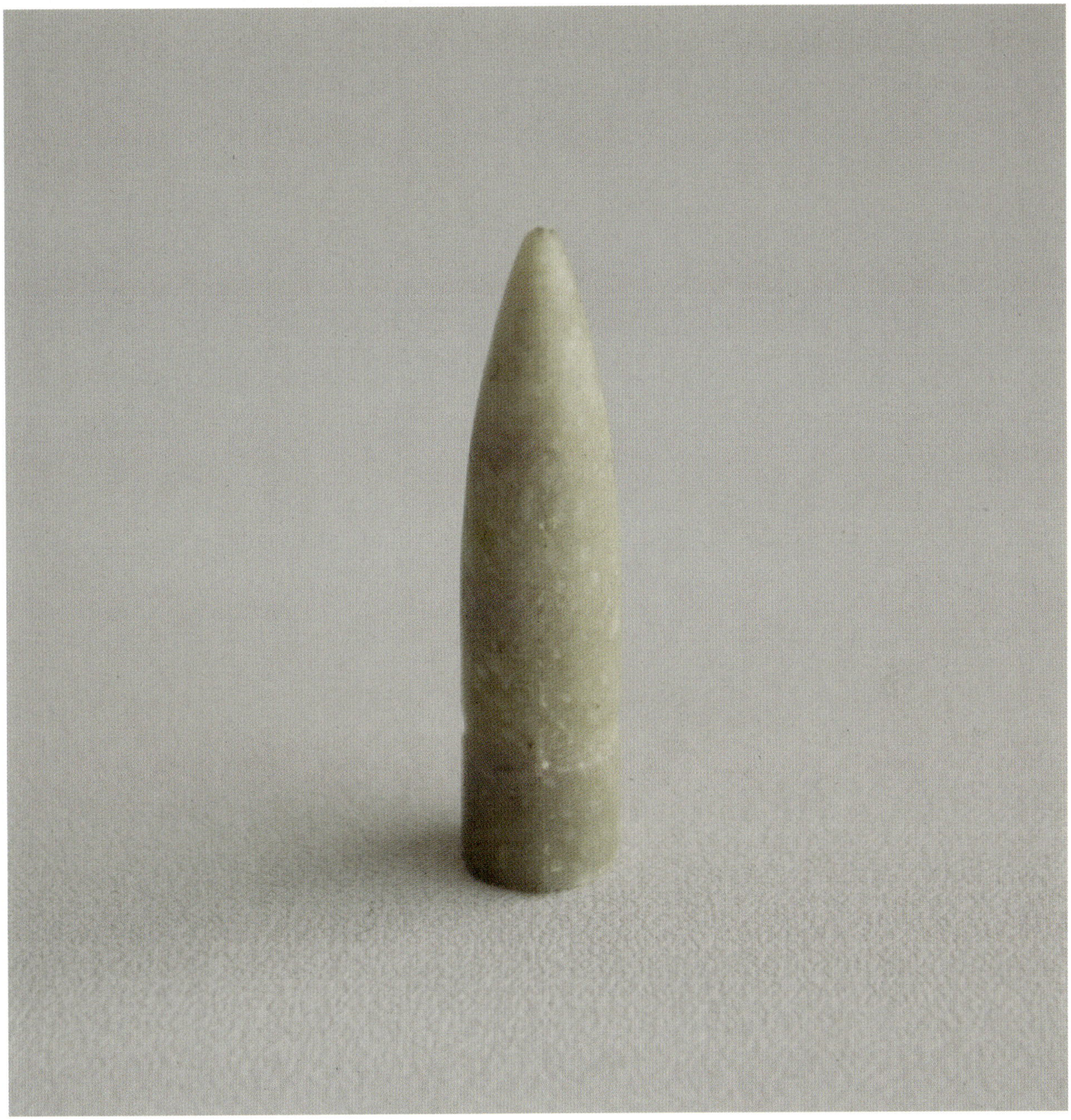

OPPOSITE
Robert Gober
Untitled Candle, 1991
beeswax, string and human hair

ABOVE
Dermot O'Brien
Untitled (Bullet), 2011
cast human bone and epoxy medium

In the late 1980s, before effective combination therapy drugs were found to treat, though not cure, HIV, New York-based artist collectives ACT UP (AIDS Coalition To Unleash Power) and Gran Fury petitioned Republican administrators to address the pandemic. (Reagan notoriously refused to publicly discuss the topic.) Against this backdrop, many artists addressed the issue of mortality, though few as succinctly as **Robert Gober**. His *Untitled Candle* with human hair at its base calls to mind the cautionary saying, 'Don't burn your candle at both ends', and questions prejudices about the sex lives of gay men.

Dermot O'Brien entitled two 2011 exhibitions 'Substance and Accident' after Aristotle's assertion that an accident is something incidental, rather than integral, to a substance. Thomas Aquinas later applied that idea to the Catholic Mass, where the accidents (the actual bread and wine consumed) do not change, but their substance does. For *Untitled (Bullet)*, O'Brien gave a real human finger bone to artist Mark Woods to grind and cast into a rifle bullet. O'Brien seeks in his work to contrast Duchampian tropes with religious belief systems.

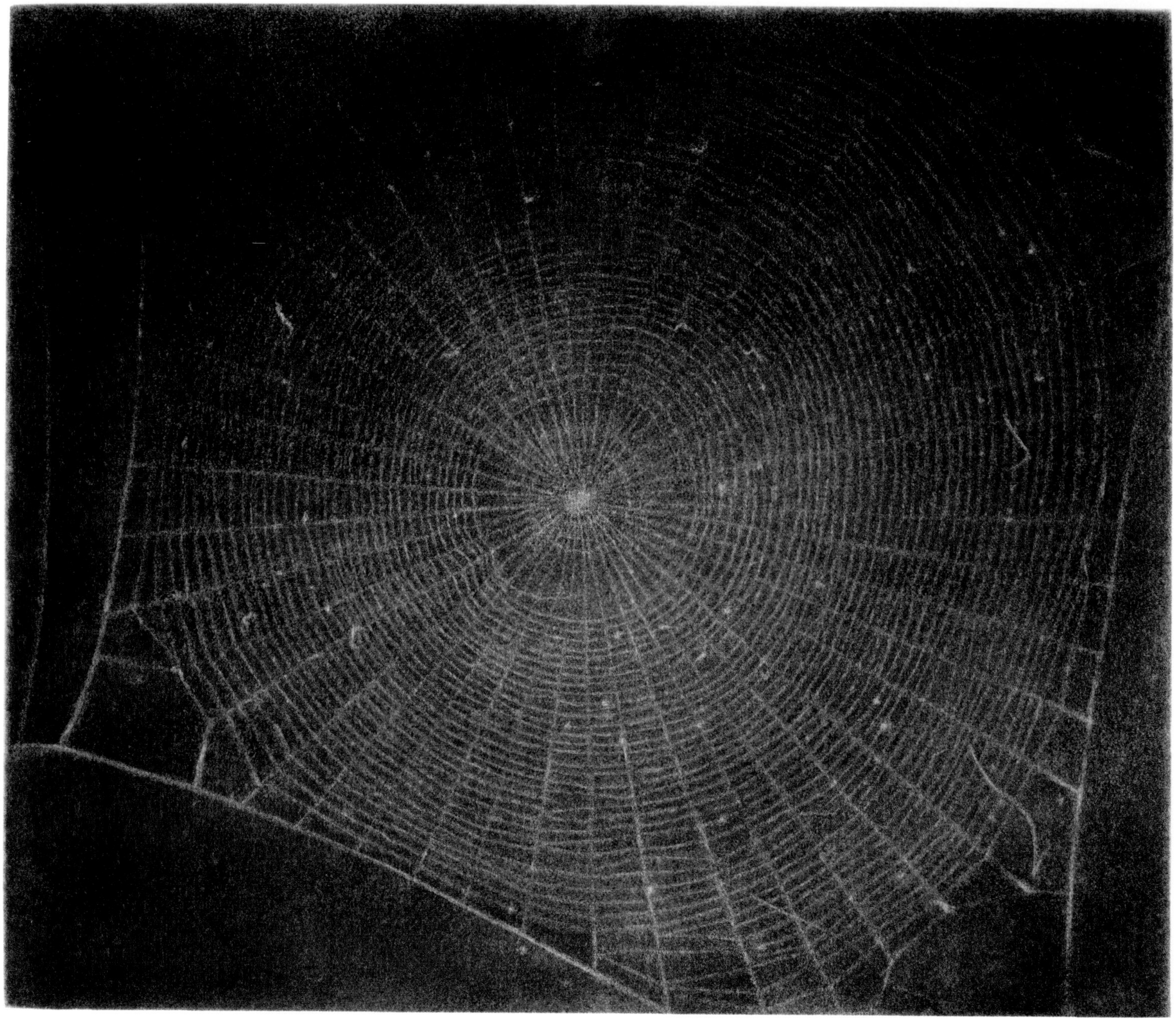

ABOVE
Vija Celmins
Web #5, 1999
charcoal on paper

OPPOSITE
Todd Hebert
Web with Snowman,
2010 · acrylic on paper

Vija Celmins uses simple drawing materials (pencil, graphite, charcoal, ink) to create extremely dense and dark images of the night sky, endless sea, vast deserts and spider webs. Celmins explains that her works are made 'not from observations of nature, but [from] "found images" from old magazines, books and photos. Thus they are already flattened and a step removed from nature. In my work, the information they hold is re-told and given a new life in a new context.'

Todd Hebert's spider web frames the soft-focus silhouette of a snowman looking out at the muted nightscape of Los Angeles, where in fact it never snows at all. Hebert's paintings often recall surreal film sets where dread mixes with an odd melancholy. In *Web with Snowman* the web functions similarly to a still-life painting, freezing time within its frame.

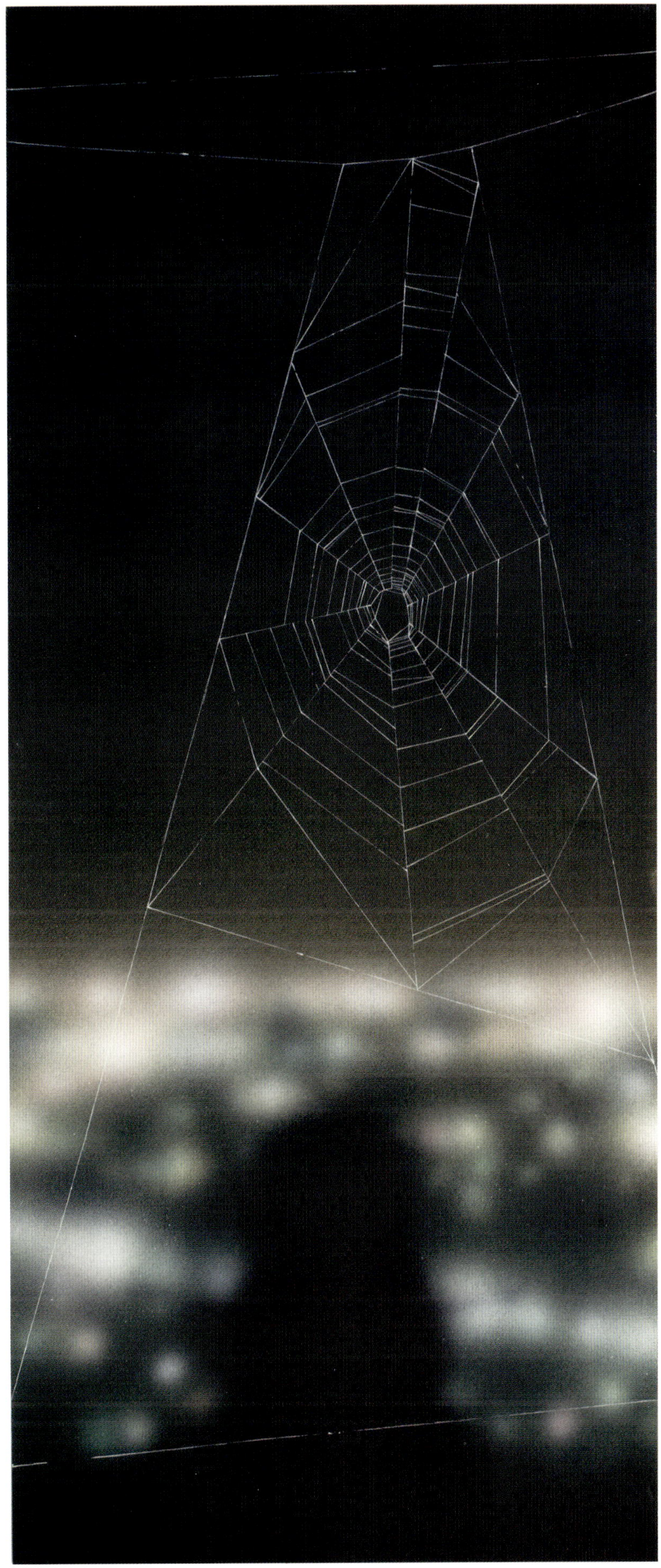

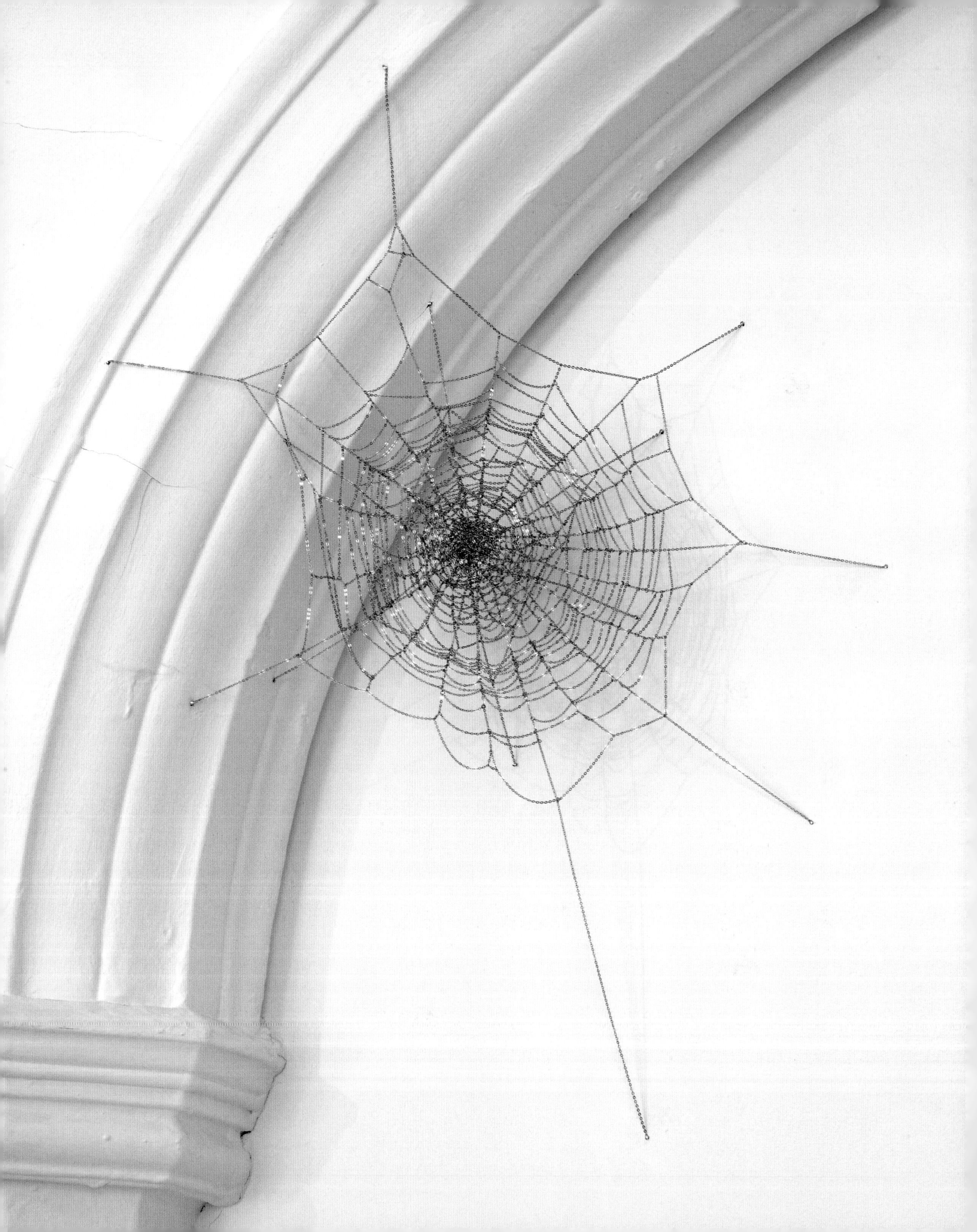

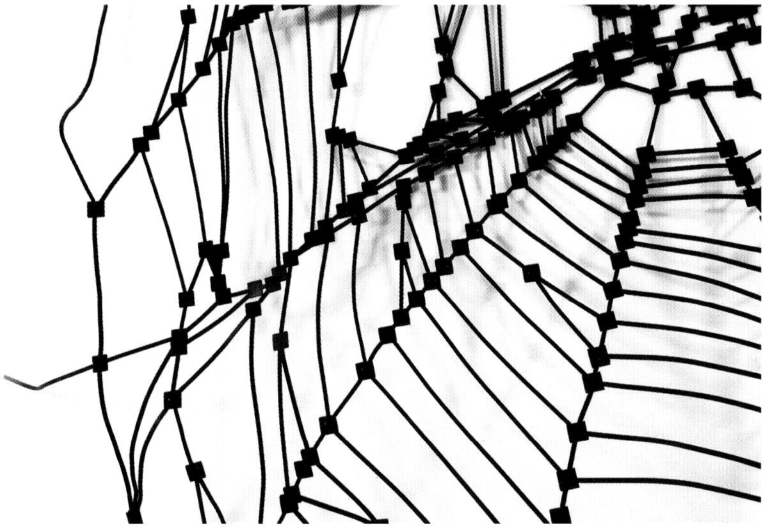

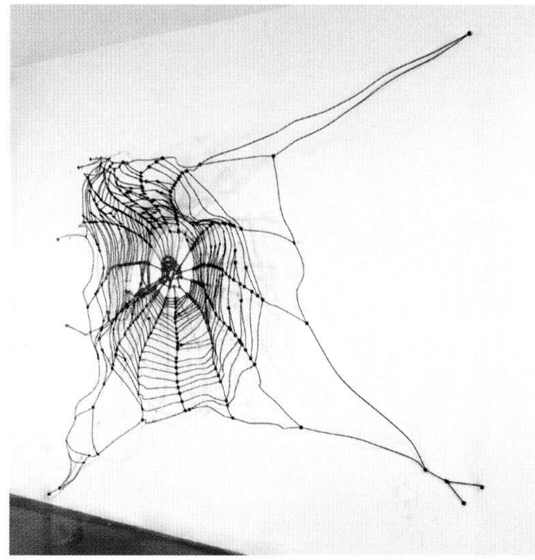

OPPOSITE
Jim Hodges
Hello, again, 1994–2003
brass chains and pins

ABOVE
Carlos Amorales
Transformable Spider web, 2008–11 (detail and installation view)
4 mm aluminium tubing and black rubber paint

The spider web, fragile and temporary, has long been a symbol of death, dread and human frailty. Not only does it catch the prey of spiders, but also the imagination and fears of humans. Many contemporary artists including **Jim Hodges** have used this latent power in their works. Hodges's *Hello, again* is one of a series of sculptural works made of shiny brass chains that, attached to a gallery wall, appear as fragile and enticing as if made of natural gossamer.

In his video *Discarded Spider* (2008), artist **Carlos Amorales** appears to be trapped in one of his own spider-web works – such as *Transformable Spider web* – perhaps rearranging its threads, perhaps fighting against their pull. His large, flexible webs of painted aluminium and rubber are one of the results of his 'Liquid Archive' of over 1,500 digital drawings, which he uses as the vocabulary for his work. He rotoscopes these found images to mere outlines, creating bare webs of information.

Reena Saini Kallat's *Untitled Cobweb (knots and crossings)* is made up of rubber stamps painted in the colours of different national flags and strung together to resemble a spider web. On the face of each stamp appears the name of a person denied a visa to travel from one country to another. Securing the right stamp on the right form (passports, birth, death and marriage certificates, immigration papers) is a bureaucratic nightmare for many, and the web metaphor effectively conveys the forces that act beyond the control of the individual.

RIGHT
Reena Saini Kallat
Untitled Cobweb (knots and crossings), 2012
acrylic paint, rubber stamps and metal

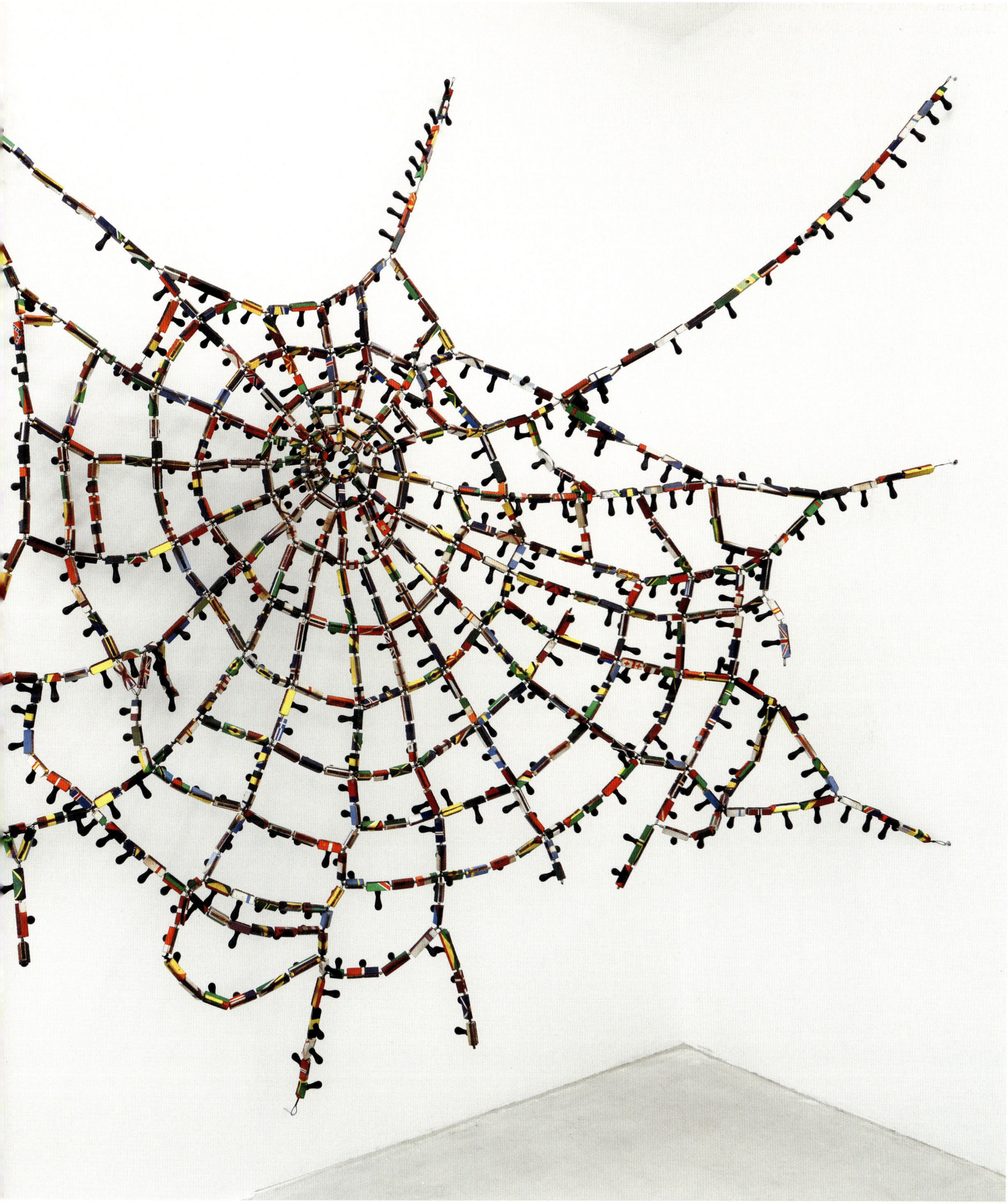

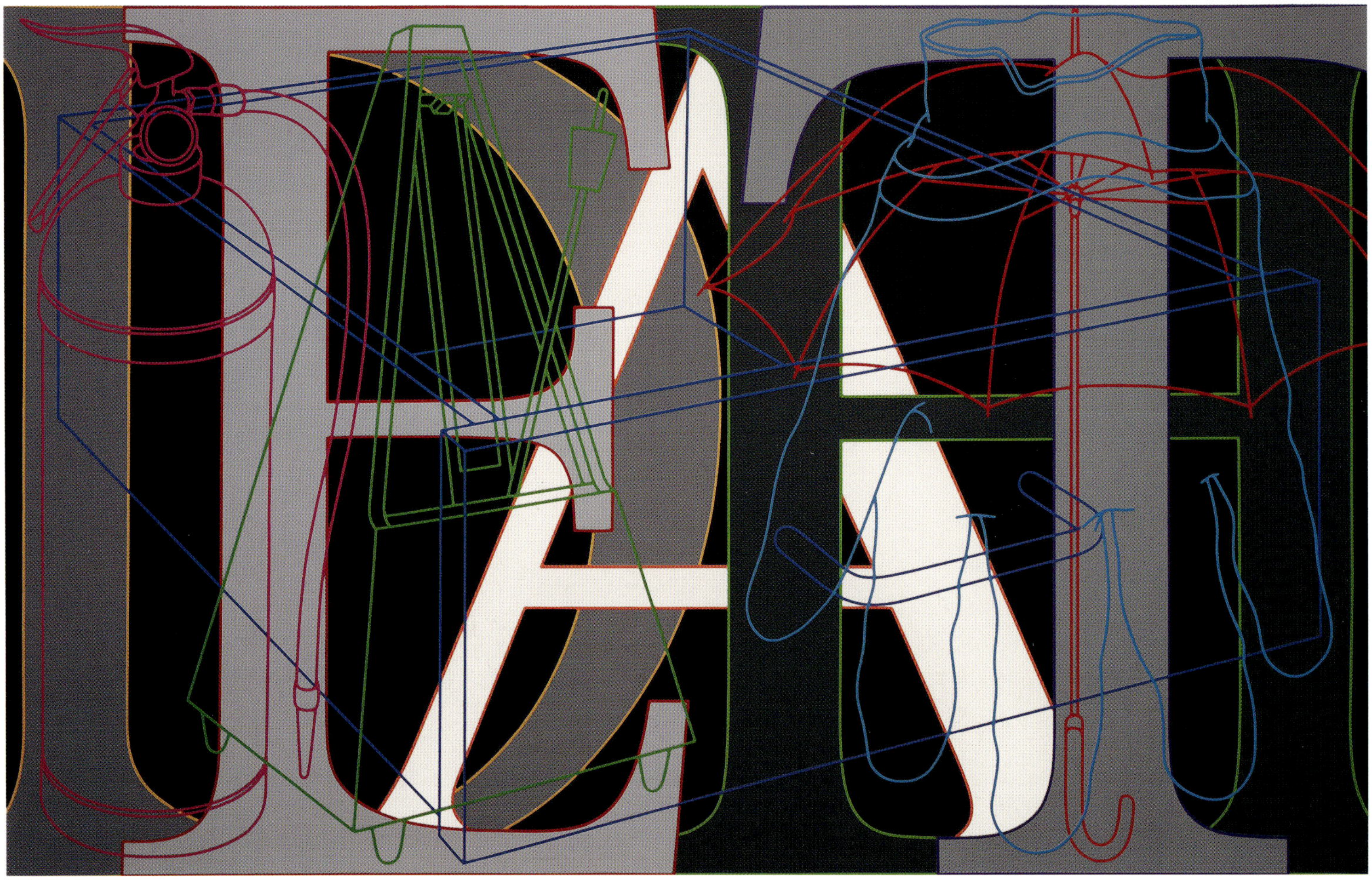

ABOVE
Michael Craig-Martin
***Untitled (death)*, 2008**
acrylic on aluminium

OPPOSITE TOP
Eric Rhein
***Leaves*, 1998**
(installation view)
wire and paper

OPPOSITE BOTTOM
Eric Rhein
***Jeff and Tim*, 1996–2012**
wire and paper

Michael Craig-Martin's painting *Untitled (death)* is much more sober than many of his works in this style, which he usually executes in brighter, more cheerful colours. His graphic sensibility remains in play, however, and the complex composition and interlinking outlines of an assortment of objects mix those of life (an umbrella, glove and drawer) with those that recall death: a metronome, a ticking clock, and a fire extinguisher, an allusion to possible tragedy.

Eric Rhein's *Leaves* was started in 1996 while the artist was recovering from an HIV-related illness. New medications had saved his life but not those of 180 friends who had already died from the disease. In their memory, Rhein began to make a unique wire leaf for each individual and named it in their honour. The resulting tributes are exhibited as a large installation, as well as in smaller sets. 'One by one,' Rhein has said, 'I picked up leaves until a host of kinsmen was gathered in my arms.' Critic Robert Atkins writes: 'an art of memory like Eric Rhein's can help harmonize our views by suggesting that honouring the past is one way to live more fully in the present.' *Leaves* continues to grow, reflecting the ongoing pandemic. It now contains more than two hundred tributes.

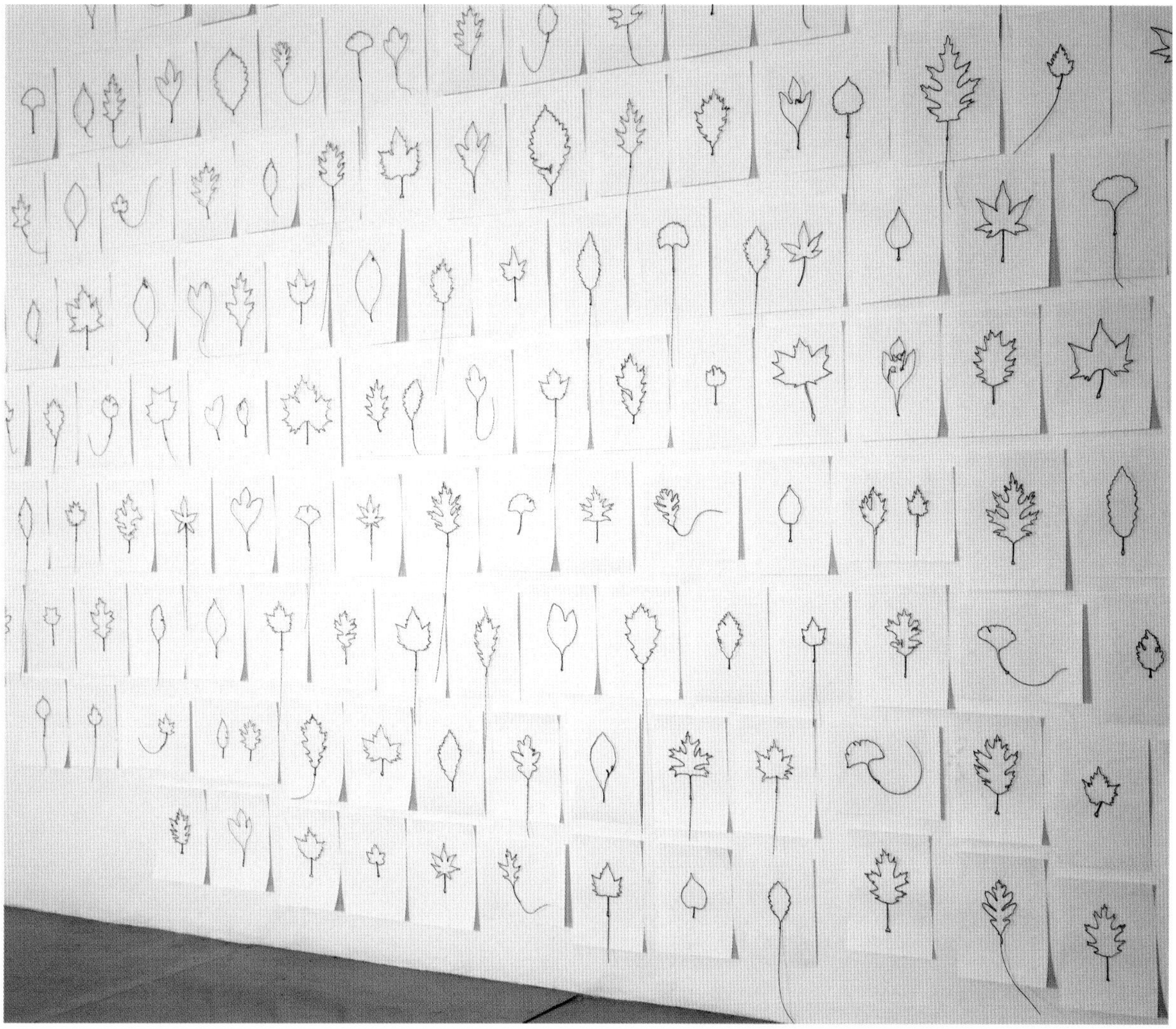

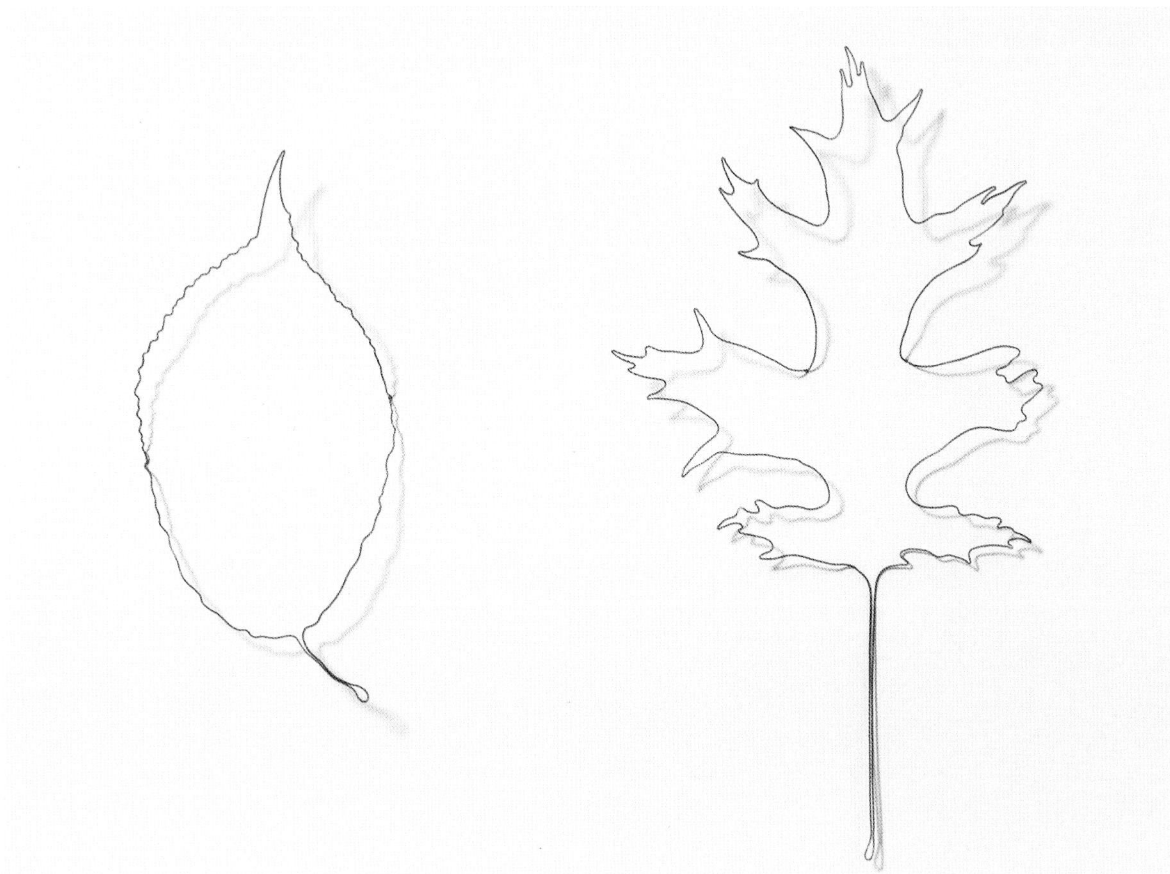

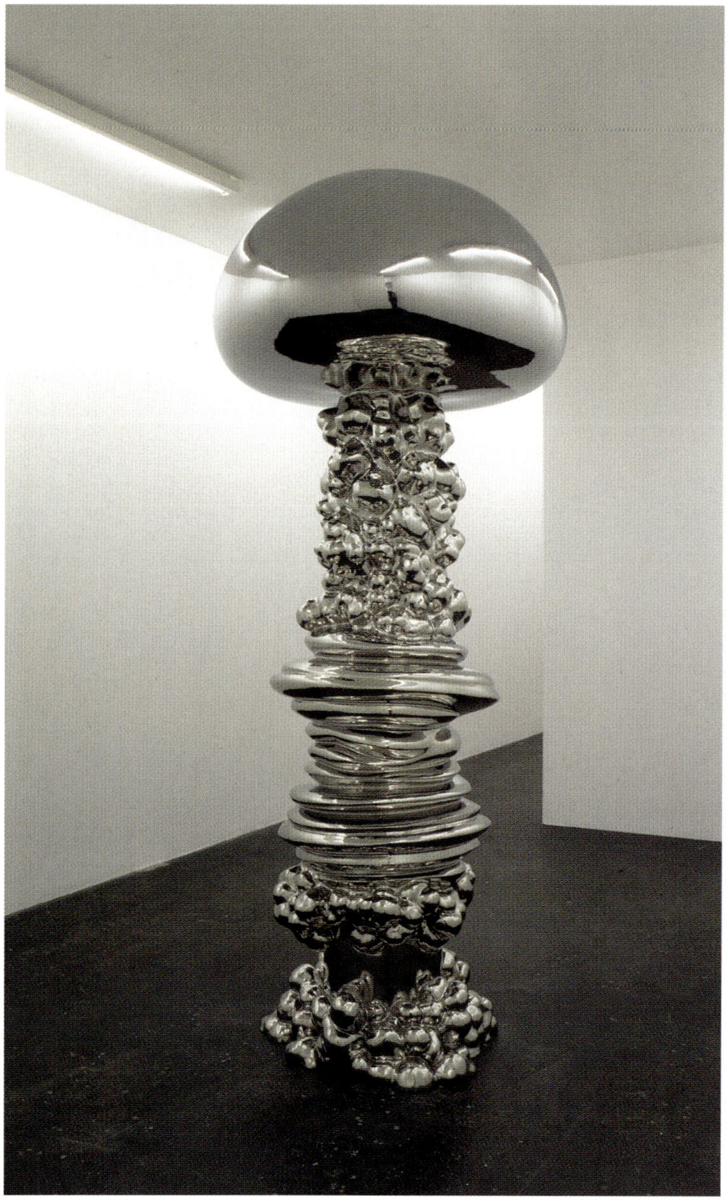

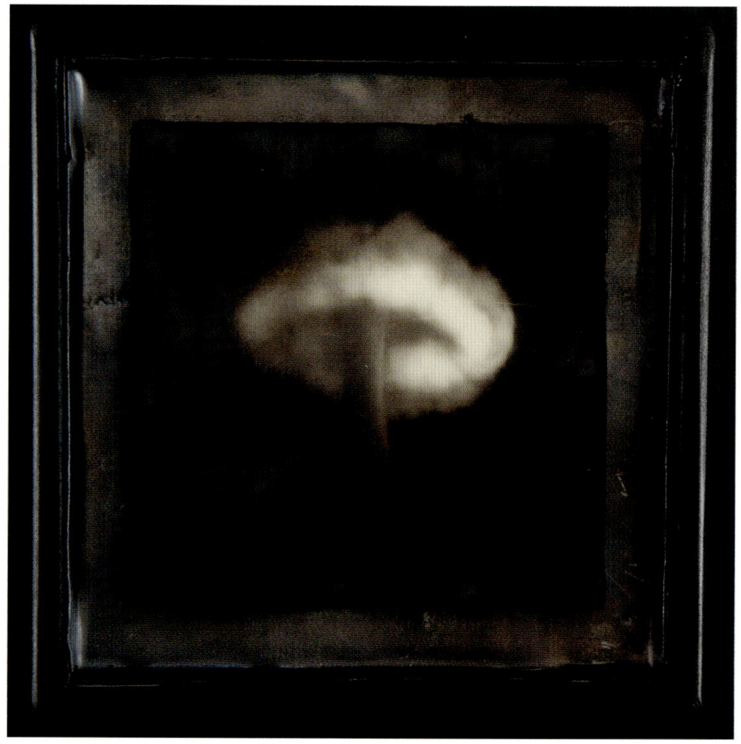

Jone Kvie and **Susan Seubert** use the frightening image of an atomic mushroom cloud to reference death in their works. Kvie's stainless steel sculpture *Untitled* dominates its physical space, an embodiment of the ever-expanding nature of the radioactive bomb and its invisible yet deathly power. Seubert incorporated the image into a series of small, delicate *Bomb* prints. To bring the impact home for the viewer, she framed each one as if for a domestic interior.

ABOVE LEFT
Jone Kvie · *Untitled*, 2002
stainless steel

ABOVE RIGHT
Susan Seubert · *Bomb #10 'Bomb in a Box'* (*tic, tac, toe*), 2008 · digital pigment print on tissue paper, encaustic wax and lead

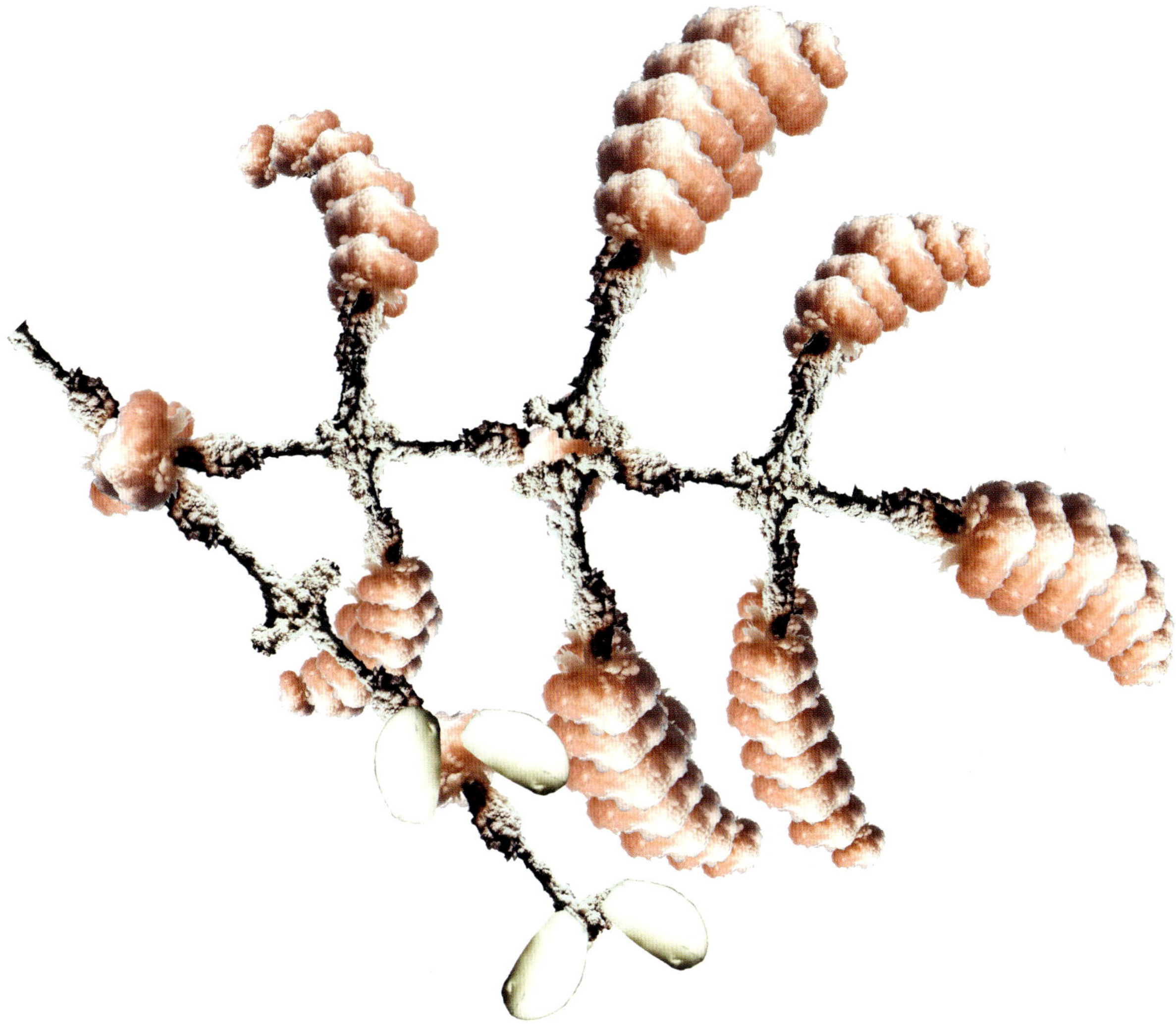

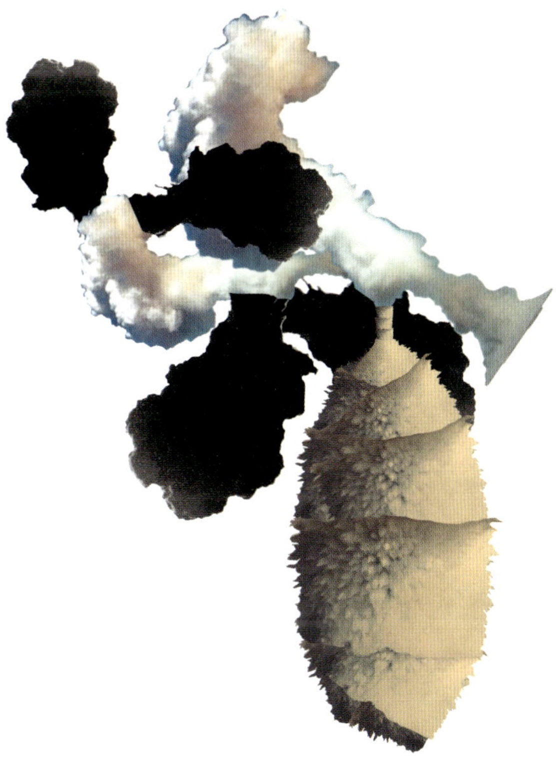

At first glance **Carlos Noronha Feio**'s series *Plant Life of the Pacific World* appears nothing more than a number of charming pressed flowers. On closer inspection, it becomes clear that they are collages of nuclear explosions. The subtitle of each work refers to a similar-looking flower found in the area where the explosion occurred, as illustrated in E. D. Merrill's 1945 book *Plant Life of the Pacific World*, which was published for the US military to aid in their nuclear testing on the Bikini Atoll. Noronha Feio transforms the nuclear bomb, symbol of destruction and death, into beautiful if *poisonous* flowers.

LEFT
Carlos Noronha Feio
Plant Life of the Pacific World, Figure 210: Durio zibethinus, 2012
photographic digital collage, printed on Hahnemühle photo rag 500 gsm

ABOVE
Carlos Noronha Feio
Plant Life of the Pacific World, Figure 70: Canarium commune, 2012
photographic digital collage, printed on Hahnemühle photo rag 500 gsm

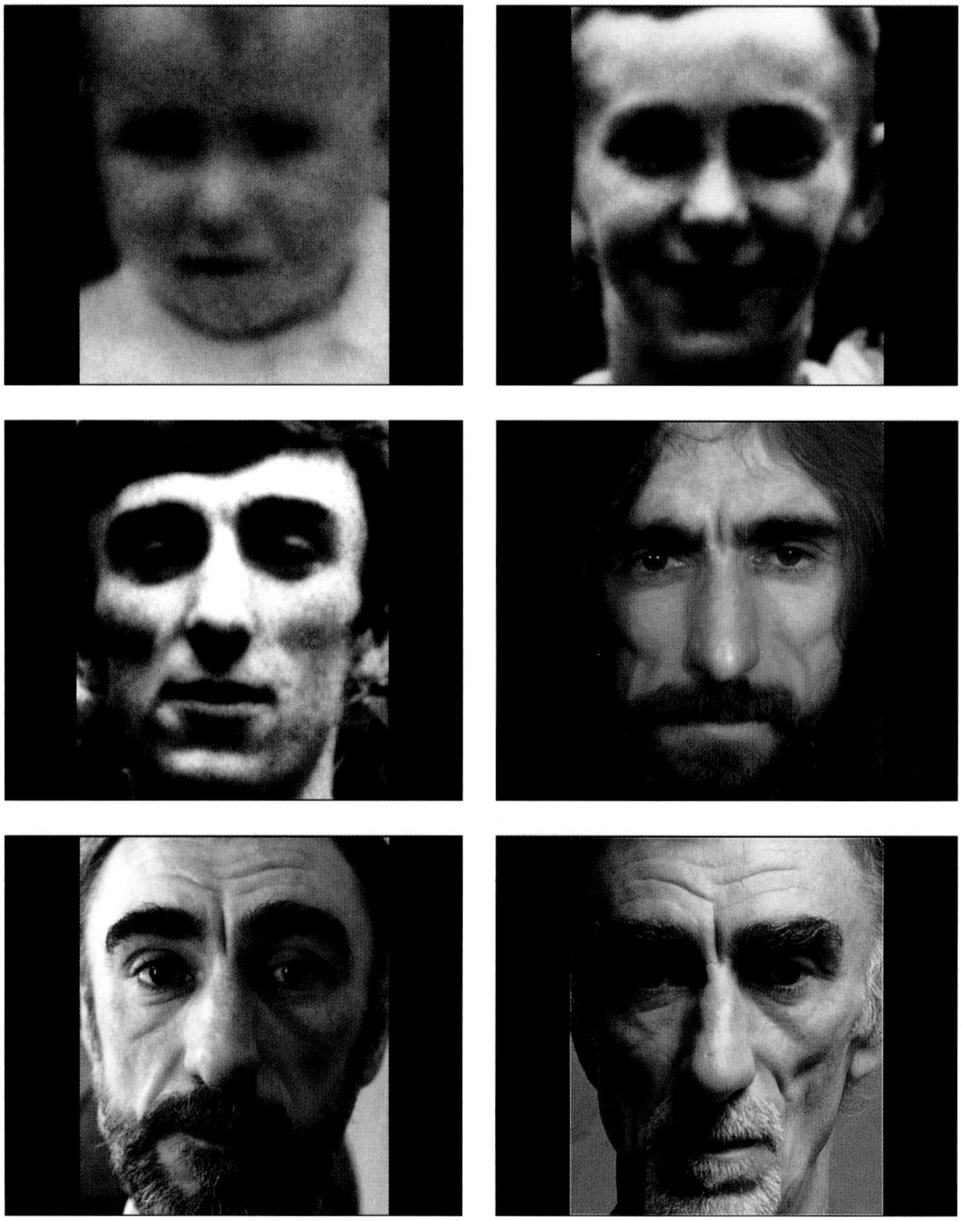

ABOVE
Ian Breakwell
BC/AD, 2005–8
(video stills)
Blu-ray, black and white, sound

In **Ian Breakwell**'s last major work – the haunting video *BC/AD* ('Before Cancer/After Diagnosis') – a series of photographs show the artist's face as he ages from infancy, through youth and adulthood, to just before his death. As a voiceover of Breakwell reading from his diary plays, viewers can clearly see how age and later his fight with cancer have worn out the artist. Created during his last days alive, the work offers the artist's thoughts as his mind turns to his imminent death. The camera acts as a mirror to his mortality and, in the playback, to that of the viewer.

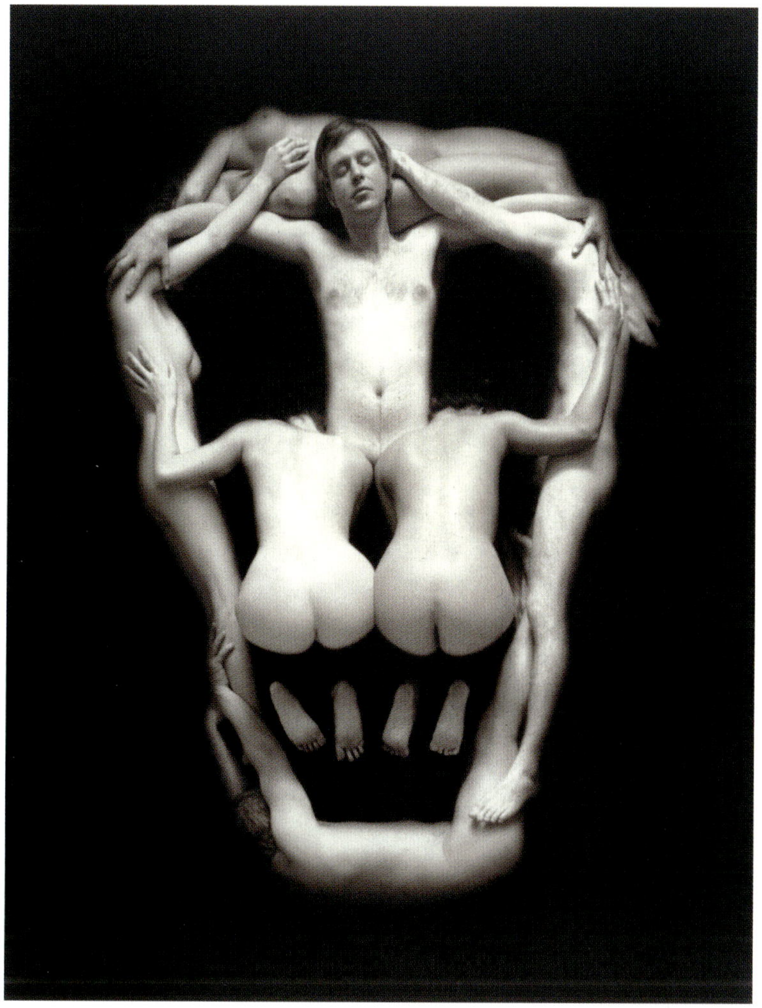

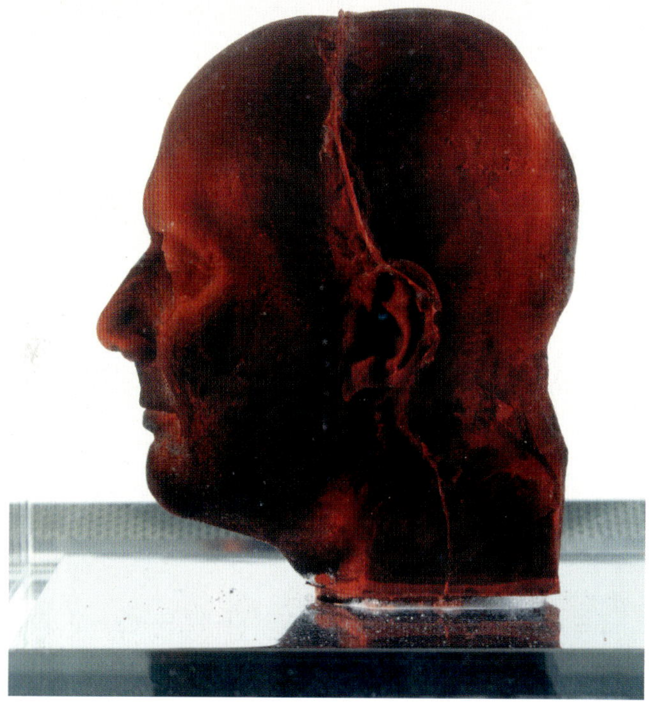

Piotr Uklański's *Untitled (The Skull)* depicts the artist with closed eyes surrounded by nude men and women (all of their faces are obscured), each posed so that as a unit they resemble a skull. The work takes inspiration from an infamous film poster for *The Silence of the Lambs* (1991) that in turn appropriated a similar skull configuration depicted in Philippe Halsman's *In Voluptas Mors* (1951), though in that photograph all the nudes are female and Salvador Dalí, in top hat and tails, looks on worriedly.

Marc Quinn's *Self* of 1991 was the first life-sized cast of the artist's head to be made from his own blood. Since then Quinn has created a new version of the work every five years, slowly collecting his blood so as to preserve his health. Each frozen sculpture differs from the last as the artist ages and his features change, making the works an evolving series of death masks. Time is seen to mark his face yet a frozen version of that self will live endlessly on, its static existence reminding viewers of the artist's (and their own) impending death.

ABOVE LEFT
Piotr Uklański
***Untitled** (**Skull**)*, 2000
platinum print

ABOVE RIGHT
Marc Quinn
Self, 2006
artist's blood, stainless steel, Perspex and refrigeration equipment

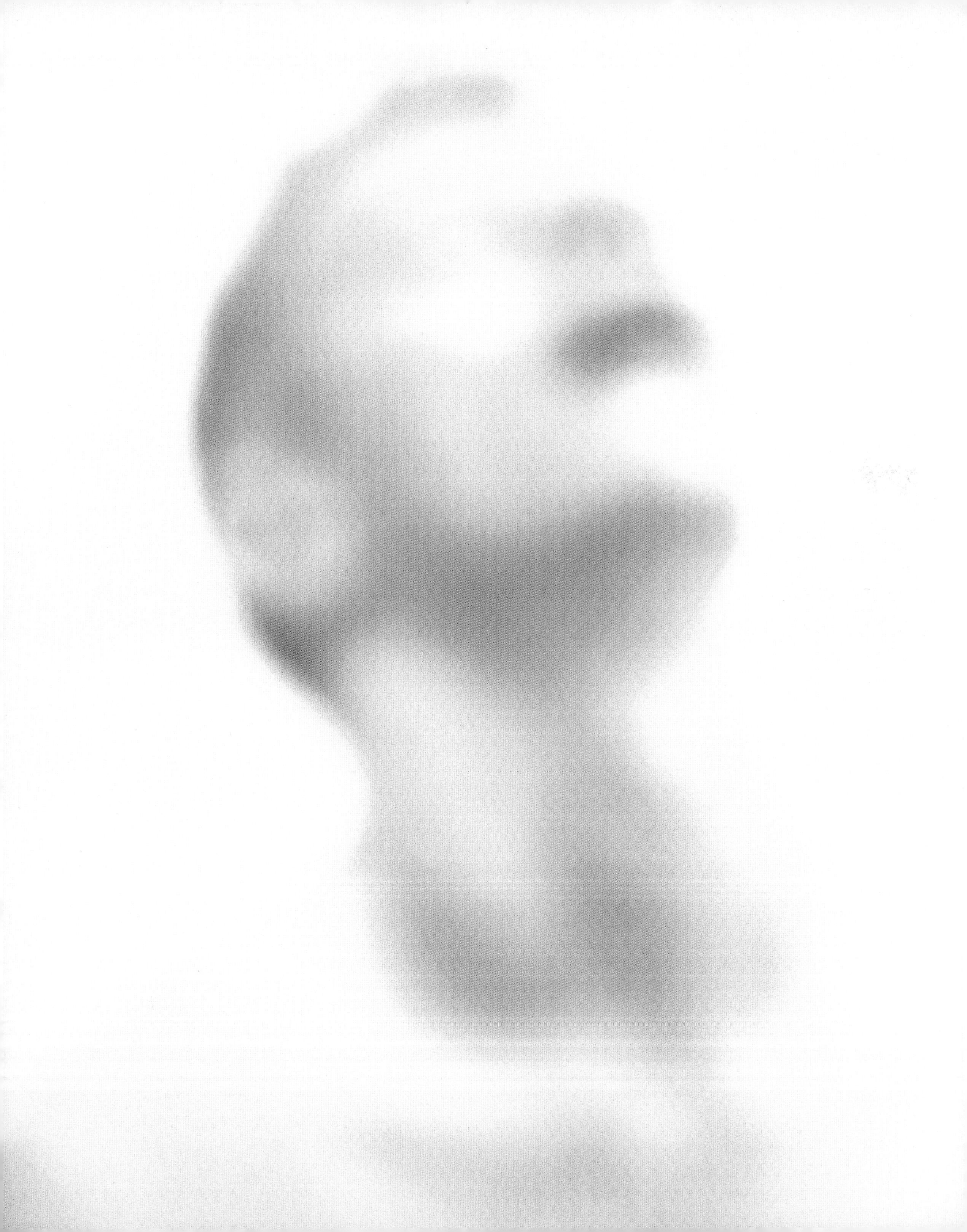

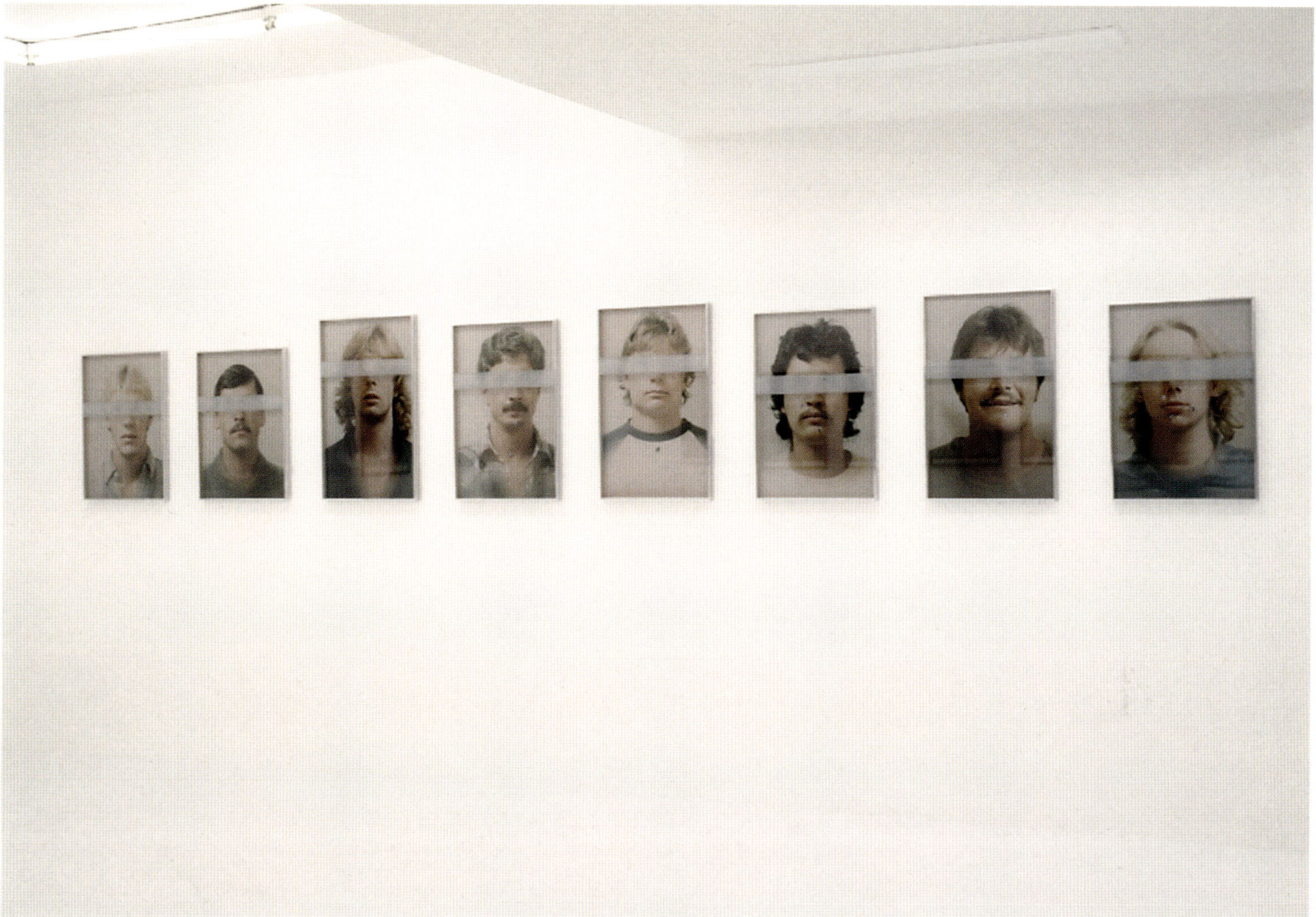

Portraits of young offenders used as targets during the training of police officers in the city of M., US

Bill Jacobson's *Interim Portrait* series (1992–94) was a personal and poetic photographic reflection on the AIDS pandemic. All of the figures are blurred and out of focus, somehow ghostly, the smudged greys fading into the white background. 'They're intended as a metaphor for an inner state or an interior way of being,' Jacobson has explained. 'The pictures denied representations of physicality in part because there was no detail.'

The title of **Sophie Calle**'s sinister *Coeur de Cible* translates as key target, core target, or even target audience. The work consists of reproductions of portraits of young offenders that were used for target practice by serving police in an American city identified only as *M*. Another possible translation of the work's title is 'on the nose' and, ironically, *Target 3* (far left) has a bullet hole directly through his nostril.

OPPOSITE
Bill Jacobson
Interim Portrait #378, 1992
C-print

ABOVE
Sophie Calle
Coeur de Cible / Target 1, Target 2 ... Target 13,
2003 (detail) · colour photographs, aluminium, frames (× 13)

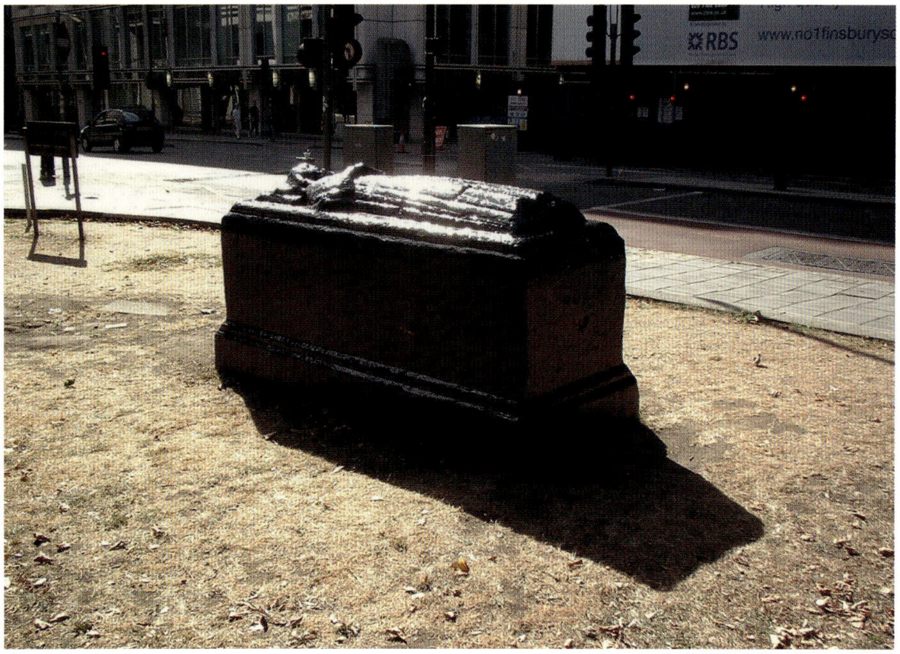

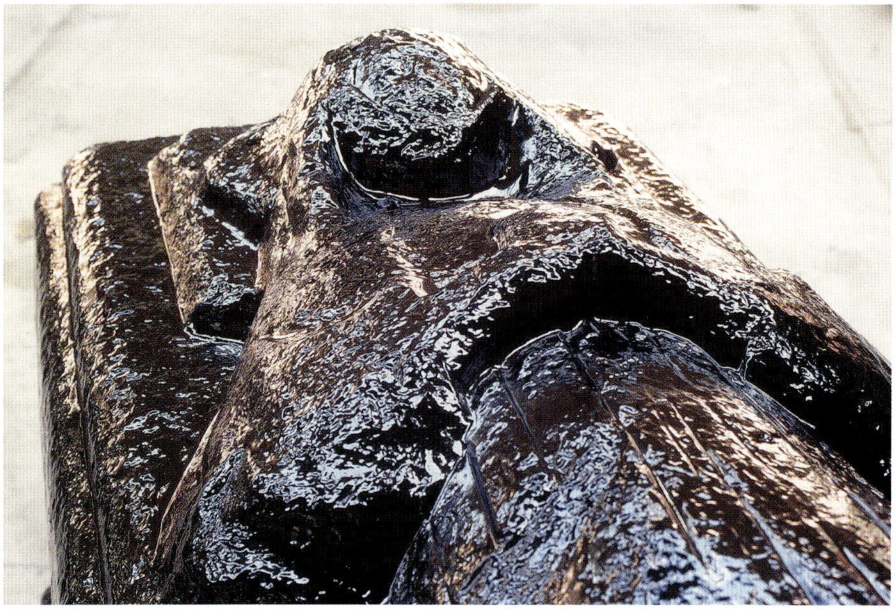

ABOVE
Ana Genovés
Effigy, 2001 (installation view and detail)
acrylic composite and gloss paint

Ana Genovés's *Effigy* is modelled on the medieval monuments that marked out the resting place of the dead, immortalizing their likeness sleeping or in repose. Genovés's work, however, is made from very modern materials: acrylic and gloss paint. Nevertheless, with its deep black surface – a colour so often associated with death – the imposing installation appears to be carved out of weathered stone.

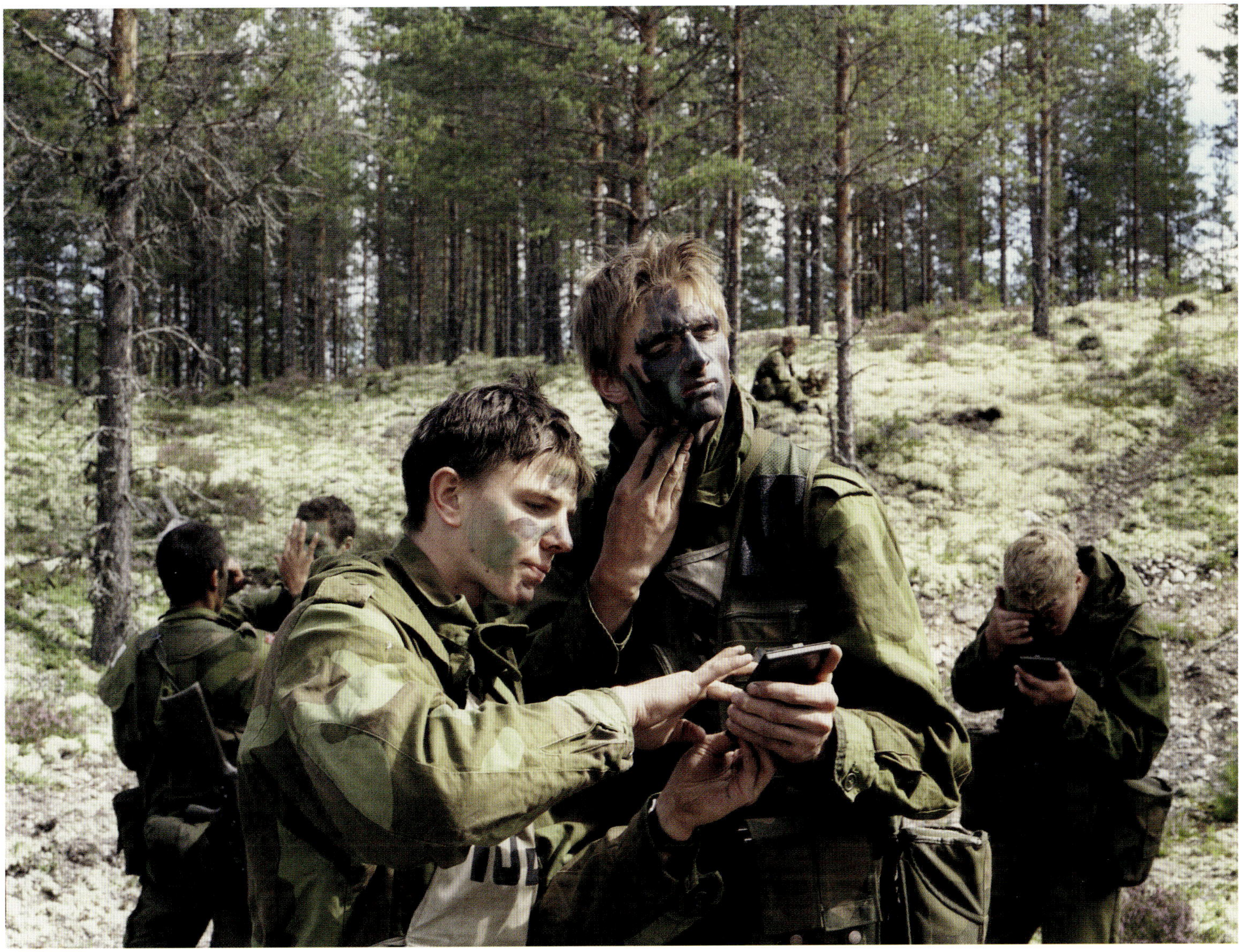

Per Christian Brown was commissioned by the Norwegian Army to photograph training at the Rena military camp and captured a number of trainees applying black-and-green camouflage paint to their faces. They are all in the process of becoming soldiers, *performing* their very masculinity (as theorist Judith Butler would posit) in preparation for war. These young men are training to be soldiers, practising how to kill, learning to hide and disguise themselves. This work captures the moment when the implication of violence and death is at its most potent, reminding viewers that the sanctioning of death via war is always artificial.

ABOVE
Per Christian Brown
Nature Vanitas 2, 2006
C-print

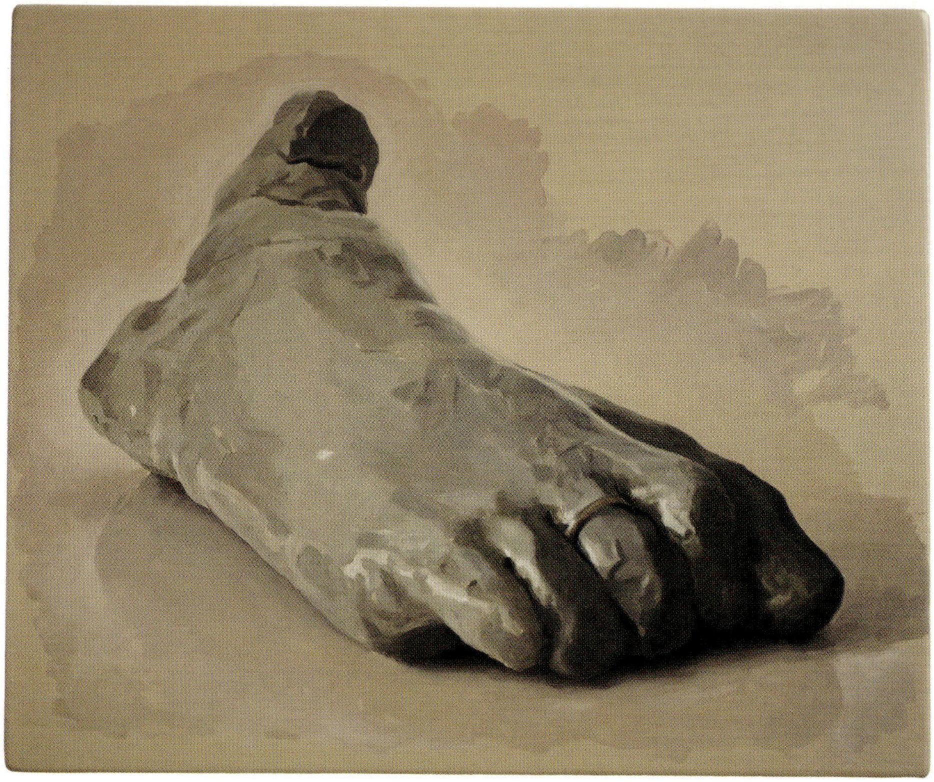

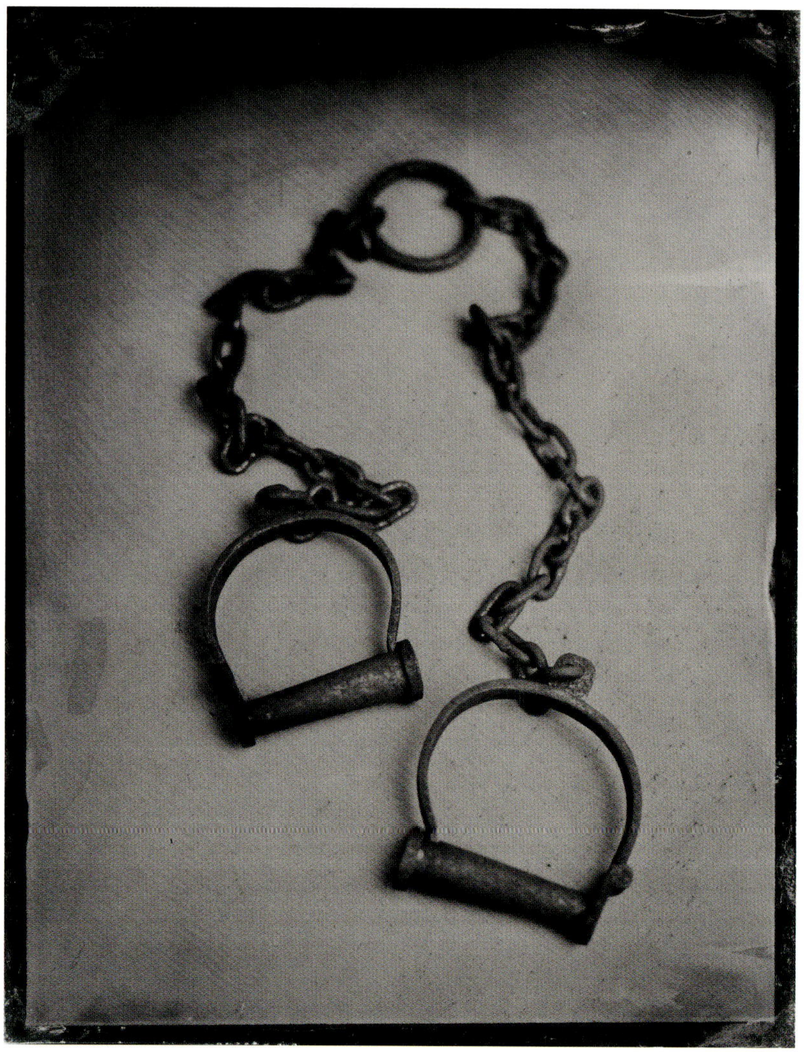

Damien Meade is a painter who sculpts objects out of wet clay before painting their likeness, creating 'artifice within artifice'. The models are allowed to dry and are discarded when they crack and break, making the act of painting them an attempt to capture a fleeting state lost in time. That the stark objects are also a bit gruesome (a sheared-off foot, a decapitated head) adds to their power as contemporary still lifes.

Susan Seubert's stark and unsentimental *Slave Cuffs* is a reminder of America's trade in humans for many centuries and the terrible legacy that still affects the country's race relations, regardless of the fact that Barack Obama is its first black president. Along with cruelty and a lack of freedom, slaves faced an almost certain death should they try to escape, and these cuffs still evoke that social depravity.

ABOVE
Damien Meade
Foot II, 2009
oil on linen on board

LEFT
Susan Seubert
Slave Cuffs, 2011
photography ambrotype

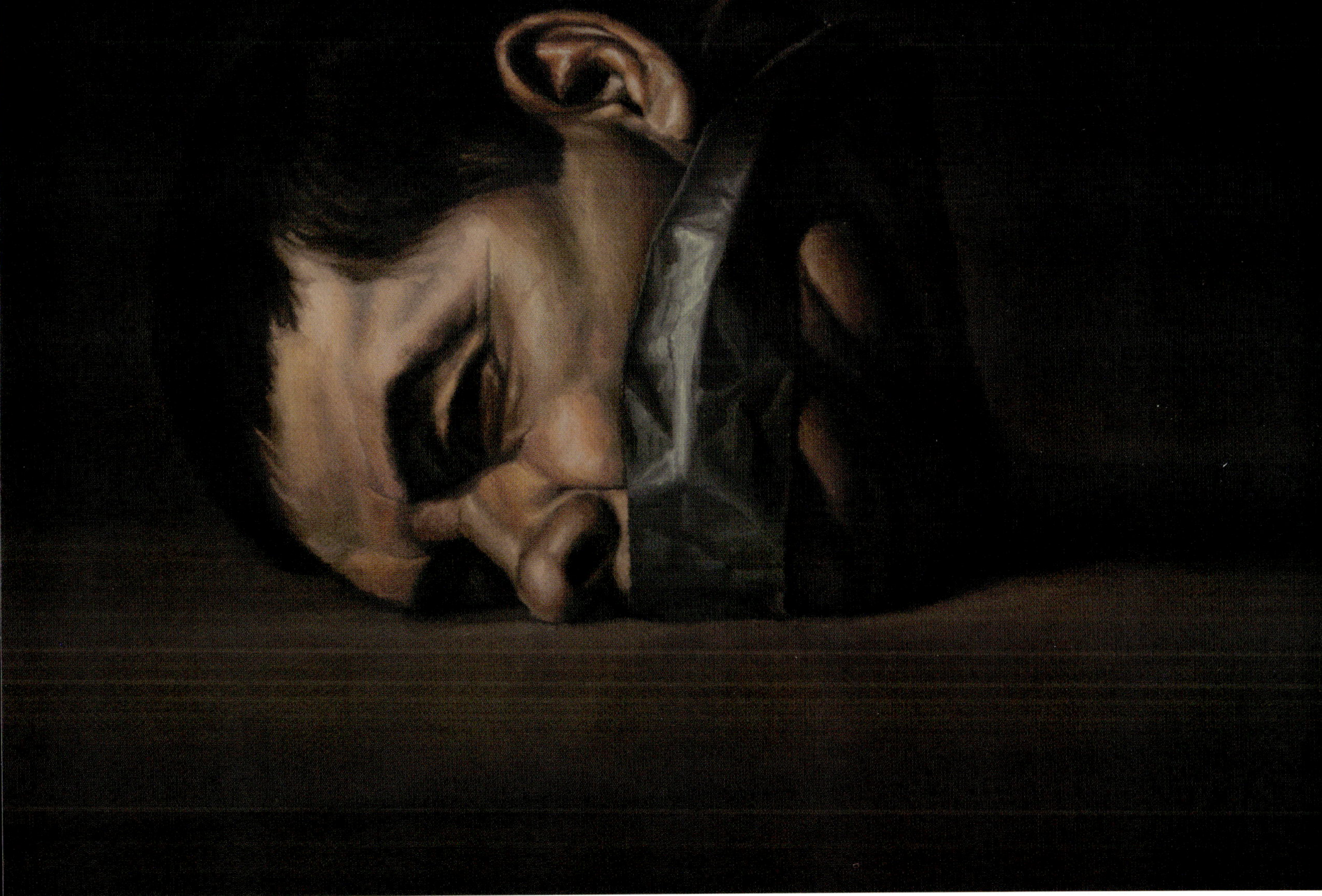

ABOVE
Rigoberto A. Gonzalez
Para Que Aprendan A Respetar (So That They Learn to be Respectful), 2009
oil on linen

Rigoberto A. Gonzalez comes from near Mexico's border with Texas where for the past ten years drug cartels have been fighting each other and the Mexican government. Death by decapitation is favoured by the cartels as an effective means of silencing those who might inform on them, or fight against them. In *Para Que Aprendan A Respetar (So That They Learn to be Respectful)*, Gonzalez depicts one such victim. Gonzalez has had such a 'lesson' inflicted on one of his own family members (his cousin's husband was murdered in this way) and he says that he is painting these stilled lives in order to 'humanize this conflict'.

LIST OF ILLUSTRATIONS

A = above · B = below · C = centre · L = left · R = right

42A, 42B · Jeroen de Rijke / Willem de Rooij · *Bouquet IV*, 2005 · flower arrangement in white ceramic vase and gelatin silver print in aluminium frame · vase: dimensions variable, print: 122.5 × 122.5 cm (48 1/4 × 48 1/4 in.) · Collection Museum für Moderne Kunst, Frankfurt · Courtesy Galerie Buchholz, Berlin/Cologne

43 · Hans-Peter Feldmann · *Flower Pot* · mixed media · dimensions variable. Courtesy of the artist and 303 Gallery, New York

44L · Jim Hodges · *ghost*, 2008 · glass sculpture in multiple components · bell jar and glass base: 89 × 56 × 56 cm (35 × 22 × 22 in.), glass base: 13 × 56 × 56 cm (5 × 22 × 22 in.) · Courtesy of the artist and private collection, London · © Jim Hodges

44R · Jim Hodges · *A Line to You*, 1994 · silk, plastic and wire with thread · Installation view of 'Jim Hodges at Camden Arts Centre', 2010 · Photo: Andy Keate · Courtesy Camden Arts Centre

45 · Jim Hodges · *Changing things*, 1997 · silk, plastic, wire and pins, 342 parts · Installation view of 'Jim Hodges at Camden Arts Centre', 2010 · Photo: Andy Keate · Courtesy Camden Arts Centre

46L · Klara Kristalova · *Black Pansy*, 2009 · glazed stoneware · 57 × 36 × 32 cm (22 1/2 × 14 1/8 × 12 5/8 in.) · Courtesy Galleri Magnus Karlsson, Stockholm, and Alison Jacques Gallery · © Klara Kristalova

46R · Georgie Hopton · *Flowers in a Bag*, 2007 · acrylic on jesmonite · 38.5 × 35 × 19 cm (15 1/8 × 13 3/4 × 7 1/2 in.) · Courtesy of the artist and Poppy Sebire

47 · Marc Quinn · *The Nurseries of El Dorado (cucumissativuspaphiopedliumsolanumlycopersicumphalenopsispotinaraanthuriumpyrus)*, 2007 · bronze with heat-treated chrome patina · 76 × 70 × 46 cm (29 7/8 × 27 5/8 × 18 1/8 in.) · Photo: Stephen White · Courtesy White Cube · © Marc Quinn

48 · Karin Broker · *Don't Lie Bouquet*, 2005–12 · metal, graphite, rhinestones and wire · 61 × 35.6 × 39.4 cm (24 × 14 × 15 1/2 in.) · Photo: Paul Hester · Courtesy of the artist

49A, 49B · Nicky Deeley · *Gardens 1 and Gardens 2*, 2009 · fabric, modelling compound, steel, vinyl, rubber and timber · 160 × 65 × 22 cm (63 × 25 5/8 × 8 5/8 in.) · Courtesy of the artist

50 · Philip Pirolo · *Velvet Orifice*, 1991 · velvet and gallery wall · diameter: 15.2 cm (6 in.) · Courtesy of the artist

51 · Rodney McMillian · *Untitled*, 2010 · vinyl and thread · 4.27 × 8.38 m (14 ft 1/8 in. × 27 ft 5 7/8 in.) · Photo: Robert Wedemeyer · Courtesy Susanne Vielmetter, Los Angeles Projects

52A · Mat Collishaw · *Infectious Orchid 2*, 2004 · digital print · 39.5 × 29.2 cm (15 5/8 × 11 1/2 in.) · Courtesy of the artist

52B · Saara Ekström · *Breeding*, 2010 · C-print · 89 × 110 cm (35 × 43 1/4 in.) · Courtesy of the artist and Helsinki Contemporary

53 · David LaChapelle · *Wilting Gossip*, 2008–11 · chromogenic print · 182.9 × 137.2 cm (72 × 51 3/4 in.) · © David LaChapelle

54 · Alana Lake · *Stilleven I*, 2011 · archival digital print · 30 × 45 cm (11 3/4 × 17 3/4 in.) · Courtesy of the artist

55 · Ori Gersht · *Time after Time: Blow up No. 3*, 2007 · light jet print on aluminium · 240 × 180 cm (94 1/2 × 70 7/8 in.) · Courtesy of the artist and Mummery+Schnelle

56 · Sharon Core · *1665*, from the series *Flowers*, 2011 · archival pigment print · 56.5 × 46.4 cm (22 1/4× 18 1/4 in.) · edition of 7 · Courtesy of the artist and Yancey Richardson Gallery · © Sharon Core

57 · Alexander James, Distil Ennui Studio · *Vanitas, 'Grace'*, 2011 · C-print on polished aluminium · 120 × 90 cm (47 1/4 × 35 3/8 in.) · Courtesy of the artist

58L · Persijn Broersen & Margit Lukács · *Time & Again*, 2011 · HD video loop · duration: 6 minutes · Courtesy of the artists and Akinci

58R · David Hockney · *Untitled, 30 May 2009, No. 1*, 2009 · iPhone drawing · © David Hockney

59L · Jennifer Steinkamp · *Rapunzel*, 2005–11 · 5000+ lumen projectors, computers · dimensions variable, height: approx. 3.05 m (10 ft) · Courtesy of the artist and Lehmann Maupin, New York and Hong Kong

59R · Jennifer Steinkamp · *Daisy Bell*, 2008 (installation view) · Mitsubishi projectors, Dell OptiPlex or Logisys computers · Courtesy of the artist and Lehmann Maupin, New York and Hong Kong

60A, 60B · Kana Harada · *Dance With Me*, 2011 · hand-cut white foam sheet and mixed media · 104.1 × 81.3 × 68.6 cm (41 × 32 × 27 in.) · Collection of Suzanne and Ansel Aberly · Photo: Makoto Takemura

61A · Ugo Rondinone · *still.life. (pine tree standing in a corner)*, 2008 · cast bronze, lead and paint, 2 parts · 328 × 508 × 11 cm (129 1/8 × 200 × 4 3/8 in.) · Courtesy Sadie Coles HQ, London · © Ugo Rondinone

61B · Jone Kvie · *Untitled*, 2009 · nickel silver and black pigment · 250 × 100 × 70 cm (98 3/8 × 39 3/8 × 27 5/8 in.) · Photo: Anders Sune Berg · Courtesy of the artist and Nils Stærk, Copenhagen

61R · Cecilia Edefalk · *Weeping Birch Stem*, 2010 · bronze · 165.7 × 14.6 cm (65 1/4 × 5 3/4 in.) · Photo: David Regen · Courtesy Gladstone Gallery, New York/Brussels · © Cecilia Edefalk

62 · Maria Roosen · *Washed Tree Fluor*, 2009/11 · glass, mirror and wood · 45 × 270 × 53 cm (17 3/4 × 106 1/4 × 20 7/8 in.) · Photo: Liedeke Kruk · Courtesy Collection Lise and Thierry Prevot, and Gallery Fons Welters, Amsterdam

63A · Per Christian Brown · *you will still be here when I am gone*, 2011 · C-print · 100 × 80 cm (39 3/8 × 31 1/2 in.) · Courtesy of the artist

63B · Cammie Toloui · *Shadow+Tree*, January 1997 · colour transparency film · Courtesy of the artist

64L · Aidan McNeill · *Non-Native Invasive No.01, (Japanese Knotweed)*, 2010 · C-print · 140 cm × 102 cm (55 1/8 × 40 1/8 in.) · Courtesy of the artist and PayneShurvell, London

64R · Mats Adelman · *Into the Dawn*, 2010 · plant sculpture in wood · 62 × 53 × 40 cm (24 3/8 × 20 7/8 × 15 3/4 in.) · Courtesy of the artist and Poppy Sebire

65A · Frank Webster · *Plastic Bags*, 2009 · acrylic on canvas · 152.4 × 203.2 cm (60 × 80 in.) · Courtesy Blackston New York · © Myriam Babin Photography

65B · Carol Marin-Pache · *Evidence no 13*, 2009 · giclée print on watercolour paper · 29.6 × 42 cm (11 5/8 × 16 1/2 in.) · Courtesy of the artist

66A · Sue Arrowsmith · *Blowin' in the wind*, 2008 · watercolour on paper · 56.5 × 75.5 cm (22 1/4 × 29 3/4 in.) · Photo: the artist

66B · Bill Richards · *Leaves and Branches*, 2011 · graphite on paper · 47 × 59.1 cm (18 1/2 × 23 1/4 in.) · Private collection · Courtesy Nancy Hoffman Gallery, New York

67 · Philip Taaffe · *Devonian Leaves II*, 2004 · mixed media on linen · 127 × 97.8 cm (50 × 38 1/2 in.) · Photo: Steven Sloman · Courtesy Gagosian Gallery

68–69 · Matts Leiderstam · *Paris, 15-03-1999 Returned, Parc des Buttes-Chaumont (Made After Nicolas Poussin's Spring or The Earthly Paradise, Rome 1660–1664)*, 2000–01 · slide projection on a freestanding wall, bench · dimensions variable · Installation view at Badischer Kunstverein, Karlsruhe, 2007 · Collection Moderna Museet, Stockholm · Photos: Torsten Hallscheidt · Courtesy of the artist

70A, 70B · Caroline McCarthy · *Floral Still Life*, 2007 · bin bags on canvas and MDF support, metal brackets · dimensions variable, image: 30 × 20 cm (11 3/4 × 7 7/8 in.) · Courtesy of the artist · Photo: Hana Vojackova

71 · Mark Flores · *Spring in Los Angeles (After Alma Tadema)*, 2009 · oil on canvas mounted on wood panel · 81.3 × 81.3 cm (32 × 32 in.) · Courtesy of the artist

72A, 72B · Rob Kesseler · *On closer inspection*, 2001 · bone china plate with magnifying lens and gold decal of pollen grain · Installation view with 19th-century porcelain modelled bird and flowers · Victoria and Albert Museum, London · Courtesy of the artist

73 · Aidan McNeill · *Australia, India, Japan, New Zealand, North and South America to GB*, 2010 · C-print · 20.3 × 25.4 cm (8 × 10 in.) · Courtesy of the artist and PayneShurvell, London

74A · Natasha Archdale · *FUCK*, 2011 · varnished fun and vintage paper · 61 × 28 cm (24 × 11 in.) · Courtesy of the artist and Alexander Fox

74BL · John Kaine · *DAFFODILS*, 2004 · aluminium, glass, Perspex (acrylic sheet) and automotive cellulose paint · 42 × 28 × 5.5 cm (16 1/2 × 11 × 2 1/4 in.)

74BR · John Kaine · *DEAD ROSES* · salt-rusted steel, blued steel, aluminium, glass and Perspex (acrylic sheet) · 43 × 33 × 9 cm (16 7/8 × 13 × 3 1/2 in.)

75 · Rob Smith · *Waterwheel*, 2002 · stone · Courtesy of the artist and MOCA London

76 · Martin Gustavsson · *Black Plums*, 2012 (detail) · oil on linen · 203 × 132 cm (79 7/8 × 52 in.) · Photo: Claire Lawrie · Courtesy of the artist and Maria Stenfors

80A · Christopher Williams · *Bergische Bauernscheune, Junkersholz, Leichlingen September 29th, 2009*, 2010 · archival pigment print · 83.5 × 94 cm (32 7/8 × 37 in.) in frame · Courtesy Galerie Gisela Capitain, Cologne

80B · Shirana Shahbazi · *[Stilleben-26-2008]* · C-print on aluminium · Courtesy Bob van Orsouw, Zurich

81 · Kraig Wilson · *Origin*, 2010 · C-print on pearlized paper · Photo: the artist · Courtesy of the artist and Platform A Gallery

82 · Cynthia Greig · *Nature Morte no · 3 (Gravitational Pull)*, 2009 · chromogenic print · 50.8 × 61 cm (20 × 24 in.) · © Cynthia Greig

83 · Lisa Milroy · *Food*, 1999 · oil paint on clay · © Lisa Milroy

84 · Klaus Pichler · *Strawberries: Sort: Strawberries 'Elsanta' · Place of production: San Giovanni Lupatoto, Verona, Italy · Transport distance: 741 km · Carbon footprint (total) per kg: 0,35 kg · Water requirement (total) per kg: 348 l · Price: 7,96 € / kg*, 2012 · digital C-print · 85 × 100 cm (33 1/2 × 39 3/8 in.) · edition of 5 + 2 AP · Courtesy of the artist

85A · Klaus Pichler · *Capsicum: Sort: Capsicum 'Kapya' red · Place of production: Souk El Khemis, Maroq · Transport distance: 3856 km · Carbon footprint (total) per kg: 0,92 kg · Water requirement (total) per kg: 384 l · Price: 3,98 € / kg*, 2012 · digital C-print · 85 × 100 cm (33 1/2 × 39 3/8 in.) · edition of 5 + 2 AP · Courtesy of the artist

85C · Klaus Pichler · *Lemons: Sort: Lemons 'Lapithkiotiki' · Place of production: Limassol, Cyprus · Transport distance: 2050 km · Carbon footprint (total) per kg: 0,72 kg · Water requirement (total) per kg: 448 l · Price: 1,99 € / kg*, 2012 · digital C-print · 85 × 100 cm (33 1/2 × 39 3/8 in.) · edition of 5 + 2 AP · Courtesy of the artist

85B · Klaus Pichler · *Tomatoes: Sort: Cuore di Bue · Place of production: Albenga, Italy · Transport distance: 1035 km · Carbon footprint (total) per kg: 0,31 kg · Water requirement (total) per kg: 215 l · Price: 0,89 € / kg*, 2012 · digital C-print · 85 × 100 cm (33 1/2 × 39 3/8 in.) · edition of 5 + 2 AP · Courtesy of the artist

86 · Daniel Gordon · *Pink Ladies and Pears*, 2012 · C-print · 76.2 × 101.6 cm (30 × 40 in.) · Courtesy of the artist and Wallspace, New York

87A · David Halliday · *Carrots, entwined*, 2007 · archival pigment print · 35.6 × 45.7 cm (14 × 18 in.) · Courtesy of the artist and Wessel O'Connor Fine Art

87B · David Halliday · *Sausage & Eggs*, 2007 · archival pigment print · 22.9 × 30.5 cm (9 × 12 in.) · Courtesy of the artist and Wessel O'Connor Fine Art

88L · Kate Joyce · *Effuse*, from the series *Aporia*, 2000 · archival pigment print on rag paper · Courtesy of the artist

88R · Kate Joyce · *Almost*, from the series *Aporia*, 2000 · archival pigment print · Courtesy of the artist

89A · Ged Quinn · *Myth of the Metals*, 2012 · oil on linen · 49.5 × 61 × 3.5 cm (19 1/2 × 24 × 1 3/8 in.) · Photo: Stephen White · Courtesy of the artist and Stephen Friedman Gallery, London · © Ged Quinn

89B · Ged Quinn · *Bunker Archeology*, 2012 · oil on canvas · 49.5 × 61 × 3.5cm (19 1/2 × 24 × 1 3/8 in.) · Photo: Stephen White · Courtesy of the artist and Stephen Friedman Gallery, London · © Ged Quinn

90 · Alan Salisbury · *Four Hundred Year Old bread Rolls with reference to works by Pieter Claesz (1597 to 1660)*, 2009 · oil on board · 90 × 73 cm (35 3/8 × 28 3/4 in.) in frame · Courtesy of the artist

91–94 · Jorge Diezma · *Bodegón del Limón*, 2010 · oil on linen · 850 × 180 cm (334 5/8 × 70 7/8 in.) · Courtesy of the artist

95 · Jefferson Hayman · *Martini*, 2006 · toned silver gelatin print, antique frame · print size: 25.4 × 20.3 cm (10 × 8 in.) · Courtesy of the artist and Wessel O'Connor Fine Art

96 · Laura Letinsky · *Untitled #28*, from the series *The Dog & The Wolf*, 2009 · C-print · 101.6 × 134.6 cm (40 × 53 in.) · Courtesy of the artist and Yancey Richardson Gallery · © Laura Letinsky

97 · Mat Collishaw · *Last Meal on Death Row, Texas. Martin Vegas*, 2011 · C-print · 64.8 × 47.5 cm (25 1/2 × 18 3/4 in.) · Courtesy of the artist

98 · Maciej Urbanek · *The Elders*, 2012 · archival giclée print · 70 × 100 cm (27 5/8 × 39 3/8 in.) · Courtesy of the artist

99A · Janice McNab · *The Bloodbathers*, 2011 · oil on linen · 135 × 180 cm (53 1/8 × 70 7/8 in.) · Courtesy of the artist and Ersatz, London

99B · Anne-Françoise Couloumy · *Réception*, 2010–11 · oil on canvas · 73 × 50 cm (28 3/4 × 19 5/8 in.) · Courtesy of the artist and Cynthia Corbett Gallery

100 · Alexander James, Distil Ennui Studio, *Vanitas, 'Multiply'*, 2010 · C-print mounted on polished aluminium · 120 × 90 cm (47 1/4 × 35 3/8 in.) · Courtesy of the artist

101 · McDermott & McGough · *Tory Fecundity, 1907*, 1988 · cyanotype · 25.5 × 20.5 cm (10 × 8 in.) · edition of 3 + 3 AP · © McDermott & McGough

102A · Ryan McLaughin · *Dinner Date (Brot)*, 2010 · oil on linen on board · 50 × 67 cm (19 5/8 × 26 3/8 in.) · Courtesy of the artist and Lüttgenmeijer

102B · Claudia Carr · ***Seraphim F***, 2010 · oil on canvas · 25.5 × 35.5 cm (10 × 14 in.) · Photo: Angelo Plantamura · Courtesy of the artist

103 · Caroline McCarthy · ***The Luncheon***, 2002 · C-type print: framed photograph of still life made from wet toilet paper, disposable tableware, real stalks, chicken bones, black bin bags and plastic flies · 183 × 122 cm (72 × 48 in.) · Courtesy of the artist

104 · Pádraig Timoney · ***Imagine this pumpkin is a superhuge concrete boat that has crashed into a small volcanic island in the bay of Naples, knocking the top off it and causing an eruption***, 2005 · oil on canvas · 70 × 90 cm (27 5/8 × 35 3/8 in.) · Nerio and Marina Fossati Collection, Italy · Photo: P. Di Stasio · Courtesy Galleria Raucci/Santamaria, Naples

105A · Craig Wylie · ***Blue***, 2010 · oil on canvas · 70 × 66 cm (24 × 26 in.) · Courtesy of the artist and Jonathan Cooper Park Walk Gallery

105B · Maryam Amiryani · ***Fish***, 2010 · oil on linen · 8.75 × 11.75 cm (3 1/2 × 4 5/8 in.) · Courtesy of the artist and Jonathan Cooper Park Walk Gallery

106A · Andro Semeiko · ***Very Big Chocolate Cake***, 2006 · acrylic on canvas · 152 × 152 cm (59 7/8 × 59 7/8 in.) · Courtesy of the artist

106B · Andro Semeiko · ***Very Big Toffee Popcorn***, 2005 · acrylic and oil on canvas · 152 × 152 cm (59 7/8 × 59 7/8 in.) · Courtesy of the artist

107 · Christopher Williams · ***RITTERSPORT Von oben nach unten/ from the top to the bottom 100 g Tafeln / 100 g Bars Offizieller Produktname / Official Product Name / EAN Code Bar / UPC Code for Case / Bars per Case Voll Nuss / Whole Hazelnuts / 4000417019004 / 050255013005 / 10 Joghurt / Yogurt / 40004170270 09 / 050255027000 / 12 Voll Erdnuss / 4000417262202 / 10 Weisse Voll Nuss / White Whole Hazelnuts / 4000417013002 / 050255013003 / ... / 10 Marzipan / Marzipan / 4000417025005 / 050255025006 / 12 Cappuccino / Cappuccino/ 4000417230003 / 0550255230042 / 12 Fotostudio Axel Gnad, Düsseldorf, October 24th, 2008 [No · 1]***, 2009 · archival pigment print · 85.2 × 94 cm (33 1/2 × 37 in.) in frame · Courtesy Galerie Gisela Capitain, Cologne

108 · Wilhelm Sasnal · ***Food***, 2008 · oil on canvas · 160 × 120 cm (63 × 47 1/4 in.) · Courtesy Sadie Coles HQ, London · © Wilhelm Sasnal

109 · Michael Hilsman · ***Still Life with Thumb***, 2011 · oil and acrylic on canvas · 91.4 × 91.4 cm (36 × 36 in.) · Courtesy of the artist

110L, 110R · Annie Attridge · ***Chocolate Chip Flirt***, 2012 · porcelain, enamel and tin glaze, 40 × 20 × 40 cm (15 3/4 × 7 7/8 × 15 3/4 in.) · Courtesy of the artist and Asya Geisberg Gallery

111 · Michael Raedecker · ***wrong***, 2009 · acrylic and thread on canvas · 138 × 110 cm (54 3/8 × 43 1/4 in.) · Photo: Peter White · Courtesy of the artist and Galerie Max Hetzler, Berlin

112 · Victoria Reynolds · ***Reindeer Voluptuary***, 2008 · oil on panel and frame · 111.8 × 81.3 cm (44 × 32 in.) in frame · Collection of Alita and Richard Rogers · Photo: Brian Forrest

113 · Rigoberto A Gonzalez · ***Cabrito Degollado (Goat Head)***, 2008 · oil on linen · 40.6 × 30.5 cm (16 × 12 in.) · Courtesy of the artist

114A · Rebecca Scott · ***Red in Tooth and Claw***, 2008 · oil on canvas · 102 × 127 cm (40 1/8 × 50 in.) · Courtesy of the artist

114B · Cindy Wright · ***Baconsquare***, 2008 · oil on canvas · 210.1 × 214.9 cm (82 3/4 × 84 5/8 in.) · Frederick R. Weisman Art Foundation · Courtesy of the artist

115 · Cindy Wright · ***Nature Morte 2***, 2010 · oil on linen · 139.7 × 139.7 cm (55 × 55 in.) · Private collection · Courtesy of the artist

116 · Paul McDevitt · ***We Must Heap Up a Great Pile of Doing, for a Small Diameter of Being***, 2008 · acrylic, gouache, colour pencil, ink and beer mats on canvas · 50 × 40 cm (19 3/4 × 15 3/4 in.) · Courtesy of the artist and Stephen Friedman Gallery

117 · Simon English · ***Forbidden Fruit***, 2008 · crayon, ink, acrylic, gouache and oil on paper · 152 × 112 cm (59 7/8 × 44 1/8 in.) · The Falckenberg Collection, Hamburg · Photo: Hugo Glendinning

118 · Julie Heffernan · ***Self Portrait as Root III***, 2006 · oil on canvas · 152.4 × 167.6 cm (60 × 66 in.) · Courtesy of the artist and PPOW Gallery, New York

119 · Thomas Woodruff · ***(Still Life Variation) Sanguinic***, 2009–10 · acrylic on linen · 152.4 × 121.9 cm (60 × 48 in.) · Courtesy of the artist and PPOW Gallery, New York

120A · Hans-Peter Feldmann · ***One Pound Strawberries*** · 34 photographs · 10.2 × 10.2 cm (4 × 4 in.) each · Courtesy of the artist and 303 Gallery, New York

120B · Andrew Guenther · ***Hotdogs***, 2011 · acrylic on unprimed canvas · 121.9 × 76.2 cm (48 × 30 in.) · Courtesy of the artist

121 · Anja Priska · ***Dance, Dance, Dance***, 2009 · oil on canvas · 190 × 160 cm (74 3/4 × 63 in.) · Photo: the artist

122 · Anya Gallaccio · ***Tense***, 1990 · 1 ton of oranges and silkscreen on paper · dimensions variable · Installation at the 'East Country Yard Show', Surrey Docks, London · Courtesy of the artist and Lehmann Maupin, New York and Hong Kong

123 · Peter Coffin · ***Untitled (Orange Pyramid)***, 2007 · table and oranges · 137.2 × 109.2 × 109.2 cm (54 × 43 × 43 in.) · Courtesy Herald St, London

124 · Robert Gober · ***Untitled***, 2005 · beeswax and human hair · 14 × 52 × 16 cm (5 5/8 × 20 5/8 × 6 3/8 in.) with hair fully extended · Courtesy Matthew Marks Gallery · © Robert Gober

125A · Robert Gober · ***Bag of Donuts***, 1989 · acid free hand-cut paper, graphite dough and synthetic resin · 28 × 16.5 × 15.2 cm (11 × 6 1/2 × 6 in.) · Courtesy Matthew Marks Gallery · © Robert Gober

125B · Yuken Teruya · ***Scarlet Birds, Crimson Sky (Bingata pattern)***, 2010 · KFC package (S) · 15.2 × 22.8 × 10.2 cm (6 × 9 × 4 in.) · Photo: Gene Ogami · Courtesy of the artist and Shoshana Wayne Gallery

126A · Kris Martin · ***Plate with milk***, 2005 · plate and milk · diameter: 16.5 cm (6 1/2 in.) · Courtesy Sies + Höke, Düsseldorf

126B · Renata Hegyi · ***Bottle and Shade***, from the series ***Waiting for time to pass by***, 2003 · gelatin silver print · 22 × 34 cm (8 5/8 × 13 3/8 in.) (M), 11 × 17 cm (4 3/8 × 6 3/4 in.) (S) · Courtesy of the artist

127 · Peter Abrahams · ***Milk and Earth***, 2009 · archival pigment print · 98 × 77 cm (38 5/8 × 30 1/4 in) · Courtesy of the artist

128 · Saara Ekström · still from the installation ***Grotesque & Arabesque (milk) I***, 2005 · MiniDV transferred on DVD · duration: 7 minutes 23 seconds · Courtesy of the artist and Helsinki Contemporary

129A, 129C · Saara Ekström · ***Domestic Nature Morte***, 2004 · digital camera stop-frame animation transferred on DVD · duration: loop · size variable · Nordic Watercolour Museum, Sweden · Photo: Thom Vink · Courtesy of the artist and Helsinki Contemporary

129B · Saara Ekström · ***Carnation***, 1997 · digital print · 104 × 128 cm (41 × 50 3/8 in.) · Courtesy of the artist and Helsinki Contemporary

130 · Saara Ekström · ***A Single Charm is Doubtful (liquids)***, 2010 (detail) · C-print · 85 × 104 cm (33 1/2 × 41 in.) · Courtesy of the artist and Helsinki Contemporary

134L · John Currin · ***Monroeville***, 2008 · oil on canvas · 121.9 × 86.4 × 3.5 cm (48 × 34 × 1 in.) · Courtesy Sadie Coles HQ, London · © John Currin

134R · John Currin · ***Urn***, 2003 · oil on canvas · 22.9 × 30.5 cm (9 × 12 in.) · Courtesy Sadie Coles HQ, London · © John Currin

135 · Charles LeDray · ***Milk and Honey***, 1994–96 · 2,000 porcelain objects, glass and wood · 195.6 × 76.2 × 76.2 cm (77 × 30 × 30 in.) · Whitney Museum of American Art, New York, purchase with funds from the Contemporary Painting and Sculpture Committee · Courtesy Sperone Westwater, New York

136 · Jane Telford · ***Porcelain Black***, 2012 · acrylic on canvas · 61 × 45.5 cm (24 × 17 7/8 in.) · Courtesy of the artist

137 · Clare Twomey · ***Monument***, 2009 · ceramic waste · dimensions variable · Photo: Dan Prince · Courtesy of the artist

138A · James White · ***Burger Box***, 2010 · oil and varnish on birch-ply in Perspex box frame · 100 × 120 cm (39 3/8 × 47 1/4 in.) · Courtesy Max Wigram Gallery, London · © James White

138B · James White · ***Afri Cola***, 2007 · oil and varnish on birch-ply in Perspex box frame · 45 × 60 cm (17 3/4 × 23 5/8 in.) · Courtesy Gerhardsen Gerner, Berlin · © James White

139 · Peter Abrahams · ***Illuminations; Coiled***, 2007 · archival pigment print · 77 × 98 cm (30 1/4 × 38 5/8 in) · Courtesy of the artist

140L · Adam Fuss · ***Untitled***, 2008 · daguerreotype · 35.6 × 27.9 cm (14 × 11 in.) · Courtesy Cheim & Read, New York

140R · John Dugdale · ***Petals***, 1998 · cyanotype · 35.6 × 27.9 cm (14 × 11 in.) · Courtesy of the artist and Wessel O'Connor Fine Art

141 · McDermott & McGough · ***18th-Century Salon as Reflected in a 19th-Century Vase, 1907***, 1988 · cyanotype · 25.4 × 20.3 cm (10 × 8 in.) · edition of 3 + 3 AP · © McDermott & McGough

142A, 142B · Tony Charles · ***Still Life Unpainted***, 2012 · steel and aluminium · dimensions variable · Photo: Cal Carey · Courtesy of the artist and Platform A Gallery

143AL · Jane Simpson · ***Baroque Bouquet***, 2006 · platinum-based silicone and Perspex · Courtesy of the artist and MOCA London

143AR · Lisa Milroy · ***Four Vases***, 2006 · oil on canvas · 203.2 × 165 cm (80 × 65 in.) · Courtesy Alan Cristea Gallery · © Lisa Milroy

143B · Jane Simpson · ***Radioactive Tupperware (revisited)***, 2012 · archival digital giclée print · 20 × 30 cm (7 7/8 × 11 3/4 in.) · Courtesy of the artist

144L · Peter Coffin · ***Untitled (Champagne Pyramid)***, 2010 · table on wheels with motor, champagne glasses · 198 × 101.6 × 101.6 cm (78 × 40 × 40 in.) · Courtesy Herald St, London

144R · Renata Hegyi · ***For Cherries***, 2003 · gelatin silver print · 80 × 116 cm (31 1/2 × 45 5/8 in.) (L), 43 × 54 cm (16 7/8 × 21 1/4 in.) (M), 25 × 31 cm (9 7/8 × 12 1/4 in.) (S) · Collection of Ernst & Young · Courtesy of the artist

145 · Matthew Darbyshire · ***Untitled: Shelves No. 8***, 2011 · various glass and plastic components, shelving units and Perspex cases · 140 × 110 × 30 cm (55 1/8 × 43 1/4 × 11 3/4 in.) · Photo: Andy Keate · Courtesy Herald St, London

146L · Wilhelm Sasnal · ***Untitled***, 2011 · oil on canvas · 200 × 160.2 × 2.5 cm (78 ¾ × 63 × 1 in.) · Courtesy Sadie Coles HQ, London · © Wilhelm Sasnal

146R · Darren Jones · ***A Time and a Place***, 2011 · various elements · dimensions variable · Courtesy of the artist

147 · Michael Craig-Martin · ***Eye of the Storm***, 2002 · acrylic on canvas · 335.3 × 279.4 cm (132 × 110 in.) · Courtesy Gagosian Gallery · © Michael Craig-Martin

148L · Jefferson Hayman · ***My Jacket***, 2010 · platinum print and artist-made frame · print size: 30.5 × 20.3 cm (12 × 8 in.) · Courtesy of the artist and Wessel O'Connor Fine Art

148R · Charles LeDray · ***Becoming/ FIGHT***, 1992 · flannel, thread, silk and cotton · 54.6 × 15.2 × 8.9 cm (21 1/2 × 6 × 3 1/2 in.) · Private collection · Courtesy Sperone Westwater, New York

149L · Colin Smith · ***Overcoat 1***, 2005 · oil on canvas · 218 × 122 cm (85 7/8 × 48 in.) · Private collection, Stockholm · Courtesy of the artist

149AR · Andro Semeiko · ***Black Shoe***, 2005 · acrylic on canvas · 62 × 62 cm (24 3/8 × 24 3/8 in.) · Courtesy of the artist

149BR · Jan Merta · ***Ambiciózní fuga / Ambitious Fugue***, 2008–9 · oil on canvas · 260 × 230 cm (102 3/8 × 90 1/2 in.) · Photo: Martin Polák · Courtesy of the artist and Galerie Martin Janda, Vienna · © Jan Merta

150L · Daniel Gustav Cramer · ***Untitled (Eusebius – Jerome)***, 2009 · C-print · 71 × 61 cm (28 × 24 in.) · Courtesy of the artist and BolteLang Gallery, Zurich

150R · Jan Merta · ***Solidarita (Polovina sebraných spisů J. W. Goetha) / Solidarity (Half of the Collected Writings of J. W. Goethe)***, 2008–9 · oil on canvas · 145.5 × 125 cm (57 1/4 × 49 1/4 in.) · Courtesy of the artist and Johnen Galerie, Berlin · Photo: Martin Polák · © Jan Merta

151L · Susan Seubert · ***Pocket Watch***, 2011 · ambrotype · 12.7 × 10.2 cm (5 × 4 in.) · Courtesy of the artist and Froelick Gallery

151R · Jefferson Hayman · ***Pocket Watch***, 2007 · toned silver gelatin print, artist-made frame · print size: 30.5 × 20.3 cm (12 × 8 in.) · Courtesy of the artist and Wessel O'Connor Fine Art

152A · Ugo Rondinone · ***still.life · (cardboard leaning on the wall)***, 2009 · bronze cast, lead and paint · 110 × 117.5 cm (43 × 46 in.) · edition 1 of 1 + 1 AP · Courtesy Sadie Coles HQ, London · © Ugo Rondinone

152B · Bill Jacobson · ***Place (Series) #58***, 2009 · pigment print · 71 × 56 cm (28 × 22 in.) · Courtesy of the artist

153 · Bruno Pacheco · ***Folding Box***, 2010 · oil on canvas · 70 × 90 cm (27 5/8 × 35 3/8 in.) · Photo: Andy Keate · Courtesy of the artist and Hollybush Gardens

154L · Aziz + Cucher · ***Plasmorphica Still-Life #7***, 1996 · C-print · 101.6 × 76.2 cm (40 × 30 in.) · Courtesy of the artists

154R · Aziz + Cucher · ***Plasmorphica Still-Life #2***, 1996 · C-print · 101.6 × 76.2 cm (40 × 30 in.) · Courtesy of the artists

155 · Shirana Shahbazi · ***[Komposition-01-2011]*** · C-print on aluminium · Courtesy Bob van Orsouw, Zurich

156 · John Dugdale · ***Empire Chair in the Gloaming***, 1994 · cyanotype · 20.3 × 25.4 cm (8 × 10 in.) · Courtesy of the artist and Wessel O'Connor Fine Art

157L · Renata Hegyi · ***Dialog***, 2003 · gelatin silver print · 86 × 106 cm (33 7/8 × 41 3/4 in.) (L), 43 × 54 cm (16 7/8 × 21 1/4 in.) (M), 25 × 31 cm (9 7/8 × 12 1/4 in.) (S) · Courtesy of the artist

157R · Michael Raedecker · ***frame***, 2008 · acrylic and thread on canvas · 148 × 124 cm (58 1/4 × 48 7/8 in.) · Photo: Peter White · Courtesy of the artist and Hauser & Wirth, Zurich/London

158A · **Derek Buckner** · ***Assemblage #2***, 2010 · oil on linen · 111.8 × 152.4 cm (44 × 60 in.) · Courtesy of the artist

158B · **Jan Merta** · ***Zátiší s nožem (Hranice spasitelnosti) / Still-Life with a Knife (The Limits of Salvationability)***, 2009 · oil on canvas · 151 × 116 cm (59 1/2 × 45 5/8 in.) · Photo: Martin Polák · Courtesy of the artist and Johnen Galerie, Berlin · © Jan Merta

159AL · **Rebecca Scott** · ***Oh, it's a perfect day***, 2005 · oil on canvas · 76 × 76 cm (29 7/8 × 29 7/8 in.) · Private collection

159AR · **Rebecca Scott** · ***The Perfect Hostess***, 2006 · oil on canvas · 188 × 151 cm (74 × 59 1/2 in.) · Courtesy of the artist

159B · **Rebecca Scott** · ***The Perfect Christmas Dinner***, 2006 · oil on canvas · 76 × 102 cm (29 7/8 × 40 1/8 in.) · Private collection

160L · **Janne Malmros** · ***Unfold***, 2007 · floral pattern on an English oak footstool, cut out in one piece and arranged on the wall · 35 × 70 × 120 cm (13 3/4 × 27 5/8 × 47 1/4 in.) · Courtesy of the artist

160–61 · **Peter Coffin** · ***Untitled (Free Jazz Mobile)***, 2007 · mobile structure and musical instruments · dimensions variable · Courtesy Herald St, London

162A, 162B · **Darren Jones** · ***Reservation***, 2007 · muslin, table settings and wine · 2.44 × 2.44 × 4.27 m (8 × 8 × 14 ft) · Courtesy of the artist

163 · **Conrad Bakker** · ***Untitled Project: LAWNCHAIR (Walden)***, 2010 · oil on carved wood · 87.6 × 61.3 × 69.9 cm (34 1/2 × 24 1/8 × 27 1/2 in.) · Courtesy of the artist and Lora Reynolds Gallery

164 · **Livia Marin** · from the series ***Broken Things***, 2011 · crockery, plaster, varnish, transfer-print, approx. 6 × 13 × 17 cm (2 3/8 × 5 1/8 × 6 3/4 in.) · Photo: Livia Marin · Courtesy of the artist

165A · **Stephanie Syjuco** · ***Blue Selection*** from 'Raiders: International Booty, Bountiful Harvest (Selections from the A____ A__ M______)', 2011 · 13 vessels, archival Epson photo prints mounted on laser-cut wood, hardware and crates · approx. 61 × 109.2 × 73.7 cm (24 × 43 × 29 in.) each · editions of 3 · Courtesy of the artist and Catharine Clark Gallery, San Francisco

165B · **Stephanie Syjuco** · 'Raiders: International Booty, Bountiful Harvest (Selections from the A____ A__ M_____)', 2011 (installation view) · archival Epson photo prints mounted on laser-cut wood, hardware and crates · dimensions variable · editions of 3 · Courtesy of the artist and Catharine Clark Gallery, San Francisco

166A · **Jan De Vliegher** · installation view of 'Treasury', New York, 2012 · Courtesy Mike Weiss Gallery

166B · **Jan De Vliegher** · ***Sèvres, White Flower***, 2012 · oil on canvas · 200.7 × 200.7 cm (79 × 79 in.) · Courtesy Mike Weiss Gallery

167 · **Ai Weiwei** · ***Coloured Vases***, 2010 · 31 Han Dynasty vessels and industrial paint · dimensions variable · Courtesy of the artist and Lisson Gallery

168 · **Elad Lassry** · ***Collie, Poodle***, 2011 · C-print, painted frame · 29 × 36.5 × 4 cm (11 1/2 × 14 1/2 × 1 1/2 in.) · Photo: Fredrik Nilsen · Courtesy White Cube, London, and David Kordansky Gallery, Los Angeles

169A · **Barnaby Barford** · ***Do it again, I didn't press record***, 2009 · porcelain, ceramic, enamel paint, wood and other media · 25 × 100 × 40 cm (9 7/8 × 39 3/8 × 15 3/4 in.) · Photo: Noah Da Costa

169B · **Matt Smith** · ***Looking for a Chicken Hawk***, 2010 · cast earthenware, underglaze and decals · 22 × 24 × 16 cm (8 5/8 × 9 1/2 × 6 1/4 in.) · Photo: David Rowan · © Birmingham Museum and Art Gallery

170L · **John Mitchell** · ***Dawn Chorus***, 2009 · ceramic and china birds, garden decking and audio birdsong · 1.83 × 0.91 m (6 × 3 ft) · Photo: Peter Anderson

170R · **Patrick Jackson** · ***Tchotchke Stack 17***, 2010 · tchotchkes, glass, mirrors, wood and coins · 142.2 × 50.8 × 50.8 cm (56 × 20 × 20 in.) · Photo: Chris Burke Studios · Courtesy Nicole Klagsbrun, and Courtney and Karen Lord

171L · **Paul Wood** · ***Domestic Slump I***, 2005 · refired found ceramic objects · 80 × 30 × 30 cm (31 1/2 × 11 3/4 × 11 3/4 in.) · Photo: Siri Hayes · Courtesy of the artist

171R · **Joan Bankemper** · ***Suzanna's Garden of Earthly Delights***, 2009/10 · ceramic and mixed media · 101.6 × 55.9 × 47 cm (40 × 22 × 18 1/2 in.) · Courtesy Nancy Hoffman Gallery, New York

172L · **Richard Stone** · ***narcissus and the ground***, 2011 · antique spelter, wood and wax · 38.1 × 12.7 × 10.2 cm (15 × 5 × 4 in.) · Photo: Original&theCopy · Courtesy of the artist

172R · **Richard Stone** · ***the day will come***, 2011 · antique parian porcelain and wax · 30.5 × 12.7 × 10.2 cm (12 × 5 × 4 in.) · Photo: Original&theCopy · Courtesy of the artist

173 · **David Edmond** · ***The Collector***, 2011 · oil on canvas · 40 × 50 cm (15 3/4 × 19 5/8 in.) · Photo: Jefferson Smith

174 · **Theodora Allen** · ***A Song For You***, 2011 · oil on canvas · 61 × 61 cm (24 × 24 in.) · Courtesy of the artist

175 · **Ernst Billgren** · ***Mermaid's View***, 2011 · 5 glass frames, objects in glass, wood · flat frames: 57 × 51 × 3 cm (22 1/2 × 20 1/8 × 1 1/8 in.), 3D frames: 57 × 51 × 110 cm (22 1/2 × 20 1/8 × 43 1/4 in.) · Photo: Francesco Allegretto · Courtesy Venice Projects / Berengo Private Collection, Venice

176 · **Cindy Wright** · ***Poisonous wave***, 2007 (detail) · oil on canvas · 180.3 × 218.4 cm (71 × 86 in.) · Frederick R. Weisman Art Foundation

180–81 · **Gabriel Orozco** · ***Dark Wave***, 2006 · calcium carbonate and resin with graphite · 304 × 392 × 1,375 cm (119 6/8 × 154 3/8 × 541 3/8 in.) · Photo: Stephen White · Courtesy White Cube

182 · **Andrew Guenther** · ***Sick Whale***, 2011 · acrylic on unprimed canvas · 304.8 × 198.1 cm (120 × 78 in.) · Photo: Adam Reich · Courtesy of the artist

183A · **Elaine Bradford** · ***Pushmi-Pullyu (Tragus januali)***, 2009 · taxidermy aoudad sheep, crocheted yarn and mixed media · Photo: Elaine Bradford · Courtesy of the artist and Art Palace Gallery

183B · **Miho Sato** · ***Monster***, 2007 · acrylic on board · 45.5 × 55.5 cm (17 7/8 × 21 7/8 in.) · Photo: Andy Keate · Courtesy Domobaal

184 · **Javier Pérez** · ***Carroña***, 2011 · Murano glass chandelier and stuffed crows · 120 × 235 × 300 cm (47 1/4 × 92 1/2 × 118 1/8 in.) / dimensions variable · Photo: Francesco Allegretto · Courtesy Venice Projects / Berengo Private Collection, Venice

185 · **Marta Klonowska** · ***Large Kitchen Still Life after Michel de Bouillon***, 2009 · glass and metal · 94 × 58 × 44 cm (37 × 22 7/8 × 17 3/8 in.) · Photo: Eric Tschernow · Courtesy of the artist and lorch+seidel contemporary, Berlin

186 · **Sam Taylor-Johnson** · ***A Little Death***, 2002 · 35 mm film/DVD · duration: 4 minutes · Courtesy White Cube · © Sam Taylor-Johnson

187 · **Shirana Shahbazi** · ***[Voegel-02-2007]*** · C-print on aluminium · Courtesy Bob van Orsouw, Zurich

188A · **Ben Reid** · ***tumu***, 2010 · drypoint, intaglio and relief print · 20 × 25 cm (7 7/8 × 9 7/8 in.) · Photo: Olivia Reid of Pulse Photography · Courtesy of the artist

188B · **Ben Reid** · ***Tibbles***, 2008 · drypoint, relief and woodblock print · 35.5 × 42 cm (13 × 16 1/2 in.) · Photo: Olivia Reid of Pulse Photography · Courtesy of the artist

189 · **Susan Silas** · ***eyes wide shut***, 2010, from ***found birds, 2000 – the present*** · giclée print on Hahnemühle photo rag · 68.6 × 43.2 cm (27 × 17 in.) · image 1 of 24 · Courtesy of the artist

190 · **Elmgreen & Dragset** · ***Somewhere in the World it's 4 o'clock – Blocking the view – Just a Single Wrong Move***, 2004 · animatronic twitching sparrow · display dimensions variable · Installation view of 'This is the First Day of my Life', Malmö Konsthall, 2007 · Photo: Andreas Sune Berg · Courtesy of the artists

191A · **Taryn Simon** · ***Contraband*** · installation image · Gagosian Gallery 2010 · © Taryn Simon · Courtesy Gagosian Gallery · Photography by the Douglas Parker Studio

191B · **Taryn Simon** · ***Bird corpse, labeled as home décor, Indonesia to Miami, Florida (prohibited)*** [detail], 2010 · 1 of 15 archival inkjet prints in 6 Plexiglas boxes · © Taryn Simon · Courtesy Gagosian Gallery

192A · **Polly Morgan** · ***Feed Me***, 2010 · taxidermy, steel, metal vase, clay and glass · Courtesy of the artist

192B · **Cindy Wright** · ***Koolmeesje***, 2010 · oil on linen · 55 × 83.8 cm (21 1/2 × 33 in.) · Tomio Koyama Collection

193A, 193B · **Daniel Gustav Cramer** · ***Cat***, 2002/11 · 2 C-prints, 1 framed text · Courtesy of the artist and BolteLang, Zurich

194–95 · **Cai Guo-Qiang** · ***Head On***, 2006 · 99 life-sized replicas of wolves (gauze, resin and painted hide) and glass wall · dimensions variable · Deutsche Bank collection, commissioned by Deutsche Bank AG · Photo: Erika Barahona-Ede · © FMGBGuggenheim Bilbao Museoa, 2009

196A · **Nancy Fouts** · ***Rabbit with Curlers***, 2010 · taxidermy rabbit, curlers and kirby grips · 10 × 15 cm (3 7/8 × 5 7/8 in.) · Courtesy of the artist and Pertwee, Anderson & Gold Gallery

196B · **Sherrie Levine** · ***Bobcat Skull***, 2010 · cast bronze · 12.7 × 8.89 × 7.62 cm (5 × 3 1/2 × 3 in.) · edition of 12 · Courtesy of Simon Lee Gallery, London/Hong Kong · © Sherrie Levine

197A · **Klaus Pichler** · ***Plastic Deers***, 2010 · digital C-print · 55 × 70 cm (21 5/8 × 27 5/8 in.) / 80 × 100 cm (31 1/2 × 39 3/8 in.) · edition of 5 + 2AP · Courtesy of the artist

197B · **Matt Smith** · ***Otters and Bears***, 2010 · taxidermy otter and salt-glazed ceramic bears · dimensions variable · Photo: David Rowan · © Birmingham Museum and Art Gallery

198 · **Elmgreen & Dragset** · ***Ganymede (Jockstrap)***, 2009 · laserchrome colour print mounted on aluminium with Plexiglas · 150 × 200 cm (59 × 78 3/4 in.) · Photo: Anders Sune Berg · Courtesy Galleri Nicolai Wallner and the artists · Exhibited at: Art Basel 2009; 'Elmgreen & Dragset', Thorvaldsens Museum, Copenhagen, 2011

199A · **Jan Kjetil Bjørheim** · ***Still Life, Nocturn- Owl in Pine***, 2007 · C-print · 42 × 59 cm (16 1/2 × 23 1/4 in.) · edition of 5 · Courtesy of the artist

199B · **Alana Lake** · ***The Closer you are the Further you Become, ii (creepy)***, 2010 · archival digital print · 30 × 45 cm (11 3/4 × 17 3/4 in.) · edition of 3 + AP · Courtesy of the artist

200A · **Maurizio Bongiovanni** · ***Bird rib, (yellow bird)***, 2011 · oil on canvas · 50 × 50 cm (19 5/8 × 19 5/8 in.) · Private collection

200B · **Maurizio Bongiovanni** · ***Bird rib, (blue bird)***, 2010 · oil on canvas · 60 × 60 cm (23 5/8 × 23 5/8 in.) · Courtesy Galleria Studio d'Arte Cannaviello, Milan

201A · **Shane Mecklenburger** · ***Treasure in Palestine***, 2011 · archival photographic print · 32 × 21 cm (12 5/8 × 8 1/4 in.) · Courtesy of the artist

201CL, 201CR · **Shane Mecklenburger** · ***Roadkill Diamond***, 2012 · diamond made from armadillo remains and glass · 30.5 × 30.5 × 15.2 cm (12 × 12 × 6 in.) · Photos: Kevin Todora · Courtesy of the artist

201B · **Shane Mecklenburger** · laser inscription on ***Roadkill Diamond***, 2012 (detail) · Courtesy of the artist

202 · **Brion Nuda Rosch** · ***Warrah or Antarctic Wolf Dusicyon australis***, 2011 · acrylic on found book page · 28 × 23 cm (11 × 9 in.) · Courtesy of the artist and Eli Ridgway Gallery, San Francisco

203L · **Karl de Vroomen** · ***Falling fox***, 2011 · oil on canvas · 122 × 122 cm (48 × 48 in.) · Courtesy of the artist

203R · **Peter Vos** · ***Untitled (canis)***, 2008 · oil on canvas · 58 × 48 cm (22 7/8 × 18 7/8 in.) · Courtesy of the artist and Gerhard Hofland, Amsterdam

204 · **Ben Reid** · ***the eileen greenwood memorial trophy***, 2010 · drypoint, relief and woodblock print · 66 × 48 cm (26 × 18 7/8 in.) · Photo: by Olivia Reid of Pulse Photography · Courtesy of the artist

205 · **George Boorujy** · ***Fugue***, 2010 · ink on paper · 96.5 × 127 cm (38 × 50 in.) · Courtesy PPOW Gallery

206 · **Madeleine Farley** · ***Tiya***, 2010 · silkscreen print on canvas with diamond dust · 88 × 100 cm (34 5/8 × 39 3/8 in.) · Courtesy of the artist and Maddox Arts Gallery

207 · **Peter Jones** · ***Ollie Monkey***, 2007 · oil on linen · 30.5 × 25.5 cm (12 × 10 in.) · Courtesy of the artist

208 · **Daniel Firman** · ***Würsa (à 18 000 km de la Terre)***, 2006–8 · taxidermy, fibreglass and polyester resin · 5.7 × 1.4 × 2.5 m (18 ft 8 in. × 55 in. × 8 ft 2 in.) · View of the exhibition 'Château de Tokyo / Palais de Fontainebleau' at the Château de Fontainebleau, France, 2008 · Collection Vranken-Pommery Monopole · Photo: André Morin · Courtesy Galerie Perrotin, Hong Kong & Paris

209 · **Bharti Kher** · ***The Skin Speaks a Language Not Its Own***, 2006 · bindis on fibreglass · 142 × 456.2 × 195 cm (55 7/8 × 179 5/8 × 76 3/4 in.) · Private collection · Photo: Bartholomew/ Netphotograph.com · © Bharti Kher

210A · **Peter Jones** · ***Lamb***, 2009 · oil on linen · 35.5 × 40.5 cm (14 × 16 in.) · Courtesy of the artist

210BL · **Filippa Barkman** · ***Disagreement***, 2008 · colour pencil on paper · 50 × 70 cm (19 5/8 × 27 5/8 in.) · Courtesy of the artist

210BR · **Filippa Barkman** · ***Still***, 2008 · colour pencil on paper · 50 × 77 cm (19 5/8 × 30 1/4 in.) · Courtesy of the artist

211 · **Tolly Nason** · ***Large Cactus Finch Geospiza conirostris***, 2009 · kiln cast glass · 38 × 30 × 23 cm (15 × 11 3/4 × 9 in.) · Photo: the artist

212 · **Joana Vasconcelos** · ***Giallina***, 2008 · Rafael Bordalo Pinheiro faience painted with ceramic glaze, handmade cotton crochet · 14 × 50 × 67 cm (5 1/2 × 19 5/8 × 26 3/8 in.) · Courtesy Galerie Nathalie Obadia, Paris/Brussels · Photo: DMF, Lisbon / Courtesy Atelier Joana Vasconcelos

213 · **Joana Vasconcelos** · ***Capote***, 2009 · Rafael Bordalo Pinheiro acrylic-painted faience, bobbin lace and handmade cotton crochet · 65 × 54 × 61 cm (25 5/8 × 21 1/4 × 24 in.) · Courtesy Galería Horrach Moyà, Palma de Mallorca · Photo: DMF, Lisbon / ©Unidade Infinita Projectos

214A · **Paul Housley** · ***Velazquez***, 2010 · oil on paper · 55 × 45 cm (21 5/8 × 17 3/4 in.) · Courtesy of the artist and Poppy Sebire

214B · **Wim Delvoye** · ***Sylvie***, 2006 · stuffed tattooed pig · 67 × 140 × 30 cm (26 1/2 × 55 1/4 × 11 3/4 in.) · Courtesy Galerie Perrotin, Hong Kong & Paris · © Studio Wim Delvoye, Belgium

215 · Paola Pivi · ***Don't disturb me***, 2007 · photographic print, aluminium, glass and frame · 140 × 187.6 cm (55 1/4 × 73 7/8 in.) · Photo: Hugo Glendinning · Courtesy Galerie Perrotin, Hong Kong & Paris

216AL, 216AR, 216CL, 216CR, 216BL · Pradeep L. Mishra · paintings from 'lovetolive', 2010 · oil on canvas · 61 × 61 cm (24 × 24 in.) each · Courtesy of the artist and Palette Art Gallery

216BR · Pradeep L. Mishra · painting from 'lovetolive', 2010 · oil on paper, 61 × 61 cm (24 × 24 in.) · Courtesy of the artist and Palette Art Gallery

217 · James Hart Dyke · ***Toy Duck***, 2010 · oil on canvas · 45 × 45 cm (17 3/4 × 17 3/4 in.) · Private collection · Courtesy of the artist

218A · Sarah Lucas · ***Cock***, 2005 · metal cockerel, cigarettes and glue · 60 × 47 × 20 cm (23 5/8 × 18 1/2 × 7 7/8 in.) · Courtesy Sadie Coles HQ, London · © Sarah Lucas

218B · Sarah Lucas · ***Coco***, 2005 · china cast dog, cigarettes and glue · 28 × 18 × 24 cm (11 × 7 1/8 × 9 1/2 in.) · Courtesy Sadie Coles HQ, London · © Sarah Lucas

219 · Edward Kay · ***Illustration from 'A Child's Guide to Rejection'***, 2005 · oil on canvas laid on panel · 37 × 53 cm (14 5/8 × 20 7/8 in.) · Photo: MOCA London

220 · Kris Martin · ***Bee***, 2009 · solid gold · 1 × 1 × 1.5 cm (1/2 × 1/2 × 2/3 in.) · edition of 3 + 1AP · Photo: Achim Kukulies, Düsseldorf · Courtesy Sies + Höke, Düsseldorf

221 · Tomáš Libertíny · ***The Seed of Narcissus***, 2011 · mirrored glass and beeswax · diameter: 100 × 38 cm (39 3/8 × 15 in.) · Photo: Francesco Allegretto · Courtesy Venice Projects / Berengo Private Collection, Venice

222 · Klara Kristalova · ***A fly on your floor***, 2010 · glazed stoneware · 19 × 23 × 17 cm (7 1/2 × 9 × 6 3/4 in.) · Photo: Inka Lindergård · Courtesy Galleri Magnus Karlsson, Stockholm · © Klara Kristalova

223AL · Lisa Sweeney · ***Fly***, 2009 · pencil on gesso board · 21 × 16 cm (8 1/4 × 6 1/4 in.) · Photo: Paul Maye · Courtesy of the artist

223AR · Cindy Wright · ***Spaceinvaders***, 2008 · oil on canvas · 269 × 179.8 cm (106 × 70 3/4 in.) · Courtesy of the artist and Mark Moore Gallery, Culver City

223B · Maryam Amiryani · ***Fly, White Plate***, 2008 · oil on linen · 8.75 × 11.75 cm (3 1/2 × 4 5/8 in.) · Courtesy of the artist and Jonathan Park Walk Cooper Gallery

224 · Roberto Ekholm · ***Mosquito Man #1 (congress)***, 2009 · archival print · 50 × 50 cm (19 5/8 × 19 5/8 in.) · Collection of Sasha Jensen, Australia · Courtesy of the artist

225 · Adam Fuss · ***Untitled***, 2003 · pigment print · 182.9 × 111.8 cm (72 × 44 in.) · Courtesy Cheim & Read, New York

226 · Paul Hazelton · ***Moth-er***, 2006 · household dust · 3.8 × 3 × 1 cm (1 1/2 × 1 1/8 × 3/8 in.) · Private collection · Courtesy of the artist

227A, 227B · Janne Malmros · ***Black-veined Whites 1906–1947***, 2010 · plywood, brown wrapping paper, nails and entomologist foam; pencil, Indian and acrylic ink on *The Butterflies of the British Isles* (Richard South, F.E.S. London, Editions 1906–1947) · 110 × 120 × 150 cm (43 1/4 × 47 1/4 × 59 in.) · Courtesy of the artist

228 · Tessa Farmer · ***The Ressurrection of the Rat***, 2008 · dried rat, mummified mouse, dried insects, hedgehog spines, wasp nest and plant roots · dimensions variable · Photo: Casino Luxembourg, Luxembourg · Courtesy of the artist and Danielle Arnaud, London

229 · Berthold Bell · ***Still Life In Plato's Cave***, 22 March 2011, Paros, Greece · digital photograph · 20 × 32 cm (7 7/8 × 12 5/8 in.)

230 · Donald Baechler · ***SKULL***, 2009 (detail) · acrylic on canvas dropcloth · 330.2 × 274.3 cm (130 × 108 in.) · Courtesy Cheim & Read, New York

234 · Damien Hirst · ***For the Love of God***, 2007 · platinum, diamonds and human teeth · 17.1 × 12.7 × 19.1 cm (6 3/4 × 5 × 7 1/2 in.) · Photo: Prudence Cuming Associates Ltd · © Damien Hirst and Science Ltd · All rights reserved, DACS 2012

235 · Gabriel Orozco · ***Black Kites***, 1997 · graphite on skull · 21.6 × 12.7 × 15.9 cm (8 1/2 × 5 × 6 1/4 in.) · Courtesy Marian Goodman Gallery, New York, and White Cube, London

236 · Elizabeth Peyton · ***Cezanne + Balzac***, 2009 · oil on linen on board · 30.5 × 23.2 cm (12 × 9 1/8 in.) · Courtesy Sadie Coles HQ, London · © Elizabeth Peyton

237A · Alexander James, Distil Ennui Studio · ***Vanitas, 'The Great Leveler'***, 2011 · C-print mounted on polished aluminium · 120 × 90 cm (47 1/4 × 35 3/8 in.) · Courtesy of the artist

237B · Shirana Shahbazi · ***[Stilleben-33-2009]*** · C-print on aluminium · Courtesy Bob van Orsouw, Zurich

238A · Sarah Elise Hall · ***Temporal***, 2010 · oil on panel · diameter: 50.8 cm (20 in.) · Courtesy of the artist

238B · Paul McDevitt · ***Mountain Flowers A***, 2005 · biro on paper · 55 × 50cm (21 3/4 × 19 3/4 in.) · Courtesy of the artist and Stephen Friedman Gallery, London

239 · Mathew Weir · ***A Fool's Life***, 2010 · oil on canvas mounted on board · 54 × 40.5 cm (21 1/4 × 16 in.) · Photo: Michael Brzezinski · Courtesy Alison Jacques Gallery, London · © Mathew Weir

240 · Cindy Wright · ***Collector's Item***, 2010 · oil on linen · 167.6 × 109.2 cm (66 × 43 in.) · Courtesy of the artist and Mark Moore Gallery, Culver City

241A · Piotr Uklański · ***Untitled (Monsieur François Pinault, President of Artemis)***, 2003 · colour photograph · 112 × 146 cm (44 × 57 in.) · edition 2 of 5 + 1 AP · Courtesy of the artist and Gagosian Gallery

241B · Guillaume Paris · ***Out of the Whale***, 2008 · real time evolving permanent video, HD plasma screen, computer; colour, silent · © Guillaume Paris

242 · Nobuhito Nishigawara · ***Skeletal Bottle***, 2009 · clay, iron, bronze and acrylic · 30.5 × 25.4 × 22.9 cm (12 × 10 × 9 in.) · Courtesy of the artist

243L · Pharrell Williams · ***Inside Out***, 2011 · glass · big skeleton: 180 × 110 cm (70 7/8 × 43 1/4 in.), small skeleton: 90 × 90 cm (35 3/8 × 35 3/8 in.) · Photo: Francesco Allegretto · Courtesy Venice Projects, Venice

243R · Marc Quinn · ***Waiting for Godot***, 2006 · patinated bronze · 77 × 36 × 76.5 cm (30 5/16 × 14 3/16 × 30 1/8 in.) · Photo: Stephen White · Courtesy White Cube

244 · Jan Fabre · ***Untitled***, 2009 · glass and Bic ink · 22 × 44 × 43 cm (8 5/8 × 17 3/8 × 16 7/8 in.) · Photo: Francesco Allegretto · Courtesy Berengo Private Collection, Venice / Venice Projects

245A, 245B · Yang Jiechang · ***Underground Flowers***, 1989–2009 · wooden cases with human bones from porcelain, hand-painted; silkscreen prints on silk · Installation at Galerie Conrads, 2010 · ©photo CONRADS Düsseldorf

246 · Hugh Hayden · ***Untitled***, 2012 · reproduction of African American male skull, human hair and adhesive · 16.5 × 17.8 × 28 cm (6.5 × 7 × 11 in.) · Courtesy of the artist

247 · Museum Clausum · ***Head***, 2012 · C-print · 100 × 67 cm (39 3/8 × 26 3/8 in.)

248 · McDermott & McGough · ***Their Distant Voices, 1883***, 2001 · painted wooden sculpture · 42 × 18.5 × 23.5 cm (16 1/2 × 7 1/4 × 9 1/4 in.) · Courtesy Galerie Jérôme de Noirmont · © McDermott & McGough

249 · Roberto Ekholm · ***Untitled (The Healer)***, 2012 · plaster, resin, neodymium magnets, iron filings, printed ink on paper · 25 × 20 × 19 cm (9 7/8 × 7 7/8 × 7 1/2 in.) · Collection of Patronia Campbell · Photo: Gunnar Tufta · © Roberto Ekholm

250 · Zhang Huan · ***49 Days No.6***, 2011 · grey brick and steel · 197 × 265 × 196 cm (77 9/16 × 104 5/16 × 77 3/16 in.) · Photo: Joshua White · Courtesy Zhang Huan Studio, Blum & Poe and White Cube · © Zhang Huan

251 · Paul Hazelton · ***Death Duster***, 2011/12 · synthetic wool duster and household dust · 64 × 17 × 20 cm (25 1/4 × 6 3/4 × 7 7/8 in.) · Private collection · Courtesy of the artist

252 · Adam Fuss · ***Untitled***, 2002 · daguerreotype · 35.6 × 27.9 cm (14 × 11 in.) · Courtesy Cheim & Read, New York

253 · Jim Skull · ***Mister Smith***, 2009 · papier maché and polyester rope · height: 100 cm (39 3/8 in.) · Photo: Christophe Lebedinsky

254 · Museum Clausum · ***Museum Clausum, Wundercamera: Malplaquet House, Diptych # 23, London, 10 August 2010*** · C-prints · dimensions variable

255A · Sherrie Levine · ***Crystal Skulls: 1–12***, 2010 · cast glass · 12 parts and 12 vitrines, 13.9 × 17.7 × 11.4 cm (5 1/2 × 7 × 4 1/2 in.) each · Installation view of 'Sherrie Levine – Crystal Skulls', Böhm Chapel, Hürth Kalscheuren, 2011 · Private collection · Photo: Farbanalyse Cologne · Courtesy Jablonka Galerie, Cologne

255B · Angela Freiberger · ***B (Brain)***, 2009 · Carrara marble · 10.2 × 15.2 × 10.2 cm (4 × 6 × 4 in.) · Courtesy of the artist

256 · Jefferson Hayman · ***The Wishbone Table***, 2010 · salt print, antique frame · print size: 20.3 × 19.1 cm (8 × 7 1/2 in.) · Courtesy of the artist and Wessel O'Connor Fine Art

257A, 257BL, 257BR · Caroline McCarthy · ***Vanitas***, 2007 · bin bag, canvas and mdf support, metal bracket · dimensions variable · Courtesy of the artist

258 · Gerhard Richter · ***Skull with Candle***, 1983 · oil on canvas · 100 × 150 cm (39 3/8 × 59 in.) · © Gerhard Richter, 2012

259L, 259R · Cynthia Greig · ***Nature Morte no. 11 (Burned at Both Ends)***, 2010 · chromogenic prints · 50.8 × 40.6 cm (20 × 16 in.) each · © Cynthia Greig

260 · Robert Gober · ***Untitled Candle***, 1991 · beeswax, string and human hair · 20.3 × 12 × 16.5 cm (8 × 4 7/8 × 6 1/2 in.) · Courtesy Matthew Marks Gallery · © Robert Gober

261 · Dermot O'Brien · ***Untitled (Bullet)***, 2011 · cast human bone and epoxy medium · approx. 2.3 × 0.8 cm (1 × 1/2 in.) · Courtesy PayneShurvell and MOCA London

262 · Vija Celmins · ***Web #5***, 1999 · charcoal on paper · 55.9 × 64.8 cm (22 × 25 1/2 in.) · Courtesy McKee Gallery · © Vija Celmins

263 · Todd Hebert · ***Web with Snowman***, 2010 · acrylic on paper · 70 × 30 (11 3/4 × 27 5/8 in.) · Courtesy Devin Borden Gallery and Jack Shainman Gallery

264 · Jim Hodges · ***Hello, again***, 1994–2003 · brass chains and pins · Installation view of 'Jim Hodges at Camden Arts Centre', 2010 · Photo: Andy Keate · Courtesy Camden Arts Centre

265L, 265R · Carlos Amorales · ***Transformable Spider web***, 2008–11 · 4 mm aluminium tubing and black rubber paint · dimensions variable · Courtesy of the artist and Yvon Lambert

266–67 · Reena Saini Kallat · ***Untitled Cobweb (knots and crossings)***, 2012 · acrylic paint, rubber stamps and metal · dimensions variable · Photo: Uwe Walter, Berlin · Courtesy Reena Kallat Studio

268 · Michael Craig-Martin, ***Untitled (death)***, 2008 · acrylic on aluminium · 200 × 325 cm (78 11/16 × 128 in.) · Courtesy Gagosian Gallery · © Michael Craig-Martin

269A · Eric Rhein · ***Leaves*** · wire and paper · dimensions variable · Installation view of 'The Course of My Life', Richard Anderson Fine Arts, New York, 1998

269B · Eric Rhein · ***Jeff and Tim***, 1996–2012 · wire and paper · 40.6 × 49 × 5 cm (16 × 19 1/4 × 2 in.) · Courtesy of the artist

270L · Jone Kvie · ***Untitled***, 2002 · stainless steel · 220 × 80 × 80 cm (86 5/8 × 31 1/2 in.) · Photo: Anders Sune Berg · Courtesy of the artist and Nils Stærk, Copenhagen

270R · Susan Seubert · ***Bomb #10 'Bomb in a Box' (tic, tac, toe)***, 2008 · digital pigment print on tissue paper, encaustic wax and lead · 14 × 14 cm (5 1/2 × 5 1/2 in.) · Courtesy of the artist and Froelick Gallery

271A · Carlos Noronha Feio · ***Plant Life of the Pacific World, Figure 70: Canarium commune***, 2012 · photographic digital collage printed on Hahnemühle photo rag 500 gsm · 29.5 × 36 cm (11 5/8 × 14 1/8 in.) · Courtesy of the artist

271B · Carlos Noronha Feio · ***Plant Life of the Pacific World, Figure 210: Durio zibethinus***, 2012 · photographic digital collage printed on Hahnemühle photo rag 500 gsm · 29.5 × 36 cm (11 5/8 × 14 1/8 in.) · Courtesy of the artist

272 · Ian Breakwell · **BC/AD**, 2005–8 · Blu-ray, black and white, sound · duration: 60 minutes · Courtesy The Estate of Ian Breakwell and Anthony Reynolds Gallery, London · © The Estate of Ian Breakwell

273L · Piotr Uklański · ***Untitled (Skull)***, 2000 · platinum print · 35.6 × 27.9 cm (14 × 11 in.) · Courtesy of the artist and Gagosian Gallery

273R · Marc Quinn · ***Self***, 2006 · artist's blood, stainless steel, Perspex and refrigeration equipment · 205 × 65 × 65 cm (80 11/16 × 25 9/16 × 25 9/16 in.) · Photo: Todd-White Art Photography · Courtesy White Cube · © Marc Quinn

274 · Bill Jacobson · ***Interim Portrait #378***, 1992 · C-print · 61 × 50.8 cm (24 × 20 in.) · Courtesy of the artist

275 · Sophie Calle · ***Coeur de Cible / Target 1, Target 2 ... Target 13***, 2003 (detail) · colour photographs, aluminium, frames (× 13) · 68 × 50.5 cm (26 3/4 × 19 7/8 in.) minimum to 79.5 × 505 cm (31 1/4 × 19 7/8 in.) maximum · Installation view of 'Dommages collatéraux', Galerie Perrotin, Paris, 2003 · © ADAGP, Paris 2013 · Courtesy Galerie Perrotin, Hong Kong & Paris

276A, 276B · Ana Genovés · ***Effigy***, 2001 · acrylic composite and gloss paint · 237 × 104 × 93 cm (93 1/4 × 41 × 36 5/8 in.) · Courtesy of the artist

277 · Per Christian Brown · ***Nature Vanitas 2***, 2006 · C-print · 140 × 120 cm (55 1/8 × 47 1/4 in.) · Courtesy of the artist

278A · Damien Meade · ***Foot II***, 2009 · oil on linen on board · 44.5 × 55 cm (17 1/2 × 21 5/8 in.) · Courtesy of the artist

278B · Susan Seubert · ***Slave Cuffs***, 2011 · photography ambrotype · 12.7 × 10.2 cm (5 × 4 in.) · Courtesy of the artist and Froelick Gallery

279 · Rigoberto A. Gonzalez · ***Para Que Aprendan A Respetar (So That They Learn to be Respectful)***, 2009 · oil on linen · 50.8 × 61 cm (20 × 24 in.) · Courtesy of the artist

SELECT BIBLIOGRAPHY

MARK BAHTI, *Spirit in the Stone: A Handbook of Southwest Indian Animal Carvings*, Rio Nuevo Publishers, 1999

LEO BERSANI, 'Is the Rectum a Grave?', *October* 43 (Winter 1987), 197–222

JOE BOVA, *500 Animals in Clay: Contemporary Expressions of the Animal Form*, Lark Crafts, 2006

JONATHAN BROWN, *Painting in Spain, 1500–1700*, Yale University Press, 1998

NORMAN BRYSON, *Looking at the Overlooked: Four Essays on Still Life Painting*, Reaktion Books, 2004

PETER CHERRY, JOHN LOUGHMAN and LESLEY STEVENS, *In the Presence of Things: Four Centuries of European Still-Life Painting,* Volume One, Museu Calouste Gulbenkian, 2010

GARTH CLARK and CINDI STRAUSS, *Shifting Paradigms in Contemporary Ceramics: The Garth Clark and Mark Del Vecchio Collection*, Yale University Press, 2012

T. J. CLARK, *The Painting of Modern Life: Paris in the Art of Manet and His Followers*, Thames & Hudson, rev. ed., 1999

EMMANUEL COOPER, *Contemporary Ceramics*, Thames & Hudson, 2009

JOHN COPLANS, *Andy Warhol*, Little Brown & Co., 1970

NEIL COX, *In the Presence of Things: Four Centuries of European Still-Life Painting,* Volume Two, Museu Calouste Gulbenkian, 2011

SUZANNE DONOVAN, 'Shadow Figures: A Portrait of Life on the Row', *Texas Death Row*, University Press of Mississippi, 1997

MARK ALICE DURANT, *McDermott & McGough: A History of Photography*, Arena Editions, 1998

SYBILLE EBERT-SCHIFFERER, *Still Life: A History*, Harry N. Abrams, 1998

GEORGE FERGUSON, *Signs and Symbols in Christian Art*, Oxford University Press, 1954

JANE FORTUNE, *Invisible Women: Forgotten Artists of Florence*, The Florentine Press, 2009

RUDI FUCHS, *Dutch Painting*, Thames & Hudson, [1978] 2000

FRANCESCA GIUBILEI, *Glasstress 2011*, Marsilio, 2011

JAN GROOVER, *Pure Invention: The Tabletop Still Life*, Smithsonian, 1990

FLAMINIO GUALDONI, *Still Life*, Skira, 2009

DAVE HICKEY, *In the Dancehall of the Dead: Robert Gober*, Dia Center for the Arts, 1993

JULIE BERGER HOCHSTRASSER, *Still Life and Trade in the Dutch Golden Age*, Yale University Press, 2007

MICHAEL JUUL HOLM, POUL ERIK TØJNER and JONAS BENCARD (eds.), *The Flower As Image*, Louisiana Museum of Modern Art, 2005

LUCIA IMPELLUSO, *Nature and Its Symbols*, J. Paul Getty Museum, 2005

WILLIAM B. JORDAN, *Spanish Still Life In The Golden Age, 1600–1650*, Kimbell Art Museum, 1987

ROBERT MAPPLETHORPE and HERBERT MUSCHAMP, *Mapplethorpe: The Complete Flowers*, teNeues, 2006

PAUL MARTINEAU, *Still Life in Photography*, J. Paul Getty Museum, 2010

HANS J. VAN MIEGROET, 'Still-life', *The Dictionary of Art* 29, ed. Jane Turner, Grove, 1996, 663–71

—, 'Vanitas', *The Dictionary of Art* 31, ed. Jane Turner, Grove, 1996, 663–71

ELAINE SCARRY, *On Beauty and Being Just*, Princeton University Press, 2001

NORBERT SCHNEIDER, *Still Life*, Taschen, 2009

JUDITH S. SCHWARTZ, *Confrontational Ceramics*, University of Pennsylvania Press, 2008

SEYMOUR SLIVE, *Dutch Painting, 1600–1800*, Yale University Press, 1998

NATO THOMPSON, *Becoming Animal: Contemporary Art in the Animal Kingdom*, MIT Press, 2005

ANNE T. WOOLLETT, *Miraculous Bouquets: Flower and Fruit Paintings by Jan van Huysum*, J. Paul Getty Museum, 2011

STEFANO ZUFFI, *Discovering Caravaggio: The Art Lover's Guide to Understanding Symbols in His Paintings*, Rizzoli, 2010

ARTISTS' WEBSITES

For artists not listed below, please see the List of Illustrations for gallery representation.

Peter Abrahams
peterabrahams.eu

Mats Adelman
matsadelman.blogspot.co.uk

Ai Weiwei
aiweiwei.com

Theodora Allen
theodoraallen.com

Maryam Amiryani
maryamamiryani.com

Carlos Amorales
estudioamorales.com

Natasha Archdale
natashaarchdale.co.uk

Sue Arrowsmith
suearrowsmith.com

Annie Attridge
annieattridge.com

Aziz + Cucher
azizcucher.net

Donald Baechler
donaldbaechler.com

Kim Baker
kimbaker.co.uk

Conrad Bakker
untitledprojects.com

Joan Bankemper
joanbankemper.com

Barnaby Barford
barnabybarford.co.uk

Filippa Barkman
filippabarkman.com

Emma Bennett
emmabennett.info

Ernst Billgren
ernstbillgren.se

Jan Kjetil Bjørheim
jankjetil.net

Maurizio Bongiovanni
mauriziobongiovanni.com

George Boorujy
georgeboorujy.com

Elaine Bradford
elainebradford.weebly.com

Robert Brinker
robertbrinkerstudio.com

Karin Broker
karinbroker.com

Per Christian Brown
perchristianbrown.com

Derek Buckner
derekbuckner.com

Cai Guo-Qiang
caiguoqiang.com

Claudia Carr
claudiacarr.com

Mat Collishaw
matcollishaw.com

Michael Craig-Martin
michaelcraigmartin.co.uk

Daniel Gustav Cramer
danielgustavcramer.com

Anne-Françoise Couloumy
couloumy.fr

Nicky Deeley
nickydeeley.com

Wim Delvoye
wimdelvoye.be

Jorge Diezma
jorgediezma.com

John Dugdale
thejohndugdaleschool.com

David Edmond
davidedmond.blogspot.co.uk

Roberto Ekholm
robertoekholm.com

Saara Ekström
saaraekstrom.com

Elmgreen & Dragset
elmgreen-dragset.com

Simon English
simonenglish.com

Paul Evans
pkevans.co.uk

Jan Fabre
janfabre.be

Madeleine Farley
madeleinefarley.com

Tessa Farmer
tessafarmer.com

Daniel Firman
danielfirman.com

Nancy Fouts
nancyfouts.com

Nick Fox
nickfoxart.com

Angela Freiberger
angelafreiberger.com

Ana Genovés
anagenoves.co.uk

Helena Goldwater
helenagoldwater.co.uk

Rigoberto A. Gonzalez
rigobertogonzalezalonso.com

Daniel Gordon
danielgordonstudio.com

Cynthia Greig
cynthiagreig.com

Andrew Guenther
guentherart.com

Martin Gustavsson
martin-gustavsson.com

Sarah Elise Hall
sarahelisehall.com

Kana Harada
kanakanakana.com

James Hart Dyke
jameshartdyke.com

Hugh Hayden
hughhayden.com

Jefferson Hayman
jeffersonhayman.com

Paul Hazelton
paulhazelton.com

Todd Hebert
toddhebert.com

Renata Hegyi
renatahegyi.com

Michael Hilsman
michaelhilsman.com

Damien Hirst
damienhirst.com

David Hockney
hockneypictures.com

Paul Housley
paulhousley.com

Patrick Jackson
patrickjacksonblog.blogspot.co.uk

Bill Jacobson
billjacobsonstudio.com

Alexander James
distilennui.com

Darren Jones
darrenjonesart.com

Peter Jones
peterjonesart.com

Kate Joyce
kate-joyce.com

Reena Saini Kallat
reenakallat.com

John Kaine
johnkaine.co.uk

Rob Kesseler
robkesseler.co.uk

Klara Kristalova
kristalova.se

Jone Kvie
kvie.nu

David LaChapelle
davidlachapelle.com

Alana Lake
alanalake.blogspot.co.uk

Matts Leiderstam
mattsleiderstam.com

Laura Letinsky
lauraletinsky.com

Tomáš Libertíny
tomaslibertiny.com

Caroline McCarthy
carolinemccarthy.net

McDermott & McGough
mcdermottandmcgough.com

Janice McNab
janicemcnab.com

Aidan McNeill
aidan-mcneill.com

Janne Malmros
jannemalmros.com

Livia Marin
tumblr.com/tagged/livia%20marin

Carol Marin-Pache
marin-pache.com

Damien Meade
damienmeade.com

Shane Mecklenburger
shmeck.com

Lisa Milroy
lisamilroy.net

John Mitchell
johnmitchell-atist.co.uk

Polly Morgan
pollymorgan.co.uk

Museum Clausum (Klaus Wehner)
museumclausum.org

Tolly Nason
tollynason.com

Nobuhito Nishigawara
nobuhitonishigawara.com

Carlos Noronha Feio
carlosnoronhafeio.co.uk

Dermot O'Brien
dermotobrien.net

Bruno Pacheco
brunopacheco.info

Guillaume Paris
guillaumeparis.com

Javier Pérez
javierperez.es

Michael Petry
michaelpetry.net

Klaus Pichler
kpic.at

Philip Pirolo
philippirolo.com

Paola Pivi
paolapivi.com

Anja Priska
anjapriska.com

Marc Quinn
marcquinn.com

Ben Reid
benreid.co.nz

Eric Rhein
ericrhein.com

Gerhard Richter
gerhard-richter.com

Maria Roosen
mariaroosen.com

Brion Nuda Rosch
brionnudarosch.com

Alan Salisbury
alansalisbury.com

Miho Sato
mihosato.co.uk

Rebecca Scott
rebecca-scott.com

Andro Semeiko
androsemeiko.com

Susan Seubert
seubertfineart.com

Susan Silas
susansilas.com

Taryn Simon
tarynsimon.com

Jane Simpson
galeriesimpson.com

Jim Skull
jim-skullgallery.com

Colin Smith
colinsmithstudio.com

Matt Smith
mattjsmith.com

Rob Smith
robsmith.me.uk

Jennifer Steinkamp
jsteinkamp.com

Richard Stone
richardstoneprojects.com

Lisa Sweeney
lisasweeney-artist.blogspot.co.uk

Stephanie Syjuco
stephaniesyjuco.com

Philip Taaffe
philiptaaffe.info

Jane Telford
janetelford.com

Yuken Teruya
yukenteruyastudio.com

Cammie Toloui
cammiet.blogspot.co.uk

Cy Twombly
cytwombly.info

Clare Twomey
claretwomey.com

Maciej Urbanek
urbanek.co.uk

Joana Vasconcelos
joanavasconcelos.com

Peter Vos
petervos.com

Karl de Vroomen
karldevroomen.com

Frank Webster
fwebster.com

James White
saatchi-gallery.co.uk/artists/james_white.htm

Pharrell Williams
n-e-r-d.com

Paul Wood
wheretheycreate.com/Paul-Wood

Thomas Woodruff
thomaswoodruff.com

Cindy Wright
cindywright.org

Craig Wylie
craigwylie.com

Yang Jiechang
yangjiechang.com

Zhang Huan
zhanghuan.com

INDEX OF ARTISTS

Page numbers in *italic* refer to illustrations.

This book is dedicated to my partner, Travis Barker.

Michael Petry is an American artist who has lived in London since 1981. He is Director of the Museum of Contemporary Art (MOCA), London, and holds a Doctor in Arts. His books include *Installation Art* (1994), *Installation in the New Millennium* (2003) and *The Art of Not Making* (2011), all published by Thames & Hudson. In 2010 he became the first artist in residence at Sir John Soane's Museum, London. In 2012 he had a solo exhibition 'The Touch of the Oracle' at Palm Springs Art Museum, California.

Picture research: Roberto Ekholm
Administrative assistants: Matteo Ferri, Guifré Jordan, Àgata Mutaneer

The author would like to thank all the participating artists, their gallery representatives and their staff, along with the Thames & Hudson and Barnbrook production teams. Particular thanks for all their help and diligence in the making of the book go to Roberto Ekholm, Jonathan Abbott, and to Laura Potter for her invaluable editorial contribution. He would also like to thank the following for their support: Travis Barker, Adriano Berengo, Devin Borden, Kathleen Boyd, Hiram Butler, Daniell Cornell, Mark Davy and Futurecity, Germaine Franco, Helene Galen, Gavin Greenaway, Katherine Hough, Molly Hubbard, James Kabler, Myrna Kaplan, Theodore J. Lee, Marilyn Loesberg, Alec Longmuir, Donna MacMillan, Melissa Morgan, Steve and Carol Nash, Ursula Neuman, Terry New, Joshua Pazda, John Powell, Faye and Herman Sarkowsky, Marc A. Sekula, Audrey Strachen, Sundaram Tagore, Eva Watne, Chris Westbrook, Randolph Wile and Sandy Zane. The author would also like to thank Constance Kaine for her ongoing support.

—

First published in the United Kingdom in 2013 *by*
Thames & Hudson Ltd, 181A High Holborn, London WC1V 7QX

Designed *by* Jonathan Abbott *at* Barnbrook

British Library Cataloguing-in-Publication Data
A catalogue record for this book is available from the British Library

ISBN 978-0-500-23906-3

Manufactured in China *by* Imago

—

ON THE COVER

Ori Gersht · ***Time after Time: Blow up No. 08***, 2007 · light jet print on aluminium · 240 × 180 cm (94 1/2 × 70 7/8 in.) · Courtesy of the artist and Mummery+Schnelle

Jan Davidsz. de Heem · ***Still Life with Flowers*** · oil on canvas · 90 × 68 cm (35 1/2 × 26 3/4 in.) · Museum der Bildenden Kuenste, Leipzig (inv. 1578) · Photo: akg-images/Erich Lessing